Political Theory and Socio-Political Philosophy

Our Other Books by the Same Author

1. Principles of Modern Political Science
2. Contemporary Political Theory
3. Comparative Politics
4. International Relations and Politics
   (Diplomatic History between Two World Wars)
5. International Relations and Politics
   (Theoretical Perspectives in the Post-Cold War Era)
6. The Constitution of India - - A Politico-Legal Study
7. Great Radical Humanist - - M.N. Roy

Hindi Translations

1. आधुनिक राजनीति विज्ञान के सिद्धात्त
2. समकालीन राजनीतिक सिद्धान्त
3. तुलनात्मक राजनीति
4. अत्तराष्ट्रीय सम्बन्ध व राजनीति
   (उत्तर-शीत युद्ध काल में सैद्धान्तिक परिप्रेक्ष्य)

Edited Books

1. Indian Freedom Movement and Thought (1919-29)
   by Dr. Lal Bahadur
2. Indian Freedom Movement and Thought (1929-47)
   by Dr. R.C. Gupta
3. Struggle for Pakistan (1906-47)
   by Dr. Lal Bahadur
4. Introduction to International Relations
   by Pierre-Marie Marin
5. Introduction to the Methods of Social Sciences
   by Jean Louis Loubel del Bayle

Political Theory and Socio-Political Philosophy

J.C. JOHARI
MA., L.L.B., PhD.

STERLING PUBLISHERS PRIVATE LIMITED
A-59, Okhla Industrial Area, Ph-II, New Delhi-110020
CIN: U22110PB1964PTC002569
Tel: 26387070, 26386209; Fax: 91-11-26383788
E-mail: mail@sterlingpublishers.com
www.sterlingpublishers.com

Political Theory and Socio-Political Philosophy

ISBN 978 81 207 9858 8

PRINTED IN INDIA

Published and Printed by Sterling Publishers Pvt. Ltd., New Delhi-110020.

Preface

The term 'political theory' is quite comprehensive, for it covers within its fold certain related fields as 'political thought', 'political philosophy','political ideology', 'political analysis', 'political inquiry' and the like. A serious student of this subject may draw lines of distinction between these terms that may, or may not, be acceptable to an equally serious student of this discipline. The fact stands out that a neat line of distinction between them cannot be drawn. The reason is that the writers take different views of politics before theorising the themes of social and political 'reality'. It depends upon the broadness of their vision and the depth of their investigation from the standpoint of normativism, or empiricism, or a curious blending of both.

The nature and ramifications of social and political issues change with the passage of time. New issues emerge which may be like the offshoots of their old forms in certain respects, or they may be quite fresh generated by the new conditions of the age. Such developments provide ample stuff for further investigation as a result of which social and political theories witness their revision or reformulation. The process of continuity and change remains at work. The new theories may have their new names, or the word 'post' may be prefixed to the new forms of the older ones. Theories made in the age of feudal society, for example, are revised or put in a new shape in the age of the capitalist society that, with the passage of time, is now called industrial, even post-industrial, society.

As generally understood, social and political theories are regarded as a contribution of the Western thinkers and scholars. Such a view needs rectification in the light of significant contributions made by the thinkers and writers of the East as well. Hence, in this book, while much space has been given to the study of political and social philosophy contributed by the Western thinkers and writers, some space has been given to the study of eminent modern Indian thinkers.

For the sake of a convenient study, the book has been divided into two parts. While Part I contains a study of concepts and ideologies in detail, Part II contains a brief study of the great social and political thinkers (Western and Indian). Some topics like the meaning and nature of political theory, and traditional and modern approaches have been discussed in detail particularly so as to make the readers aware of the latest ways of understanding and critically explaining the themes of social and political philosophy. All important themes of social and political philosophy, including contemporary ideologies and important social and political ideas of great thinkers (Western and Indian) have been analysed and discussed in easily intelligible language.

I have taken due note of all such salient points and thus ventured to present this useful textbook for those studying this course at the degree and post-graduate levels or preparing for various competitive examinations conducted by the Universities, University Grants Commission, and Union and State Public Service Commissions. I hope that this venture of mine shall meet the requirement of the students/candidates to whom it is addressed and thereby my humble efforts shall be suitably rewarded. I shall feel thankful to my readers who convey their critical comments to me in the light of which necessary changes or improvements shall be made in the next edition or print of this book.

—J.C. Johari

Contents

Part-II: Great Social and Political Thinkers (Western and Indian)

PART I

CONCEPTS AND IDEOLOGIES

Political ideas are not merly a passive reflection of vested imterest or personal ambition, but have the capacity to inspire and guide political action itself and so can shape material life. At the same time, political ideas do not emerge in a vacuum; they do not drop from the sky like rain. All political ideas are moulded by the social and historical circumstances in which they develop and by the political ambitions they serve. Quite simply, politicial theory and political practice are inseparably linked. Any balanced or persuasive account of political life must, therefore, acknowledge the constant interplay between ideas and ideologies on the one hand, and historical and social forces on the other.

—Andrew Heywood

Political Ideologies; An Introduction, pp. 2-3.

1
Political Theory

The term 'political theory' interchangeable with other terms like 'political thought', 'political philosophy', 'political ideas', 'political analysis', 'political inquiry', 'political ideology', 'theories of the political system' etc., is that branch of political science which "attempts to arrive at generalisations, inferences, or conclusions to be drawn from the data gathered by other specialists, not only in political science, but throughout the whole range of human knowledge and experience."[1] It may rightly be regarded as the most comprehensive branch of this discipline in view of the fact that here we study the momentous theme of man in relation to his fellow beings under some form of control exercised by those in 'authority roles'. Moreover, as the dimensions of such a relationship change from time to time and, moreover, as these have different images in the minds of different students of this subject, political theory comes to have its different forms. It leads to the emergence of its different varieties ranging from purely abstract and hypothetical on the one side to perfectly causal and empirical on the other. Taking such a consideration in his view, Prof. F.W. Coker incisively sums up the meaning of political theory in these words : "When political government and its forms and activities are studied not simply as facts to be described and compared, or judged in reference to their immediate and temporary effects, but as facts to be understood and appraised in relation to the constant needs, desires and opinions of men—then we have political theory."[2]

Meaning and Nature

The English word 'theory' originates from the Greek word 'theoria' which suggests a well-focused mental look taken at something in a state of contemplation with an intent to grasp it. In this sense, it covers an understanding of being (ontology) as well as a causal explanation that may be in the nature of a theological, philosophical, empirical or logical thought. If so, the term 'theory' may be studied in wider as well as narrower senses. In the former sense, it may be taken as a proposition or a set of propositions designed to explain something with reference to data or inter-relations not directly observed, or not otherwise manifest. Mere description is not theory, nor are the proposals of goals, policies, or evaluations. Only the explanations, if any, offered for

---

1. C.C. Rodee, T.J. Anderson and C.Q. Christol : *Introduction to Political Science* (New York ; McGraw Hill. 1957), p. 11.
2. F.W. Coker : *Recent Political Thought,* p. 3.

descriptions or proposals may be theoretical; the descriptions or the proposals as such do not make theory. On the other hand, theory does include 'prediction' provided it so follows from an explanation. Then, in the latter sense, it "comprises a thinker's entire teaching on a subject (his *Lehre),* including his description of the facts, his explanations (whether religious, philosophical or empirical), his conception of history, his value-judgements, and his proposals of goals, of policy and of principles."[3]

In simple terms, theory "is always used to designate attempts to 'explain' a phenomenon especially when that is done in general and abstract terms."[4] But it is also usual to admit that it may be 'scientific' or 'non-scientific' according to whether or not scientific rules are followed. It is true that scientific theorising may be differentiated from non-scientific theorising, but theory in either of its forms may not be identified with 'law'. The term 'law' connotes something clear, fixed and binding, while a theory is just an explanation of some phenomenon. It may suggest the existence of a law without being itself identifiable by a law. As Norman Campbell says, it may try to explain a law of course, but if that is the intention, the theory must refer to some more general law. Exactly speaking, a law can never be deduced directly from a theory; it can be deduced only from a more general law offered in theory.[5] Conversely, a law "is not a theory, it is rather a fact, namely with which some other facts are associated either as a rule or in general. In another sense, it may refer to a legal, moral, aesthetic or procedural norm."[6]

It implies that theory covers both 'values' and 'facts' that determine its normative or speculative and causal or empirical character. It is the field where the investigations and findings of a writer or a researcher are tied together, cross-referenced, weighed, contemplated and churned so as to lay down certain conclusions in regard to the proper relationship between man and authority (power). An investigator may be mainly a political scientist, or an economist, or a psychologist, or a sociologist, or a historian, even an anthropologist; what is essential is that his conclusions must touch the fundamental issue of man in relation to authority under which he has to survive, or his association with a community in which he desires to seek power or, his struggle for, what Hobbes calls, 'some future apparent good'. Here it should be stressed that facts — even if demonstrably incontrovertible — 'do not by themselves', point to any single, inescapable course of action. The function of the political theorist is to consider facts in all their varied ramifications and at least suggest conclusions, remedies and public policies."[7]

---

3. Arnold Brecht : "Political Theory" in David I. Sills (ed.) : *International Encyclopaedia of the Social Sciences* (New York : Macmillan and Free Press, 1969), p. 307.
4. Arnold Brecht : *Political Theory : The Foundations of the Twentieth-Century Political Thought,* p. 14.
5. *Ibid.,* p. 15.
6. *Ibid.,* Also see Campbell : *What is Science*?, pp. 89-91.
7. Rodee and others, *op. cit.,* p. 11.

A student of this subject should, therefore, be concerned with both the aspects of political theory—value-laden and fact-laden. As such, political theory, for better or worse, has two distinct meanings:[8]

1. It stands for the history of political ideas. Starting with Plato, these ideas are regarded as contributions to an intellectual tradition. They are studied with due regard for the historical circumstances which produced them, and their influence on political practice is a matter of constant speculation. This understanding of political theory is the more traditional of the two and an honourable tradition of scholarship supports it.
2. The other conception of the theory is newer and, in consequence, less sure of its methods and purposes. Nevertheless, it can be said that this approach calls for the systematic study of political behaviour in the modern world.

Obviously, the field of political theory includes both the traditional and modern spheres in spite of the fact that the two may be distinguished from each other on certain valid grounds. Thus Hacker continues: "Whereas the older conception has as its subject matter the historical texts and the conditions which surrounded their writing, the more recent approach to theory sees as its subject the actual behaviour of men and institutions in our own time. Systematic theory is, then, concerned to create generalisations which describe and explain contemporary political phenomena. By and large, it places great importance on the method of collecting data, for systematic knowledge must be founded on evidence rather than intuition. On the whole, this approach to theory tries to avoid making value-judgements or enter into ethical controversies."[9]

From what we have said above about the meaning and nature of political theory, two impressions must be formed before we go ahead with the study of this theme in other relevant directions. First, political theory, in the main, "stands for an abstract 'model' of the political order" which a professional student of this subject "is examining, a guide to the systematic collection and analysis of political data."[10] Second, it, as it is today, has become like "a blend of philosophy, scientific theory and description with far more space and emphasis given to non-scientific philosophical aspects than to strictly scientific ones."[11] Keeping all these points in view, the term 'political theory' has been defined, rather explained, in these words: 'Political theory is trying to weld together the insights, data and understandings of those who study the actuality of political life into a coherent explanatory theory or the theories of political behaviour capable, even, of generating predictions. Traditionally, the classical political theorists like Plato and Hobbes, in fact, did both jobs. Ideally, political theory should probably be defined as trying to combine the empirical truths about human political reactions with the moral truths of what is politically desirable by designing institutions and constitutions which

---

8. Andrew Hacker : *Political Theory — Philosophy, Ideology, Science,* p. vii.
9. *Ibid.*
10. W.T. Bluhm : *Theories of the Political System : Classics of Political Thought and Modern Political Analysis,* p. 3.
11. Brecht "Political Theory" in *International Encyclopaedia, op. cit.,* p. 310.

Some Definitional Statements

- ***Theory:*** It refers to sets of systematically related generalisations, and involves viewing and thinking. It also generates insight. Loosely conceived, it comprises sets of systematically related generalisations. More specifically, it is a coherent body of generalisations and principles associated with the practice of a field of inquiry.
- ***Method:*** It is the procedure or process that involves the techniques and tools utilised in inquiry for examining, testing and evaluating theory.
- ***Methodology:*** It consists of methods, procedures, working concepts, rules and the like used for theory and guiding inquiry, and the search for solutions to problems of the real world. It is a particular way of testing, viewing, organising and giving shape to inquiry.
- ***Inquiry:*** It involves four steps—description, classification, explanation and confirmation. The collection and description of facts are drawn from some classificatory scheme. The uniformities and differences are identified and described. Tentative hypotheses about the inter-relationships in the political process are formulated. These tentative hypotheses are verified through rigorous empirical observation. Then, the acceptable findings are set forth.
- ***Analysis:*** It is the separation or breaking up of the whole into its fundamental parts and subjecting them to detailed qualitative or quantitative examination. It may involve clarification and explication.

will generate the desirable by harnessing human political nature. That is clearly a massive job, perhaps never capable of more than limited achievement, but it is increasingly the goal of united and coherent political science."[12]

Social and Political Philosophy

Philosophy is described as the 'science of wisdom', though here the word 'science' is not used as generally understood by the students of natural sciences. Newton and Einstein were natural scientists who studied what could be observed, or felt, or measured and tested by the instruments and on that basis solid and irrefutable laws of the material world could be discovered and laid down. But social and political scientists study what is related to human life in numerous social and political institutions. They study what may, or may not, be observed, but that may be seen or perceived by intellectual power. Moreover, they seek to study things not only as they are but also as they ought to be in their ideal form. However, as their viewpoints and approaches vary, so they offer different formulations. As this process continues, their formulations undergo revisions

12. David Robertson : *A Dictionary of Modern Politics,* p. 266. The word 'theory' is full of ambiguity. It is often employed as a synonym for thoughts, conjectures or ideas. Thus, political theory is political thought or political speculation, and all three terms involve the expression of political ideas or 'philosophising about government'.

as a result of which different theories come up with a perplexing stock of further elaborations, explanations, complications, contradictions and repudiations.

To an average reader philosophy looks like a dull and monotonous subject, but its lover may appreciate it like sieving sand in a desert to find out the particles of gold and silver. A natural scientist may feel happy at the discovery of the law of gravitation, a social scientist may feel so after discovering a solution to the malady of alienation. A natural scientist gets happiness of a materialistic nature, but a social scientist receives inner bliss pertaining to the realm of spiritualism. The concern of a natural scientist is confined to the realm of reality or empiricism, the concern of a social scientist transcends the realm of reality and finds its culmination in the realm of glorious human values which would prevail in an ideal society of human beings. Such conclusions of a social scientist may be utopian of course, but they hint at, what the English poet William Wordsworth says, the 'inner bliss of solitude'.

Social and political philosophy may be distinguished from each other on some counts as society and state are different entities. While society means peaceful, collective and organised life of the people, state signifies power that keeps the social life in order. A social philosopher may study certain institutions having nothing to do with power such as family, school, church or the usages and customs of the people, but he jumps into the realm of politics if he thinks in terms of the necessity of state interference in the affairs of family, school or church. For instance, Bodin is a political philosopher who advises his ruler not to meddle in the affairs of a household, Hobbes makes his ruler so powerful that his rule pervades all spheres of the life of the people.

As man cannot live without society and the society cannot exist without state, the two are closely inter-retated in a way that a watertight division cannot be made. The political structures stand on a social base. Hence, the knowledge of sociology becomes essential if one wants to understand the nature and working of political structures and, more than that, if he seeks to replace the present model with a new one in the conceptual frameworks of Plato, Aristotle, Rousseau, Hegel, Marx and Gandhi.

Indeed, it is a perplexing as well as an interesting feature of the subject of social and political philosophy that its field has ever been expanding. With the passage of time, patterns of social life change and as a result of that new theories come up which either refute or rectify the older ones. The capitalist society ridden with the evils of exploitation and oppression of the working class provided ample material for the formulation of theories of socialism ranging from utopian socialism, revisionism and Fabianism or democratic socialism to syndicalism, anarchism and communism. The industrial society, as called by Herbert Marcuse, has provided stuff for the formulation of new theories as environmentalism, feminism, communitarianism, multiculturalism and post-modernism. New left has replaced the traditional left; neo-liberalism has replaced positive liberalism. The trend of globalisation has eroded the dimensions of sovereignty and paved the way for the emergence of 'states without frontiers'. Such instances may be multiplied, but the fact stands out that now traditional categories within which social and political theories were discussed and evaluated "are increasingly becoming inadequate."[13]

Sociology and political philosophy have penetrated into each other to an extent that a new discipline with the name of 'political sociology' has come up. August Comte is known as the 'father of sociology', but his positivism has been borrowed by a number of political philosophers, particularly the behaviouralists of the United States. A study of important themes like rights, law, liberty, equality, justice, property etc., has its place in the domain of sociology as well as politics. Can there be a society without a state? It has attracted the attention of many social and political theorists ranging from liberals like Mill, Spencer and Nozick to socialists and anarchists like Proudhon, Bakunin and Marx. D.D. Raphael well observes that one should not try to maintain a rigid separation between social and political philosophy. Some of the time-honoured subjects of political philosophy such as nature of state, sovereignty and the grounds of political obligation clearly belong to the political domain, but others such as authority, equality and justice have a wider application and are best considered as belonging to the sphere of the social in the sense of the term which includes the political.

Approaches and Methods

In simple terms, an approach may be defined as a way of looking at and then explaining a particular phenomenon. The perspective may be broad enough to cover a vast area like the world as a whole in the study of politics, or it may be very small embracing just an aspect of local, regional, national, and international politics. Besides, it also covers within its fold every other thing related to the collection and selection of evidence followed by an investigation and analysis of a particular hypothesis for an academic purpose. Thus, an approach "consists of a criteria of selection—criteria employed in selecting the problems or questions to consider and in selecting the data to bring to bear; it consists of standards governing the inclusion and exclusion of questions and data."[14]

It is for this reason that approaches to the study of politics are so many. As the criteria for selecting the problems and data or issues seeking answers to some questions are determined by the standpoint that a scholar adopts or makes use of, so there may be several approaches. However, when a scholar seeks to channelise his efforts into a presentable form, the same approach leads to the utilisation of a particular method. In this way, approaches and methods become closely interrelated themes; the latter becomes an integral part of the former. Thus, Van Dyke observes: "In brief, approaches consist of criteria for selecting problems and relevant data, whereas methods are procedures for getting and utilising data."

However, with a view to bring about a subtle distinction between an approach and a method, we may say that the latter is commonly used either to denote epistemological

---

13. Will Kymlicka: *Contemporary Political Philosophy,* p. 1.
14. V.V. Dyke : *Political Science : A Philosophical Analysis* (Stanford : Stanford University Press, 1962), p. 114.

assumptions on which the search for knowledge is based, or the operation and activities that occur in the acquisition and treatment of data. It is because of the use of varying methods generally borrowed from other social and natural sciences that modern political science looks like moving closer to the domains of other disciplines such as economics, psychology, sociology, biology and anthropology. It is all done to fit better the specific problems of data collection and interpretation faced in political studies. As a result of this, political science "seems to some like history or sociology or economics applied to political data."[15]

Sometimes, the word 'methodology' is used. It means the study of method, though some writers mistakenly use it as a supposedly learned synonym for the word 'method' itself. Scientists, including social scientists, often use this term to mean the study of particular methods of research that are appropriate for particular kinds of investigation. The philosophers use the term in a broader sense so as to mean the study of methods of inquiry that are common to all the sciences. This is regarded as a philosophical problem because the idea that the main scientific method of reasoning was induction could be justified. Obviously, the term 'methodology' is too narrow to cover the philosophical questions having their natural connection with man as a part of his community, the various facets of which constitute the subject matter of 'social sciences'.[16]

While the term 'approach' may be, though rashly or mistakenly, identified with another term like 'method' or 'technique', it is certainly different from 'theory'. An approach looks closely related to a theory in view of the fact that its very character determines the way of generalisation, explanation, prediction and prescription—all of which are the main functions of a theory. But a line of difference between the two may also be drawn. The term 'theory' is so vague that its real meaning becomes indeterminable in some critical situations. It may be identified with anything like idea, thought, trend, tendency, conjecture, principle, doctrine, hypothesis, speculation, explanation, even interpetation of some kind.[17] Different is the case with approach that may be defined as the creator of or a precursor to a theory. An approach is transformed into a theory if and when its functions extend beyond the selection of problems and data about the subject under study.

In brief, an approach is a way whereby a student manages to understand and explain the 'reality' of his concern and, for that, wins the credit of formulating a particular theory that may be abstract or concrete, utopian or realistic, normative or empirical, or a combination of both. When applied to political science, it refers to the way a

15. S.L. Wasby: *Political Science.,* p. 7.
16. D.D. Raphael : *Problems of Political Philosophy,* p. 25. So conceived, a method may also be called a 'technique'. The difference, if any, between the two is that the latter "may be more susceptible to routine or mechanical application and more highly specialised, depending less (once they are mastered) on imaginative intelligence." See Van Dyke, *op. cit* , p. 114.
17. M.H. Marx: "The General Nature of Theory Construction" in his *Psychological Theory,* p. 6.

particular thinker or a theorist has the understanding of 'political reality' and then offers something in his aspiration to be "a guide of the statesmen and of the citizens."[18]

Traditional Approaches and Methods

Approaches to and methods of the study of politics are many and most of them seem to overlap each other in varying measures. However, the distinguishing feature of the traditional approaches and methods should be traced in their heavily speculative and prescriptive nature. In contrast to it, the hallmark of the modern approaches is to give to the study of politics the character of a science as far as possible. Thus, leaving aside the behavioural and other empirical approaches like the systems approach with its offshoots in the form of structural-functional and input-output approaches, simulation approach, decision-making approach, communications approach, etc., all other approaches may be treated as 'traditional' in terms of their non-scientific nature and non-revolutionary expression. Mention, in this regard, may be made of the philosophical, historical, institutional, and legal approaches that may be briefly discussed as under:

Philosophical Approach: The oldest approach to the study of politics is philosophical. It is also known by the names of speculative, ethical and metaphysical approaches. Here the study of state, government, power and man as a political being is inextricably linked with the pursuit of certain goals, morals, truths or high principles supposedly underlying all knowledge and reality. A study of politics from this approach assumes a speculative character, because the very word 'philosophical' "refers to thoughts about thoughts; a philosophical analysis is an effort to clarify thought about the nature of the subject and about ends and means in studying it. Put more generally, a person who adopts a philosophical approach to a subject aims to enhance linguistic clarity and reduce linguistic confusion; he assumes that the language used in description reflects the conceptions of reality, and he wants to make conceptions of reality as clear, consistent, coherent and helpful as possible. He seeks to influence and guide thinking and the expression of thought so as to maximise the prospect that the selected aspect of reality (politics) will be made intelligible."[19]

It is for this reason that the theorists subscribing to this approach move closer to the world of ethics and look like counselling the rulers as well as the members of an organised community to pursue certain higher ends understandable by our rational faculty. Obviously, the great works of Plato, More, Bacon, Harrington, Rousseau, Kant, Hegel, Green, Bosanquet, Nettleship, Lindsay, Hobhouse, Oakeshott, Leo Strauss, John Rawls and Robert Nozick take the study of politics to a very high level of abstraction, and they also try to mix up the system of values with certain high norms of an ideal social and political order. Of course, normativism dominates, but empiricism (as contained in the works of Aristotle, Machiavelli, Bodin, Hobbes, Locke, Montesquieu, Marx, etc.,) looks like integrating the study of politics either with ethics, or with history, or with psychology, or with law, in an effort to present the model of a best-ordered political community.

---

18. W.T. Bluhm : *Theories of the Political System,* p. 3.
19. V.V. Dyke, *op. cit.,* p. 129.

The study of politics with the use of such an approach converts it into 'political philosophy'. Here an endeavour is made to comprehend reality hidden behind the apparent reality. The objective reality is a concern of the science, the subjective reality is the concern of philosophy. Naturally, political philosophy is deeper than pure science.

The philosophical (ethical or metaphysical) approach is criticised for being speculative and abstract. It is said that it takes us far away from the world of reality. At the hands of Rousseau and Hegel, it culminates in the exaltation of the state to mystical heights. Instead of seeing things as they are, it seeks to examine things in their abstract nature and purpose. The result is that politics becomes incomprehensible to a man of average understanding who may probably find comfort in the study of politics from a historicist or a positivist approach.

The philosophical approach to the study of politics may, however, be appreciated from another angle of vision. It is correct to say that every philosopher tries to seek answers to the questions that arise before him. The conditions of ancient Greece informed Plato and Aristotle to find out philosophical solutions to their contemporary social and political problems. Likewise, the struggle between an obdurate monarchy and the rising middle class of England inspired Hobbes and Locke to find out the legitimate basis of political obligation. In other words, it is correct to say that Machiavelli wrote for a specific 'prince' who could restore the grandeur of the great Roman state, Hobbes discovered a 'leviathan' who could maintain law and order in his country, and Locke imparted a philosophical justification to the supremacy of 'parliament' in England. But the real merit of all these philosophical discourses is that the solutions offered by them may be applied to a similar situation wherever it comes up. "Our distance in time from these philosophers may make us see their work only as philosophy and not as a partisan argument."[20]

Historical Approach: The distinguishing feature of this approach is to throw light on the past or on a selected period of time as well as on a sequence of selected events within a particular phase so as to find out "an explanation of what institutions are, and are tending to be, more in knowledge of what they have been and how they came to be, what they are than in the analysis of them as they stand."[21] It may also be added that here a scholar treats history as a genetic process—as the study of how man got to be, what man once was, and now is." A study of politics with such an approach also informs him to look into the role of individual motives, actions, accomplishments, failures and contingencies in historical continuity and change.[22]

The historical approach stands on the assumption that the stock of political theory comes out of socio-economic crises as well as the reactions they leave on the minds of the great thinkers. It implies that in order to understand political theory, it is equally necessary to understand clearly the time, place and circumstances in which it evolved.

20. Wasby, *op. cit.*, p. 39.
21. Sir Fredrick Pollock : *An Introduction to the History of the Science of Politics,* p. 126.
22. Louis Gottschalk: "A Professor of History in a Quandary" in *The American Political Science Review,* Vol. 59 (January, 1964), p. 279.

It is not at all required that a political theorist may actually take part in the creation of events or in the solution of problems. However, what is necessary is that he must be affected by it and he may try to affect it in any way. Sabine thus affirms that political theories "are secreted in the interstices of political and social crisis. They are produced not indeed by the crisis as such, but by the reactions on minds that have the sensitivity and the intellectual penetration to be aware of crisis. Hence, there is in every political theory a reference to a pretty specific situation, which needs to be grasped in order to understand what the philosopher is thinking about."[23]

It may, however, be added at this stage that the historical approach to burning political questions varies in certain ways depending upon the range of choice that a scholar adopts for his purpose. If Machiavelli could make a perceptible use of history for exalting the achievements of the Romans and thereby exhorting his rulers to restore the glory of the great Roman Empire, Burke and Oakeshott adhere to the historical approach so as to provide a philosophical justification for their conservative impressions. Burke forcefully criticised the philosophy of the French revolution of 1789 and instead eulogised the British political institutions for their stability, the reason for which he could trace in their prescriptive character. Likewise, Oakeshott says: "What we are learning to understand is a political tradition, a concrete manner of behaviour. And for this reason it is proper that, at the academic level, the study of politics should be a historical study."[24]

The historical approach suffers from certain weaknesses. For instance, as James Bryce says, "it is often loaded with superficial resemblances. As such, historical parallels may sometimes be illuminating, but they are also misleading in most of the cases."[25] Likewise, Prof. Ernest Barker holds: "There are many lines—some that suddenly stop, some that turn back, some that cross one another, and one may think rather of the maze of tracks on a wide common than of any broad king's highway."[26] Holding a less favourable view of this approach, Sidgwick maintains that the primary aim of political science is to determine what *ought to be* so far as the constitution and action of government are concerned and this end cannot be discovered by a historical study of the forms and functions of government. In very clear terms he observes: "I do not think that the historical method is one to be primarily used in attempting to find reasoned solutions to the problems of practical politics."[27]

However, the real significance of the historical approach cannot be denied. It has its importance in studying the relevance of the origin and growth of political institutions. Works on political theory like those of G.H. Sabine, R.G. Gettell, C.H. Mcllwain, R.W.

---

23. Sabine: "What is Political Theory?" in Gould and Thursby, *Contemporary Political Thought,* p. 10.
24. Michael Oakeshott: "Political Education" in Peter Laslett (ed.): *Philosophy, Politics and Society* (New York : Macmillan, 1956), p. 12.
25. Lord James Bryce: *Modern Democracies,* Vol. I, p. 16.
26. Barker : *Political Thought in England,* p. 166.
27. Henry Sidgwick : *The Development of European Polity,* p. 5.

Carlyle, A.J. Carlyle, G.E.G. Catlin, W.A. Dunning, T.I. Cook and C.E. Vaughan, for this reason, have an importance of their own. Such an approach has its own usefulness in understanding the meaning of great social and political theorists from Plato and Aristotle in the ancient to Leo Strauss and Lasswell in the present times. If political theory has a universal and respectable character, its reason should be traced in the affirmation that it is rooted in the historical traditions. Studying the growth and survival of political theory in recent times, Watkins confidently opens his paper with these words: "Whether we like it or not, the existence of political theory is a fact. Ever since the beginnings of history, and perhaps even from the days of prehistory, men have been speculating about the nature and justification of political authority. A large mass of written documents survive to record a substantial part of this speculation."[28]

Legal Approach: Here the study of politics is linked with the study of legal or juridical processes and institutions created by the state for maintaining a political organisation. The themes of law and justice are treated not as mere affairs of jurisprudence, rather political theorists look at the state as the maintainer of an effective and equitable system of law and order. Matters relating to the organisation, jurisdiction and independence of judicial institutions, therefore, become an essential concern of a political theorist. Analytical jurists from Cicero in the ancient to Dicey in the present times have regarded state as primarily a corporation or a juridical person and, in this way, viewed politics as a science of legal norms having nothing in common with the science of the state as a social organism. Thus, this approach treats the state primarily as an organisation for the creation and enforcement of law. That is, it describes the constitution and activities of the state in terms of their legal or juristic nature. It "treats organised society, not as a social or a political phenomenon but as a purely juridical regime, an *ensemble* of public law, rights and obligations, founded on a system of pure logic and reason."[29]

In this connection, we may refer to the works of Jean Bodin of the early modern period who propounded the doctrine of sovereignty and of others like Grotius and Hobbes who clarified its premises. In the system of Hobbes the sovereign of the state is the highest law-maker and his command is law that must be obeyed either to avoid punishment following its infraction, or to keep the dreadful state of nature away. The works of Bentham, Austin, Savigny, Sir Henry Maine and A.V. Dicey may be referred to in this connection. The result is that the study of politics is integrally bound up with the legal processes of the country, and the existence of a harmonious state of liberty and equality is earmarked by the glorious name of the 'rule of law'.

Applied to national and international politics, the legal approach stands on the assumption that law prescribes action to be taken in a given situation and also forbids the same in some other situations; it even fixes the limits of permissible action. It also emphasises the fact that where the citizens are law-abiding, the knowledge of

---

28. Fredrick M. Watkins : "Political Theory as a Datum of Political Science" in Ronald Young, (ed.): *Approaches to the Study of Politics,* p. 148.
29. J.W. Garner: *Political Science and Government,* p. 22.

law provides a very important basis for predictions relating to political behaviour of the people. A distinguished student of this approach like Jellinek advises us to treat organised society not as a mere social or political phenomenon but as an ensemble of public law, rights and obligations founded on a system of pure logic or reason. It implies that the state as an organism of growth and development cannot be understood without a consideration of those forces and factors that constitute the domain of law and justice.

It may, however, be pointed out that this approach has a very narrow perspective. Law embraces only one aspect of a people's life and, as such, it cannot cover the entire behaviour of the political man. As the idealists can be criticised for treating state as nothing else but a moral entity, so the analytical jurists commit the mistake of reducing every aspect of a political system to a juridical entity. As Garner says: "The state as an organism of growth and development, however, cannot be understood without a consideration of those extra-legal and extra-social forces which lie at the back of the constitution and which are responsible for many of its actions and reciprocal reactions. Any view which, therefore, conceives the state merely as a public corporation, is as narrow and fruitless as the Hegelian doctrine which goes to the opposite extreme and considers it merely as moral entity."[30]

Institutional Approach: Here a student of politics lays stress on the formal structures of a political organisation like legislature, executive and judiciary. This trend may be discovered in a very large number of political thinkers and theorists from Aristotle and Polybius in the ancient to Laski and Finer in the present times. However, the peculiar thing about modern writers is that they also include party system as the 'fourth state' in the structures of a political system. More important thing in this direction is this that a large number of writers like Bentley, Truman, Key, Jr., Latham, Beer, Eckstein, etc., go a step further by including numerous interest groups that constitute the infrastructure of a political system. Since the emphasis is on the superstructure and infrastructure of a political system, this approach is also known by the name of 'structural approach'.

We may trace this approach in the writings of a very large number of theorists like Walter Bagehot, F.A. Ogg, W.B. Munro, James Bryce, Herman Finer, H.J. Laski, Harold Zink, C.F. Strong, R.G. Neumann, Maurice Duverger, Giovanni Sartori, etc. The striking feature of these works is that the study of politics has covered the formal as well as informal institutional structures of a political system. Moreover, in order to substantiate their conclusions, a comparative study of the major governmental systems of certain advanced countries has also been made. The new trend in this direction is to throw light on the political systems of the Afro-Asian and Latin-American countries (also known by the name of the developing countries of the Third World) where writers like G A. Almond and J.C. Coleman find abundant raw material for the study of politics.

Like other approaches, this approach is also criticised for being too narrow. It ignores the role of the individuals who constitute and operate the formal as well as informal structures and sub-structures of a political system. Another difficulty is that

30. *Ibid.*

the meaning and range of an institutional system varies with the view of a scholar. Those who have conceived governmental institutions, offices and agencies have been inclined to teach and write about government, accordingly; organisation charts being suggestive of much of what they have done. Under this conception, the study of politics becomes, at the extreme, the study of one narrow, specific fact about another. It is also criticised as "a routine description and pedestrian analysis of formal political structures and processes based on the more readily accessible official sources and records."[31]

However, this approach has come to have an importance of its own in an indirect way. It has found its assimilation into the behavioural approach. The structural-functionalists have made an improvement upon it by laying focus on the role of political parties and pressure groups as agencies of interest aggregation and interest articulation respectively. Thus, the study of political processes has been supplemented with the study of political institutions. New terms have been coined or old terms have been given a new version so as to describe political reality in a scientific way as far as possible. The state has its equivalent in a political system; the organs of a government (like legislature, executive and judiciary) have been given the name of formal structures of a political system, while political parties, pressure groups, channels of communication, leadership, elites, factions, etc., have been put into the category of informal or infrastructure of a political system. Moreover, the role of these infrastructural agencies in the decision-making process of formal institutions of a government and the continuation of this chain due to the role of the feedback mechanism has led new theorists to formulate the input-output approach. Viewed thus, we may come to point out that the structural-functional and input-output approaches of a political system (as devised by Easton and Almond) are an extension of, or an improvement upon, the institutional approach.

Modern Approaches and Methods

From the above, it is evident that the study of politics, in the context of philosophical-ethical, institutional-structural, historical and legal-juridical approaches cannot assign to it the character of, what the behaviouralists call, a 'pure science'. Their contention is that normativism should be replaced by empiricism to the best possible extent. It may, however, be reiterated, at this stage that modern approaches have their roots in the traditional approaches. The distinction between the two is that while the former are mainly value-laden, the latter are fact-laden. In other words, it implies that while normativism dominates the former, empiricism dominates the latter. It may also be said in this connection that what really characterises modern approaches is their 'scientific' nature and 'revolutionary' expression. These are marked by empirical investigation of the relevant data and have arisen from the realisation that "a search for fuller integration was not thought of or even hinted at by the political scientists belonging to the old order and, for this reason, the positivism of this science was not dreamt as posing a challenge to the already age-worn methods of study and approach."[32]

31. Albert Somit and Joseph Tanenhaus: *The Development of American Political Science: From Burgess to Behaviouralism*, p. 70.
32. Frank Thakurdas: "The Expanding Frontiers of Political Sceince" in the *Indian Journal of Political Science,* Vol. XXXIV, No. 4, 1973, p. 420.

Sociological Approach: Ever since Comte of France and Spencer of England made their contributions to the discipline of sociology, political theorists have realised the relevance of sociological approach to the study of politics. In contemporary times it has witnessed remarkable development in the United States where R.M. Maclver, David Easton and G.A. Almond have taken into their recognition this essential point that ample data is available in the realm of sociology with the help of which empirical rules of political behaviour can be laid down. A leading German sociologist (Max Weber) has treated sociology as the basis of politics and Easton has managed to develop certain theories of the political system on the basis of the Weberian formulations as reinterpreted and redevised by Talcott Parsons and Robert Merton. As a result of this, a new discipline, known by the name of 'political sociology', has come up.

This approach emphasises that social context is necessary for the understanding and explanation of political behaviour of the members of a community. It is the social whole in which we may find individuals having their status and playing their role that is determined by certain traits and that are transmitted from one generation to another with necessary modifications. It is called 'political socialisation'. Its objective manifestation is the 'political culture' of the people that shows their commitments to and convictions in certain political values as those of liberty, equality, rights, justice, democracy, rule of law and the like. The political system of every country is influenced by the political culture of its people. For instance, a bloody revolution aiming at the total change of social and political institutions is not possible in a country like England because of the conservative nature of the people. Democracy has been a failure in most of the Asian and African countries for the reason its values do not find coherence with the tenets of the political culture of the people.

It is, therefore, obvious that this approach considers the state primarily as a social organism, whose component parts are individuals and seeks to deduce its qualities and attributes from the qualities and attributes of the men composing it.[33] "Society should be treated as the basis of political as of all other sciences; it is a network of numerous associations and groups which play their own part in the operation of the politics of a country. Factors like kinship, racialism, tribalism, religion, caste, linguistic affinity and the like, form part of the study of sociology, but their role in the political process of a country cannot be ignored in an empirical study of a political system. The law of the state is binding either because of the force of some 'myth' working in the background or because of the fear of punishment entailing from its infraction. The structuralists, therefore, advise us to study the social system of a people before understanding and explaining the political reality of a country.

The sociological approach is appreciated for being comprehensive. Since it studies society in all its aspects and then seeks to link politics with those sociological forces, it cannot be criticised for being narrow like other approaches discussed earlier. The only fear is that by laying so much emphasis on the role and usefulness of sociology, it goes to the extent of playing with the autonomy of the discipline of political science.

33. Garner, *op. cit.,* p. 20.

It may be feared that such a study may convert politics into a handmaid of sociology. The problem of the relative autonomy of the discipline is, therefore, raised. The new advocates of this approach dismiss such apprehensions and instead contend that the theories of great sociologists (like Emile Durkheim, Malinowski, Shils, Eisenstadt, Parsons and Merton) provide useful tools and materials with the help of which we may take the study of politics to the level of a 'science'. If the purpose of politics is to deal with 'conflicts', as J.D.B. Miller says, sociology helps us to know the causes of such tensions and their possible solutions.

Psychological Approach: Political Science has moved very close to the discipline of psychology in modern times at the hands of Graham Wallas, Charles Merriam, Harold Lasswell, Robert Dahl, Eric Fromm, etc. In early modern times, Machiavelli and Hobbes had stressed the point of security of life and material possessions as a motivating force and held that the desire for it was inseparable from the desire for power. Recently a good number of political theorists have borrowed material from the writings of eminent psychologists like Freud, Jung, Eyesenck and McDougall so as to lay down certain valid rules of political behaviour. A study of politics is, therefore, made by these writers in a way so as to deal with the role of emotions, habits, sentiments, instincts, ego, etc., that constitute essential elements of human personality.

The writers subscribing to this approach try to study and explain social and political institutions and phenomena through psychological laws. To them politics, whether national or international, is structured. If one knows as to how it is structured, then it is possible to locate gaps in one's knowledge or missing pieces. For this sake, they take the help of Freud who developed a set of rules describing the structure of personality. By doing so he located the boundaries of knowledge in such a way as to project new knowledge; something must be going on just beyond what we know. Structuralism frames this potentiality in terms of *functions*. While Freud gave the names *ego, id* and *super-ego* to psychological functions, political functionalists have used other names instead like information, communication and aggregation.

The tools of psychoanalysis can be made use of in the study of politics. Thus, Lasswell has sought to apply Freudian psychology to the study of political behaviour. According to him, the psychoanalysis of political leaders reveals significant knowledge about politics. It tells us as to why some leaders are conservative and others are radical, or why some politicians are agitators and others like to be administrators. The significance of political opinions is not to be grasped apart from the private motives which they symbolise. Since political movements derive their vitality from the displacement of private effects upon public objects and since primitive psychological structures, in more or less disguised form, control individual thought and effort, we can discover significant knowledge about political beliefs and behaviour through the use of psychoanalysis. As this fact becomes increasingly accepted, the social psychiatrists will replace the social philosopher and the politics of the future will be more 'preventive' in character.[34]

34. J.H. Hallowell: *Main Currents in Modern Political Thought,* p. 532.

By way of criticism, it may be said that this approach is partially correct. It is right in enabling us to study politics with the help of psychological tools, but it cannot be treated as a comprehensive approach in view of the fact that it does not take into account some other essential elements covered by the approaches discussed earlier. That is, the role of sociological, legal, and economic factors cannot be ignored entirely in an empirical study of politics. It may also be said that this approach seeks to accommodate normativism in empirical political theory in its own way by throwing light on the role of 'belief system' in the operation of the political system of a country. As Apter says: "In political science terms, the structuralist is interested in belief systems not simply as a distribution of public opinions, but as a way of ordering the world according to the principles of equity, or moral right and wrong. One aspect of structuralism is that it restores the normative, or moral side of reciprocity and obligation. In this it resembles political philosophy."[35]

Economic Approach: Matters relating to the production and distribution of goods have an economic character. But as their regulation is done by the state, they are very much involved in the process of politics. The prominent schools of liberalism, socialism and communism emerged because of the divergent interpretations of the role of state in regulating economic matters. Eminent political theorists like Mill, Marx, Mitchell, Schumpeter, Friedman and a host of others have written volumes having a relevance of their own in the domain of political economy. However, in this regard the most outstanding name is that of Karl Marx who has built his political theory on the basis of the criticism of the prevailing capitalist system. It is contained in his well-known assumption: "The mode of production of the material means of existence conditions the whole process of social, political and intellectual life."[36]

Economic affairs are inextricably involved in the political process when we find that the public issues in connection with which political actors pursue conflicting desires, are parts of their economic activity. Thus, those adopting an economic approach to politics feel particularly inclined to raise questions about interrelationships of the economic and the political life of human beings. "Out of all the varied activities of the government, they will be inclined to examine particularly those pertaining to economic relationships, *e.g.,* monetary and tax policies, legislation concerning relationships between management and labour, relative roles of governmental personnel and private persons in making crucial decisions. Further, out of the various factors that motivate the behaviour of persons and groups and that provide a basis for explaining and predicting that behaviour, those taking an economic approach will be inclined to examine the desire for wealth—for control over the production and distribution of the comforts and luxuries of life."[37]

Thinkers like Machiavelli and Hobbes treat man as a selfish creature. Economists interpret the same thing in terms of man's *interests.* Man has certain interests and he

35. David Apter, *An Introduction to Political Analysis,* p. 380.
36. Alexander Gray: *The Socialist Tradition,* p. 303.
37. V.V. Dyke, *op. cit.,* pp. 123-24.

wants to protect as well as promote them. For this he forms groups and associations. The result is that every society has a number of conflicting interests and the people form associations for the sake of their protection and promotion. It creates stuff for the study of organised groups in a political community. Obviously, the interest or interest-group conception of politics is closely associated with an economic approach. "Those who take an economic approach are likely to seek to relate economic interests to all major public policies and events, wondering, for example, whether the American armament programme may not be designed as much to keep the economy operating at a high level as to promote security and peace. And they are likely to take the view that coherence within political parties and struggle among them reflect common and conflicting economic concerns. An economic approach frequently takes on a psychological colour, for it is frequently based on an assumption about human motivation: that people commonly act in such a way as to promote their own economic gain."[38]

Although economic problem-solving is still dominated by piecemeal and incrementalist schemes, econometric techniques have long been used to determine linear cause and effect relationships. However, these techniques tend to be restricted to mechanistic systems which do not account for the processes of change and lose touch with such reality. In recent years, computer simulation has begun to supplant many of the econometric techniques. Game theory has generated mathematical explanations of strategies, especially for marketing and advertising in business firms. It has had an impact on economics, and it has been widely used in political science analyses of international confrontations and electoral strategies. In fact, game theory has been used extensively by political scientists in the testing and implementation of rational choice theory, which assumes that the structural constraints of society do not necessarily determine the actions of individuals and that individuals tend to choose actions that bring them the best results. Cooperative and competitive relations in one's bargaining with best allies and opponents are emphasised by the political scientist "in a fashion modelled after the economist's attention to exchange, especially through competitive market systems."[39]

Behavioural Approach: Modern empirical approaches have found their best manifestation in the trend of behaviouralism where a host of leading American writers have laid emphasis on the collection and examination of 'facts' relating to the actual or observable behaviour of man as a social and political being. This approach has emerged on the scene in the midst of a large amount of turmoil and controversy within the profession widely lauded by its protagonists as a 'revolution' in the realm of political science. E. Kirkpatrick, the then Executive Director of the American Political Science Association, explained its meaning thus: "Between World War II and the midfifties the term 'political behaviour' represents both an approach and a challenge, an orientation and a reform movement, a type of research and a rallying cry, a 'hurrah' term and a 'boo' term. Debate about the behavioural techniques and methods was often accompanied by

38. *Ibid.,* p. 124.
39. R.H. Chilcote : *Theories of Comparative Politics,* p. 57.

vituperations, discussions were more often aimed at vanquishing adversaries than at clarifying issues."[40]

The credit for popularising the behavioural approach, or approaches, is ascribed to the Ford Foundation of the United States. With a view to make social sciences useful to the task of human welfare, it set up a committee that recommended the use of interdisciplinary focus to understand and explain political reality. It suggested five important 'programme areas'—establishing peace, strengthening economy, stabilising democracy, providing education in a democratic order, and understanding properly human behaviour and relations. It attracted wide attention in the period following World War II, since it emphasised the need for a scientific approach to the study of human behaviour. A new trend was thus set in, whose ardent advocates rejected the study of formal political institutions or structures as the basic unit of research and instead, advised us to study the behaviour of the individuals in political situations. As a result, this new approach is concerned with acts, attitudes, preferences and expectations of men in political contexts.

The 'newness' of the behavioural approach may be said to lie in its four broad goals that may be put as under:[41]

1. The behaviouralists, first of all, want to explore a new kind of data that has not been attended hitherto. They want to study politics by focusing attention on the individual and group behaviour and also what goes on in the political process and within political institutions.
2. They advocate a new method. They insist upon survey research and the application of statistics to the data observed and other field work exercises.
3. They invent many interpretative categories largely borrowed from the social sciences, particularly sociology, and even to a certain extent from natural sciences. These concepts like elite, role, influence, decision-making, policy-making, systems, sub-systems, structures and functioning of structures, political culture etc., have all passed into very wide currency in the political literature of our times. These concepts are the essence of contemporary empirical political theory and are related to the type of question which the theorist has in mind.
4. Neo-empiricists are concerned with drawing generalisations from the data collected and also constructing models through which interpretation of the political process could be made with scientific accuracy. All this was done with a view to establish a science of politics; to infuse a new spirit in the study of the subject and to make the approach as realistic (scientific) and precise as possible so that it could be almost parallel to the natural sciences.

---

40. Kirkpatrick: "The Impact of Behavioural Approach on Traditional Political Science" in Austin Ranney (ed.): *Essays on the Behavioural Study of Politics,* p. 11.
41. Heinz Eulau, S.J. Eldersveld and M. Janowitz (ed. s): *Political Behaviour. A Reader in Theory and Research,* pp. 3-4.

It is true that as a result of the utilisation of the behavioural approach, the scope of political science has widened, and the nature of this discipline has improved in understanding and explaining political reality. However, it may be criticised on these grounds:

1. It is based upon a false theory of knowledge. It takes facts alone as real. On the contrary, universal norms are as real as facts and facts can have meaning only in connection with the universal values.
2. It is based on a false conception of scientific method. Even after collecting facts and doing their measurement and quantification, the writer cannot free himself from the limitations of subjectivity or his own sense of value-judgements while making some observations on their basis. Thus, fixity and finiteness of a natural science cannot be infused in the discipline of a social science.
3. It circumscribes the scope of political science by advising us to study only those aspects of political life that are amenable to measurement and quantification. In this way, the significance of speculative political theory is sacrificed at the altar of 'a dry, barren and mad craze of scientism'.
4. It lacks orientation regarding all political matters. It has no protection whatsoever except by recourse to commonsense against losing itself in the study of irrelevances.
5. It makes political science a handmaid of sociology by laying down that all political activities and institutions reflect the nature of society and are determined and patterned to a large extent by divisions within society.
6. It is unmindful of the chief difficulty confronting social sciences in general — the large number of variable factors, which make control and finding difficult, but also unlike the natural sciences, there is no agreement yet between either methods to be adopted or procedures to be followed, which has resulted in a large variety of empirical research studies, whose techniques vary considerably allowing for considerable differences.
7. Above all, normativism cannot be discarded from the study of politics in entirety. Facts make sense only when there is an ideological conceptual framework. Mere facts without such a framework would become incoherent data. The very collection of data itself requires a value framework. In other words, without a value framework, it is impossible to ferret, search out and collect facts.[42]

No doubt, the behavioural approach has its own strong and weak points. It has widened the horizons of the study of politics by taking resort to the interdisciplinary focus. At the same time, it has done a sort of disservice to the subject of political science by sticking to the side of facts and thereby discarding the place of norms, goals and values. A balanced evaluation of this approach is contained in these words: "Whether

---

42. See R.A. Dahl: "The Behavioural Approach in Political Science: Epitaph for a Monument to a Successful Protest" in *American Political Science Review* (December, 1961), pp. 763-72.

they (behaviouralists) succeeded or failed in clarifying or understanding is a matter of individual judgement, but it could be said in fairness with the new perspectives that some of the interpretative categories and empirical studies have thrown a flood of light on many problems and processes of politics which the older theories were either not able to explain or explained inadequately. In this respect, their work has been illuminating even if their final objective of providing an overall theoretical edifice of universal validity has not been achieved, or if at all is highly controversial."[43]

Neo-Institutional Approach: "Neo-Institutionalism combines older institutionalist concerns with developmentalism."[44] State is no longer a police institution, it is concerned with the welfare and development of the people. So, it is a social welfare and a democractic organisation. Dahl, Rokkan, Dogan, Benedix, Inkeles and Apter are its main advocates who lay stress on their concern with 'transitions' to democracy. They touch many new issues such as termination of authoritarianism and its replacement by a liberal-democratic order, link between industrial capitalism and parliamentary democracy, and the nature of a pluralist society. The operation of party system and voting behaviour of the people are other areas of their concern. They think about the prospects and possibilities of 'consociationalism' with its emphasis on how to establish viable democratic institutions in the face of deep-seated social cleavages.

Neo-institutionalism is less constitutional than its older form. It is more prone to economic analysis in so far as it deals with fiscal and monetary policy, banks, markets and globalisation. It is also concerned with locating changes in the legislative and administrative processes, shifts in long established party politics, working of coalitions, etc., as these impinge on the state. Like its old form, it is concerned with the state as an instrumentality in its own right, with its own tendencies and needs, and as a configuring power, how it determines the nature of civil society. "In general, one can say that new institutionalism is more connected to social and political theory and less to political philosophy, than its predecessor, and also more engaged in political economy."[45]

Marxist Approach: In this direction, the Marxist approach has a place of its own that may be regarded as basically different from both traditional and modern approaches in several important respects, though we may also discover certain points of resembance with both. The astonishing feature of this approach is that here the 'state', being the central theme of political science, is conceived as an inevitable consequence of class contradictions. As such, the system of Marxian dialectics culminates in the justification of a stateless condition of social life that would come into being as the final stage of social development. Moreover, economics dominates the scene so much so that all other disciplines like history, sociology, psychology and ethics become its offshoots. Politics is integrally connected with the basic economic structure finding its manifestation in the forces and relations of production. Thus, it is stressed that in the

43. Frank Thakurdas, *op. cit.,* p. 9.
44. David Apter: "Comparative Politics: Old and New" in R.E. Goodin and Hans-Dieter Klingemann (eds.): *A New Handbook of Political Science,* p. 386.
45. *Ibid.,* p. 389.

real world "economic and political forces and factors are constantly interacting and are extremely hard to disentangle one from the other."[46]

The significance of the Marxist approach is traceable in the fact that its utilisation calls for a deeper scrutiny of the meaning and nature of politics. Instead of keeping the focus of study confined to the formal structures and sub-structures of a political system, it lays emphasis on going to the roots. Thus, it holds that the economic system determines the class structure and as there is a change in the means of production, so there is a corresponding change in the relations of the free men and the slaves, the feudal lords and the serfs, the capitalists and the workers—the dominant and the dominated classes. Struggle for power constituting the bedrock of politics should, therefore, be studied in the context of the conflict between two antagonistic classes. This state of contradictions can end only in the establishment of a socialist society. Obviously, this approach not only lays stress on the fact of social contraditions, it also finds out the way of their reconciliation. In this way, it assumes a deterministic character.

If so, the Marxist approach becomes like an ideology. It stands on a particular set of propositions that are not open to question and that call for a concerted action for the sake of their realisation and implementation so as to change the world and not merely interpret it. It not only exposes the inherent weaknesses and defects of the existing capitalist system, it also informs the exploited and the oppressed class of the workers, peasants and toilers to unite so as to break the chains of slavery and win the whole world. Thus, it treats the state as an instrument of exploitation and oppression by one class over another and lays down that class character of the state cannot come to an end until the classless society is culminated in the stateless condition of life signifying complete emancipation of man.

As given by Marx and his collaborator (Engels) and developed by Lenin, this approach claims itself to be both scientific and progressive. It rejects the present system as oppressive, exploitative and inequitable and instead, desires a new setup in which exploitation and oppression are replaced by the glorious virtues of harmony and cooperation. Politics is treated as a manifestation of class antagonisms and its end is conceived in the culmination of social development when the phase of class identification and resolution of conflicts would unleash glorious human values. Thus, this approach, that has been empirical so far, assumes a normative character in the end. In short, the whole approach "looks like a theory which *qua* theory provides a broad-based vision of society in all stages of development; at its base lies the fundamental importance of production, and from there the economic substructure of society and the crucial role of the class."[47]

---

46. S. Strange: "The Study of Trans-National Relations" in *International Affairs* (London), July, 1952, No 3, 337.
47. Tony Throndike: "The Revolutionary Approach: The Marxist Perspective" in Trevor Taylor (ed.): *Approaches and Theory in International Relations,* pp. 61-62.

An English writer mentions these critical points against the Marxist approach to the study of politics:[48]

1. It pays very little and superficial attention to psychological analysis. This, sometimes, seems to be claimed as a virtue, and it is argued that the so-called 'objective' factors are of more importance than what is going on in individual human minds. But, in fact, institutions and the like are just as much psychological facts as are impulses and desires. They are really, if fully analysed, just sets of acquired habits, and habits have no existence outside human beings.
2. The economic structure of any society is not something fixed and unalterable, nor is it something that we simply have to accept as a given fact.
3. Further Marxist deductions are equally lacking in cogency. They seem to consist of taking certain influences or tendencies which are observable at certain limits and showing what would happen if they were developed to their logical extremes and no counter-influences arose to check or modify them. It is only one among many influences and the extent of it varies enormously from country to country and from time to time.
4. The prophecy that the division into two classes will become harder and sharper and that the differences in wealth and status will continually increase has been falsified by events.

The paramount weakness of the Marxist approach may be traced in its rigid and deterministic character. By treating economic factors as 'decisive', it discards the place of other factors of non-economic character (like religion, morality, emotions, patriotism, etc.) whose role in the politics of a country has its own significance that should not altogether be lost sight of by a student of empirical political theory. Moreover, its deterministic character renders to it the character of an ideology that blinds its subscriber to comprehend social and political reality in a detached manner. However, the merit of this approach lies in the fact that it seeks to study and explain political reality in realistic terms, though in its own way. It exposes the hollowness of the present bourgeois system that perpetrates social and economic evils for its vested interest. We may take note of the fact that "many of the predictions that Marx, Engels and Lenin made have come true compelling us to study the framework of analysis which Marx has left behind."[49]

Some Other Modern Approaches and Theories

In the later part of the twentieth century, some new approaches and theories came into currency which may be included in the category of mainstream empirical formulations. Their foundations are quite old that may be traced in the assumptions of Machiavelli, Hobbes, Montesquieu, Bentham and Marx, but the superstructures have a modern look reinforced by the trend of behaviouralism and interdisciplinary focus. Once again, it

---

48. G.C. Field: *Political Theory,* pp. 258-61.
49. Frank Thakurdas, *op. cit.,* p. 47.

appears that such theorists have sought to push traditional approaches and theories aside in certain factual contexts or perspectives with the help or use of 'discourses' about preference or choice of the analytical frameworks or designs.

Rational Choice Approach: Known by various names as public choice theory, social choice theory, game theory, formal political theory, spatial model political behavioural theory, institutional public choice theory and preferential behaviour theory, this theory (popularly known as rational choice theory) has come to have a significant place in political science since the 1950s at the hands of economists like Buchanan and Downs and political scientists like Olson and Riker. Having its source in the conceptions of economics and mathematics, it provides insights into the actions of the traders, consumers, voters, lobbyists, bureaucrats, players and politicians. A mathematician may solve the puzzles of individual behaviour of the players involved in a game,[50] or the dilemma of two prisoners[51] may make us conclude that rationally self-interested behaviour can be generally less beneficial than cooperation.[52]

Faint reflections of this approach may be traced in the assumptions of Hobbes and Bentham who consider individuals as utterly selfish creatures, always seeking fulfilment of ends that would give them anything like felicity or happiness. However, associated in particular with the Virginia School of the United States, it became very popular in the economic sphere. It draws heavily upon the examples of economic theory in building models based on procedural rules usually about the rationally self-interested behaviour of the individuals. James Buchanan, in his *Fiscal Theory and Political Economy* (1960), applies it to the economic sphere for the sake of defending free market and arguing in favour of a minimal state in spite of his admission that many interest groups manage to reap benefits at the expense of the interest of the community as a whole. Anthony Downs in his *An Economic Theory of Democracy* (1957) develops

---

50. Game theory deals with rationalist choice where there is strategic interdependence. As a sub-field of rational choice theory, it had its development when the economists asked whether any satisfactory or broadly democratic way could be found out for segregating the preference of individual citizens to arrive at the social ranking of the alternatives.
51. The 'prisoners' dilemma' is the study of two prisoners, each being interrogated separately for an alleged crime. The interrogator tells each prisoner that if one of them confesses and the other one does not, the one who confesses will be acquitted and the one who keeps silent will get a long term of imprisonment. If both confess, both will get somewhat reduced prison terms. If neither confesses, both will receive short prison terms based on lack of evidence. What is the solution to the dilemma of the prisoners? Both prisoners will confess, and thus each will serve a longer sentence than if they had cooperated and kept silent. Why did cooperation fail to occur? Each prisoner is faced with a one-time choice. Neither prisoner knows how the other will respond; the cost of not confessing if the other confesses is extraordinarily high. So both will confess, leading to a less than optimal outcome. But if the game is repeated, the possibility of reciprocity makes it rational to cooperate. Had the two prisoners cooperated with each other by remaining silent, then the outcomes would have been much better for both. It was actually in the self-interest of each to cooperate. Karen Mingst: *Essentials of International Relations,* pp. 68-69.
52. Andrew Heywood: *Political Theory: An Introduction,* p. 246.

a theory of democracy based on the assumptions of economics. It presupposes a policy space in which voters, candidates and political actors of all sorts can measure where they stand in relation to other political actors in competition with each other. The case of party politics naturally figures in, because the role of political parties is very crucial in determining the behaviour of the individuals.[53]

Mancur Olson is a political scientist whose work *The Logic of Collective Action* (1968) analyses the behaviour of many interest groups. Individuals form and join interest groups to secure public goods. As the indiviuals become free riders by reaping the benefits of group action without incurring the cost of membership, there is no guarantee that the existence of a common interest will lead to the formation of an organisation to advance or defend that interest. He questions pluralist assumptions about the distribution of group power and suggests that strong networks of interest groups can threaten a nation's performance. W.H. Riker applies it to the study of political coalitions and finds the source of the merit of democratic system here. In his *Liberalism Against Populism,* he says: "Democracy is the implementation of the popular will, represented by a social preference ranking." Like others, he defends the case of a minimal state and cautions that "the innovations of the democratic governments to repair market failures often creates more problems than it solves."[54]

Rational choice as a positive approach to political explanations is based on the following assumptions:

1. There are important forms of political behaviour that are the results of the choices made with a view to the efficient achievements of given ends.
2. Individuals are essentially self-interested, but the concept of self-interest is potentially extremely elastic.
3. All individuals have the rational capacity, time and emotional detachment necessary to choose the best course of action, no matter how complex be the choice.
4. Its object is strategy equilibrium.

This theory or approach may be criticised for laying too much stress on the rationality of the individual. A political psychologist like Graham Wallas may argue that most of the actions of man are irrational, than being rational. It is a fact that human beings are psychologically complex. They frequently act irrationally; they operate within many systems which cannot be easily comprehended fully when seen from a rational choice perspective. In proceeding from an abstract model of the individual, it "pays insufficient attention to social and historical factors, failing to recognise, among other things, that human self-interestedness may be socially conditioned, and not innate."[55]

53. *Ibid.,* p. 247.
54. Hugh Ward: "Rational Choice Theory" in David Marsh and Gerry Stoker (eds.): *Theory and Methods in Political Science,* p. 79.
55. Heywood, *op. cit.,* p. 247.

Discourse Theory: The concept of discourse includes all types of social and political processes, institutions and organisations within its frame of reference. Hence, discourse theory draws inspiration from interpretative sciences such as hermeneutics, phenomenology, structuralism and deconstructivism. For instance, Michael Foucault in his *The Archeology of Knowledge* (1972) endeavours to use discursive formations which refer to a regular set of ideas and concepts and which claim to produce knowledge about the world. In his historical accounts of scientific discourses, he endeavours to sketch out their underlying discursive regularities and connects their production and transformation to the broader social and political processes of which they are a part. In his case, discourses are a form of power in that they set up antagonisms and structure relations between people who are defined as subjects and objects, as insiders and outsiders. Ernst Laclau and Chantal Mouffe have developed a concept of discourse that is concerned specifically with the analysis of political processes. They have attempted to deepen the Marxist category of ideology by utilising the insights of 'post-modernist' philosophy and theory.

This theory constitutes a relatively new approach to political analysis, although it has its strong roots in the past theoretical traditions and perspectives. Drawing on and extending the approaches of the Marxist theorists like Gramsci of Italy and Althusser of France, and while taking on broad issues and assumptions put forward by the political modernist theorists, it "examines the logics and structures of discursive articulation."[56]

The term 'discourse', as used here, implies "human interaction, especially communication, that may disclose or illustrate power-relationships."[57] Thus, discourse theory analyses all the practices and meanings shaping a particular community of social actors. It assumes that all objects and actions are meaningful and that their meaning is the product of historically-specific systems of rulers. "Discourse analysis refers to the analysis of linguistic and non-linguistic material as texts that enable subjects to experience the world of objects, words and practices."[58] The overall aim of social and political analysis from a discursive perspective is to describe, understand, interpret, and evaluate carefully constructed objects of investigation. Hence, instead of applying theory mechanically to empirical objects, or testing theories against empirical reality, discourse theories argue for the articulation and modification of concepts and logics in each particular research context."[59]

---

56. David Howarth: "Discourse Theory" in Marsh and Stoker, *op. cit.,* p. 132.
57. Andrew Heywood: *Politics* (Houndmills, Basingstoke: Palgrave Foundations, 2005), p. 17.
58. Howarth, *op. cit.,* p. 10.
59. R.A.W. Rhodes: "Old Institutionalisms" in R.E. Goodin (ed.): *The Oxford Handbook of Political Science,* p. 150.

Contextual Approach: In a certain sense, this approach may be taken as an extension or elaboration of the discourse theory.[60] Adopted by many theorists and analysts like Butler, Stokes, Marsh, Ward, Miller and Sanders, it contends that the individuals must be correctly assigned to the context of time, place and environment. Despite certain difficulties, contextual models are important, because there is a clear evidence that the same persons behave differently at different times and in different places and circumstances. Political behaviour is very much a matter of individual response to an environment that includes family, friends, neighbours, workplace associates, state of the economy and the like.

It may be pointed out here that a completely comprehensive account of all contexts is neither desirable nor possible. Contextual accounts typically work by helping the analyst to get a grip on some puzzling phenomenon. To understand how social power is exercised, one needs to understand both technology of ideas or strategy. To understand why certain social forms are widely acceptable in one time and place but not another, one may need to understand differing social ontologies.

As contextual analysis does not require a complete and comprehensive account of all contexts to be used as correctives for the purpose of the analysts, it differs fundamentally from the search for general laws. The analysts may prefer commonsense division of the contextual areas as under:[61]

1. **Philosophy:** As so many disputes and confusions in political science actually pivot on epistemology, ontology, logic and general conceptions of argument, so philosophy demands its place at the contextual table.
2. **Psychology:** Political analysts may employ conceptions of political psychology to make serious reflections on relations between individual psychological processes and the collective phenomena.
3. **Ideas:** Political analysts may attribute importance to ideas about liberty, equality, justice, democracy and social order. Contextual analysis helps them see how to take ideas into account as contexts for the understanding of political processes, evidence available for empirical examination of the political processes, and influences on or components of the processes themselves.
4. **Culture:** Culturally embedded ideas, relations and practices profoundly affect the operation of superficially similar political processes. Even within the same politics, analysts sometimes object that linguistic, ethnic, religious, and regional cultures differ so dramatically that all efforts to direct general political principles in those polities must fail.
5. **History:** In all three types of contextual effects on analysts' understanding of political processes, on the evidence available for empirical examination of political

60. "At the heart of the approach is an analogy with language. Just as we understand the meaning of a word from its context, so we understand a political institution as sedimented beliefs within a particular discourse." Rhodes, *op. cit.*, pp. 150-51.
61. *Ibid.*, pp. 453-55.

processes, and on the processes themselves, history figures significantly. The knowledge of historical context provides a means of producing more systematic knowledge of the political processes.

6. **Place:** In some definitions, history as location in space and time exhausts the influence of place. Yet geographically attuned political analysis detect effects of adjacency, distance, environment, and climate that easily escape historians who deal with the same time and places.
7. **Population:** The demographic tools can advance political analysis. The discipline of demography does, indeed, offer a number of formal techniques such as life tables and migrant stream analyses that bear directly on political processes and suggest valuable analogies for political analysis.
8. **Technology:** In contemporary political analysis, technology often appears as a black box, a demonic force, or an exogeneous variable that somehow affects politics, but does not belong to politics as such.

Such a view is hard to sustain, however, when the subject is war or economic imperialism. In fact, technologies of communication, production, distribution, organisation and of rule pervade political processes, and receive insufficient attention for their specific properties.

Like the two other modern approaches or theories discussed earlier, this theory may be subjected to attack. A pertinent question arises as to how a researcher or a theorist may cover all possible or available contexts in the presentation of his analysis or in the formulation of his theories. He has to adopt the strategy of 'pick and choose'. That is, he may take some and ignore some other contexts as a result of which his conclusions may not be thoroughly empirical.

Empirical approaches or theories dominated the scene in the period following the Second World War in the form of behavioural, positivist and neo-positivist trends. The trend of empiricism, however, saw its decline after 1970 when the trend of normativism had its resurgence. What was lauded by the empiricists in the recent past was denounced by the normativists in the last phase of the twentieth century as is evident from Ada Finifter's *Political Science: State of the Discipline* (1983) and David Ricci's *The Tragedy of Political Science* (1984). "Among contemporary political scientists, there is prevailing, perhaps, predominant view of the history of the discipline that we are now in a post-positivist, post-scientific, post-behavioural stage."[62]

Concluding Observations

A detailed study of the major traditional and modern approaches, as contained in the preceding sections, leaves following important impressions:

1. While several approaches to the study of politics may be broadly grouped into two categories—traditional and modern—a sort of overlapping cannot be lost sight of.

---

62. R.E. Goodin and Hans-Dieter Klingemann (eds.) *A New Handbook of Political Science*, p. 81.

It is a different matter that we treat the former as loaded with normativism and the latter with empiricism. The fact stands out that empiricism is available in the traditional approaches of great political theorists from Aristotle and Polybius in the ancient to A. de Tocqueville and James Bryce in the modern ages. Similarly, normativism has not been discarded by the most prominent figures subscribing to modern approaches. Even Marxism has a normative orientation in the end when it conceives of an era of emancipated humanity wedded to the observance of glorious human values. Thus, it may be asserted that the label of traditionalism is neither a criticism nor a refutation of the patent fact that norms still play an important role in modern political studies, although no longer monopolising the avenues of approach. It also follows that several approaches to the study of politics should not be treated as mutually exclusive. Most of them are interrelated in some respects.

2. Every approach, or method, or methodology has its own use and value. Even the rationalistic, deductive, *a priori* method provides hypotheses and frames of reference which can readily be discarded if and when scientific method proves them wrong. The historical and philosophical methods have their advocates even now. The legalistic-juristic approach to the state, closely linked with political theory, is still vital. The empirical and scientific methods have helped to replace dogma with fact, despite the lack of sufficiently precise standards of measurement.
3. It is good that the study of politics, as desired by the behaviouralists and the Marxists, should be made on scientific lines as far as possible. But it should also be remembered that scientific method has its own limitations. It cannot be applied to political science in a way it is done in the field of natural sciences.
4. On the whole, traditional and modern approaches have a relevance of their own in the study of political phenomena. The purpose is to understand and explain political reality and, as such, it should not be tried to achieve it in a way that the conclusions become thoroughly abstract or too mechanistic and not at all applicable to the life of a living and dynamic people. It is permissible to doubt the all-embracing sufficiency of a single approach which is presumed to solve all the myriad questions presented by the state and its politics. Many 'moderns' who smile tolerantly at the idealism of the Greek, Stoic, and medieval Catholic philosophers and as such 'naive' notions as those of 'natural law' and 'natural rights' ('excogitated ideas', impossible to substantiate or prove) are themselves easily hypnotised by a new 'scientific explanation, especially if replete with tables of statistics. It is well to remind ourselves that man is a complex as well as a perverse creature and that we are still far from having all the answers which will explain even the political phases of his behaviour, let alone the whole man.

A student of this subject should, therefore, be guided by two important considerations. First, the way of eclecticism is desirable. That is, he may borrow from different approaches and mix them up in his study of politics in view of the fact that no approach can serve his purpose in an exclusive manner. Second, the object of a researcher should be to give due importance to both facts and values so as to develop theories applicable to all questions concerning the explanation, and also prediction, to the possible extent, of events having their connection with the political reality of a place. This should be done with a sense of humility and this is sure to lead to the growth and development of this discipline.

2
Sovereignty

Sovereignty is an essential attribute of the state. It is the only element that disinguishes state from any other association like a family or a school, or from a whole set of associations and relations like a society or a nation. It finds its place in the supremacy of the will and power of the state.[1] We may take note of the fact that "in every fully independent state there is some person, assembly or group (*e.g.,* the electorate) who or which has the supreme power of formulating in terms of law, and of executing the collective will; that is, the final power to command and enforce obedience to its authority. Other associations have collective wills, and may formulate opinions, but it is the peculiar characteristic of the state that its will alone dominates and over-rides in the event of conflict with other wills, whether of persons or of associations. To it all other wills are potentially subject. The will of the state, once declared represents the last word regarding the matter upon which it has made a decision."[2]

Meaning: Sovereignty is a concept of modern political theory. The Greeks had no idea of this term. We may take note of the fact that Aristotle used the term 'supreme power' of the state in a different sense. During the middle ages the jurists, the theologians and other writers used terms like *summa potestas* (highest power of the state) or *plenitudo potestatis* (supreme authority of the state) in a sense different from what we mean now by the term sovereignty. The credit for using and also defining this term goes to Bodin of France who in his *Six Books on the Republic* (1576) used the term *souverainete* that came to have its English equivalent in the word 'sovereignty'. In his words, "sovereignty is the supreme power of the state over citizens and subjects unrestrained by law."[3]

Sovereignty, in simple terms, signifies supreme power of the state. It has two dimensions—internal and external.

1. The idea of sovereignty in the internal sphere means that the state has highest power within the area under its control. All people and their associations are under the control of the state. In patent terms, it signifies power of the state to make and enforce a law throughout its territory. It is the final power to command and enforce obedience, and is subject to no legal limitations.

---

1. According to Prof. C.H. McIlwain, sovereignty "is the central formula under which we may try to rationalise the complicated facts of our modern political life." *Constitutionalism and Changing World.,* p. 47.
2. J.W. Garner: *Political Science and Government,* p. 156.
3. *Ibid.,* p. 157.

Some Important Statements

- Sovereignty is the supreme political power vested in him whose acts are not subject to any other and whose will cannot be over-ridden.

  –Grotius

- Sovereignty is the supreme, irresistible, absolute, uncontrolled authority in which the highest legal power of the State resides.

  –Blackstone

- Sovereignty is that characteristic of the State by virtue of which it cannot be legally bound except by its own will or limited by any other power than itself.

  –Jellinek

- The sovereignty of the State issues orders to all men and all associations within its area; it receives order from none of them. Its will is subject to no legal limitations of any kind. What it proposes is right by mere announcement of intention.

  –H. J. Laski

Keeping it in his view, Gettell says: "Sovereignty, properly speaking, deals with the internal relations of a state to its inhabitants; it is a term of constitutional law rather than of international law. It is a legal concept and deals with positive law only. It would be conducive to clearness of thought and would avert much controversy if the term 'sovereignty' were applied only to what is usually called internal sovereignty and the term 'independence' were used for what is sometimes called external sovereignty."[4]

2. The idea of sovereignty in the external sphere implies freedom of state from any alien subjection or control. Dependent people cannot be called a state, because they live and have to act according to the will of some other state. But if a state accepts limitations on its freedom of action in pursuance of some international treaty or agreement, it does not amount to the loss or destruction of its sovereignty. These may be treated as self-imposed limitations. The association of a sovereign state with the Commonwealth of Nations or with the United Nations may be referred to in this connection. If so, external aspect of sovereignty is just an extension of its internal aspect in the international sphere.

The two aspects of sovereignty should not be distinguished inasmuch as both are two sides of the same attribute. In order to avoid confusion of any kind about the meaning of sovereignty, we may say that it has its expression in the form of a 'command' given by the state that is binding on all concerned with it. It issues forth in the form of the

4. R.G. Gettell: *Political Science,* p. 123.

law of the state. Thus, from the legal standpoint, the state is a total order, and the only total order precisely because the state and the law are identified."[5]

Characteristics: The essential characteristics of sovereignty may be enumerated as under:

1. **Absoluteness:** The authority of the state is supreme as well as absolute. It knows no limits on the formulation, expression and realisation of its will. Translated in terms of law, it may be said that the state may make and enforce any law and it is binding on all concerned. There can be no other authority that may revoke or rescind the law of the state. It is a different thing that a state denies to itself some area of action by the logic of self-imposed limitations as specified in its constitution or in the text of some international treaty or convention. Sir Henry Maine refers to social customs and traditions as important limiting factors on the power of the sovereign. Laski says that in purely juristic terms this implies that, in practice, legally unlimited power "turns out to be power exercised under conditions fairly well-known to each generation."[6]
2. **Universality:** The highest power of the state covers all people and their associations living under the area of its control. As such, it is all-comprehensive. It is co-extensive in its operation with the jurisdiction of the state and comprehends within its scope all powers and things within its territory. One may say that this provision does not apply to the embassies, consulates and legations where the law of the foreign country is applied. But we may repeat the point that it all takes place according to the will of the state that accepts some principles of international law for manifesting its commitment to the behaviour of the civilised nations of the world. In a different way, it shows the quality of exclusiveness. It implies the quality by virtue of which there "can be one but supreme power in the state, legally entitled to the obedience of the inhabitants. To hold otherwise would be to deny the principle of the unity of the state and to admit the possibility of an *imperium* in *imperio* (state within a state)".[7]
3. **Permanence:** Sovereignty is the permanent quality of the state. The holder of sovereignty may die, but the power of the state survives that is passed on to his successor. A state may lose its sovereignty only when it is conquered by some other state and then converted into a colony or a dependency. So the English people have their national anthem, 'God save the King'. The word 'king' signifies both the mortal person as the head of the state and the immortal authority as supreme power of the state. It is evident from their celebrated phrase, 'King is dead, long live the King'. It all implies that "sovereignty does not cease with the

5. Benn and Peters: *Social Principles and the Democratic State,* p. 63.
6. H.J. Laski: *A Grammar of Politics,* p. 52.
7. Garner, *op. cit.,* p. 170.

death or temporary dispossession of a particular bearer on the reorganisation of the state, but shifts immediately to a new bearer, as the centre of gravity shifts from one part of a physical body to another when it undergoes external change."[8]

4. **Inalienability:** This essential attribute of state cannot be alienated. Sovereignty is the very essence of the personality of the state. When a sovereign dies and his office is given to his successor, it amounts to a change in the government and not to an abdication or surrender of sovereignty. It is a different thing that a state may cede away a part of its territory to another state by some voluntary or involuntary agreement. But such an act does not amount to the surrender of its whole sovereignty. Lieber says that sovereignty can no more be alienated than a tree can alienate its right to sprout, or a man can transfer his life or personality to another without self-destruction.[9] Thus, by the quality of inalienability "is meant that attribute of the state by virtue of which it cannot cede away any of its essential elements without self-destruction."[10]

5. **Indivisibility:** Then, the sovereign power of the state cannot be divided. The state has its own will that cannot be divided into many wills. Hobbes, Rousseau, Hegel and Austin are very clear on this point and so they are called monists. Calhoun says that "sovereignty is a whole thing; to divide it is to destroy it. It is the supreme power in a state, and we might just as well speak of half a square, or half a triangle, as of half a sovereignty."[11] Sometimes, a point of difficulty arises when we misconstrue a federal system as one based on the division of sovereignty. Different from a unitary system, in a federal system the powers of the government are divided between a central (national or federal) government on the one hand and provincial (regional or constituent) governments on the other. But such an interpretation should be made with this important point in view that a federal system stands on the principle of the distribution of governmental powers and not that of sovereignty of the state. As Gettell says: "What is divided in a federal system is not sovereignty which resides as a unit in the state as a whole, but the exercise of its various powers, which are distributed in accordance with a constitutional system among various governmental organs."[12]

It shows that sovereignty is the exclusive, all-comprehensive or universal, inalienable, permanent and indivisible power of the state. The pluralists repudiate indivisible characteristic of sovereignty on the basis of some arguments to which we shall refer afterwards.

---

8. *Ibid.*
9. Lieber: *Political Ethics,* Vol. I, p. 219.
10. Garner, *op. cit.,* p. 171.
11. Calhoun: *Works,* Vol. I, p. 146.
12. Gettell, *op. cit.,* p. 125.

Kinds: Since the term 'sovereignty' is used in different senses and thereby it becomes a source of confusion, it shall be worthwhile to understand its various forms. These are:

1. **Nominal and Real Sovereignty:** In some states, sovereignty may be seen in two forms. A nominal or titular sovereign is one whose authority is in name only; a real sovereign is one who actually uses his powers. The English monarch is the best example of a titular sovereign who reigns but does not govern. All administration is done in his name. But the real exercise of powers is vested in the ministers (under the Prime Minister) who are collectively responsible to the Parliament. Hence, this is a popular saying that 'king can do no wrong'. Gone are the days of absolute monarchy when the king was the real ruler or sovereign of his state. The President of India also belongs to this category. But the Presidents of the United States and France belong to the category of a real sovereign. It is due to the fact that they exercise the power of the state according to their best judgement and may be held accountable for any wrong entailing from an act of their commission or omission. They govern in the real sense of the term.
2. **Legal and Political Sovereignty:** A legal sovereign is one who has the highest power of making and enforcing a law. A law made by such a sovereign is binding on all concerned people and parties; it may be changed or repealed by the same authority. The British Parliament is the best example of a legal sovereign that may make any law as per its best judgement. Legally speaking, it is omnipotent, in that it "can adjudge an infant of full age; it may attain a man of treason after death; it may legitimise an illegitimate child, or, if it sees fit, make a man judge in his own case."[13] But political sovereignty signifies the power of the electorate. The voters can make and unmake a parliament. The members of the parliament cannot make a law that is not acceptable to the voters and, if it happens, the voters may rise in revolt and thereby change their parliament. It is, for this reason, said that political sovereignty lies behind legal sovereignty. According to Gilchrist, "political sovereignty is the sum-total of influences in a state which lie behind the law."[14] It may, however, be conceded at this stage that while the idea of legal sovereignty is a patent fact and so easily intelligible, the idea of political sovereignty is a fiction and so a matter of confusion and controversy. In other words, it may be said that while the will of the legislators may be manifest through their resolution in the form of a law, the will of the electorate cannot be so ascertainable. So Gettell remarks that "any attempt to find a political sovereign at the back of a legal sovereign destroys the value of the entire concept and reduces sovereignty to a mere catalogue of influences."[15]
3. **De Jure and De Facto Sovereignty:** Sometimes a distinction is made between a *de jure* (legal) and a *de facto* (factual) sovereign. A *de jure* sovereign is one

13. A.V. Dicey: *An Introduction to the Study of the Law of Constitution,* p. 66.
14. R.N. Gilchrist: *Principles of Political Science,* p. 94.
15. Gettell, *op. cit.,* p. 98.

who occupies his office according to the well-established laws and practices of his state and by virtue of that he has the authority to issue commands and secure their obedience by the persons concerned. It means that his occupation of the office and then exercise of all power rests on the authority of the law of the land. But a *de facto* sovereign is one who occupies the highest office of the state in an illegal or unconstitutional manner and then makes use of force to enforce his will. It may be as a result of war or revolt in the country. As Bryce says: "The person or body of persons who can make his or their will prevail whether with the law or against the law, he (or they) is (or are) the *de facto* ruler (or rulers), the person to whom obedience is actually paid".[16] History is full of such instances when some ambitious person seized power in a revolt and then declared himself as the real ruler of the country. In England Cromwell became the *de facto* ruler after the execution of King Charles I and dissolution of the Long Parliament in 1649; Napoleon became the *de facto* ruler of France after overthrowing the Directory in 1796. Ayub Khan became the *de facto* sovereign of Pakistan after wresting power from President Iskander Mirza in 1958. Such a distinction between *de jure* and *de facto* sovereigns goes on for some time and then it disappears either when the deposed sovereign gets back his power, as Emperor Haile Selaisse of Ethiopia (who had taken asylum in England in 1936) returned to his country and once again became the Emperor after the defeat of Italy in 1945, or when the *de facto* ruler legitimises his authority by changing the constitutional law of the land as was done by President Daoud in Afghanistan in 1973 and by Khomeini in Iran in 1979 after overthrowing the system of monarchy in their respective countries.[17]

4. **Popular Sovereignty:** It implies highest power of the people. Obviously, it constitutes the foundation of a democratic order. In ancient times the Romans held the view that the authority of the commonwealth was derived from the corporate power of the people. During the later medieval period it was reiterated by the precursors of the conciliar movement like William of Ockam and Marsiglio of Padua. However, its best exponent is Rousseau of France who idealised the theory of social contract by holding that the authority of the state was based on the 'general will' of the people. Among the nation-builders of the United States, Thomas Jefferson harped on the theme of the highest authority of the people. Since then, this idea has become an integral part of democratic theory, though in actual practice it assumes the shape of political sovereignty. So says Garner: "Unorganised public opinion, however powerful, is not sovereignty unless it is clothed in legal form, no more so than the informal or unofficial resolutions of the members of a legislative body in law. The sovereignty of the people, therefore, can

---

16. James Bryce: *Studies in History and Jurisprudence,* Vol. II, pp. 513-16.
17. Garner well says: "On account of the manifest advantages which flow from the exercise of power resting on strict legal right rather than upon physical force, the new sovereign sometimes has his *de facto* claim converted into a legal right by election or ratification." *op. cit.,* p. 168.

mean nothing more than the power of the majority of the electorate, in a country where a system of approximate universal suffrage prevails, acting through legally established channels, to express their will and to make it prevail."[18]

Theory of Jean Bodin

The most important feature of Bodin's political philosophy is his doctrine of sovereignty. Indeed, it is not merely the fundamental part of his political philosophy, it is his unique contribution to the subject of political science. Bodin rightly claims that no philosopher or jurist before him could propound this concept. The 'supreme power' of Aristotle cannot be identified with the concept of sovereignty, because the Greek philosopher confined its scope by the bonds of law which had its source in reason. Likewise, the Romans and the medievalists failed to propound the doctrine of sovereignty. Living in a period of political chaos and conceiving that religious and other disturbances of the time were attributable in the last analysis to impotence of political authority, Bodin naturally arrived at a view of the state which exalted its unity and power.

According to Bodin, "sovereignty is supreme power over citizens and subjects unrestrained by law."[19] He argues that this power is not only supreme but perpetual; for, if it be limited as to time or so to scope, it cannot be supreme. It is a power which has its origin in the people acting as a corporality, and orginates in the will of the people who may themselves retain it. It is customary, however, to commit this power in whole or in part, temporarily or permanently, to the custody of prince and other functionaries of government. He further argues that if it is bestowed, for any term of years, at the pleasure of anyone or in any form so that the possessor is not the supreme legislator-unrestrained by laws–that functionary, no matter how great the power he enjoys, does not possess sovereignty, for only he has sovereignty who after God acknowledges no one greater than himself."[20]

It implies that sovereign being the creator of law cannot be subject to law. Law is the command of the sovereign. Bodin very carefully rules out the considerations of metaphysical and theological elements by explicitly pointing out that when he speaks of 'supreme power' (*legibus solutus*), he regards it unrestrained by civil laws. He says: "As for the laws of God and of nature, princes and people are equally bound by them, so that no one who attempts to abrogate or weaken them can escape the judgment of divine sovereignty. What we have said as to the freedom of sovereignty from the binding force of law does not have reference to divine or natural law."[21] He clearly stresses that the law which has its origin in definite human sources and is executed by human agencies does not come within these categories and such a law sovereignty necessarily transcends. Sovereignty alone is the supreme legislative authority and its

18. *Ibid.,* p. 165.
19. F.W. Coker: *Recent Political Thought.,* p. 374.
20. *Ibid.,* p. 375.
21. *Ibid.,* p. 376.

first and foremost function "is to give laws to citizens generally and individually, and, it must be added, not necessarily with the consent of superiors, equals or inferiors."[22]

Besides, in Bodin's view, sovereignty is the highest will that can exist in a society. The human society consists of individuals associated in groups each having a capacity for ultimate and indefeasible volition with respect to the affairs of that groups. But the state being an all inclusive entity possesses such a volitional capacity that it overmatches all other groups of the society. Thus, sovereignty represents the human will at its highest point of development. It is unity which stands above all diversity in human society, the centripetal force which exceeds any countervailing centrifugal force.

Hence, according to Bodin, sovereignty has the traits of being absolute, perpetual and unrestrained by laws. On account of being absolute, it is supreme both internally and externally and so it does not recognise the authority of any external power like the Pope or the Holy Roman Emperor or any internal force like feudal lords and corporations. Similarly, on account of being perpetual, it cannot be limited by the duration of time and so it does not inhere in regents, viceroys and dictators vested with temporary powers. Finally, its characteristics of legislative supremacy or legal omnicompetence manifests the peculiar position of the state in relation to its subjects and other associations. By virtue of it the state is excepted from all sorts of legal compulsion, owes obedience to no earthly superior and can be subjected to no will but of its own. Without its own consent it may not be used or made responsive to any legal process whatsoever, internal or external, because its fiat is law, binding upon all subjects under its jurisdiction regardless of ethical or any other consideration.[23]

Again, while the sovereign is the creator of every positive law, he is not bound by them either enacted by him or by his predecessors. He is hardly bound to observe them even if he has taken an oath to that effect or given any specific condition or commitment or made some such contract with his people. The sovereign must rule with reason in the interest of justice. Bodin says: "A state is an association of families and their common. possessions, governed by a supreme power and by reason."[24]

One noteworthy aspect of Bodin's theory of sovereignty is that he points out some restrictions on the scope of sovereignty. Although the sovereign is the creator of the laws and, as such, he stands above all laws, he is bound by the laws of God, the laws of nature and the laws of nations. The sovereign must respect the law of private property, because without a good cause no citizen can be deprived of his natural rights. Property is very essential for the maintenance of the family and even any taxation over it without

---

22. *Ibid.*, p. 379.
23. Sir F. Pollock thus summarises Bodin's view: "In every independent community governed by law there must be some authority whether residing in one person or several whereby the laws themselves are established and from which they proceed. And this power, being the source of law, must itself be above the law". *An Introduction to the History of the Science of Politics,* p. 47.
24. Coker, *op. cit.*, p. 370.

the consent of the people is not justified. If the sovereign violates the laws of God and of nature, he becomes a tyrant. Likewise, the sovereign must respect the laws of the constitution which determine the very existence of the state.

It is quite clear that the enumeration of above restrictions reduces the real value of Bodin's theory of sovereignty. The limitations of divine law, natural law and constitutional law make his theory full of contradictions, confusions and inconsistencies. The inalienable right of the family to property, the superiority of the law of the constitution and the sanctity of divine law and natural law clearly contradict the salient traits of sovereignty. By observing fidelity to the constitutional law of France and by asserting inviolability of private property, Bodin makes his whole theory confusing and inconsistent and it remained for later philosophers, like Hobbes, to formulate a correct theory of sovereignty. W.T. Jones thus comments: "Hence, Bodin does not make his sovereign supreme in the Hobbesian sense that whatever he does is right simply because he wills it. Rather, in the ultimate analysis, the supreme sovereign's decisions are not absolutely final, since they are subject to divine law. But how this restriction is to be effective or who is to recognise it and put it into operation. Bodin does'nt tell us."[25]

As Bodin imposes certain restrictions on his sovereign, some critics feel that he stands at the cross-roads between the medieval notion of the ruler as subject to the directive although not to the coercive power of human law and the modern notion of the sovereign as completely free from any law on earth.[26] Contrary to this, Maritain contends that Bodin may rightly be considered as the 'father of modern theory of sovereignty'. While constructing Bodin's definition to mean freedom of the sovereign from the human law, he asserts that this is the essence of the absolute rule, and absolutism is alien to medieval political thought. As he says: "Yet the fact remains that Bodin's sovereign was subject only to natural law, and to human law whatsoever, as distinct from natural law, and that is the core of political absolutism."[27]

Juristic Interpretation of John Austin

No doubt, the best exposition of the idea of sovereignty can be seen in its legal or juristic form. The reason is that the will of the state has its best manifestation in the law of the state that has a binding character. It is for this reason that the study of sovereignty from a strictly legal point of view, as given by Hobbes and Bentham, has an importance of its own. In this connection the best explanation of this term is furnished by an English jurist John Austin (1790-1859) who in his work *The Province of Jurisprudence Determined* (1832) defines this term in these words: "If a determinate human superior, not in the habit of obedience to a like superior, receives habitual obedience from the bulk of a given society, that determinate human superior is the sovereign in that society and that society (including the superior) is a society political and independent."

25. W.T. Jones: *Masters of Political Thought,* Vol. II, p. 62.
26. M.A. Shepard: "Sovereignty at the Cross-Roads: A Study of Bodin" in *Political Science Quarterly,* 1930, pp. 580-603.
27. Jacques Maritain: "The Concept of Sovereignty" in *American Political Science Review* (June, 1950), p. 344.

According to Henry Sidgwick, Austin's view may be briefly stated thus: "Positive law of any state is a general command to do or abstain from certain acts which is issued directly or indirectly by the sovereign of the state to a person or persons subject to his authority; the sovereign being that determinate person, or body of persons combined in a certain manner that the bulk of the members of the state habitually obey, provided that he or it does not habitually obey anyone else. It is implied in the conception of sovereign that the community, that has a sovereign, is independent in the sense that its government does not habitually obey a foreign power, and orderly in the sense that the bulk of the community habitually obeys the laws."

From this definition together with the assumption that facts exist corresponding to the definition, two important consequences are inferred:

(a) The power of the sovereign cannot be legally limited—for, obviously, the sovereign cannot be coerced to act in a certain way by any command of his own;

(b) Sovereignty cannot, strictly speaking, be legally divided between two or more persons, or bodies of persons acting separately, because any such person or bodies of persons must have *ex hypothesis* powers legally limited in certain directions—these are certain things which each of them is by law prevented from doing; but if so, they are in habitual obedience to the authority that laid down the law, and it is this latter that is the real sovereign. For example, in a federal state, such as the USA, sovereignty, strictly speaking, does not belong to the Central Government nor to the separate governments of the federated states, but to the body, whatever it may be, that is recognised as having authority to alter the conditions of federation."[28]

Following important conclusions may be drawn from what Austin has said about the nature of the sovereignty of the state:

1. That in every independent political community or state, there is a supreme and absolute power in the hands of some person or persons (institution) whose will is the law of the state and, as such, is binding on all concerned persons and their associations.
2. That the sovereign is a determinate person. It means that the highest authority of the state is vested in the hands of some person or persons who may be identified and who may exercise it as per his or their best judgement. That is, he or they may formulate, express and realise his or their will. If so, sovereignty can be only in the legal form; to talk of anything like political sovereignty (supreme power of the people), or popular sovereignty (supreme power of the electorate) is to play with a fiction. The vast electorate or the vast multitude of people cannot be identified with the sovereign of a state, nor can they formulate and express their resolve in

28. Sidgwick: *Elements of Politics,* pp. 651-52. It may be seen in the statement of Stephen Leacock: "The moment one passes from the dry certainty of the Austinian conception of legality, all is confusion." *Elements of Political Science,* p. 61.

the form of a law. It also follows that human laws and nothing else in the form of natural or divine law may be the proper subject of study in this connection.

3. That sovereignty is indivisible, because sovereign does not obey any other authority. The will of the sovereign is supreme over all persons and their associations living in the state, but he is under nobody's control or subjection. The determinate human superior may act unwisely or unjustly in an ethical sense, but his action is unimportant for the purpose of legal theory on this subject. The laws emanating from the authority of the state are like commands that must be obeyed so as to avoid the agony of suitable punishment.
4. That the sovereign receives habitual obedience from the bulk of a given community, means that obedience must be a matter of habit and not merely of an occasional ritual. It must be regular, undisturbed and continuous. It is not necessary that society as a whole must render obedience because in every society there may be a small section of the dissenters; it is enough that it comes from the bulk or the major part of the community.
5. That command is the essence of law. Whatever the sovereign wills is law. Failure to do so invites punishment. Hence, law of the state may be distinguished from a usage and a custom. The former has a mandatory character, the latter's character is volitional. The people may observe their customs or not, but obedience to law is not a matter of volition.

In short, the whole argument of Austin has a juristic complexion. The idea of sovereignty is expressed in a juristic form. The sovereign power of a state manifests itself in the form of a law that is a command to be obeyed by the persons and groups concerned. As he says: "Every positive law, or every law, simply and strictly so called, is set by a sovereign person or a sovereign body of persons to a member or members of the independent political society wherein that person or body of persons is sovereign or supreme." He further says: "To that determinate superior the other members of the society are dependent. The position of its other members towards that determinate superior is a state of subjection or a state of dependence. The mutual relation which subsists between that superior and them may be styled as the relation of sovereign and subject, or the relation of sovereignty and subjectivity." In short, law is the regulator of the behaviour of the people and sovereign is the maker and enforcer of this law. There can be no political society without a sovereign power which "is the centre of gravity in a mass of matter."[29]

The interpretation of sovereignty, as given by Austin, obviously assimilates all its five characteristics—absoluteness, all-comprehensiveness, inalienability, indivisibility, and permanence—as discussed earlier. As such, it is regarded as the best exposition of the idea of sovereignty in juristic terms. But it has some weak points that may be enumerated as follows:

---

29. Sir Henry Maine: *The Early History of Institutions,* p. 339.

1. The sovereign of Austin is not only a determinate human superior, he is the wielder of highest and absolute authority. It is said that so far there has been no sovereign in the world that may be truly identified with the model of the Austinian sovereign. A leading light of the historical school like Sir Henry Maine contends that even the great Tartars of China and the Mughals of India could not be taken as the concrete examples of the Austinian sovereign. Even the case of Maharaja Ranjit Singh of Punjab cannot be invoked in this connection. The reason is that even the most power-drunk rulers of the world have bowed their heads before the might of some natural or supernatural agency. The power of the sovereign has certain limits that may be in the form of some religious or social customs having their sustenance in the deep-rooted convictions of the people. "Only a despot with a 'disturbed brain' may be the sole conceivable example of Austin's sovereign. We cannot ignore the existence of a vast mass of influences which we may call for shortness moral, that perpetually shapes, limits, or forbids the actual direction of the forces by its sovereign."[30]
2. The Austinian view of sovereignty is immersed in the world of law. It ignores the importance of social usages and customs that definitely have a binding character. The sociologists contend that people obey their established practices in the same way they obey the laws of the state. Machiavelli understood this fact and he cautioned the ruler against playing with the customs of the people. It is also said that the law is nothing but a custom translated into the form of a written command of the state. A wise sovereign would never commit the mistake of playing with the customs of the people and imposing upon them a law that is opposed to the well-established practices and sentiments of the people. Custom is not a deliberate statute; it is the outcome of ages and even an autocrat, like Peter the Great, is expected to be the guardian and servant of the customs of the people. R.M. MacIver says that all customary laws are in their origin spontaneous, not created by any deliberate will to organise, certainly not created by the will of the state. "The state has little power to make custom and perhaps less to destroy it."[31] Again: "For custom, when attacked, attacks law in turn, attacks not only the particular law which opposes it, but, what is more vital, the spirit of law-abidingness."[32]
3. Austin's argument that the sovereign obeys none and receives habitual obedience from the bulk of a given society is disputed. In every political community there is a division of functions, though not of will, and without such division no government can be conducted effectively. There is not one sovereign but three sovereigns like the executive, the legislature and the judiciary, and these three ultimate authorities are so far independent of each other that the executive sovereign alone continues

---

30. *Ibid.*, p. 359.
31. R.M. MacIver: *The Modern State*, p. 160.
32. *Ibid.*, p. 161.

without intermission, whilst the legislature may be dissolved temporarily and the supreme judiciary is not always in session.[33]

4. The interpretation of Austin covers the case of legal sovereignty alone; it rejects the cases of political and people's (popular) sovereignty. In Austin's view, sovereignty cannot be vested in the people as a whole or even in the body of the voters, because both have an indeterminate character. The vast body of the voters or of the people of a country cannot have a will of their own that may be translated into the law of the land. Such a view is not acceptable to the scholars of political theory who laud democratic system as one based on the 'will of the people'. The popular saying is 'voice of the people is the voice of God'. We may give numerous instances to prove that even the autocratic legislators have had to bow their heads before the voters (or the people) of their country. Laski has given a challenging observation that even the so-called sovereign British Parliament cannot make a law that is taken as 'uncivilised' or 'barbarian' by the voters (people) of the country. It is a different matter that the people in general may not recognise their real force that is visible to them in the times of a popular uprising. As John Chipman Gray says, "the real rulers of a society are undiscoverable."[34] So Laski says that it "is impossible to make the legal theory of sovereignty valid for political philosophy... A realistic analysis would probably content itself with saying that the will of the State is, for practical purposes, the will which determines the boundaries within which other wills must live. The will of the State, in fact, is the will of government as that will is accepted by the citizens over whom it rules."[35]

5. A difficulty arises when we try to study a federal system in the context of the Austinian theory of sovereignty. In such a system the powers are divided between the central and provincial governments and each is taken as autonomous in the sphere allotted to it. In a sense, it looks like the division of sovereignty. The provincial governments have the status of coordinate governments vis-a-vis the central government. It shows that neither the central nor provincial governments have an authority that may be termed absolute, exclusive and indivisible to be treated as essential qualities of sovereignty as given earlier. We may also take note of centre-state controversies and confrontations in which victory may rest with either side. A study of this kind may inform a student of political theory that either the interpretation of Austin applies to a country with a unitary system, or it should be revised so as to be also applicable to a federal system. The problem stands as to how the Austinian theory can be reconciled with a federal polity in which neither the central nor the regional governments can be termed 'sovereign'. So Laski

33. A.R. Lord: *Principles of Politics,* p. 89.
34. Laski, *op. cit.,* p. 55.
35. *Ibid.,* pp. 55-56. "The electorate is a component part of the sovereign and its election of representatives is only the adoption of a certain mode of exercising its powers." Sidgwick, *op. cit.,* p. 656.

says: "It has been pointed out that the discovery of sovereignty in a federal State is, practically, an impossible adventure."[36]

6. A powerful attack on the Austinian theory comes from the side of the pluralists who desire to pluralise the concept of sovereignty. In this connection we may refer to a very large number of social thinkers like Duguit, Durkheim, Figgis, Lindsay, Barker and Laski who contend that the sovereign state has no right to discard the real significance of numerous social groups and associations that have a 'personality' of their own and also play a quite important part in satisfying the needs of the people. It will be in the interest of individual liberty if some portion of sovereignty is shared by these social groups and associations of the people. As Laski says: "Men are members of the State; but they are members also of innumerable other associations which not only exercise power over their adherents, but seek also to influence the conduct of government itself... But not less important as a limitation upon its power to determine itself is the control exercised over their own sphere of activity by different associations."[37]

7. Finally, we may refer to the attack of the internationalists on the Austinian theory of sovereignty. Like Hobbes and Rousseau, Austin denies the existence of any authority outside and above the state. The state knows no power above it and, as such, it is the master of its own will. In clear terms, it implies that every state has the right to produce weapons of mass destruction, or to settle its disputes by means of force, or to do anything in violation of the principles of international law and international morality. The disasters of the two World Wars tell us that such a view of the sovereignty must be discarded. It is required that the power of the state must be regulated, even controlled, by some international authority so as to save this mankind from the scourge of another great war that would bring untold sufferings. It implies that the whole idea of sovereignty should be restated in the light of the canons of internationalism. As Laski forcefully argues: "In such an aspect the notion of an independent sovereign State is, on the international side, fatal to the well-being of humanity. The way in which a State should live its life in relation to other States is clearly not a matter in which that State is entitled to be the sole judge... International government is, therefore, axiomatic in any plan for international well-being. But international government implies organised subordination of States to an authority in which each may have a voice, but in which also, that voice is never the self-determined source of decision."[38]

All these points of attack have their significance. But the fact stands out that Austinian interpretation of sovereignty has its own significance if attention is kept confined to its purely juristic character. We may find fault with it by studying it from sociological, political and other standpoints. Garner is correct in his assessment that "as

---

36. Laski, *op. cit.*, p. 53.
37. *Ibid.*, p. 59.
38. *Ibid.*, p. 65.

a conception of strict legal nature, Austin's theory is, on the whole, clear and logical, and much of the criticism directed against it has been founded on misapprehension and misconception."[39]

Laski's Attack on Monistic Theory of Sovereignty

There are two theories on the nature of sovereignty—classical and modern. Bodin, Hobbes and Austin are the great advocates of the classical or traditional theory according to which all powers reside in and are vested in the state; the pluralists like Lindsay, Figgis, Barker and Laski subscribe to the modern or pluralistic view of sovereignty. They distinguish between state and society and try to bring down the state from a place of supremacy to that of servitude. A.D. Lindsay says: "If we look at the facts, it is clear enough that the theory of sovereign state has broken down." In the view of J.N. Figgis, sovereignty is like 'a venerable superstition' and it would go like the dogma of 'the divine rights of kings'. Likewise, E. Barker contends: "We see the state less as an association of individuals in a common life, we see it more as an association of individuals already united in various groups for a further and more embracing common purpose." In very harsh terms, H.J. Laski says that it "would be of lasting benefit to political science if the whole concept of sovereignty were surrendered."[40]

But the most important of all is Laski whose ideas in this connection may be seen in his *A Grammar of Politics* published in 1925 and also in some other writings that had appeared earlier. The main arguments of Laski are:

1. The state is only one of the social associations. It meets our requirements, but other social groups also do the same in varying measures. Thus, the state cannot exhaust the associative impulses of man and it cannot lay its claim for man's total allegiance to itself.
2. If society is federal, authority should also be federal. It implies that society is a network of numerous groups and associations and each group has its autonomous and corporate character, the state should have its own area of activity without grabbing the areas of other social groups and associations.
3. The area of state authority must also be determined in the light of moral adequacy and free conscience of the individual. The claim of authority upon the individual is legitimate proportionately to the moral urgency of its appeal. The only state to which a man owes allegiance is one in which he discovers moral adequacy. Man's first duty is to be true to his conscience.
4. The state should compete with other social groups and associations in serving man and winning his allegiance; it has no right to destroy or encroach upon the autonomy of other social groups and associations. We live not in a universe but in a multiverse. Anything like Rousseau's general will is an impossibility. Thus, no association's will can be given the credit of finality.

---

39. Garner, *op. cit.,* p. 181.
40. Laski, *op. cit.,* p. 55.

5. The monistic view of sovereignty is inimical to the liberty of the individual. It supports the case of an all-powerful state. An omnipotent state is the offspring of the religious struggles of the early modern age. But facts show that never in history has sovereignty existed as an absolute power and there have always been limitations on the scope and exercise of the power of the state.
6. The real function of the state is to set conditions within which other associations move, because its mission is to enable the people, through these associations, to have their best selves which they are capable of. It coordinates the activities of the groups with a view to that end.
7. Though the state is an association for political purposes, it is not coextensive with society. It may set the keynote of social life, but it is not coextensive with it. It is a *communitas communitatum* and not the crowning point of a hierarchical structure. The state may be the regulator of a community, it is not the coordinator of all that a community includes.

However, the astonishing feature of the political thought of Laski is that he discards the case of pluralism after 1930. Once a diehard pluralist, then a modified pluralist, then a Marxist, he ends as a Fabian socialist supporting the case of increasing state activity in the public interest. In the fourth edition of his *A Grammar of Politics* (1934) he added a preliminary chapter titled 'Crisis in the Theory of State' wherein he frankly said: "The weakness, as I now see it, of pluralism is clear enough. It did not sufficiently realise the nature of the state as an expression of class-relations. It did not sufficiently emphasise the fact that it was bound to claim an indivisible and irresponsible sovereignty, because there was no other way in which it could define and control the legal postulates of society."[41] It shows that while Laski "expressed himself enthusiastically in favour of the groups particularly in his earlier writings under the influence of James, he became more and more critical of the pluralist attitude in his later writings. The attempt to dethrone the state or to expunge sovereign authority from the community was abandoned, and the necessity of state regulation of individual and group life came to be increasingly recognised."[42]

Kautilya on Supremacy of Royal Power

According to Western political theory, state is an association having four essential elements—population, territory, government, and sovereignty. Sovereignty is the last essential element that was invented by Bodin of France in the later part of the sixteenth century. It is certainly the hallmark of the modern state. If so, the idea of sovereignty was unknown during ancient and medieval times. Viewed thus, sovereignty has no place in the political ideas of Kautilya who occupies the highest place in ancient Indian political thought. According to Kautilya, state has seven organic elements—*swami* (ruler), *amatyas* (ministers), *janapada* (land), *durg* (fort or abode of the ruler), *kosh* (treasury), *danda* (system of punishment) and *mitrany* (statecraft or diplomacy).

41. Laski, *op. cit.*, pp. xi-xii.
42. G.N. Sarma: *Political Thought of Laski*, p. 67.

It is true that in ancient times the concept of sovereignty "was not known, but its content and character were very different from those of its modern counterpart. That was due to the peculiar circumstances amidst which it arose and developed."[43] As a matter of fact, Bodin exalted the power of the king to demolish the hold of the Pope in the external and of his agents (bishops and clergies) in the internal spheres. He committed the mistake of placing his ruler under three laws—law of God, law of nature and law of nations. But Hobbes of England rectified this mistake by exalting the absolute power of the king in executive, legislative and judicial spheres. Austin described the ruler as 'a determinate human superior, not in the habit of obedience to a like superior, but receiving habitual obedience from the bulk of a given society.'

If sovereignty implies absolute power of the ruler (king), it is very much contained in the political ideas of Kautilya. His king has absolute power by the exercise of which he can terminate the condition of *matsya nyaya* (utter lawlessness or anarchy). Kautilya is the first great Indian political thinker who mentioned rights and duties of the king in quite clear terms. Sinha wel points out: "As the duties of the king became more and more clear and precise, so did the conception of the contents of the sovereignty. Of course, the content of sovereignty is always power: but before Kautilya there was hardly any clear conception of what constituted that power."[44] The noticeable point here is that while Bodin, Hobbes and Austin exalt the case of absolute monarchy without confining it to the norms of public good, Kautilya establishes certain checks to prevent the misuse of the royal power. It is well pointed out: "Howsoever autocratic the king was in some matters, he could not by the established precepts in the *Dharamshastras* and the *Nitishastras* afford to play the part of a Greek tyrant without losing his kingdom and his life at the hands of people. Although the king was exalted, he was neither apart from nor alien to the people, who were never mere subjects of his will."[45]

It is obvious that Kautilya idealises absolute monarchy that had its representative manifestation in the rule of Emperor Asoka who adopted the Buddhist ways of life. He is admired for being a 'great ruler' of ancient India. He regarded himself as an agent of the people and resolved to abide by the law as laid down in the *Shastras* or embodied in the customs of the land which constituted both a political constitution and an ethical law of the realm. With these checks operating on the system of government, it "was very difficult for any king to make himself absolute and wield despotic authority."[46] One may say that Asoka 'is the best representative of the Indian kingship or royal sovereignty."[47]

It may well be concluded that modern conception of sovereignty was not fully developed in the age of Kautilya. Altekar aptly observes: "There is no Sanskrit term exactly corresponding to it (sovereignty), though *Swamittva* in the *Arthasastra* may be

43. H.N. Sinha: *Sovereignty in Ancient Indian Polity* (London: Luzack & Co. 1938), p. 111.
44. *Ibid.,* p. 150.
45. B.A. Saletore: *Ancient Indian Political Thought and Institutions,* pp. 319-31.
46. M.V. Krishna Rao: *Studies of Kautilya,* p. 93.
47. Sinha, *op. cit.,* p. 191.

partly approaching its meaning. But though the king was below the *Dharma* and was bound by it, though it was the law (*Dharma*) which made the king, the ancient Indian polity provided no constitutional means or checks to call the king to account if he transgressed the law."[48]

48. A.S. Altekar: *State and Government in Ancient India,* p. 62.

3

Rights, Liberty and Equality

Rights, liberty and equality are inter-related themes. Possession and enjoyment of certain rights makes up the case of liberty; possession and enjoyment of such rights by all without any distinction on some artificial ground makes up the case of equality. To talk of liberty means to talk of rights; to talk of liberty for all means to talk of equality. It means that the three concepts (rights, liberty and equality) exist together. Moreover, a discussion of the three concepts must be made in a particular order. If liberty involves rights, the latter must be discussed first; and since real liberty means liberty for all, a discussion of liberty must be followed by a discussion of equality and the relationship between the two. Hence, in this chapter an attempt has been made to discuss the three important concepts in this particular order. We may well endorse the view of Laski that "without rights there can be no liberty"[1] and that "every State is known by the rights it maintains."[2]

Rights

In order to live, a man must have some rights; in order to develop his personality to the best possible extent he must have some particular rights. If state is the first condition of a civilised life, the civilised life requires a set of special rights that a man must have. We may differentiate between governments in the context of their relative merits and demerits taking into account the rights of the people. A discussion of such a problem involves the issue of proper relationship between the individual who has to pattern his life according to the rules and the state that has to ensure their due enforcement. In this way, the concept of rights finds its broad manifestation in the liberties of the individual on the one hand and in the scope of state activity on the other.

Meaning and Nature: Simply stated, a right is a claim of an individual recognised by the community and the state. Obviously, a proper definition of the term 'right' has three ingredients. First, it is a claim of the individuals. However, not every claim can be a right. It is required that a claim should be like a disinterested desire, or something which is capable of universal application. The guiding factor is that what an individual wills should be of common interest. That is, in asserting a claim, one should feel like rendering a public service. In other words, the motivating force should be a rational consideration and not a personal caprice of the individual. Paraphrasing the idea of T.H. Green, Barker says that the will that issues in the form of a claim to something

---

1. H.J. Laski: *A Grammar of Politics,* p. 142.
2. *Ibid.,* p. 89.

not only wills the good of itself, it wills the goodness of itself in relation to others. "It wills the goodness of society which is constituted by such relations. The goodness of the relations which constitute society means a system of rights."[3]

It is also required that a claim of the individual must receive social recognition. Since an individual's claim is backed by a disinterested desire, it receives social recognition. For instance, an individual's claim that none should take his life, receives social recognition as every individual wills in the same direction. A recognition of the claim of this type leads to the creation of right to life. Likewise, an individual's desire that none should take away his property creates in him a sense that he should not take away the property of others. When this claim gets social recognition, it becomes right to property. "Claims thus recognised are translated into rights, and it is such recognition that constitutes them rights. Thus, if we care to make the distinction, we may say that rights have a double aspect. On the one hand, a right is a claim of an individual arising from the nature of self-consciousness for permission to will his own ideal objects, on the other hand, it is the recognition of that claim by society and, therein and thereby, the addition of new power to pursue these objects."[4]

Finally, we come to the point of political recognition. Rights are like moral declarations, until they are protected by the state. Individuals are guided by their real wills when they think in terms of patterning their conduct according to the rules of 'common behaviour.' However, in actual practice, they are motivated, in most of the cases, by their selfish wills. The result is the violation of the system of rights. Naturally, there must be some coercive force to ensure the exercise of these rights. The state translates socially recognised claims of moral rights into terms of law and thereby accords them legal recognition. It, therefore, acts like a coercive agency to prevent the operation of selfish wills of the individuals. Rights, therefore, have a three-fold nature. They are ethical when we deal with claims of the individuals based on their real wills and, therefore, recognised by the community. They are legal when translated into law by the state. In the sphere of politics, we are concerned with 'moral rights' which would be legally enforceable if law were what it ought to be.

A proper definition of the term 'right' should, therefore, involve all the three ingredients. However, in the realm of political theory, the most important ingredient is the fact of political recognition that connects the element of disinterested claims of the individuals with the sovereign authority of the state. The version of Gilchrist, for this reason, is partly correct when he says: "Rights arise, therefore, from individuals as members of society and from the recognition that for society there is ultimate good which may be reached by the development of the powers inherent in every individual."[5] We may instead appreciate the view of Laski: "Rights, in fact, are those conditions of social life without which no man can seek, in general, to be himself at his best. Since

3. E. Barker: *Political Thought in England* (1848-1914), p. 25.
4. *Ibid.*
5. R.N. Gilchrist: *Principles of Political Science*, p. 135.

the State exists to make possible that achievement, it is only by maintaining rights that its end may be secured."[6]

However, one point relating to the development of the concept of rights in recent times is that the 'claim aspect' has overshadowed the 'duty aspect' of this important term. It may be seen in the marked tendency to inflate the notion of rights. Now the rights are not merely asserted defensively against state action, they are rather interpreted as legitimate claims on government to satisfy human needs. Thus, the distinction between rights as 'liberties' and rights as 'claims' has become a matter of its own importance in social and political theory.[7] Such an assertion has put a premium on the ideal relationship between rights and duties in view of the fact that the 'claim rights' entitle their holder to limit the liberty of another person. In the case of certain rights, the argument that duties and rights are logically linked seems to be water-tight, but there are uses of the word 'duty' which do not imply correlative rights.[8] Sometimes, this is put in the form of distinction between 'special' and 'general' rights. The former, which arise out of specific undertakings and agreements between individuals, presuppose the existence of general rights, because one needs a special right or a claim to justify a limitation on another's freedom, and in the absence of such a right, everyone has the general right not to be coerced.[9]

Theories of Rights: From time to time, various explanations regarding the origin and nature of rights have been given that have led to the emergence of different theories in this direction. These are:

In the first place, we take up the *theory of natural rights*. It holds that rights being rationally deducible from man's nature have their universal application irrespective of the difference of place, time and environment. The nature is the author of certain rights that have a universal, rational, eternal and immutable character. The Stoics of ancient Greece upheld the right to equality as given to us by nature. The Roman thinkers like Polybius and Cicero emphasised the existence of law of nature to which the laws of the state must conform. The principles of the law of nature may be understood by man by his rational power. But these principles are of a universal and eternal character. In modern times, Thomas Hobbes defined right to life as a natural right which even the sovereign of the state could not jeopardise. But the name of John Locke is important who treated three rights (relating to life, liberty and property) as natural rights. Effective protection of the natural rights is the responsibility of the state. In case the sovereign authority is incapable of fulfilling the trust of the people, the contract may be dissolved and a new sovereign may be chosen instead for securing effective protection of natural rights.

6. Laski, *op. cit.*, p. 91.
7. D.D. Raphael: *Political Theory and the Rights of Man,* pp. 56-57.
8. N.P. Barry; *An Introduction to Modern Political Theory*, pp. 186-87.
9. H.A.L. Hart: "Are There Any Natural Rights?" in Anthony Quinton (ed): *Political Philosophy,* pp. 60-64.

The doctrine of natural rights became so popular in the early phase of the modern age that it saw its incorporation into important declarations as those of the American independence in 1776 and of French Revolution in 1789. The Universal Declaration of Human Rights adopted by the General Assembly of the United Nations in 1948 invokes the spirit of this theory when it says: "All human beings are born free and equal in dignity and rights." In short, the whole idea of natural rights is based on the assumption that irrespective of his merit as an individual in his personal or moral capacity, man is at least equal to all others in human worth. Even convicted criminals who have violated the rights of others and, therefore, do not score highly in moral grading, still have the right not to be treated in cruel or inhuman ways by the jail staff.[10]

The theory of natural rights may be criticised on some important grounds. First, it is incorrect to say that rights may be available in the pre-political stage. To say that some rights are created by nature is to say that some rights are available to man just after his birth. But, as we have already seen, there are no rights unless there is some machinery to give them effective recognition or protection. The second difficulty is that rights are created in a well-organised social system. A man living in a forest or in some unknown island has no rights of his own. Robinson Crusoe had no rights until he met Man Friday.[11] Third, it is impossible to prepare a list of natural rights. We may refer to the names of Cicero, Hobbes and Locke, but we may not offer a precise definition of the term 'natural right', nor can we prepare a catalogue of such rights. The fact is that there "is no official, or complete, or generally agreed upon list of natural rights."[12] Last, to treat rights as pre-political is to make them absolute or beyond the control of the state. The doctrine of natural rights becomes like a dogma at the hands of anti-statists. The new notion is that all rights are subject to the consideration of social welfare. The state may impose reasonable restrictions on the exercise or enjoyment of any right that a man possesses. That is, our rights must be associated with the consideration of usefulness or utility to the community. Jeremy Bentham, therefore, scoffed at the doctrine of natural rights by calling them as 'rhetorical nonsense upon stilts'.

Then, we come to the *legal theory of rights*. It holds that a right is a creation of law. If there is no law, there is no right. Custom may sanction some right, but it is no right as there is no law to enforce it. Hobbes is a powerful advocate of this theory in whose view people make a social contract and thereby establish a Leviathan to protect their rights by the force of law. So Bentham holds that rights are the creatures of law and of organised society. The best exponent of this theory is John Austin who says that every right, whether divine, legal or moral, "rests on a relative duty; that is to say, a duty lying on a party or parties other than the party or parties in whom the right resides. And manifestly that relative duty would not be a duty substantially if the law which affects to impose it were not sustained by might."[13]

---

10. Barry, *op. cit.,* p. 192.
11. Benn and Peters: *Social Principles and the Democratic State,* p. 97.
12. E. Asirvatham: *Political Theory*, VIII Ed., p. 163.
13. Austin: *The Province of Jurisprudence Determined,* edited by H.A.L. Hart, p. 285n.

This theory has its weaknesses. First, to say that law alone creates right is to dismiss the importance of custom in the life of a community. We know that people have so many rights because of the force of customs behind them. It is true that law of the state protects the system of rights, but to dismiss the value of customs altogether is not justified. Second, to say that law is the creator of rights and that the state is the possessor of legal sovereignty is to make the state omnipotent and the people helpless in fighting for their rights in the event of any encroachment upon them by the action of the state. Such a view deprives the people of their right to resist state absolutism. Last, this theory totally discards the place of ethical considerations. "It does not help us to make the state what it should be."[14]

The *historical* or *prescriptive theory of rights* puts emphasis on the factor of time in the creation of rights. Every right is based on the force of long observance. The essential sanction behind a right is, for this reason, a tradition or custom on account of its long observance. A sociologist like R.M. MacIver says that law is nothing else than an action of the state in the form of the crystallisation of the age-old custom into a legal sanction. However, a better affirmation of this view can be seen in the ideas of Edmund Burke relating to his theory of prescriptive institutions. The burden of his argument is that people have a right over anything that they exercise or enjoy uninterruptedly over a fairly long passage of time. With this point of view, he condemned the philosophy behind the action of French revolutionaries who desired to uproot the established system of institutions and suddenly erect a new one in its place.

This theory has its weak points. It is true to say that rights are created by the force of time, they do not have an eternal character just by virtue of their force of long observance. Had it been so, the system of slavery would have been in practice even in modern times. There was a time when the masters had rights over their slaves. Times change and with that changes the whole pattern of social life. So the system of rights also undergoes a change. Then, it is also possible that the rulers may abolish a particular system of rights and instead impose a new one in the light of new conditions without bothering about the factor of prescription or long observance. For instance, the British rulers finished some rights of the Indian people (as those burning alive a widow, settling disputes in a panchayat, excommunicating a person by the head of particular caste or community, etc.) and instead introduced a new system of rights that had to be accepted by the people of the country. However, to a certain extent it is plausible that rights are created by the passage of time. We may appreciate the view that history "cannot be ignored, but history cannot be relied on alone."[15]

The *idealistic theory of rights* depends upon the factor of man's rational will that issues in the form of claims and that leads to the creation of a system of rights when moral recognition of such claims is converted into legal sanction. Its best presentation is contained in the political philosophy of T.H. Green who begins with this assumption that human consciousness thinks of the goodness of the 'self' as well as of other human

14. Asirvatham, *Political Theory,* p. 167.
15. Hocking: *Law and Rights,* p. 7.

beings and thus the recognition of a claim as conducive to common interest brings about a system of rights. It is thus summed up by Barker: "Human consciousness postulates liberty: liberty involves rights; rights demand the state."[16] Same thing may be noted in the affirmations of Prof. Bernard Bosanquet that a right is both a legal and a moral reference. "It is a claim which can be enforced at law, which no moral imperative can be; but it is also recognised to be a claim which ought to be capable of enforcement at law; and thus it has a moral aspect... A typical right unites the two sides."[17]

In this way, this theory looks at rights from a highly moral point of view. Rights are rooted in the mind of man; they are powers granted to him by the community in order that he with others may realise a common good of which his good is an intrinsic part. A right must establish two things—the individual claiming it must be able to convince society that in doing so he is not interfering with like claims of his fellow beings, and that he must be able to convince society that his claim is absolutely necessary for the sake of his self-development. Thus, a right "is a freedom of action possessed by a man by virtue of his occupying a certain place and fulfilling a certain function in a social order."[18]

Like other theories on this subject, it also suffers from some weaknesses. First, the idealistic interpretation of the origin and nature of rights is too abstract to be understood by a man of average comprehension. The whole idea of the 'best possible development of a man's personality' is so vague that the state cannot prescribe a particular pattern that may be equally relevant for all. Then, it may also be commented that this theory seems to sacrifice social good for the sake of individual good. However, the merit of this theory lies on the theoretical plane where we find that it furnishes a safe test of rights which can be applied at all times, and herein it is superior to the legal, historical, and social welfare theories. "The one absolute right of all human beings is the right of personality."[19]

We may also have a peep into the *social expediency* or *social welfare theory* on this subject. It implies that the rights are the creation of the society inasmuch as they are based on the consideration of common welfare. Rights make what is conducive to the greatest good of the greatest number; they are the conditions of social good. Thus, claims not in conformity with the general welfare would not be recognised by the community and thus fail from being rights. It has its best manifestation in the works of Jeremy Bentham who developed the principle of utility so as to show that the system of rights is beneficial both to the individual and to the society. But the best exponent of this theory is Laski who reinterprets the premises of Benthamite utilitarianism in the fashion of his positive liberalism. As he says: "We are making the test of rights utility; and that, it is clear, involves the question of those to whom the rights are to be useful. There is only one possible answer. In any state the demands of each citizen for the

16. Barker, *op. cit.*, p. 23.
17. B. Bosanquet: *The Philosophical Theory of State*, p. 188.
18. N. Wilde: *The Ethical Basis of the State*, p. 12.
19. Asirvatham, *op. cit.*, pp. 175-76.

fulfilment of his best self must be taken as of equal worth; and the utility of a right is, therefore, its value to all the members of the State."[20]

But this theory has certain weaknesses. First, it dwells on the factor of social welfare—a term that is too vague to be put into a precise form. The Benthamite formula of 'greatest good of the greatest number' may mean something quite different to the Marxists. Then, if carried to extremes, the point of individual welfare may be lost, as it seeks to sacrifice individual good at the altar of social welfare. Thus, a critic like N. Wilde is of the view that if rights are created by the consideration of social expediency, the individual is without an appeal and helplessly dependent upon its arbitrary will.[21] However, the essential merit of this theory lies in its linking the idealistic version of rights with its utilitarian counterpart and thereby making it a commendable affair so far as liberal political theory is concerned.

Finally, we may refer to the *Marxian theory of rights* that links the case of rights with the prevailing economic system of the society. It holds that rights cannot be understood in isolation from the pattern of social classes and struggle going on between them as a necessary consequence of the laws of dialectical materialism. The dominant class owns the means of production and distribution and just to keep itself in power, it creates a system of rights. It is due to this that the dominant class has the right to exploit and oppress the dominated class that has no control over the means of production and distribution. The working class cannot have rights until the capitalist system is replaced by the system of socialism. The whole set up would change after the successful revolution when the proletariat has a new kind of social life in which its rights shall be associated with the set of duties so as to consolidate the new (socialist) order. For instance, the people would have rights like those relating to work and social security, they would also be tacked with duties like obedience to law and protection of the socialist system. It follows that with the advent of the socialist system the society would be able to dispense with the idea of rights prevailing in the bourgeois society.[22]

It is quite obvious that the Marxian theory of rights is unique in telling us about the meaning and nature of rights. Critics may, therefore, pick up holes in it. For instance, it may be remarked that every system, whether pre-feudal, feudal, bourgeois or socialist, has its own code of rights. Thus, it cannot be accepted that the whole system of existing rights would disappear with the establishment of socialist society. To say that rights must be tacked with duties is a good idea, but to destroy the whole system of rights in the name of the fulfilment of duties by the role of an omnipotent state is equally bad. Some recent critics like Milovan Djilas and Stojanovic of Yugoslavia had rabidly denounced the Soviet political system for allowing no meaningful rights to the people.

Kinds of Rights: Rights are of different kinds. A classification of rights in a water-tight form is not possible owing to the fact that some of the specific rights overlap their

---

20. Laski, *op. cit.*, p. 92.
21. Wilde, *op. cit.*, p. 124.
22. J. Plamenatz: *Karl Marx's Philosophy of Man*, p. 312.

categories. But in order to discuss them in a simplified form, we may categorise them in the following manner:

1. **Moral Rights:** These rights are the claims of the individuals based on the conscience of the community. In other words, these are the claims recognised by the good sense of the people. For instance, a teacher has the moral right to be respected by his students. But the difficulty with such rights is that they cannot be enforced by the state. Their enforcement depends upon the good sense of the community. When moral rights are converted into legal rights, they become enforceable by the action of the state.
2. **Legal Rights:** Moral rights become legal rights when they are enshrined in law and, for this reason, are enforceable through the courts. They are also taken as 'positive rights' in that they are enjoyed or upheld regardless of their moral content, in keeping with the idea of the law of the state or 'positive law'. It is possible that some legal rights may remain in force for some time in spite of being regarded as immoral.
3. **Civil Rights:** These rights relate to the person and property of the individuals. They are called civil or social, as they are related to the essential conditions of a civilised life. This broad category includes a number of rights like those relating to life, personal liberty, thought and expression, property, religion and the like. Of all civil rights, right to life is most important, since enjoyment of all other rights depends upon it. It implies that no person can take the life of another person. Not only this, a person has the right to save his life even by killing another person in case his opponent makes an attempt with the intention to kill him and he has no other way to save himself. It is called 'right to self-defence.' So significant is right to life that suicide is a crime. Allied to this, is the right to personal liberty. It includes right to live like a free citizen. A person cannot be detained without a proper cause and that he cannot be punished physically or economically unless he is held guilty by a court of competent jurisdiction. The trial of the accused must also be free and open. Right to think and express views falls in this category. So is the case with right to keep arms and property. In legal parlance, it means equality before law and its equal protection for all. Right to religion is also a civil right.
4. **Political Rights:** These rights are related to a man's participation in the affairs of the state. This category includes rights relating to exercise of vote, fighting elections, taking public employment, supporting or opposing the government and changing it by constitutional means. Moreover, these rights enable a person to send petitions to the government for the redressal of certain wrongs, following or abandoning a particular policy, making or unmaking a particular law, and expressing views for the creation of a healthy public opinion. Democracy is regarded as the best form of government for the obvious reason that it ensures all such rights.

5. **Economic Rights:** These rights are related to a man's vocation, his engagement in a gainful employment so as to solve the problem of food, clothing and shelter. It implies right to earn livelihood by proper means. Right to work falls in this category. Allied to this is the right to rest and leisure so that a person may take relief for the sake of maintaining and increasing his efficiency. So the workers must have the right to form unions and associations for protecting and promoting their interests, they should have right to bargain freely for remunerative work and have some share in the management of industry. The socialists go to the extent of including right to social insurance and self-government in industry in this category.
6. **Human Rights:** A modified version of what was once termed 'natural rights' coupled with certain civil rights has assumed a significance of its own since the formulation of the Universal Declaration of Human Rights by the Human Rights Commission and their adoption by the General Assembly of the United Nations in December, 1948. The Declaration is quite comprehensive. It incorporates a host of rights that have a necessary connection with moral and civil rights pointed out above. It says that all human beings are born free and equal in dignity and rights; they are endowed with reason and conscience and should act towards one another in a spirit of brotherhood. It also speaks of the right to security in the event of unemployment, sickness, disability, old age, or other conditions of destitutehood beyond one's control.

Human rights are rights to which people are entitled by virtue of being human. They are, therefore, universal rights in the sense that they belong to all human beings rather than to the members of any particular nation, race, religion, gender, social class and the like. "Human rights are also 'fundamental rights' in the sense that they are inalienable; they cannot be traded away or revoked... Many have further suggested that human rights are 'absolute' rights in the sense that they must be upheld at all times and in all circumstances. However, this view is more difficult to sustain, since in practice rights are often balanced against one another."[23] It means that human rights cannot be thoroughly likened with natural rights which have an absolute and transcendental character. The Protection of Human Rights Act (1993) made by the Parliament of India defines human rights as "rights relating to life, liberty, equality and dignity of the individual guaranteed by the Constitution or embodied in the International Covenants and enforceable by courts in India." The British Parliament made the Human Rights Act in 1998 that protects important rights of the citizens, but it made the Anti-Terrorism Act in 2001 that places severe limitations on the rights of a person detained under this law.

Rights and Obligations: Simply stated, a right is a power or a privilege or an entitlement to act or to be treated in a particular way. But as man lives in society and all members of the society have their rights, each right has a corresponding duty or

23. Andrew Heywood: *Political Theory,* p. 188.

obligation. If I have a right to live, it becomes my duty to let others live. If I want that nobody should take away my property, I am also bound to honour such a right of others. The exercise of a particular right requires a duty to act in a particular way so that the whole system of rights safely prevails. So Heywood says: "In a sense, rights and obligations are the reverse sides of the same coin... However, if citizens are bearers of rights alone and all obligations fall upon the state, orderly and civilised life would be impossible: individuals who possess rights but acknowledge no obligations would be lawless and unrestrained. Citizenship, therefore, entails a blend of rights and obligations; the most basic of which has traditionally been described as 'political obligation'; the duty of the citizen to acknowledge the authority of the state and obey its laws."[24]

Not only this, since people are expected to lead a 'good life', it also becomes essential that rights should be exercised in a proper way so as to make the performance of corresponding duty equally well. It implies that proper exercise of rights leads to proper discharge of corresponding duty. Problems arise when the balance between the two is broken down or disturbed. In the present age of globalisation its meaning should be expanded to cover the world as a whole. As Mahatma Gandhi says: "I learnt from my illiterate but wise mother that all rights to be deserved and protected come from duty well done. Thus, the very right to life accrues to us only when we do the duty of citizenship of the world. From this one fundamental statement, perhaps, it is easy enough to define duties of men and women and correlate every right to some corresponding duty to be first performed. Every other right can be shown to be a usurpation badly worth fighting for."

Protection of Rights: Mere conferment of rights on the people is not enough. What, in addition to this, is required is their proper protection. For this, following measures may be suggested:

1. The rights of the people must be enshrined in the constitution of the state so that they have the character of fundamental rights. By doing so the state accords them constitutional protection and empowers the courts to issue prerogative writs for their enforcement.

2. Another safeguard is the rule of law as available in Britain. There is no written constitution in Britain and yet the people enjoy their rights. It is due to the fact that this country is known for having, in the words of Dicey, the 'rule of law.' It has two essential features: First, every citizen is under the same law of the land irrespective of his social, economic or political status. Second, a person cannot be arrested without sufficient cause and he cannot be made to suffer in body or in goods unless declared guilty by a court of competent jurisdiction after a fair trial.

3. It is also necessary that there should be a free and honest press in the country so that the people may have a straightforward dissemination of news and views. If there is any encroachment on the rights of the people, the press would highlight

24. Heywood, *op. cit.,* p. 197.

it and then a healthy public opinion would be created for the protection of their rights against encroachment of any kind.

4. There should be decentralisation of powers. Concentration of powers creates conditions under which the rights of the people are in jeopardy. But decentralisation of powers creates conditions that minimise the possibility of the abuse of power.
5. The existence of an independent and impartial judiciary is also necessary for the same purpose. If the people feel aggrieved by any action of state or some other institution, they may move the courts for the protection of their rights. It is for this reason that in democratic countries the courts are given special power of issuing prerogative writs for the enforcement of constitutional provisions.
6. It is also suggested that the state should not extend its area of activity into the legitimate domain of voluntary groups and associations.
7. But the most important of all is the condition of eternal vigilance of the people. If the people are apathetic or indolent, their rights can never be secure. It is well said: "It is the proud spirit of the citizens, less than the letter of the law, that is their most real safeguard."[25]

Liberty

A discussion of the idea of liberty in its various aspects looks like an extension of what we have said in the preceding section in view of the fact that the theme of rights is integrally connected with the theme of liberty. It is the provision of rights with their due enforcement by the state that ensures freedom to a citizen and thereby enables him to seek the best possible development of his personality. The purpose of the state is not confined to the maintenance of law and order, or the protection of the weak against the strong, it is also concerned with the creation and preservation of that atmosphere in which an individual has the opportunity to sharpen his constructive initiative. The subject of rights naturally ushers in the form of one of the essential ingredients of a liberal political order attaching significance to the continuous initiative of man.

Real Meaning and Nature: The meaning of liberty is generally taken in a wrong way as it is identified with the absence of restraints and limitations. It is taken synonymously with man's right to 'do what he likes'. Hobbes calls it 'license' or 'a condition to do what you like' that prevails in the hypothetical state of nature. In a correct sense, liberty means man's right to do what is worth doing. Social life is regulated by a set of principles or norms that make man's life civilised. These restraints lay down the line of distinction between good and bad, right and wrong, moral and immoral, legal and illegal. Thus viewed, liberty means man's right to do what he wants to do for the sake of making the best possible development of his personality by following a course that is good, or right, or moral, or lawful. In short, the real meaning of liberty should be understood with this point in view that the liberty of an individual is relative to that of others.[26]

---

25. Laski, *op. cit.,* p. 104.

The meaning of liberty has two dimensions—negative and positive. In a negative sense, it implies the absence of restraints as far as possible. Here the point of stress is that restraint is bad, because it effects curtailment or diminution of individual freedom. But as liberty lives within restraints, these should be as few as possible. Here the burden of argument is to accept the fact of restraints with a sense of compulsion. A classic defender of this argument like John Stuart Mill says that "all restraints *qua* restraints is an evil...leaving people to themselves is always better than controlling them."[27] In order to make his meaning more clear, he divides man's actions into two parts—self-regarding and others-regarding. The state has no right to interfere with the liberty of man if his actions affect himself alone. Professing any religion, worshipping the deity, and reading a book may he cited as examples of man's strictly self-regarding actions. However, the state may intervene in the liberty of a man if he harms the liberty of his fellow-beings. If a man does something that has its effect on others, it pertains to the realm of others-regarding actions. As he forcefully asserts: "The sole end for which mankind are warranted, individually or collectively, in interfering with the liberty of action of any of their member, is self-protection. The only purpose for which power can be rightfully exercised over any member of a civilised community against his will is to prevent harm to others. His own good, either physical or moral, is not a sufficient warrant... Over himself, his own body and mind, the individual is sovereign."[28]

Among the recent exponents of this view we may refer to F.A. Hayek who says that every individual has some assured area of personal freedom which others cannot interfere with. The element of 'choice' should be taken as decisive. The rock climber on a difficult pitch who sees only one way to save his life is unquestionably free, though we could say that he has hardly any choice. A man is really free when he is not subjected to coercion of any kind and coercion means subjection to the arbitrary will of others. Coercion occurs when an agent's actions are made to serve the will of another, not for his own but for others' purposes. Coercion implies action in the sense that a person, who is coerced, chooses to be what he does. It occurs only when one person threatens with the intention of thereby getting the other to act in conformity with his will."[29]

The negative view of liberty is not appreciated in present times. Now individual liberty is sought to be reconciled with the growing authority of the state. Restraints are essential if the state desires to achieve the goal of public welfare. It is said that human actions cannot be divided into water-tight forms as was done by Mill more than a hundred fifty years back. Since man lives in society, his actions have an effect on the liberty of others. There can be nothing like a strictly private or self-regarding sphere. Man cannot be allowed to commit suicide or produce obscene literature. The acceptable view is that there "is no side of man's life which is unimportant to society,

26. Barker: *Principles of Social and Political Theory,* p. 145.
27. Mill: *Essay on Liberty,* pp. 150-51.
28. *Ibid.,* pp. 72-73.
29. Hayek: *The Constitution of Liberty*, p. 13.

for whatever he is, does, or thinks may affect his own well-being, which is and ought to be a matter of common concern, and may also directly or indirectly affect the thought, action and character of those with whom he comes into contact."[30]

However, the meaning of liberty in its positive aspect is a contribution of T.H. Green. He defines it as a positive power of doing or enjoying something that is worth doing or worth enjoying in common with others. Since man is a social creature, his life should be regulated by certain social bonds. Liberty of the individual should be considered in relation to these norms of good will. Paraphrasing the meaning of Green, Barker says: "Liberty can only be liberty for this good will; it can only be liberty for the pursuit of objects which a will presents to itself. It is, therefore, no negative absence of restraints any more than beauty is the absence of ugliness. Inhering as it does in the good will and in that will only, it is not a power of pursuing any and every object, but a power of pursuing these objects which the good will present to itself. In a word, it has two qualities. It is positive—a freedom to do something, not a freedom from having something done to one. It is determinate—a freedom to do something of a definite character, something which possesses the quality of being worth doing, and not any and everything."[31]

As a result of this, the meaning of liberty has come to involve within itself both the individual and social sides of man's existence. Moreover, as social life requires a network of regulations, the idea of liberty has, therefore, come to have a derivative value arising ultimately from the supreme value of the moral personality acting and developing its capacities as such. If so, liberty which the state upholds and makes a principle of its action must be a liberty relative to and, therefore, regulated by the nature of such a personality. A powerful defender of this view like Prof. Leo Strauss says: "There is no relation of man to man in which man is absolutely free to act as he pleases, or as it suits him... By virtue of his rationality man has a latitude of alternatives such as no other earthly being has.... The sense of the latitude of this freedom is accompanied by a sense that the full and unrestrained exercise of that freedom is not right. Man's freedom is accompanied by a sacred awe, by a kind of divination that not everything is permitted. Restraint is, therefore, as natural or as primeval as freedom."[32]

It follows that the real meaning of liberty has its negative and positive dimensions. While, the negative view disfavours the case of restraints on the liberty of man as far as possible, the positive view appreciates the system of reasonable restraints in the name of public good. If Mill and Hayek subscribe to the former view, Green and Strauss do the same for the latter. But Isaiah Berlin of the Oxford University has an interpretation of his own. In his view, the real meaning of liberty involves both sides, and the two cannot be separated from each other. There is some area of a man's life in which he must be free from the restraints of any kind whatsoever so that he may wish to determine the course of his action without any direction from the side of others, no matter how

30. L.T. Hobhouse: *Liberalism,* p. 65.
31. Barker: *Political Thought in England,* p. 24.
32. Strauss: *Natural Right and History,* pp. 129-30.

benevolent. As he affirms: "The extent of my social or political freedom consists in the absence of obstacles not merely to my actual, but to my potential, choices to my acting in this or that way if I choose to do so."[33] The state may impose some fetters on the freedom of man, but no fetter should be like one killing his area of choice. "Liberty is increased when sovereignty is put into right hands."[34]

Berlin is regarded as a 'liberal pluralist' who holds that as moral beliefs cannot be susceptible to rational analysis, there are innumerable values that cannot be reconciled with each other. There is no standard for determining the pattern of 'good life.' That is, people always differ from each other on the ultimate ends of life. On this basis, he attacks the notion of positive liberty that entitles the state to place a number of restraints on the liberty of the individual and thereby, in the words of Hayek, opens the 'road to serfdom'. "Whereas positive liberty can be used to map out the potentially totalitarian idea of a rationally ordained human future, negative liberty, understood as non-interference, is the best guarantee of freedom of choice and personal independence."[35]

Kinds: Simply stated, liberty implies a condition "especially opposed to political subjection, imprisonment, or slavery."[36] However, in a wider sense, it is a multiple concept having these important varieties:

1. **Natural Liberty:** It implies complete freedom for a man to do what he wills. It is another name for the liberty of the woods, called 'licence' by Hobbes. It means no restraint of any kind whatsoever on the doings of a man. Just as all creatures live according to their will in the world of nature, so should be the pattern of a man's life. Let a man do what he wills. We have already made it clear that liberty lives within restraints. The idea of natural liberty is, therefore, an arrant nonsense; it cannot prevail in a society of human beings. As a social creature, man should lead a life regulated by social restraints. Thus, we find that Rousseau who begins with the assumption that 'man is born free, he is everywhere in chains' ultimately stresses the point that "what man loses by the social contract is his natural liberty and an unlimited right to everything he tries to get and succeeds in getting; what he gains is civil liberty and the proprietorship of all he possesses."[37]
2. **Social Liberty:** What we really mean by liberty lies in its civil or social variety. It has its wider ramifications in personal, political, religious, economic, national and international spheres. It is related to man's freedom in his life as a member

33. Berlin: *Four Easays on Liberty,* pp. xxxix-xl.
34. *Ibid.,* p. 166. The element of 'choice' is very important in the meaning of liberty. N.P. Barry says: "The old lag may deliberately commit a crime in order to recapture the security of prison life, but it would be absurd to describe his resulting condition as one of liberty." *Op. cit.,* p. 160.
35. Heywood, *op. cit.,* p. 261. Such a view takes inspiration from Benjamin Constant who distinguishes between 'liberty of the ancients' and 'liberty of the moderns', identifying the former with the ideas of direct participation and self-government and the latter with non-interference and private rights.
36. *Encyclopaedia Britannica*, Vol. 13, 1967 Ptg., p. 1029.
37. Rousseau: *Social Contract,* Book I, Ch. VIII.

of the social organisation. As such, it refers to a man's right to do what he wills in compliance with the restraints imposed on him in the general interest. In other words, this kind of liberty consists in the rights and privileges that the society recognises and the state protects in the spheres of private and public life of an individual. Its sub-varieties may be put as under:

(a) **Personal Liberty:** Private liberty "is that aspect of which the substance is mainly personal to a man's self. It is the opportunity to be fully himself in the private relations of life."[38] According to Blackstone, this kind of liberty consists in three directions—(i) personal security not only of health and life but also of reputation, (ii) personal freedom especially of movement, and (iii) personal property or the free use and enjoyment and disposal of all acquisitions.

(b) **Domestic Liberty:** Prof. Hobhouse talks of domestic liberty which means a responsible and respectable position of the wife and children in the family, freedom for the members of the family to have marriage of their choice, and responsibility of the parents to seek moral and mental development of the members of their family.

3. **Political Liberty:** It refers to the power of the people to be active in the affairs of the state. Thus, it is integrally connected with the life of man as a citizen. It consists in the provisions for universal adult franchise, free and fair elections, and freedom for the avenues that make a healthy public opinion. The existence of this kind of liberty shows that the people may curb, control and change their government.

4. **Economic Liberty:** It pertains to the individual in his capacity as a producer or a worker, whether manual or mental, engaged in some gainful occupation or service. It means security and opportunity to find reasonable significance in the earning of one's daily bread. The individual should be free from the constant fear of unemployment and insufficiency which, perhaps, more than any other inadequacies, saps the whole strength of personality. In a wider sense, it stands for the establishment of industrial democracy enabling the workers to participate in the management of industry. The case of economic freedom is, however, a matter of controversy. While the liberals desire a free and competitive economic system, the socialists advocate the system of state controls, even nationalisation of private property in the public interest. The communists go to the last extent of abolishing private economy and defining economic freedom as man's emancipation from evils like unemployment and exploitation. Absence of unemployment and provisions for social security are taken as the bold marks of economic freedom in the country.

5. **National Liberty:** It is another name for national independence. It rejects the case of colonial or imperial subjection of one nation by another. Thus, freedom struggles are regarded as national movements. For instance, the Americans gained

38. Laski, *op. cit.*, p. 146.

national liberty in 1776 and the Indians in 1947. Historical evidence shows that love for one's country is so deep-seated in human hearts as a result of which millions of people lay down their lives for the sake of protecting the honour and security of their motherland.

6. **International Liberty:** The ideal of liberty covers the world as a whole. Thus, in the international sphere, it implies renunciation of war, limitation on the production of armaments, abandonment of the use of force and stress on pacific settlement of international disputes. The ideal is based on this pious assumption that in proportion as the world becomes free, the use of force becomes irrelevant and that there is no sense in aggression if it is not an issue of national subjection in one form or another.

7. **Moral Liberty:** This type of freedom is contained in the idealistic interpretations of thinkers from Plato and Aristotle in the ancient to Rousseau, Kant, Hegel and Green in modern times. In this context, it is suggested that though a person may have all kinds of freedom, as described above, he lacks the essential quality of a human being in case he does not have moral freedom. This kind of freedom lies in man's capacity to act as per his rational self. Every individual has a personality of his own and unless he seeks best possible development of his personality and, at the same time, he desires the same thing for others and, more than this, he pays sincere respect for the real worth and dignity of his fellow beings, he is not free in the moral sense. Kant calls it the 'fulfilment of the will to categorical self-imposed imperative of duty' and the 'autonomy of the rational will.' To Hegel such freedom has its objective realisation in the state and has its place in the observance of complete loyalty to the state. In other words, it is necessarily connected with man's self-realisation that has a meaning only in the context of the common good.

Liberty and Authority: Whether liberty of the individual and authority of the state are exclusive of, inimical to, or complementary with each other is a very delicate question. It has engaged the attention of many social and political thinkers and theorists. Different views are available in this regard:

1. The classical individualists like John Stuart Mill, Adam Smith and Herbert Spencer take liberty of the individual incompatible with the authority of the state. The two are antithetical. But as the state is a 'necessary evil,' there should be as little interference of the state as possible so that the individuals may have the maximum possible amount of liberty. They appreciate the system of *laissez faire* implying minimum possible area of state interference.

2. The anarchists go a step ahead in denouncing the state as an unnecessary evil that should go root and branch. Authority of any kind is bad, because it restricts liberty of the individual. As advocated by great anarchists like Proudhon, Bakunin and Kropotkin, there should be no authority—whether economic, political or religious—so as to emancipate man from the yoke of the capitalists, the state and the religion respectively.

3. The Marxists treat the state as an instrument of exploitation and oppression by one class over another. The state deprives the class of the have-nots to enjoy liberty in the midst of numerous restraints imposed by it to protect and promote the interest of the class of the 'haves'. The authority of the state shall survive during the transitional stage so as to deal with all reactionary and counter-revolutionary forces, but when the socialist system is finally established, it shall wither away entailing complete emancipation of man.
4. The view of the democratic socialists is different from all the views given above. To them the state is a welfare agency that may restrict liberty of the individuals in the name of public welfare. Liberty lives within restraints. The state, therefore, makes laws for the protection of individual liberty. The violators of laws are punished. The liberals support the view that law protects liberty of the individuals. To Hobbes and Locke, the distinction between the state of nature and civil society is that in the latter there is a system of restraints imposed by the sovereign authority in the form of laws. But positive liberals like Hobhouse and Laski take the point to the extent of appreciating more and more reasonable restraints in the public interest.
5. The Fascists go to the extent of adulating the system of restraints to any extent whatsover. In their view, liberty of the individual lies in rendering complete obedience to the authority of the state. This view takes inspiration from the idealistic interpretation of Rousseau and Hegel that the state can do no wrong. Hence, Mussolini of Italy and Hitler of Germany justified their totalitarian system as the best safeguards for individual liberty.

We may take note of the variations in all the arguments given above. But we must also bear in mind that, as a matter of fact, liberty by its very nature involves restraints. Two points should, therefore, be borne in mind in this connection. First, there can be no liberty in the absence of authority. That is, state intervention is necessary in the sphere of individual liberty in order to keep it within reasonable limits. Second, the authority of the state should not be absolute so as to menace or even destroy, every iota of liberty as happens under a Fascist or a Communist system.

Equality

Like liberty, equality is an equally important theme of normative political theory. Moreover, like liberty, it is also a subject that cannot be studied in isolation to other related themes like fraternity (cooperation) and justice. As a matter of fact, the concept of equality constitutes a concomitant of the principle of liberty, on the one hand, and of justice, on the other. It is due to this that great thinkers as well as revolutionaries have treated it as an integral part of their movement for liberty and social transformation. For instance, the representative thinker of the social contract school (John Locke) held that the "Law of Nature teaches all mankind who will but consult it, that being all equal and independent, no one ought to harm another in his life, health, liberty or possessions."[39] The Founding Fathers of the American nation adopted Declaration of Independence in 1776 that *inter alia,* said, "... all men are created equal, that they are endowed by their

Creator with certain unalienable rights." Likewise, the National Assembly of France adopted the Declaration of the Rights of Man and Citizen in 1789 which, *inter alia,* said that "all human beings are born free and equal in dignity and rights."[40]

Real Meaning and Nature: Eminent social and political thinkers have realised the difficulty of offering a precise definition of the term 'equality'. According to Laski, no idea is more difficult to be defined in the whole realm of political science than the concept of equality.[41] So says Ernest Barker: "Equality is a Protean notion; it changes its shape and assumes new forms with a ready facility."[42] The reason behind it is that equality has become like a multi-dimensional concept. It possesses more than one meaning, and that the controversies surrounding it arise partly, at least, because the same term is employed with different connotations. That is, it may either purport to state a fact, or convey the expression of an ethical judgement. On the one side, it may affirm that men are, on the whole, very similar in their natural endowments of character and intelligence; on the other side, it may assert that while they differ profoundly as individuals in capacity and character, they are equally entitled as human beings to consideration and respect, and that the well-being of society is likely to be increased if it so plans its organisation that, whether the powers are great or small, all its members may be equally enabled to make the best of such powers as they possess."[43]

And yet some serious efforts have been made to offer a definition of the term 'equality'. According to *Oxford English Dictionary,* it implies (i) the condition of having equal dignity, rank or privilege with others; (ii) the condition of being equal in power, ability, achievement of excellence; (iii) fairness, impartiality, due proportion, proportionateness. That is, this term is defined in the light of equal conditions guaranteed to each for making the best of himself. In the words of Barker, it implies that "whatever conditions are guaranteed to me in the form of rights, shall also, and in the same measure, be guaranteed to others, and that whatever rights are given to others shall also be given to me."[44] So says Laski: "Undoubtedly, it implies fundamentally a levelling process. It means that no man shall be so placed in society that he can over-reach his neighbour to the extent which constitutes a denial of the latter's citizenship."[45]

In very simple terms, the idea of equality refers to the equality of rights and opportunities so that each member of the civilised community may have the best possible scope for the development of his personality. It obtains insofar as, and only insofar as, each member of a community whatever his birth or occupation, or social position, possesses in fact and not merely in form equal chances of using to the full his natural endowments of physique, of character, and of intelligence."[46] In other words,

39. Locke: *Second Treatise of Civil Government*, Ch. II, paras 18-19.
40. See Benn and Peters, *op. cit.,* p. 107.
41. Laski, *op. cit.,* Ch. 3.
42. Barker: *Principles of Social and Political Theory,* p. 151.
43. R.H. Tawney: *Equality,* p. 22.
44. Barker, *op. cit.,* p. 151.
45. Laski, *op. cit.,* p. 153.

it desires a state of life in which the strong and the weak share same privileges for the development of their personality irrespective of any artificial distinction like that of wealth, religion, colour of the skin, domicile, language, descent, sex and the like. Keeping it in view, Laski asserts: "It means that my realisation of my best self must involve as its logical result the realisation by others of their best selves. It means such an ordering of social forces as will balance a share in the toil of living with a share in its gain also. It means that my share in the gain must be adequate for the purpose of citizenship."[47]

Viewed thus, the idea of equality has two sides—positive and negative:

1. In a positive sense, equality means the provision of adequate opportunities for all. But it does not mean simply identical treatment for all. Since men differ in their needs and capacities and also in their efforts, they require different opportunities for their self-development. The native endowments are by no means equal. The goal of 'equality of opportunities' is achieved only when there is an appropriate opportunity for each; what is to be equalised is not the opportunity to enter professions or to be successful in business but the opportunity to lead a good life, or to fulfil one's personality."[48]
2. In a negative sense, equality means no discrimination on some artificial ground like that of religion, caste, wealth, creed, domicile, descent, sex and the like. A discrimination can be made if the reason behind it is valid. For instance, very hazardous jobs cannot be given to the females. A distinction on the basis of sex in such a case would not be against the principle of equality. But discrimination on the basis of caste (as in Hindu society) cannot be justified by any rational standard. It all implies that there should be no arrangement whereby the authority of few is qualitatively more than that of the many.[49]

One important point that should be touched at this stage is the case of discrimination on the basis of merit, efficiency or excellence. It is known by the name of the doctrine of the desert. The idea behind it is that the principle of equal opportunities for all should be qualified by the maxim of 'deserving'. The doors of progress must be open for all in an equal measure, but due consideration must be given to the factor of talent or ability that a person has in comparison to others.

On a theoretical plane, the doctrine of the desert has sense. But the difficulty arises when we try to look into its practical implications. It is quite likely that a discrimination in the name of talent or special merit may not be wholly fair and impartial and thereby the whole sanctity of the principle of equal opportunities may be destroyed. But in a poor and backward country some other criterion may be adopted. For instance, the Constitution of India sanctions special reservations and safeguards for the upliftment

46. Tawney, *op. cit.*, pp. 103-04.
47. Laski, *op. cit.*, p. 153.
48. Benn and Peters, *op. cit.*, p. 119.
49. Laski, *op. cit.*, pp. 153-54.

of socially and educationally backward sections of the community. The State may provide special benefits to the persons belonging to Scheduled Castes and Scheduled Tribes. Obviously, such an arrangement is a violation of the principle of equality. But it may be justified on two grounds. First, it is meant for the benefit of those sections of the society which, for many centuries, have suffered the pangs of social injustice and now some special facilities must be given to them for the sake of the betterment of their lot. Second, it is a temporary affair that is to be abolished after some time when the contemplated goal of social justice is happily achieved. That is why, it is known by the name of 'compensatory' or 'protective discrimination'.

Kinds: Since equality is a multi-dimensional concept, it has its different kinds that may be put as under:

1. **Natural Equality:** It implies that nature has made all men equal. In ancient times, the Stoics of Greece and then Roman thinkers like Polybius and Cicero contradicted the principle of natural inequality of mankind as advocated by Plato and Aristotle. Cicero said: "For no one thing is like as equal to another one as we human beings are like and equal to one another." The Stoics and the Romans took the argument of the 'law of nature' that was equally applicable to all people irrespective of their country or race. The Christian thinkers identified the 'law of nature' with the 'law of God' and thereby upheld the principle of natural equality of mankind as sanctioned by the Biblical injunction of the 'Fatherhood of God and brotherhood of man'. In modern times, Rousseau and Marx may be taken as the best exponents of the case of natural equality of mankind. It may, however, be said at this stage that the natural equality of mankind is a very noble idea which constitutes one of the two foundations of democracy (the other being liberty), in practice things are not so. It is like an ideal to say that 'all earth is surface'.[50]
2. **Social Equality:** While natural or moral equality is just an ideal, the social or civil equality is an actuality. What we have said about the real meaning of equality applies here. It implies that the rights and opportunities of all are equal so that each may have the best possible development of his personality. Its best manifestation can be seen in the world of law where we come across the principle of equality before law and its equal protection for all. The law of the land is applicable to all from the President or Prime Minister at the top to a constable or a watchman at the bottom. The judicial system protects the rights of all irrespective of anybody's social and economic position. The noted English jurist (Dicey) defines it as one of the two essential principles of the 'rule of law'.[51]
3. **Political Equality:** It means the access of all to the avenues of power. All citizens irrespective of their differences in matters of religion, caste, creed, race, wealth, sex, language, and the like should have equal voice in the management of public

---

50. A. Appadorai: *The Substance of Politics*, p. 81.
51. A.V. Dicey: *An Introduction to the Study of the Law of the Constitution,* p. 202.

affairs, or in the holding of public offices. Thus, every adult citizen should have rights like exercising franchise, fighting elections, securing a public employment, opposing or supporting some official policy or activity, changing the government by constitutional means and the like. If there are severe restrictions on the freedom of franchise, thought and expression, or where such privileges are available to a very limited section of the community, there is no political equality as we could once see in the case of South Africa. Impressed with the case of implications of political equality, Laski insisted on the abolition of the privileges of the Lords in England. Carl J. Friedrich rightly says that "political equality is increased by the degree to which democratic legitimacy is embodied in the political order."[52]

4. **Economic Equality:** It implies that there should be no concentration of economic power in the hands of a few persons. The distribution of national wealth must be such that no section of the people becomes over-affluent to the detriment of others; no section of the community must be forced to reach the margin of starvation or economic want. There should be 'a specific civic minimum' in the realm of economic benefits accruing to all. In a technical sense, it implies the case of the 'equality of proportions'. But the difficulty with the case of economic equality is that it has different implications according to different thinkers. While the classical liberals take it as equal opportunities to all in the spheres of production, consumption and distribution of goods with least possible intervention of the state, to the socialists it means economic freedom to all subject to rules and regulations imposed by the state in public interest so that the rich may not exploit the poor. The Marxists go to the final extent of establishing a 'classless society' in which all property would be under the control of the state and the ideal of economic equality would mean complete absence of the exploitation of man by man just by the use of economic power. Taking the view of a positive liberal or a democratic socialist, Laski says: "State divided into a small number of rich and a large number of poor will always develop a government manipulated by the rich to protect the amenities represented by their property."[53]

5. **Legal Equality:** Though we have given a hint of the meaning of legal equality while discussing the case of social or civil equality, it shall be worthwhile to discuss it under a separate heading. It has three implications. First, all citizens are alike in the eye of the law of the land. (Only the head of the state may be its exception). Second, the protection of the life and property of each citizen is guaranteed by law and this facility is available to all without discrimination of any kind. Last, justice is available to all at a low cost and without undue delay so that everyone irrespective of his social or economic position may get it according to the established procedure of the land. But there would be no violation of the

52. C.J. Friedrich: *"A Discourse on the Origin of Political Inequality"* in Nomos, IX, p. 222.
53. Laski, *op. cit.*, pp. 157-58.

principle of equality if law guarantees different sets of privileges for persons belonging to different positions in the society. For instance, the privileges of a member of Parliament cannot be made equal to the privileges of a cabinet minister by the system of law. In other words, it implies the case of equality at equal levels. And yet it implies that the privileges of one must be legally equal to the privileges of others if they stand at the same level. An English writer is, therefore, right in his assessment that it "is in the spirit of modern law to hold certain fundamentals of rights and duties equally applicable to all human beings."[54]

6. **Material or Distributive Equality:** Also known as the 'equality of outcomes,' it implies that "all runners finish the race in line together, regardless of their starting point and the speed at which they run."[55] It goes much beyond what Rousseau says, "No citizen should be rich enough to buy another, and none so poor as to be forced to sell himself". It negates the principle of equality of opportunities which allows room for the display of one's merit. Rather it places the deserving and the undeserving on the same pedestal by arguing that all citizens should have equal share in the resources as well as in their outcomes. The equality of opportunities results in the inequality of the outcomes. The diehard Maoists (Red Guards) created an upheaval in China by demanding abolition of wage differentials and they banned competitive sports like football during the days of, what they called, 'great proletarian cultural revolution'. A liberal like David Miller puts that "a society of social equals is a community in which people's dealing with and emotional attachments to others are not inhibited by the barriers of class."[56] Even an English New Fabian like Crossland argues that the goal of social justice "is to weaken the existing deep-seated stratification, with its concomitant feelings of envy and inferiority, and its barriers to uninhibited minglings between the classes."[57]

7. **International Equality:** Last, we may refer to international equality. It means that all nations of the world must be treated equally without any consideration of any nation's demographic, geographical, economic or military potential. The fact that each member-state of the United Nations has one vote in the General Assembly represents the case of equality in the international sphere. But with the growth of internationalism, this term has acquired some more implications. It is also desired that nations must not resort to force; they must make use of pacific means for the settlement of their disputes. Gigantic evils like those of slavery and racial segregation must disappear from the face of the earth. Above all, it implies

54. L.T. : Hobhouse: *The Elements of Social Justice,* p. 104.
55. Heywood, *op. cit.,* p. 291.
56. David Miller: "Equality and Market Socialism" in Pranab Bardhan and John Roemer (eds.): *Market Socialism: The Current Debate* (Oxford: Oxford University Press, 1993, p. 302.
57. C.A.R. Crossland: *The Future of Socialism* (London: Cape, 1964), p. 77.

distribution of scientific and technological achievements among all nations of the world so as to usher in a new international social and economic order.

Affirmative Action of the State: The principle of equality implies that there should be no discrimination among the people on artificial grounds as those of religion, race, caste, sex, language, place of birth, wealth, colour of the skin, etc. However, discrimination on any logical or scientific ground is not a violation of this principle. Admissions to educational institutions or recruitment to public services should be open to all citizens, but rules for minimum eligibility or competence may be laid down. Physically unfit persons cannot be recruited in defence services. Local persons should be given preference in recruitment to menial jobs as those of peons, sentries, drivers, postmen, etc.

The idea of the affirmative action of state implies that discrimination may be done in favour of socially and educationally backward classes or weaker sections of the community. All persons enjoy equality of rights and opportunities, but those belonging to depressed castes or tribes cannot take the benefit of this principle. The case of negroes in the United States may be taken up for this purpose. Same thing can be said about the minorities in any state such as the Hindus and Buddhists in Pakistan and Christians in a Muslim country like Lebanon or Sudan. In India we may refer to the case of Scheduled Castes, Scheduled Tribes, and other socially and educationally backward classes. The case of women and children may also be counted here. The affirmative action of the state can be helpful to those who have suffered injustice for centuries. This historic injustice must be undone to place the unprivileged sections of the people on a pedestal of equality with the rest of people. It is an attempt not only to eliminate discrimination but to redress the wrongs done in the past.

Also known by the name of protective or compensatory discrimination, affirmative action of the state does not violate the principle of ideal equality if its implications are sythesised with the norms of social justice. For instance, the US Rights Act of 1964 secured civil rights to the negroes. It prohibited discrimination in voting, public education, accommodation and employment. The Indian Constitution sanctions reservations in favour of Scheduled Castes, Scheduled Tribes and other socially and educationally backward classes. Discrimination may be made by the state in favour of women and children also. Preference may be given to the local people in recruitment to lower posts. State may adopt social security measures to help the sick, aged and physically handicapped or destitute people.

However, it is also essential required that some reasonable limits be fixed so that the system of reservations does not become inconsistent with the standards of efficiency in administration. Taking it in view, the Courts in India have repeatedly ruled that the number of seats reserved for any category of persons should not exceed fifty per cent of the total number of seats. In the *Indra Sawhney Case* (1992), the Supreme Court has further ruled that this benefit should not be given to those belonging to the backward classes if they come into the 'creamy layer', that is, they are economically well off. And yet this fact cannot be overlooked that by having such benefits, the recipients develop a sort of vested interest and so they feel happy in remaining backward or depressed.

Liberal and socialist thinkers have different views about the existence and retention of the system of affirmative action of the state. For instance, while F.A. Hayek calls it as something against the law of nature, John Rawls sanctions it for a very limited section of the people. Many others like Laski and Nehru argue that "affirmative action programmes are required for economically and culturally disadvantaged groups, if their members are to have a genuinely equal opportunity to acquire the qualifications necessary for economic success."[58]

Relationship between Liberty and Equality: Now we turn to the most complex theme of relationship between liberty and equality. The difficulty, in this direction, arises from the fact that, historically speaking, the glorification of liberty precedes that of equality and until recent times many thinkers can be seen assigning a higher and superior position to the former. For instance, ancient Greek and Roman ideals of liberty were not coupled with the notion of equality, as not all men were free in slave societies. Though the Stoics preached the principle of natural equality of mankind, it received limited response. Moreover, when thinkers like Polybius and Cicero of the Roman period repeated the Stoic doctrine, they did so just to make their political philosophy consonant with the changing conditions of the empire. The whim of difference between a Greek and a barbarian and subsequently between a Roman and a non-Roman continued until Christianity became the official religion that preached the doctrine of 'Fatherhood of God and brotherhood of man'.

Liberty remained a privilege of the aristocratic section of the society. A great social contractualist like John Locke described liberty as a natural right, but he excluded the case of right to equality. It is the American Declaration of Independence of 1776 that, for the first time, incorporated the idea of equality and that saw its shining repetition in the slogan of 'Liberty, Equality, Fraternity' during the days of French Revolution in 1789. Since then the relationship between liberty and equality has been a matter of controversy that has two sides:

1. The negative view is that liberty and equality are incompatible terms. An English poet Matthew Arnold spoke strongly about the incompatibility of the attitude of equality with the spirit of humanity and a sense of dignity of man which are the marks of a true civilised society. Lord Birkenhead declared that 'all men are equal' is a poisonous doctrine. Sir Ernest Benn writes that economic equality is a 'scientific impossibility'.[59] It is based on the Aristotelian notion that mankind are unequal by nature; that equals should be treated equally and unequals unequally. A modern protagonist of this view like F.A. Hayek says: "From the fact that people are very different, it follows that if we treat them equally, the result must be inequality in their actual position, and that the only way to place them in an equal position would be to treat them differently."[60] Lord Acton of England and Alexis de Tocqueville of France subscribe to the same view that liberty is a privilege of

58. Will Kymlicka: *Contemporary Political Philosophy,* p. 58.
59. Tawney, *op. cit.,* p. 19.

Relationship Between Liberty and Equality

Negative View

All men are not equal, nor can they ever be. The argument of natural inequality of mankind still stands valid in the light of the 'rule of the privilege'. The number of persons competent to share in social, economic and political affairs is limited. Government is an expert undertaking that requires highly specialised technical competence and consequently demands of its practitioners more than ordinary qualities of character or mind. Let the deserving get more than those who deserve less or none at all.

1. Aristocracy and priesthood, a governing class and a teaching class ... there did no society exist without these two vital elements, there will none exist.

—Thomas Carlyle

2. The parliamentary principle of decision by majority, by denying the authority of the person and placing it instead in the number of crowd in question, sins against the aristocratic basic idea of nature.

—Adolf Hitler

3. Society is always a dynamic unity of two component factors—minorities and masses. The minorities are individuals or groups of individuals which are especially qualified. The mass is the assemblage of persons not specially qualified.

—O.Y. Gasset

Positive View

It is only in their skill, intelligence, strength, or virtue that men are equal, but merely in their being men; it is their common humanity that constitutes their equality. On this interpretation, we should not seek for some special characteristics in respect of which men are equal, but merely remind ourselves that they are all men, because:

1. All are human beings; all belong to the same species, can speak a language, use tools, live in societies, can interbreed despite racial differences, etc.
2. 'Treat every man as an end in himself and not as a means'. (Kant). Each man is to be, as were, free from certain conspicuous structures of inequality in which we find him.
3. The notion of inequality is invoked not only in connections where all men are claimed in some sense to be equal, but in connections where they are agreed to be unequal as in situations of need and merit.

—Bernard Williams

the few that cannot be reconciled with the liberty of all that means equality. A recent American writer says that equality "can be reached only by massive external intervention in people's lives."[61] The acme of such an affirmation can be traced in the interpretation that the pursuit of equality has in practice led to inequality and tyranny. Bringing about a condition of equality results in the coercion of the many at the hands of the few. "A society in which the choices fundamental to human existence are determined by coercion is not a free society. It follows irresistibly that egalitarianism must choose between liberty and equality."[62]

2. The positive view takes liberty and equality as compatible terms. It was reiterated by the Stoics and the Roman lawyers in the ancient period that 'all are equal in the eye of nature'. The Christian thinkers repeated the same point by replacing nature with God. But in the present century it has seen its reaffirmation at the hands of many positive liberals. For instance, Hobhouse says that 'liberty without equality is a high sounding phrase with squalid results'. In the words of Tawney, 'a large measure of equality, so far from being inimical to liberty, is essential to it'. While lamenting over the 'religion of inequality', he says that the people "accepted the *mana* (a mysterious wisdom) and *karakia* (a magical influence) of social and economic inequality in the same way that primitive people accepted the ritual of tribal society. There is no rational justification for social inequality; its survival is a matter of prejudice."[63] So says Barker: "It remains to add that equality is not an isolated principle. It stands by the principle of liberty and fraternity."[64]

The positive view is really convincing. If the aim of normative political theory is to seek and analyse the avenues relating to the development of human personality, it is required that the ideals of liberty and equality should have a simultaneous flow despite the fact that in terms of historical evolution the latter is older than, and no matter now outshone by, the former. Both are necessarily connected with the supreme worth and dignity of human personality and the spontaneous development of its capacities. The modern age is not prepared to tolerate the fact that the boons of liberty and with that of equality remain confined to the world of the 'peers'. While paraphrasing the ideas of Laski, Deane says: "Liberty and equality are not in conflict, nor even separate, but are different facets of the same ideal.... Indeed.... Since they are identical, there can be no problem of law or to what extent they are or can be related to. This is surely the nearest, if not the most satisfactory, solution ever devised for a perennial problem in political philosophy."[65]

---

60. Hayek: *The Constitution of Liberty,* p. 87.
61. Richard Norman: "Does Equality Destroy Liberty?" In Keith Graham (ed.): *Contemporary Political Philosophy,* p. 85.
62. K. Joseph and J. Sumption: *Equality,* p. 47.
63. Tawney, *op. cit.,* p. 13.
64. Barker, *op. cit.,* p. 159.
65. H.A. Deane: *The Political Ideas of Laski,* p. 46.

4
Justice, Crime and Punishment

The three terms—justice, crime and punishment—are inter-related. Violation of the norm of justice makes a crime and its indictability involves punishment. Although it is difficult to offer a precise or standard definition of all the three terms, the problem may be solved if our attention remains confined to their juristic interpretations involving empirical as well as normative aspects.

Justice

If political theory is studied in purely normative terms, one comes to this important conclusion that what really connects the themes of law, rights, liberty and equality (including fraternity or cooperation) is the element of justice. In every organised community these themes have their value and there must be something to bring them together so that we may understand the nature of a well-ordered community. As we shall see, justice is one of the important themes of political theory that "is the reconciler or synthesiser of political values; it is their union in an adjusted and integrated whole: it is, in Aristotle's words, 'what answers to the whole of goodness...being the exercise of goodness as a whole... towards one's neighbours."[1] It is obvious that the theme of justice has a significance of its own in the realm of political theory in view of the fact that among the proper ends of state and government, it has been given a high rank at all times. "Two axioms have been generally accepted without question; first, that government's own actions ought to be just; second, that governmental institutions such as law courts, ought to ensure the preservation of justice."[2]

Meaning and Nature: It is a difficult task to offer a precise definition of the term 'justice' for some reasons. First, the term 'justice' is given different meanings by different people at different times. Not only this, its implications vary from man to man and from situation to situation. Second, the idea of justice is a dynamic affair. As such, its implications change with the passage of time. What was justice in the past may be injustice today or *vice versa*. A further difficulty arises in reconciling the abstract notion of justice with its practical manifestation. For instance, one may talk of moral justice or divine justice, but it will hardly be conformable to any set of empirical standards and, for this reason, not capable of practical application. Due to this, we may appreciate the view of Potter that "most men think that they understand the meaning of justice, but, in fact, their notions prove to be vague."[3]

---

1. E. Barker: *Principles of Social and Political Theory.*, p. 102.
2. Arnold Brecht: *Political Theory,* p. 136.
3. Harold Potter: *The Quest of Justice,* p. 3.

The concept of justice has these important implications. First, it requires a just state of affairs. That is, it is impossible to assess the justice of actions without a prior identification of the just state of affairs.[4] Second, it is aligned with the conditions of morality. For instance, a fair race is one in which a person who wins morally deserves to win but one in which there is no cheating, nobody jumps the gun, or has an unfair advantage through the use of bad things like drugs.[5] Third, it carries the sense of proper distribution of favours and losses. It means that it is primarily concerned with the way rewards and punishments are distributed among the individuals in a rule-governed practice and its intimate connection with fairness indicates that if a ruler were to boil his subjects in oil, jumping in afterwards himself, it would amount to an act of injustice though there would be no inequality of treatment.[6] Fourth, it normally prevails in a congenial atmosphere that is provided by a democratic set-up, but it may also survive in a non-democratic set-up as an exception. "Fair rules may be impartially enforced in regimes which allow little political participation and majority rule democracies may generate arbitrary treatment of individuals and minorities."[7]

While dealing with the problem of offering a precise definition of the term 'justice', we should, however, keep this paramount fact in our mind that "not only do different individuals hold various ideas about the ideal state of affairs they would consider really just; every individual is capable of several such ideas. Our ideas and feelings of justice may be two-fold, or three-fold, or manifold in accordance with different systems of values to which we respond positively at different times, or even simultaneously. Justice, in the light of personal ideas, is, or at least may be a barrel with several bottoms."[8]

Theories: What is the real nature of justice? Different theories have come up ranging from philosophical theory that studies it in quite abstract or metaphysical terms to the Marxian theory that identifies it with class domination in a society. First of all, we take up the *philosophical theory of justice* finding its place in the religious injunctions, or in the highly abstract ideas of philosophers. Hindu scriptures identify justice with *Dharma* or righteousness that involves duties in the category of actions. Plato in his *Republic* treats justice as the principle of right ordering of human personality so as to have a right ordering of social classes. In the case of individual the principle of justice means that he should discover his place according to the best element of his personality (reason, courage, appetite); in the case of society it means that it should have three classes (ruling class, military class, economic class) and in each class individuals should be accommodated according to the best element of their personality. There should be no interference of one element or of one class into the domain of another. Only this shall open the way for proper division of labour and specialisation of functions. Here

---

4. David Miller: *Social Justice,* pp. 17-18.
5. Brian Barry: *Political Argument,* p. 103.
6. W.K. Frankena: "The Concept of Social Justice" in R. Brandt (ed.): *Social Justice,* p. 17.
7. N P. Barry: *An Introduction to Modern Political Theory,* p. 116.
8. Brecht, *op. cit.,* pp. 147-48.

is the profile of a just man and a just society and, for this reason, justice means proper ordering of the three elements of human personality and reorganisation of society in three classes in correspondence to these three elements of human personality. A critic may say that all this is too abstract to be understood by a man of average comprehension and that it is too difficult to be put into practical terms.

Then, there is *natural theory* of justice. Man should follow the principles of a moral life as sanctioned by the law of nature. For instance, the observance of the principle of natural equality of mankind is a precept of natural justice. Slavery is not a natural but a conventional institution. With the advent of Christianity the word 'nature' came to have its substitute in God. Therefore, natural justice came to be identified with divine justice. The law of nature became the law of God. As such, not law of nature but law of God (as contained in the holy books) became the determinant of justice. Even in modern times, the canons of natural (or divine) justice are invoked as the strong should not oppress the weak, the victor should not kill the vanquished when the latter surrenders, even criminals should be treated in a humane way inside the jail. Once again, a critic may say that, like philosophical justice, the idea of natural or divine justice is a matter of myth. It is too abstract and metaphysical in nature.

But the most clear-cut and widely understood theory on this subject pertains to the realm of law. The *legal theory* of justice identifies the whole idea of justice with the working of the courts. The magistrate is the administrator of justice and, as such, he should interpret the meaning of law and then pronounce a verdict whether the accused is guilty of a certain crime or not and, if guilty, what punishment should be given to him. The advocates of imperative theory of jurisprudence like Hobbes, Bentham, Austin and Dicey fully endorse this view. The legislature has the authority to make a law and the courts have the authority to administer justice according to the law of the land. In a situation where law is silent, the courts may act according to the norms of natural justice. Out of it arises a new kind of law based on the principles of equity. It is required that a dispute must be settled by a court of competent jurisdiction; the accused must be given opportunity to defend himself; the procedure of trial must be fair and open; the judges hearing the case should act freely and honestly; the accused should be given punishment according to the nature and magnitude of the wrong. It is obvious that this theory is the best of all theories on this subject and it constitutes the basis of Western jurisprudence. Proper implementation of this theory leads to the creation of an ideal situation what Dicey calls the 'rule of law'.

But the *Marxian theory of justice* is different from all theories discussed above. Here law and justice are identified with the fact of class domination. To the Marxists, state is an instrument of exploitation and oppression by one class over another and, as such, law and justice are nothing else than a part of the entire state structure. The legislature makes a law that is in the interest of the ruling class; so the courts act in a way that strengthens and defends the interests of the class in power. If the instruments of law and justice may protect and promote the interests of the bourgeois class, they will serve the purpose of the proletariat after the successful socialist revolution. It means that judiciary has a 'committed' character. It defends the system of exploitation in a bourgeois society; it finishes the class of exploiters in a socialist society.

It shows that while the liberal interpretation of justice is quite flexible and places judiciary in an impartial and independent position, the Marxist notion desires its committed form. The result is that while the former is too flexible and, for this reason, amenable to diverse, even conflicting, interpretations in various important directions, the latter is inherent with very rigid postures. Highlighting this essential point of distinction between liberal and totalitarian (including Fascist and Communist) varieties, an eminent writer says: "In modern democratic society the judge must steer his way between the Scylla of subservience to government and the Charybdis of remote lies from constantly changing social pressures and economic needs... the administration of law under these systems becomes a predominantly political function and an instrument of government policy."[9]

Kinds: What is known by the name of justice in common parlance relates to the settlement of disputes through judicial bodies. It is in this respect that this term has a positive character and by virtue of which the law of the state and the justice of the courts become very close affairs. However, with the penetration of democracy into social and economic spheres, the meaning of justice has expanded itself so as to cover all walks of human life. A new awareness has developed that informs that the rights of an individual should be reasonably restricted in the wider interests of his community so that the ends of social justice are properly achieved. In other words, it is widely recognised that the well being of society depends on the coordination and reconciliation between the rights of the individual and interests of the community. Not only this, if there is a conflict between the two, the latter should prevail over the former. Thus figures in the issue of justice in social, economic and political spheres.

First of all, we take up the case of *social justice*. It is related to the balance between an individual's rights and social control ensuring the fulfilment of the legitimate expectations of the individual under the existing laws and assures him benefits thereunder and protection in case of any violation or encroachment on his rights, consistent with the unity of the nation and needs of the society. Undoubtedly, the idea of social justice requires the sacrifice of certain rights of an individual at the altar of general interest. However, viewed in a wider perspective, the idea of social justice not only aims at the proper reconciliation of the interest of an individual with the over-all interest of the community or prevalence of the latter over the former in the event of any conflict, it also constitutes "an essential part of the great complex of social change, for which something may have to be sacrificed for a greater good."[10]

It is evident that the concept of social justice is a very wide term that covers within its fold everything pertaining to the norm of general interest ranging from the protection of the interests of the minorities to the eradication of poverty and illiteracy. It is not merely related to the observance of the principle of equality before law and

9. W. Friedman: *Law in Changing Society,* pp. 65-66.
10. Boalding: "Social Justice in Social Dynamics" in R. Brandt (ed.): *Social Justice,* p. 92.

independence of judiciary as we find in the developed countries of the West, it is also related to the eradication of gigantic social evils like those of pauperism, disease, unemployment and starvation which have their stigmatic expression on the face of the developing countries of the East. Moreover, all this is also related to the liquidation of vested interests that obstruct the achievement of common good and have their interest in the maintenance of the status quo to their own advantage. As such, in the backward countries of the world, the idea of social justice enjoins upon the state to make concerted efforts for the improvement of the lot of the down-trodden and weaker sections of the community. Its area widens itself so as to cover the economic domain of a people's life for the obvious reason that it demands non-exploitation of the working class.

The difficulty about defining the theme of social justice and its proper realisation by the state is that it lacks a precise connotation on account of varying social and economic theories and, more than that, in view of the conflicting interpretations of thinkers and jurists belonging to the liberal and the Marxist schools. It is owing to this formidable difficulty that the ideal remains such a variable from Robinhood to the levellers and to those conducting the 'gherao' (i.e., encirclement of a person for coercing him to accept the demands) all declare themselves to be in pursuit of social justice. An eminent writer on this subject thus observes: "We hear much today of 'social justice'. I am not sure that those men who use the term most glibly know very clearly what they mean by it. Some mean distribution or redistribution of wealth; some interpret it as 'equality of opportunity'—a misleading term, since opportunity can never be equal among human beings who have unequal capacities to grasp it. Many, I suspect, mean simply that it is unjust that anybody should be fortunate than themselves and the more intelligent mean that it is just—I would rather say benevolent—that every effort should be made at least to mitigate the asperities of natural human inequality and that no obstacle should be offered, but rather help offered, to practicable opportunities of self-improvement."[11]

The case of *economic justice* should be treated as a corollary to what we have said above. As a matter of fact, the two are closely related so much so that a discussion of one covers much what comes within the fold of the discussion of another. It is owing to this that while social justice demands eradication of gigantic social evils, most of them (as exploitation of the workers by the capitalists or concentration of national wealth in fewer hands) find their place, in particular, in the economic sphere. Thus, the whole idea of liberty issuing forth in the form of economic justice crosses the domain of politics and enters into those of economics and sociology. It is well said: "Freedom is meaningless if it prevents the achievement of economic justice. To a hungry man or to a man who is denied human dignity, political freedom is an empty word. The problem of today is how to bring about economic and social justice without sacrificing the individual to the ever-increasing power of the state."[12]

Simply stated, the idea of economic justice means non-discrimination between man and man on the basis of economic values. In positive terms, it implies adequate

---

11. C.K. Allen, *Aspects of Justice.*, p. 3.
12. M.C. Chagla: *The Individual and the State*, p. 8.

payments for work without any discrimination on some artificial ground. It also enjoins freedom for all in the sphere of production and distribution of goods subject to the conditions of social welfare. It also demands that the state of national economy be reshaped in a way that the benefits are made more and more available to the common man. In this way, the idea of economic justice comes to imply a socialist pattern of society. What Nehru said about the case of economic justice in a poor and backward country like ours applies to the case of economic justice in general that it necessarily relates itself with feeding the starving and clothing the naked masses, providing them shelter, and affording them all opportunities of progress.

We may easily take note of the fact that, like social justice, the case of economic justice is a matter of acute controversy between the liberal and Marxist thinkers. Not only this, it is a matter of acute controversy among the proponents of liberalism too in view of the fact that their commitments vary from the canons of classical individualism to those of democratic socialism. Thus, we find that while the Communists desire to abolish the institution of private property for the sake of bringing about an era of economic justice, the liberals invoke varying standards ranging from the maintenance of private property system to the imposition of reasonable restrictions on its use and enjoyment by the people. As a result both notions suffer from inherent fallacies. For instance, while one may say that the Marxist formula 'from each according to his ability, to each according to his work' in the era of socialism and 'from each according to his ability, to each according to his need' in the final stage of socialism (communism) would be contrary to the just principle of distribution as well as to the humanistic norm of helping the weak and the disabled even when they do not work. Likewise, we may say that the norm of regulatory legislation of reasonable restriction as laid down by the courts of free and democratic countries would make the whole idea of economic justice fluid, perhaps touching the verge of meaninglessness. "He may have to come to appreciate the view that justice and ideas about it are having, therefore, to seek a new balance and a new harmony in the present conflicts between large national economic and social interests, on the one hand, and the individual or group rights and interests on the other."[13]

However, the idea of *political justice* is not a matter of controversy so far as its theoretical expression is concerned. It stands for a free and fair participation of the people in the political sphere. As such, it involves the guarantee of universal adult franchise and no distinction on some artificial grounds in matters of recruitment to public services. What the policy of the state should be, and how the society should be organised in political and economic directions are matters which should be decided by the people themselves according to the prevailing needs and circumstances. Here the idea of the preservation of political rights of the individual dominates the scene so much so that the very notion of justice, by and large, assumes an individualistic tenor in view of the fact that, despite being a social creature, some of his deeper pursuits in the field of knowledge, mind

13. P.B. Mukharji: *Three Elemental Principles of Indian Constitution*, pp. 12-13.

and spirit are individual affairs. As a matter of fact, they "are the springs from which civilisation grows."[14]

In other words, the notion of political justice requires that the state must protect and preserve certain valuable rights of the individual so that he may develop his personality as a citizen and thereby contribute his share to the welfare of the political community. It desires a liberal-democratic order in which rights of the individuals, including those of the minorities, are well protected. Viewed in a wider perspective, it naturally covers much of what falls under the category of social and economic justice. Moreover, it makes itself coterminous with the case of a full-fledged democratic order. It involves not merely recognition and protection of rights relating to the maintenance of a political creed, it also enjoins the prevalence of right to dissent and duty to tolerate.

Apart from discussing the three kinds of justice in the social, economic and political spheres, we may also look into its two other varieties—distributive and corrective. The concept of *distributive justice* has assumed an importance of its own in the present age of 'socialist democracy' or 'revisionist liberalism' as traceable in the writings of J.W. Chapman and John Rawls. The earliest notion of distributive justice is given by Aristotle who says that equals should be treated equally and unequals unequally. Injustice arises when the reverse comes to take place. In other words, this idea establishes an organic relationship between the norms of justice and the principle of equality. The modern interpretation of this term is, however, different which establishes an organic relationship of a juristic norm with a particular system of economy. In this sense, distributive justice desires equal distribution of income among the equals only.

But *corrective justice* is contained in the verdict of the judicial bodies that is delivered after hearing the statement of parties in a dispute. The aim of this norm is to correct the erratic behaviour of the party in dispute. Obviously, it emanates from the decisions of the courts in which we find an interpretation of the law of the land, a wise distinction between 'just' and 'unjust' situations, award of punishment to the wrong-doer, strictures passed against the delinquent authority and the like. It is possible that, in certain cases the courts may significantly reduce the scope of inequality created by the statutory provisions of the land. In brief, what is done by the courts to correct the erratic behaviour of a person by following the law of the land constitutes the case of corrective or 'positive' justice.

On the whole, what we have seen so far leaves an impression that justice is essentially a normative concept having its place in various spheres like religion, philosophy, ethics and jurisprudence, though its ramifications also cover social, political and economic spheres. So great is the diversity of its connotations that it becomes difficult to lay down its precise meaning. It is, however, for the sake of convenience that justice is necessarily related with the function of judicial organisations. But, as pointed out in the beginning, in the realm of political theory, justice is the bond that connects important political values like those of rights, liberty, equality and fraternity. For instance, there can be no liberty if there is no equality; and there can be no equality if there is no

14. *Ibid.*, p. 20.

justice. Likewise, we may say that there can be no liberty if there are no rights, and there can be no protection of rights if there is no well-organised system of law so as to ensure proper administration of justice. In short, justice is the synthesiser and reconciler of great political values. Daniel Webster is right when he holds that "justice is the chiefest interest of man."[15]

Views of Rawls: In 1958 and thereafter, John Rawls wrote some papers with the title of 'justice as fairness' which were elaborated in his *A Theory of Justice* published in 1971. Since, he has followed the style of great contractualists like Hobbes and Locke in arriving at a conclusion on the basis of a hypothetical situation, what he calls 'original position', this theory is known as the contractarian theory of justice. He rejects the utilitarian argument that justice implies 'greatest good of the greatest number' and instead holds that in the 'original position', each individual is a 'rational agent' who knows his interest and for its sake he intelligently negotiates with other individuals who are equally selfish and behave like 'intelligent negotiators'. It is a different thing that some individuals may not be aware of this fact that the distribution of offices or rewards is justly done according to the results of a competition conducted in a fair manner.

Rawls takes up the issue of 'primary goods' or needs-resources which are to be distributed fairly. It is based on the maintenance of two principles:

1. Each person is to have an equal right to the most extensive liberty compatible with a similar liberty for all.
2. Social and economic inequalities are to be arranged so that they are both: (a) to the greatest benefit of the least advantaged, and (b) attached to positions and offices open to all under conditions of fair equality of opportunity.

While the first principle reflects a traditional liberal commitment to formal equality, the second principle (the so-called difference principle) points towards a significant measure of social equality.[16]

Justice requires that all individuals have basic or primary goods in the nature of equal rights and opportunities and some income. Each individual should have some income and for this sake the state should eradicate economic inequality. Only then the least advantaged person may have the benefit of improving his lot so as to become the highest member of his society. Such a situation shall strengthen incentives and enlarge the size of the social cake. In his view, the people would support it if they were not placed behind 'a veil of ignorance' which deprives them of the knowledge of their own social position and status. The people cooperating together for mutual advantage should have an equal claim to the fruits of their cooperation and should not be penalised as a result of factors such as gender, race and genetic inheritance over which they have no control. Redistribution and welfare are, therefore, 'just', because they conform to a widely held view of what is fair.[17]

15. Mukharji, *op. cit.,* p. 29.
16. Andrew Heywood, *Political Theory: An Introduction,* p. 297.
17. *Ibid.,* p. 298.

The theory of justice as given by Rawls may be criticised on some grounds. The communitarians (as A. MacIntyre, Michael Walzer, Michael Sandel and Charles Taylor) accuse the makers of such theories of treating individual as a purely selfish creature having no obligations or responsibilities towards the community. Individual is taken as an 'unencumbered self' interested in his own good without having anything to do with the public good. Moreover, the norms of justice differ from one community to another. Hence, there can be no universal theory of justice. The idea is abstract that cannot be applied to the life of the communities as given by Hobbes and Locke. "The weakness of such a notion is that it abstracts the individual from his or her social context, and so ignores the contribution which society has made to cultivating individual skills and talents in the first place. Some would go on to argue further that to treat individuals in this way is to reward them for selfishness and actually to promote egoistical behaviour."[18]

It is true that Rawls is an egalitarian and he is an advocate of a liberal democratic order suitable to rich and advanced countries of the world. In the system of Rawls, the state may correct economic imbalance or eradicate economic inequality, but it cannot play the role of a welfare agency the type of which is advocated by the democratic socialists. He lays stress on the point of individual as a selfish creature and desires a system with as little control of state as for as possible. Such a view cannot be acceptable to the people of poor and backward countries who desire a social and economic revolution in the country by the active role of the state.

Crime

The conception of crime "is an unusually difficult one, since it is difficult to find any definition of crime that does not have a larger element of circularity. In general, crimes are defined as events and actions that are proscribed by the criminal law of a particular country. This reduces the definition of a crime to being 'what the criminal law says it is'."[19] However, this definition cannot be of universal application in view of the fact that the boundaries of a legal system are usually those of the nation-state, but the national boundaries are not exactly similar to cultural boundaries.[20]

Crime is a misdeed or a wrong action of indictable nature that invites punishment. It consists in the violation of a rule or law made by the state or some authority in whose favour the state delegates such power. Crime is, however, different from a sin that consists in the violation of a religious code and for which punishment may be

---

18. Heywood, *op. cit.,* p. 300.
19. L.T. Wilkins "Offence Patterns" in David I. Sills (ed.): *International Encyclopaedia of the Social Sciences,* Vol. 3, p. 476.
20. The sociologists identify crime with 'deviancy' and call a study of crimes scathingly as the 'sociology of nuts, sluts and perverts'. Some of them as Howard Becker of the United States are called 'label theorists, because they attribute labels to wrong doers as 'criminals' or 'non-criminals', 'murderers' or 'innocents' just to throw light on the stigmatised behaviour of a person. Stephen Moore and Barry Hendry: *Sociology,* p. 188.

awarded by God in this life or hereafter or by the 'custodians of the public conscience'. Following points may be noted in the definition of a crime:

1. Crime is always defined in terms of social institutions and their organisations. A wrong committed by a slave could be a crime in a slave or feudal society, but not so when slavery is abolished in the capitalist society.
2. Crime involves at least two essential actors the victim and the sufferer. Crime may be perceived or defined differently according to the role of either of the two. If one party is a person, the other party may be a person or an institution like a corporation or a state.
3. Crime is a kind of human behaviour subject to the canons of public behaviour as laid down in a statute. For instance, polygamy is a crime in Hindu society, but not in a Muslim society.
4. A crime is no crime unless it is detected or cleared up.
5. Some acts of misdeed may be a crime against the state like assassination of the alien rulers for which the guilty persons are awarded long terms of imprisonment, or are even executed. But after independence such persons are honoured as martyrs and, if languishing in jail, they are granted amnesty by the government of the national leaders.
6. Crimes are of many kinds as civil, criminal, and constitutional. Non-payment of rent is a civil wrong, committing theft or burglary is a criminal wrong, violation of the oath of office by the head of the state or government is a constitutional wrong. Since embezzlement or misappropriation of state funds by the bureaucrats is different from the misdeeds of murder or dacoity, some writers prefer to call them 'white collar crimes' just for the sake of giving a refined name to something that is basically bad.
7. A crime is an illegal and indictable act, but action must be taken within time. A crime is no crime if its indictability expires with undue passage of time as specified in the law of limitation.

The social and political philosophers have different views about the nature and causes of crimes as well as about the punishment to be awarded to the guilty persons. The causes may be of any kind like social, cultural, economic, psychological, political and the like. A pauper may feel forced to commit theft, or the exploited people may rise in revolt at the behest of a leader like Lenin or Mao. Emile Durkheim of France holds that a certain amount of crime is a factor in public health, an integral part of all societies, and that crime performs an important function in bringing about social change. His argument is based on his theory of division of labour in a society that creates the line of distinction between good and bad as laid down by the 'collective conscience' of the society. If a person breaks the permissible line, he commits a crime for which he must be punished.[21] As sunshine informs us about the difference between light and darkness, so crime specifies the line of distinction between permissible and non-perminsble actions of a person or persons.

21. *Ibid.*, p. 191.

Some Important Statements

A crime is a breach of criminal law, which is law that establishes the relationship between the state and the individual, and thus lays down the conditions for orderly and peaceful social interactions. Criminals persons convicted of a crime) are usually seen as being motivated by self-gain of some kind, rather than broader political or moral considerations, as in the case of civil disobedience.

—Andrew Heywood

Politics, p. 390.

The term 'punishment', in its psychological sense, is most commonly and appropriately applied to a situation in which a privation or an unpleasant experience is deliberately imposed by one party or another because of an actual or supposed misdeed which is knowingly and intentionally committed by the latter. The misdeed may be the violation of a rule or law, a command or an expectation and may consist either of an act or of inaction when action is called for.

—A.R. Lindesmith

"Punishment" in David I. Sills (ed.): *International Encyclopaedia of the Social Sciences*, Vol. 13, p. 217.

The argument of Durkheim may be empirically correct, it cannot be appreciated in ideal terms. Crime is a misdeed which reflects the bad side of human behaviour. According to Gandhiji, a crime is a consequence of the 'mental illness' of a person. The argument of Goebbels that 'a lie is a lie if spoken by one person, it is no lie if spoken by many people', cannot stand in the face of Gandhiji's assertion that 'untruth is untruth and it cannot become truth if spoken by any number of people'. Hence, to say that 'upto a certain level, crime may be useful and healthy in society' is absurd. The weight of this maxim cannot be refuted that crime never pays.

Punishment

The essence of the concept of political obligation is that man should obey the state; the essence of the theme of political resistance is that man can disobey the state under some conditions. But a question arises whether the state has a right to punish the wrong-doer. Redressal of the wrong must be done. One may say that it may be done by the individuals themselves. But the act of determination of the wrong and the award of punishment should not be in the hands of the individuals, as it would amount to the prevalence of the state of nature in which, as Locke says, everyone is a policeman as well as a magistrate. What is, therefore, needed in a civil society is that the state must take upon itself the task of determining the nature of the wrong and also setting up a suitable machinery for the award of punishment given by one of its competent authorities. Only then the liberty of the individual can be protected or his rights secured by the actions of the wrong-doers. So 'rights demand the state', says Green. The whole idea may be put in these words: "A criminal displays an anti-social will and, therefore, society is justified in interfering with his right to free life. In the interest of society it is necessary that the criminal tendencies in everyone of its members be curbed. To neglect this will lead society back to primitive chaos and anarchy."[22]

Meaning: The word 'punishment' literally means torture that a person should undergo on account of doing a wrong. Hence, it may be seen from a religious or an ethical point of view. The religious injunction is that God being the ruler of this world punishes those who break His laws. 'The mills of God grind surely, though slowly'. A moralist would say that a man should always act according to his best rational judgment and if he makes a wrong by default, he should correct it by undergoing a self-imposed penance or remorse. But different is the viewpoint of a jurist who desires positive role of the state in a matter relating to the determination of the guilt and award of suitable punishment according to the law of the land. It shows that there are different views about the meaning of punishment. Prof. Flew has suggested five criteria for the use of this word (punishment) in its primary sense as:[23]

1. It must involve an evil or an unpleasantness to the victim.
2. It must be for an actual or supposed offence.
3. It must be for an actual or supposed offender.
4. It must be the work of personal agencies (i.e., not merely the natural consequences of an action).
5. It must be imposed by authority (real or supposed), conferred by the system of rules against which the offence has been committed.

But Benn and Peters add one more item to the above list: that the unpleasantness should be an essential part of what is intended and not merely incidental to some other aim.[24]

Justification: Punishment is a matter of necessity. It may be justified on two important grounds:

1. The utilitarian argument as advanced by Jeremy Bentham is that by violating a law of the state, the wrong-doer adds to the unhappiness of the society and, for that reason, he must be punished. But the nature of punishment should be such that the wrong-doer is reformed so that the stock of social happiness is increased by excluding the possibilities of a greater evil. While dealing with the subject of penology, Bentham suggests the scheme of having a semi-circular jail (Panopticon) with the seat of the jailor in the centre and the rooms of the prisoners on the periphery so that the jail staff may keep a close watch on the activities of the jail inmates. The aim of the jail staff should be to convert the criminals into

---

22. E. Asirvatham, *Political Theory.,* p. 248.
23. A. Flew: "The Justification of Punishment" in *Philosophy*, Vol. XXIX (1954), pp. 291-307.
24. Benn and Peters, *Social Principles and Democratic State,* p. 174.

better citizens. As he says: "All punishment is mischief, all punishment in itself is an evil. Upon the principle of utility, if it ought at all to be admitted, it ought only to be admitted in as far as it promises to exclude some greater evil."[25]

2. But the argument of the idealists is peculiarly harsh. Rousseau says that a state has every right to punish the wrong-doer in the interest of protecting a system based on the 'general will of the community'. A wrong-doer may be forced to be a good man, or 'he must be forced to be free.' Kant says that a 'penal law is a categorical imperative of duty'. Hegel says that a state can do no wrong and if a criminal is punished, he should be happy to feel that he is being made a free or an intelligent member of the civil society. So Green and Bosanquet contend that the aim of punishment should be 'removal of obstacles' in the way of the 'good life' of the people by very harsh means. It shows that, in the view of the idealists, "punishment, like all State action, has a moral purpose and a positive quality."[26]

In order to justify punishment, it should be differentiated from anything like revenge or retribution or vengeance. It refers to a penalty inflicted on a person for a crime or wrong or offence, but it should not be random or arbitrary. The wrong action of a person should be linked to a specific crime and the punishment to be awarded should also be proportionate to the guilt committed by him. Moreover, it "has a moral character that distinguishes it from simple vindictiveness. Punishment is not motivated by spite or the desire to inflict pain, discomfort or inconvenience for its own sake, but rather because a wrong has been done. That is why, what are thought of as cruel or inhuman punishments such as torture and perhaps the death penalty, are often prohibited."[27]

Theories: From such a justification of punishment, we may trace three important theories on this subject. In the first place, there is *retributive theory*. According to it, a wrong-doer must be punished because he has done a wrong. It is based on the old saying—'an eye for an eye and a tooth for a tooth'. Obviously, it imbibes the element of revenge or retaliation with this difference that while the action of an individual can be taken as revengeful, it cannot be so in the case of the state. The guilty should suffer pain for an act that gives pain to the society. The guilty should get punishment as a matter of his right in such a situation "of which he must not be defrauded."[28]

Then there is the *preventive* or *deterrent theory* of punishment. It is an extension of the above theory to the last extent. It tells us that the punishment given to a wrong-doer must be as hard as possible so that it may set an example and thereby possibly deter other persons to commit the same in time to come. That is, it not only punishes a particular person, it also directs punishment against other possible criminals. Thus, public execution of a person is justified who commits an act of murder. In this way, this theory "regards punishment as a measure of social hygiene. Punishment is a display of the power of society in the service of social self-preservation."[29]

25. Bentham: *An Introduction to the Principles of Morals and Legislation,* edited by W. Harrison, p. 281.
26. Barker: *Political Thought in England,* p. 38.
27. Heywood, *op. cit.,* p. 169.
28. B. Bosanquet: *The Philosophical Theory of State*, p. 211.

Finally, we may refer to *reformatory theory* on this subject. Here the burden of argument is that a criminal is like a patient and he needs proper cure. Instead of killing a patient, efforts should be made to cure his disease. So the criminal should be punished in a way that his character is reformed and he becomes a good member of the community.[30] Gandhiji also laid emphasis on this kind of punishment. The purpose of punishment should be to enlighten the soul of the criminal in a way that after completing the term of sentence he engages himself in an act of social service. One may say that such a view is thoroughly ethical and, therefore, amenable to be misunderstood by those who see things in their practical perspective alone.

All the three theories on the subject of punishment have their own points of merit and demerit. For instance, while the retributive and preventive theories are appreciated for discouraging persons from committing a crime and thereby protecting the system of rights in an effective way, the reformatory theory is criticised for being too idealistic and thereby encouraging the tendency of committing crimes. Let the punishment be as harsh as possible so that its repetition may not take place. But the demerit of the retributive and deterrent theories is that they hurt the norm of a civilised way of thinking. The merit of the reformatory theory is that it treats crime as a conventional affair that may be checked by reforming the character of the individual with the force of love and fellow-feeling.[31]

It is not only desirable but essential that the award of punishment should be backed by a moral purpose for the sake of reform or rehabilitation of the wrong-doer. This is what Michael Foucault of France says in his *Discipline and Punishment* (1975). In his another work *Power/Knowledge,* (1980) he defines the term power in such a comprehensive way that, apart from being an instrument of exploitation and oppression, its exercise may also reform a person. For instance, when a criminal is put in jail and there he has to bear tortures, then he inculcates the feelings of being a good person. If a bad man is thus rehabilitated, it may be said to constitute the case of restorative justice.

---

29. Asirvatham, *op. cit.,* p. 249.
30. However, the utilitarian and the idealist arguments are not basically different from each other. It is evident that while the utilitarian can provide some sort of justification, the retributivist is either offering utilitarian arguments in disguise, or virtually denying that punishment in general needs any justification at all." Benn and Peters, *op. cit.,* p. 181.
31. Though reformative treatment "might cure criminal inclinations by relaxing the rigours of punishment, it might still defeat the ends of punishment, if it reduced the deterrent effects for other." *Ibid.,* p. 180. The deterrence theory of punishment cannot be defended on any ground. "The severity of the penalty imposed upon one individual must be balanced against the benefit of preventing similar crimes occurring in future. The problem, however, is that the idea of deterrence comes dangerously close to divorcing the wrong that has been done from the punishment meted out, and so runs the risk of victimising the initial wrong-doer. Indeed, deterrence theory sets no limits to the form of punishment that may be applied even for the most trivial offence." Heywood, *op. cit.,* p. 171.

What should be the best form of punishment? On this subject we may say that it should imbibe the essential elements of all the theories briefly discussed above. Sidgwick says: "I conclude, then, that from a political point of view, it is evidently necessary to take the primary end of punishment as prevention of mischiefs and not the retribution of wickedness; and to decide on this principle any doubtful question as to the allotment of punishments."[32] For this sake, he offers a set of following important principles.[33]

1. To realise the principle of justice that similar cases should be treated similarly, it is important that the punishment should be equal, e.g., if imprisonment then the same kind of imprisonment to all the delinquents.
2. Avoidance of excess in punishment is impossible not only in order to inflict no more pain than is needed but even more in order that different degrees of punishment may all be adequately deterrent, where the criminal has choice of alternatives differing in degrees of mischievousness. Punishment should be so chosen that clearly greater punishments may be allotted to more mischievousness.
3. Punishment should be of an exemplary kind–more in appearance less in reality, as appearance is more deterrent. But it should be offensive to public feeling and so likely to arouse aversion to the administration of law and dangerous sympathy with the criminal punished.
4. Punishment should be as little burdensome to the community as possible.
5. Punishment should be remissible if possible in the name of humanity.

Thus, a union of the elements of retribution, deterrence and reformation may be suggested as the best form of punishment. James Seth uses the word 'discipline' for punishment, but what he says is worth quoting at this stage that it should have no trace of vengeance or vindictiveness. "The goal of punishment should be to bring home to a man such a sense of guilt as shall work in him a deep repentence for the evil past, a new obedience for the time to come."[34]

---

32. Henry Sidgwick: *Elements of Politics*, p. 114.
33. *Ibid.*, pp. 123-25.
34. Seth: *Study of Ethical Principles*, p. 323.

5
Political Power, Hegemony, Ideology and Legitimacy

Political power is the central theme of political hegemony or ideology. Power may reside in the hands of one person, or few, or many persons, but it is required to secure and ensure political legitimacy and effectiveness. Hence, in this chapter an attempt has been made to discuss these important and inter-related concepts. The entire discussion is centred on this issue that "political ideas are, then, the theories and doctrines about how institutions are, can, and should be worked."[1]

Political Power

Ever since the *Leviathan* of Hobbes appeared in 1651, the concept of power in the realm of national and international politics has become a momentous subject of investigation so much so that now it is regarded as the key area of fundamental research. Curiously, it is so in spite of the fact that the real meaning of this term has been a matter of controversy on account of its social, economic, political, psychological and metaphysical ramifications. Recently the idea of power has assumed an importance of its own in the realm of political theory. The reason for this should be traced in the fact that the meaning of politics has now changed from one of being 'a study of state and government' to that of being a 'study of power'. As Curtis says: "Politics is organised dispute about power and its use, involving choice among competing values, ideas, persons, interests and demands. The study of politics is concerned with the description and analysis of the manner in which power is obtained, exercised, and controlled, and the purpose for which it is used, the manner in which decisions are made, the factors which influence the making of those decisions, and the context in which those decisions take place."[2]

Meaning: The problem of defining the term 'power' in a quite precise manner arises from the fact that different writers have taken different views about it. The result is that its real meaning seems to range from Friedrich's description of it as 'a certain kind of human relationship'[3] to Tawney's emphasis on the identification of power with the capacity of an individual or a group of individuals to modify the conduct of others

---

1. Bernard Crick: "The Tendency of Political Studies" in *New Society* (November, 1966), p. 683.
2. Michael Curtis: *Comparative Government and Politics,* p. 1.
3. Carl J. Friedrich: *Constitutional Government and Democracy,* pp. 12-14.

in the manner which one desires.'[4] Not merely this, while a great political thinker like Hobbes identifies power with some 'future apparent good', a modern psycho-analyst like Harold Lasswell likens it with 'influence'. We also find that while a great communist leader like Mao of China says that 'power flows from the barrel of a gun', an apostle of peace, truth and non-violence like Mahatma Gandhi substitutes the force of gun and bomb with the power of love and truth emanating from the hearts of the people.

If so, the sense of the term 'power' becomes interchangeable with several related themes like control, influence, authority, force, might, persuasion, coercion, domination and the like irrespective of the fact that different writers make use of different terms at different places and in different situations in their peculiar ways with the result that it becomes a highly tedious job to say as to what the word 'power' precisely conveys. Some other writers, however, warn against the insidious tendency of equating power with other kindred themes like influence, force, control and authority in order to have a proper understanding of each term. For instance, Max Weber says that power and authority are different things inasmuch as the latter invariably conveys within its fold the sense of 'legitimacy'. Likewise, force necessarily involves some brutal manifestation which may, or may not, form an integral part of the idea of power, no matter we invoke the observation of Bertrand Russell who takes power as 'the capacity to influence the actions of other.'[5]

Among the recent writers, we may refer to the contribution of Michael Foucault of France who integrates knowledge with power. In his book *Power/Knowledge* (1980), he says that knowledge is deeply enmeshed in power, truth always being a social construct and that power can be productive, prohibitive and transformative. The omnipresence of power is a solid fact. It is with the free man who exploits the slave, it is also with the slave who raises his voice against any torture. It never stands on a particular centre; it is always moving from one situation to another. It has a transformative feature as well in the sense that the behaviour of a criminal is reformed in the prison when he is punished by those who exercise power according to the rules and regulations of the state. The exercise of power by one invites opposition from the other side. As a result of this, social conflicts take place. An understanding of power in this way adds to the stock of our knowledge. Foucault calls it 'discourse of power.'

Through the idea of 'discourse of power', we may discover the link between power and systems of thought. As Heywood says: "A discourse is a system of social relations and practices that assign meaning and therefore identities to those who live or work within it. Anything from institutionalised psychiatry and the prison service to academic disciplines and political ideologies can be regarded as a discourse in this sense. Discourses are a form of power in that they are antagonisms and structure relations between people who are defined as subjects or objects, as 'insiders' or 'outsiders'.[6]

---

4. R.H. Tawney: *Equality,* p. 230.
5. Russell: *Power*, p. 1.
6. Andrew Heywood: *Political Theory: An Introduction*, p. 128.

In this way, Foucault agrees with as well as differs from Marx and carves out a place for himself in the category of post-modern thinkers. As Heywood continues: "These identities are internalised, meaning that those who are subject to domination, as in the Marxist view, are unaware of the fact or extent of that domination. Whereas Marxists associate power as thought control with the attempt to maintain class inequality, post-modern theorists come close to seeing power as ubiquitous, all systems of knowledge being viewed as manifestations of power."[7]

In short, power "is the ability to determine the behaviour of others with one's own wishes."[8] That is, a man is said to have power to the extent that it "influences the behaviour of others in accordance with his own intentions."[9] Likewise, we "ascribe power to those who can influence the conduct of others even against their will."[10] Again, it "is simply the probability that a man will act as another man wishes. This action may rest on fear, rational calculation of advantage, lack of energy to do otherwise, loyal devotion, indifference, or a dozen of other individual motives."[11] Certainly, it is because of this diversity in the meaning of the term 'power' that its whole study has become like a 'bottomless swamp'.[12]

Power Theory of Politics: As pointed out above, this theory has its first brilliant expression in the *Leviathan* of Hobbes. The grandest conclusion of the Hobbesian politics is his clearest and most perfect expression of the naturalistic conception of human nature. Hobbes tells us that man desires power and ever greater power, spontaneously and continuously in one set of appetite, and not by reason of summation or innumerable isolated desires caused by innumerable isolated perceptions.[13] According to him, search for power is the root cause of competition among the individuals. Interests collide in the race to acquire more and more riches, honours and commands and, for this sake, the competitors take to the means of killing, subduing, supplanting and repelling their opponents. Though the struggle for power has its incessant play among the competitors, it is also true that men like to live in peace in order to enjoy the iota of power they possess, it disposes them to live under a common power. The nature of the civil society is such that everyone, whether with moderate or immoderate desires, "is necessarily pulled into a constant competitive struggle for power over others, or at least to resist his powers being commanded by others."[14]

---

7. *Ibid.*
8. Coser and Rosenberg: *Sociological Theory,* p. 123.
9. Goldhamer and Shils: "Types of Power and Status" in *The American Journal of Sociology,* Vol. XLV, No. 2, 1939, pp. 171-82.
10. Gerth and Mills: *Character and Social Structure,* pp. 193-95.
11. *Ibid.*
12. R.A. Dahl: "The Concept of Power" in Roderick Bell, D.V. Edwards and R.H. Wagner (eds.): *Political Power,* p. 79.
13. Leo Strauss: *The Political Philosophy of Hobbes,* p. 10.
14. C.B. Macpherson: "Introduction" to *Leviathan,* p. 37.

After Hobbes, the idea of power had its powerful reiteration in the works of Hegel who absolutised sovereign power of the state to the extent of discarding all ethics of international morality. Power and the urge towards it were very much extolled in the nineteenth century by a good number of writers. In this direction, we may, in particular, refer to great German thinkers like Nietzsche, Treitschke and Bernhardi who elaborated what was given by Hegel. This power current of thought witnessed its ardent protagonist in the twentieth century in Eric Kaufmann, a young German student of international law, who found the essence of the state in *Machtentfaltung* meaning anything like development, increase and display of power, along with the will to maintain successfully and assert itself.[15]

Among the leading advocates of this theory in the twentieth century, we may also refer to Prof. H.J. Morgenthau who says that politics is nothing but struggle for power. In one of his writings titled *Scientific Man Versus Power Politics,* he says that the re-examination of the Western tradition "must start with the assumption that power politics, rooted in the lust for power which is common to all men, is, for this reason, inseparable from social life itself. In order to eliminate from the political sphere not power politics–which is beyond the ability of any political philosopher of system–but the destructiveness of power politics, rational faculties are needed which are different from and superior to the reason of the scientific age... Contemptuous of power politics and incapable of statesmanship which alone is liable to master it, the age has tried to make politics a science."[16]

The power theory found its concrete manifestation in the emergence of Fascism in Italy in 1922 when Mussolini declared 'nothing against the state, nothing above it'. As a reaction against such an affirmation, Prof. Charles Merriam sought to examine the premises of power theory in detail. He undertook to mark out the situation in which power "comes into being; that plurality of competing loyalties; the sham of power and some of credanda, miranda and agenda of authority; some of the techniques of power holders who survive; and some of the defence mechanism of those upon whom power is exercised; the poverty of power; the integration, decline and overthrow of authority, the emerging trend of power in our time."[17]

Though the element of truth in power theory cannot be denied, it may still be said that it lays too much reliance on the fact of power in physical terms alone. As a matter of fact, power is a very broad concept that includes within itself much that may not be covered by the compass of physical power. One may also refer to the power of soul, power of mind, power of ideas and thus justify what great sages from Buddha to Gandhi have uttered. Catlin is of the view that even cooperation may be a form of power perhaps more subtle and difficult to construct, but also more subtle than domination.[18]

---

15. Arnold Brecht: *Political Theory,* p. 345.
16. G.E.G. Catlin: "What is Political Theory?" in Gould and Thursby (eds.): *Contemporary Political Thought,* p. 35.
17. Charles Merriam: *Political Power*.
18. Catlin, *op. cit.,* p. 36.

Political Power

Hobbes	:	Man wants peace, peace enables him to achieve power, power creates pride or vainglory. Being a selfish creature, man has lust for power. It is like a ceaseless and restless desire that goes with the end of life.
Hegel	:	State is the embodiment of power, nothing above it. Fall down and worship it. It is a divine idea, an ethical substance, march of God on earth.
Marx	:	Power is always with a social class by which it dominates and exploits the other class. It is a class instrument that would wither away in the communist society.
C.B. Macpherson	:	Power signifies ability of the individual to develop his personality or to extract advantages from the like ability of others.
R.H. Tawney	:	Power is the capacity of an individual or a group of individuals to modify the conduct of others in a manner as one desires.
C.J. Friedrich	:	Power is a certain kind of human relationship.
H.J. Morgenthau	:	Lust for power is common to all men and thus it is indispensable for social life itself.
Michael Foucault	:	Power is omnipresent; it has a transformative character; it is aligned with knowledge.
Mao Zedong	:	Power flows from the barrel of a gun.
Gandhi	:	Power means soul-force.

Brecht appreciates the view that even people's sense of justice is power as emphasised by Otto Wels who, in opposition to what was said by his leader (Hitler), went to the extent of saying: "No enabling act can give you the power to destroy ideas that are external and indestructible."[19]

Marxian View: Here power is treated as an instrument that connects economics with politics. Politics signifies a sphere of social activity in which two contending classes are engaged in a struggle for the control of the state—the organised force of society. It is the means of production whose ownership involves control over the labour power of those who own little or no means of production and it is this fact that determines the distribution of political power or, what Marx calls, the 'relations of production'. In this sense, property ownership involves control over production as well as political control. Only a class whose members are aware of their objective class interest, who have a will to forward that interest and who possess a political organisation, can be said to act

19. Brecht, *op. cit.,* p. 347.

politically. Hence, political power, properly so called, is merely the organised power of one class oppressing another.[20]

Political power, or class power as it may be called in the strict Marxian sense, is the general and pervasive power which the dominant class exercises in order to maintain and defend its predominance in the society. The class power is challenged by a counter-power. Thus, class war takes place in which the contending classes as well as their subordinate allies take part. In the present society it may be traced in the conflict between the capitalist and the labour classes having their subordinate allies—the former in the family, school and churches and the latter in the socialist and communist parties and trade unions. Marx also tells us that in the period of acute social crisis and conflict, class power "does tend to be taken over by the state itself, and indeed gladly surrenders to it; and it may well be argued that even in the normal circumstances of advanced capitalism, the state takes over more and more of the functions hitherto performed by the dominant class, or at least takes a greater share in the performance of these functions than was the case in the previous periods."[21]

However, the peculiar feature of the Marxian theory of power should be traced not in the integration of the case of political power with the prevailing socio-economic system as in the disappearance of the political power with the ushering in of a new society having its hallmark in the emergence of a stateless pattern of collective life. Like politics, power also becomes a transient phenomenon. In a capitalist society, out of the separate economic movements of the workers, there grows up everywhere a political movement, that is to say, a movement of the class, with the object of enforcing its interests...in a form possessing general, socially coercive, force. However, in a full communist society private property would be abolished and that would entail the disappearance of classes and hence class conflict. And when class rule has disappeared, no state would exist in the current political sense. In this way, the 'public power' would lose its political character.[22]

The Marxian theory of power may be criticised on some grounds. First, it "is grasped as a mechanical theory in which the economy determines absolutely the political structure."[23] One may refer to the various theories on the subject of power and then assert that the source of power lies not only in the realm of economics but also very much in the realms of psychology and sociology. Lust for power is a psychological fact. Second, Marx wrongly argues that power is an essential instrument of class war and, as such, in the capitalist society state is a class institution that serves and protects the interests of the dominant bourgeois class in an exclusive manner. State is a welfare agency. It has its ethical end also that consists, as Aristotle said, in the realisation of the ideal of 'good life'. Thus, Marx may be accused of not working out a satisfactory theory of power in a capitalist society. Finally, Marx fondly hopes for the emergence

20. Marx-Engels: 'Communist Manifesto' in *Selected Works,* Vol. I, p. 36.
21. Ralph Miliband: *Marxism and Politics,* p. 56.
22. Marx-Engels: *Selected Works,* Vol. IV, p. 482.
23. Alan Swingewood: *Marx and Modern Social Theory,* p. 138.

of a stateless pattern of collective life in which there would be no place for state or political power. Hence, Marxism becomes utopian in the end.[24]

Liberal View: Power is not merely a fact having its manifestation in the forms of control, influence, coercion, persuasion and manipulation, it is a value also. Essentially speaking, power signifies the capacity of an individual which may either refer to his ability to develop his personality or to extract advantages from the like abilities of others. In this way, power has both developmental and extractive capacities and thereby it has a normative dimension in the former and an empirical dimension in the latter. It should always be borne in mind that if power refers to the capacities, the capacities of man are more and higher than those of an animal. Moreover, the norms of social life require that the use of such capacities be made for the betterment of the personality of man as well as of his community. Whether the existence of especially human capacities "is attributed to divine creation, or to some evolutionary development of more complex organism, it is a basic postulate. It is at the same time a value postulate in the sense that rights and obligations can be derived from it without any additional value premise, since the very structure of our thought and language puts an evaluative content into our descriptive statements about man."[25]

Though Western political theory studies the case of power in its normative as well as empirical dimensions, most of the literature from Machiavelli and Hobbes to Weber and Lasswell concerns itself with the latter dimension. It dwells on man's ability to get what he wants by controlling others. However, as the power of money has become the most important of all powers in modern market societies, the idea of political power has become essentially connected with the theme of 'economic power'. Keeping this fact in view, Easton refers to a long line of modern writers who see that the characteristic of political activity, the property that distinguishes the political from the economic or other aspects of a situation, is the attempt to control others.

But the essential feature of the liberal view is that the normative aspect of power cannot be thoroughly discarded. Man is not merely a power-hungry creature, he is also a value-loving fellow. He not only fights for power, he has a sense of discrimination too. Thus, while extracting benefits from others by virtue of his capacities, he is also expected to care for his as well as his fellow beings' development. The developmental and extractive aspects of human capacities should be joined in a way so that the maximisation of democracy takes place without causing loss or destruction of the values of humanism. Impressed with this assumption, Macpherson counsels: "We must attend to the developmental concept of power, and the democratic claim to maximise that power, if our political science is to be analytically adequate."[26]

Hegemony

The value pattern of the life of a people, also known as their culture, plays an important role in their social make-up and the operation of their political system. Liberal writers

24. Michael Evans: *Karl Marx,* p. 162.
25. Macpherson: *Democratic Theory,* p. 53.
26. *Ibid.,* p. 50.

like G.A. Almond and Sidney Verba call it 'civic culture' that has its synonym in 'political culture. It is of three kinds. A *participant political culture* is one in which citizens pay close attention to politics and regard popular participation as both desirable and effective. A *subject political culture* is characterised by more passivity amongst citizens, and the recognition that they have only a very limited capacity to influence the government. A *parochial political culture* is marked by the absence of a sense of citizenship, with people identifying with their locality rather than the nation, and having neither the desire nor the ability to participate in politics. The civic culture "is a blend of all the three in that it reconciles the participation of the citizens in the political process with vital necessity for government to govern. Thus, "democratic stability is underpinned by a political culture that is characterised by a blend of activity and passivity on the part of citizens, and a balance between obligation and performance on the part of government."[27]

However, the Marxists study the case of psychological dispositions of the people in a different way. To them the ideas of the ruling class constitute its ideology or a system of values that is imposed by the dominant class over the dominated class by force. The dominated class accepts it on account of living in a condition of exploitation and oppression. Thus, Engels calls it 'false consciousness of reality', though Gramsci calls it 'cultural hegemony' of the bourgeois class that surprisingly involves the elements of force and persuasion or consent. The bourgeois class purchases the acquiescence of the people of the dominated class in a way that the elements of force and consent are amalgamated. The intellectuals, writers, artists, clerics, professionals and the leaders of political parties accept the legitimacy of the 'capitalist state'. Moreover, as a sworn Marxist, Gramsci further says that bourgeois hegemony can be overthrown by the 'organic' intellectuals of the working class. They would unleash a new kind of cultural revolution in the bourgeois society and thereby create a favourable situation for a socialist revolution. He calls the first step as the 'war of position' and the latter one as the 'war of manoeuvre'.

In simple terms, hegemony implies ascendancy or domination of one element of system over others. In the view of the liberal writers, it signifies 'relative stability of political authority in a capitalist country'.[28] But the Marxists give a peculiar twist to its implications for the sake of condemning the capitalist system on ideological grounds and seeking its replacement by a socialist system having a new form of civic culture. The important line of distinction between the two may be traced in that while the capitalists manage to legitimise their system based on a particular ideology by the use of brute force as well as cunning persuasion, the Marxists desire to bring about a different system based on the culture of the proletariat. The dictatorship of the proletariat established after the successful socialist revolution would be like an iron rule for the enemies of all hues of socialism; it shall be a real democracy for the hitherto exploited and oppressed sections of the people professing a new variety of civic or political culture.

27. Andrew Heywood: *Politics,* p. 200.
28. Martin Griffiths: *Encyclopaedia of International Relations and Global Politics,* p. 363.

Political Ideology

Meaning: The word 'ideology' was used for the first time by a French theorist Destutt de Tracy in 1797 who introduced it as a newly conceived science in opposition to the subject of metaphysics. By ideology he meant the science of ideas—a fresh discipline intended to be the basis of an entirely new social and political order. As he said, it "does not hint of anything doubtful or unknown.'[29] In this way, he took ideology as 'the modern answer to the unscientific past'.[30] Since then the term 'ideology' has assumed an importance of its own in spite of the fact that Karl Marx denounced it as 'false consciousness of reality', Karl Mannheim called it 'utopia', and Daniel Bell spoke of the 'end of ideology'. As now understood, ideology "is a type of theory which upholds a certain political system (in its broadest sense) and the values and ideals that sustain it, as the final approximation of the human mind to an ideal arrangement and, therefore, claiming this finality seeks to realise it."[31]

In a broad sense, the term 'ideology' signifies a set of ideas ranging from one desiring change in the prevailing order to another crying for a total transformation of society. Moreover, it includes the refutation of one and the justification of another set of ideals irrespective of the fact that a critic may call a particular ideology as a 'utopia' or 'false consciousness'. The ideas may also be in the form of an explanation of some fact, or a justification of some claim or a quest for some truth, or a manifestation of some conviction and the like. Keeping all these dimensions in view, an eminent writer says: "I take ideology to any more or less systematic set of ideas about man's place in nature, in society, and in history, i.e., in relation to particular societies, which can elicit the commitment of significant numbers of people to (or against) political change. This does not exclude a set of ideas essentially concerned with merely a class or a nation if it relates the place and needs of that section of humanity to the place of man in general. Thus, liberalism, conservatism, democracy (in various senses), Marxism, Populism, Nkrumahism, pan-Africanism and various nationalisms are all ideologies. Ideologies contain, in varying proportions, elements of explanation (of fact and history), justification (of demands), and faith or belief (in the ultimate truth or rightness of their case). They are informed by, but are less precise and systematic than, political theories or political philosophies. They are necessary to any effective political movement, hence to any revolution, for they perform the triple function of simplifying, demanding and justifying."[32]

However, the most important thing about ideology is its action-oriented character. Its test lies in its application. Thus, Preston King says that an ideology "will either involve the actual application of a coherent system of political ideas to a political system in such a way as to direct its activities, or it involves the serious distinction of making this application."[33] In other words, ideology refers to an action-related system of political ideas in the sense that these are sets of ideas concerning the change or

29. Drucker: *The Political Uses of Ideology,* p. 3.
30. *Ibid.*
31. Frank Thakurdas: *Essays in Political Theory,* p. 40.
32. C.B Macpherson: *Democratic Theory,* pp. 157-58.
33. Frank Thakurdas, *op. cit.,* p. 41.

Ideology

Marxism : While it deprecates ideology as 'false consciousness of social reality', it presents an ideology of its own. It is more or less a coherent set of ideas which purport to explain and justify social position of the two rival classes. In political terms, it seeks to change the status quo by overthrowing the rule of the dominant class of the exploiters and the oppressors. Revolution can usher in the socialist society alone. The state known as the 'dictatorship of the proletariat' is an all-powerful institution to protect the interest of the class of the workers and the toilers that would wither away in the final stage of social development. Socialism would replace capitalism and eventuate into communism. Marxism-Leninism may be described as totalitarianism of the left.

Fascism : It seeks to maintain the status quo so as to protect the interests of the affluent and privileged sections of the society. The state is omnipotent, nothing against it and nothing above it. It may be described as totalitarianism of the right.

Liberalism : It stands for the values of liberty, democracy and humanism. It has a flexible character by virtue of which it cannot be taken as an ideology. And yet its stern commitment to the norms of freedom and tolerance makes it so. 'Give me liberty or give me death', says Thomas Jefferson.

defence of the existing political structures and relationship.[34] It may or may not possess a logical or philosophical character at all, but it must possess a political character, i.e., a content without which it cannot be described as an ideology—a guide to direct political action."[35] If so, political philosophy and political ideology may be differentiated in the sense that while the former "evokes reflection and understanding," the latter "is more likely to imply commitment and action."[36]

Liberal View: Liberalism as an ideology stands for the values of freedom, democracy and humanism. Its basic assumptions lie in the entire paraphernalia of a democratic order having representative government, responsible executive, political checks and balances, rule of law, independence of judiciary, free press and socio-economic justice. It is said to have three fundamental postulates—limited government, pluralistic society, and unlimited scope for free choices. The government operates in the midst of autonomous, spontaneously self-creating, voluntary associations. The society has a pluralistic character which implies that it "is made up of a host of autonomous sections and associations, but to believe that each enshrines values or interests dear to its members."[37]

---

34. Carl J. Friedrich and Z.K. Brzezinski: *Totalitarian Dictatorship and Autocracy,* p. 88.
35. Preston King in Frank Thakurdas, *op. cit.,* p. 41
36. Preston King and B. Parekh (eds.): *Politics and Experience,* p. 351.
37. S.E. Finer: *Comparative Government,* p. 77.

Tolerance is the hallmark of the liberal ideology. It believes that a decent life for all is best protected in a society in which every interest is allowed free expression and access to power. The case of political pluralism is justified whereby community is said to exist in a large number of such groups. Thus emerges the classical liberal notion of a free, substantially equal and ferociously competing interest groups with the provision that the liberty of the individual is not trampled as a matter of deliberate action or policy of any group, including the government. It stands on the assumption that truth is a matter of individual conscience where all consciences are held by an act of faith, to be equal either in the eyes of God or of man. Two practical conclusions follow from this, namely, toleration and the qualification of majority rule.[38]

It is owing to a stern emphasis on the elements of freedom and tolerance that liberalism decries totalitarianism of any kind as 'anti-ideology.' The set of ideas, norms or values should not be converted into a rigid framework with the result that respect for certain norms becomes a matter of blind faith. That is, ideology should not be converted into a 'religion.' Totalitarianism may be thus said to be devoid of any ideology in as much as it points to the fact that the ruling group endeavours to spread its fiat by every possible means at its command throughout the country. In a different way, it may be said that the assertion that the ideology is nothing but an intolerant political thinking leads liberals "to write of religion as a kind of ideology. For them the battle against ideology today is but an echo of battle against religion yesterday."[39]

However, the real difficulty about the ideology of liberalism is that it is too fluid and flexible to be designated as such. One may say that its essentially flexible character takes it from one pole of liberal democratic to the other pole of liberal-authoritarian orders. A sort of ideas which cannot at all be subjected to very specific and concrete programmes and where even action-orientedness is missing cannot be designated as an ideology. The Fascists and the Communists alike denounce the liberals as 'deluded idealists or incompetent intellectuals."[40] Lenin calls liberals 'arm chair fools.' Oswald Spengler says that the liberal's concern for individual or minority rights and freedoms leads only to blindness, cowardice and spiritual indiscipline.'[41]

Marxian View: The fascinating point of Marxian theory on this subject is that while it decries every existing ideology as 'false consciousness' of social reality, it instead offers an ideology of its own. One may marvel at the fact that Marx never defined the term 'ideology' in quite explicit terms, though, in general, he used to refer to a more or less coherent system of ideas which purported to explain and justify the social position of a class. Hence, the important thing to be taken note of here is that the implications of the term 'ideology' are involved in the doctrine of the class and, since class has a place within the society and its standpoint determines the angle from which it sees society

38. *Ibid.*, p. 88.
39. Drucker, *op. cit.*, p. 137.
40. F.W. Coker: "Some Present-Day Critics of Liberalism" in Stankiewicz (ed.): *Political Thought Since II World War*, p. 379.
41. Spengler: *The Hour of Decision*, p. 119.

and thereby what it sees, the notion of social position becomes analogous to that of physical position.[42]

Marx's theory of ideology begins with his criticism of Feuerbach's *Essence of Christianity* wherein he denounces the significance of religious myths in understanding the reality of man's life. Marx carries his point further in his *Economic and Philosophic Manuscripts* wherein he says that man is the sole object of ultimate value and that the distinctly human quality is reason or consciousness. He emphasises practical nature of thought and denies importance of unpractical thinking. To him it is the thought or consciousness which can change the world, but consciousness is governed by the laws of objective reality. In his *German Ideology* Marx frankly condemns prevailing ideology as 'false consciousness' and also links it up with the fact of 'class domination.' He emphatically asserts that German thinkers "failed to realise the fundamental advance made by the materialist philosophy and still talked of revolutions in thought. Hegel is declared as the source of all error from whom German thinkers have learned the art of changing real objective chains that exist outside 'me' into 'mere ideals', 'mere objective chains' existing in 'me' and thus to change all 'exterior' palpable struggles into pure struggles of thought. Against this sort of inversion, so characteristic of all prevailing ideologies, Marx suggests that all ideas and all words are the products of society. That is, we must return to the study of real individuals, since the basis of the study of man must be man; active, working, breathing, man and nothing else."[43]

Ideology is integrally connected with the interest of the ruling class. Its basis is the interest of the class in dominance. "When the forms of material means of production are no longer able to meet the demands of an expanding population, the social system is bound to be overthrown. But before this occurs, a new ideology, one setting forth a programme favourable to the interest of a different class, will emerge."[44] It follows that the system of ideas which tends to justify and further the aims of the ruling class are the predominant ideas of the age. The dominant class is able to impose its ideas upon the dispossessed class. According to Marx, the objective interests of the working class is what it is to become in the future and, as such, a major function of political and social theory is to combat the so-called contributions of the ruling ideologists who "make the perfecting of the illusions of the class about itself their chief source of livelihood."[45]

The function of ideology is thus to understand social and political reality in terms of the doctrine of class war according to which class conflicts between the haves and the have-nots would inevitably end in the victory of the larger class, the proletariat, and this triumph would usher in the classless society.[46] Obviously, such an interpretation may not be acceptable to those who believe in human liberty and on that basis strongly advocate the case of a free and divergent pattern of social life. The men of liberal

42. Plamenatz: *Ideology*, p. 50.
43. Marx: *The German Ideology*, p 37.
44. Michael Evans: *Karl Marx*, p. 83.
45. Marx-Engels: *Collected Works*, Vol. III, p. 46.
46. A. R. Ball: *Modern Politics and Government*, p. 257.

ideology cannot accept the Marxian contention that whatever we think and offer in the form of a set of ideas is 'false' and whatever is said by Marx is true and scientific. The obnoxious part of the Marxian ideology is that it subordinates the personality of man under an all-powerful ruthless system called 'dictatorship of the proletariat.'

Fascist View: An extension of as well as a total opposition to the Marxian theory should be traced in the case of totalitarianism as an ideology which takes ideas as weapons either to reconstruct a new society or to save an existing one from total destruction. As an ideology of the 'left,' totalitarianism advocates the case of a communist state; as an ideology of the 'right,' it advocates the case of a fascist state. The noticeable thing at this stage is that the ideology of fascism not only stands for the preservation of the status quo, it declares communism as its arch-enemy and includes within itself a feature of destroying it (communism) by all means. However, as fascism is a totalitarian ideology, this definition will apply to it that it stands for an official ideology consisting of an official body of doctrines covering all vital aspects of man's existence to which everyone living in that society is supposed to adhere, at least passively; this "ideology" is characteristically focused and projected towards a perfect final state of mankind, that is to say, it contains a chiliastic calm, based upon a radical rejection of the existing society and the conquest of the world for the new one."[47]

The ideology of fascism desires an all-powerful state which is all-absorbing and to which no opposition of any kind can be tolerated. The entire state apparatus must be in the hands of a political party under a great leader through which all political and economic programme shall be effectuated. The life of the people must be bound by a chord of common faith in the excellence and infallibility of the rule of a single party under a single leader. There must be no place for competing interests, because the state represents 'general will' of the community. The life of the people must be in a period of highest ideal tension.[48] All particularistic interests of the individuals must be suppressed by an omnipotent, hierarchical organisation of the nation."[49] An absolute state and an irresistible government are the main features of fascist ideology. In other words, it may be defined as a coherent body of ideas concerning practical means of how totally to change and reconstruct a society by force, or violence, based upon an all-inclusive or total criticism of what is wrong with an existing or antecedent society."[50]

The real difficulty about totalitarian ideology is that it either becomes a 'myth' or a 'utopia.' It becomes a myth when it is imposed on the people by means of force; it becomes a utopia when the people are indoctrinated to cultivate faith in the advent of a contemplated golden age of human life. In other words, a definition of ideology comes to have its 'exclusive' instead of 'inclusive' connotations, to posit and explain

47. Friedrich and Brzezinski: "The General Characteristics of Totalitarian Dictatorship" in Stankiewicz, *op. cit.*, p. 40
48. Finer, *op. cit.*, p. 88.
49. Martin Seliger: *The Marxist Conception of Ideology*, p. 1.
50. Coker: *Recent Political Thought*, pp. 482-83.

and justify ends and means of organised social action, especially political action, irrespective of whether such an action aims to preserve, amend, destroy, or rebuild any given order.

End of Ideology Debate: A new theory on this subject has recently come up in which the names of Daniel Bell and Robert E. Lane have a special mention. In their view, ideology has come to an end. The contention is that Western societies have developed in such a way and to such an extent that no ideology is any more required. The function of ideologies or their programmes of action have now been taken over by a scientific social technology. The burden of the argument is that Marx died long back and much has happened since then. As a matter of fact, bourgeois system has acquired several improved forms, which Marx and his ardent followers could never imagine with the result that the life of the people, including the proletariat, has improved considerably in social and economic terms. Hence, has happened the 'end of ideology.'

Bell thinks of ideologies as systems of ideas which serve to 'concretise' social values. He believes that all societies need ideologies and that they are all equally successful. The issue of economic development has come to stay in the forefront as the problem of political stability has almost become a well settled phenomenon. The people have developed firm faith in the free institutions of their political culture and they have nothing to fear in this regard in the era of 'welfare state.' Moreover, the issue of economic development has come to be their main goal that they want to achieve by living within the broad framework of their well-established political system. It is for this important reason that there is hardly any difference of opinion between the Democratic and Republican parties of the United States. It all shows that ideology, 'which was once a road to action, has come to a dead end.'[51]

Lane has thrown light on this theme from a different standpoint. He has sought to give a peculiar twist to the argument of Lenin by adding that now even the working class is faced with a number of 'socialist' ideologies that automatically strengthens the case of 'bourgeois' ideology. While referring to the case of the working class of any industrial country, it may be said that it is split up among a number of ideologies. Since there can be no talk of an independent ideology formulated by the working class itself in the process of its movement, the only choice is either bourgeois or socialist ideology. There is no middle course, for mankind has not created a third ideology and, moreover, in a society torn by class antagonisms there can never be a non-class or above-class ideology. Hence, to belittle the socialist ideology in any way is to turn aside from it in the slightest degree, means to strengthen bourgeois ideology."[52]

As a matter of fact, the aim of the American social theorists is to beat the concept of ideology with the stick of sociology in this age of democracy. The burden of their argument is that democracy being a system of consensus allows no room for the politics of conflict (class struggle). It requires organisations which sustain legitimacy

51. Bell: *The End of Ideology,* p. 252.
52. Lane: "The Decline of Politics and Ideology in a Knowledgeable Society" in *American Sociological Review,* Vol. XXXI, No. 5, 1966, pp. 649-62.

and consensus, or general agreement. Barrington Moore, Jr. observes that as we reduce economic inequalities and privileges, we may also eliminate the sources of contrast and conflict that put 'drive' into genuine political alternatives. He concludes that the driving force of discontent disappears and a society settles down for a time to a dull acceptance of things as they are. Following this line, Lipset highlights the end of ideology in these words: "The democratic class struggle will continue, but it will be a fight without ideologies, without red flags, without workers' May Day Parades."[53]

The critics of this theory, particularly the Marxists, have looked at it with apprehension and come to decry it as the resurgence of a 'new bourgeois ideology'. They are of the view that the acceptance of welfare state, desirability of decentralised power, mixed economy, political pluralism and the like are just concrete evidences so as to cry for the end of ideology. As a matter of fact, the advocates of the end of ideology theory draw inspiration from pragmatism and status quoism and then, instead of exposing the hollowness of their intellectual systems, endeavour to distract the attention of the progressive thinkers. "The adjustments made among the diverse elites to the exclusion of the masses without breaking the structure of society and disturbing its hierarchical class nature by peaceful parliamentary methods exclusively is traded off as 'end of ideology'. In fact, it is an ideology of an end to maintain the base intact by slight modifications in the superstructures."[54]

Convergence Theory: The idea of the convergence of two systems—capitalist and socialist—looks like a continuation of the theory of de-ideologisation. Here we may take note of a kind of anchorage in the idea of an integrated type of society to which socialism and capitalism supposedly and eventually have to come. To a critic it looks like an attempt to get the working people to believe that socio-political distinctions between capitalist and socialist societies are being erased as a result of industrial development especially in the era of technological revolution. The two systems are becoming loose, more and more, with the result that they are moving closer to each other in a way that may culminate in the formation of a kind of 'hybrid society' with identical social and economic features.

The convergence theory refers to the structural changes in modern industrially developed societies, the increase in the proportion of the wage earners, the growth of education and skills of the labour forces, transition to control by machines and so on. The theory is also based on the hope that rising standards of living in the socialist countries will allegedly lead to the formation of a consumer psychology among the people there which will force socialism to meet the bourgeois mass consumption society half the way.

The closer move of the two systems towards a hybrid society would inhere the best that has been achieved by capitalism and socialism in a way that the common merit of the two would replace their demerits. An American economist Peter Drucker hopefully visualises that the free industrial society is certainly very different from what the

53. S.M. Lipset: *Political Man,* p. 197. (Abridged Edition)
54. K. Seshadri: *Marxism and Political Science,* pp. 190-91.

common merits of the two would replace their demerits we have traditionally considered to be 'Capitalism'. It is also very different from what we have considered traditionally to be 'Socialism'. An industrial society is beyond Capitalism and Socialism. It is a new society transcending both.[55]

In an integrated or hybrid society socialism is not entirely merged with capitalism. It has a right to exist to an extent that it gradually evolves into an industrial society after the capitalist model. An American economist W.S. Buckingham, Jr. asserts that "three of the four foundations of capitalism seem likely to be carried over from capitalism and incorporated into the newly emerging economic system: (1) Private property in capital plant and equipment may even grow as industry expands into consumer goods and services, although this could be partially offset by further expansion of public power and transportation services. (2) Economic incentives and profit motivation are well established and future tax policies seem to favour strengthening them. (3) The market system is everywhere reasserting itself as the principal mechanism for controlling the allocation of goods and services.[56]

In the 1960s the convergence theory could carve out a place of its own. Huntington and Brzezinski hopefully projected that the fundamentally important aspects of the democratic system would be retained after America and Russia 'converge' at some future indeterminate historical juncture. It may assume the shape of such merger, not just convergence of the two opposite systems.[57] But A.C. Meyer is more forthright when he hints at the end of both dictatorship and ideology. As he says: "There is implicit in a good deal of convergence theory the assumption that Western society and specifically the United States is the model towards which all contemporary societies are striving."[58]

The views of these noted American writers look like a discourse about industrial society suggesting complete reliance on technology. To the people of the socialist countries they appear in the form of various democratic, liberal and humane modifications of socialism calculated to undermine the socialist system. It is closely intertwined with an attempt to kindle nationalism by any means. Herbert Marcuse says that whether it is dictatorship or democracy, high level of technological development requires and secures integration of the mass of population, not only into work but mentally into functionally useful patterns of feeling and thought.

Curiously the trend of convergence touched the sphere of world politics as well. The American administration embarked on the path of building peace with the association

---

55. P.F. Drucker: *The New Society: The Anatomy of Industrial Order,* 1962, p. 351.
56. W.S. Buckingham, Jr.: *Theoretical Economic Systems: A Comparative Analysis,* New York 1958, p. 485. James Burnham in his *Managerial Revolution* (1941) had visualised that regardless of their ideological differences all industrial societies "are governed by a class of managers, technocrats and state officers whose power is vested in their technical and administrative skills." See Andrew Heywood: *Politics,* p. 359.
57. Zbigniew Brzezinski and S.P. Huntington: *Political Power: USA/USSR,* 1964, p. 419.
58. A.C. Meyer: "Theories of Convergence" in Chalmers-Johnson (ed.): *Change in Communist System,* Stanford, California, 1970, pp. 320-24.

of the socialist countries. In 1960 President Kennedy thus affirmed: "In Poland and in any other crack that appears in the Iron Curtain, we can then begin to work gradually, carefully and peacefully to promote closer relationship and nourish the seeds of liberty".[59] His successor L.B. Johnson gave the concept of peaceful involvement or building bridges. On 23 May, 1964 Johnson affirmed: "We will continue to build bridges across the gulf which has divided us from Eastern Europe. They will be the bridges of increased trade, of ideas, of visitors and of humanitarian aid."[60]

Such affirmations are taken by the Marxists as another attempt towards de-ideologisation. The end is the same as was with the 'end of ideology' debate. It may be interpreted as replacement of one ideology by another. The bourgeois intellectuals and theorists pay no attention to their diametrically opposed class structures and relations of production. They prefer to deal only with surface features characteristic of industrially developed societies distorting the facts of present-day reality. They magnify the state of crisis in socialist society so as to highlight the achievements of a liberal-democratic order with a view to put a mask on the old vices of capitalism or to equate the vices of their system with the failure of the socialist system. At the level of international politics, the convergence of the two systems is seen as involving the only alternative to a military confrontation with the socialist powers. If the 'end of ideology' debate raised the banner of 'de-ideologisation', the convergence theory raises the banner of re-ideologisation by acknowledging the importance of ideology. They are like two sides of anti-communism. Both are an attempt to mobilise the entire apparatus of ideological influence on the masses for a vigorous struggle against the communist ideology.[61]

Political Legitimacy and Effectiveness

Meaning: The stability of a popular or democratic political system depends not only upon economic development, as is generally understood, but also upon its legitimacy and effectiveness. While effectiveness is judged according to how well a political system performs its basic functions as measured by the reactions of most of the people and their powerful groups, legitimacy includes the capacity to produce and maintain a belief that the existing political institutions, or forms, are most appropriate for the society.[62] Legitimacy "is the foundation of political power in as much as it is exercised both with a consciousness on the government's part that it has a right to govern and with some recognition by the governed of that right."[63]

The idea of political legitimacy should be studied in the context of 'usurpation' and 'revolution'. While usurpation of power is always an illegitimate act, revolution may,

59. John F. Kennedy: *The Strategy of Peace,* edited by Allan Nevins, New York, 1960, p. 18.
60. Adam Westoby: "The Anatomy of Communist States" in Gregor McLennan, David Held and Stuart Hall (ed.s): *The Idea of the Modern State,* p. 144.
61. V. Kortunov: *The Battle of Ideas in the Modern World* (Moscow: Progress Publishers, 1979), pp. 104-08.
62. Lipset, *op. cit.,* p. 229.
63. Dolf Sternberger: "Legitimacy" in *International Encyclopaedia of the Social Sciences,* edited by David I. Sills, Vol. 9, p. 244.

and also may not, belong to such category, though one may find fault with the personal or subjective attitude of the observer. Simply stated, the ideal of political legitimacy is integrally associated with a successful revolution that exhibits its appreciation by the masses. If a revolution succeeds, it introduces a new principle of legitimacy that supersedes the rightness of the former system. Under such circumstances, recognition by the people will often be acquired only as the new regime begins governing and the process of becoming legitimate may include violence and terror. Foreign diplomatic recognition, while not essential, may help internal consolidation and therefore expedite acceptance of the new pattern of legitimacy.

The idea of political legitimacy and effectiveness is also organically related to the problem of political change. "Governments, whether following traditional principles of legitimacy or established revolutionary ones, may lose their legitimacy by violating these principles. The desire for having the stamp of legitimacy is so deeply rooted in human communities that it is hard to discover any form of government that does not try to win such a recognition by any possible means whatsoever. Legitimacy is so universal a phenomenon that it is continuously endangered by the plurality of its patterns and sources. Rivals for power often automatically consider themselves legitimate and their opponents illegitimate. It is, therefore, difficult to talk about legitimacy in general terms, the different types must be discussed separately and specific examples given."[64]

It may, however, be added that as a crisis of legitimacy is a crisis of change, its genesis should be traced in the character of the transformation that affects the social life of the people. It does not matter whether the status of major social institutions is threatened, or if the political system is not open to all major groups in society during the phase of transition, or the time when they have developed critical demands. It is also possible that a new crisis may develop after a new social structure is established if the new system is unable to sustain the expectations of major groups for a period long enough to develop legitimacy upon the new basis."[65] The basic question stands: How people choose to accept, or not to accept, a particular government? It may be answered with two main theses: "First that people make political decisions, including even decisions about support for government, rationally or at least act as if they did; and second, that the ethnic and occupational divisions of any society are the principal information on which its members would have to base a rational choice among forms of government."[66]

Obviously, the idea of political legitimacy and effectiveness is integrally connected with the new interpretation of the concept of political power characterised by its potential effect through the role of government in matters of making and implementing its policy. It expands the study of political behaviour so as to include all forms of social relations which 'effect', 'influence', 'control' and 'support' the decision-makers. The concern of a political scientist is limited not only to the problems of franchise,

64. *Ibid.*
65. Lipset, *op. cit.,* p. 29.
66. David E. Apter: *The Politics of Modernisation,* p. 236.

freedom of speech and expression, making laws and securing their due enforcement, preservation of the neutrality of public servants and independence and impartiality of the judges and the like. In other words, the idea of political 'power' is bound with the notion of political legitimacy and effectiveness that covers within its fold the entire stuff of social psychology with reference to group behaviour and political socialisation implying internalisation of the values of a free and open governmental system. In this way, the study of politics "is the study of the legitimisation of social power in situations of social interaction."[67]

Weber's Analysis: The idea of political legitimacy and effectiveness is associated with the name of a German sociologist Max Weber. He holds that in a legitimate dominion of any type, legitimacy "is based on belief and elicits obedience."[68] If so, the ruling group in a state must be legitimate. The fact of legitimacy may be ascribed to an order by those acting subject to it in the following ways:[69]

1. by virtue of tradition, a belief in the legitimacy of what has already existed;
2. by virtue of affectual attitudes, especially emotional, legitimising the validity of what is newly revealed or a model to imitate;
3. by virtue of rational belief in its absolute value, thus lending the validity of an absolute and final commitment; and
4. because it has been established in a manner which is recognised to be legal, this legality may be treated as legitimate in either of the two ways: on the one hand, it may derive from a voluntary agreement of the interested parties on the relevant terms, and on the other hand, it may be imposed on the basis of what is held to be legitimate authority over the relevant persons and a corresponding claim to their obedience.

Weber emphatically notes that the basis of every system of authority and correspondingly of every kind of willingness to obey "is a belief by virtue of which persons exercising authority are lent prestige."[70] His classification of the type of legitimacy is regarded as the basis of a noble investigation of the nature of authority in contemporary civilisations. He mentions three types of legitimate authority as:[71]

1. Rational-legal authority: It is said to rest on a belief in the legality patterns of normative rules and the right of those elevated to the authority under such rules to issue commands.
2. Traditional authority: It is derived from an established belief in the sanctity of immemorial traditions and the legitimacy of the status of those exercising authority over them.

---

67. H.V. Wiseman: *Political Systems,* p. 172.
68. Sternberger, *op. cit.,* p. 246.
69. Ilsa Dronberger: *The Political Thought of Max Weber,* p. 197.
70. *Ibid.*
71. *Ibid.*

3. Charismatic authority: It rests on the devotion to the specific and exceptional sanctity, heroism or exemplary character of an individual person and of the normative patterns of order revealed or ordained by him. Charisma, literally meaning 'gift of grace', in order that it may become a permanent structure, would have to assimilate itself to modern institutions. All types of authority require administrative staff by efficiency and continuity.

It may be pointed out that rational legitimacy, which Weber identifies with legality, "is the only type of legitimacy to survive in the modern world. In it every single bearer of the power of command is legitimated so far as it corresponds with the norms."[72] A critic may, however, add that the relations between the psychologist and nominalist interpretation of a phenomenon like authority is strikingly illustrated in the approach of Max Weber who, while compromising authority with legitimacy, "misses one of the key aspects of authority by maintaining its rational aspect."[73]

New Theories of Legitimacy: Legitimacy signifies rightfulness of political power. It creates a line of distinction between power and authority in spite of the fact that both are used interchangeably. Power may be used rightly as well as wrongly, but its proper exercise makes it authority. Hence, there is no difference between power and authority if the former is exercised in a proper way. The rules and regulations, whether written or unwritten, create a framework within which power is to be exercised. "Whereas power can be defined as the ability to influence the behaviour of another, authority can be understood as the right to do so. Power brings about compliance through persuasion, threats, coercion or violence. Authority, on the other hand, is based upon a perceived 'right to rule' and brings about compliance through a moral obligation on the part of the ruled to obey."[74]

The basic issue is as to how this compliance can be achieved. In the view of Antonio Gramsci, the capitalist state manages to secure legitimacy by establishing its 'hegemony' over all important sections of the people. The scholars, intellectuals, religious heads, teachers, party leaders, press barons and all others are 'purchased' by the capitalist class who appreciate the capitalist system in a way and to an extent that the 'discredited state of the bourgeois class' secures the title of legitimacy. Thus, the prospects of a socialist revolution are 'killed'. Whatever happens in fact makes up the case of a 'passive revolution'. The dialectical process, which can bring about the socialist revolution, is thereby blocked.

Likewise, Ralph Miliband in his *State in the Capitalist Society* (1978) hints at the shrewd ways whereby the state manages to resolve the contradictions in the bourgeois class. Jurgen Habermas in his *Legitimation Crisis* (1975) hints at the 'crisis tendencies' in liberal democracies which threaten to undermine their legitimacy. But the politics of electoral mechanism allows liberal regimes to adjust their policies and

---

72. Alexander Passerin d' Entreves: *The Notion of State,* pp. 153-54.
73. Friedrich: *Authority,* p. 32.
74. Andrew Heywood: *Political Theory,* p. 130.

programmes in response to competing demands of the people. The waves of popularity and unpopularity of the regimes flow side by side and the state shifts its policies from time to time ranging from more and more interventionism to more and more free market system just to retain and maintain its legitimacy. The cause of the rise of Neo-Liberalism or the New Right after 1970 may be traced here. In his book *Manufacturing Consent* (1994) Noam Chomsky dwells on the 'propaganda model' of the mass media that imparts legitimacy to the existing capitalist state. It looks like a reinterpretation of the argument of Gramsci.[75]

Legitimacy and Ideology: Now we may look into the issue of the role of ideology and leadership in the acquisition of political legitimacy. Parties committed to a particular ideology try to create an environment in which a definite set of rules endeavours to determine the lives of the people. A line of basic distinction may thus be drawn between the parties of 'representation' (those trying to represent diverse political beliefs and convictions) and parties of unification (those trying to make all others conform to their own convictions). A democratic system loses its legitimacy if there is coercion or imposition of some particular kind of political discipline on the people. Hence, the parties of unification or integration are the exponents of a pattern that smacks of totalitarianism. Parties hoping to gain majority by democratic methods cannot ultimately be parties of integration or complete unity.[76]

We find that in a political system leaders strive to ensure that the decisions taken by them are widely accepted by the people not only due to fear of violence and coercion but also due to a conviction that men-in-authority have done things well and in the right manner. Thus, the leadership of the men-in-power is said to be 'legitimate' if the people, to whom the orders are directed, believe that the structures, procedures, acts, decisions, policies, etc., possess the quality of 'rightness', propriety or moral goodness. As such, the decisions taken by the officials have a binding character. The issue of ideology also figures in, since the leaders "usually espouse a set of more or less persistent, integrated doctrines that purport to explain and justify their leadership in the system."[77]

That is, ideology serves the purpose of a convenient tool to endow leadership with the mark of legitimacy. The leaders realise that by means of some ideology or 'political formula' (as called by Mosca), they would be able to convert their political influence into a valid authority and that it is far more economical to rule by means of authority taken as legitimate by the people than by means of coercion that leads to the resurgence of people's resentment in the form of agitational and insurrectionary politics. Not only this, the invocation of, and adherence to, a particular ideology is done so as to accord legitimacy to the political system itself. In this way, different ideologies are espoused by different leaderships which "are like suitable garments which can, and should, be

75. *Ibid.,* p. 147.
76. Lipset, *op. cit.,* p. 35.
77. Dahl, *op. cit.,* p. 60.

changed according to the exigencies of a situation in order that leaders might retain their leadership and constantly legitimise their power into authority—legal and rational component being supplied by the bureaucracy of the Weberian model.[78]

Obviously, such an approach cannot satisfy those against whom it is really directed. To a Marxist, ideology is like a 'false consciousness of reality' and no political system is legitimate unless it strives for the 'emancipation of man'. Only to men of bourgeois orientation, different ideologies may persist at one and the same time. Not only this, even different political parties interested in the maintenance of the status quo may be seen involved in capturing power and seeking legitimisation of their authority in the name of their respective ideologies. To say, for instance, that the Conservative Party of England at the time of governing was espousing a reigning ideology and that the Labour Party in opposition was espousing a rival one 'may satisfy a structural-functionalist but not a Marxist. It is not leaders who seek an ideology for perpetuating and legitimising their authority. "It is the social relationships at a given time that generate corresponding ideologies. Leaders cannot be chameleons changing their ideological colour and yet remaining in their positions."[79]

On the whole, a study of the idea of political legitimacy and effectiveness takes us into the realm of sociology and then inspires us to examine the relationship of political authority with the political culture of the people. It is due to this that the people not only oppose their rulers for violating their pledges or commitments made particularly on the eve of the polls, they also oppose organisations having no legitimacy at all and yet trying to play their part in the political process of the country. An association of a minister with some secret organisation like CIA of the United States or with some multinational corporation like Lockheed in Japan thus becomes a matter of wide condemnation. It has its peculiar importance in a democratic system that remains undoubtedly involved in solving the problem of remaining legitimate as well as effective in the midst of many social tensions and conflicts.

78. K. Seshadri: *Marxism and Political Science,* pp. 187-88.
79. *Ibid.,* p. 188.

6

Monarchy, Theocracy and Democracy

Many are the forms of government which may be distinguished on two grounds–residence of power and the mode of its operation. If the power of the state is vested in one person, it is monarchy. From the operational viewpoint, it may be further pointed out that if the weilder of this power (monarch) reigns as well as rules, i.e., he exercises that power himself, it is absolute or unlimited monarchy as it prevailed during ancient, medieval and early modern ages. With the growth of democracy, this system saw its rapid decline. It has, however, come to stay if the monarch simply reigns, he does not rule. It is called limited or constitutional monarchy and its best example may be seen in the British system. In an aristocracy or oligarchy, power resides in the hands of few persons who are very influential or powerful by virtue of their birth, wealth, status or physical strength. In a democracy, power resides in the people. So it is also known as popular government. If the people exercise their power themselves, it is called direct or pure democracy and its example may be seen in Switzerland which has been lauded by Lord James Bryce as 'the ancestral home of democracy'. In most countries of the world, it has its indirect or 'representative' form in which power is formally vested in the people, but they delegate it to their elected representatives who are accountable to them for their acts of commission and omission. Any form of government may be theocratic if it operates according to the laws, rules or injunctions of a particular religion. But if all religions are treated at par and no discrimination on the basis of religion can be made, then it is called secularism.

Monarchy

Meaning: It is the oldest form of government in which the ruling power is vested in a single person who wears a crown. He holds his office by virtue of hereditary succession, though we may trace some instances of his election by the influential sections of the community as well. He may be having the title of a king, an emperor, a czar and the like, but the essential point is that the government works according to his will. So Garner says: "In its widest sense, any government in which the supreme and final authority is in the hands of a single person is a monarchy, without regard to the source of his election or the nature and duration of his tenure. In this sense, it is immaterial whether his office is conferred by election (by parliament or people) or is derived by hereditary succession, or whether he bears the title of emperor, king, czar, president or dictator. It is the fact that the will of one man ultimately prevails in all matters of government which gives it the character of monarchy."[1] So Jellinek defined monarchy as a government by a single physical will and he emphasised that its essential characteristic "is the competence of the monarch to express the highest power of the state."[2]

Since monarchy is the oldest form of government, its prevalence may be seen in the history of all states of the world. It declined with the growth of democracy in modern times. For instance, France, Spain, Portugal, Germany, Italy, Russia, Turkey, etc., became republics. Another significant development in this regard is that while some European countries desired to retain their monarchical system, they preferred to harmonise it with the institutions of parliamentary democracy. Its best example can be seen in Britain where constitutional monarchy enables the people to call their system 'crowned republic'. Similar is the case with other monarchies as of Belgium and the Netherlands. So it is said: "Modern Europe's monarchs are ceremonial heads of their respective states, often loved and respected by their people, but actually devoid of political power. Such constitutional monarchs are symbols of the unity of the nation or empire; as such, they are useful, visible personifications of the state."[3]

Viewed thus, monarchy in fact may be differentiated from the monarchy in name. While the former signifies a system in which the monarch acts according to his will, in the latter the monarch is like a symbol of the headship of the state. In other words, while the monarch reigns as well as rules in the former position, he merely reigns in the latter capacity. Thus, some writers make an attempt to identify monarchy of the latter type with a democratic system in which, as the English proverb goes, 'the king can do no wrong'. Behind such an attempt, the motive of immunising the system of monarchy from its inherent stigma of 'despotism' may also be traced.

Kinds: Keeping in view the manner in which a monarch occupies his office, the system of monarchy may be categorised as hereditary and elective. Most monarchies of the world are and have been of a hereditary character in view of the fact that the office goes by the fixed law of succession. Thus, the office remains confined to a particular dynastic house or family as of the Bourbons in France or the Hanoverians in England. But the instances of an elective monarchy may also be seen in history. The early Roman kings were elected and so were the kings of Poland. The emperors of the Holy Roman Empire were chosen by a small college of electors, usually from the same family. During the days of feudalism, the kings were elected by the nobles, the barons and the lords. Speaking of the election of early English monarchs, it was observed that the king "was in theory always elected and the fact of election was stated in the coronation service throughout the Middle Ages in accordance with the most ancient precedents."[4] Even in early modern times, the first monarchs (as of Belgium and of

---

1. J.M. Garner: *Political Science and Government,* p. 305.
2. *Ibid.*
3. Rodee, Christol and Anderson: *Introduction to Political Science,* p. 37.
4. Stubbs: *Constitutional History of England,* Vol. I, pp. 520-28.

some of the Balkan states) were chosen by election. But in due course the system of election was superseded by the system of hereditary succession.

The distinction between hereditary and elective monarchies is hardly of any practical significance, since in most of the cases the institution of monarchy has a hereditary character. What is of real importance at this stage is that monarchy may be classified into absolute and limited varieties. In case the monarch acts according to his will and caprice and, in the words of Louis XIV of France, he is 'the state', then it is the case of absolute or unlimited monarchy. Hobbes defends such a system in his *Leviathan*. In Austin's words, law of the state is the command of such a monarch (sovereign). The examples of such a system can be seen in the rule of the Tudors and the Stuarts of England, Mughals of India, Ottomans of Turkey, Czars of Russia, etc. Such a monarchical system, as said above, has now declined, though its instances may still be seen in the autocratic behaviour of the kings of Saudi Arabia and Jordan. While defining such a system, Garner says: "An absolute monarchy is one in which the monarch is not merely the titular head of the state, but is actually the sovereign; that is, his will is the law in respect to all matters upon which it is proclaimed. In short, he is bound by no will except his own. Under such a system, the state and the government, legally speaking, are identical, the monarch being not only an organ of government and the sole organ, but also the sovereign."[5]

Basically different from this is the case of limited or constitutional monarchy in which the position of the monarch is like that of a titular head of the state. He simply reigns; all orders are issued and all laws are made in his name. But it is the will of the popular ministers that counts. For this reason, a constitutional monarch is lauded as the 'dignified executive' and also satiricised as 'magnificent cipher'. Locke in his *Second Treatise of Civil Government* justifies the case of such monarchy.

Criticism: We may briefly discuss the merits and demerits of monarchy. Its merits are:

1. Monarchy should be given the credit for establishing a strong political order. In ancient times when man was almost a savage, it was the prowess of the monarch that could tame man into a political animal. By virtue of his family or clannish traditions, the force of local customs, and his intrinsic mettle, the ruler could prove equal to the occasion in establishing conditions of peace and security. The heavy hand of the monarch could deal with the ways of the barbarians. Order was established and normalcy restored by the hand of a powerful ruler like Charlemagne and Peter the Great.
2. Monarchy means a stable government. The monarch lives in office for a long period. He is a much experienced man in the administration of public affairs. He cannot be removed by anything like impeachment or vote of no confidence. By virtue of living in office for about half a century even, a ruler like Queen Elizabeth I in England and Akbar in India could give stability to administration

5. Garner, *op. cit.,* pp. 307-8.

that may hardly be seen in a democratic system where government depends upon the vagaries of an elected legislature and executive.

3. A monarchical system should also be appreciated for promptness and vigour in actions. The policies made by the monarch are implemented quickly. No time is wasted on lengthy discussions and deliberations as we see in a democratic system. The word of the monarch is the law that must be followed faithfully. It is for this reason that the rule of a benevolent monarch like that of Asoka or Akbar in India is described as 'golden period' in the history of the country.
4. Since the rule of the monarch runs for a fairly long time, a consistent policy, home as well as foreign, is followed. There is no scope for sudden or unexpected change, because the ruler does not change his views with the shift in the public opinion the kind of which may be seen in a democratic system.
5. Above all, the monarch recognises the talents of the artists, poets, painters, musicians, architects and the like. He honours and patronises a galaxy of such talented persons as a result of which great works in the form of books, paintings, buildings and fine arts come into being.

But monarchy has its demerits too that may be briefly enumerated as under:

1. In most of the cases a monarch acts like a despot or a tyrant. His word is law that is enforced with the might of the sword. We have numerous examples of corrupt, incompetent, feeble-minded and callous kings who ruled tyrannically. Such a king has no regard for the rule of law. Anyone speaking against the 'wisdom' of the monarch is taken to task and may be put to any degree of torture. The names of Queen Mary of England, Changez Khan of China and Aurangzeb of India may be referred to in this regard.
2. A monarchical system gives no place for self-rule. The people have no voice in the administration of their country. It is the will of one man that counts. The apologists of monarchy say that the rule of a benevolent king is the best form of government. But an apologist of democracy would say with greater force that a good monarchical government can be no substitute of self-government.
3. A monarchical system inheres the danger of imperialistic tendencies of the ruler. Generally, the kings remain keen on acquiring more authority and expanding their kingdom so that it may be converted into an empire. The result is a war. The history of the world is full of such wars which have proved utterly destructive for the common people. It is also possible that an ambitious ruler may involve his country into a war for the sake of distracting the attention of his people and may thus bring great harm to the people by implementing his hazardous expansionist schemes.
4. Inefficiency, corruption and dishonesty prevail in a country having monarchical system. The sycophants thrive on the patronage of the king. Spoils system prevails in matters of recruitment to government posts. All benevolences are showered on the 'favourites' of the monarch indiscriminately.

5. Above all, the monarch has to live under a fear of perpetual revolt from the side of his opponents. He is always afraid of sinister conspiracies and intrigues by his enemies, including his courtiers. The result is that the monarch adopts a very repressive policy in dealing with such elements. Such acts of repression breed discontent and ultimately lead to rebellions in which a monarchical system may find its doom.

As a matter of fact, monarchical system is said to inhere tendency of despotism that is the very negation of a popular government. The office of a king, howsoever benevolent he may be, is taken for granted as the symbol of autocracy based on the whims and caprices of the ruler.

Theocracy

Theocracy is a form of state and government in which all public affairs are managed according to the laws, rules, regulations or conventions of a particular religion. It sanctions the rule of a person who claims to owe his authority to God or some supernatural being. The holy book is the highest law of the land and that can be authoritatively interpreted by the religious heads like bishops and caliphs. State has a relgion of its own. Hence, all privileges are available to the 'faithfuls', while any kind of injustice may be done to the pagans. It is a different matter that the clergies or the caliphs are the rulers themselves, or the rulers live under their thumb implying subordination of the state to the dictates of the church. This system prevailed in ancient and medieval times in many countries of the world.

Thus, theocracy "is a form of state in which the ultimate sovereignty was assumed to rest in God or some other super-human or spiritual being."[6] It had two forms—pure and dualistic or limited. As Garner says: "The pure theocracy was one in which the supernatural person to whom the sovereignty was attributed was alleged to rule directly or immediately without the aid of human intermediaries; that is, the monarch was considered to be God himself. The limited or dualistic theory was described as one in which the immediate ruler was not God, but a human being who ruled as his viceregent and acted as the interpreter of the divine will, which was made known to him by revelation. As such, he was divinised and sacred."[7]

Throughout the Middle Ages, the basis of the state was theocratic. In all European countries of the Christians, state was like a department of the church. The pope of Rome had both swords in his hands—religious (spiritual) and political (temporal)—and so all the bishops and the kings had to obey his 'bull' (order), or he could punish any violator by ex-communicating him from the Christian community. It is rightly said that then the church was not only a state, it was the state; the state in so far as it had an existence as the 'police department' of the church."[8] Church Fathers (like St. Augustine, St. Ambrose and St. Thomas) coined arguments to justify the doctrine of

6. J.W. Garner, *op. cit.*, p. 247.
7. *Ibid.*
8. J.N. Figgis: *From Gerson to Grotius*, pp. 4 and 6.

plenitudo potestatis (absolute and unrestrained powers) so as to divinise the spiritual and temporal supremacy of the Pope. But the trend declined after the thirteenth century when anti-papalists (like Marsiglio, Dante and William of Occam) coined equally powerful arguments to justify the separate and independent position of the state. Machiavelli of Italy and Hobbes of England condemned the supremacy of the church in very harsh terms. The emergence of the nation-state in modern times having the attributes of nationalism and secularism made the state 'sovereign' and thus theocracy saw its replacement by secularism. It is a different matter that it still prevails in the Muslim countries of West Asia and Africa. If monarchy is anywhere (like Britain and Sweden), it is 'limited' and so the people are under a man-made constitution, not under any revealed book or a ruler owing his power to some supernatural being. For this reason, now theocracy is regarded as a form of government, not a form of state.

Historical facts show that theocracies and despotisms lived together. The rulers did what they liked by claiming themselves as the vicars of God. James I and Charles I of England invoked what is known as the theory of 'divine rights of kings'. Louis XIV of France could say that he was the state. As a result of the persecutions on a very large scale, the people rose in revolt. The people of England executed their king, Charles I in 1649, and the people of France executed their emperor, Louis XVI in 1791. Gradually the vestiges of the theocratic order went into the pages of history. Democracy replaced monarchy and the constitution of the state became the highest law of the land. Now religion cannot interfere in the domain of state, though the state may take measures to remove the evils of the religious order. Obviously, now state is a sovereign entity and the church is under its control. Now theocracy even as a form of government has lost its shine and has no place in a discussion on political theory.[9]

Democracy

Meaning: Democracy is now the most popular form of government, though it is as old as the Greeks. The peculiar thing about democracy is that it is a form of state, a form of government, a form of society, and, above all, an ethical idea or a way of life. In the first place, as a form of state, democracy prevails where people are powerful or the sovereign authority is vested in the people. In case the constitution declares residence of sovereignty in the people and ensures the boons of liberty and equality, it becomes a democratic state irrespective of the fact that the form of government may, or may not, be democratic. This is a peculiar interpretation whereby a country like the USSR was described as a democratic state with an undemocratic government.[10] Such a distinction may be made on theoretical grounds; practically speaking, a democratic state implies a democratic government that acts according to the will of the people. The government is constituted by the people and is accountable to them.

---

9. Garner, *op. cit.*, p. 249.
10. Garner says that the Russian Soviet system was a good example of a government which claimed to be based on the representative principle, but which even according to the admission of its leaders was not democratic. It was confessedly a dictatorship of the proletariat. *op. cit.*, p. 316 n. 2.

Democracy as a way of life has its own significance in the realm of sociology. A society is democratic if it stands on the pillars of liberty and equality. There are no social distinctions making a particular part of the community high or low in relation to other parts; the worth and dignity of the individual are recognised; people understand the nexus between their rights and duties and very carefully try to maintain it; violence and extremism are avoided and differences are resolved through peaceful and constitutional means. Thus, Bryce could visualise that in some advanced countries like the United States, Britain, Canada and Australia the terms 'democracy' and 'democratic' "have acquired attractive associations of a social and, indeed, almost a moral character." In his view, "a democratic person is one who is friendly, genial or a good mixer, regardless of his wealth or social status."[11]

However, what has engaged general attention is the meaning of democracy as a form of government. Since it is a combination of two Greek words 'demos' (people) and 'kratia' (rule), it implies the rule of the people. Thus, the great Greek leader Pericles could define it as 'a government in which people are powerful'. Aristotle defined it as 'the rule of many'.[12] In modern times, its best manifestation can be seen in the Gettysberg oration of President Lincoln of the United States that concluded with designating it as 'government of the people, by the people, and for the people'. An English writer Seeley defined it as 'a government in which everyone has a share.'[13] To Dicey, it 'is a form of government in which the governing body is a comparatively large fraction of the entire nation.'[14] Bryce affirms that since the time of Herodotus the word 'democracy' has been used to denote that form of government "in which the ruling power of a state is largely vested, not in any particular class or classes, but in the members of the community as a whole."[15]

Kinds: If democracy means a government in which political power is vested in the people, a question arises as to how it is exercised. From this standpoint, democracy has two forms—direct or pure and indirect or representative. In the former form, democracy means a government in which the residence as well as exercise of power is in the hands of a large and powerful section of the people like the freemen in Athens and the patricians in Rome. Manifestly democracy in its pure type is practicable only in very small and relatively undeveloped communities where it is physically possible for the articulate section of the community to assemble at a public place and deliberate and decide public affairs. This form prevailed in ancient city-states, but today its form may be seen in five very small cantons (provinces) of Switzerland where the voters meet in 'open-air parliament' (*landsgemeinde*) for the purpose of electing their public officers, voting taxes, and adopting legislative and administrative regulations.[16] Thus, Garner

11. James Bryce: *Modern Democracies,* Vol. I, p. 23.
12. Aristotle: *Politics,* Book III, Sec. 8.
13. John Seeley: *Introduction to Political Science,* p. 324.
14. A.V. Dicey: *Law and Opinion in England,* p. 350.
15. Bryce, *op. cit.,* p. 20.
16. These cantons are Appenzell, Uri, Glarus, Unterwalden (Upper) and Unterwalden (Lower).

says: "A pure democracy, so called, is one in which the will of the state is formulated or expressed directly and immediately through the people in mass meeting or primary assembly, rather than through the medium of delegates or representatives chosen to act for them."[17]

It is true that direct democratic system of the ancient Athenian or Roman type cannot prevail in modern country-states, some institutions of direct democracy have come up in modern times. These are:

1. **Initiative:** The device of initiative prevails in Switzerland at the national as well as cantonal levels. It means power in the hands of a specified number of voters to prepare a bill or a resolution and then ask their government to make a law on that point. In the case of national legislature, such a resolution must be signed by at least 100,000 voters. Thus, initiative "is an arrangement whereby a specified number of voters may prepare the draft of a law and may then demand that it either be adopted by the legislature or referred to the people for acceptance at a general or special election. If approved by the required majority, it then becomes a law."[18]
2. **Referendum:** It also prevails in Switzerland whereby an important bill passed by the legislature must be put to the voters for final ratification. In case it is adopted by the majority, it becomes a law. Thus, the veto power is in the hands of the voters. In this way, the will of the legislature is subservient to the will of the people. "Thus, while initiative is the sword, referendum is the shield of democracy in Switzerland. In a word, they exhibit the uncontested and direct sovereignty of the people."[19] The constitutions of other countries like France and Australia also provide for referendum in case of bills of constitutional amendment.
3. **Plebiscite:** As a synonym of 'referendum', it means that any important issue that cannot be solved by the government for some reason should be decided by the votes of the people. Let the decision of the people be final. Obviously, it is a device of direct democracy. History has many instances when ticklish questions could be settled by means of a plebsicite. For instance, plebiscite was held in 1935 whereby Saar area was given back to Germany.
4. **Recall:** It means that the voters have the right to call back their elected representative in case they are not satisfied with his role or behaviour and then elect someone else instead. The system of recall was provided in the electoral law of the USSR. It prevails in some States of America.

A new kind of democracy has come up after the English Glorious Revolution of 1688, the American Revolution 1776, and the French Revolution of 1789, in particular. It means that while the political power should be vested in the people, its exercise should

17. Garner, *op. cit.*, pp. 314-15.
18. W.B. Munro: *The Governments of Europe,* p. 746.
19. A.V. Dicey: *An Introduction to the Study of the Law of the Constitution,* p. 608.

be given to the representatives chosen by and accountable to the people. Thus, it is also known as representative democracy, what J.S. Mill calls 'representative government'. In such a system, the will of the state is formulated and expressed through the agency of a relatively small and select body of persons chosen by the people to act as their representatives. It is based on the idea that while the people cannot be actually present in person at the seat of government, they "are considered to be present by proxy."[20]

Indirect or representative democracy has some essential features that may be enumerated as follows keeping in view the fact that their existence and operation differ from one country to another in varying degrees:

1. **Universal Adult Suffrage:** The first and foremost requirement of indirect democracy is that all adults of the state should have the right to vote. The minimum age of a voter may be anything like 21 years as in France, 20 years as in Japan, 18 years as in Britain, USA, Australia and India. There should be no artificial restrictions in matters of suffrage based on the factors of religion, caste, wealth, sex, colour of the skin, language, domicile and the like. It is, however, a different matter that a very negligible section of the people may be deprived of the privilege of franchise on the grounds of lunacy, undischarged insolvency, heinous crimes and the like.
2. **Free, Fair and Periodic Elections:** The, elections should take place from time to time so that the voters may choose and change their representatives. It is necessary that the elections should be free from corruption or rigging of any kind. Let the voters vote in a free and frank manner so as to register their will in the battle of the ballot box. And it is equally necessary that the elections should be contested periodical, after every four or five years. In case the holding of elections is delayed for very long durations without any reasonable cause, it amounts to the negation of a democratic system.
3. **Role of Parties and Interest Groups:** There should be a number of political parties and interest groups in the country to take part in the political process. They may form a healthy public will or opinion. The power should alternate between these parties and groups so that it may not be monopolised by a particular section of the people as happens in a fascist or in a communist country.
4. **Freedom of the Press and Mass Media:** It is also necessary that all channels of information should be open so that people may have a correct 'image' of the news and views about great matters of public concern. The freedom of the press is, therefore, an essential requirement of a democratic system. So other mass communication agencies like broadcasting and telecasting should be free to play their part in the making of the public opinion.
5. **Independence of Judiciary:** Above all, the courts should be free to decide matters according to the law of the land. There should be no coercion or compulsion

20. Ford: *Representative Government,* p. 3.

over the judges in matter of adjudication. Their selection should be made on the basis of merit; they should get promotions on the basis of seniority as well as efficiency; their tenure should be fixed; their emoluments should be attractive; the mode of their removal on some charge should be tedious; they should not be allowed to maintain public contacts. These measures are required to maintain the independence of judiciary that has its own role to play in the maintenance of a democratic system.

In short, a representative government is one that establishes, what A.V. Dicey calls, the 'rule of law'. It guarantees essential liberties of the people and also honours the principle of equality of mankind. It is a 'limited government' bound by the principle of the 'separation of powers'. Thus, according to F.G. Wilson, its essential requirements are (i) a constitution specifying the rules of the composition and working of the government, (ii) constitutionalism implying the rule of laws and not of men, (iii) a declaration of the fundamental rights of the people, and (iv) a democratic structure of government.[21]

Criticism: A very large number of writers have expressed their views to laud democracy as the best possible form of government that man has been able to design for himself. At the same time, there is no dearth of critics who have denounced it in equally strong terms. First, we shall look into the merits of democracy. These are:

1. Democracy is the best form of government for the reason that it ensures popular participation. It is the only government that stands on the will of the people and stimulates them to take part in the political affairs of the country. The people choose their representatives and force them to act according to their will. The rulers act with a sense of responsibility towards their elections. They cannot ignore the weight of public opinion. Thus, the leaders have their rise and fall according to the winds of public mind. It cannot occur in any other form of government like monarchy, aristocracy or dictatorship.
2. The case of democracy can be defended from a psychological point of view. Since the people have power and they make use of it not only through their representatives but also through numerous parties and groups, they have a feeling of satisfaction. They do not think in terms of a revolutionary or bloody agitation the kind of which may be seen in the smouldering resentment of the people towards their king or dictator. They may wait for the elections, and then easily change their rulers. "Popular governments, resting as they go on the consent of the governed and upon the principle of equality, are also likely to be more immune from revolutionary disturbances than those in which the people have no right of participation.
3. The case of democracy should also be appreciated from the educational point of view. Every form of government gives some kind of political education and

21. Wilson: *The Elements of Modern Politics,* pp. 210-13.

training to its people. But its best manifestation can be seen in a democratic system. The holding of elections, the working of the legislature, the role of parties and groups, the opposition of the people in the form of strikes and demonstrations and the like impart a good deal of political education to the people. The people are inspired to understand the implications of terms like rule of law, accountability of the rulers, motions of impeachment and no-confidence, enforcement of judicial decisions for the protection of fundamental rights, etc. In this way, democracy becomes a system of self-education for the people of the country.

4. The case of democracy is strongly defended on moral grounds as well. It is said that democracy makes the character of the people noble. It inculcates in them the feelings of hard work and enterprise, it sharpens their sense of responsibility and patriotism. It makes them self-reliant and enthuses them to undertake big projects for the development of the country. Lowell says that democracy nurtures a people strong in moral fibre, in integrity, in industry, in self-reliance and in courage. Mill lays great stress on the influence of democracy in elevating the character and political intelligence of the people in general. As he says: "The most important point of excellence which any form of government can possess is to promote the virtue and intelligence of the people themselves, and the first consideration in judging the merits of a particular form of government is how far they tend to foster intellectual and moral qualities in the citizens."[22]

5. Above all, democracy is the only form of government that acts in a self-correcting manner. The formula of trial and error has its operation here. The government commits many acts of commission and ommission and the process of self-correction is at work simultaneously. People know that they are the real rulers of the country; they choose their rulers and when they desire to change the government, they can do it without destroying the constitutional system. As a machinery can be repaired by replacing its defective part, so the government can be corrected by the replacement of a particular organ like the chief administrator or the body of legislators.

On the contrary, the system of democracy has been denounced for various reasons. Aristotle described it as 'the degenerated form of polity'; Talleyrand defined it as 'aristocracy of blackguards'; Carlyle sneeringly referred to the people as 'a certain number of millions, mostly fools'; Ludovici said that 'democracy means death, while aristocracy means life'; Maine found it greatly 'fragile' making all forms of government insecure; Barker discovered the weakness of democracy in the 'role of few manipulators'; Giddings could trace the two serious dangers of democracy in 'unbridled emotionalism' leading to the occurrence of violence and 'absolutism of the multitude' that tramples all rights of the minorities'. The main points of attack on democracy may be enumerated as follows:

22. Mill: *Considerations on Representative Government,* pp. 27-29.

1. A democratic system works on the basis of quantity; it ignores the side of quality. All decisions are taken by the majority that, as the critics say, consists of 'fools'. The sycophants, the clappers, and the hand-raisers have an upper hand over those who think and speak in the real interest of the people. Thus, merit and wisdom weep unknown. It is for this reason that Plato and Aristotle condemned democracy. Modern critics like Lecky and Maine stress the point that democracy means rule of the majority. It entails suppression of the voice of those who are intellectually and morally superior to those who constitute 'manipulated' majorities. The principle of 'one person, one vote' is wrong in view of the fact that all persons can never be of equal worth. Thus, a defender of the privileges of the British peers like Lecky condemns democracy as "the government by the poorest, the most ignorant, the most incapable, who are necessarily the numerous."
2. Politics becomes a profession in a democratic system with the result that crafty leaders excite popular passions to serve their nefarious purposes. Innocent people are hoodwinked by the demagogues; agitations become the order of the day. Numerous groups take part in political affairs as a result of which politics becomes like a tug-of-war between conflicting interests. The net result of all this is that public peace remains disturbed and prevalence of chaotic conditions becomes the order of the day. Government loses its stability and revolutions become a matter of frequent occurrence. In other words, a democratic system is always subject to popular upheavals that makes its existence greatly fragile or ephemeral.
3. Democracy is a very expensive form of government. A lot of national wealth is squandered on lengthy discussions. It is a luxury for the rich people. We may take note of the fact that millions are spent on the sessions of the national legislature and, in fact, very little useful comes out of that. Carlyle thus debunked the parliament as a 'talking shop' and Gandhiji decried it as a 'sterile woman'. Much amount of money is spent on duplication and triplication of work. Enormous wealth is spent on elections and propaganda work. A dictator like Mussolini could, therefore, correctly say that "democracy is not suited to a poor country."
4. In a rich country like the United States, democracy is degenerated into plutocracy or the perverted rule of the wealthy persons. Politics becomes a brisk profession for those who can spend a lot and thereby manage to secure what they desire. It is said that the entire wealth of the United States is concentrated in nine families and the office of the President may be captured by one who belongs to one of them. Lobbying is a good business, but it is money that runs the institution of lobbying. Elections are a gigantic fraud, because the rich manage to get votes of the poor and thereby enter into the portals of power. By the power of money political favours are grabbed.
5. A democratic system brings about instability in the sphere of legislation and administration. The rulers change very quickly and every leader tries to run the

administration according to his choice. The personal interest of the leader or his group is exhibited as the national interest. Laws are enacted or changed, policies are adopted, appointments are made, and all important decisions are taken to suit the purpose of the leaders in power. It is due to this that many writers "have pointed out the difficulty of carrying out a consistent policy over a period of years under a democratic system. The frequent changes in administration and in policy resulting from the overthrow of the party in power make it difficult to secure continuities of political purpose or to plan for the future. This weakness is considered especially dangerous in foreign affairs."[23]

6. The working of a democratic system reveals many serious defects such as loss of the sense of responsibility in the rulers and bureaucrats, groupism and factionalism, distribution of the spoils, political corruption, manipulations of party politics, more of a show and very little of a reality, wasteful expenditure of propaganda work, loot of national wealth, suppression of the minorities, no respect to the men of talent and merit, primacy to local considerations over national interest, violence of the mob, etc.

However, a look at the demerits of democracy should not become a source of discouragement. Every government has its points of strength and weakness, so is the case with democracy. But the apologists of democracy have their strong points to justify the excellence of this system alone. Lord Bryce puts a pertinent question as to which form of government is better than democracy. C.D. Burns says: "No one denies that existing representative assemblies are defective; but even if an automobile does not work well, it is foolish to go back into a farm cart, however, romantic."[24]

Future of Democracy and Conditions of Its Successful Working: It is now universally acclaimed that democracy is the best form of government and though it has some defects, they may be removed in course of time. It is better to bear with the defects of democracy than to replace it by any form of authoritarian system like fascism or communism. Dictatorship is no substitute of democracy. Sidgwick's comment is laudable that 'democracy is now a widely and enthusiastically accepted political ideal.'[25] Laski's remark is equally significant that 'people who have once tasted power will never surrender it.'[26] We are free to criticise democracy as much as we may, but, as Bathelemy remarks, it is as vain to criticise the course of the seasons or the laws of attraction of the stars. "Whatever may be the weaknesses of democracy, and they undoubtedly exist, it seems destined to become universal. In fact, it has already nearly become such."[27]

---

23. R.G. Gettell, *Political Science,* p. 203.
24. Burns: *Democracy,* p. 80.
25. Sidgwick: *Elements of Politics,* p. 608.
26. Laski: *A Grammar of Politics,* p. 17.
27. Garner, *op. cit.,* p. 403.

Taking for granted that democracy alone is the good form of government and also taking into account that it has some defects that may either be removed or borne with, it may be suggested that democracy requires certain prerequisites or conditions for its successful working. According to Mill, the three prerequisites of democracy are that the people should be willing to receive it, that they should be willing and able to do what is necessary for its preservation, and that they should be willing and able to fulfil the duties and discharge the functions which it imposes.

As a matter of fact, different writers have laid stress on different points in the direction of specifying conditions for the successful working of a democratic system. Though critics of democracy, like Lecky and Maine, have suggested the existence of a 'written constitution' to keep the rule of the many within bounds, Laveleye and Mill have laid stress on 'elementary education of the people; and Bryce has laid all emphasis on the 'moral and intellectual progress of mankind.' In the words of Garner: "It is hardly necessary to say that perhaps the most fundamental of all conditions to the successful working of democratic government is that the people who work it shall possess a relatively high degree of political intelligence, an abiding interest in public affairs, a keen sense of public responsibility, and a readiness to accept and abide by the decisions of the majority. The majority in turn must be willing to recognise that strong minorities have rights which are entitled to respect and cannot be disregarded without violating one of the fundamental principles of popular government. The distressing indifference of the electors in many countries is undoubtedly a danger to democracy."[28]

Theories of Democracy

After discussing at length the case of democracy as a form of government, we may now pass on to the study of democratic theory as espoused by the classical liberals, the neo-liberals (including pluralists and elitists) and the Marxian socialists. Two points baffle us at this stage. First, democracy is no longer a political contrivance; it has penetrated into social and economic spheres. As such, a theory of democracy should be broad enough to cover all these directions in a consistent form. Second, a study of this subject should be made in the light of all available classical and modern interpretations so as to present a full picture of the view its advocates take about its dimensions in theoretical as well as practical perspectives. As we shall see, such theories may be grouped broadly into two parts—liberal and socialist—and while they have their strong and weak points, an ideal situation would be to harmonise their strong points at the cost of their weak elements so as to offer the most plausible theory of democracy.

28. Garner, *op. cit.*, pp. 405-06.

Some Important Statements

- I believe that the most defensible and attractive form of democracy is one in which citizens can participate in decision-making in a wide array of spheres – political, economic and social.

  — David Held

- Democracy is a political method or an institutional arrangement for arriving at political, legislative or administrative decisions by vesting in certain individuals the power to decide on all matters as a consequence of their successful pursuit of the people's vote.

  — Joseph Schumpeter

- Liberalism is a doctrine about what the law ought to be; democracy is a doctrine about the manner of determining what will be the law.

  — Fredrick von Hayek

- Democracy is perhaps the most promiscuous word in the world public affairs.

  — Bernard Crick

- The most essential point to be taken note of is that in a democracy, important public decisions or questions of law and policy depend, directly or indirectly, upon public opinion, formally expressed by citizens of the community, the vast bulk of whom have equal political rights.

  — Albert Weale

Classical Theory: Democracy is a very old form of government and so its theory dates back to the days of the Greeks who identified it with 'people's power' (Pericles), or a system in which 'rulers are accountable to the people for what they do therein' (Herodotus). Such a view saw its reaffirmation in modern times when Abraham Lincoln in his Gettysberg oration of 1864 called it 'a government of the people, by the people, and for the people'. Great liberals like John Locke and Edmund Burke developed the same theme in the laws of the land. Later on, utilitarians like Bentham and James Stuart Mill justified the case of democratic government in the name of their formula of the 'greatest good of the greatest number', and John Stuart Mill did the same on the basis of his moral or ethical argument. This trend continued in the present century and saw its powerful reiteration at the hands of Dicey, Bryce and Laski. Apart from this, the idealistic argument of democracy prevailed side by side that had its brilliant manifestation at the hand sof Rousseau, Green and Lindsay. All such affirmations constitute, what is now called, the classical theory of democracy.

The classical theory of democracy as advocated by the liberals and the idealists of the modern age has these salient features:

1. Power is vested in the people and its exercise is given to them or to their chosen representatives accountable to them for their acts of commission and omission. All decisions must be based on the consent of the people, whether expressed or

implied, which, in practical terms, means the will of the majority. Thus, it stands on the premise that 'people are always right' (in theory), or the 'decision of the majority is always correct' (in practice). We may take note of the fact that, though a great idealist, Rousseau also went to the extent of laying down that, for all practical purposes, the general will should be taken as the will of the majority. So James Bryce defined democracy as "a government in which the will of the majority of qualified citizens rules, taking the qualified to constitute the great bulk of the inhabitants say, roughly, at least three-fourth so that the physcial force of the citizens coincides (broadly speaking) with their voting power.[29]

2. The people have certain natural and inalienable rights which the government cannot abrogate or diminish. The doctrine of 'natural rights,' as it came to be known, emerged as the most powerful instrument at the hands of the democrats who struggled for the rights of the people against arbitrary power of the kings. Reacting against the arbitrary powers of the king, John Milton asserted that "all men are naturally born free" and from this principle he derived "the liberty and right of free-born men to be governed as seems them best." Most powerful was the argument of John Locke coined to justify the Glorious Revolution of 1688-89 that "to understand political power right, we must begin with the recognition of a natural and original freedom of all men to order their actions and dispose of their possessions as they think fit, with the bounds of the laws of nature, without asking leave or depending upon the will of any other man."[30]
3. The doctrine of 'natural rights' lost its significance with the growth of the idea of positive liberalism that sought to reinterpret the relationship between individual liberty and state activity. Thus, Bentham offered his principle of utility that sought to give a new interpretation to the justification of democracy. The doctrine of natural rights was rejected, rather replaced by the doctrine of the happiness of man measured in terms of material pleasures. He gave the formula of 'one man, one vote'. It implied that "although all persons are not naturally the same in intelligence, energy, thrift, inventiveness, and perseverance, yet all normal men – just as they have equal rights to life, freedom and access to the courts of law–have equal rights to a voice in government because they have equal stakes in the justice and efficiency of governmental action."
4. If Benthamite utilitarianism displaced the line of 'natural rights', a revisionist of the utilitarian creed like Mill replaced the materialistic content of Bentham by the force of his ethical argument in favour of democracy. The argument of Bentham was based on the self-interest of the individual that ought to be harmonised with the interest of the society in the framework of the 'greatest good of the greatest number'. The defenders of Bentham called it enlightened or benevolent hedonism. But Mill defended the case of democracy as the best form of government on moral grounds. As he says, "The most important point of excellence which any form of

29. James Bryce: *Modern Democracies,* Vol. I, p. 22.
30. Locke: *Second Treatise of Civil Government,* Book II, Sections IV and XCV.

government can possess is to promote the virtue and intelligence of the people themselves. The first question in respect to any political institution is how far they tend to foster in the members of the community the various qualities... moral, intellectual and active."[31]

5. The classical theory of democracy has a peculiar dimension when we examine the view of the idealists like Rousseau and Green. To Rousseau, democracy alone ensures prevalence of the 'general will'. In every community there is a section of really selfless and enlightened people who think in terms of public interest and it is the inherent force of their selfless argument that ultimately prevails in any matter under discussion before a body of the people. Through the process of cancellation, good would set aside the bad; all contradictions would be resolved and in the end only 'dominant good' would emerge. This good, which would be what was left at the will of all becomes integrated, would be in effect the same as the general will."[32] Influenced by the idealistic interpretations of Rousseau, Green says that 'will, not force, is the basis of the state.'
6. Above all, democracy has no substitute in terms of excellence from a practical point of view. Every form of government has its merits and demerits. But peculiar is the case of democracy where merits far outweigh its demerits. Hence, it is the substituteless form of government. Bryce goes to the last extent of posing a question that if democracy "has not brought all the blessings that were expected, it has in some countries destroyed, in others materially diminished, many of the cruelties and terrors, injustices and oppressions of former times. However, grave the indictment that may be brought against democracy, its friends can answer, 'What better alternative do you offer?"[33]

In short, the classical or traditional doctrine of democracy has been in part a theory of certain original rights of men – a view that government is made by virtue of those rights and must conform to them. The men have a natural right to participate equally in political power, just as they have a natural right to be free from enslavement or to appeal on equal terms to judicial tribunals for protection of their lives and property against assaults, trespass or encroachment of any kind. What is known as 'democratic method' is that institutional arrangements for arriving at political decisions which realises the common good by making the people itself decide issues through the election of individuals who are to assemble in order to carry out its will.

The classical theory of democracy has been criticised on many counts.

1. It is thoroughly normative. It is loaded with high ideals and bombastic propositions like 'general will', 'people's rule', 'people's power', 'common good', and the like that cannot be subjected to empirical verification. All these terms are quite elusive.

---

31. John Stuart Mill: *Considerations on Representative Government,* pp. 39-40.
32. A.M. Osborn: *Rousseau and Burke,* pp. 169-70.
33. Bryce, *op. cit.,* Vol. II, pp. 669-70.

2. It attaches no importance to the role of numerous interest groups and organisations that play their part in the struggle for power, or which compete among themselves and all that constitutes the stuff of a democratic system in practice. The utilitarians talked about 'greatest happiness of the greatest number' without taking into consideration the powerful role of groups, factions and elites that ever strive to protect and promote their specific interests.
3. The socialists and the Marxists have their own version of democracy that stretches the system of political democracy into social and economic spheres. To the Marxists, it is all like a defence of the discredited bourgeois system.

And yet the classical theory of democracy has its own salient merits which are thus summed up by Schumpeter:

1. Though the classical doctrine of collective action may not be supported by the results of an empirical analysis, it is powerfully supported by its association with religious beliefs. The very meaning of a term like 'equality' may be in doubt; there is hardly any rational warrant for exalting it into a postulate, so long as we move in the sphere of empirical analysis. Christianity harbours a strong equalitarian element. Any celebrated word like 'equality' or 'freedom' may become a flag, a symbol of all a man holds dear, of everything that he loves about his nation whether rationally contingent to it or not.[34]
2. It is a fact that forms and phrases of classical democracy are for many nations associated with events and developments in their history which are enthusiastically approved by large majorities. Any opposition to an established regime is likely to use these forms and phrases whatever its meanings and social roots may be. Under these circumstances a democratic revolution has meant the advent of freedom and decency, and the democratic creed meant a gospel of reason and betterment. To be sure, this advantage was bound to be lost and the gulf between the doctrine and the practice of democracy was bound to be discovered. But the glamour of the dawn was slow to fade.[35]
3. It must not be forgotten that there are patterns in which the classical doctrine will actually fit facts with a sufficient degree of approximation. It provides an effective mechanism for talking and implementing decisions whether it is a small and primitive society of Switzerland or a big and industrialised society of the United States. This is the case with many small and primitive societies which, as a matter of fact, served, as a prototype to the authors of that doctrine of classical theory. It may be the case with those societies also that are not primitive, provided they are not too differentiated and do not harbour any serious problems.[36]

---

34. J.A. Schumpeter: *Capitalism, Socialism and Democracy.*, pp. 265-66.
35. *Ibid.,* pp. 266-67.
36. *Ibid.,* pp. 267-68.

4. Of course, the politicians appreciate a phraseology that flatters the masses and offers an excellent opportunity not only for evading responsibility but also for crushing opponents in the name of the people.[37]

Therefore, the intrinsic merits of the democratic system cannot be denied.

Neo-Liberal Theory: This theory of democracy is a modification, not a mutilation, of the classical or traditional liberal theory on this subject with a view to approximate to reality what it seeks to profess. In other words, the neo-liberals like to abjure the use of terms as 'general will,' 'common interest,' 'people's rule' and the like on account of their being of a non-verifiable nature and instead prefer to offer an explanation about the nature and working of democracy with the use of a new vocabulary loaded with causal and practicable implications. An attempt may also be seen in the direction of narrowing down the gulf between the liberty of the individual and the authority of the state in a democratic set up. Thus, instead of treating the two as basically antithetical terms, the neo-liberals like to establish a sort of happy and workable compromise between them. Moreover, it is taken into account that although democracy may be available in many countries of the world, it differs from place to place and, as such, a uniform theory of democracy of universal application cannot be formulated.

The salient features of the neo-liberal theory of democracy may be enumerated as follows under:

1. Democracy has different forms of its own in different parts of the world. It is also known by many labels as pure democracy, liberal democracy, socialist democracy, guided democracy, participatory democracy, etc. Surprisingly, the word 'democracy' may be recklessly applied to a system that has hardly anything like democratic in it. Hence, the first step in such an analysis is to dispel the illusion that democracy always stands for that which is good and virtuous about a political system. "If democracy is used to describe the 'good society,' then there will, indeed, be as many types of democracy as there are visions of utopia and the word will lose all descriptive meanings."[38]
2. Classical theory of democracy stands on the principle of natural equality of mankind – a doctrine given by the Stoics, followed by the Romans, preached by the Christians, and forcefully advocated by those who fought against royal despotism in the seventeenth and eighteenth centuries. The neo-liberals accept this doctrine with a reservation. Though they do not frankly subscribe to the rule of natural inequality of mankind, as stressed by Aristotle, they make a dexterous attempt to do so by sticking to the practical side of things. They discard the meaning of equality in ideal or absolute terms. As Barry says: "Democracy implies some commitment to political equality, not an absolute equality, since any form of rule necessarily involves some political inequality, but in the sense of no race, class, or individual being arbitrarily deprived of the opportunity of participating in the political process."

37. *Ibid.*, p. 268.
38. N.P. Barry: *An Introduction to Modern Political Theory,* p. 208.

3. An inference from the above would be that democracy is neither the rule of all, nor of many, it is the rule of a section of the political people. It has created a sort of dilemma for political theory and in order to solve it, an attempt has been made to harmonise the law of oligarchy with the premise of the rule of the people. Thus, Barry feels that the prevailing problem is that of reconciling the aim of government by the people with the obvious fact that "the government itself is a minority activity."[39] A powerful advocate of this view like Schumpeter, therefore, says, "To put it differently, we now take the view that the role of the people is to produce a government, or else an intermediate body which in turn will produce a national executive or government. And we define: the democratic method is that institutional arrangement for arriving at political decisions in which individuals acquire the power to decide by means of a competitive struggle for the people's vote."[40]
4. The neo-liberal theorists of democracy like Giovanni Sartori and Joseph Schumpeter summarily reject the doctrine of natural rights as a dogma, or rule of people as a myth on the plea that it "is both unsustained and also unsustainable by any possible evidence and without practical value in solving any of the actual problems of political life." His more detailed attack is directed against the democratic assumptions as to "the equality of men in political capacity."[41] Thus, the case of position and role of man in a 'market society' has come up. To an economist, a market works according to the law of supply and demand; to an empirical theorist, politics means exercise of 'extractive' and 'developmental' capacities of man (Macpherson). Politics is struggle for power, it is like a competition in which many actors are involved. The merit of democracy is that it opens doors for all to enter into the arena of struggle or competition for power. The result is that numerous organisations play their part for the sake of protecting and promoting their interests in a 'plural society'. Democracy thus becomes an 'elective polyarchy'.[42]
5. If so, a realistic theory of democracy must frankly highlight the role of numerous interest groups, factions, elites, leadership and the like including their techniques and tactics (such as strike, demonstration, petition-mongering, lobbying, blackmailing, log-rolling, pork-barrel, violence etc.) for the protection of their specific interests. Due significance should be given to the 'iron law of oligarchy' as laid down by Robert Michels. Thus, taking the line of Schumpeter and Dahl, Sartori subscribes to the doctrine of calling democracy 'elective polyarchy' without bothering for the fact that some critics would call it 'an aristocratic theory of democracy' as against its 'demolatric version.'[43]

---

39. *Ibid.*, p. 212.
40. Schumpeter, *op. cit.*, p. 269.
41. Coker, *op. cit.*, p. 353.
42. R.A. Dahl: *A Preface to Democratic Theory*.
43. Sartori, *op. cit.*, p. 127.

We may easily form an impression that the empirical theory of democracy discards the normative premises of its classical counterpart. As true to its creed, it takes into account those aspects of political life that are a reality in the working of a democratic system. In this way, it becomes an improvement upon what the classical theorists of democracy say. And yet it does not altogether dismiss the sanctity of the phrases used in classical theory of democracy like residence of power in the hands of the people and decision-making by the majority. Schumpeter, Dahl and Sartori seek to accommodate the facts of political life into the body of classical doctrine of democracy. One may, however, discover some points of differences among the empirical theorists, of course, on the issue of giving any place, or not, to the normative premises of the traditional doctrine of democracy.

The neo-liberal theory of democracy may be criticised on two grounds. First, it discards the place of norms and goals in the operation of a democratic system. It takes things in their crass materialistic forms, and thereby takes away the freshness of the idea of democracy that comes from its normative version. Second, it becomes a vulgar instrument for the justification of the discredited bourgeois system in which society is taken as a multitude of numerous interests competing and conflicting with each other. Such an interpretation brings a bad name to the case of liberal democracy that must be revised in the light of prevailing economic inequalities calling for social and economic justice in a free and humanistic order. Thus, while being a critical advocate of the empirical theory of democracy, Macpherson would appreciate a model of democratic theory that "provides conditions for the full and free development of the essential human capacities of all the members of the society."[44]

Elitist Theory: This theory is a reinterpretation of the liberal theory of democracy in a strictly empirical direction. The elite theorists like Pareto, Mosca, Michels, C. Wright Mills and Haorld Lasswell lay stress on the point that what is known as the rule of the people, in a practical sense, it is the rule of the elites. It discards normative expressions like 'voice of the people' or 'rule of the general will' and instead stands for the 'rule of the chosen few' with the consent or acquiescence of the many. Even if all men are taken as equal according to the Biblical injunction of the 'Fatherhood of God and the brotherhood of man', some are more equal than others with the result that few have a position of advantage over the many. Inequality is a universal fact making every political system 'oligarchical', though in varying degrees. Thus, the empiricists would say that all people are always governed by an elite, or by 'a chosen element of the population'. In this sense, democracy is the government of the people in theory, in practice it is the 'government of an elite sprung from the people'.[45]

It follows that classical affirmations highlighting the fact of 'power with the people' have a normative or idealistic connotation. In terms of practice, it is the body of the very few that takes all important decisions and plays its part in the political process of the country. The people may think that they may participate in political process,

44. Macpherson: *The Real World of Democracy,* p. 36.
45. Maurice Duverger: *Political Parties,* p. 425.

but in reality, so the argument runs, their influence is largely confined to elections. At the centre of power there is a social elite which "wields considerable influence."[46] All wars, all revolutions, all elections, all parliamentary discussions leading to some decisions and the like are effected by the role of elites. And as every elite is formed around a leader, the credit or discredit for all acts of triumph or disaster is given to him. So it is affirmed: "By this time recognition is widespread that the world-inclusive study of power elites is indispensable to all serious inquiry into political processes."[47]

The elite theory of democracy should be taken as a peculiar mixture of the classical theories of democracy and aristocracy. It has a democratic content in the sense that it accepts residence of power in the people; its aristocratic content lies in its assertion that only a few persons under a leader are capable of exercising power. However, its democratic content should also be viewed with this line of distinction that while classical theorists of democracy would appreciate the growing role of the people in the sphere of political process, the elite theorists would like to keep the distribution of power in a limited circle of the most influential, most intelligent, most shrewd, most cunning and most competent people. That is, classical theorists of democracy would say that public policy should result from extensive and informed discussion, the elite theorists would contend that it is neither possible nor desirable. By extending general participation in decision-making, the classical theorists hoped to increase the awareness of the citizens towards their moral and social responsibilities, reduce the danger of tyranny, and improve the quality of government. Public officials acting as agents of the public at large would then carry out the broad policies decided upon by majority vote in popular assemblies."[48]

But the elite theorists look at such idealistic affirmations of the classical advocates of democracy with ample apprehension. In their view, the involvement of as many people in the decision-making process as possible would be dangerously naive in view of the fact that it would create demagogic leadership, mass psychology, rise of sycophancy, group coercion and the influence of those who control concentrated economic power. The affirmations of the classical theorists are, therefore, either utopian as they cannot be realised or, if put into practice, would lead to the disintegration of a good political system. According to such theorists, a revisionist movement should be started so that democratic theory may be reformulated in tune with the reality of an empirical analysis. The fact stands out that every political system is divided into two groups—the elites or the political entrepreneurs who have ideological commitments and manipulative skill, and the citizens at large, the masses or the apolitical clay of the system, a much larger class of passive, inert followers who have little knowledge of public affairs and even less interest.[49]

---

46. D.V. Verney: *An Analysis of Political Systems,* p. 166.
47. Lasswell and Lerner: *World Revolutionary Elites.,* p. 3.
48. See G.H. Sabine: "The Two Democratic Traditions" in *Philosophical Review,* Vol. 61, 1952, pp. 451-74.
49. R.A. Dahl: *Who Governs?,* pp. 25-27.

A good political system is one that enjoys stability and stability requires limited political participation. The classical theorists hoped that growing political participation would be a blessing for the success of democracy elite theorists contend that call for more and more political participation should be treated as essentially a noble myth. Only limited political participation would give stability to a democratic system. Democracies have good reasons to fear increased political participation. A successful or stable democratic system depends on widespread political apathy and general political incompetence. The ideal of the democratic participation is thus transformed into a 'noble lie' designed chiefly to insure a sense of responsibility among political leaders. "It is important to continue moral admonishment for citizens to become more active in politics, not because we want or expect great masses of them to become active, but rather because the admonishment helps keep the system open and sustains a belief in the right of all to participate which is an important norm governing the behaviour of political elites."[50]

But the elite theorists do not reject the central idea of democracy as affirmed by the classical theorists. They maintain that democracy is an 'open system' which allows struggle for power. Let there be as many groups and elites to compete as possible. Voting provides the electors with an opportunity to change their leaders and competition among the candidates for office. These two key institutional devices are taken for granted by the elite theorists. As Bottomore says: "The significance of political democracy is primarily that the positions of power in society are open, in principle, to everyone, that there is competition for power, and that the holders of power at any time are accountable to the electorate."[51] And in spite of this, there is no harm if the actual shaping of policy is in the hands of elites; but this does not mean to say that the society is not democratic. For it is sufficient for democracy that the individual citizens... have at least the possibility of making their aspirations felt at certain intervals."[52]

The elitist theory of democracy, though loaded with verifiable assumptions, may be criticised on these grounds:

1. Although an extension of the liberal theory of democracy, it inheres a conservative character. It affirms that in case the uninformed masses participate in large numbers, the network of democratic restraints will break down and peaceful competition among the elites, the central element of elitist theory, would become impossible. Thus, by revising the theory to bring it into closer correspondence with reality, the elite theorists have transformed democracy from a radical into a conservative political doctrine, stripping away its distinctive emphasis on popular political activity so that it "no longer serves as a set of ideals towards which society ought to be striving."[53]

---

50. L. Milbrath: *Political Participation,* p. 152.
51. T.B. Bottomore: *Elites in Society,* p. 168.
52. Karl Mannheim: *Essays on the Sociology of Culture,* p. 179.
53. J.L. Walker, "A Critique of the Elitist Theory of Democracy" in T.J. Bellows, S. Erikson and H.R. Winter (ed.): *Political Science: Introductory Essays and Readings,* p. 64.

2. The elite theorists discard moral or ethical aspect of democracy that is so powerfully stressed by the classical theorists like Mill and Bryce. To them democracy is a mere mechanism with no morality of its own, or with the set of its existing morality that pertains to a bourgeois system. In the version of the elitists, emphasis has shifted to the needs and functions of the system as a whole, there is no longer a direct concern with human development. It has no place for ideals or noble directions towards which a democratic system must move. The central question is not how to design a political system which stimulates greater individual participation and enhances the moral development of its citizens but how to combine a substantial degree of popular participation with a system of power capable of governing effectively and coherently.[54]

3. In a valid sense, the elite theory of democracy is the negation of the system of democracy. Democracy is the only system that stands on the 'will of the people'. As such, growing participation of the people in the political process should be desired and appreciated. Contrary to this, it assumes a distinctly oligarchical complexion by denying in practice what it accepts in theory. It allows the citizen only a passive role as an object of political activity. A citizen exerts his influence on policy-making only by rendering judgments at the time of elections. Obviously, political participation "is reduced to the manageable task of periodic choices in elections."[55] The elitists "forget that the safety of contemporary democracy lies in the high-minded sense of responsibility of its leaders, the elements of society who are actively striving to discover and implement the common good."[56]

4. The elitist theory of democracy looks for the principal source of innovation in the competition among rival leaders and the clever manoeuvring of political entrepreneurs which is in its view the most distinctive aspect of a democratic system. The primary concern of the elitists is maintenance of 'stability', or the status quo, or the preservation of democratic procedures, and the creation of a machinery which would produce efficient administration and coherent public policies. With these goals in mind, social movements have usually been pictured as threats to democracy or as manifestations of political extremism. We may easily take note of the fact that elite theorists are status quoists; they are faithful disciples of Burke and Hegel. They deliberately ignore the fact that every political system undergoes changes from time to time and the requirement of the present age is to make democracy in tune with the good of the people in general. Instead they take it for granted that "one major consequence (function) of social movements is to break society's log jams to prevent ossifications in the political system, to prompt and justify many innovations in social policy and economic organisation."[57]

---

54. S. Beer: "New Structure of Democracy: Britain and America" in J.W. Chambers and R.H. Salisbury (eds.): *Democracy in the Mid-Twentieth Century*, p. 46.
55. P. Bachrach: *The Theory of Democratic Elitism*, p. 38.
56. Walker, *op. cit.*, p. 65.
57. *Ibid.*, p. 75.

5. Above all, this theory commits an act of self-contradiction by adulating democracy as an 'open system' and, at the same time, by justifying the way of manipulation and secrecy in which elites remain involved all the time. Elite politics is never open politics, and yet it requires a democratic system that is invariably an open system. Politics should be open and clean and if a politics of this kind prevails, democratic system would be an ideal for humanity. Only in that case the working of Rousseau's 'general will' may be seen. Leadership should not be mere transactional or based on the principle of give and take; it should be of a transformational kind correcting the behaviour of the followers.[58] The elite theorists would defend the ways of a leader like Lenin, they would certainly disdain to laud the ways of a leader like Gandhi.

In short, the elitist theory of democracy reveals a political truth and therein its real value can be assessed. It is thoroughly empirical. It takes democracy as a mechanism, the essential function of which is to maintain an equilibrium.[59]

Pluralist Theory: Like elitist theory of democracy, this theory believes in the system of limited political participation. But the essential point of distinction between the two is that while the elitists lay all emphasis on the role of the chosen few, the pluralists do the same for the numerous groups that play their part in the struggle for power. An open society is also a plural society; it recognises the existence of varied interests of the people and their groups formed for the sake of protecting and promoting their specific interests. Thus, in a democratic system all such groups should be allowed to take part in the political process which operate either singly or in combination with other groups, either directly and autonomously or in alliance with some political party.

Liberalism defends self-interest of the individual. As such, the pluralist theory of democracy stands on the premise of individual interest and thereby becomes a part of the liberal theory on the subject of democracy. It is the cardinal factor of self-interest that forces persons to be in unison with other like-minded ones in order to enhance their position and power to the point of gaining recognition, legitimisation and realisation of their specific interest. That is, it depends upon the fact that a man's skin is closer to him than his shirt.

The theory of pluralism saw its emergence in the 19th century when some students of history and sociology like O.V. Gierke of Germany, F.W. Maitland of England and Emile Durkheim of France appreciated the medieval social system recognising autonomy of the groups. In the 20th century a good number of American social theorists like Arthur Bentley, David B. Truman, V.O. Key, Jr., James Burnham and H.D. Lasswell made a serious attempt to examine the working of a democratic system in the light of the role of numerous groups, big and small, which have a definite role in the sphere of making and implementation of policy decisions. In recent times a good number of empirical theorists like S.H. Beer, Harry Eckstein, Joseph la Palombara,

58. J.M. Burns: *Leadership,* p. 15.
59. C.B. Macpherson: *Democratic Theory,* p. 78.

Myron Weiner, Earl Latham, etc., have thrown much light on the need for revaluating the meaning and role of government in democratic countries.

The advocates of this theory reject the contention of the monists (like Hobbes and Austin) that state alone is the repository of sovereign authority. If society is federal, authority should also be federal, says Laski. Thus, pluralist democracy means a political system in which policies are made by mutual consultation and exchange of opinions between various groups. The sovereign power of the state should be distributed in a way that the groups have a share in it. All important decisions on social, economic and political matters should be taken by the officials of state after consulting groups whose interests are involved in it, or who might be affected by the implementation of such decisions. Thus, democracy, apart from being a rule of the people, or of the majority, is a socio-political system in which the power of the state is shared with a large number of private groups, interest organisations and individuals represented by such organisations.... Pluralism is a system in which political power is fragmented among the branches of government; it is, moreover, shared between the State and a multitude of private groups and individuals."[60]

A degree of superficial similarity between the elitist and the pluralist theories of democracy may be established on the ground that both desire an 'open' system in which struggle for power witnesses the role of limited persons. But the essential point of distinction between the two is that while the former desires to keep the privilege of political participation confined to the minimum possible extent, the latter seeks to see its proliferation confined to the interest groups of the individuals. More than this, while the elitists do not appreciate the fact of growing politicisation of the people, the pluralists have no such reservations. The elitists are committed to the aristocratic approach and, as such, they want to keep the scope of political participation confined to the chosen few; the pluralists have a democratic approach and, as such, they favour extension of group competition to any possible extent.

In this way, despite being an extension of the liberal democratic theory, pluralist theory takes a turn in a direction opposed by the elitists. Political alienation is something good to the elitists; it is undesirable to the pluralists. Thus, by taking such a turn, the pluralist theory moves closer to the classical theory of democracy which desires more and more politicisation of the masses. Elections are not meant for the recruitment of the elites, or for the circulation of power among the elites, rather they are the vital instruments of mass participation in political decisions. If democracy means rule of the consensus, it must not be a narrower consensus of the elites, it must be the wider consensus of the groups.

The burden of the argument of the pluralists is that the state must recognise the personality and autonomy of social groups and allow them to take part in the political process of the country. The main function of the state is to deal with social conflicts in

60. R. Presthus: "The Pluralistic Framework" in H.S. Kariel (ed.): *Frontiers of Democratic Theory,* p. 280.

a way that the competitive struggle for power is regulated. The state is a harmoniser of social relations, it is the adjustor of conflicting social claims. The groups fill up the gap between the individuals and social and political systems. It is through their leaders that such groups mediate between individuals and all organised forms of power. In this way, government "is kept close to the people, and decisions benefit from the skill and interest which such groups provide."[61]

The pluralist theory of democracy may be criticised on these grounds:

1. It undermines the sovereign position of the state by laying too much stress on the personality and autonomy of social groups. It ignores the salient fact that state alone can deal with the conditions of anarchy in which the hands of some rebellious and irresponsible groups may be traced. It is true that the role of many groups would act as a check on the abuse of power by the government, but it is also true that in case groups are given the kind of autonomy as desired by the pluralists, they would create many serious problems of law and order. It is a pity that while the pluralists say so much about the necessity of the role of these groups in an open society, they hardly say anything in so forceful terms about the legitimate control of the state over them.
2. The elitists make their own point that looks like an improvement upon what the pluralists assert. Let there be as many social groups as possible to take part in the political process of the country, but it is the role of the elites that must be given all significance. The iron law of oligarchy stands to demonstrate the point that elites control power and power shifts among them. If political theory is to be made empirically correct, the emphasis must switch from the role of the social groups to those of the elites.
3. The argument of the Marxists is that pluralist theory of democracy is a justification of the discredited bourgeois system. Political pluralism prevails only in a society in which there are different classes. Since a socialist society would be singular, there would be no need for contending classes and groups. Thus, a new kind of democracy is needed to save man from exploitation and coercion of any kind. It shall be a classless society in which power would be in the hands of the working class and, as such, its main object would be to liquidate capitalist and feudal systems by all possible means, it would be designated as the 'dictatorship of the proletariat.' In this way, the Marxists reject both the elitist and the pluralist versions of democracy after condemning them as contributions of the bourgeois social and political theorists.

We may say that after the decline of the doctrine of pluralism in the period following the Second World War, the pluralist theory of democracy has lost its weight. Its central theme (that struggle for power should be open for all interests) has been stolen by the elitists and their interpretation has come to be accepted by the empirical social

61. *Ibid.*, p. 228.

and political theorists. The Americans have appreciated the model of 'polyarchical democracy' as given by Robert A. Dahl. The operation of 'mass democracy' is no longer possible in modern times. The new awareness is that not all groups but only a few groups count and even there the elites take part in the struggle for power. Power, in fact, has been monopolised by a few groups and their elites.[62]

Empirical Theory: Here we may refer to the views of Downs, Macpherson and Hayek. Inspired by the 'social choice theory' of his teacher (Kenneth Arrow), Anthony Downs presents economic theory of democracy. His purpose is to provide 'a behaviour rule for a democratic government and to trace its implications.' He constructs a model of 'rational political behaviour' in terms of economic costs of alternative choices and within the framework of a democratic system of government. In other words, his object "is to specify the principles of the rules of behaviour which are implied by the notion of rationality in the pursuit and use of power in a democratic order."[63] The case of a democratic system is examined in the light of 'economic rationality of the individual'. Like Hobbes, he asserts the point of human selfishness and, like Adam Smith, he sticks to the case of an 'economic man'. He, therefore, comes to hold that consideration of public welfare as espoused by the rulers of a democratic state are tricks to catch votes and influence the people in their favour. Such ethical affirmations have no normative concern; they are just factual parameters.[64]

However, like Bentham, Downs masks the selfish part of human behaviour with the thin layer of altruism. In his view, utility which the citizen seeks, need not be selfish in the narrow sense of the word, because self-denying charity is often a great source of benefit to oneself. Thus, his model leaves room for altruism in spite of its basic reliance upon the self-interest axiom. From such a primary axiom that democratic governments act rationally to maximise political support and from his definition of democratic procedures, he proceeds to deduce an entire theory of rational political behaviour, an elaborate set of 'positive' norms which describe how rational men behave under specified conditions.[65]

It follows that democracy is the best form of government in terms of man's rational behaviour, both political and economic. Man is a selfish creature; he remains involved in the struggle for power. The problem arises as to how man's essentially selfish search for power or interest be reconciled with the standard of social good as espoused by the normativists. The answer is that such a complementarity of interests is provided by the democratic system. "It is perhaps only this assumption of politically performed majority opinions that allows Downs to hold that purely selfish rulers will always, in a democratic system, produce government policy in the interest of the majority of the ruled. There is a perfect complementarity of interest between 'rational rulers' and

62. See K. Lowenstein: *Political Power and Governmental Process*.
63. W.T. Bluhm: *Theories of the Political System,* p. 274.
64. Anthony Downs: *An Economic Theory of Democracy,* pp. 18-19.
65. *Ibid.,* p. 54.

'rational subjects'. It is in the interest of the rulers to govern in the majority interest, for if they did not, they would not stay in power. Thus, enlightened selfishness produces the results of unselfish government, and without the aid of a social welfare function or any moral standard other than the rulers' greed."[66]

On the whole, the model of Downs, as he claims, approximates to the world of reality. It is not a utopian model of democracy as conceived by Rousseau, it is a normal model of a democratic system tending to conform to a kind of Aristotelian entelechy with the conception of perfection expunged from it. What is new about it, in the view of Downs, is that he has been able to introduce the tinge of altruism, though of a superficial kind, in the theory of democracy. It, however, leads to a condition of ambiguity which Downs realises but discards in order to demonstrate his arrival at a scientific mode of analysis adapted from the non-rational world. A critic may say that while Hobbes and Adam Smith remained consistent in developing their theories on the basis of individual behaviour, Downs committed an act of inconsistency by introducing the element of superficial normativism in a thoroughly empirical theory of democracy.

A peculiar feature of such an interpretation is that its exponent seeks to introduce an element of so-called normativism in the thoroughly empirical theory of democracy. It has, however, a better and more sensible manifestation in the works of C.B. Macpherson who examines the case of liberal democracy in the context of his thesis of 'possessive individualism'. His thought looks essentially practical in that its ultimate aim is the resolution of moral problems which emerge with social changes. As he contends: "The trouble with the equilibrium theory of democracy is that, like the economists' managerial utility theory, it leaves out of account the historical determinants of effective demand. It treats class interests in advanced countries and national aspirations in advancing countries, as just one among many kinds of political pressures. In doing so it averts its thoughts from the most serious problems of democracy."[67]

In a candid way, Macpherson finds faults with the way the case of liberal theorists is so ardently defended. This trend has been in acceptance curiously since the days of Locke and Burke who regarded individual as essentially the proprietor of his capacities and in return owing nothing to society. His basic argument is that liberal democracy is based on the assumption of possessive individualism and that the persistence of this assumption is in some measure responsible for the difficulties of liberal democratic theory in our time. In other words, his aim is to reveal the directions and limits of a social thinker's vision of the prevailing human conditions. The liberal view of democracy is a justification of the way of possessive individualism which constitutes the moral foundation for alienation of labour. It is not sufficient to account for the dynamics of a bourgeois society. In addition to possessive individualism, the assumption of a drive for unlimited appropriation underlines the capitalist model. It is this acceptance of

66. Bluhm *op. cit.*, p. 280.
67. Macpherson: "Market Conceptions in Political Theory" in *Canadian Journal of Economics and Political Science,* Vol. 27, No 4, November, 1961, p. 496.

the principle that makes it difficult to justify severe inequalities of wealth and status on utilitarian grounds. But Macpherson is happy to visualise that "today bourgeois individualism is in retreat possessed by socialist and other humanisms."[68]

Such an interpretation of democracy should, however, be evaluated objectively. While it has the merit of introducing an element of superficial normativism in the premises of a theory of democracy, it ultimately goes in favour of retaining the present 'capitalist' model of democracy with an appealing touch of renovation. Its essentially practicable feature lies in the affirmation that freedom and equality cannot be reconciled in absolute terms. The 'true democracy' held up against the liberal 'sham democracy' continues to haunt all theoretical and ideological endeavours for a non-antagonistic model of democracy closed within itself. "It is based on the premise that the three great fundamental principles of all democratic theory–majority, liberty and equality can be reconciled and indeed brought into full congruence. History, however, teaches that under human conditions this is possible only within limits and that any pretension to a perfect solution of the basic conflict between freedom and equality leads to inhuman tyranny with a preponderance of the one over the other."[69] It may also be added that the profound shift from a liberal to a social form of democracy, needless to say, "implies neither the refutation nor the end of its fundamental libertarian concept. It is, of course, true that an increasingly complex social and economic society leads to a network of dependences, state intervention and economic-democratic postulates."[70]

Hayek is known as the philosopher of individual freedom and limited state. He presents the model of liberal democracy that is quite different from the models of Mill, Laski and Rawls. He does not support the case of a *laissez faire* state whose aim is 'to protect, not to promote'. At the same time, he rejects the idea of Laski and Rawls that the state should eradicate social and economic inequality. According to him, the central concept of liberalism is that under the enforcement of universal rules of just conduct, protecting a recognisable private domain of individuals, a spontaneous order of human activities of much greater complexity "will form itself than could be produced by a deliberate arrangement, and that in consequence the coercive activities of government should be limited to the enforcement of such rules."[71]

The state should not do anything for the public welfare by coercing the individuals in any way. Liberty means that a person is not coerced by the arbitrary will of another person and liberalism is a doctrine which emphasises the restriction to a minimum of the coercive powers of government. In the Kantian fashion, he subscribes to the view that the function of the state is to hinder hindrances to good life. Liberalism "derives from the discovery of a self-generating spontaneous order which makes it possible

68. Macpherson: "Progress of the Locke Industry" in *Canadian Journal of Political Science,* Vol. 3, No. 2, June, 1970, p. 326.
69. Karl Dietrich Bracher: *The Age of Ideologies: A History of Political Thought in the Twentieth Century,* p. 231.
70. *Ibid.,* p. 239.
71. F. A. Hayek: *Studies in Philosophy, Politics and Economics* (London: Routledge, 1967), p. 162.

to utilise the knowledge and skill of all members of society to a much greater extent than would be possible in any order created by central direction and (reflects) the consequent desire to make as full use of these powerful spontaneous ordering forces as possible."[72]

An all-round development of man's personality is possible only in a liberal democratic order where the government is non-coercive and the conditions of 'rule of law' prevail. The rule of law is concerned not with all the functions of government, but only with the limitations on its coercive activities. The rule of law is not a rule for the law, but a rule concerning what the law ought to be—a meta-legal doctrine or a political ideal. It "would be more correct to think of progress as a process of formation and modification of the human intellect, a process of adaptation and learning in which not only the possibilities known to us but also values and desires continually change."[73]

A liberal democratic state is one which ensures a spontaneous or non-coercive order based on the *nomos* or the rules of liberty of universal significance. A *nomos* aims at securing the formation of an abstract order of its actions only through its universal and perpetual application. Such a rule is subject to revision in the light of better insight into its interaction with other rules, and it will be valid only as part of a system of mutually modifying rules. This cannot be achieved by means of legislation. Hayek calls law of the state a 'thesis' that has a coercive nature. The system of laws creates a gigantic administrative machinery that instead of doing good to the people acts as an impediment in the way of spontaneous human activity. The principle of 'evolutionary rationalism' based on *nomos* should prevail for the sake of all round progress of the individual. The course of 'constructive rationalism' established by the system of laws in the name of people's welfare is thoroughly unjustified.

With such a standpoint, Hayek attacks the model of a liberal democratic state as it exists now. In his words, such a form of government is like 'a tragic illusion'. The people elect their representatives who do not bother for the wishes of their electors. They have their place in the legislature and then they make laws which circumscribe the liberty of their electors. The very meaning of the term 'rule of law' is subverted. The legislators may go to the extent of making any coercive law in the name of the 'sovereignty of parliament'. The result is the creation of a 'totalitarian democracy' or 'plebiscitary dictatorship'. Instead of democracy as it exists now, he prefers a system based on the rule of law what he calls 'demarchy'.[74]

In a liberal democratic order there is nothing but scramble for power that can be eradicated only by a 'model constitution' guaranteeing limited government and operation of the 'rule of law'. The government should be such that serves the good of all, but caters to the special interest of none. The true value of democracy is to serve as a 'sanitary precaution' that may protect the people against any abuse of power. It

72. *Ibid.*
73. Hayek: *The Constitution of Liberty* (London: Routledge, 1960), p. 40.
74. Hayek: *Law, Legislation and Liberty* (London: Routledge, 1979), Vol. III, p. 124.

is a pity that the liberal democratic state "has become the main cause of a progressive and accelerating increase of the power and weight of the administrative machine."[75] The myth of social justice should be broken down so as to curtail the role of the so-called welfare state. Thus, he "attempts to bring about strict separation between the articulation of principle and the shaping of policy and to protect the rule of law by entrusting its care to persons of maturity and good character rather than to party leaders and inexperienced youths."[76]

As Berlin desires that sovereignty should be in the 'right hands', so Hayek desires that the government should take its support from the expectations that it will enforce the prevailing opinions concerning what is right. Only in such a situation scramble for power shall have no place and then would occur the 'dethronement of politics'. It is clear that Hayek is a libertarian and so his ideas may be criticised from the angle of egalitarianism. The case of social justice as defended by the democratic socialists and positive liberals, like Laski and Rawls has no appreciation at his hands. The state is required to maintain a 'spontaneous social order'. It has nothing to do with the rendering of socially useful services. So Galeotti comments that Hayek's state "is indifferent to any social question that would trespass the borderline of political power."[77]

Marxist Theory: The generally mistaken notion is that Marxism is anti-democratic, but the fact is that it has its own conception of democracy, though basically at variance with the model of a liberal (bourgeois) democracy. Marx and Engels never lost their faith in democratic system; they desired to replace the existing pattern of democracy by a new pattern what may be termed 'socialist democracy'. They accepted the basic point that democracy is the rule of the people, but they questioned the implications of the word 'people'. If this term meant all people to the liberals, whether capitalists and workers, feudal lords and serfs, exploiters and exploited, oppressors and oppressed, to Marx and Engels it included only the latter—'proletariat'. As such, the meaning and operation of democracy must change with a change in the nature of the word 'people'. So Engels says: "The concept (democracy) changes every time the 'demos' changes and so does not get us one step further.... The democratic republic is the logical form of a bourgeois rule."[78]

If so, the first requirement of a democratic system is to give power to the workers and peasants and a government in their hands must liquidate all exploiters and oppressors. The existence of a classless society is the condition-precedent for the advent of a democratic system. Moreover, as this form of government would be faced with a dual mission of establishing socialism at the debris of capitalism and feudalism and as it would have to realise its task by means of all possible force, it would be the dictatorship of the proletariat.

---

75. *Ibid.*, p. 138.
76. Prakash Sarangi: *Liberal Theories of State* (New Delhi: Sterling Publishers, 1996), p. 131.
77. A.E. Galeotti: "Individualism, Social Rules, Tradition: The Case of F.A. Hayek" in *Political Theory,* 15, 1987, p. 167.
78. Engels: *Selected Correspondence,* p. 445.

The Marxist theory of democracy has some important features. First, it appreciates the liberal democratic system for terminating the era of feudalism and instead introducing the system of parliamentary democracy. It is true that liberal democracy is another name for the capitalist system, but its emergence should be appreciated in the name of a bourgeois democratic revolution—a big change that terminated the medieval system of feudalism and paved the way for the advent of socialism. The liberal democracy has to be replaced by the socialist democracy, because then the meaning of the word 'people' would be a reality.

Second, such a democracy is designated as 'socialist democracy' or 'people's democracy' having its distinctive characteristics. It implies the rule of the working class. "It not only guarantees the rights of the working class, but also provides conditions for the people to exercise them. Under the dictatorship of the proletariat, as it should be called, the working people possess not formal rights, but they actually govern the country and, either directly or through their representatives, manage its entire social, economic, political and cultural life. They own all means of production that enables them to manage the country's economy. Schools, universities, scientific and cultural institutions, health and holiday homes give them the opportunity to exercise their rights to education, rest and leisure. They have at their disposal press, radio and television centres, which ensure their freedom of thought and expression. They actively take part in the political life of the country and in all public affairs through their wide participation in the Soviets or other State bodies, in numerous committees and commissions set up by the Soviets and also through their own social organisations. In a word, proletarian democracy, as Lenin said, "is a million times more democratic than any bourgeois democracy."

Third, the Marxian concept of democracy not only covers the political aspect, it lays equal emphasis on its social and economic dimensions. That is, socialist democracy not merely means political power in the hands of the people, it also means absence of class distinctions and exploitation of any kind. It desires social equality ensuring dignity of labour and worth of the individual. In the economic sphere it means removal of all gigantic social evils like unemployment, disease, starvation, squalor, poverty and the like.

But the most astonishing feature of the Marxian view of democracy is that it changes its complexion in the final stage of socialism. To Marx and his ardent followers, democracy has three phases—during the phase of liberalism it guarantees rights to all in a formal manner, but it creates conditions so that the rights may be exercised only by a limited section of the bourgeois class. In the second phase of socialism, it means that rights are formally guaranteed to all and they must also be enabled to exercise them so that a really people's rule comes into existence. Finally, in the age of communism, democracy becomes a social affair as the classless society is converted into the stateless condition of life. The vision of Marx and Engels included the negation of the capitalist and the socialist states, the society in that phase of its development "would have no institution of government separate and estranged from the people, and it would have no organised coercive force, for none would be needed. Human emancipation and human freedom would be attained when no external or coercive power existed, and when the *res publica* became the part time collaboration of all the people rather than the full time profession of a special body of coercers."[79]

The Marxist theory of democracy, it is obvious, cannot be appreciated by the people of liberal disposition who frankly condemn it as the justification of totalitarian system. The state after the successful socialist revolution is a dictatorship of the communist party. The people are deprived of all political and economic rights. Opposition is prohibited. There is no freedom of press, no independence of judiciary, no place for other political parties and groups to function. Man is sacrificed at the altar of a 'red state'. Karl Popper has, therefore, ranked Marx among the enemies of an open (free) society. The leaders of the Euro-communist movement like Carrillo and Berlinguer appreciated the view of Milovan Djilas and Stojanovic who had described the Soviet system as the ruthless dictatorship of a communist clique led by a Lenin or a Stalin. It is the rule not of the working class as desired by Marx and Engels, it is the iron dictatorship of a 'new class' (clique of the communist party). An advocate of liberal democracy like Giovanni Sartori had denounced the Soviet system as 'phantom alternative'.

The noticeable point is that the Marxian model of democracy, as established in the former Soviet Union, had been denounced not only by the liberals (anti-communists) but also by the revisionists and the Eurocommunists who vehemently attacked the whole set up called 'dictatorship of the proletariat'. The contention of such leaders is that democracy and socialism should live together and a state of socialism can be brought about by peaceful means, and by using democratic devices. The working class may capture power by aligning itself with other like-minded parties and groups and that too by winning elections on the basis of specific programmes. Thus, according to this view, socialism recognises multi-party system, liberties of all kinds, rights of free expression, etc. There can be no democracy under the dictatorship of the proletariat that "means complete subordination of the working class and the masses to the monopolistic authority of an elite of the 'wisest'... the maximum centralisation within that system... and the subjection of the whole field of science and ideas of the interests of the system's survival."[80]

Post-Liberal Theory : All theories of democracy studied so far take it for granted that democracy means a system in which sovereign power resides in the people and the government functions for the good or welfare of them. The real point of difference lies in the actual operation of this system. To the pluralists, it is the role of numerous groups in the competition for power that should be stressed; to the elitists, it is the role of the elites and the leadership that should be given all importance in a theory of democracy without bothering for the charge that such a version would lead to the justification of an oligarchical model of democracy; to the socialists, democracy has social and economic aspects as well. It is not merely a political contrivance, it has social and economic

---

79. R.N. Carew Hunt: *Theory and Practice of Communism.,* p. 130.
80. E. Kardelj: *Socialist Democracy,* p. 23.

dimensions too and, as such, the working of democracy should cover economic and social spheres as well. In other words, a proper theory on this subject should align democracy with the case of socialism.

Thus, to find fault with the pattern of liberal democracy and to correct it with the infusion of socialistic content in it, constitutes the profile of a new theory of democracy that, in the words of Macpherson, may be called 'post-liberal democracy'. Laski is the most powerful advocate of this theory who sought to revise liberalism in the light of socialistic achievements and thereby he drew close to the world of democratic socialism. It is worth noting that the application of Marxian analysis to the elucidation of the concept of democracy and liberalism has revealed that whatever claims may be made on their behalf in theory, they are in fact so intimately connected with the prevailing economic system that they are, in their working, political expressions of economic reality."[81]

Though an English liberal, Laski was so much influenced with the rising tide of socialism that he criticised the model of liberal democracy. He desired nationalisation of important industries, social control over the means of production, narrowing down gap between the rich and poor, abolition of absolute right of inheritance and the like. He frankly stressed the point that bourgeois society with its formal equality before law was in reality based on a glaring material and economic inequality of classes. By leaving inviolable, by defending and strengthening the monopoly of the capitalist and the landlord classes over the vital means of production, bourgeois democracy, as far as the exploited classes and especially the working class are concerned, converts the formal equality before law and the whole set of rights and liberties into a judicial fiction and consequently into a means for deceiving and enslaving the masses. The equality proclaimed by liberal democracy is a formal and superficial affair. Parliamentary democracy serves the capitalist system and enables it to preserve its substance by making political concessions to the electorate when it becomes unavoidable. Laski contends that wider disparities of wealth, being incompatible with the system of democracy, are inherent with the conditions of a revolution. So he warns that if the state "remains divided into rich and poor, men, after a period, refuse to suffer quietly. The revolution supervenes to alter the balance in the State."[82]

However, a better manifestation of such a version of democracy may be seen in the writings of C.B. Macpherson keeping which in view a critical commentator has observed: "The chief concern of Macpherson has been with the problem of democracy in the contemporary world."[83] We may take note of the fact that while Laski desires to attach democracy with socialism, Macpherson seeks to integrate the thought of liberal democracy with prevailing human conditions. Looking like a follower of the post-behavioural tradition, Macpherson tries to reaffirm the place of humanistic values into the corpus of liberal democratic theory so as to reinforce empiricism with changing

81. G.N. Sarma: *Political Thought of Harold J. Laski,* p. 13.
82. Laski: *A Grammar of Politics,* p. 177.
83. M.A. Weinstein: "C.B. Macpherson: The Roots of Democracy and Liberalism" in Anthony de Crespigny and Kenneth Minnogue (ed.): *Contemporary Political Philosophers,* p. 252.

social relations of human beings. This is the fault of the contemporary liberal theory that must be corrected. As he forcefully argues: "The new matter which the accepted political theory cannot accommodate is not only simply new factual phenomena, but new moral problems which have been brought into existence by changed social relations."[84]

To hit at the basic feature of contemporary liberal society, Macpherson has coined a new term 'possessive individualism'. It is the image of human nature generated by a competitive capitalist or market society. It signifies that man is the proprietor of his own person. He is what he owns. The human essence is freedom to do what one wills with one's own, or freedom properly limited only by such rules as are needed to secure the same freedom for others. On these assumptions, the best society (indeed the only possible good society) is one in which all social relations between individuals are transformed into market relations, in which men are related to each other as possessors of their own capacities and of what they have acquired by the exercise of their capacities.

A liberal society is marked by a liberal state which has become a liberal-democratic state. This state arose to protect the interests of those who controlled the means of production and distribution. At first, it was not a democratic state and only became so through the growth of pressure from below. Its another essence became the growth of multiple party system whereby government could be held responsible for different sections of the class or classes that had political power in their hands. The two functions of the state became to adjust conflicting interests held by different sections of the dominant class and to provide a check on arbitrary uses of state power. "By admitting the mass of people into the competitive party system, the liberal state did not abandon its fundamental virtue; it simply opened the competitive political system to all the individuals who had been created by the competitive market society."[85]

The tendency of possessive individualism is responsible for enabling the few (rich) to alienate the many (poor), and since the liberal state is committed to maintain the existing pattern of society, economy and polity, one small class (bourgeoisie) manages to exploit the other big class of the society (proletariat). As capitalist society has matured and the means of production and distribution become progressively concentrated in the hands of the small class, the liberal state has come to play, more and more, an exploitative rather than a coordinative role. The dilemma of modern liberal democratic theory is that it must continue to use the assumptions of possessive individualism at a time when the structure of market society no longer provides the necessary conditions for deducing a valid theory of political obligation from these assumptions."[86]

84. Macpherson: "World Trends in Political Science Research" in *American Political Science Review,* Vol. 48, No. 2, June, 1954, p. 434. Elsewhere, Macpherson says: "The purpose of scholarly re-appraisals of political theory is to help us to see the limits and possibilities of a great tradition as applied to our own day."
85. Macpherson: *The Real World of Democracy,* p. 11.
86. Macpherson: *Political Theory of Possessive Individualism,* p. 275.

Macpherson is no advocate of the case of 'people's democracy' as established in the communist countries for the reason that in a classless society there can be nothing like 'one general will.' A good government is one that is run by the choice of the consumers. In his view, people's democracy is now faced with the problem of transforming itself into a form that debases human beings through the efforts of those who have been debased by it. But even such a democracy can be converted into a real democracy under the conditions of full intra-party democracy, open party membership, and a price of membership in the party that involves no greater degree of activity than an average person can reasonably be expected to contribute. He goes to the length of predicting that people's democracies "are likely to retain their moral advantage in future, while the liberal democracies are likely to progressively lose their advantage as the police states in the East loosen up. This means that we in the West decline in power unless we can discard our possessive market morality."[87]

Liberal democracy is a special case of democracy, rather than the essence of democracy itself. The adjustment of multitudinous group interests is the primary task of democratic political institutions. But in a democracy, such an adjustment of multitudinous group interests is possible only in a peaceful and expanding society the economic and political relations of which are generally acceptable, so that there is no strong or urgent pressure to establish or having established, to consolidate a new structure of economic class relationships. It is for such a society that the need of an alternative party system can be shown. The ultimate value is the value of a full self-developing individual. To some extent Macpherson looks like sticking to the moral argument of John Stuart Mill in defence of democracy. So he argues that "revaluation of democratic consciousness is needed in liberal democracies."[88]

The post-liberal democratic theory has some good points. It seeks to realise what is so confidently asserted by the positive liberals of the twentieth century. The English Fabians would naturally appreciate the model of integrating democracy with socialism. The latest trend is that while liberalism is moving towards socialism, socialism is happily moving towards liberalism the best instances of which could be seen in the *glosnost* (openness) and *perestroika* (reconstruction) programme of the erstwhile Soviet Union. Both liberalism and socialism have some strong and weak points. It shall be an ideal situation if the good points of both are harmonised with each other frankly at the cost of their weak points. Liberal society cannot be morally satisfied, because it frustrates the development of human capacities through the alienation of labour and fosters a money grubbing maximising behaviour. But this malady can be done away with if the rich people humanise their political, social and economic behaviour so as to correct the pattern of present democratic system. Besides, the rich states "should give massive aid to poor nations so that economic development will be speeded and the moral stature and power of the liberal democracies preserved."[89]

---

87. Macpherson: *The Real World of Democracy,* p. 66.
88. Weinstein, *op. cit.,* p. 268.
89. *Ibid.,* p. 269.

Polyarchy

- It may be understood as a rough or crude approximation of democracy, in that it operates through institutions that force rulers to take account of the interests and wishes of the electorate. Its main features are:

1. The government is in the hands of the elected officials.
2. Elections are free and fair.
3. Practically all adults have the right to vote.
4. There is free expression of views, and the people have the right to criticise the administration and also to protest for its sake.
5. The citizens have access to alternative sources of information.
6. Groups and associations enjoy at least relative independence from the government.

But such a version of democracy may not be acceptable to the negative liberals wedded to the tradition of Adam Smith and Herbert Spencer, and to the socialists committed to the line of Marxism-Leninism. While the former would not like to see alignment of democracy with socialism, the latter would not agree with the existence of democracy in a society ridden with class conflicts and contradictions. However, leaving aside the element of bias of Macpherson in favour of Western democracy, we should stress the point that the need of today is to humanise people's democracy and to socialise liberal democracy in a way that a better and more equitable pattern of democracy comes to prevail.

Polyarchy

The name of R.A. Dahl may also be included in this category who coined the term 'polyarchy'. It is another name for a liberal-democratic system as prevailing in the United States and other advanced democratic countries of the West like Britain and France. In such a system power is widely diffused and the government is based on the separation of functions. Dissent is allowed and numerous political parties and interest groups take part in the political process of the country. The state acts like a neutral arbitrator or referee. Its job is to maintain coordination among such parties and groups. For this sake, it makes laws, rules and regulations within which all parties and groups have to operate. If any party or group breaks the network of laws and rules, it is pushed out of the arena. As all such laws and rules are based on the consent of the people, the political order has its 'legitimacy'.

Thus, a polyarchical regime has two special features. "First, there is a relatively high tolerance of opposition that is sufficient at least to check the arbitrary inclinations of government. This is guaranteed in practice by a competitive party system, by institutionally guaranteed and protected civil liberties, and by vigorous and healthy civil society. The second feature of a polyarchy is that the opportunities for participating in politics should be sufficiently widespread to guarantee a reliable level of popular responsiveness. The crucial factor here is the existence of regular and competitive elections operating as a device through which the people can control and, if necessary, displace their rulers."[90]

We may conclude our study with these words of Prof. Joad: "The task (defence of democracy) is not an easy one. When he comes to defend his belief, the advocate of democracy finds himself at a disadvantage. Whereas the authoritarian doctrines of the State are clear-cut, definite and systematic, the theory of democracy is vague, tentative and fragmentary. Indeed, it is not a theory at all so much as a number of principles, each of which the democrat takes it to be true, but which he would be hard put to substantiate. He believes in individual freedom and self-development; he believes that the State is made for man and not man for the State, and he has an instinctive distrust of the State. If, however, he is asked for a theory of State, it is feeling rather than reason that is apt to reply. And his feeling is that the beginning and end of the State's functions is to give individuals the equipment, the scope and the leisure to develop the best that is in them. The democrat does not, at any rate, in the twentieth century regard democracy as an ideal form of government that is practicable. It is not best so much as a second-best, embraced because of the frailties of human nature and accepted less for its own merits than for fear that worse may befall, if it be rejected. Thus, no systematic defence of democracy is possible, for the reason that democracy is not itself the product of a systematic theory."[91]

---

90. Andrew Heywood: *Politics,* p. 33. For a detailed study see Dahl's *Polyarchy; Participation and Opposition* (1971). Polyarchy is certainly a developed form of liberal democracy, though the course of its development has not been uniform. It had its appearance in the period before the Second World War in countries like America, Canada, Britain and France. It had its appearance in other countries after the Second World War as in West Germany, Italy, Japan and in some countries of the Third World like India. Huntington, therefore, calls it as 'two waves' of polyarchical regimes.
91. C.E.M. Joad: *Guide to the Philosophy of Morals and Politics,* p. 770.

7
Secularism

Secularism is the anti-thesis of theocracy. It desires a system in which religion and politics are kept apart; there is no official religion, hence, no discrimination among the people may be made on religious basis. Theocracy prevailed during ancient and medieval ages when the ruler belonged to a particular religious order and the entire administration was conducted according to its dictates and injunctions. Thus, all privileges were available to the believers, while the non-believers were discriminated against. Not only this, the infidels were deliberately tortured and persecuted by the rulers as well as by the people subscribing to the official faith. Sometimes, there were cases of forced conversion of the non-believers and those who opposed or disliked it, were compelled to leave that country. With the downfall of the Papacy in the fifteenth century the trend of secularism emerged in Europe which ensured freedom of faith to all in hitherto dominant Christian countries. Thus, secularism became an essential attribute of modern state along with the attributes of sovereignty and nationalism. In 1920 Mustafa Kemal made Turkey a secular state, but this wave could not affect other Muslim countries which are still under a theocratic order.

Meaning and Nature: The term 'secularim' means "non-spiritual, having no concern with religious or scriptural matters, anything which is distinct, opposed to, or not connected with religion, or ecclesiastical things, temporal as opposed to spiritual or ecclesiastical."[1] According to Eric S. Waterhouse, secularism is 'an ideology' which provides 'a theory of life and conduct' as against one provided by religion.[2] According to *A New English Dictionary,* secularism denotes 'the absence of connection with religion'. Secular literature means a literature that is not concerned with or devoted to the service of religion. Likewise, secular education maens a curriculum where religious education is excluded; and a secular attitude is one which progressively tends to isolate religion from the more significant areas of common life.

In very simple and widely understood terms, secularism signifies the separation of state and church. Obviously, it "is materialistic in tone and holds that human improvement can be sought through material means alone."[3] In the words of Smith, "The secular state is a state which guarantees individual and corporate freedom of religion, deals with the individual as a citizen irrespective of his religion, is not constitutionally connected to a particular religion, nor does it seek either to promote or interfere with religion.

---

1. *Encyclopaedia Britannica,* Vol, XX, 1967, p. 264.
2. *Ibid.,* Vol. XI, p. 348.
3. V.P. Luthera: *The Concept of Secular State and India,* p. 19.

Some Important Statements

- Every religion has its full and equal place. We are all leaves of a majestic tree whose trunk cannot be shaken off its roots which are deep down in the bowels of the earth. The mightiest of winds cannot move it.

  — Mahatma Gandhi,

  ***Harijan*, 28 July, 1946, p. 236.**

- Dharma is something much more than religion or creed; it is a conception of obligations, of the discharge of one's duties to oneself and to others.

  — Jawaharlal Nehru

  ***The Discovery of India*, p. 90.**

- When India is said to be a secular State, it does not mean that we reject the reality, or the unseen spirit, or the relevance of religion to life, or that we exalt irreligion. It does not mean that secularism itself becomes a positive religion, or that the State assumes divine prerogatives..... We hold that not one religion should be given preferential status..... This view of religious impartiality or comprehension, or forbearance, has a prophetic role to play within the National and International Life.

  — S. Radhakrishnan,

  ***Recovery of Faith*, p. 184.**

Upon closer examination, it will be seen that the conception of a secular state involves three distinct but inter-related sets of relationships concerning the state, religion and the individual."[4]

It is obvious that secularism "is a belief that religion should not intrude into secular (worldly) affairs usually reflected in a desire to separate church from state."[5] However, a deeper study of the term shows that it has these implications:

1. The state has no religion of its own and, for this reason, all faiths are treated equally in the eye of law. Equal protection of law is also guaranteed to all.
2. A secular state is not irreligious. It ensures that all religions have equal respect. Freedom of conscience is guaranteed and conversion of religion by choice or will is allowed.
3. As religion is a private affair, people freely observe the canons or customs of their religion. No religion can interfere in the affairs of the state, but the state can interfere in the affairs of any religion for the sake of social reform or public good.
4. A secular state ensures certain privileges to minorities. A democratic system implies rule of the majority, it is also obligated to protect the rights of the religious, social and cultural minorities.

---

4. D.E. Smith: *India as a Secular State,* p. 4.
5. Andrew Heywood: *Politics,* p. 64.

5. A secular state requires a democratic order. Hence, people of all faiths enjoy freedom of thought and expression. The people are exhorted to cultivate faith in the composite culture of the country and to establish communal unity and harmony.

In short, secularism implies that religion is a private affair and so people must have freedom of conscience. No discrimination among the people should be made on religious, racial or communal basis. The state is not a department of the church, but it can meddle in the religious affairs of any community for the sake of social reform or in the name of national interest.

Views of Gandhiji: Secularism finds an enlightened place in the ideas of Gandhi. Machiavelli of Italy and Hobbes of England established the trend of secularism by thoroughly separating religion and politics. As a result of this, they treated man as a selfish and wicked creature to whom politics meant struggle for power by all possible means. Gandhiji realised that the only way to save politics from vulgarisation was to mix it with religion, better called *Dharma*. As he says: "To me there is no politics without religion. Politics without religion is a death trap that kills the soul." He cautions: "To try to root out religion itself from society is like a wild goose chase. And were such an attempt to succeed, it would mean destruction of society."

However, one should study such affirmations of Gandhiji with a clear and open mind. His view of religion should not be taken in the light of the observance of the rituals or blind adherence to certain tenets leading towards obscurantism, even fundamentalism. His religion has its essence in the Hindu concept of *Dharma* or ideal righteousness that must govern the conduct of human beings. As he says: "By religion I do not mean formal religion or customary religion, but that religion which underlies all religions and which brings us face to face with our Maker."

Religion means Truth, and Truth and God are synonymous. His techniques of *ahimssa* and *satyagraha* can be utilised only by those who have firm faith in God. He could demonstrate it on many occasions in the course of the Indian freedom struggle. No doubt, his views on secularism aim at the purification or spiritualisation of politics. As Pattabhi B. Sitaramayya observes: "By the practice of *satyagraha* our country was plunged into a world of new values in which hatred and abhorrence, fear and cowardice, anger and vengeance were at once to yield place to service and in which the enemy is not to be conquered but converted."[6]

Case of India: The Constitution of India establishes a secular polity. The ideal of secularism is contained in the Preamble. Then, there are numerous provisions to give effect to it. All people are equal in the eye of law and equal protection of law is guaranteed to all. Discrimination on the ground of religion or creed is prohibited in matters relating to the use of things of public utility, admissions in educational institutions, and recruitments to public services. Untouchability is prohibited. All citzens have a fundamental right to religion. Freedom of conscience is guaranteed.

6. P.B Sitaramayya: *The History of the Indian National Congress,* Vol. I, p. 614.

People may establish their religious, charitable and denominational institutions. Religious instructions cannot be imparted in state institutions.

Some other important points should also be noted in this direction. The state can interfere in religious affairs for the sake of social reform. For instance, temple entry may be opened for all sections of the Hindu community. The Sikhs have the right to carry *kripans.* Religious and linguistic minorities have the right to preserve and conserve their distinct language, script and culture. The state cannot interfere in the management of educational institutions run by the minority communities. However, educational institutions established by minority communities may have their heads belonging to their own community. The provisions are so comprehensive that, according to Basu, they "make our state more secular than even the United States of America."[7]

Critical Appreciation: Following conclusions may be drawn from what we have said in the preceding sections:

1. Secularism stands for the separation of religion and politics, but it does not mean thorough or total separation to an extent that the place of religion is altogether dismissed. The barren secularists forget that religion or faith in the Supreme Being has been as old as humanity itself and hence to repudiate the existence of God may carry conviction only with men of negative and destructive thinking. For instance, bloody anarchists like Proudhon of France and Bakunin of Russia condemn the institution of church and desire to emancipate man from the yoke of God. Such blunt affirmations not only vulgarise secularism, rather make it barren and inhuman.
2. Secularism emerged in the modern age when renaissance resuscitated the trend of humanism. Thus, secularism and humanism became interlinked. At the same time, scientific inventions had their effect on the rational approach of the people. As the enlightened people appreciated scientific approach, secularism, humanisn and rationalism became inter-linked.
3. Indian leaders like Rajendra Prasad and Jawaharlal Nehru and a host of others who took active part in the making of the Constitution, reiterated what was uttered by Gandhiji. Hence, India offers the shining example of enlightened and dynamic secularism. All religions enjoy equal respect, but, as Dr. B.R. Ambedkar warned, 'let no community be in a state of mind that they are immune from the sovereign authority of Parliament.'

The fact stands out that in the present age of triumphant liberalism, the three ideals of secularism, humanism and rationalism are inter-linked. Here is a standard by which we may examine the foundations and superstructures of a modern state which claims itself to be 'democratic' in the real sense of the term.

---

7. D.D. Basu: *Introduction to the Constitution of India,* XII ed., 1989, p. 115.

8
Theories of State

Social and political thinkers have given their views on the themes of nature, functions and end of the state, out of which many theories have come up ranguing from those aiming at the belittlement of the state to its justification and glorification, thereon to its eventual withering away. While the classical or negative liberals regard state as a 'necessary evil' with a function 'to protect and not to promote', the positive or modern liberals take it as an agency of public welfare meant for rendering socially useful services. The neo-liberals look like hovering between the two poles. The pluralists subscribe to the doctrine of liberalism, but they regard the state as an instrument that permits numerous social groups and associations to play their part in the political process of the country within well-defined limits. Different from all is the view of the Marxists who regard state as an instrument of exploitation and oppression by one class over another that would have its eventual withering away in the final stage of social development. The post-colonialists study the case of state in poor and backward countries of the Third World where it is faced with the grim problem of its identity on account of the dialectical struggle going on between the forces of colonialism and nationalism. The feminists have no theory of state as such, though they desire a system in which women are empowered and thereby feel emancipated from all sorts of gender inequality and injustice.

Liberal and Neo-Liberal State: Liberalism stands for the liberty of the individual. As state imposes restraints on the liberty of the individual, it is an evil. However, as it alone can provide protection to the life and property of its people, it is a necessity. Hence, state is a 'necessary evil'. It should leave the individual alone (*laissez faire*) so that he may have the best possible development of his personality. According to John Stuart Mill, a state must perform only essential functions such as protection from foreign aggression, maintenance of internal peace, administration of justice, circulation of currency and management of the means of communication. It has nothing to do with any activity of public welfare, as it is a concern of the people themselves. Such a state is called a 'police state'. Herbert Spencer says that every law is a sin and so the state must make as few laws as are very necessary. He cautions that 'the ultimate result of shielding fools from folly would be to fill the world with fools'. Robert Nozick goes to the extent of treating state as a 'night watchman'.

The line of classical liberalism faded after the First World War. A host of modern or positive liberals like J.M. Keynes and H.J. Laski of England and R.M. MacIver of the United States regarded state as an agency of public welfare and they sought to reinterpret the domains of the liberty of the individual so as to harmonise them with expansion of the sphere of state activity in the public interest. They discarded the axiom of *laissez faire* and instead argued that the liberties of the individual could be circumscribed for the sake of bringing about a new social order as far as possible free from the gigantic evils of poverty, unemployment, disease, ignorance, starvation, squalor, etc. Since the Labour Government formed in England in 1945 adopted the programmes of Laski and Keynes, Britain was widely hailed as the 'home' of the welfare state. In the United States MacIver insisted that protection of the weak against the strong was the function of the modern state.

The idea of the welfare state became popular more and more as a result of which it could be seen as a fine alternative to a communist state formed in Russia by Lenin in 1917. This model of state was basically liberal, but it had the mixture of the content of socialism. So this line of thought was given the name of democratic socialism. It may be pointed out that "the genesis and development of the concept of welfare state lay in the interaction of the ideas mainly conservatism, liberalism and socialism, in the unique British historical setting of a qualitative change from administrative to ameliorative legislation."[1]

The liberal-democratic state of the nineteenth century became a liberal-democratic-socialist state in the twentieth century after the First World war. By absorbing the content of socialism, this state also absorbed the fallacies of a socialist system. It widened the scope of state activity to an extent that it became 'over-worked' or 'over-loaded'. The result was bureaucratisation at a very large scale and the entire system of administration became rampant with corruption and misappropriation of funds. The emerging menace could be diagnosed by Prime Minister Margaret Thacher of Britain who took to the ways of 'rolling back' the state. Now the ideas of F.A. Hayek and C.B. Macpherson became the source of inspiration. Liberalism now took a new turn and in its modified form came to be known by many names as 'new right,' 'new conservatism', 'new individualism' and 'neo-liberalism'.

The neo-liberal state as preferred by Prime Minister Thatcher of Britain and President Reagan of the United States aims at curtailing its public welfare functions and instead meeting new challenges posed by nuclear proliferation, environmental pollution, cross-border terrorism, ethnic conflicts, genocide, suppression of human rights, etc. It does not stand for the minimisation of its activity as conceived by the classical liberals, nor does it endorse to make itself strong so as to effectively meet the new challenges of the time. More than this, it desires to remove unnecessary restrictions imposed on the economic sphere so as to make itself market-friendly. "Nothing should be done at the cost of authority, order and discipline. The state should be strong enough to play its role in the domains of law and order, defence and public morality."[2]

1. M.M. Sankdher: *The Welfare State*. p. 17.
2. Andrew Heywood: *Political Theory,* p. 149.

Some Important Statements

- The sole end for which mankind are warranted individually or collectively in interfering with the liberty of action of any of their member is self-protection. The only purpose for which power can be rightfully exercised over any member of a civilised community against his will, is to prevent harm to others. Over himself, his own body and mind, the individual is sovereign.

  — John Stuart Mill

- But the order so understood is a larger task. Order within the community is justified only as it serves the needs of the community. It is not order for the sake of order, but for the sake of protection, conservation and development.

  — R.M. MacIver

- The promise of neo-liberalism seems to be that a just society (narrowly defined) is achieved by uncoerced market exchanges. More markets lead to less state both in totality and in its potential to intervene. If there are no goods for social distribution in a market-led society, the role of the state is limited to the protection of property rights and other related tasks, *e.g.*, national security and external defence.

  — Fraser King

The model of a liberal or a neo-liberal state is appreciated for defining the role of state in a way and to an extent that essential liberties of the people remain well protected. A welfare state may curtail the scope of freedoms of the individuals in the name of public good, but it is done carefully with a view to maintain his freedoms as much as possible. The socalist and communist thinkers wrongly call welfare state a capaitalist state in disguise. The liberal state is so flexible that it may well absorb the contents of a socialist state without losing its identity. However, this much may be said in criticism of this model of state that it is too flexible and so too indeterminate as a result of which its definite contours cannot be laid down. As people are the lovers of liberty, so this model of state is regarded as the best of all.

Marxist State: According to Marx and his ardent followers like Lenin, Stalin and Mao, state is a class institution that came into being with the emergence of class war. There was no state in the primitive society, for there were no two contending classes. With the invention of means of production, the classes of the freemen and the slaves came into being in the slave society. Since state is an instrument of exploitation and oppression by one class over or against another, it was in the hands of the freemen who exploited the slaves. In the feudal society the landlords exploited the serfs. In the capitalist society, same exploitation may be seen of the workers (proletariat) at the hands of the capitalist class (bourgeoisie).

Some Important Statements

- Between capitalist society and communist society lies the period of the revolutionary transformation of the one into another. There corresponds to this also a particular transitional period in which the state can be nothing but the revolutionary dictatorship of the proletariat.

—Karl Marx

- Since the state is only a temporary institution which is to be made use of in the revolution in order forcibly to suppress the opponents, it is perfectly absurd to talk about a free and popular state. So long as the proletariat needs the state, it needs it not in the interest of freedom, but in order to suppress its opponents; and when it becomes possible to speak of freedom, the state as such ceases to exist.

— Fredrick Engels

- But, indeed, from the moment the dictatorship of the proletaraint is acknowledged to be a kind of state, freedom is excluded; while the state exists there is no freedom; when freedom exists, there will be no state.

— V.I. Lenin

State is neither a necessary evil as advocated by the classical liberals, nor is it a public welfare agency as advocated by the positive liberals. It is a class institution by which the dominant class exploits and oppresses the dominated class. After the successful socialist revolution, state would be in the hands of the workers and the toilers. Then, its main function would be to liquidate the class of the landlords, capitalists and all enemies of socialism so as to establish a classless society. The rule shall prevail: 'He who shall work, shall eat.' It would be a state of a new type called 'dictatorship of the proletariat'. In the real sense of the term, it would be a dictatorial system for the enemies of socialism, it would be a democratic system for the class of the workers and the toilers.

Since state is a class institution and since it came into being after the emergence of two contending classes, it would have its natural end in the final stage of social development. When the socialist society is firmly established, state would wither away and the hitherto classless society would eventuate into a stateless condition of life. For this reason, Lenin calls dictatorship of the proletariat as a 'quasi-state.' After the liquidation of the state, 'glorious human values' would prevail and the new rule would be: 'From each according to his capacity, to each according to his need.' Thus, human life would pass on from the 'kingdom of necessity' to 'kingdom of happiness'. It would be the communist society, classless as well as stateless, signifying complete emancipation of man from the evils of exploitation, oppression and alienation.

The Marxian theory of state is full of weaknesses. The whole idea of class war is absurd. Society has never been ridden with class conflicts. It is also absurd to treat the state merely as an instrument of exploitation and oppression in view of the irrefutable fact that it is the 'first condition of a civilised life'. In the words of Aristotle, it alone can ensure 'good life' to its people. Man is a social and political creature by his nature and necessity. The state is an instrument of protection as well as promotion. It is quite utopian to think of a stateless society in which man would enjoy complete freedom and happiness. It is well observed: "The state is the keystone of the social arch. It moulds the forms and substances of the myriad human lives with whose destinies it is charged."[3]

Pluralist State: The theory of pluralism treats sovereignty of state as divisible. It lays stress on the significance of numerous social groups and associations which must have their share of the supreme and absolute power of the state in view of the fact that they, in their own ways, meet the requirements of the people. The state is like 'an association of the associations of the society' (J.N. Figgis), and, as such, 'we give to it no peculiar merit'. (H.J. Laski) All pluralists harp on the theme of the value of numerous social groups and associations that should entitle them for a share of sovereignty of the state. The essence of all discussions is that state "is confronted not merely by un-associated individuals but also by other associations evolving independently, eliciting individual loyalties, better adapted than the state because of their select membership, their special forms of organisation and action for serving various social needs."[4]

Obviously, a pluralist state is one that allows numerous social groups and associations to play their part in the political process of the country. All such bodies have a share of the sovereignty of the state. The state lays down frontiers within which these bodies should play their part. In case any association crosses the arena, the state may warn it or outlaw it. Thus, the state plays the role of a coordinator and an impartial referee in dealing with these social groups and associations. This point should, however, be noted that while the early pluralists like Barker, Laski, Cole, Lindsay, Figgis and MacIver directly attacked the case of a sovereign state and indirectly they laid stress on the importance of social groups and associations, later pluralists, particularly of the United States, like Arthur Bentley, David B. Truman, V.O. Key Jr., Earl Latham, G.A. Almond, etc., built their superstructures on the foundations of the early pluralists.

However, the neo-pluralists argue that while numerous social groups and associations play their part in the political process of the country, equal significance cannot be attached to all. A study of numerous groups in the political process of a democratic state with special stress on the powerful role of some of them constitutes the case of a neo-pluralist state. This line is taken by a number of writers like R.A. Dahl, Charles E. Lindblom and C.W. Mills who lay stress on the fact that the existence of many other centres "hardly guarantees that government will (a) listen to them equally; (b) do anything other than communicate with leaders of such groups; (c) be susceptible to influence by anybody other than those in powerful positions; (d) do anything about the issues under discussion, and so on."[5]

---

3. H.J. Laski: *A Grammar of Politics,* p. 21.
4. F.W. Coker: *Recent Political Thought,* p. 508.
5. David Held: *Political Theory and the Modern State,* p. 45.

Thus, R.A. Dahl calls democracy 'polyarchy' in which numerous groups and associations compete for power by operating within a frame-work of rules and regulations which are acceptable to them, or which are based on the consensus of the people. Lindblom throws special focus on business groups which virtually deteremine the shape of the policies of the state. Constraints are imposed on the institutions of government by the requirement of private accumulation which systematically limits policy options. C.W. Mills reveals the fact that those groups have an extraordinary influence which meet the immediate requirements of the state like those manufacturing arms and ammunition. Taking it into view, he described America as 'military-industrial complex'.

The views of the pluralists and the neo-pluralists are emprically correct. But a critic may say that a pluralist state is a capitalist state in which groups of the industrial magnates play the decisive role. Anthony Downs in his 'economic theory of democracy' has proved that only very rich people manage to win elections and then they run the government. They reap the dividends of their 'economic rationality' and thereby create the 'mammon state' loaded with "disproportionate influence of major corporations."[6]

Post-Colonial State: Post-colonialism refers to the case of many poor and backward countries of the Third World which, after their independence from foreign rule, are struggling to have an identity of their own and, for this sake, facing the grim problem as how to reconcile the alien impositions of the past with the native or indigenous institutions of the present. The new leaders in power look like drifting in different directions. It is well observed: "Post-colonialism is neither Western nor non-Western, but a dialectical product of interaction between the two, articulating new points of counter-insurgency from the long-running power struggles that predate and postdate colonialism."[7]

The models of a post-colonial state may be briefly described as under:

1. The obdurate and fanatic leaders want to have a political system having nothing to do with the institutions imposed by the colonial masters. That is, the model of their state should be strictly indigenous. As Frantz Fanon says: "Total liberation is that what concerns all sectors of the personality."[8] He exhorts his Algerian people to shun the culture of the whites and feel pride in being black and loving all that is a part of their black culture. This is called 'Negritude'. In Muslim countries religious fanaticism creates problems of its own kind. The leaders of a country like Uganda or Nigeria try to synthesise Western political institutions with the dictates of Islam. As such pursuits fail, the result is the emergence of a dictatorial state. Rejection of the vestiges of colonialism may be possible for them, but the more serious problem is how to create something out of the discordant forms of nationalism, or the discordant notes of Islamic theologians. The traditional hold of bureaucracy coming from the days of colonialism cannot be erased by them,

6. Andrew Heywood: *Politics,* p. 90.
7. R.J.C. Young: *Post-Colonialism: An Historical Introduction,* p. 48.
8. Frantz Fanon: *The Wretched of the Earth,* p. 63.

rather emergence of military dictatorship becomes a natural affair owing to the failure of the 'imported' democratic system. The net result is a nexus between the bureaucrats and the military leaders that makes the state, in the words of Hamza Alvi, not 'over-loaded' but 'over-developed' as may be seen in the cases of Pakistan and Bangladesh.

2. In some countries post-colonial state becomes the victim of a new kind of colonialism what Kwame Nkrumah of Ghana calls 'neo-colonialism'. In appearance state is free from all sorts of alien trappings or control and yet its sovereignty is mortgaged to a foreign power on account of receiving massive financial and military assistance. The iron hold of the ruler creates a situation in which colonialism itself becomes a type of nationalism'.[9] Anderson calls it birth of 'official nationalism.'[10]

3. The colonial powers managed to keep under their control different segments of the people having different cultures and mores of life. After independence, the rulers of many states were confronted with the problem of nation-building. Indian leaders could tackle the problems created by hostile Nagas and Mizos, but the government of Sri Lanka had to take to the ways of genocide to suppress the movement of the Tamils. The leaders of Congo and Pakistan failed to patch up with dissident elements as a result of which a part of their country had its secession. It is well observed: "Post-colonial states demonstrate the potential to assemble the new communities and networks of people who are joined by the common political and ethical commitments to challenging and questioning the practices and consequences of domination and subordination."[11]

4. It is also a fact that colonial aftermath does not signify the end of colonialism. As the foreign rulers governed the native people in a way that was denounced as a form of 'exploitation', so the new rulers of the post-colonial era govern some segments of their own people in a way that they raise their voice against such forms of maltreatment. Voices of dissent sometimes get public as those of the Karens in Myanmar, Kurds in Iraq and Chakmas in Bangladesh. The noticeable point is that they do not take to the course of secessionism on account of their weak position in their country, or their wounds are not so festering. They remain content with their lot as 'subalterns' and yet they express their resentment in tolerable terms that wins the sympathy and support of other segments of the people. It shows that post-colonialism "has blossomed into a garden where the marginals can speak and be spoken, even spoken for."[12]

---

9. Leela Gandhi: *Post-Colonial Theory: A Critical Introduction,* p. 115.
10. Benedict Anderson: *Imagined Communities,* p. 86.
11. John McLeod: "Introduction" in his (ed.): *The Routledge Companion to Post-Colonial Studies,* p. 6.
12. Gayatri C. Spivak: *Outside in the Teaching Machine,* p. 56. Edward W. Said in his *Culture and Imperialism* writes about relentless disavowal of the Third World's post-imperial regression into combative and dissonant forms of nationalism.

5. However, a fine model of a post-colonial state may be seen in some countries like India, Malaysia, Indonesia and South Africa where the national leaders have successfully sought to synthesise the alien past with the native present. They realised that the roots set by foreign masters were very deep and so, instead of uprooting them, they should build new structures and superstructures upon them. Such leaders rejected the critical views of their seniors or elders that such structures or superstructures be built on entirely new foundations. For instance, Nehru did not appreciate Gandhi's comment that 'structural violence of modernity existed everywhere' or his warning that by importing Western institutions 'Indians would develop tiger's nature without being tigers'.[13] Such a state becomes a 'developing state' in course of time and surprisingly some states as Malaysia, Singapore and Indonesia have become 'economic tigers' of the South-East Asian region.

In short, the state in most of the Third World countries is in search for its identity. Progress is going on through the process of trial and error. The colonial hold of bureaucracy still persists that converts the superficially democratic state into an 'administrative state' and thereby hampers the rise and growth of civil society.

Feminist State: The feminists have no theory of state of their own, though they insist that the state must eliminate the conditions of gender inequality and injustice. Feminism is a form of identity politics in a general sense and an examination of the concept of woman in an effort to understand, reveal or subvert the sexist practices. The feminists react against the trend or tendency of treating women as 'exchange objects' and in very clear terms, ranging from soft and modest to harsh and immodest, they desire to eliminate the evil of gender inequality and injustice coming down since ancient times. A common point of all feminist ideas is the belief that women are disadvantaged in comparison with men and this disadvantage is not a natural and inevitable result of biological differences but something that can and should be challenged and changed. Unlike traditional political theories and ideologies, feminism provides a way of looking at the world that sees women's situations and inequalities between men and women as central political issues; as such, it provides a fundamental challenge to dominant assumptions about the scope and nature of politics. All feminists "call for changes in the social, economic, political and cultural order to reduce and eventually overcome the discrimination against women."[14]

All feminists lay stress on the role of the state to eliminate gender inequality and injustice. They also want that the state should ensure conditions in which women may be immune from anything like exploitation, oppression, torture, indignity and insecurity. They also demand that the state should punish those who commit crimes against women as molestation, rape, dowry-demanding, bride-burning and their obscene displays in films or advertisements etc. The women may feel free and safe in their offices or public places. The solution to all such problems of women lies in effective arrangements made by the state ranging from their enfranchisement to empowerment.

---

13. M.K. Gandhi: *Hindi Swaraj,* p. 27.
14. Jane Freedman: *Feminism,* p. 1.

The number of the feminists is quite large and it is growing, but divergence in their views may also be noted that confuses their claims to be met by the state. For instance, the liberal feminists as Betty Frieden and Susan Muller Okin lay stress on the enfranchisement of women and their equal rights with men in all spheres that would automatically clear the way for their empowerment. The socialist (Marxist) feminists as Clara Zetkin, Alison Jaggar and Dalla Costa denounce the state as a capitalist institution in which workers, including women, are exploited. Class war is converted into 'sex war'. This bad state of affairs may see its end in a socialist system. Then, the radical feminists like Simone de Beauvoir and Kate Millet demand that all male-dominated centres from the family to the state must be dismantled. There should be no discrimination between the personal and public spheres of women's life. Finally, eco-feminists like M. Mies and Vandana Shiva integrate environmental degradation with women's exploitation. Both nature and women should be saved from exploitation and damage, for both are essential for the preservation of human life and bio-diversity.

Politics is an activity centred on the theme of power. It is power and struggle for its sake. Hence, feminist movement has a patently political character. Since it aims at the presence of women in all spheres of state activity, it is also known as the 'politics of presence'. The empowerment of women can replace the 'politics of ideas' or mere debates on the social status or issues of women. A male-dominated family is patriarchal, a male-dominated state constitutes the model of public patriarchy. Even in the welfare state, hierarchies of power are male-dominated. "So women have moved out of their position of private dependency as men in the house into a position of public dependency on the male-controlled state."[15]

By way of criticism, it may be said that the feminists demand too much from the state and if their all demands are conceded, it would be detrimental to their own cause. Women are biologically weak; they need protection which can be provided only by the males. A feminist may easily refute the dictum of Nietzsche that 'men are trained for war, and women for the procreation of the warriors', or may dismiss the slogan of Mussolini that 'war is to man what maternity is to woman.' But this sane comment cannot be set aside that 'all families need fathers'. Family life as coming down from ancient times, has really been a source of comfort, support and fulfilment for women. To say that in a capitalist state women are exploited like the workers and this evil would go in a socialist society is also a utopian idea. The women would like to have administrative and police offices, but would shirk in leaving their homes after sunset. A French writer Chantal Mouffe calls it 'Wollstonecraft's dilemma'. Another French writer comments: "In a nutshell, many contemporary women would like to have their cake and eat it too, share with men the status, power and privileges that they apparently enjoy in social and professional life, while keeping all the special privileges that were allotted to women as compensation for having been virtually idled by the machine. This, of course, will never come to pass."[16]

15. Freedman, *op. cit.*, p. 44.
16. A. de Reincourt: *Woman and Power in History,* p. 316.

9
Socialism and Its Varieties

The present age is proudly known as the age of 'democracy' and 'socialism'. But to a student of political theory the problem that baffles is as to what these two terms really mean. We have already studied democracy in all its essential aspects; now we take up the matter of socialism known by various names like democratic socialism, state socialism, evolutionary socialism, Fabianism, scientific socialism and the like. Allied with it is the problem that the varieties of socialism have their sub-varieties that interact, interclash, as well as overlap each other. Thus, to a beginner socialism looks like a storehouse of confusion. One may say that the two broad categories of socialism may be seen in its Marxist and anti-Marxist dimensions. But it shall be too simplistic a statement to offer in view of the fact that even these two varieties of socialism are ridden with numerous differences on the point of their exposition and interpretation.

Socialism

Since socialism is the most popular as well as the most abused term in modern times, it is a matter of great difficulty to offer its precise and universally acceptable definition. According to Joad, we are here faced with three difficulties. First, socialism signifies both a body of doctrine and a political movement going on all over the world. That is, it has its theoretical as well as practical aspects and a proper definition of the term should cover both. Second, socialism has two more aspects—political and economic. That is, it not only desires to seize the power of the state, it also seeks to give a new shape to the system of national economy. Moreover, the two sides are so closely interwoven that it is neither practicable nor even desirable to confine our description solely to the political aspect of socialism. Last, it has its advocates all over the world armed with their own expositions and interpretations with the result that there are astonishing varieties of socialism so much so that it is hard to say what exactly socialism means. Keeping all these difficulties in view, Joad comes to this conclusion: "Socialism, in short, is like a hat that has lost its shape, because everybody wears it."[1]

---

1. C.E.M. Joad: *Introduction to Modern Political Theory*, p. 40.

Some Definitional Statements

- Socialism means four closely connected things—a human fellowship, which denies and expels distinctions of class, a social system in which no one is so much richer or poorer than his neighbours as to be unable to mix with them on equal terms, the common ownership and use of all vital instruments of production, and an obligation upon all citizens to serve one another according to their capacities.

—G.D.H. Cole

- By socialist society we shall designate an institutional pattern in which the control over means of production itself is vested with a central authority or, as we may say, in which as a matter of principle, the economic affairs of society belong to the public and not to the private sphere.

—Joseph Schumpeter

- Socialism, in fact, seeks to free the individual from the pressure of material cares, in order that he may live his life in his own way and freely develop his personality. But because the Socialist holds an organic view of the State as an entity composed of mutually dependent units, he believes that such freedom can only be achieved as the result of elaborate social organisation.

—C.E.M. Joad

Meaning: However, one should not feel discouraged or dismayed. Every term has its essential implications on the basis of which some workable definition may be evolved and that may be acceptable to a large number of people, if not to all of them. Here we shall like to keep our attention confined to the non-Marxist variety of socialism where it is easy to mark out some common features of socialism. Thus, Garner says: "Directly opposed to the *laissez faire* theory of state functions is what, for lack of a more suitable term, we may call the socialistic theory, which contends for a maximum rather than a minimum of government. The supporters of this theory instead of distrusting the state and looking upon it as an evil whose functions should be restricted to the narrowest possible limits, regard it as a supreme and positive good; and hence its mission should include the promotion of the common economic, moral and intellectual interests of the people."[2]

The subscribers to this variety of socialism take state as an instrument of positive good and lay all stress on narrowing the gulf between the rich and poor sections of the society as much as possible or practicable. For this they advocate the case of public ownership over the means of production, exchange and distribution of goods, elimination of competition, social justice and the like. Thus, Kirkup says: "A socialist society is one based on the system of public or collective ownership of the material instruments of production, democratic administration of the industries, and cooperative labour."[3] The whole idea is contained in the 6E's programme of Prof. F.J.C. Hearnshaw:

2. J.W. Garner: *Political Science and Government,* p. 476.
3. Kirkup: *Socialism in Theory and Practice,* p. 87.

1. Exaltation of community above the individual,
2. Equalisation of human conditions,
3. Elimination of capitalism,
4. Expropriation of landlordism,
5. Extinction of private capital, and
6. Eradication of competition.

In short, socialism "is that policy or theory which aims at securing, by the action of the central democratic authority a better distribution, and in due subordination thereto, a better production of wealth than now prevails."[4]

Arguments: The meaning of this variety of socialism may be more clear if we look at its essential arguments which, according to Garner, are as follows:[5]

1. Under the present system of economic organisation, the labouring man does not receive the fruits of his toil. A large part goes to reward capital or to pay for the services of those who direct and supervise the employment of labour, or to speculators and middlemen, and too little to those who are the real producers. In short, society under the present system is organised in the interests of the rich and leads to grave inequalities of wealth and of opportunity.
2. The means of production are being monopolised by the few who exploit the masses. The state should, therefore, take control of all the land and capital or means of production now being used for the exclusive benefit of the owning class.
3. The theory of socialism is founded on the principles of justice and right. The land and the mineral wealth contained therein should belong equally to all, not to few. They are nature's gift to the human race, and ought not to be appropriated by the few any more than sunlight, air, or water. The same is true as regards the instruments of production.
4. Competition under the present system not only leads to injustice and the crushing out of small competitor, but it involves enormous economic waste and extravagance in the duplication of services. The system of unrestricted competition leads to lower wages, over-production, cheap goods, and unemployed workers. The only remedy for such a condition is the abolition of competition and the substitution of the cooperative principle under which equality of opportunity and equality of reward and economy of production will be secured.
5. The doctrine of socialism is in harmony with the organic theory of the nature of state which teaches that society is like an organism, not a mere aggregation of individuals, that the good of all is paramount to that of a few, and that in order to secure the good of the greatest number, the welfare of the individual as such must be subordinated to that of the many.

---

4. *Encyclopaedia Britannica,* XI Ed.
5. Garner, *op. cit.,* pp. 478-80.

6. The state has already abolished competition in certain fields and introduced in its place the cooperative principle and has demonstrated its success as an industrial manager to the entire satisfaction of all candid and thoughtful men.
7. Collective ownership and management is thoroughly democratic; indeed, socialism is the economic complement of democracy; it rests upon both ethical and altruistic principles and is the only system under which efficiency and justice in production can be secured and under which a full and harmonious development of individual character can be realised.

A learned authority on socialism enumerates these essential features of socialism:[6]

1. As the words are commonly understood, socialism is ordinarily regarded as opposed to individualism.
2. Socialism demands the abolition of private ownership of much (if not all) wealth, and requires that the wealth so transferred should in some way be vested in, and operated by the community as a whole. It denies individual private property, and affirms that society organised as the State should own all wealth, direct all labour and compel the equal distribution of all produce.
3. Socialism aims at ends, and is actuated by motives that are ultimately incompatible. Broadly speaking, one would not be far wrong in saying that socialism has two main springs of inspiration. It is, in the first place, a protest against the injustice of this world; witnessing the grinding of the faces of the poor and the monstrous inequalities in the conditions of men, it contrasts this repulsive reality with a better world where justice will prevail. But socialism is also a protest against the inefficiency, the mess and the incompetence of the present competitive world.
4. Socialism invariably represents itself as a liberating force; its purpose is to deliver the proletariat from his chains, to give real content to rights which may be ineffective and nominal in the present conditions.

The gist of all such arguments and affirmations is that socialism "regards individuals as being primarily constrained in the full realisation of their freedom by arbitrary and capricious economic power in the form of the private ownership of the means of production. The practical problem, as the socialists see it, is to find some way of destroying this power or transforming it. They believe that they have found the answer in the common ownership of the means of production and of exchange."[7] It is true that several schools of socialism differ considerably in their programmes of action, but they "agree in certain of their theoretical assumptions and also in their general aim—all seek to secure, through some substantial limitations on the private ownership of property, a fairer and practically more satisfactory apportionment of wealth and economic opportunity."[8]

---

6. Alexander Gray: *The Socialist Tradition.*, pp. 487-94.
7. J.H. Hallowell: *Main Currents in Modern Political Thought,* p. 368.
8. F.W. Coker: *Recent Political Thought,* p. 37.

Criticism: The theory of socialism with its meaning and arguments, as given above, may be criticised on these grounds:

1. It is said that socialism starts from a false premise. It takes it for granted that private ownership of the means of production and distribution is all bad and its substitution by public ownership would solve all problems. Private property is a very old institution and it has played a very important part in the making of human civilisation. Any arrangement in the direction of collective ownership would tend to destroy one of the most powerful mainsprings of human endeavour and the chief incentive on which the success of the economic world depends. All men cannot be equalised in a way desired by the socialists and, if it were done, it would lead to social disaster. Society, according to the saying of J.F. Stephen, is like a pack of cards which remain the same after any number of shuffles. Thus, any move in the direction of socialism would go to benefit the inefficient and the idlers at the cost of those who are industrious, enterprising, efficient and adventurous and on whose sacrifices depends the all-round development of society. All liberal thinkers from Locke and Burke to Hayek and Rawls contend that the idea of economic equality, as so powerfully espoused by the socialists, is not only untenable, it is nonsense.
2. On the political side, it is said that socialism over-estimates the capacity and efficiency of state. The functions of the state should be maximised to a certain extent. To say that state can manage all affairs and so it should be a total state is to vitiate the entire scope of state activity. It would naturally lead to over-taxational and a paternalistic system of government. All would depend upon the will of the men in power who would give a shape to national economy as suits their whims and caprices. A diminution in the quantity and quality of production might be expected to result from the withdrawal of the stimulus of private incentive. Government managers would be languid and without interest in the result, and labourers would be without incentives, from which there would result, a diminished rate of progress, decreased production of wealth, with, finally, in all probability, a diffused poverty, which besides being an evil in itself, is one that threatens all the higher human interests. Moreover, the increasing area of state activity would amount to the curtailment of the liberty of the individual.
3. Since socialism accepts the organic theory of the nature of state, it makes itself liable to criticism that is levelled against the organic view of relationship between man and society (political community). An organicist would say that each organ is an integral part of the body and as the interest of the body should prevail over the interest of any individual part, so a socialist would say that an individual is an integral part of the society. As such, individual interest should be subordinate to the social interest. To say that much is not so objectionable as to draw its further inferences. An extension of this argument would lead to this conclusion than individual has no separate and distinct identity of his own and as such he can be sacrificed at the altar of the state.

Utopian Socialism

Socialistic ideas are very old. We may find their traces in religious scriptures where norms of social justice have been laid down. A detailed description of such ideas may be seen in the *Republic* of Plato where he sanctions a communistic pattern of life for the Guardians and Auxiliary Guardians in the ideal state. In the Old Testament as well as in the New Testament socialistic thoughts may be traced. Some such ideas may be seen in More's *Utopia,* Bacon's *New Atlantis* and Campanella's *City of the Sun*. However, it is France of the eighteenth century where a good number of socialist writings appeared; and since they dwelt on the rosy picture of a future society guaranteeing equality and social justice for all, it came to be nicknamed as 'utopian socialism'. The names of Babeuf, Cabet, St. Simon, Fourier and Blanc became well-known in this important direction, though the name of an English thinker Robert Owen is also included in this category. "The real home of what has come to be called Utopian Socialism was eighteenth century France."[9]

The main features of utopian socialism may be thus enumerated:[10]

1. The thinkers started with the premise that all human beings possess the same dignity by virtue of their humanity, and whatever the innate difference among the individuals, they are identical so far as their rights and duties are concerned.
2. They tried to visualise an industrial society wherein equality of economic opportunity would prevail and wherein no man would be able to live on the labour of his fellows.
3. They regarded poverty as the principal source of the ills of society and private property as the chief cause of poverty. They made elaborate analyses of the emotional and national qualities of men and gave some realistic description of the ways in which these qualities showed themselves in the actual life of a society where the traditional moral code and the whole legal cover accorded a particularly privileged position to private property. They believed that the changes they desired could be achieved through appeals to the reason and sense of justice of influential members of the community.
4. They did not look at all to revolutionary action or to revolutionary reconstruction of society, nor primarily to political action for bringing about the changes. They sought rather to set up select communities in which principles of justice, benevolence and intelligence would rule and from the example of which the whole of society would be gradually converted to their ideas.

We may now examine the ideas of leading utopian socialists. The first and foremost place should be given to St. Simon of France who argued that the new industrial state must take the place of the church as the supreme authority among men to bring harmony into their lives. Society must be reorganised into a "productive association" with an economic rather than a political form of government. Representation in the

9. Hallowell, *op. cit.,* p. 379.
10. Kolakowski: *Main Currents in Marxism,* Vol. I, p. 218.

government should be in terms of economic interests, and occupation and the supreme task of government should be the development of the nation's economic resources.

The socialism of Charles Fourier of France is saturated with the doses of over-optimism. He looked at the fact of social inequality and injustice with great concern and discovered its solution in the life of mutual attraction available in a phalanx. At least seven persons or more bound together by similar tastes and desiring to be united in the pursuit of some common art, science or industry should form a "group" and a series of such groups should form a bigger gathering called phalanx. It would be a community of about 1,500 people, occupying about 500 acres of land, all living in a big house Palace) containing dining halls, furnaces, library, study rooms, worship corners, carpentry, smithy, etc. The main idea is that a phalanx should be a perfect social community and an economically self-sufficient unit. Here the division of labour should be according to the aptitude of persons, there should be equality of education for all children with special training for skills and professions. In short, a phalanx is like a perfect city of a poet's imagination in which every animate has everything for the satisfaction of his wants, material as well as spiritual, and there is complete equality and justice in all walks of life. The associative impulse of man would play all sorts of social and economic ills. It may, however, be pointed out that Fourier does not propose abolition of private property, since each phalanx is to be organised very much like a joint stock corporation.

As Fourier span his fantasies and developed his over-confidence to the extent that he could claim himself as the Newton in underlying fixed principles of social relations, in England, Robert Owen came forward with his own design of a future society based on the principles of complete equality and justice. Like Fourier, Owen discovers the alternative to the evils of a capitalist society in establishing cooperative village societies averaging about 1,000 persons and including both agricultural and industrial workers. Rather than spending vast sums of money on poor relief which offers "greater reward for idleness and vice than for industry and virtue", the money should be used for the establishment of cooperative villages the existence of which in time will make poor relief in any form unnecessary." These communities would be self-sufficient economic units with the advantages both of city and country life. Since the spirit of brotherhood would prevail among the inhabitants, poverty and exploitation would be unknown. All such settlements would be financed by the state in one way or another with a population of at least 300 and at most 2,000. The inhabitants would be occupying large blocks arranged in "parallelograms" pleasantly decorated with the works of diligent persons. Owen is commendably vague as to how his parallelograms are to be run, but it is perhaps of the essence of dreams that they achieve their effect by the vividness of the general impression rather than by consistency of operative detail."[11]

The ideas of these socialists are dubbed as "utopian" in view of the obvious point that they take matters to the world of unreality. Both Fourier and Owen could see the failure of their socialistic experiments in their own life. Marx and Engels studied critically

11. Coker, *op. cit.*, p. 108.

the ideas of such socialists and rejected them in the name of utopianism. As they say in the *Communist Manifesto:* "Hence, they (utopian socialists) reject all political, and especially all revolutionary action; they wish to attain their ends by peaceful means and endeavour by small experiments, necessarily doomed to failure, and by the force of example, to pave the way for the new social Gospel. Such fantastic pictures of future society, painted at a time when the proletariat is still in a very underdeveloped state and has but a fantastic conception of its own position, correspond with the first instinctive yearnings of that class for a general reconstruction of society."[12]

Revisionism or Evolutionary Socialism

A new kind of socialism known as "scientific socialism" of Marx and Engels appeared in the later part of the nineteenth century whose acceptance here and rejection there made the case of a new variety of socialism called 'revisionism." Its best exponent is Edward Bernstein of Germany and his book *Evolutionary Socialism* attributes to it that name also. The beginning of this trend can be seen in the ideas of Ferdinand Lassalle, Babel and Liebknecht and other leading lights of the German social democratic movement who drew their programmes first at Gotha in 1875 and then at Erfurt in 1891. A new situation arose indicating that while both the revisionists and the staunch Marxists alike regarded socialism as mainly a doctrine and a programme for the working class and they sought to find the policy that would serve best the interest of workingmen in improving their physical, economic, and cultural well-being and strengthening their political position, the dispute between them "arose chiefly out of their opposing ideas as to the present economic situation of the wage-earners, the tendencies under way towards a change in that position, and the political tactics a socialist party should pursue in order to enable the workers to take full advantage of the actual movement of events."[13]

The Erfurt Programme incorporate in most of the tenets of liberal political philosophy and, as such, its authors provided a radical revision of the line laid down by Marx and Engels. This programme did not mention the formation of "producers' cooperatives" as the Gotha Programme had done, nor did it assert that labour was the source of all wealth. Naturally, different interpretations came and Bernstein emerged as a revisionist Marxist at the Stuttgart Conference of the German Social Democrats in 1898. The main points of Bernstein's "revisionism" are:

1. The materialistic or economic interpretation of history may be correct in some respects, but it is incorrect also in some other respects. He does not reject it, he rather likes to reform it by adding that the non-economic factors must also be taken into account in explaining past history and in forecasting future development. In his view, one who over-simplifies the situation and concentrates only on the economic factor is bound to prove a false prophet. He also objects to the phrase "materialist conception" on the ground that the theory is not based on philosophical materialism.

12. Gray, *op. cit.,* p. 216.
13. Marx and Engels: *Selected Works.* Vol. I, p. 135.

2. The theory of value, as given by Marx, is also wrong in as much as it is based on a wrong understanding of the role of labour and capital in the production of value. The Marxian view appears again as the measure of the actual exploitation of the workers by the capitalists. The theory of value gives a norm for the justice or injustice of the partition of the product of labour just as little as does the atomic theory for the beauty or ugliness of a piece of scripture.
3. The prediction of Marx that wealth would be concentrated in fewer and fewer hands and that such a concentration would be necessarily antecedent to the advent of socialism, Bernstein rejects it as manifestly untrue.
4. Bernstein was also skeptical of the Marxian contention concerning the increasing severity of economic crises in the capitalist economies and declared that at least for some time general commercial crises similar to the earlier ones are to be regarded as improbable.
5. Bernestein is also opposed to the establishment of the dictatorship of the proletariat by bloody means. In his view, universal adult franchise is the alternative to bloody or violent revolution.
6. The socialists should be less critical than they frequently are of the institutions and values associated with liberalism, for socialism does not aim to destroy the principles upon which liberalism is based. In his view socialism is based on liberalism and the purpose of socialism is to extend the scope of liberalism so as to develop the personality of the individual.
7. Bernestein also rejects the Marxian view that society is invariably divided between two hostile classes and there is no place for a third or middle class in it. He argues that if the collapse of modern society is dependent upon the disappearance of the middle classes and their absorption by the extremes above and below them, then the realisation of the new world (of socialism) is so near in England, France or Germany today than at any earlier time in the nineteenth century. "The squeezing out of the intermediate classes is, indeed, the unhappiest of all the forecasts of the *Communist Manifesto;* and what was true in the closing decades of the last century is still more abundantly true today."[14]

We may thus come to hold the view that while Bernstein rejects Marxism at so many places, he accepts it at very few places and even there he makes some qualifying interpretations. The net result of all his exercise is that he accepts Marxism in a very low measure. One may, therefore, take Bernstein more as a mutilator than a modifier of Marxism. "So much for the 'revision'—the less mealy mouthed might say the 'refutation' of Marx. It contains little that may now not be regarded as the somewhat

14. Edward Bernstein: *Evolutionary Socialism,* pp. 71-72. The doctrine of class war is the key tenet of Marxism and that is totally rejected by Bernstein. He says that modern wage-earners are not a homogeneous mass, there is vast differentiation among the different kinds of workers. "The feeling of solidarity between groups of workers is only very moderate in amount. There is no working class bound together as a unity by eternal and inexorable Marxian decree." *Ibid.,* pp. 71-72.

hackneyed and obvious criticism of a literal Marxism, but coming as it did in 1898 from among the ranks of the faithful, it was something of a portent."[15]

Fabianism or English Variety of Democratic Socialism

If the revisionists accept some content of Marxism and reject its principal tenets, the English Fabians reject Marxism altogether. Instead they present a new variety of socialism drawing sustenance from the ideas of John Stuart Mill of the post-1860 period. The establishment of the Fabian Society in 1884 and the publication of the *Fabian Essays* in 1889 represented the trend of collectivism in English political thought—a trend that should be regarded as an alternative to the line shown by the leading lights of scientific socialism.[16]

An aggressive model of socialism could never develop on the English soil. The English middle class could feel greatly satisfied after the triumph of the Chartists in 1848. Though Marx lived in England from 1849 till his death in 1883 and a small section of the English labour class joined his First International (International Workingmen's Association) formed in 1864, the labour movement of this country adhered to the lines of individualism and gradualism or incrementalism. The Social Democratic Federation formed in 1881, chiefly through the efforts of H.H. Hyndman, William Morris, Helen Taylor (step daughter of J.S. Mill), E.B. Bax, Edward Avelling and Eleanor Avelling (daughter of Marx and wife of Avelling) drew inspiration from Marx and talked in terms of "energetic class war" without advocating the means of revolutionary extremism. But the members of this body had wide differences over the use of parliamentary action ranging from liberalism to anarchism.

The Fabian Society was an organisation of the leading English intellectuals of that time who drew inspiration from the social and economic theories of Henry George, David Ricardo and John Stuart Mill. They also appreciated some of the British interpretations of Marx relating to the usefulness of the system of parliamentary democracy. But they were mainly influenced by the theory of "economic rent" as developed by John Stuart Mill in the fourth edition of his *Principles of Political Economy* published in 1864. However, the striking feature of Fabian socialism appeared in the rejection of all tenets of Marxism and instead in the presentation of an alternative variety of socialism compatible with the system of British parliamentary democracy. For this they looked towards Mill as the prophet of collectivism. It is, therefore, rightly said that not Marx but Mill was the "starting point of the English Fabians."[17]

Three years after its formation, the Fabian Society hammered out its "basis" in chosen words that reflected the faith of the members in democratic socialism. Fabian socialism adheres to these important beliefs:

15. Gray, *op. cit.,* p. 404.
16. The Fabian Society was a body of distinguished leaders and intellectuals as G.B. Shaw, Sidney Webb, Beatrice Webb, Sidney Olivier, Graham Wallas etc. Later G.D.H. Cole and H.J. Laski also joined it.
17. E. Barker: *Political Thought in England from 1848 to 1914,* p. 189.

1. It asserts that the competitive system assures the happiness and comfort of the few at the expense of the suffering of the many and that society must be reconstituted in such a manner as to secure the general welfare and happiness.
2. Land should be "nationalised" in some form and that the state should compete with all its might in every department of production.
3. Socialist ideas should "permeate" political parties and, if necessary, the Fabians should have their own political organisation. Mainly their work should be confined to the publication of tracts, books, monographs and the like so as to make a "public point" in favour of socialism.
4. As Shaw said, "the Fabians agreed to give up the delightful case of revolutionary heroics and to take to the hard work of practical reform on ordinary parliamentary lines."[18]
5. Webb said that history constantly demonstrated the irresistible progress of democracy and the almost continuous process of socialism. Now socialism as a fact had become a part of the constitution of modern society.
6. The Fabians reject the theory of value as given by classical economists in defence of capitalism as well as of Marx in defence of scientific socialism and instead appreciate the views of Ricardo and Mill. In their view, value is creation of society rather than of the labourers. Since value is a socially-created thing, it should be controlled by the society. So the case of "economic rent" is advocated. The object of socialism is to obtain for all members of society the values which society creates, and this object is to be achieved by gradually transferring land and industrial capital to the community, while making the state more representative of the community.
7. The Fabians reject the doctrine of class war. The conflict is not between those who work for wages and those who employ wage-workers, it is rather between the community and those who grow richer through investment. The transfer of ownership of the means of production and distribution should be made not in favour of the workers but in favour of society. Moreover, this transfer should be done gradually, applied at any time only to such industries as can then be successfully administered by the community and with compensation and such relief to the expropriated individuals as may seem fair to the representatives of the community in the parliament.
8. The state is neither an evil, whether necessary (as stated by the individualists) nor unnecessary (as contended by the extremist anarchists); it is a welfare agency. It is a representative and a trustee of the people, their guardian, their man of business,

18. In 1912 the Society established its Fabian Research Department which in 1916 was transformed into the Labour Research Department under the joint control of the Fabian Society and the British Labour Party. The idea behind such efforts was to offer a scientific as well as an ethical justification of a socialistic policy definitely related to the social and economic facts of the country at that time.

their manager, their secretary, even their stock-holder. The social and economic evils can be removed by the action of the state. Moreover, the existing stae can be made, without radical transformation, if not absolutely perfect, at least trustworthy. Suffrage should be broadened, educational opportunities be equalised, and social and economic inequalities be terminated.

9. Socialism can be brought about by means of "social legislation." The state should make laws for regulating working hours and bettering service conditions of the workers, it should lay down minimum standards for public health, safety and wages, it should establish public ownership over national or municipal public utilities, it should impose taxes on inheritance, buildings, land and other investments in the light of the gains accrued to their owners by virtue of social development; it should also improve educational opportunities.

10. Above all, constitutional and democratic methods should be applied for the realisation of the goals of socialism. The agency through which the Fabians propose to effect the change in the existing state, the state being influenced by a gradual alternation in public opinion brought about by intensive socialist propaganda and exercised through the ballot box.

In short, the Fabians offer a kind of socialism that is anti-Marxist, anti-utopian as well as anti-revisionist. It is anti-Marxist, because the Fabians reject all the tenets of Marxism; it is anti-utopian socialism because they do not ramble in the world of dreams, they see things in practical perspectives and come forward with a practicable programme; they are anti-revisionists in the sense that they desist from making a hotch-potch of things by accepting Marxism here to this extent and rejecting Marxism there to that extent.

Fabian socialism saw its criticism at the hands of the Marxian socialists as well as the individualists. The former denounced it as another name for bourgeois socialism. Engels, who was alive at that time, condemned it as "rotten socialism." The liberals belonging to the school of Adam Smith and Herbert Spencer deprecated it for extending the scope of state activity at the expense of individual liberty. The Fabians were also accused of being idealists like Rousseau and Green, and utopians like Fourier and Owen. It was said: "Suffering from the Narcissus complex, they were rather too much given to contemplating themselves. In their missionary zeal for truth or self-advertisement, they were perhaps too adept to winnow with every wind and to go into every way. And perhaps in half-conscious ways their intellectual top-heaviness reveals itself in a certain aridity. They were more grieved by the world's mess than hurt by the world's wrongs; that the world was run with so little wisdom reflected little credit on the intelligence of homo sapiens."[19]

But it is also said, and said well, that the Fabians were practical reformers. Like Bentham they advocated many important reforms in social, economic and political spheres through their writings. Their "resolute constitutionalism" was the necessary ally of their incremental socialism or practical progressivism. What they said and did

19. Gray, *op. cit.*, p. 400.

was taken over by the leaders of the labour movement and that ultimately went into the philosophy of the Labour Party. Thus, it "may be said generally that the Fabian socialists have contributed more to practice than to theory. The diligence and intelligence with which they have assembled and explained facts about the actual economic and social conditions of Great Britain have contributed substantially to the success with which national and local governments in that country have gradually and cautiously put into actual operation a very moderate sort of socialism."[20]

Syndicalism

Syndicalism is another variety of socialism that looks like a hybrid of the socialism of Marx and the anarchism of Proudhon. Since it begins with Marxism, it is taken as a variety of socialism; and since it ends with anarchism, it is also nicknamed as "anarcho-syndicalism" or "organised anarchy." By its advocates, it is defined "as a trade union reading of the Marxist economic doctrine and the class war."[21] Joad says: "Syndicalism may be defined as that form of social theory which regards the trade union organisation as at once the foundation of the new society and the instrument whereby it is to be brought into being. It is frankly socialistic in the sense that it adopts the general socialist view of capital as theft, endorses or rather extends the notion of the class war as fundamental in capitalist society, and proposes to abolish the private ownership of the means of production and to substitue ownership by the community."[22]

Here the main reliance is on the role of the syndicates or unions of the workers which would stage a successful revolution and after that create a new social order by violent means in which all power would be vested in these organisations. Taking inspiration from Marxism, the syndicalists say that since the workers are the real producers of value, they should be the masters of entire production. But taking inspiration from anarchism, they contend that in the future society all power should be given to the syndicates. Thus, while the collectivists (including the Fabians) talk of social control and social welfare, the syndicalists talk of the control and welfare of the workers through their trade union organisations.

Syndicalism arose from the trade union movement of France whose most important leader was Georges Sorel. But the organisational heart of the movement was the General Confederation of Labour (C.G.T.) established in 1895. It was largely due to the endeavours of Pelloutier and the adoption of a Syndicalist policy, but it was mainly due to his influence. After some time, the influence of Sorel prevailed who asserted that the "whole future of socialism resides in the autonomous development of workingment's syndicates." Thus the amalgamation of a very large number of bourses (labour exchanges) into a general confederation strengthened the position of the

20. Coker, *op. cit.,* p. 107; J.A. Schumpeter holds that the Fabians were a small group of "bourgeois intellectuals." *Capitalism, Socialism and Democracy,* p. 322.
21. Hallowell, *op. cit.,* p. 460.
22. Joad, *op. cit.,* p. 63. A syndicate is a body of syndics. A syndic is an official of kinds in different countries and times. But here we take a syndicate as a trade union. Thus, syndicalism originates from a French word 'syndicate'.

workers' unions to an astonishing degree. In all this Pelloutier played a very important part and then came Sorel with his philosophy of revolutionary violence. In this way, Pelluotier and Sorel are the two great exponents of this theory who preached that social transformation sought by the proletariat "must be a self-transformation and that the institutions through which existing society is to be displaced by a new society are institutions that grow out of and are built up by the working class through its unaided efforts and in defiance of political authority."[23]

According to Joad, the objections of the syndicalists to the state and consequently to any form of its organisation of society may be briefly stated as follows under:[24]

1. There is a generalised, though somewhat vague, hostility to the state as a bourgeois and middle class institution. The state is not only the instrument of capitalist exploitation in society, but from its very nature it would and must remain necessarily a middle-class institution. The service of the state makes men bureaucratic and unsympathetic to the needs and aspirations of those who are engaged in the actual work of production, and it would continue to have this effect under any system of society that retained the state. Even a benevolent state, therefore, would be inimical to progress if left in the control of industry.
2. It has a distrust for middle-class socialism. It claims to be the only school of socialism that is the product of the workers themselves; and all other forms of socialism have emanated from the brains of clever middle class theorists and betray their origin. They have a tendency to regiment the workers in conformity with some pre-arranged system of society which has seemed good to a clique of intellectuals. They are accordingly out of touch with the needs of the workers which can only be adequately expressed by a system devised by the wokers.
3. In favour of a system of producer's control, it is argued that it will lead to an increase both of freedom for the workers and of the efficiency in industry. Where industry is owned and controlled by the trade unions, each worker participating therein has a direct voice in the management. He, therefore, enjoys the substance of democracy in every act of his working life, as compared with misleading shadow which is offered to him once every few years under a political system, when he is invited to cast a vote into the ballot box to enable the least unsuitable of three or four unsuitable candidates, none of whom he has selected for himself to represent him in national parliament. Having a personal interest in the conduct of industry he will take pride in his work, and the quantity and quality of his output both will be improved.

However, what makes syndicalism a special and sinister variety of socialism is the advocacy of revolutionary means. The syndicalists reject all peaceful and constitutional methods and instead advocate the use of very revolutionary means what they term "direct action." It may assume any form like a general strike, sabotage, boycott, libel and go-slow work. Here they take inspiration from the ideas of a French socialist

23. Coker, *op. cit.,* p. 234.
24. Joad, *op. cit.,* pp. 64-66.

Blanqui. In their view, the general strike is not a strike in all industries of the country, it must cover very 'key' industries to paralyse the system of capitalism. The workers should take it as "myth".

Sabotage is another method that may involve acts of breaking machinery, damaging premises of work, spoiling manufacture and the like. It may cover any act of destruction that aims at paralysing the capitalist economic system. Let the building and machinery be destroyed so that the capitalists are put to any amount of harm. Apart from this, the workers may also resort to the ways of unpopularising the production of their industries. They may use blackmail tactics, or they may indulge in very slow work process or "ca canny' so that the capitalist system is destroyed. That is, the syndicalists prefer to follow a policy of injuring an employer's property or business through sluggish bungling, wasteful or positively damaging acts — done either while the worker remains on the job or in connection with strikes. It may take non-violent forms of slow work for long hours, poor work for low pay, meticulous observance of instructions so as to increase costs of production, or telling the truth to customers so as to injure the sale of articles, or it may take the violent form of destroying materials and mutilating machines and tools.[25]

Like the anarchists, the syndicalists have a picture of their own about the future society in which all power would be with the trade unions. Here they dwell on the elaboration of Emile Patuad and Emile Pouget who have given such a picture in their book *How We Shall Bring About the Revolution.* The syndicalist revolution will be followed by the permanent constructive tasks of syndicalism. Ordinary functions of management will be in the hands of industrial unions, which will have possession of buildings, machinery and equipment in the several industries and will exercise immediate direction of production and execute general rules for special cases. The authors appear to have generally in their mind the local unions, but they assign certain nation-wide services such as post offices and rail roads to national federations to supply technical information and expert advice to the local bodies. Finally, a comprehensive national body like the C.G.T. would have the function of deciding matters that demand uniform treatment in all industries such as the care of children, the aged and the sick, the determination of minimum and maximum ages for work and the length of the normal work-day, and the definition of standards of remuneration.[26]

It is, therefore, obvious that syndicalism is in its early part Marxian and in its later part anarchistic.

The theory of syndicalism may be subjected to the following lines of criticism:

1. Like Marxian socialists, the syndicalists denounce the state as a class institution and go in favour of total destruction of the state. Such a view is wrong. The state should not be condemned in such harsh terms. Due significance should be attached to such statements that the state is a moral organisation, an ennobling institution, a positive good, a welfare agency and the like that has played a very

25. Coker, *op. cit.,* p. 240.
26. *Ibid.,* p. 243.

important part in making man a good citizen. it is true that the syndicalists do not advocate abolition of the state like the anarchists, but the logical conclusion of the application of their doctrine would be the same.

2. It is true that syndicalism is not a theory as such as it is a mode of action. Let the workers take everything given by a syndicalist leader as a "myth." It shows that syndicalism is another name for political irrationalism. As Lagardelle says, it is a philosophy not of thought but of action, and it gives top place to "intuition." What is required is not foresight, planning, preparation or much goods laid up in brains. What is needed to storm the barricades is "adventurous energy." "Attack, audacity, surprise—such are the keys of success in the eyes of the syndicalists who, forgetful of the Baconian dictum that boldness is the child of ignorance, accord a place of honour to the untrimmed lamp and the ungirt loin".[27]
3. The syndicalists may also be criticised for not giving a clear picture of the future society. Like anarchists they contemplate the possibility of a golden era in which all affairs would be dealt with by the trade union organisations. But the details are missing.[28]
4. Above all, the methods of the syndicalists are very dangerous. To say that a general strike is all good and the workers must take it as a "myth" is unjustifiable on any count. So to advocate the ways of sabotage like destruction of the building and machinery of the capitalists is absurd on all counts. To teach the workers to adopt the tactics of "go slow" in work or to do anything to unpopularise the production of an industry just to harm the capitalists is wrong as well as immoral by all means. It is for these reasons that the governments of France, Italy, USA and Britain put a heavy hand on the activities of the syndicalists and virtually suppressed the movement of the unions of the workers. The syndicalists forget that the leaders of the trade unions may go to any extent in abusing their authority which they set up in the contemplated future society. Thus, Gray says that the syndicalism "is a political theory, which with little modification, may be used to defend any tyranny, any dictatorship, or any other manifestation of gangsterdom."[28]

Guild Socialism

Guild socialism is another variety of socialism that may be taken as a curious mixture of French syndicalism and English Fabianism. It is distinctly anti-Marxian, for it rejects all the important tenets of Marxism like materialistic interpretation of history, class war, labour theory of value, dictatorship of the proletariat and withering away of the state. It does not appreciate the view that state is a class institution, or that it is an instrument of exploitation and oppression by one class over another. In that respect, it is anti-syndicalist as well. While it agrees with the Fabians in fighting for the cause of labour welfare and using peaceful and constitutional means for the realisation of the aims, it goes much ahead of the syndicalists in making the workers

27. Gray, *op. cit.*, p. 426.
28. *Joad, op. cit., p. 63.*

really powerful. While the Fabians desire to establish social control over the means of production and distribution, the guild socialists, like the syndicalists, desire to abolish the notorious wage system that is the symbol of labour slavery. Thus, the National Guilds League formed in 1915 described its goal as "abolition of the wage system, and the establishment by the workers of self-government in industry, through a democratic system of national guilds, working in conjunction with other democratic functional organisations in the community".[29]

The guild socialists want to deprive the owners of capital of both the powers to determine the conditions under which labourers work and their right to derive profits out of what labourers produce. There should be self-government in industry. It means that the workers of an industry should be the masters in matters relating to recruitment of staff, production of goods, determination of price, distribution of profits among themselves and the like. All workers engaged in an industry would constitute a union (called guild) that would control and manage its affairs. Thus, like syndicalists, the guild socialists talk about welfare of the workers, not of the masses like the Fabians and other collectivists, with this line of difference that while the syndicalists talk about trade unions, the guild socialists go a step onward in talking about the guilds. So Joad syas: "The Guild Socialists may, then, best be described as a small body of intellectual theorists working within the labour movement with the object of converting the influential men of the movement to their views, but not as a general rule making any direct appeal for the support of the masses."[30]

The story of guild socialism starts from 1906 when A.J. Penty brought out his book titled *The Restoration of the Guild System.* In this book he advocated a return to the medieval principle of self-government in industry whereby a craftsman who was a member of an autonomous guild owned the instruments with which he worked, and determined the nature and extent of his production. Around these years S.G. Hobson and A.R. Orage wrote a series of papers that appeared in the *New Age.* It all led to the emergence of a new idea that appealed to the leaders of the trade unions. Their plea was for self-government in industry by the workers concerned in the industry, grouped together in a system of industrial guilds, of which the existing trade unions would form the germ. As a result of this, the National Guilds League came into being with the object of initiating propaganda in favour of the guild idea throughout the labour movement.

The most distinctive feature of this variety of socialism appeared in the form of abolition of the notorious wage system. The most powerful advocate of this kind of socialism (G.D.H. Cole) enunciated four points that marked the degraded status of labour.[31]

---

29. Joad, *op. cit.*, p. 75.
30. *Ibid.*,
31. Cole: *Self-Government in Industry,* pp. 154-55. Niles Carpenter calls Cole 'the most effective and most prolific thinker and populariser'. *Guild Socialism,* p. 18.

1. The wage system abstracts labour from the labourer so that one can be bought and sold without the other.
2. Wages are paid only when profitable to the employer.
3. In return for his wages the worker surrenders all control over the organisation of production.
4. The worker surrenders all claims of the product of his labour. Accordingly, the wage system requires the removal of these marks of "degraded status." Consequently, it is the task of the National Guilds to assure the workers four things—(i) payment as a human being, (ii) payment in employment and unemployment, in sickness and in ill-health, (iii) control of the organisation of production by the workers, and (iv) a claim upon the product of his work.

It was during the first and second decades of the twentieth century that the guild socialist movement began to take root with its idea of social midway between syndicalism and older socialism, its emphasis on producers' control and its criticism of programs favouring too great a development of state functions. Its main features are:

1. **Functional Democracy:** In a favourite dictum of the guild socialists, true representation must be functional. It implies that any representation that is not functional but purports to be general and universal, is bound to be merely misrepresentation. It is clear that the guild socialists do not appreciate the system of territorial representation prevailing almost universally on the plea that under this system representation means non-representation. The national legislature is a body of those who know nothing about the professions they represent. The interest of the businessmen can be represented only by the men of business. A member of the workers' union may represent the interest of the workers, but he cannot represent all functions of society.
2. **Self-Government in Industry:** All industry must be in the hands of the guilds. A guild is a body of all persons engaged in that industry from the manager at the top to a peon at the bottom. In this respect a guild is different from a trade union in which only workers, not officers, are engaged. The second point of difference between a guild and a trade union is that while the latter simply fights for the protection and promotion of the interests of the workers, the former is concerned with the entire management of the industry. The guild would determine the amount of production and its sale at a particular price; it would decide as to how much and in what manner the profit money is to be distributed among all the workers of industry not in the form of wages but as a share of each member in the industry. Then, all the members of the guild from top to bottom should be elected by and be accountable to itself. In order, then, the industry may be really democratic, it must be organised from below.
3. **Guild Commonwealth:** The guild socialists, as stated above, desire to have a new society like the syndicalists and the anarchists. That is, they do not want to abolish the state as such, they desire its abridgement. The state should have "an important

place but not a solitary grandeur."[32]The whole society should have guilds of the producers, manufacturers, agriculturalists and the like and all guilds should be "autonomous" or "free to make what goods they pleased, pay what wages they pleased, and make what provisions for capital they pleased, or could."[33] These guilds would be regulated and controlled by the 'communes' working at local, regional and national levels. The functions of the present day state would be performed by the communes. At the apex would be national commune giving adequate representation to all guilds of the country. The functions of the communes would be:[34]

(a) financial problems especially allocation of national resources, provision of capital and, to a certain extent, regulation of incomes and prices.
(b) differences arising between functional bodies on policy questions,
(c) constitutional questions of demarcation between functional bodies,
(d) questions not falling within the sphere of any functional authority, including several questions of external relations, and
(e) coercive functions.

Cole says that guilds would be linked together in a guilds congress that would in effect be a guilds legislature laying down and interpreting essential principles of guild organisation and practice. He frankly admits that the inter-relationship of the guilds is, however, a matter of admirable complexity.[35]

The guild socialists frankly reject all extremist means to bring about the desired socialism. Like syndicalists they place reliance on the role of existing trade unions, but they frankly reject the means of "direct action." Since the trade unions of today have to be the guilds of tomorrow, they have to act as the instruments of change. The union of the workers should adopt the policy of "encroaching control" which means gradual displacement of the hold of the capitalists. The workers may come forward with a big charter of demands and then strike a compromise with the capitalists on the basis of their meeting some of the demands. Such an agreement would be like a "collective contract." After some time, they may agitate for more concessions and have another agreement as a result of collective bargaining. For instance, the workers may force the capitalists to transfer in their favour some of their powers like control of industry, appointment and dismissal of personnel, fixation of the price of manufactured goods, distributions of profits, etc.

Such a method of gradual and peaceful displacement and dispossession of the capitalists has the practical advantage of saving the workers, the public and the innocent capitalists from unnecessary suffering. It also has a moral and psychological value in progressively demonstrating the usefulness of any capitalistic participation in

32. Cole: *Self-Government in Industry,* p. 82.
33. Niles Carpenter, *op.cit.,* p. 181.
34. Cole: *Self-Government in Industry,* p. 125.
35. Cole: *Guild Socialism Restated,* pp. 67-70.

control. The state should come to the help of the guild socialists. It should nationalise private industry and deprive the capitalists of their rights of ownership over the means of production and distribution by giving them "compassionate allowance." The guild socialists, particularly Cole, made it very clear that the state should not take revolutionary steps in the dispossession of the capitalist class.

The theory of guild socialism may be criticised on the following grounds:

1. This variety of socialism is like a curious hotch-potch of the English and the French activists so much so that the whole picture is extremely blurred. The guild socialists take something from the English Fabians and something from the French syndicalists and then add something of their own (in the form of functional democracy and guild cooperative commonwealth) whereby a clear picture does not emerge. Rather what emerges is a very confused model of a labyrinth.
2. Though guild socialism draws much from the practical part of Fabianism and syndicalism, it ultimately becomes utopian. Its hope for the advent of a future society with all powers to the guilds and gradual displacement of the capitalist class are quite utopian. The National Guilds League formed in 1915 failed to have a life of more than ten years. Even Cole felt disillusioned after the Second World War and he became a Fabian in the end. Guild Socialism expected too much from the community of the workers. It fondly hoped that a system of guilds would be all good and the workers' guilds would be able to work in a state of complete harmony and coordination.
3. The guild socialists may also be accused of being reactionary social thinkers. They draw inspiration from the medieval system that had its own problems and whose resuscitation is no longer possible. They forget that the guilds had created a lot of problem of law and order which could be dealt with only by a powerful state. It may, therefore, be feared that to talk about restoration of the guild system would amount to the revival of the conditions of anarchy and lawlessness.
4. Another difficulty about guild socialism is that it plays fast and loose with the existence of the state. On the one hand, it talks of an abridged state and makes itself different from the anarchists; on the other hand, it submerges the state into the whirlpool of numerous guilds and communes. Cole wants to get rid of "the omnicompetent, omnivorous, omniniscient, omnipresent sovereign state." It is also asserted that the guild commune (virtually state) would organise people on the basis of their different and divergent interests, would give them an opportunity to thwart each other, and would give nobody, not even the population as a whole a chance to make them compose their differences. The omnicompetent state admittedly works badly at times, but it does work which is more than the impotent "commune" would be likely to do.[36] The state is retained in name but disappears in fact.[37]

---

36. Carpenter, *op. cit.,* p. 273.
37. R.M. MacIver: *The Modern State,* p. 466.

Anarchism

Anarchism should be taken as a special variety of socialism for two main reasons. First, most of the anarchists like Proudhon and Bakunin had a socialist background. They were very close to Marx and became the subject of uncompromising attack by him when they expressed their divergent views not appreciable to the father of scientific socialism. Second, anarchism is the complementary part of scientific socialism in the sense that what the Marxian socialists desire in the last stage of social development is elaborately given not by them but by the anarchists. Thus, while the socialism of Marx in the form of communism is the means, anarchism is the end. To put the matter in another way, "most communists would now subscribe to the Anarchist ideal of society, while many Anarchists would probably agree that the methods advocated by the Communists are those most calculated to realise their ideal."[38]

Anarchism has a long intellectual lineage extending to the earliest beginnings of Western political thought, but it acquired a special attention in the nineteenth century. The anarchists like other revolutionary socialists attacked the capitalist system in the name of its being a source of exploitaiton and oppression of the bourgeois class over the working class and, for that reason, advocated its replacement by a new society in which the individual shall have complete emancipation in three important directions—"as a producer from the yoke of the capitalist, as a citizen from the yoke of the state, and as an individual from the authority of religious morality derived from hypothetical metaphysical entities, such as omnipotent God."[39]

The word "anarchism" originates from a Greek word "anarchia" meaning "non-rule." It is obvious that the anarchists want no authority of any kind so as to ensure complete liberty of man. Coker defines anarchism as "the doctrine that political authority, in any of its forms, is unnecessary and undesirable" and he adds that, in recent anarchism, "theoretical opposition to the state has actually been associated with opposition to the institution of private property and also with hostility to organised religious authority."[40] Its chief literary exponent, Prince Peter Kropotkin, defines it as "a principle or theory of life and conduct under which society is conceived without government, harmony in such society being obtained not by submission to law, or by obedience to any authority, but by free agreements concluded between various groups, territorial and professional, freely constituted for the sake of production and consumption as also for the satisfaction of the infinite variety of needs and aspirations of a civilised being."[41]

However, the difficulty about offering a precise definition of the term "anarchism" is that the exponents of this theory may be grouped into two parts—the violent or revolutionary and the peaceful or religious—each detesting state, government and

38. Joad, *op. cit.,* p. 87.
39. *Ibid.* p. 102. David Robertson says: "Anarchism is a political theory based on two propositions: that society does not need government, and that no government is legitimate unless truly and in detail, consented to by the individuals governed." *A Dictionary of Modern Politics,* p. 7.
40. Coker, *op. cit.,* p. 192.
41. Joad, *op. cit.,* pp. 100-101.

authority in any form but differing on the point of liquidation of state to what extent and with what means. "The points of disagreement may be traced even in the exponents of the same variety of anarchism. The anarchists, while differing among themselves in respect to certain details are in agreement in their hostility towards what they call a coercive state, and in their desire to see it abolished. One group, the revolutionary anarchists, would go to the length of employing violence to get rid of it; consequently they advocate assassination of government officials, destruction by bombs or otherwise of government buildings and the like. The other group, the philosophical anarchists, consisting mainly of intellectuals would limit their activities to argument and propaganda, in the effort to convince mankind of the uselessness of the state and the superiority of the regime of anarchy. The claim to be opposed not to all government as such, but only to that which is founded upon principle of coercion or compulsion; in short, it is to government to which they have not freely given in their consent that they object."[42]

It is obvious that anarchism is an anti-state theory. It regards the state as an unnecessary evil. As such, the state should go and a stateless society be created in which man is under no authority and all social affairs are managed by free and voluntary associations of the people. Their main arguments are:

1. **Superfluousness of State:** The state is superfluous as it does no good to the individuals. It perpetrates conditions of economic and social inequity and injustice as a result of which crimes take place. Moreover, the state by denying justice converts an ordinary criminal into a hardened criminal. Even the argument of defence offered in favour of the state is absurd. Kropotkin says that standing armies are beaten by the invaders who have historically been repulsed only by spontaneous uprisings unorganised by the state. However, although the *raison d' etre* of political authority is the penetration of an oppressive economic condition, its essential vice, according to Bakunin, lies even more in its moral and intellectual features.
2. **Class Character of State:** The authority of the state is due to its class character. It is an instrument of exploitation and oppression. The capitalist class makes use of this instrument to oppress the working class. It protects the monoply of those things which rightly belong to all. As Kropotkin says: "Individual appropriation is neither just nor serviceable. All belongs to all. All things are for all men, since all men have need of them, since all men have worked in the measure of their strength to produce them, and since it is not possible to evaluate everyone's part in the production of world's wealth. If the men and women bear their fair share of work, they have a right to their fair share of all that is produced by all, and that share is enough to secure them well-being. No more of such vague formula as such as 'the right to work' or 'to each the whole result of his labour.' What we proclaim is "the right to well-being, the well-being for all."[43] The system of capitalism is against the principle of natural justice.

42. Garner, *op. cit.,* p. 447.
43. Kropotkin: *The Conquest of Bread,* pp. 10-11.

3. **Fallacy of Democratic Institutions:** The anarchists reject the whole concept of the liberal-democratic system. To them representation is absurd, because one person cannot represent the will of another. It creates a body of professional politicians who thrive on the ignorance of the electorate. The legislature consists of inexperienced and incompetent persons who know how to spoil things. The politicians draw boundary lines without any proper knowledge of ethnology or geography and lawyers decide questions of will, purpose and motive with the crudest knowledge of psychology. The idea of general or common will of the community is either nonsense or the representatives make it so. They either fail to understand as to what the common will is, or they twist it to suit their personal interests.
4. **Effect of Power:** The anarchists endorse the dictum of Lord Acton that "power corrupts and absolute power corrupts absolutely." The exercise of power makes man selfish, arrogant, oppressive, inhuman. "This or that despicable minister might have been an excellent man, if power had not been given to him." (Kropotkin). It is the element of force that disrupts social unity. Humanity is fragmented into hostile groups, classes, nationalities due to the role of force that is in the hands of self-seeking politicians. "The politician, for example, is wicked not because he is a man, but because he is a politician. No man and no body of men should, therefore, be entrusted with the governmental authority over their fellows."[44]
5. **Attack on Religion:** The anarchists are very critical of religion and of the name of "God" that is exploited by the capitalists so as to perpetrate their system of social injustice. In their view, religion is an evil both because it sanctions bad institutions and because it is incompatible with man's true nature. It is consciously used by the possessors of economic and political privileges to sanctify an unnatural superiority. Kropotkin rejects religion on both scientific and natural grounds. Bakunin very outspokenly identifies the state with the church, the former as the younger brother of the latter, as they owe their origin to the same causes and being alike instruments of the enslavement of humanity. Attack on both must be made. Hence, anarchism and atheism become inter-changeable terms in the social philosophy of Bakunin.[45]

The earliest reflections of anarchism as a social and political theory may be traced in William Godwin's *An Enquiry Concerning Political Justice* published in 1791. By virtue of being the first frank critic of the system of private property and of political authority, he is regarded as the "first modern anarchist."

But Joseph Proudhon of France should be taken as the father of anarchist thought.[46] In his work *What is Property?* he frankly calls property as "theft."[47] His most specific

44. Joad, *op. cit.*, p. 105.
45. Kropotkin: *Anarchist Communism,* pp. 32-35.
46. Gray, *op. cit.*, p. 355. Gray says: "The revolt against God (or the idea of God) and the rebellion against the State—his atheism and his anarchism—may, in a sense, be regarded as the two phases of Bakunin's gospel of disobedience." *Ibid.*, p. 354.
47. Proudhon himself declares: "I am, in the full sense of the word, an anarchist." *What is Property?* (Eng. Tras. by Tucker), p. 272.

complaint against the state is that it has evolved out of the system of private property and sustained the inequitable incidents of that institution. He condemns political authority on the broader ground that it implies the dominance of passion over reason, justice and understanding. He draws up a plan for the "Bank of the People" to issue labour notes which would represent units of labour, measured solely by duration, and would be loaned, without interest to anyone offering his capacity and promise to work as security. His more elaborate fiscal proposals constitute a system of "mutualism" under which individuals and voluntary associations would be enabled to engage in productive enterprise through gratuitous credit supplied by cooperative banking associations. He calls this "mutualism" as "positive anarchy." His most uncompromising attack on state is contained in these words: "The State becomes a monster; it is that fictitious being, without intelligence, without passion, without morality that we call the State."[48]

The name of Bakunin of Russia is very important in this direction. The peculiar feature of his anarchism is that his starting point is Marxist in nature. He repudiates the state because, like the Marxists, he sees it as an instrument of class coercion for the exploitation of the working class, and because it demoralises the governors as well as the governed by ruling with compulsion rather than with persuasion. Liberty, morality and the human dignity of man consist precisely in this that he does good, not because it is commanded, but because he conceives it, wills it, loves it. The state is not identical with society but represents only an historical form of it, as brutal as it is abstract. The state "is born of the marriage of violence, war and conquest with the gods created by the theological fantasy of nations. It is the embodiment of brutal force and triumphant inequality and religion serves only to lend it divine sanction."[49]

However, a softer version of anarchism may be seen in the writings of Kropotkin. His treatment of political authority is offensively inoffensive. He says that history reveals both the state's incompetence for the achievement of any high purpose and its positive contribution to human suffering and injustice. The state has not protected the factory labourer and the peasant from exploitation by the capitalists and the landlords or secured food for the needy, or work for the unemployed. Neither the protective nor the beneficient services of the state are either necessary or effective. The people acting spontaneously can defend themselves against domestic brigands and foreign aggressors. Nor is government successful in protecting us against ill-disposed persons at home; prisons are more effective in spreading vice than in checking it. Finally, the cultural and benevolent activities of government are superfluous; when men are released from their economic and political dependence, voluntary activity will supply all that is needed for both education and charity.

Different from this is the tradition of peaceful anarchism, also known as religious or Christian anarchism, represented by Ruskin of England, Thoreau of America and Tolstoy of Russia. Ruskin in a very sophisticated manner challenges the assumptions of modern political economy that is founded on the "ossifant theory of progress." He treats

48. Proudhon: *General Idea of Revolution,* p. 208.
49. Bakunin: *Oeuvres.* (French) Vol. I, p. 288.

it as almost a negation of the human soul. He advocates the moralisation of commerce and suggests that even the merchant should be ready to die for the community. In his view, "the largest quantity of work will be done only when the motive force, that is to say, the will or spirit of the creature, is brought to its greatest strength by its own proper fuel, namely, by the affection."[50]

Thoreau challenges the foundation of state in the name of reason and wisdom. He says that a wise man would only be useful as a man and not submit to be clay. He puts a pertinent question: Must a citizen ever for a moment, or in the least degree, resign his conscience to the legislator? Every law that kills liberty of man should be disobeyed. "If injustice is of such a nature that it requires you to be the agent of injustice to another, then, I say, break the law. Let your life be a counterfiction to stop the machine of government."[51]

The anarchism of Tolstoy is contained in the reinterpretation of the doctrines and injunctions of Christianity. He says that the private property system and political authority are incompatible. Under the former a few are enabled to enjoy superfluous comforts and luxuries made possible by the labours of the many who live in want. This is an offence against Christ's exhortations to charity and human brotherhood. Under the latter, the state is based on force and executes its will through armed men, policemen and soldiers trained to kill whom they are commanded to do so. It transcends the command of Christ not to resist evil by force. He hopes for the regeneration of human race by its own free will. "The future will only be what men and circumstances make it."[52]

The merit of anarchist theory should be traced not in its consistent attack on political authority and the system of capitalism, it should be seen in its projection of the design of a future society which would be classless and stateless both. There would be no contending classes, and there would be no authority of the state and also of religion (that is an ally of the state). Thus, man in this "golden era" would enjoy complete emancipation from the yokes of the state, the capitalists, and the church. All public affairs would be managed by free and voluntary associations of the people. Each public activity would be conducted by a group of people voluntarily formed by all those who choose to engage in it, that would elect and remove its own officials, determine its own policy, and co-operate by free arrangements with other similar bodies. "A complex inter-weaving of associations with order everywhere and compulsion nowhere, forms the stuff of which an Anarchist society will be made. For Anarchy, as Mr. Lowes Dickinson puts it, is not the absence of order, it is the absence of force."[53] Above all, anarchism desires abolition of the state all over the world along with elimination of

50. John Ruskin: *Unto this Last.*, p. 120. He also says: "Whereas riches are a power like that of electricity acting only through inequalities or negations of itself. The force of the guinea you have in your pocket depends wholly on the default of a guinea in your neighbour's pocket."
51. Henry David Thoreau: *Civil Disobedience,* p. 95.
52. Count Leo Tolstoy: *The Kingdom of God is Within You,* p. 326.
53. Joad, *op. cit.,* p. 107.

the national lines. As Bakunin hopefully visualises: "There will be a free union of individuals into communes, of communes into provinces, of provinces into nations, and finally of nations into the United States of Europe and later of the whole world."[54]

How is the goal to be achieved? The anarchists suggest both non-violent or peaceful and bloody or revolutionary means. The peaceful or religious anarchists like Tolstoy would appreciate that people should be more and more self-dependent and adopt virtues of a saintly life so that the goal of future society may be achieved by the forces of love and persuasion. But, in the main, anarchism is known as a revolutionary and extremist tendency. Its two great protagonists (Bakunin and Kropotkin) suggest the use of revolutionary means. Kropotkin says: "A frightful storm is needed to sweep away all this rottenness, to vivify torpid souls with its breath, and to restore to humanity the devotion, self-denial, and heroism, without which a society becomes senile and decrepit, and crumbles away."[55]

The theory of anarchism may be subjected to these lines of criticism:

1. The anarchists take a very wrong view of the origin and nature of state and of authority of any kind. Their basic assumption that the state is by all means a coercive and oppressive organisation and that only a stateless condition of life would ensure absolute liberty to the individual is wrong and unconvicing. We should take it for granted that man is a political creature by his nature and necessity and that the liberty of man always lives within restraints.
2. In a sense, anarchism should be taken as another variety of utopian socialism. While its indictment of the state on several grounds can be said to have some logical foundation, its hope for a golden era ensuring total emancipation of man is nothing short of a utopia. Like Plato, More and Rousseau, the leading lights of the anarchist school fondly hope for an age of perfect bliss entailing from the non-existence of authority of any kind. The anarchists forget that after the abolition of the state as such, immediately some other form of authority would come up to manage public affairs, or to save people from the ordeals of savagery and barbarism. Men have always lived under some form of authority and they shall so continue to live in time to come. The result is that anarchism has remained like a theory.
3. The methods of violence as suggested by revolutionary anarchists should not be appreciated. Violence begets violence. The taste of blood can never be forgotten. Those who once indulge in the acts of violence, develop a liking for it. It may be feared that a violent revolution would lead to bloodshed and destruction of public property. To adopt the path of violence is to tread the path of fire.

The proper course is, however, to pay attention to the arguments of the anarchists on which the indictment of political institutions is based and then try to correct them so as "to make them more worthy of popular allegiance."[56]

54. Bakunin, *op. cit.,* pp. 16-17.
55. Cited in Coker, *op. cit.,* p. 449.
56. Ivor Brown: *The Underlying Principles of Modern Legislation,* p. 31.

10
Marxism

Marxism is a variety of socialism given by Karl Marx (1818-1883) in which the role of his friend and collaborator Fredrick Engels (1820-1895) has its own place. Known as Marxism, it appeared as a merciless criticism of all forms of socialism that it reproached as 'utopian'. It started with the publication of *Communist Manifesto* in 1847-48 at the behest of a small international workingmen's organisation that "was at once an interpretation of the role of the working class in the past and future history and a clarion call to labour to unite for the purpose of securing its emancipation and, through that emancipation, the freedom of all mankind. It marked a definite decline of the leadership of the utopian school of thought among the advocates of a new social order. It marked, at the same time, the advent of Marxian or 'scientific socialism', a social philosophy which has exerted such a powerful influence on the political, social, economic and cultural thought of the last half century and which seems destined to play a still larger role in future historical developments."[1]

The main tenets of Marxian socialism are dialectical materialism, materialistic interpretation of history, class war, labour theory of value and inevitability of revolution.

Dialectical Materialism: The word 'dialectic' originates from a Greek word 'dilego' meaning dialogue or discussion. Plato used it as a method of discussion, argumentation and disputation so as to arrive at a definite conclusion or perfect truth. But credit goes to Hegel for inventing a formula of social change that became popular by the name of dialectical method. The formula is: thesis × anti-thesis=synthesis. It implies that whatever exists today is like a thesis; its contradiction develops within itself that may be taken as its anti-thesis. The inevitable clash between the two results in the destruction of both and the emergence of a new thing that may be taken as the 'synthesis' which is the higher stage of development. It has the qualities of both (thesis and anti-thesis), it represents something higher as well.

The moving force is the 'idea', 'mind', 'spirit', 'geist' or 'immanent God' and, for this reason, Hegel is regarded as an idealist or a metaphysicist. It follows that history, according to Hegel, is the realisation of the 'Absolute Idea' (anything like Reason, Mind, God, World Spirit) that works itself out in both—life of man and inanimate nature according to inexorable laws of evolution. In this process of realisation man plays his part unintentionally and unconsciously. Thus, according to Hegel, 'ideas' are predominant in the movement of history and they exist apart from reality and

1. H.W. Laidler: *Social-Economic Movements, p. 121*. It is said that *Communist Manifesto* is 'the best thing that Marx ever wrote.' Coker: *Recent Political Thought*, p. 40.

experience which they create. Opposed to it, is the materialism of Marx where matter by virtue of being original, indestructible and self-operating is regarded as the moving force. Thus, Marx says: "My dialectical method is not only different from the Hegelian, but is its direct opposite. To Hegel, the life process of the human brain, i.e., the process of thinking which under the name of the 'idea,' he even transforms into an independent subject, is the demi-urge of the real world, and the real world is only the external, phenomenal form of the 'idea.' With me, on the contrary, the ideal is nothing else than the material world reflected by the human mind, and translated into forms of thought."[2]

The ultimate reality is matter in motion. But this process is dialectical signifying reconciliation of opposite movements in an endless effort to achieve more perfect harmony. Matter contains within itself the energy necessary to transform it; matter is self-moving or self-determining. The universe is self-sufficient, self-creating, self-perpetuating. Marx borrows the formula from Hegel, but he changes the moving force; he dissociates it from God and locates it in matter itself. As Engels says: "According to Hegel, the dialectical development apparent in nature and history, i.e., the causal interconnection of the progressive movement from the lower to the higher, which asserts itself through the zigzag movements and temporary setbacks, is only a miserable copy of the self-movement of the concept going on from eternity, no one knows where but at all events independently of any thinking human brain. This ideological reversal had to be done away with. We comprehended the concepts in our heads once more materialistically—as images of real things instead of regarding the real things as images of this or that stage of development of the absolute concept."[3] Elsewhere in his *Anti-Duhring*, he says: "Dialectic is nothing more than the science of the general laws of motion and development of nature, human society and thought."[4]

The essential implications of the law of dialectical materialism are as follows:

1. The phenomena are generally connected with, dependent on and limited by each other. They are interdependent.
2. The phenomena should be considered from the standpoint of their movement, change and development.
3. Change is not more quantitative, as a result of gradual accumulation, it becomes qualitative as well at certain stage of development.
4. The internal contradictions are inherent in all things, for all things have a past and a future, something dying away and something developing. The struggle between these opposite forces constitutes the internal content of the process of development and of the transformation of quantitative changes into qualitative ones.
5. Finally, the laws of evolution and change are discoverable by man.

---

2. Marx: *Capital,* Vol. I, 'Preface,' p. 25.
3. Engels: "Ludwig Feuerbach" in Emile Burns (ed.): *A Handbook of Marxism,* p. 224.
4. *Ibid.,* p. 266.

There is no hand of any mystical force in the movement of things. In short, it is not the consciousness of man that determines his being, rather it is his being that determines his consciousness. The philosophy of Marx is materialistic, because in solving the fundamental question of philosophy it proceeds from the premise that matter or being is primary and consciousness is secondary. It recognises the materiality and knowability of the world, and examines the world as it really is. It is dialectical also, because it examines the material world in constant motion, development and regeneration."[5]

The Marxian theory of dialectical materialism may be subjected to these lines of criticism:

1. The Marxists claim that at the hands of Marx and Engels, "the dialectic became a scientific method of highest potency. By its means they revolutionised the social sciences where experimentation is impossible and the sheer force of the thought must take its place."[6] But a critic may find fault with both Hegel and Marx who adopt dialectical method just to serve their purpose. If change occurs due to the application of this formula, how can this come to an end after the desired aim of the author is achieved. To Hegel there is nothing after the evolution of nation-state; to Marx and Engels no change after the advent of socialism. It all becomes eschatological. "The law of dialectic will stop to operate the moving finger having writ, stops writing. This apocalyptic note is a heritage from Christianity which has always emphasised a final judgment or an ultimate end to man's history on earth."[7]
2. An idealist would stick to his position and say that not matter but spirit is the moving force in evolution. Matter is a dead weight; it cannot work unless it is moved by the spirit that is not matter. Marx followed Hegel in using the dialectical formula; and, in spite of repudiating, he followed Hegel in converting the science of wisdom (philosophy) into the science of faith (religion) by attaching all significance to 'matter' what Hegel does to 'spirit.' It is merely an act of substitution; the end of both is the same—formulation of an ideology, As a critic says: "Marx rejected Hegel's divine spiritualisation of the world and the historic process; he declared the essential thing to be solid, stubborn, unconscious and unconsoling matter. And then he proceeded to read into that matter the very essence of the Divine Spirit as it had been conceived in Hegel's consoling system, its self-active motion by an inherent logical necessity with which in a debating mind the conclusion follows from the premise towards an ideal end. The end was different, and so were the actions and emotions of one who participated in its evolution towards them, but the concept of the universe was essentially the same.[8]

---

5. V.G. Afanasyev: *Marxist Philosophy,* p. 21.
6. Herman Simpson: "In Support of the Marxian Dialectic" in Michael Curtis (ed.): *Marxism,* p. 193.
7. H.B. Mayo: "Marxism as a Philosophy of History," *Ibid.,* p. 205.
8. Max Eastman: "Against the Marxian Dialectic," *Ibid.,* p. 181.

Historical Materialism: The doctrine of historical materialism (also known as materialistic or economic interpretation of history) is the application of dialectical materialism to the study of social development. Here the main argument of Marx and Engels is that economic forces make the history of a people. The *means of production* (like land, machinery, tools and technology) and the *relations of production* (the two classes—one that owns the means of production, exchange and distribution and the other that is dependent upon them to earn its livelihood) provide stuff that makes the story of social change. The material forces mean the 'powers of production' like (*i*) natural resources including land, climate, fertility of soil and mineral resources like coal, iron, water, power etc., (*ii*) machinery, tools and techniques inherited from the past, and (*iii*) mental and moral qualities of the men of the time. The powers of production are the active determinants of historical development. So Marx says: "The mode of production and the material means of existence condition the whole process of social, political and intellectual life."[9]

Under the weight of new requirements, these means of production change and with them occurs a change in society. 'The hand mill gives you a society with the feudal lord, the steam mill gives a society with the industrial capitalist' (Marx). "In the social production of their means of existence men enter into definite, necessary relations which are independent of their will, productive relations which correspond to a definite stage of development of their material productive forces. The aggregate of these productive relationships constitutes the economic structure of society, the real basis on which a juridical and political superstructure arises, and to which definite forms of social consciousness correspond."[10] Thus, in simple terms, the economic interpretation of history "means that in any given epoch the economic relations of society, the means whereby men and women provide for their sustenance, produce, exchange and distribute the things they regard as necessary for the satisfaction of their needs, exert a preponderating influence in shaping the progress of society and in moulding political, social, intellectual and ethical relationships."[11]

Bringing out the meaning of Marx, Engels says: "The materialist conception of history starts from the principle that production, and with production the exchange of its products, is the basis of every social order; that in every society which has appeared in history the distribution of the products, and with it the division of society into classes or estates, is determined by what is produced and how it is produced, and how the product is exchanged. According to this conception, the ultimate causes of all social changes and political revolutions are to be sought, not in the minds of men, or in their increasing insight into eternal truth and justice, but in changes in the mode of production and exchanges; they are to be sought not in the *philosophy*, but in the *economics* of the period concerned."[12]

9. Marx: *Capital,* Vol. I, p. 25.
10. *Ibid.,*
11. H.W. Laidler: *Social-Economic Movements,* p. 160.
12. Engels: *Anti-Duhring,* p. 294.

By way of criticism, it may be remarked that the 'materialist conception of history' "is not too happy in its baptismal name."[13] All events of social history, great and small, cannot be interpreted in terms of economics alone. The force of non-economic factors like religion, culture, philosophy, language, nationalism and the like cannot be thoroughly ignored. So the doctrine of Marx is too lopsided to explain all the facts of experience. The history of the world is full of events having their source in religious dogmatism, or racial instincts for warfare, or extension of their cultural influence and the like. Thus, to say that economics alone makes history is not a tenable proposition. Economics may be said to play a very important part, but it cannot be taken as decisive. "Marx was quite right in drawing attention to the importance of economic factor, which had been seriously neglected, but he gave it an undue prominence and thus oversimplified the complexity of the social situation as his followers have continued till this day."[14]

Class War: The doctrine of class war is a corollary to the doctrine of historical materialism. The two are inextricably connected and have their foundation in the doctrine of dialectical materialism whereby every change is regarded as a consequence of struggle between contending elements. If the thesis has its anti-thesis and the inevitable conflict between the two leads to the disintegration of both and their eventual replacement by a synthesis, the role of contending social classes should be looked into. While the dominant class is the thesis, the dominated class is its anti-thesis; and as a result of the inevitable conflict between the two, a new stage of social development takes place. Applying it to the present society, Wayper says that capitalism being the thesis calls into being its anti-thesis (organised labour) and from the resultant clash the final synthesis of the classless society will result when pre-history ends and history begins. It is true that St. Simon and Guizot had thrown some focus on the nature of class divergences, but the original feature with Marx is 'the union of the idea with Hegel's dialectic.'[15]

Marx and Engels affirm in the *Communist Manifesto*: "The history of all hitherto existing society is the history of class struggle. Freeman and slave, Patrician and Plebian, lord and serf, guildmaster and journeyman, in a word, the oppressor and the oppressed, stood in constant opposition to one another, carried on an uninterrupted, now hidden, now open fight, a fight that each time ended either in a revolutionary reconstruction of society at large or in the common ruin of the contending classes." It shows that there "is no history apart from the record of class struggles; and presumably what is

---

13. Alexander Gray: *The Socialist Tradition,* p. 301. Even Cole's suggestion of designating it as a 'realist conception of history' would be inadequate.
14. R.N. Carew Hunt: *The Theory and Practice of Communism,* pp. 78-79. We may also endorse the view of Laski: "The impulses of men are, in fact, never referable to any single source. The love of power, herd instinct, rivalry, the desire of display, all these are hardly less vital than the acquisitiveness which explains the strength of material environment." *Karl Marx: An Essay.*
15. C.L. Wayper: *Political Thought,* p. 207.

left of history when the class struggle is decanted is but the record of insignificant trivialities."[16]

As social movements are class movements, the term 'class' occupies a particular connotation for Marx. By the term 'class' he means a collection of people who feel a sense of solidarity created by the consciousness of their very position in the economic order of the day. It signifies that the members of a class entertain sentiments, illusions, forms of thought and views of life not as individuals but as members of the class. The people having the ownership of the means of production, exchange and distribution constitute the dominant class of the exploiters and the oppressors, on the other hand, those who earn their living by selling their labour power constitute the class of the oppressed and the exploited people. So feudal lords and the serfs constituted two contending classes in the feudal society, the capitalists and the workers constitute two such classes in the present capitalist society. Marxism, however, is particularly concerned with the class of the workers (proletariat) that is to be freed from all sorts of oppression and exploitation and given the power with which it has been deprived so far.

If social history is studied from the viewpoint of class struggle, society, according to Marx and Engels, has passed through four stages so far. First, there was *primitive communism* in which society was free from any class antagonism. There was common possession over things. But the second stage of social development took place when *slave society* came into being in which freemen became the masters and they exploited the slaves. With the invention of agriculture, society changed. The freemen constituted the dominant class and the slaves belonged to the dominated class. So the class war started. Then came the *feudal society* as the third stage of social development. Now the landlords and the nobles constituted the dominant class, and the peasants or the serfs belonged to the exploited class. With the success of the industrial revolution came into being the fourth kind of society—the *capitalist society*—in which the bourgeoisie and the proletariat became the two contending classes. On this basis, Marx and Engels could predict that *socialist society* would replace the capitalist society in the next stage of development. And as the socialist society would effect an end of class contradictions, the process of class war would come to an end. The socialist society would eventually become the communist society having neither classes nor state.

The termination of the feudal society was a great event that opened the way for the emergence of capitalism. So it was a 'bourgeois democratic revolution'. But a socialist revolution would also occur as a result of the inevitable application of the law of dialectical materialism and then capitalist system would go. It would be the first revolution of its kind. As Marx and Engels affirm in the *Communist Manifesto*: "All previous historical movements were the movements of the minorities, or in the interest of the minorities. The proletarian movement is the self-conscious, independent movement of the immense majority, in the interest of the immense majority."

---

16. Gray, *op. cit.,* p. 305.

The doctrine of class war, being the core of Marxism, may be criticised on these grounds;

1. It teaches the lesson of class hatred and class enmity. All classes should live in peace and harmony, but Marx and Engels take a wrong view of man's social life and also seek to vitiate it by injecting the poison of irreconcilable class antagonisms. The element of divergence of interests may be traced, but to take them as patent symbols of class enmity is not justified. As Popper says: "The divergence of interests with the ruling and the ruled classes goes for that Marx's theory of classes must be considered as a dangerous over-simplification even if we admit that the issue between the rich and the poor is always of fundamental importance."[17] The Marxian theory of class war "justified hatred and aggressiveness on the part of those who hold such views towards their political opponents.... It does suggest that those who concentrate blindly upon the existence of this phenomenon who deny historically the possibilities of cooperation and goodwill among persons and groups of conflicting economic interests, are conditioned to do so by the necessities of their emotional life, and by an over-powering desire to find a scapegoat upon which to lay down their aggression."[18]
2. The history of a people has a record of many changes which may be due to different reasons and the role of class war may not at all be traceable in them. Quite obviously, it "is absurd to seek to show that there must be an economic occasion to every conflict in history. Perhaps ultimately the moral factor is a more potent divider of men than is the economic; men consciously engage in conflict, in defiance of the dictates of their economic interests."[19] This doctrine suggests that the true element lies in the certainty that group acquisitiveness and the canalisation of personal aggressiveness through group life and particularly through group acquisitiveness, is a frequent source of conflict and change in history. But conditions differ from people to people and from country to country. On the basis of a psychological investigation it is said that the balance of conflicting forces "is extremely likely to vary from group to group, and from nation to nation. Upon psychological grounds alone, it is in the highest degree unlikely that the tradition of emotional education should be identical for all nations and all classes."[20]
3. It is also said that Marx has taken a wrong view of the term 'class'. In order to have the application of his dialectical formula, he has blinded himself to the existence of only two hostile social classes. He has not only ignored the facts of harmony and cooperation among the people, he has also deliberately discarded the existence of the 'middle class', a class that is neither very rich so as to be taken as an ally of the capitalist class, nor so poor to be included in the class of those to whom the law of increasing misery and degradation certainly applies. The neo-

---

17. Karl Popper: *The Open Society and Its Enemies,* Vol. II, Ch. 16.
18. E.F.M. Durbin: *Politics of Democratic Socialism,* p. 190.
19. Gray, *op. cit.,* p. 508.
20. Durbin, *op. cit.,* p. 189.

Marxists like Herbert Marcuse of the United States and Jean-Paul Sartre of France have frankly taken into account this fact. The liberal economists also throw ample light on the role of joint stock enterprises in which the increasing role of the middle class is too obvious. A critic rightly feels that as propaganda the doctrine of class war "is excellent, if for no other reason than that it puts the worker on the side that it informs him is sure to win. As science, it is considerably less satisfactory, since there are grave difficulties about the term 'class' and thereafter about the reality of the class struggle."[21]

4. The prediction that Marxism makes on the basis of the doctrine of class war may also be wrong. It is not certain that after the successful overthrow of the hold of the bourgeoisie, the power may fall into the hands of the proletariat. "The breakdown of capitalism might result not in communism but in anarchy from which there might emerge some dictatorship unrelated in principle to communist ideals."[22] It is also possible that a tottering capitalist system may create condition for the rise of fascism that would be a still more cruel state of affairs for the working class as happened in Italy in 1922. And so it is also possible that a successful socialist revolution may occur in a country without having a fully developed capitalist system as happened in Russia in 1917, or in China in 1949.

Labour Theory of Value: The doctrines of economic interpretation of history and class war form part of the Marxian sociological system, the labour theory of value constitutes the economic base of Marxism. But all the three are inter-related. It is here that we may trace the cause of exploitation and oppression of the working class at the hands of the capitalists. Marx takes from the early economists (like Adam Smith, David Ricardo and Ferdinand Lassalle) the idea of labour power that creates value in the commodities, but what he finally contributes is the antithesis of liberal economics. The economic analysis of Marx on the issue of 'value' has two parts—the labour theory of value and the theory of surplus value.

1. The labour theory of value regards labour as the sole creator of value in a commodity and holds that the value of a commodity is determined by the amount of labour power spent over the production of that commodity. Marx uses the term 'exchange value' to denote the worth of an article in terms of its relation to other articles. This exchange, commonly represented by the price, may fluctuate according to market conditions, but these fluctuations are accidental and do not eliminate or even obscure the real influence which determines both the value and ultimately the exchange value of a commodity. Thus the labour time which is socially necessary for the production of commodities asserts itself like an over-riding law of nature in spite of superficial variations in exchange values, as the real standard or measure of exchange value. As Marx says: "A commodity has

21. Lancaster: *Masters of Political Thought,* Vol. III, pp. 179-80.
22. Laski: *Communism,* pp. 87-88.

a value, because it is a crystallisation of social labour... The relative value of commodities is, therefore, determined by the respective quantities or amounts of labour, worked up, realised, fixed in them."[23]

2. As a result of the inventions in science and technology, the instruments of production (like machinery, steam power, factories, electricity etc., enormously increased both in number and efficiency) are owned by a relatively small class of the capitalists. The capitalist buys the labour power of the destitute workman, applies it to the machinery and raw materials which he owns and as a result produces a commodity having exchange value. The commodity is sold at a price which is greater than the amount expended on the amount of the workmen's wages and the upkeep of the factory. This difference between the exchange value of the manufactured commodity and the price paid to the workmen who produced it, is called the surplus value. Marx contends that in each factory or enterprise the wages paid to the workers "are not equivalent of the full value they produce but only equal to about half of this value or even less. The rest of the value produced by the worker during his working days is taken out right by his employer."[24]

The availability of surplus value to the capitalists enables them to exploit the workers and thereby accumulate more and more capital. Inflationary trends are encouraged so that the level of price goes up that results in the increasing misery and degradation of the working class. A situation comes when the working class reaches the last point of economic degradation and the way for a revolution is opened. In the language of the *Communist Manifesto:* "The knell of capitalist private property sounds. The expropriators are expropriated."

The Marxian theory of value suffers from some weaknesses. First, it is wrong to say that labour alone is the creator of value in a commodity. The liberal economists take five agents of production and labour is one of them (others being land, capital, organisation and enterprise) and, as such, labour cannot have more than a share of the total dividend. Second, the prediction of Marx that the law of increasing misery and pauperisation would inevitably apply has not been proved by actual developments of many capitalist states. The poor have not become poorer; rather in some leading capitalist countries we may take note of the embourgeoisment of the working class. It is due to this that in such countries there exist no prospects of a socialist revolution. Last, Marx has taken a wrong view of the work that a capitalist performs for increasing the production of his goods. He may be a hard-working and an honest man doing for the good of the country. On the other hand, the workers for whom Marx has done so much of hard thinking, may be idlers and shirkers. To say that all good shall follow from the abolition of capitalism and the advent of socialism in its place, is to talk like a utopian social thinker. Thus, a liberal economist of England like Prof. J.M. Keynes

---

23. See Laidler, *op. cit.,* p. 164.
24. Emile Burns: *What is Marxism?* , p. 21.

described the *Capital* of Marx as "an obsolete text book on economics..., not only scientifically erroneous, but without interest of application for the modern world."[25]

Inevitability of Revolution: The law of dialectical materialism tells us that no social system can exist forever. The antithesis would work to destroy the thesis and a new thing in the form of a synthesis would emerge. Thus, Marx and Engels could declare in the *Communist Manifesto* that 'capitalists dig their own graves'. In their view, the inevitable trend of development in the existing economic system is in the direction of a constantly greater intensification of the inexorable warfare between the owners of industrial property and the propertyless workers. At the same time, the trend is towards the overthrow of capitalism. Capitalism constantly generates the needs of its own destruction. The instruments which the owners use to enlarge their profits and rents are the instruments which, when perfected, fall inevitably into the hands of the workers, to be used by them to demolish the whole capitalist system."[26]

What does inevitably lead to all this? The following factors may be enumerated:

1. The tendency under capitalist production is towards large scale production and monopoly. As a result of this tendency manifested in the form of partnerships, joint stock companies and corporations, wealth becomes concentrated in fewer and fewer hands, so that smaller capitalists are more and more crowded out and pushed down into the proletarian class. Thus, along with the increase in great capitalist fortunes the number of capitalists decreases, while the working class gains in numbers.
2. The tendency is towards local concentration. Large-scale production necessitates the bringing together of thousands of workers into small areas, and by these contacts they become more fully conscious of their common hardships and needs; their class consciousness is strengthened and their means of cooperation are facilitated.
3. The tendency of capitalist production is towards the attainment of ever wider fields for markets. This requires a high development of the means of communication among different parts of the industrial world and this, in turn, facilitates inter-communication among the workers distributed through the industrial world.
4. The capitalist system produces recurring economic crises. The labourers, who constitute the great body of consumers, are paid enough to purchase only a very limited portion of what they produce; the products accumulate and crises of extreme over-production take place. The recurring crises, becoming more acute as capitalism develops, make the domination of capitalists more insecure; and the means which the latter adopt to avoid the crises—such as acquiring new markets—only pave the way for severer and more extensive crises and destroy the means whereby they may be prevented.

---

25. Keynes: *Essays in Persuasion,* p. 300.
26. F.W. Coker, *Recent Political Thought,* pp. 50-51.

5. The tendency under capitalism is towards a steady increase in the misery, ignorance and dependency of the workers; and this aggravates their hostility and discontent. Throughout the whole process, capitalism, while always increasing the number of the propertyless, is always by its development of labour-saving machinery, reducing the number of labourers that it needs; in other words, it constantly brings down the number of those who are able to purchase its constantly increasing products.

"Thus, the capitalist system enlarges the number of workers, brings them together into compact groups, makes them class conscious, supplies them with means of inter-communication and cooperation on a world-wide scale, reduces their purchasing power, and by increasingly exploiting them arouses them to organised resistance. Capitalists, acting persistently in pursuit of their own natural needs and in vindication of a system dependent upon the maintenance of profits, are all the time creating conditions which stimulate and strengthen the natural efforts of workers in preparing for a system that will fit the needs of a workingman's society."[27]

The most distinctive aspect of Marxism should be seen in its being a theory of action. Unlike utopian socialists, Marx offers a programme of action so that the workers may win the 'battle for democracy'. In 1875, he strongly condemned the Gotha programme adopted by the German social democrats in the name of its being a pro-bourgeois exercise and also for keeping the working class in a condition of inaction. His main argument was that "every step of real movement is more important than a dozen programs."[28] But his programme is both revolutionary and evolutionary. It is given in the *Communist Manifesto* that the workers disdain to hide their views and aims; they openly declare that their aims can be achieved only by violent means. But elsewhere Marx also appreciates peaceful and democratic methods in advanced democratic countries like Britain, America and France. It shows that the view of Marx on the methods of revolution is not vague but 'pragmatic'. "He would advocate organised violence where conditions indicated that socialists could obtain political supremacy in that way.... He opposed, on the one hand, an untimely revolution, and, on the other hand, all attempts, even through legitimate means, to establish a socialist regime before the conditions were ripe."[29]

But a question arises as to what would occur after the successful revolution. On two occasions Marx speaks of a transitional state as 'dictatorship of the proletariat.'[30] In the view of Marx, a state is not a voluntary association of community cooperation but a compulsive force—employed organisation and, indeed, an instrument of exploitation

27. *Ibid.*, p. 52.
28. Earlier in 1871 Marx said: "The workers have no ready-made utopias to introduce by order of the people. They know that in order to work out their emancipation, and along with it that higher form to which society is irresistibly tending by its own economic agencies, they will have to pass through long struggles, through a series of historic processes, transforming circumstances and men." *Civil War in France,* p. 50.
29. Coker, *op. cit.,* p. 59.
30. For this see *Class Struggle in France* of 1850 and *Critique of the Gotha Program* of 1875.

and oppression by one class over another. But the state during the period of transition would be a state of its own kind, it would be a 'dictatorship' by all means but not like that of a bourgeois state in the hands of a dictator. It would be a state in the hands of the working class committed to eliminate the class of the exploiters and the oppressors by all forcible means so that a classless condition of life eventually comes into being signifying prevalence of sovereignty of the people basically different from the 'vague idea of popular sovereignty' given in a bourgeois state.[31] In the final stage of socialism (communism) there would be no classes, no state, and so the law of dialectic would cease to operate. The society will inscribe on its banners: 'From each according to his abilities, to each according to his needs'. In short, the complete application of socialism will allay all class antagonisms. The dialectic of thesis and antithesis will be resolved in a final synthesis. Through socialism, mankind will make the ascent 'from the kingdom of necessity to the kingdom of freedom.'[32]

Marx died in 1883 and Engels died in 1895, leaving behind a new kind of social theory as well as a programme of action laudably known as 'scientific socialism'. It had its revision or reinterpretation at the hands of great leaders like Lenin and Stalin of Russia and Mao of China who earned the distinction of applying it to their respective countries. Thus, in its applied form, Marxism became 'communism'. Marxism has, as we have seen, its strong and weak sides and so numerous are its friends and foes. But the peculiar thing about Marx is that he is regarded as the greatest of all social scientists by his admirers, the criticism of his foes indirectly places him in the same position. Laidler says: "The years that have intervened since his (Marx's) death have shed new lustre on his name, and have given him a secure place as one of the great economists, social scientists, historians, and leaders of the working-class movement of all time. He made his mistakes in calculating the speed with which the great change was to be brought about, but he prophesied with remarkable insight the general direction of the change."[33] So says Laski: "Where Marx was also irresistibly right, was his prophecy that the civilisation of his epoch was built upon sand. And even the faults of his prophecy may be pardoned by an agitator in exile to whom the cause of the oppressed was dearer than his own welfare."[34]

---

31. Marx: *Eighteenth Brumaire of Louis Bonaparte,* p. 52.
32. Engels: *Socialism: Utopian and Scientific,* p. 135. *The Communist Manifesto* also says that the ultimate goal is the condition in which all class warfare, all authority, all authority of one group over another, will have disappeared, since the circumstances which create hostile or competing classes will have disappeared.
33. Laidler, *op. cit.,* p. 158.
34. Laski: *Karl Marx,* pp. 47-48. Paying his tribute at the grave of Marx, Engels compared him with Newton in laying down fixed laws of social change. He went to the length of saying: "We are what we are because of him; without him we should be still sunk in slough of confusion." See Isaiah Berlin: *Karl Marx,* p. 229.

11
Liberalism, Neo-Liberalism and Fascism

After studying the theories of socialism and its several varieties, we may now have a study of other political theories ranging from liberalism on the one extreme to totalitarianism on the other. That is, now our study would cover political theories ranging from those of the defence of individual liberty at the expense of state authority to the justification of absolute state authority at the expense of individual liberty. While the former would include a detailed discussion of liberalism with its old as well as new interpretations, the latter would have a discussion of totalitarianism of the right—fascism.

Liberalism

Meaning: Liberalism may be regarded as an idea, an attitude, a philosophy, a disposition, even an ideology, the heart of which is contained in recognising the significance of the liberty, the worth and the dignity of the individual. It may be defined "as an idea committed to freedom as a method and policy in government, as an organising principle in society, and a way of life for the individual and the community."[1] In other words, it is the voice of a free life—a life in which freedom is maximised to the extent that the individual may think, believe, move, express, discuss, associate and so on. As such, it serves the purpose of numerous thinkers ranging from the economists who desire man's freedom to produce or distribute goods, or import and export commodities to the men of politics who lay emphasis on people's right to choose and remove their rulers, or form and change their government by persuasion if possible and by revolution if necessary. In fine, carnal to the whole idea of liberalism is the principle of liberty; moreover, so crucial "is the idea of liberty that liberalism might be quite summarily defined as the effect to organise liberty socially and to follow its implications."[2]

The implications of liberalism may be seen in three important directions—social, economic and political:

1. In the social sphere, liberalism stands for secularism, i.e., man's freedom from the shackles of religious orthodoxy. It enjoins that man should have a scientific temper and a critical disposition. He should change his habits, customs and

---

1. *Encyclopaedia Britannica,* Vol. 13, 1967 Ptg., p. 1017.
2. *Ibid.,* p. 1018. According to Derek Heater, "Freedom is the quintessence of liberalism.... For the liberal it is the individual who counts not society at large or segment of it, for only by placing priority on the rights of the individual can freedom be ensured." *Contemporary Political Ideas,* pp. 22-23.

institutions which have outlived their usefulness, or which act like a chain on his real freedom. The social aspect of liberalism has its particular concern with man's freedom in relation to religion and morality.

2. In the economic sphere, liberalism means freedom to produce, exchange and distribute goods, carry on any trade or profession, keep or dispose off his property. Here a line of distinction should be drawn between negative and positive liberalism. While the former desires least possible state interference in the economic sphere, the latter desires more and more reasonable restrictions on man's economic freedom in the social interest. It is for this reason that positive liberalism draws close to democratic socialism.
3. Finally, in the political sphere, it desires a democratic system with separation of powers and checks and balances, free and fair periodic elections, accountability of the rulers to the people, universal adult franchise, freedom of the press and judiciary, protection of the rights of the minorities, freedom of thought and expression and the like.

In a word, liberty of the individual is the heart of liberalism. The worth and dignity of the personality of an individual can be secure only when he is free from coercion and oppression of any kind. He has the right to live according to his choice so that he may have the best possible development of his personality. "Liberalism is the belief that society can safely be founded on this self-directing power of personality, that it is only on this foundation that a true community can be built, and that so established its foundations are so deep and so wide that there is no limit that we can place to the extent of building."[3] Another writer says: "Liberalism denotes an attitude which seeks to make possible those social conditions in which the individuality of all men may be best realised."[4]

Classical Versus Modern Liberalism: Liberalism is a very old idea and we place those figures in the category of great liberals who lived and died for the cause of liberty. The name of Socrates comes first who died for the cause of freedom of thought and expression. Lincoln and Gandhi were great liberals who paid with their life for the cause of human liberty and dignity. The victory of the people against royal despotism meant victory of liberalism and thus the names of Locke, Rousseau, Voltaire, Burke and Montesquieu are placed among the great liberal thinkers of the eighteenth century. The names of Bentham, Mill and Green have the same place in the galaxy of the liberals of the nineteenth century. Among the great liberal thinkers of the twentieth century we may refer to the names of Wallas, Laski, Cole, Barker, Russell, MacIver, Keynes, Friedman, Hobhouse, Macpherson, Lasswell, Hayek, Rawls and Nozick.

---

3. L.T. Hobhouse: *Liberalism,* p. 66.
4. A.P. Grimes: "The Pragmatic Course of Liberalism" in *Western Political Quarterly,* Vol. XI, No. 3 (September, 1956), pp. 633-40.

Four Features of Liberalism

1. It is *individualist*, in that it asserts moral primacy of the person against any collectivity.
2. It is *egalitarian*, in that it confers on all human beings the same basic moral status.
3. It is *universalist*, in that it affirms the moral unity of the species.
4. It is *ameliorist*, in that it asserts the open-ended improvability by the use of critical reason of human life.

John Gray: *Liberalism,* (Delhi: World View, 1998), p. 86

The difference between old or negative and modern or positive liberalism lies in its stress on the degree of restraints that should be imposed on the freedom of man. The view of the old liberals was to treat liberty of the individual and authority of the state as antithetical and thus to identify liberty of the individual with minimum possible restraints. An eminent writer sums up the assumptions of classical liberalism as 'beliefs' in:[5]

1. the absolute value of human personality and the spiritual equality of all individuals,
2. the autonomy of the will of the individual,
3. the essential rationality and goodness of man,
4. the existence of certain inalienable rights like those relating to life, liberty and material possessions,
5. the creation of state of mutual consent for the sole purpose of preserving and protecting natural rights of the individuals,
6. the contractual relationship between the state and the individual and that when the terms of the contract are violated, individuals have not only the right but the responsibility to revolt and establish a new government,
7. the law being superior to command as an instrument of social control,
8. the limit and negative functions of government which is the best if it governs the least,
9. the affirmation that the individual is, and should be, free in all spheres of life such as political, economic, social, intellectual, religious, and
10. the existence of a supreme truth based on reason which can be achieved by individual thought and conscience that plays an important role in man's choice between order and anarchy.

It is clear that the basis of classical liberalism is the principle of *laissez faire* or 'leave man alone'. It implies that the interference of state should be as little as possible so that man may enjoy as much liberty as possible.

5. J.H. Hallowell: *Main Currents in Modern Political Thought,* pp. 110.11.

A marked change took place after 1860 when even Mill revised his views in a way that became the basis of the philosophy of English socialism. A new awareness developed that desired more and more state interference in the liberty of the individual in the name of public interest. Thus, Mill supported state regulation of private property according to the principle of economic rent, and he went to the length of sanctioning public ownership and control over natural resources of the country. Though an idealist, T.H. Green desired positive action of the state in the eradication of three gigantic social evils—ignorance, intemperance and pauperism. This trend became more manifest in the twentieth century when Laski in England and MacIver in the United States desired positive role of the state in rendering socially useful services. Hobhouse, Barker and Keynes, likewise, preferred more and more regulations by the action of the state in eradicating great evils like those of unemployment, disease, starvation, ignorance and squalor. Since the Labour Government of Attlee undertook several measures to implement the recommendations of the Beveridge Report (1943), Britain got the credit of being the home of the 'welfare state.'

The main principles of positive or modern liberalism may thus be enumerated:[6]

1. Freedom is not just freedom from want. The individual must be able to exercise effective political influence through properly constituted constitutional machinery.
2. Modernise the machinery of government by bringing new life to the neglected sections and dispelling present political apathy.
3. There should be constitutional reforms involving devolution of power to give effective power to regional councils.
4. Decline of parliamentary system is a serious ill and efforts should be made to revise the constitutional system for producing a parliament reflecting popular will.
5. In the international field, state sovereignty should be restricted to strengthening supra-national bodies like the United Nations.

It shows that positive liberalism has a socialistic content. So a writer says: "By a positive liberal I mean a person who holds an empirical conception of liberty, but together with this accepts a view of society which is somewhat different from that of a negative liberal."[7]

Criticism: The philosophy of liberalism suffers from some weaknesses. First, it is so flexible that its implications cannot be put in a precise form. It may mean anything in the name of man's liberty from this much to that much of the action of the individual. Everyone is a liberal from Locke to Lasswell if he shows his concern with the problem of individual liberty vis-a-vis state authority while keeping himself committed to the cause of preserving, defending and valuing the worth and dignity of the individual.[8]

6. Derek Heater, *op. cit.,* pp. 23-24.
7. David Nicholls: "Positive Liberty" in *The American Political Science Review,* Vol. LXI, No, I (March, 1962), p. 117.

That is, liberalism is a very loose and amorphous idea. Second, it is taken as the philosophy of the 'bourgeois' class in spite of the fact that positive liberalism advocates state interference in the liberties of the individual in the name of public interest. The reason is that basically liberalism disfavours stringent state regulations that are ardently desired by socialism. The spirit of liberalism is individualism and, as such, it lays more emphasis on the interest of the individual and not of the society. Liberal thinkers are, therefore, criticised for being arm-chair social theorists.

In spite of all this, it cannot be denied that the principal postulates of liberal movement—individual freedom, human rights, political rights, and rule of law—are today at least nominally the accepted common ground of all democratic forces. Undoctrinaire, tolerant, jealous of the rights of the individual, it is precisely this quality that has provided it resilience and flexibility—perhaps the most precious political quality there is, enabling change to be brought about without crisis. These values have pervaded all sections of the society and the British writers endorse it with a sense of pride: "There is not a single institution in the country which has not felt the impact of these ideas while at the deeper level of instinctive feeling they have become a part of the national character, finding expression in the tradition of fairplay."[9] It is well observed: "The importance of the liberal temper and of liberal principles applied to politics has not diminished; probably it has increased. Liberalism thrives on material prosperity, social peace and common enlightenment."[10]

Neo-Liberalism

Also known by different names as 'new individualism', 'new-conservatism', or 'new right,', neo-liberalism , as advocated by President Reagan in the United States and Prime Minister Margaret Thatcher in Britain, seeks to replace the 'welfare state' by a 'strong state'. The model of a welfare state, as given by Laski and Keynes, and established in Britain, West Germany and Sweden after the Second World War, revealed its inherent fallacies after about three decades. The liberal-democratic state expanded its area of activity in the name of rendering socially useful services. In course of time, such a state became an 'over-loaded state' ridden with rampant corruption and maladministration. In such a situation, the ideas of the negative liberals like Hayek and Nozick justifying the case of a 'minimal state' came up to pave the way for 'rolling back' the welfare state.

---

8. Such a deceptive meaning of liberalism creates confusion in the sphere of state activity. For instance, it may be said that if the test of a liberal government is that the rule of law should be secured and that the area of private independence be respected strictly, even an enlightened despot can satisfy that test. Fredrick of Prussia was highly praised by Kant precisely on that score; for having enabled his subjects to use their reason and to speak their mind, thus removing all hindrances to the spread of enlightenment. Alexander Passerin d'Entreves: *The Notion of the State,* p. 211.
9. Alan Bullock and Maurice Shock: *The Liberal Tradition (From Fox to Keynes),* p. liv.
10. W.G. Smith: 'Liberalism' in E.A.R. Seligman (ed.): *Encyclopaedia of the Social Sciences,* 1968 Ed., Vol. 9, p. 282.

The essential features of neo-liberalism may be enumerated as follows under:

1. Individuals are 'rational creatures' who know their interests. Only they can decide as to what they need or desire, hence lesser the state intervention in their life, the better for them. The neo-liberals desire extension of 'market' to more and more areas of life and the creation of a state stripped of 'excessive involvement' both in the economy and in the provision of opportunities.
2. If so, the state should reduce its burden of rendering useful public services as the individuals may manage these affairs themselves. State and market should be taken as friendly to each other. Hence, private initiative should be given encouragement. The activities of the labour unions and all other bodies supported by the socialists demanding more and more restrictions on the private sphere should be restrained.
3. It may be inferred that the neo-liberals desire a return to the *laissez faire* model as advocated by Adam Smith and Mill. But such an inference is misfounded. The neo-liberals desire to curtail the welfare state and replace it by a 'strong state' in the light of the requirements of the day. Now the state is required not to eradicate the gigantic evils of poverty, ignorance, disease, starvation, unemployment and squalor as recommended in the Beveridge Report of 1943, rather its essential function is to deal with the new challenges posed by the new gigantic evils as nuclear proliferation, cross-border terrorism, environmental pollution, serious epidemics and racial and ethnic conflicts. For this purpose, not a weak or a minimal but a strong and hegemonic state is required.

It shows that the neo-liberals, in general, "are committed to the view that political life is, or ought to be, a realm of individual freedom and initiative."[11] Thatcher appreciated the view of Hayek that a welfare state clears the 'road to serfdom' and it should be taken as 'state-administered socialism'. The role of the state should be minimised in the political and economic spheres of course, but it should be maximised for the sake of defence of the realm and preservation of the civil society. In this way, neo-liberalism "is committed to the classic liberal doctrine that the collective good (or the good of all individuals) can be properly realised in most cases only by private individuals acting in competitive isolation and pursuing their sectoral aims with minimal state interference. This commitment to the market as the key mechanism of economic and social regulation has a significant other side in the history of liberalism; a commitment to 'strong state' to provide a secure basis upon which, it is thought, business, trade and family life will prosper."[12]

The New Rightists are said to present a 'hegemonic project' that divides them into two categories. "While the neo-liberals attempt to reassert the autonomy of the market by proclaiming, in essence, that the economy works best when left alone by the government. In this way, economic and social life is portrayed as a private sphere over

11. David Held: *Political Theory and the Modern State,* p. 139.
12. *Ibid.,* pp. 139-40.

Essential Features of New Right

1. **Belief in Freedom:** They place tradition at the top of their values and what they mean by this term is the absence of coercion.
2. **Freedom, Democracy and Equality:** They deny that democratic government is a means of extending freedom. All legislation reduces freedom irrespective of whether it is enacted by elected assemblies or dictatorships. Democratic government is often a means by which majorities can impose their will on minorities and from the viewpoint of the minority the fact that the decision has been arrived at 'democratically' offers little consolation for the loss of individual liberties. It follows from all this that freedom and equality are, to some extent, incompatible objectives. To make people equal is to prevent some of them from doing what they want, since it would benefit them more than others.
3. **Personal responsibility:** Enjoyment of liberty also entails responsibility for the consequences that follow when we exercise these liberties.
4. **Competition and innovation:** Innovation will not occur in a society where the state owns or controls the means of production or where higher rewards are prohibited in the name of social justice. A state monopoly has no spur to innovate.
5. **Planning versus market:** Markets are not chaotic or anarchist, for firms plan to meet anticipated demands, workers plan career moves to enhance their prospects and so on. A state planned system puts all eggs into one basket.

Jean Dearlove and Peter Saunders: *Introduction to British Politics* (Cambridge U.K.: Polity Press, 2000), pp. 409-13.

which the state exercises no rightful influence. Neo-conservatives, on the other hand, call for the restoration of authority, order and discipline. In particular, this reflects a desire to strengthen the authority of the government, at least in relation to what the New Rightists regard as its proper role: law and order, public morality and defence."[13]

One may ask as to where do the neo-liberals stand? Their attack on the 'nanny state' (welfare state) is understandable in that it makes the people indolent and helps the undeserving people at the cost of the deserving ones. Such a state promotes wrong ethos of equality. It repudiates the sane view of Herbert Spencer that 'the ultimate result of shielding fools from folly would be to fill the world with fools'. To overcome

13. Andrew Heywood: *Political Theory: An Introduction:* p. 149. According to Fraser King, the "promise of neo-liberalism seems to be that a just society (narrowly defined) is achieved by uncoerced market exchanges. More markets lead to less state both in totality and in its potential to intervene, if there are no goods for social distribution in a market-led society, the role of the state is limited to the protection of property rights and other related tasks, e.g., national security and external defence." Refer to his paper "Neo-Liberalism: Theoretical Problems and Practical Inconsistencies" in Mike Mills and Fraser King (eds): *The Promise of Liberalism: A Comparative Analysis of Consensus Politics* (1995), p. 12.

these failings of the welfare state, the neo-liberals suggest that "we must go 'beyond entitlements', and focus instead on people's responsibility to earn a living. Since the welfare state discourages people from being self-reliant, the safety net should be cut back, and any remaining welfare benefits should have obligations tied to them."[14]

Such an affirmation makes the neo-liberals faithful disciples of Hayek and Nozick who are regarded as libertarian thinkers. But the difficulty arises when the neo-liberals want to defend the case of a mini-welfare state that takes them close to the idea of an egalitarian like Rawls. Their aim is to 'roll back' the welfare state, not to roll it out. The advocates of this trend look like hovering between the poles of libertarianism and egalitarianism with a definite slant towards the former which is vitiated by the 'neo-conservatives'. They certainly fail to draw a clear picture of their attempt to reconcile the model of free economy with a strong state. A line of political and ideological tension between neo-liberalism and neo-conservatism may be seen that enables a critic to say that it "does not so much constitute a coherent and systematic philosophy as an attempt to marry two distinct traditions."[15]

Fascism

Meaning: Fascism is the antithesis of liberalism and socialism; it is another name of the totalitarianism of the right.[16] Though basically a creation under the leadership of Mussolini of Italy, it saw its repetition in Germany under Hitler and also in other countries as in Spain under Gen. Franco and in Japan under Prince Fuminaro Konoe in the pre-II World War period. It had its inglorious manifestation in the period following the Second World War, though in varying degrees, as Salazarism in Portugal, Peronism in Argentian, Gaullism in France, and in the form of military rule in many countries of the Third World. The most striking feature of fascism is that it has assumed the shape of an ideology negating the principles of liberalism, socialism and internationalism and thereby posing a very serious challenge to those who desire to make the world 'safe for democracy'.

Fascism is primarily used to identify the social, economic and political system that was established in Italy in 1922 under the leadership of Benito Mussolini of the Fascist Party. It is also used to identify a prototype of totalitarianism that had its equally vigorous manifestation in Germany in 1933 under the leadership of Adolf Hitler of the Nazi Party.

14. Will Kymlicka: *Contemporary Political Philosophy: An Introduction* (New Delhi: Oxford University Press, 2002), II ed., p. 157.
15. Andrew Heywood: *Politics,* p. 49.
16. According to William Kornhauser, totalitarian dictatorship involves total domination limited neither by received laws and codes (as in traditional authoritarianism) nor even by the boundaries of governmental functions (as in classical tyranny), since they obliterate the distinction between state and society." *The Politics of Mass Society,* p. 23.

Totalitarianism

Implications[1]

Totalitarian ideologies provide the justificatory arguments in support of a type of society nominally characterised by:

1. an official or highly specific official ideology based upon a radical rejection of some aspects of the past and chiliastic claims for the future,
2. a unitary mass movement of solidarity, hierarchically organised as a single party under the authoritarian leadership of a charismatic (or pseudo-charismatic) leader and a directive and tutelary elite,
3. a technologically conditioned near monopoly of the means of communication and coercion, and
4. a centralised direction under bureaucratised control of the entire economy.[1]

Features of Totalitarian State[2]

1. It is a repudiation of reason and glorification of instincts and impulses. It is anti-intellectual. Instinct and will are given priority over reason.
2. It is dictatorial in character. It is opposed to liberalism and parliamentary government. It vests supreme power in the hands of one individual or one party. Parliamentary democracy is criticised as being stupid, corrupt and slow-moving. Parliaments are looked down upon as mere talking shops, incapable of accomplishing results.
3. It combines the aristocratic principle of government by a privileged elite with a democratic width on the basis of election.
4. It crushes individual liberty. It tolerates no political opposition.
5. It glorifies the nation and emphasises the idea of state as a power system. It adulates war and condemns peace.[2]

1. A James Gregor: *The Ideology of Fascism: The Rationale of Totalitarianism*, p. 7.
2. Asirvatham: *Political Theory*, 1988 Ed., pp. 690-93.

Though Nazism is the German version of Fascism, the common point is that both stand for the ideology of the totalitarianism of the right.[17] Thus, fascism is defined as "a political attitude which puts the nation-state or race, its power and growth, in the centre

17. Totalitarianism of the right is pro-capitalism and anti-communism; totalitarianism of the left is pro-communism and anti-capitalism. But the element of totalitarianism is common whereby both stand for the negation of the values of democracy in national and of pacifism in international spheres. H.R. Kedward: *Fascism in Western Europe. 1990-1945,* p. 240. Totalitarianism is an all-encompassing system of political rule that is typically established by pervasive ideological manipulation and open terror and brutality. Totalitarianism differs from both autocracy and authoritarianism in that it seeks total power

of life and history. It disregards the individual and his rights, as well as humanity, in the exclusive interest of the nation. As a political technique, it follows the lead of the totalitarian bolshevism as a single-party state with a strict regimentation of all aspects of national life."[18]

The word 'fascism' is derived from an Italian word 'fascio' or 'fasci' literally meaning a well-tied bundle of rods. As legend goes, in ancient times, the Roman army moved with a lictor's fasces in which an axe was inserted into a bundle of well-tied sticks. This emblem signified unity, strength and solidarity of the Roman army. Mussolini invoked this emblem and made it the symbol of his party. The word 'fascism' is said to have been invented by Mussolini; it became the name of his movement after March, 1919 and of his government after October, 1922. What Mussolini did in Italy was followed in other countries as in Germany, though the German fascists had their party called National Socialists and they used the symbol of 'swastika'. The fascist leaders prescribed a particular uniform as the 'black shirt' of the followers of Mussolini in Italy and 'brown shirt' of the followers of Hitler in Germany. "The notable point is that all these organisations stood for a government with strong centralised power, permitting no opposition or criticism, controlling all affairs of the nation (industrial, commercial, etc.) emphasising an aggressive nationalism, and often anti-communist."[19]

Features: What Mussolini did in Italy and then Hitler did in Germany, some important tenets have come out of that in the form of the ideology of fascism. Its main features may be summed up briefly as under:

1. It stands for an omnipotent state. The authority of the state is absolute, unlimited and indivisible. 'Nothing outside the state, nothing against it, nothing above it', says Mussolini. The interest of the individual is secondary to the interest of the state. The individual is commanded to have full faith in the dictum of state absolutism and for that sake, in Treitschke's words, 'he should fall down and worship the state'. Fascism may thus be defined positively as 'the unlimited sovereignty of the state over all phases of national activity.'[20]

through the politicisation of every aspect of social and personal existence. Autocratic and authoritarian regimes have the more modest goal of monopoly of political power, usually achieved by excluding the masses from politics. Totalitarianism thus implies the outright abolition of civil society: the abolition of the private. Andrew Heywood: *Politics,* p. 29. Identification of a totalitarian system may be made through a six-point syndrome: (1) an official ideology, (2) one-party state, usually led by all-powerful leaders, (3) system of terroristic policing, (4) monopoly over the means of mass communication, (5) monopoly over the means of armed combat, and (6) state control of all aspects of economic life. C.J. Friedrich and Z.Brzezinski: *Totalitarian Dictatorships and Autocracy* (1963).

18. *Encyclopaedia Britannica,* 1967 Ptg., Vol. 9, p. 103.
19. *The American College Dictionary,* p. 438.
20. Mario Einaudi: "Fascism" in David I. Sills (ed): *International Encyclopaedia of the Social Science,* 1968 Ed., Vol. 5, p. 337.

2. If the state is an omnipotent institution in the hands of the ruling party, there is no place for opposition of any kind to it. Freedom of thought and expression is crushed; opposition is outlawed, press and other mass information agencies have to work under strict censorship of the state. The slogan of 'liberty, equality, fraternity' is replaced by the slogan of 'responsibility, discipline and hierarchy'. Democracy is condemned as a luxury for the rich nations of the world; parliamentary institutions, in the words of Carlyle, are debunked as 'talking shops'. The whole idea of liberty is identified, in the vein of Hegel, with complete obedience to the state. In the words of Mussolini's minister (Gentile), 'always the maximum of liberty is coincided with the maximum of state force.'[21]
3. A fascist state is not a state of the people; it is not even dictatorship of any particular social class. Though sovereignty is said to be vested in the nation, its exercise is in the hands of a small section of the ruling party or junta that may be defined as its elite formed around the personality of a charismatic leader. The elite is always right. Charisma is attached to the personality of the great leader. Hero-worship becomes the order of the day. The supreme leader is addressed in colourful terms as "Il Duce' (Mussolini) and 'Fuhrer' (Hitler). In the words of Fichte, the personality of supreme leader is filled with the 'divine idea of the world.'[22]
4. It has no doctrinal basis. It is essentially empirical and pragmatic. Mussolini often declared: 'My programme is action, not talk'. In the words of Mussolini's minister Alfredo Rocco: "It is true that fascism is, above all, action and sentiment and as such it must continue to be." It is owing to its highly practical nature that its followers may combine the elements of any social and political theory with their own ideology at any stage of its development. Mussolini diluted many important socialistic principles of his Charter of Labour of 1927 so as to win over the sympathy of the native bourgeois class; Hitler adopted many anti-labour measures in spite of the fact that his was the National Socialist Party by its name.[23]
5. On the economic front, it is certainly a pro-capitalist ideology. It wants to establish a completely authoritarian system in which there is no opposition of any kind from any section of the community. The result is that the workers are deprived of their basic rights to stage a strike or a demonstration. Economic policies are framed and implemented so as to benefit the class of the capitalists. Laski goes to the extent of saying that fascism is the last remedy to save a tottering capitalist system. The two most important features of fascist economy are the establishment

---

21. F.W. Coker: *Recent Political Thought.,* p. 476.
22. M. Palmieri, while keeping the image of Mussolini in his view, in 1936 said that "a hero is one who can pierce with the mystic light of inner vision to the very heart of things." *The Philosophy of Fascism.*
23. Throwing light on the intensely practical nature of fascism, and thereby distinguishing it from Lenin's Bolshevism, Mussolini said: "We want to come out of the cloud of discussion and theory." Coker, *op. cit.,* p. 473.

of a cooperative state and the realisation of the goal of 'autarchy' or economic self-sufficiency."[24]

6. The pro-bourgeois character of fascism can be traced in its stern anti-socialist orientation. Both Mussolini and Hitler made public utterances to finish communism from the world. It is for this reason that the capitalist powers of Britain, France and the United States adopted the policy of 'appeasement' to strengthen the hands of fascists so that eventually they would destroy the communist state of the USSR. In 1924 the Italian fascists assassinated the great socialist leader (Matteoti) and in 1936 Mussolini put great Marxist theoretician (Gramsci) behind the bars where he died due to tortures. Even contemporary fascist rulers have very close relations with the United States. So, the communists describe fascism as "a blood-thirsty, terrorist dictatorship of the most reactionary, chauvinistic and aggressive factions of the exploiting classes, engendered by the general crisis of capitalism."[25]

7. Fascism also believes in the myth of racial purity. The German Nazis proudly declared themselves as the most civilised people of the world. Hitler called Nordic people as the race of the Aryans and condemned the Jews as people with adulterated blood. The Nazis persecuted the Jews in the most inhuman way. Although Mussolini was not in favour of the myth of racialism, after 1936 he also subscribed to it and he proudly spoke of the excellence of the Roman race. 'The fascists seek to justify their imperial aggrandisements in the name of 'civilising the barbarians'.[26]

8. Fascism also cultivates faith in the course of blind and aggressive nationalism that manifests itself in the form of territorial aggrandisements. The fascists exhort their people to be united, strong and disciplined so as to create a mighty state capable of restoring the grandeur of the past. The glorious past of the community is invoked to sharpen the feelings of patriotism. Thus, Mussolini invoked the name of great Roman empire of the ancient period and inspired his people to re-establish the grandeur of the Roman empire in the present century. Hitler did the same in the

24. Mussolini established a network of corporations in which the fascists dominated. The association of the manufacturers and others with these bodies was of a superficial kind. At the top was the national corporation of the fascists in which Mussolini himself played the leading role. The philosophy of the 'corporate state' rests on two assumptions. First, man should not only be politically articulate as a citizen but also as a worker, entrepreneur, farmer, doctor or lawyer; general political problems are assumed to be too complicated for the mass of the people who are only expected to understand issues that bear directly on their vocational or professional work. Second, members of the small ruling elite are supposed to understand broad problems that affect the whole society, and they alone are, therefore, qualified to govern the community." William Ebenstein: *Today's Isms,* p. 73.
25. *A Dictionary of Scientific Communism,* p. 90.
26. Hitler not only eulogised th e German race, in very harsh terms he also denounced the Jews as a community of usurers, liars, and cultureless. He compared them with parasites that destroy any organism. Says he: "For the sham culture which the Jew possesses today is the property of other peoples and is mostly spoiled in his hands." Carl Cohen (ed.): *Communism, Fascism and Democracy,* p. 382.

name of his pan-Germanism and for that sake he destroyed the independence of Austria and Czechoslovakia. 'Expand or perish' becomes the motto of the fascist state and, with a view to realise it, the fascist rulers play with the independence of poor and weak states of the world.

9. Above all, the fascists believe in the way of brute force and violence. They condemn peace as the dream of the cowards and instead admire the way of war. They have no faith in the method of pacific settlement of international disputes and instead love to follow the policy of 'blood and iron'. Mussolini said that 'war is to man what maternity is to woman' and 'I want to make my mark on the pages of history like a lion with his claws'. Like Hegel, Hitler compared the life of peace-loving people with the rotten water of a stagnant pool. He withdrew his country from the League of Nations and frankly discarded the principles of internationalism that led to the outbreak of Second World War.

It all demonstrates that the ideology of fascism "is dominated by the dogmas of sovereign state and irresistible government."[27]

Criticism: The protagonists of fascism offer some arguments to justify its excellence. In their view, a fascist system gives to the people what they really need particularly in times of crisis. It provides safety and security in homes and factories, punctuality in the running of public transport, orderly management of industrial concerns and a sense of pride in the destiny of the people what they really need particularly in times of crisis. It creates a new awareness in the minds of the people towards their public duties and replaces the evils of corruption, inefficiency and treason with the virtues of efficiency, integrity and patriotism. The progress made by a country in a very short span of time and the elevation of national status in the comity of nations are also cited as strong points in defence of fascism.[28]

But all these points of defence lose their significance in the face of its demerits that may be counted as follows under:

1. Fascism is not a coherent ideology. It is another name for the course of political opportunism in which any principle can be accommodated if it goes to serve the interest of the power-drunk leader and his loyal organisation. The fascists may boast much about their democratic and socialistic affirmations, but when the time comes they have no hesitation in doing anything in clear contravention of their professions. Fascism thus means sheer opportunism for the sake of winning and retaining power. It is a 'revolution of nihilism', 'dynamics in vacuo', action for the sake of action alone, power sought for its own sake.[29]
2. Fascism is the enemy of democracy. It crushes liberty of the individual. State becomes an end in itself and individual a means. Terror stalks the land and any kind of opposition is sternly repressed. There is no right to dissent. The party or

27. Coker: *Recent Political Thought,* p. 482.
28. Martin Seliger: *Ideology and Politics,* pp. 200-01.
29. Harman Rauschning: *The Revolution of Nihilism,* p. 24.

the junta in power under the leadership of a 'supremo' is glorified. There is no freedom of press due to strict censorship. So there is no independence of judiciary. Elections are not held, or they are held for the sake of show alone. Hence, it is commented: "If liberalism is a combination of two principles of democracy and individualism, the Fascist tradition is an expression of the two opposing principles of autocracy or authoritarianism and state worship."[30]

3. Fascism is the enemy of socialism. It suppresses the legitimate rights of the workers and instead protects the interests of the capitalist class. The capitalists support the dictator with their financial resources for the reason that his iron rule manages to place a heavy hand on the workers as well as on the smugglers who harm their economic interests. In this sense, fascism is not a progressive but a reactionary ideology.
4. Fascism discards internationalism. It has faith in the course of blind and aggressive nationalism. It exalts collective ego of the nation and sacrifices liberty of the individual at its altar. The people are taught to hate other races and nations and sacrifice themselves for the myth of national solidarity, discipline and greatness. The principle of war is appreciated and the way of peace is condemned. It is good that a state should strive for its economic self-sufficiency, but the principle of 'autarchy' implies economic isolationism that is detrimental to the way of a happy international economic order. By all means a fascist state undermines the existence of an international organisation and pacific settlement of disputes under its auspices.
5. Fascism feeds itself on the myth of racial superiority. It hates people of other races and nationalities. Not only that, it takes pride in humiliating and torturing the people it condemns as 'barbarians' or of 'mixed blood'. But it is all done to hoodwink the people and thereby to arouse their sentiments for a definite purpose—consolidation of power by all possible means.
6. Above all, fascism is another name of a dictatorial system in the hands of a single ambitious and power-drunk leader. He declares himself as the 'supreme leader', rather the 'superman' of the land, and seeks to deify himself by means of hypocrisy and demagogy. Sycophancy is rewarded with the result that merit and virtue weep unknown. As Schapiro says: "And, it is, indeed, to the mass that the Leader's main effort is directed: he woos, cajoles, bewitches, befuddles and blinds the mass with all the instruments which his skill, his imagination, his resources, above all, his style make possible. Mussolini, in this sense, was a showman, he acted on his part in front of a people whom in his heart he despised for the credence which they bestow on his histrionics. The more hysterical Hitler used the methods of necromancy to mobilise mass hysteria and to induce crowd hypnosis on a scale hitherto unknown in the modern history of mankind, and, be it said, with a degree

30. William McGovern: *From Luther to Hitler,* p. 14.

of success among the civilised people comparable only to the manifestation of religious dementia in the Middle Ages."[31]

On the whole, fascism is a very pernicious tendency. The essential fact stands out that it is a curse. The ideology is based on 'the irrationalisation of society.' (Talcott Parsons) The people should know that it "has striven, somewhat paradoxically, to unite philosophy with a bias towards conservatism and one that glorified revolutionary violence, an ethics that regarded conformity as a chief virtue and one that saw 'sacred egotism' as the highest form of character."[32]

31. Leonard Schapiro: *Totalitarianism,* pp. 52-53.
32. G.H. Sabine: *A History of Political Theory,* p. 757.

12
Gandhism

Though too rational, spiritual and metaphysical, Gandhi's place in the world of political theory is definitely unique. The value of his social, economic and political ideas does not lie in proposing institutional devices which might help reduce social conflicts and tensions; it consists in providing clear moral goals for the people who aspire to realise them. As we shall take note of, his social and political philosophy is inseparably associated with his saintly life and, for this reason, it may be said that Gandhi is a politician among the saints and a saint among the politicians. It is well observed: "Gandhism, like Hinduism, is a spirit, not a dogma; it is an attitude, not a creed; it is a process of thinking and living and not a hidebound organisation. Gandhi himself is an erring follower of Gandhism, a devoted worshipper of the eternally valid, and yet eternally elusive ideals of the love of God and the love of truth. Gandhism is, therefore, not a formula; it is an age-long passion for God directing Gandhi, in ways peculiar to him, to realise Him in his service of humanity and of India."[1]

Philosophical Anarchism: Gandhism cannot be identified with any school of Western political philosophy like liberalism, socialism, anarchism and communism in spite of the fact that the features of all such theories may be traced in his social and political philosophy. And yet we may place Gandhism in the category of religious or philosophical anarchism in view of the fact that he denounces the nature and character of political authority and instead ultimately goes in favour of an ideal society without any instrument of coercion. As an eminent writer says: "Gandhi is a philosophical anarchist, because he believes that his end can be realised only in a classless and stateless democracy of autonomous village communities based on non-violence instead of coercion, on service instead of exploitation, on renunciation instead of acquisitiveness, and in the largest measure on local and individual initiative instead of centralisation."[2]

The religious or philosophical anarchism of Gandhiji can be traced in these features:

1. **Denunciation of State:** Gandhiji looks at the state as an engine of violence and exploitation that kills the sentiments of service and sacrifice. He repudiates the usefulness of state on every ground—philosophical, ethical, historical, economic and political. His argument is based on the point that the compulsive nature of

---

1. M.S. Buch: *Rise and Growth of Indian Nationalism: Non-Violent Nationalism: Gandhi and His School,* pp. 4-5.
2. G.N. Dhawan: *The Political Philosophy of Mahatma Gandhi,* p. 3.

political authority mutilates the moral value of human actions. The state destroys what otherwise comes from the force of conscience or consciousness. As he says: "The state represents violence in a concentrated and organised form. The individual has a soul, but the state is a soulless machine; it can never be weaned from violence to which it owes its very existence."[3] Again: "I look upon an increase in the power of state with greatest fear, because while although apparently doing good by minimising exploitation, it does the greatest harm to mankind by destroying the individuality which lies at the root of all progress."[4]

2. **Indictment of Parliamentary Democracy:** Gandhiji rejects the system of parliamentary democracy. He ridicules parliament as a 'sterile woman.' Like Carlyle, he calls it a 'talking shop' or an institution consisting of self-seekers and hypocrites. It is an organisation that has done nothing useful of its own accord and always suffered from fickle-mindedness and uncertainty. As he says: "Today it is under Mr. Asquith, tomorrow it may be under Mr. Balfour.... What is done today may be undone tomorrow. It is not possible to recall a single instance in which finality can be predicted for its work."[5]
3. **Appreciation of Ram Raj:** Gandhiji desires a new kind of social and political order ensuring complete justice and equality. In such an ideal condition of life there would be no discrimination between a prince and a pauper, a barrister and a scavenger (sweeper) and 'justice would be done even to the dog.' The state would continue to exist in this society, but it would be a perfectly non-violent organisation. The scope of state activity would be reduced to the minimum possible extent. Some institutions like army, police, bureaucracy, courts, heavy transport and industry, big hospitals and gigantic machinery would continue to function not for the sake of suppression of individuality but for the sake of common welfare. The Kingdom of God on earth would come to prevail; there would be sovereignty of the moral authority of the people and the state as a structure of violence would go. It would entail the kingdom of love, justice and righteousness and stand on the basis of complete non-violence. There would be fructification of moral spirit and the abolition of tensions, conflicts and egotistic interests. Sympathetic accommodation, non-coercive organisation and spontaneous cooperation would be the characteristics of this ideal society. Everyone would earn his honest living by the sweat of his brow and there would be no distinction between big and small labour. The society would be classless and also without violent state. It would consist of a number of self-contained and self-regulated village communities. Every village would have a panchayat having full powers of administration and capable of meeting all its essential needs even to the extent of defending itself. The pattern of life would be simple and civilisation would have a rural character. Moreover, there would be complete decentralisation of authority. Voluntary cooperation would inform the institutions of social life and it would appear that

3. N.K. Bose: *Studies in Gandhism,* p. 202.
4. *Ibid.,* p. 204.
5. Gandhi: *Indian Home Rule or Hind Swaraj,* pp. 15-16.

men have acquired complete personal swaraj or grown accustomed spontaneously to observe their social obligations without the operation of the existing violent state.

It is obvious that, like anarchists, Gandhiji desires a new social system ensuring complete freedom, equality and justice to all with capacity of man to resist the abuse of authority, wherever it occurs, by means of *ahimsa* and *satyagraha*. However, while realising that this condition of life would always remain an unrealised and unrealisable ideal in its entirety, Gandhiji "indicates the direction rather than the destination, the process rather than the consummation. The structure of the state that will emerge as a result of the non-violent revolution will be a compromise, a *via media*, between the ideal non-violent society and the facts of human nature."[6]

Gandhiji's theory of state may be criticised on certain grounds. First, we may not agree with the indictment of the anarchists that the state has been, and also is, an instrument of exploitation and oppression. If it has destroyed liberty of man, it has also provided protection and welfare. The fact that the state is the first condition of a civilised life, cannot be refuted. Second, Gandhiji places too much reliance on the change of human nature. Madison said that 'if men were angels, no government was needed.' The fact is that man can never be as good as Gandhiji visualises and, as such, the state would continue to exist. If man by his nature is a social, rational and cooperative being, he is also a self-seeker. The competitive instincts in man are strong and powerful as the instincts of love and friendship. But the fault of Gandhiji is that he looks only to one side of the picture and places utmost reliance on it in the fashion of an idealist. Last, the picture of the ideal society or Ram Raj may be very attractive, but it is all hypothetical. The form of social organisation as given by him would be wholly inadequate to deal with the complex problems of the modern world. What Joad has said about the criticism of Western anarchism applies here also that the whole theory "is necessarily vague, because, though simple in outline, it exists in outline only."[7]

Non-Violence: One of the distinctive contributions of Gandhiji is that he gives a comprehensive meaning to the concept of *ahimsa* (non-violence). Instead of regarding it as a tenet of personal motivation and action like that of Buddha or Mahavira, he could transform it into a successful technique of direct mass action. That is, here we find that the individualistic message of non-violence is transformed into a twofold phenomena—personal as well as institutional. Evil thoughts, sentiments of revenge, brutality, verbal pugnacity, accumulation of unnecessary things, falsehood, trickery,

---

6. Dhawan, *op. cit.,* p. 291. According to V.P. Varma, Ram Raj means the realisation of universal peace and humanitarian ethics. There is no place in it for pungacity, barbarity and war. The realisation of the Kingdom of God would depend, however, on a sincere faith in the Supreme Spirit by millions. It is evident that this Ram Raj will be more cohesive than the formal bonds of legal organisation." *The Political Philosophy of Mahatma Gandhi and Sarvodaya.,* p. 295.
7. C.E.M. Joad: *Modern Political Theory,* p. 111.

intrigues, chicanery, deceitfulness, economic exploitation and stranglehold of others, excess of emulation and destructive competition, etc., are the examples of violence at the personal level. So physical punishment, conscription, compulsory recruitment in armed forces, wars, etc., are the instances of violence at the institutional level—violence committed by the state.

The salient features of Gandhi's concept of non-violence may be put as follows:

1. Literally, non-violence means doing no harm or injury to others. But, in a wider sense, it implies a positive quality of doing good to others instead of merely refraining from doing bad. Its aim is to love the opponent and to win him over by the force of heart. It means goodwill towards all in its active form.
2. Normally a man should abstain from committing violence, but there may be a situation in which doing violence would be like observing non-violence. It is the right of a person to save his life and honour. So is with the case of a country. It would be an act of non-violence to beat and kill a person who runs amuck and may kill anyone with a sword in his hand. So a country has every right to beat the foreign aggressor by the force of arms.
3. Non-violence means doing no injury to the person of others. But Gandhiji sanctions the idea of killing a living creature in case there is no way to cure its agony and killing is the only way to relieve it of that unbearable agony beyond the help of any kind of service. A reference to both intent and deed is thus necessary in order to decide whether a particular act of abstention can be classed as non-violence.
4. Non-violence is not the weapon of the weak; it is the weapon of the strong. Taking a sword is the symbol of cowardice, observing non-violence is the summit of bravery. A coward never risks his life. A non-violent person's life is always at the disposal of him who would take it. The more a man gives his life, the more he saves it.
5. Non-violence is an effort to abandon the violence that is inevitable in man's life. The quality of non-violence that is calculated to take us on the onward path, must be spontaneous, must be the lowest minimum, must be rooted in compassion, and must lead us every moment on the path of good.

It is obvious that though Buddha, Mahavira and Christ have laid stress on the principle of non-violence, Gandhi's interpretation is different from all. Their non-violence is of a non-resisting kind in any case whatsoever, but the non-violence of Gandhiji is of a persuasive nature. We may give three reasons for this.'[8]

1. Non-violence is held to be superior to violence, because it is an expression of love that accepts punishment upon itself rather than imposing it upon the opponents. Such self-sacrificing love is held to be redemptive to both parties in the dispute—

---

8. W.R. Murthy: "Non-Violence, Violence and Reason" in *Journal of Politics,* Vol. 33, No. 1 (February, 1971), pp. 3-24.

morally and psychologically to the sufferer and persuading and converting to the opponent.

2. Non-violence persuades a man by appealing to his conscience and better impulses, rather than of coercing him against his will. In this way, respect is shown to the opponent's freedom and dignity and the chain of violence—hatred leading to hatred, violence to revenging violence—is broken.
3. Because it is spiritual or soul force rather than physical force, the former is considered to be the law of civilised man, whereas the latter is the law of the brute.
4. Adherence to non-violence is sometimes held to be a commandment of religious faith.

The whole meaning of non-violence, as preached and acted upon by Gandhiji, may be thus summed up: "Gandhi's greatness as a leader and a thinker lay in his transformation of the individualistic message of non-violence into a successful technique of direct mass action... Ahimsa is not merely the negative act of refraining from doing offence, injury and harm to others, but really it represents the ancient law of positive self-sacrifice and constructive suffering... Ahimsa is vitally integrated with Truth or God... The social application of ahimsa is postulated upon the acceptance of spiritual metaphysics and the implied necessity of the growth of social charity. The law of love and respect for life, if courageously practised, is bound to lead to the elevation of the accent, quality and character of politics and civilisation... Thus, the basis of the Gandhian philosophy of politics consists in stressing the persistent, over-powering and resolute power of love as a significant factor which can solve group and national tensions and antagonisms through non-constrained conversion."[9]

Gandhiji's concept of non-violence may be criticised on the following grounds:

1. The concept of non-violence is too spiritual to be relevant in the sphere of politics where resort to violence often becomes a necessity. It may be practised to a limited extent. The concept of Gandhiji has more relevance in the theoretical sphere of politics; in the practical sphere of politics the laws of Machiavelli and Hobbes have a relevance of their own which cannot be overlooked.
2. While the doctrine of *ahimsa* is comprehensive enough to cover so many directions, it is also narrow enough to exclude the unbelievers in God or those who do not profess faith in any religion. It cannot appeal to the athiests who discard religion as 'the opium of the people', deny the existence of God and want to emancipate man from the yoke of religion.
3. Though Gandhiji affirms that his concept of *ahimsa* has national as well as international relevance, it is said that it has hardly any relevance in the sphere of international politics. The British government dismissed the suggestion of Gandhiji in 1940 that world war should be waged by non-violent means. Even an

9. V.P. Varma, *op. cit.,* pp. 118-19.

admirer of Gandhi says: "Some of the suggestions of Gandhi for the use of *ahimsa* in world diplomacy appear unrealistic and unconvincing to me."[10]

Satyagraha: Like *ahimsa* the concept of *satyagraha* (insistence on truth) has very comprehensive connotations. It is moral pressure for the sake of truth. If truth is the ultimate reality, then it is imperative for its votary to resist all encroachments on it. According to Gandhiji, it is the imperative duty of the *satyagrahi* (civil resister) to make endless endeavours for the realisation of truth through non-violence. As Prof. Varma says: "It signifies a genuine, intense and sincere quest for truth which is God. It means an assertion of the power of the human soul against political and economic domination. Satyagraha is the vindication of the glory of the human conscience. Conscience does not stand for abstract inwardness or withdrawal from the world. Satyagraha is based on the invincible belief in the ultimate triumph of divine justice and right."[11]

The main ingredients of the doctrine of *satyagraha* are following:

1. It denotes the operation of soul force against all forms of injustice and oppression. It is inconsistent with jealousy towards or hatred of the opponent, for the opponent has to be converted, not coerced. The active non-violent resistance of the 'heroic meek' makes an immediate appeal to the heart, for it constitutes the gentle process of conversion by love. As such, it is the inherent birth right of a person. However, its practice requires self-discipline and a readiness to bear all kinds of suffering.
2. The operation of *satyagraha* is a twofold blessing. It is a like a double-edged sword that blesses both the killer and the killed. If it elevates the character of the petitioner, it also brings a change in the heart of the opponent. If it purifies the sufferer, it also intensifies favourable public opinion. It makes a direct appeal to the soul of the oppressor.
3. The *satyagraha* is the weapon of the strong, not of the weak. To be a passive onlooker to tyranny and to allow untruth to prevail over truth is the negation of the capacity of *satyagraha*. It has no room for timidity and violence, and if there is a choice between cowardice and violence, Gandhiji prefers the latter, because the use of violence shuns the situation of timidity.
4. The concept of *satyagraha* should not be identified with the idea of passive resistance as preached by the Quakers and also by Sri Aurobindo during the days of anti-Bengal partition agitation in the first decade of the twentieth century. Passive resistance is a weapon to face the enemy, but it does rule out the necessity of having a pure and clean heart, nor can it be contemplated at a level other than political. But *satyagraha* presupposes the existence of a pure heart and its use can be contemplated at any level—social, economic, political. As Gandhiji says:

---

10. *Ibid.*, p. 137. The critics have regarded Gandhi's concept of non-violence as a doctrine of negation and exclusion. Lord Chelmsford went to the extent of calling it as 'the most foolish of all schemes'. Romain Rolland: *Mahatma Gandhi,* p. 81.
11. Varma, *op. cit.*, pp. 185-86.

"Satyagraha differs from passive resistance as North Pole from the South Pole. The latter has been conceived as a weapon of the weak and does not exclude the use of physical force or violence for the purpose of gaining one's end, whereas the former has been conceived as the weapon of the strongest and excludes the use of violence in any shape or form."[12]

5. The practice of *satyagraha* may take any form such as strike, demonstration, non-cooperation, *dharna* (squatting), fasting, picketing, civil disobedience, non-payment of 'black taxes,' surrendering honorary posts and titles, not taking part in 'official functions,' boycott of foreign goods, and *hijrat* or leaving the place of extreme injustice. But it is necessary that all or any of the means of *satyagraha* should be reinforced by the practice of non-violence.

Gandhiji's doctrine of *satyagraha* may be criticised on certain grounds. First, it is too spiritual, even metaphysical, whose implications may not be understandable to a man of average comprehension. C.M. Case points out that *satyagraha* may be a superior method theoretically, in practice it is too idealistic as it "demands a stronger self-control, a more enduring solidarity of purpose, of greater capacity for passive suffering, a higher ethical development than most human beings have thus far attained."[13] Second, Gandhiji wants no coercion of any kind, but a *satyagrahi* may create a situation in which the other party feels so. What would happen in a state of confrontation when both sides observe *satyagraha* for the sake of 'justice' and both claim their stand as based on truth and soul force. Thus, Case regards various means of *satyagraha* as the instances of coercion because in them suffering, though self-inflicted, "aims at producing a dilemma in the mind of the opponent. Neither of the alternatives appeals to his desires or his judgment, yet he is compelled by the situation to choose between them."[14]

Trusteeship: Gandhism is neither capitalism nor socialism. It is not even a mixture of the two. Both systems, as developed in the West, have their inherent limitations. As such, a third method should prevail. It is the system of trusteeship which desires that property should be under the control of a private person, but he should regard himself as its protector not its master. It is based on the ideal of non-possession (*aparigraha*) as given in the *Isopanishada*. It also conforms to the idea of the *Bhagwata* which holds

---

12. *Ibid.,* p. 195. In the words of Pattabhi Sitaramayya: "As passive resistance, it was a movement of bitterness and pride which had perhaps even a tinge in it of hatred and violence. In non-cooperation, it was an attitude of sulky and sullen people, angry with their rulers and anxious to wound but unwilling to strike.... Erelong we saw that the basis of *satyagraha* was nothing short of love and non-violence. Non-violence was not merely to be a negative factor, but a positive force and was equivalent to that love which does not burn others, but burns itself to death..... Satyagraha is really a compendium of all the virtues known to man for Truth is the mainspring of such virtues, and non-violence or love is its envelope." *The History of the Indian National Congress,* Vol. I., pp. 613-14.
13. C.M. Case: *Non-Violent Coercion,* pp. 406-7.
14. *Ibid.,* p. 402.

that we have a claim only to so much as would satisfy our hunger, otherwise desiring more than that is like theft deserving punishment. While acknowledging his debt to the ***Bhagwad Gita,*** Gandhiji once said: "I understand the *Gita* teaching of non-possession to mean that those who desired salvation should act like a trustee who, though having control over great possessions, regards not an iota of them as his own."[15]

This theory of trusteeship has some important implications. First, it applies with regard to accumulated wealth and earnings beyond one's needs. It desires that any superfluous wealth should be held in trust. It also implies an ideal of economic equality in the ideal state. Second, it implies the case of equality of rights, not of rewards. More talented people have a right to keep greater amount of wealth. Gandhiji does not like to cramp the intellectual attainments of the people and allows them to make full use of their talent in the interest of the community. Third, it discards the case of nationalisation or abolition of private property. Instead it desires a change of heart or mentality. The property-owners should not consider themselves as the absolute lords of what they possess; instead they should regard themselves as the custodians of social wealth or trustees utilising their property for the good of the whole community. Fourth, Gandhiji is not in favour of the modern capitalist system, because he rejects the law of inheritance. The choice of a trustee or his successor should be subject to the final approval of the community. The misuse of trust property may be set right by the action of the state. The state may make a law for the regulation of private property system, or it may confiscate it with minimum use of violence.

The salient implications of Gandhian concept of trusteeship may be put as follows:

1. Trusteeship provides a means for transferring the present capitalist order of society into an egalitarian one.
2. It does not recognise any right of private ownership of property except in as much as it may be permitted by the society.
3. It does not exclude legislative regulation of the ownership and use of wealth.
4. Thus, under state-regulated trusteeship an individual would not be free to hold or use his wealth for his own satisfaction or in disregard of the interest of society.
5. Just as it is proposed to fix a decent minimum living wage, even so a limit should be fixed for the maximum income that could be allowed to any person in society. The difference between such minimum and maximum incomes should be reasonable and equitable and variable from time to time so much so that the tendency would be towards obliteration of the difference.

---

15. Gandhi: *The Story of My Experiments with Truth,* pp. 221-22. Gandhiji is much influenced with the teaching of Christ who said: "Persons, then being God's one real concern and their welfare being the end for which everything can become human property exists and is held in trust from God, all life becomes a proving of loyalty and love to him through loyal love to one's brother man."

6. Under the Gandhian economic order, the character of production would be determined by social necessity and not by personal whim or greed.

A critic may say that Gandhi's theory of trusteeship is quite utopian. Man's love for wealth is so ingrained that, in Machiavelli's words, he may forget as to who had killed his father but not as to who usurped his property. It may be taken as an idealistic defence of the private property system. A democratic socialist would scoff at such an idea and he would, like Laski, frankly advocate the way of state control over public property, while a communist would discard it as a tenet of utopian socialism. Even Jawaharlal Nehru could raise this question: "Is it reasonable to believe in the theory of trusteeship to give unchecked power and wealth to an individual and to expect him to use it entirely for the public good? Are the best of us so perfect as to use it entirely for the public good? Are the best of us so perfect as to be entrusted in this way? Even Plato's philosopher-kings would hardly have borne this burden worthily. And is it good for others to have even these benevolent supermen over them?"[16]

End and Means: In the view of Gandhiji, means and end are organically related so much so that the latter grows out of the former. He dismisses the contention of the Machiavellians and the Marxists that 'end justifies the means' and instead insists that 'as means so the end'. In his own words: "The means may be likened to a seed, the end to a tree, and there is just the same inviolable connection between the means and the end as there is between the seed and the tree."[17] It is for this reason that he immediately suspended the non-cooperation movement in the wake of February 1922 when a section of the ***satyagrahis*** indulged in burning a police station in Chauri Chaura. He asserts that the state cannot attain its ideal character as long as the means are tainted with violence. He said: "For me Ahimsa comes before Swaraj. So close and inseparable is the connection between the two that if one takes care of the means, the end will take care of itself. The realisation of goal is in exact proportion to that of the means." Hence, he affirms that "the attempt made to win swaraj is swaraj itself."[18]

It follows that in the system of Gandhiji, end and means are inter-related and convertible terms. "Ends which are sought in human affairs are matters of growth and inevitably absorb and embody the means which are used to produce them, just as a plant absorbs water, minerals and the energy of the sunshine which are the means of its growth."[19] While highlighting the importance of this feature of Gandhian social and political philosophy, an American writer says: "In the realm of political philosophy, as in the field of action, the dynamic technique of satyagraha suggests a re-examination of the means-end relationship. Satyagraha, claiming to be more than means, to be, indeed, end-creating, introduces dynamic element with challenging implications for political method. If the cry of Spengler that man needs above all a noble end, with the

16. Nehru: *An Autobiography,* p. 528..
17. Gandhi: *Hind Swaraj,* p. 39.
18. *Ibid.,* p. 40.
19. Richard B. Gregg: *Which Way Lies Hope,* p. 24.

inerrant proposition that what political man needs is not a noble end but constructive and creative means."[20]

Internationalism: Gandhiji is not only a staunch nationalist, he is also an internationalist. The spirit of sacrifice underlying his movement is that a man should go beyond his own community (nation) and embrace the whole mankind. The logical conclusion of self-sacrifice is that the individual should sacrifice himself for the sake of the family, the family for the district, the district for the province, the province for the country, and the country for the whole world. Thus, a person can serve his neighbours and humanity at the same time, the condition being that the service of the neighbours is in no way selfish or exclusive. The spirit of self-sacrifice implies that a nation is bound to help others in the times of distress. Gandhiji discards the case of blind and aggressive nationalism that creates artificial barriers along different peoples of the world and that informs them to settle their differences by the force of arms. So he says: "It is not nation that is evil, it is the narrowness, selfishness, exclusiveness which is the bane of modern nations, that is evil."[21]

The greatness of Gandhi's thought is that he desired to integrate the case of Indian freedom with the emancipation of the entire mankind. As he said: "I want the freedom of my country so that the resources of my country might be utilised for the benefit of mankind. Just as the cult of patriotism teaches us today that the individual has to die for the family, the family has to die for the village, the village for the district, the district for the province, and the province for the country, even so a country has to be free in order that it may die, if necessary, for the benefit of the world."[22]

Gandhi wants a world where real peace and cooperation prevail. There should be a world organisation based on the principle of non-violence. It should include representatives of all states believing in the way of non-violence. There should also be an international non-violent police force to prevent sporadic outbreak of conflicts among the peoples of the world. This non-violent international organisation would recognise the principle of equality and freedom of all peoples of the world and, for this reason, it would work for the elimination of imperialism, racialism, war and other evils that stand in the way of a happy international life. In his own words: "Isolated independence is not the goal of world states. It is voluntary independence. The better mind of the world desires today not absolutely independent states warring one against another, but a federation of friendly independent states."[23]

Religion (Dharma) and Politics: Since Gandhiji believes in truth and non-violence, he takes politics as inseparably linked with the force of religion that is the English equivalent of the word 'Dharma'. He says: "To me there is no politics without religion. Politics bereft of religion is a death-trap that kills the soul." It is for this reason that he denounces all contemporary philosophies based on the way of atheism. But,

20. Joan von Bondurant: *Conquest of Violence.,* pp. 230-31.
21. Gandhi: *Young India,* Vol. II, p. 1292.
22. Mahadev Desai: *Gandhi in Indian Villages,* p. 170.
23. Gandhi, *op. cit.,*

in this direction, the meaning of Gandhiji should be understood correctly. His is not a dogmatic approach to religion as we may see in the case of fundamentalists. In his view, true religion implies an unbending stress on the moral values of man. Religion means firm faith in the existence of God and love for all mankind. One may be a Hindu or a Muslim or a Christian or of any faith or creed, but his faith in God and love for mankind should be unshakable. Hence, human behaviour should be informed by the canons of true religion. On one occasion, he said: "To try to root out religion itself from society is a wild goose chase. And were such attempt to succeed, it would mean the destruction of society."

We may comment that Gandhiji's approach to politics is in tune with the doctrine of enlightened secularism. He equates all religions of the world and identifies them with Truth or God. One may have faith in any religion but what is required is that he should not use it as an instrument of hatred, enemity, or ill-will. He frankly suggests that we should give up all religious injunctions that create social ill-will or hatred by virtue of drawing sustenance from the misinterpretations of the meaning of a true religion. In an address to the Christian missionaries assembled in Calcutta at the YMCA on 28 July, 1925 he said: "I did not stop studying the Bible and the commentaries and other books on Christianity that my friends placed in my hands; but I said to myself that if I was to find my satisfaction through reasoning, I must study the scriptures of other religions and also make my choice. And I turned to the Quran. I tried to understand what I could of Judaism as distinguished from Christianity. I studied Zoroastrianism, and I came to the conclusion that all religions were right, and everyone of them imperfectly because they were interpreted by our poor intellects, sometimes with our poor heart, and more often misinterpreted.... If I want the satisfaction of my soul, I must feel my way."[24]

Obviously, Gandhiji is a religious secularist. To him religion is identifiable with a pious force that should inform all human action. The techniques of *ahimsa* and *satyagraha* cannot be utilised in a successful way unless sharpened by the force of religion. The true religious attitude means voluntary acceptance and enthusiastic fulfilment of *swadharma*. It also desires performance of a selfless service in accordance with the principle of *Bhagwad Gita*. It is called *karmayoga*. Such an attitude leads to the progressive expansion of the human self till it comes to comprehend almost the whole of humankind. So J. von Bondurant holds: "Gandhi's religious predilections did not obscure his reasonableness nor his willingness to accept the results of empirical tests. The element of appeal to reason is essential for the functioning of satyagraha."[25]

24. J. von Bondurant, *op. cit.*, pp. 129-30.
25. *Ibid.*, p. 130.

Gandhian Pattern of Ideal Life

Commitment to Eleven Core Values (Ekadashavrat)	**Avoidance of Seven Evils**
1. Truth (Satya)	1. Wealth without work
2. Non-Violence (Ahimsa)	2. Pleasure without conscience
3. Non-possession	3. Politics without principles
4. Non-stealing	4. Knowledge without character
5. Fearlessness	5. Commerce without morals
6. Celibacy	6. Science without humanity
7. Swadeshi	7. Worship without sacrifice
8. Bread Labour	
9. Temperance or self-control	
10. Eradication of untouchability	
11. Equal respect for all religions	

Swaraj: It literally means 'self-rule'. But in the system of Gandhiji it has different meanings. First of all, it means national emancipation. In the case of our country it meant termination of the British Raj. Tilak gave the slogan 'Swaraj is our birth right'. Others repeated it many a time. But in the case of Gandhiji, the meaning of Swaraj is tied to the attainment of freedom by means of *ahimsa* and *satyagraha*. It is for this reason that he abruptly suspended the non-cooperation movement in 1922. Second, Gandhiji also interpreted Swaraj as independence within the British empire if possible and without it if necessary. It meant that while he frankly called the alien rule as 'satanic' in 1920, he had no reservations in making peace with the English people if some form of real partnership could be devised between the British Empire and Indian independence. On one occasion he said: "It (Swaraj) means a state such that we can maintain our separate existence without the presence of the English. If it is to be a partnership, it must be a partnership at will."[26]

But the term 'swaraj' has a metaphysical implication also in the system of Gandhiji. It is the name of a hypothetical condition of human life in an ideal society in which everyone has the capacity to resist the abuse of power. That is, Swaraj becomes

26. As a matter of fact, while the leaders of our freedom movement often used the word 'swaraj', they were not very clear in their minds about its implications. At the special Congress session of Calcutta (September, 1920), Lala Lajpat Rai said that this word was deliberately chosen for its ambiguity in order to enable the Indians to remain within the projected commonwealth or to leave it according to their own preferences." While referring to the period of 1920-21, Jawaharlal Nehru recalls: "It was obvious that to most of our leaders Swaraj meant something much less than independence. Gandhi was delightfully vague on the subject and he did not encourage clear thinking about it either." *Autobiography.*, p. 76.

identifiable with Ramraj. On one occasion he said: "By Ramraj I do not mean Hindu raj. I mean by Ramraj divine raj, the kingdom of God... the ancient ideal of Ramraj is one of true democracy."[27] In this way, swaraj implies the reign of complete social justice, equality and freedom. Ramraj is the acme of swaraj. It is not merely a political spirit. It also desires a social order without egotistic interests that cause social conflicts and tensions. Thus, Ramraj is regarded as the kingdom of dharma, non-violent (*ahimsatmak*) swaraj, swaraj of the people, and the final goal of swaraj.[28]

Swadeshi: It literally means something indigenous or home-made. The leaders of the extremist school staged a movement to boycott the use of foreign-made goods and instead desired use of goods made in the country. It was a very powerful instrument used by the early nationalist leaders to defeat the economic or the backbone side of British imperialism. But Gandhiji adopted it as one of his non-cooperation techniques that covered the injunctions of swadeshi and boycott movement. His emphasis on plying *takli* and wearing *khadi* was in tune with the spirit of swadeshi movement. But what is really significant here is that Gandhiji developed this term so as to mean much what we do not find in the case of his predecessors. It is clear from his statement: "After much thinking I have arrived at a definition of Swadeshi that perhaps best illustrates my meaning. Swadeshi is that spirit in us which restricts us to the use and service of our immediate surroundings to the exclusion of more remote. Thus, as for religion, in order to satisfy the requirements of the definition, I must restrict myself to my ancestral religion. This is the use of my immediate religious surroundings. If I find it defective, I should serve it by purging it of its defects. In the domain of politics I should make use of the indigenous institutions and serve them by curing them of their proved defects. In that of economics I should use only things that are produced by my immediate neighbours and serve those industries by making them efficient and complete where they might be found wanting."[29]

Gandhiji takes a very broad view of swadeshi. While an individual should stick to the use of home made goods, he should understand the meaning of *Vasudhev Kutumbkam*. (The whole world is my family.) In fact, he reconciles the idea of swadeshi with the high ideal of cosmopolitanism.

Oceanic Circles: While travelling to England from South Africa by a ship, Gandhiji saw rising tides creating circles within circles and yet all remaining in the same ocean. With this he developed the idea of harmonising his concept of swadeshi with universalism. A person should love his family at the base and the whole universe at the top with his village, city, province, country and state in the middle. All units should be tied to each other with the bond of sacrifice. So in his *Hind Swaraj,* he says that a person should be prepared to sacrice himself for the family, the family for the village, the village for the city, the city for the province, the province for the country and the country for the whole world.

27. Gandhi: *Young India,* 28 May, 1931.
28. K.G. Mashruwala (ed): *Gandhi-Vichar-Dohan,* (Hindi), p. 61.
29. J. von Bondurant, *op. cit.,* pp. 106-7.

Significance: Critics may find faults with the social, economic and political ideas of Mahatma Gandhi, but the following contributions of Gandhism cannot be minimised:

1. The trend of crass materialism as set by Machiavelli and Hobbes has now become so dominant that all aspects of a noble and ideal life have been sacrificed at the altar of an artificial and inhuman way of life. The need of the hour is, therefore, to re-emphasise the value of goals, norms and ideals of human life. The meaning of politics should not be kept confined to the mere scramble for power without any regard for the high principles of life. Viewed thus, we may appreciate this argument: "The fundamental value of Gandhism lies in its stress on the incorporation of moral and spiritual categories in human action which are sadly neglected in materialistic and atheistic civilisation."[30]
2. Gandhiji's unbending resolve to stick to the way of non-violence has an eternal significance. Much damage has been done and is still being done by resorting to violence whose most sinister instances can be seen in the rise of terrorism all over the world. In such a horrible atmosphere, we may feel relief in the way of non-violence that inheres within itself the traits of love, truth and self-sacrifice.
3. Gandhiji's technique of satyagraha has its own significance in that it offers us a new way of solving disputes and redressing grievances in consonance with the way of spiritual salvation. "It may not supersede the method of force but as men grow more powerful in the art of destruction, must supersede it if civilisation is to survive.[31]
4. The critics may scoff at the highly idealistic affirmations of Gandhiji. They may dub his theories as 'utopian'. But we may put aside such accusations. We have already said that political theory should not only deal with things as they have been in the past or exist at present, it should have an ethical overtone. That is, it should be goal-oriented as well. Only such a political theory can show us the way to improve our existing social and political institutions.[32]
5. Above all, the significance of Gandhian social and political philosophy should be understood in the context of its blending of idealism with realism. As a practical idealist, the Mahatma could prove the practicability of his ideas. In this way, Gandhian social and political theory shows a new direction having no parallel

---

30. Varma, *op. cit.,* p. 350. As Pattabhi Sitaramayya says: "By the practice of satyagraha our country was plunged into a world of new values in which hatred and abhorrence, fear and cowardice, anger and vengeance were at once to yield place to service, and in which the enemy is not to be conquered but convereted." *op. cit.,* p. 614.
31. C.E.M. Joad: "The Authority of Detachment and Moral Force' in Radhakrishnan (ed): *Mahatma Gandhi: Essays and Recollections,* p. 171.
32. Realising the limitations of his ideal society, Gandhiji said in 1946: "If Euclid's point, though incapable of being drawn by human agency, has an imperishable value, my picture has its own for mankind to live. Let India live for this true picture though never realisable in its completeness. We must have a proper picture of what we want, before we can have something approaching it."

in the world. An American writer frankly admits: "The search for constructive, creative means has been pressed forward in fields of inquiry peripheral to the study of politics. The political philosopher who would pursue the search for an adequate technique of action can view the Gandhian philosophy of conflict as little more than a point of departure."[33]

We may, therefore, come to endorse the view that the political philosophy of Mahatma Gandhi is very important, because it "is the most original contribution of India to political thought and practice."[34]

33. J. von Bondurant, *op. cit.,* p. 232.
34. Dhawan, *op. cit.,* p. 4.

13
Feminism

Feminism is a form of 'identity politics' in a general sense and an examination of the concept of woman in an effort "to understand, reveal or subvert the sexist practices."[1] The feminists react against the trend or tendency of treating women as 'exchange objects' and in very clear terms, ranging from soft and modest to harsh and immodest, they desire to eliminate the evil of gender inequality and injustice prevailing since ancient times. "A common point for all feminist ideas is the belief that women are disadvantaged in comparison with men, and this advantage is not a natural and an inevitable result of biological differences but something that can and should be challenged and changed. Unlike traditional political theories and ideologies, feminism provides a way of looking at the world that sees women's situations and inequalities between men and women as central political issues; as such, it provides a fundamental challenge to dominant assumptions about the scope and nature of politics."[2]

Nature and Ramifications of the Movement

Among the 'new social movements', feminism has an importance of its own. We may take note of the divergence of views of the leading feminists with regard to the nature and categories of this movement, but all "concern themselves with women's inferior position in society and with discrimination encountered by women because of their sex."[3] Furthermore, all feminists "call for changes in the social, economic, political and cultural order to reduce and eventually overome the discrimination against women.[4] The protagonists of this movement reject the contention that "whereas women have been seen as closer to 'nature', men have been perceived as closer to 'culture', more suited to public role and political association. This is the reason that women have been relegated to a secondary status in society, often confined to the role in homes rather than able to accede to powerful public positions."[5]

Feminism as a movement has both empirical and normative aspects. It is a critique as well as an ideal and, surprisingly, it assumes the form of an ideology in its own right

---

1. Carol Mastrangalo: "Feminism" in Christopher John Murray (ed.): *Encyclopaedia of Modern French Thought,* p. 217.
2. Valerie Bryson: "Feminism" in Roger Eatwell and Anthony Wright (eds.): *Contemporary Political Ideologies* p. 206.
3. Jane Freedman: *Feminism,* p. 1.
4. *Ibid.,*
5. *Ibid.,* p. 10.

in view of its stress as a programme of action aimed at the eradication of all forms of injustice and oppression so that women enjoy a life of security, equality and dignity. As Robert Leach says: "Like other ideologies, feminism involves a critique, an ideal and a programme. The critique contains an analysis of the discrimination and injustices suffered by women in existing society; the ideal is justice for women, generally but not exclusively interpreted to mean sexual equality. The practical programme has included action to achieve political and legal rights, equality in the economic sphere, the elimination of sexual discrimination in education, the workplace and the home, and protection against physical and sexual violence. All political ideologies contain implications for political action, but feminism is markedly action-oriented."[6]

The feminists charge that all social sciences have been designed by men so as to establish and exalt the place of 'man' to the exclusion of 'woman'. In theology God is celebrated as the Father or the Lord. Aristotle's view of natural inequality of mankind confines the life of woman to her household. Weber's theories do not take cognisance of the existence of women. Durkheim's figures for suicide rates do not exclude women, but they are incorporated without any distinct recognition of gender as a meaningful category in their search for variation, proof or validity of his theory of suicide. Surprisingly, Marx's conceptualisation of labour value and work insufficiently recognise women's contribution to the process of social life, to production and social re-production. So in economic theories, concepts and techniques of analysis are generally premised on the insignificance and, indeed, the absence of women. Comte's is only a romanticised exaltation of women's role in the historical process. Malinowski says that 'anthropology is the science of man embracing woman'. In short, in all theories of social sciences, it may be taken note of that man in the sense of 'male' overshadows man in the sense of 'human being' inasmuch as all theories are characterised by their forms of female invisibility—exclusion, pseudo-exclusion and alienation.

Examined from a juristic-cum-sociological standpoint, the same fact stands out. The feminists endorse the view that while inequality between man and woman in many matters has been abolished, the domestic factor has been logically left untouched. So C. Mackinnon complains: "In spite of legal equality injustice remains, because all important roles and positions in the society are gender-based. Every quality that distinguishes man from woman goes in favour of man. For example, men's psychology defines most sports, their needs define auto and health insurance coverage, their socially designed biographies define workplace expectations and successful career patterns, their perspectives and concerns define quality in scholarship, their experiences and obsessions define merit, their objectification of life defines art, their military service defines citizenship, their role in wars and rulership defines history, their image defines God."[7]

As we shall see, the feminist movement is more than two centuries old and its appearance may be noticed in the Western countries like France, Britain and the

6. Robert Leach: *Political Ideology in Britain,* p. 143.
7. Mackinnon: *Feminism Unmodified: Discourses on Life and Law.*

United States. It covered other countries of the world as well in the twentieth century. However, it may be noted that the ramifications of this movement in the West somewhat differ from their counterparts in the East. In the East, the movement has put particular emphasis on crimes against women, surprisingly and shockingly, having their sanction in nasty social traditions such as female infanticide, bride-burning, dowry-demanding and a housewife's suicide owing to family tortures. In such countries, discrimination against women starts in the foetus, proceeds through systematic under-nourishment in childhood and thereafter, deprivation of education in adolescence, and it ends in all sorts of domestic violence done shockingly by the 'femi-nazists' and 'femi-terrorists'. Unfortunately, the degree of discrimination bears no relationship with economic prosperity of the people. Some crimes as those of sexual harassment, assault or molestation may be common to the West and the East. However, the common point in both may be noted in their gender struggle against gender-powerplay or gender politics going to the detriment of the basic interests of women.

We may also take note of this significant fact that the feminist cry for justice forms part of the modern, even post-modern, social and political theory. It takes the movement of women from their 'emancipation' to their 'empowerment'. It hinges on the maxim that their liberation means empowerment and the means to a 'power for' not 'power over'. It signifies honour not domination and, as such, it transcends the phenomenon of leadership. It desires to bring about a new pattern of social order governed by a different set of values and ethos in which equality means no discrimination on the basis of sex in all spheres of public life. The focus is shifted from mere liberation of women to their social, cultural and political empowerment so as to blend their distinct identity with their distinct place in a civilised society. This is the only way to align the ideal of 'good life' with the reality of the 'goodness of life'.

The views of the liberal, socialist (Marxist) and radical feminists followed by those of the black and conservative feminists may not be alike on certain women-related issues, but their common concern with the following points may be noted:

1. Gender-based discrimination should be eliminated. Thus, women should have equality in all spheres which are open to men. It will dispense with their inferior or subordinate position in the society.
2. Women should be liberated from servitude, exploitation and injustice of all kinds. They should be able to lead a life of security and dignity. For this education is very important as it creates such a consciousness in them.
3. Male dominance in the family, in the community and in the state is responsible for the weak position of women. Hence, it should be terminated as far as possible.
4. Women alone can understand and appreciate their problems. They may represent and safeguard their interests themselves.
5. Crimes against women as those of molestation, rape, sexual assault or harassment, dowry-demanding, bride-burning, pornographic displays, etc. can be checked and the grievances of women can be redressed if the women have power. So women

should have proper representation in the national legislature and in all important decision-making bodies.

A woman is a woman and so everywhere the problems of women are the same. Their solution can be sought in the recognition of their identity, in the security of their dignity, and in the elimination of all kinds of discrimination and torture. It is gender bias that "views woman as basically different from man—psychologically, physiologically and often intellectually."[8] This is the way to universalise the feminist movement. It constitutes the case of the 'essentialism' of this movement, but the cracks and contradictions in this movement negate it. It is particularly noticeable in the role of the black feminists who deprecate 'essentialism' as false universalism.

Categorisation of Feminism—Liberal, Socialist (Marxist) and Radical

Feminist movements, as we shall see in due course, transcend national boundaries and touch sensitive issues like those of gender inequality, sexual harassment, exploitation and oppression of women and the like. The question is as to how the problems of women should be solved? For this, feminists have come forward with their demands which range from their enfranchisement to their empowerment. It is in the sphere of their action programme that their agitations are characterised as liberal, socialist (Marxist) and radical. There are sharp differences among the feminists on the nature and ramification of the issues and their proper solution, though all are unanimous on achieving the goal of gender equality and justice.

First of all, we take the case of 'liberal' feminism. It includes all those feminists who campaign for equal rights for women within the framework of a liberal political order. The leaders of this movement argue that the theoretical basis of the state is sound, but the rights and privileges it confers must be extended to women in the same manner as they are available to men. As a matter of fact, in its initial stages, the movement was launched by the leaders of liberal disposition like Olympe de Gouges in France and Mary Wollstonecraft, Harriet Taylor and Lydia Becker in England. They sought equality for both the sexes in matters of civil rights and economic opportunities and considered education as the best means to achieve their objective. Mill's work on the subjection of women was one of the landmarks of British feminist movement in which he provocatively claimed that 'no slave is a slave to the same length and in so full a sense of the word as a wife is'. He demanded women's admissibility to all the functions and occupations hitherto retained as a monopoly of the stronger sex.

The second wave of liberal feminism includes figures like Betty Friedan, Janet Radcliffe Richards and Susan Moller Okin. Friedan advocated the cause of women having a career in the public share without abandoning the traditional values of motherhood and family.[9] In her work *The Skeptical Feminist* (1982) Richards reaffirmed traditional liberal feminist support to reason, equality and social justice. Moller Okin in her work *The Subjection of Women* (1988) sought to extend the Rawlsian theory of justice to the

8. K. Claire Fullenwider: *Feminism in American Politics: A Study of Ideological Influence.*
9. Robert Leach, *op. cit.,* pp. 145-46.

family.[10] Since such demands raised by the earlier leaders of the movement (as equality before law and right to vote) were conceded by the liberal-democratic state of many countries of the West, the modern leaders now came forward with new demands for the empowerment of women in social, cultural and political spheres as the panacea for the elimination of all kinds of discrimination and injustice on the basis of sex. Success could be achieved to a certain extent. For example, in Britain, Equal Pay Act came into being in 1970 and in order to implement it Equal Opportunities Commission was set up.

Liberals are generally criticised by the radicals and the extremists of any hue for being soft and slow-movers. Hence, their achievements are not much appreciated. It is contended that neither rational persuasion nor legal compulsion may be adequate to secure justice for women. Their approach is taken as flawed and inappropriate for the purpose of bringing about radical changes in the desired direction. The distinction between civil society and state, as made by the liberals, is also criticised in the name of narrowing the scope of the movement. Thus, modern feminists "criticise liberals for concentrating on discrimination and injustice in the public sphere of law, politics, school and work, and neglecting women's role in the private world of home and family, to many feminists the very centre of women's exploitation and subordination."[11]

Then, 'socialist' (Marxist) feminism links gender inequality and women's oppression to the capitalist system of production and the division of labour consistent with this system. The division between male and female is merely a product of social power-relations with no basis in nature of human biology. Taking the Marxist line, Wittig argues: "There is no sex. There is but a sex that is the oppressor sex and that oppresses. It is oppression that creates sex and not the contrary."[12] Thus, women are nothing but an oppressed social class. The disappearance of oppression and, therefore, of the dominant and the dominated, will see the elimination of women and of men as distinct groups of human beings. In this world of nature, sex and classes will no longer exist, freedom for all human beings will be attained beyond the categories of sex and both the concept and the real existence of men and women will give way to the advent of individual subjects.[13]

Since Marxism studies politics in terms of class war, these feminists regard women as belonging to the exploited and oppressed class of the society. They refute the argument of an anarchist like Joseph Proudhon that women should not work outside their homes for the obvious reason that it prevents them from securing public employments and working there in a secure and dignified manner. A German socialist Clara Zetkin who had once argued that women needed no special protection other than one given to the

10. *Ibid.*, p. 146.
11. *Ibid.*, pp. 147-48.
12. Monique Wittig: "The Category of Sex" in D. Leonard and L. Adkins (eds.): *Sex in Question: French Materialist Feminism*, p. 25.
13. *Ibid.*, p. 20.

workers in general, changed her view and demanded protectionist legislation in favour of women.[14] The grouse of such feminists is that the women are either denied jobs in public concerns, or they are not paid adequately. Moreover, they suffer from sexual harassment in places of work. They work in very humiliating conditions which open the way for the occurrence of bad events like molestation, torture and rape.

Among other socialist feminists, we may refer to Alison Jaggar who integrates plight of women with the Marxian concept of 'alienation'.[15] Dalla Costa and James give a new twist to the Marxian theory of value by pointing out that the males working in an industry really work for their capitalists and it is possible only due to the fact that the women do much work at home which remains unpaid and unrecognised. The males have abundant time for work, but their work goes to the benefit of the capitalists. It is for this reason that the feminists desire to bring about significant changes in the household and the relationships between men and women in the family.[16]

Not only this, in the poor and backward countries of the world, the women of the lower castes or classes go out for work and the capitalists engage them at a very low payment. The result is that manpower is not fully utilised, while women labour is engaged at a very cheap rate. It certainly goes to the benefit of the capitalist class whether native or foreign. Mies and Shiva call it 'externalisation of costs'.[17] In their view, women in the industrialised world are exploited through 'housewifisation'—a historical process necessary for the growth of industry through which women were and are mobilised as the primary consumers of the products of this industry. These two processes of colonisation and housewifisation are closely and causally interlinked. Firestone coins a term 'cybernetic communism'. In her view, women's liberation is at the very heart of a communist revolution and so cybernetic communism would be achieved only by the abolition of sex class which, in her view, goes deeper than the economic class of traditional Marxist analysis.[18]

The socialist and the Marxist feminists have played a leading role in women's liberation movement by raising the consciousness of women and stimulating their fight in this regard. The demands of the founding conference at Ruskin in 1970, in a large part, reflected such an agenda by including such themes as equality in respect of education, opportunities and payments, 24-hour nurseries, and free contraception and abortion demand. But both the liberal and the radical feminists "contend that socialism and feminism do not invariably go together."[19] Sargent highlights it in his work *The Unhappy Marriage of Marxism and Feminism* (1981). By picking up some threads from this work, Mackinnon argues that while Marxism focuses on work, feminism

14. S. Rowbotham: *Women in Movement: Feminism and Social Action,* p. 146.
15. Alison Jaggar: *Feminist Politics and Human Nature.*
16. Dalla Costa and Selma James: *The Power of Women and the Subordination of the Community* (1972).
17. Maria Mies and Vandana Shiva: *Eco-feminism,* p. 98.
18. S. Firestone: *The Dialectic of Sex,* p. 12.
19. Leach, *op. cit.,* pp. 150.

focuses on sexuality. That is, it lays more emphasis on class exploitation and less on gender discrimination as a result of which the issue of class becomes primary and the issue of gender secondary.[20]

In the end, we take up the case of 'radical' feminism. It may be taken as an extension of liberal feminism with its special stress on the destruction of male dominance in every sphere of social and cultural life whether it is family or the community or the state. Since patriarchal family system is the base of male dominance, it should go. Simone de Beauvoir argues that 'one is not born as a woman, but becomes so'. It implies that woman's inferior position in the society is a social construct and not a natural fact. The liberation of woman thus depends on freeing women from their social construct of the eternal feminine which has reduced them to a position of social and economic inferiority'.[21]

Similar line of thought may be seen in the work of Oakley who explains: "Many classics of feminist writing during this period are hard-hitting elaborations on the basic themes of social construction—society, psychology, sociology, literature, medicine, science, all construct woman differently, slipping cultural rhetoric under the heading of biological fact."[22] In the view of the radical feminists, the problem is neither an adequate legal or political framework as argued by the liberals, nor is it the capitalist system as explained by the socialist and the Marxist feminists but just male domination. Kate Millett gives the slogan: 'Personal is political'. All others cry out: "Everywhere man exploits woman. It is the sex war, not the class war, what is fundamental."[23] Its another characteristic may be seen in its style as its advocates freely to use the language of revolution rather than reform; they challenge and set out to shock. The prevailing time is anger and outrage, and there is a clear difference in approach from that of the liberals. The enemy is male power, embodied in the universal institution of patriarchy.[24]

So the radical feminists widen the implications of the term 'dignity of woman'. They attack pornography which stimulates men to rape woman, or it excites them to do sexual violence againt women. In Britain the leaders of an association named Women Against Violence Against Women (WAVAW) attacked cinema halls and shops selling porn literature. Their argument is that 'pornography is theory, rape is its practice'. Such feminists desire to put woman in the form of a 'new man' that entails the positive exclusion of men. They revolutionise thinking on gender relations and thus convert their commitments into a distinctive political ideology. But the radical forms of this movement have done much harm to it by alienating the support of both the liberal and the socialist (Marxist) feminists. So Friedan claims that their shock tactic has made

20. C. Mackinnon: "Feminism, Marxism, Method and the State: An Agenda for Theory" in *Signs,* 1982, Vol. 7, No. 3, pp. 530-45.
21. Simone de Beauvoir: *The Second Sex* (1949), p. 13.
22. A. Oakley: *Sex, Gender and Society*, (1972), p. 33.
23. Leach, *op. cit.,* p. 152.
24. *Ibid.*

sexual politics a red herring. Radical feminists forget the unforgettable fact that male domination, though ridden with some evils, cannot be dispensed with totally. The truth of the old saying cannot be thoroughly dismissed that 'families need fathers'.[25]

Sub-categorisation: Black Feminism, Conservative Feminism, Eco-Feminism and Post-Feminism

Apart from the three categories of feminism, as discussed above, we may also have a brief look at its allied varieties which are regarded as its 'subsets' and cover the spheres of colour of the skin, attachment with the past, environmental protection and post-structuralism. It should be taken as an extension of what we have said in the preceding section in view of the fact that here we come across a situation comparable with that of wheels within wheels, though connected with each other in some respect like concentric circles. A critic may say that such a categorisation followed by a sub-categorisation of the feminist movement does no justice to the complexity of this momentous subject in spite of the fact that, in the words of A. Nye, it is like 'a tangled and forbidden web'.[26] However, a broad view of this movement shows that it is ridden with multiplicity and so it would not be wrong to use the appellation of feminisms.

First of all, we take up the case of 'black feminism.' The champions of this movement not only fight for the rights of women and their liberation from social injustice like the feminists in general, but they also challenge the superiority of white women and their competence as well as their right to speak for the black women. Its glimpse may be seen in the cry of the American negro women who criticised the role of white women, who even after the abolition of slavery by President Lincoln in 1863 and the sanction of civil rights to them by President Kennedy a century later, still maintained the old psyche in treating black women as 'fallen women, whores and prostitutes'.[27] The state of the devaluation of black womanhood persists and so the feminism of the white and black women cannot be theorised in the same manner.

It follows that the black feminists attack the superiority complex of their white counterparts and desire to fight for their demands after rejecting the claim of 'universal sisterhood' as made by the white women. Audre Lorde, a black lesbian feminist,

25. The radical feminists do injustice to Marx by placing him in an anti-feminist category like Rousseau and Proudhon. Marx says that the modern family "contains in germ not only slavery but it also contains in miniature all the contradictions which later extend throughout society and its state." One may argue that the treatment of Marx is casual, but Engels in his monograph (*The Origin of Family, Private Property and State*) says something for the purpose of the radical feminists. The idea does not seem to have struck Marx very forcibly, but Engels looks into the problem of women and develops a comprehensive theory on this subject. In the *Communist Manifesto* (1848), Marx and Engels say: "The bourgeois sees in his wife a mere instrument of production. He hears that instrument of production are to be exploited in common, and naturally he cannot imagine, but that the women will share the same fate." A. de Reincourt: *Women and Power in History.*, pp. 365-66.
26. A. Nye: *Feminist Theory and the Philosophies of Man*, p. 1.
27. Jane Freedman, *op. cit.*, p. 77.

says: "By and large within the women's movement today, white women focus upon the oppression as women and ignore differences of race, sexual preference, class and age. There is a pretence to a homogeneity of experience covered by the word 'sisterhood' that does not, in fact, exist.[28] Not only are white feminists accused of a false universalisation which hides women's different experiences and situations under the blanket concept of sisterhood, but perhaps even more importantly, they are charged with failure to acknowledge their part in the racist structure of society. Similarly, Herzel Carby argues: "Black feminists have been and are still demanding that the existence of racism must be acknowledged as a structuring feature of our relationships with white women. Both white feminist theory and practice have to recognise that white women stand in a power-relation as oppressors of black women. This compromises any feminist theory and practice founded on the notion of simple equality.[29]

In the light of what we have said above, it may be argued that black feminism has demonstrated the impossibility of untangling race and gender and shown that although dominant discourses may have tried to separate them, the two are inextricably intertwined. So Valerie Smith argues: "Within dominant discourse, race and gender are treated as if they are mutually exclusive categories of experience. In contrast, black feminism presumes the 'inter-sectionality' of race and gender in the lives of black women, thereby rendering inapplicable to the lives of black women any single axis theory about racism or sex."[30]

The black feminists repudiate the contention that the movement for women's liberation was invented in the West, or it has been imposed by the Westerners on the people of the East. Feminist movements have had their own history in the countries of the East like China and India, though it must be admitted that they had an impact on their Western counterparts in the twentieth century particularly during the days of anti-colonial resistances. Kumari Jayawardena of Sri Lanka claims that the struggles for women's emancipation were an essential and integral part of the national movements.[31] Likewise, Uma Narayan of India says: "I am arguing that Third World feminism is not a mindless mimicking of Western agendas in one clear and simple sense that, for instance, Indian feminism is clearly a response to issues specifically confronting many Indian women like dowry-related harassment, rape of women in police custody, poverty, etc."[32] But Cynthia Enloe takes a different view and holds the system of colonialism for being the arch-culprit in this regard. She says: "Colonised women have served as sex objects for foreign men."[33]

---

28. Audre Lorde: *Sister Outside*, p. 116.
29. H.V. Carby: "White Women Listen: Black Feminism and the Boundaries of Sisterhood" in H.S. Mirza (ed.): *Black British Feminism*, p. 46.
30. Valerie Smith: "Split Affinities: The Case of Inter-racial Rape" in M. Hirsch and E. Fox Keller (eds): *Conflicts in Feminism*, p. 272.
31. Jayawardena (ed.): *Feminism and Nationalism in the Third World*, p. 8.
32. Uma Narayan: *Dislocating Cultures: Identities, Traditions and Third World Feminisms*, p. 13.
33. C. Enloe: *Bananas, Beaches and Bases: Making Feminist Sense of International Politics*, p. 44.

One thing is, however, certain that black feminism rejects the case of 'essentialism' of this movement. Essentialism is, of course, a precondition of any kind of normative social and political theory or, indeed to any theory that intends to mobilise people in order to effect social change.[34] A woman is a woman whether white or black, rich or poor, Western or Eastern and the like and only on this basis feminist movement can be universalised. But to create conflicting layers within this movement, as done by the radical and socialist (Marxist) feminists, is to contradict the feature of its essentialism. The black feminists militate against white feminists who, in their view, are not concerned with the similar oppression of all women. If the case of all women is the same, there can be no essential differences between them, but as the white and the black feminists have divergent views, the factor of 'difference' supervenes to negate the feature of similarity. For instance, in Britain black and Asian women have pointed out their distinctive problems and injustices they suffer, leading to claims that the women's liberation movement as a whole is irrelevant to the needs and demands of most black women.[35]

Now we take up the case of conservative or new right feminism. Feminist movement all over the world has been both progressive and reactionary, both leftist and rightist. Mary Wollstonecraft mixed herself with French revolutionaries and yet she married William Godwin, a British anarchist and an anti-feminist. Many nineteenth century women feminists of America were closely associated with the anti-slavery movement. The British Tories always deprecated the moves of the liberal feminists and Margaret Thatcher could agree to assign some subordinate places to women in her Conservative Party. And yet the English feminists appreciate the new right approach of economic liberalisation as it would open avenues of employment for women in the labour market, particularly in the new meritocratic competition for career advancement. As a result of the market-friendly attitude of the state, "the economic position of the women in general has been transformed; their purchasing power in the economy is increasingly evident not only in the advertising of traditional female products but in the promotion of cars, banks and insurance policies."[36]

The new right feminists deplore disintegration of traditional family life and condemn recourse to easy divorce or sexual permissiveness. Family life as coming down from the ages is really a source of comfort, support and fulfilment for women and, as such, family values must be endorsed. Their slogan is 'families need fathers'. At the same time, they join hands with radical feminists in attacking pornography that stimulates

34. This type of essentialism is necessary for social mobilisation and can be a strategic tool to create group identity. And for those who find themselves in dominated or marginalised positions in society, the adoption of fixed or 'essentialised' identities can and does serve as an important strategic tool in their struggle against oppressions". D. Fuss: *Essentially Speaking Feminism, Nature and Difference*.
35. Leach, *op. cit.*, p.156.
36. *Ibid.*, p. 159.

activities of molestation and rape of women. A critic may, however, say that neo-conservative feminism dwindles between the poles of liberal and radical feminisms and stands in the danger of falling between the two stools. Their affirmations on certain points look problematic. So Nietzsche Walter strenuously argues that the feminists "can be conservative" and concedes that "individual women, who are both conservative and feminist, feel isolated and misrepresented by a culture that denies the compatibility of the two creeds."[37]

Some feminists like M. Mies and Vandana Shiva have integrated the issue of environmental pollution with the case of women suffering from social injustice. In their view, ecology is specifically feminist issue. Nature and women are the procreators and sustainers of human beings. Natural forces should be regarded as feminist in view of the fact that they have powers of fertility and birth. If woman gives birth to a child, nature sustains and helps in his healthy development. Exploitation of women and ecological destruction are thus twin evils; woman's knowledge is vital to the maintenance of biodiversity. The feminists argue that 'return to nature' is the only panacea for the ills created by gender discrimination and ecological destruction. "If the world's eco-system and biodiversity are to be conserved, it is, therefore, vital to start listening to women and taking their knowledge seriously.[38] As Mary Mellor points out: "The case made by both eco-centrists and eco-feminists is that the Western model of modernity based on this 'human' is achieved at the expense of both women and nature."[39]

If so, it is clear that women are prominently involved in the Green movement for the simple reason that there is a clear link between their feminist values and their Green commitments. "There is a strong female presence likewise in the associated animal rights and vegetarian movements. It may be that experience of pregnancy, giving birth and child nurture do give women a closer sense of kinship with the natural and animal world. Concern for the health of their children entails perhaps a greater awareness of the possible dangers in the environment and in the food chain. Women's nurturing role also gives them a greater felt stake in the future."[40]

Finally, we take up the case of 'post-feminism'. It is said that the feminist movement is ridden with certain conflicts and contradictions on account of the divergence of views and emphases of the liberal, socialist (Marxist), radical and conservative or new right feminists. At the same time, it is argued by some recent writers that this dilemma may be resolved if we study the case of feminism in the light of post-structuralism or post-modernism. That is, the tenets of the feminist movement should be reconciled with the features of post-modernism and that would lead to the emergence of post-

37. *Ibid.*, p. 160.
38. M. Mies and Vandana Shiva: *Eco-feminism*, p. 167. These two writers regretfully note that the "invisibility of women's work and knowledge arises from the gender bias which has a blind spot for realistic assessment of women's contribution." *Ibid.*
39. Cited in Freedman, *op. cit.*, p. 57.
40. Leach, *op. cit.*, p. 157.

feminism. The post-structuralists segregate what cannot be otherwise segregated; they negate what is universally or generally accepted. They disagree with the finality of any accepted creed or doctrine and so they may find out 'differences' within a woman.[41] They reject the notion of a fixed female identity and, in this way, believe that they overcome the problems of 'essentialism' which other feminists have had to face. For some feminists this move away from fixed knowable identities is a way forward that can overcome the seemingly never-ending debate over equality and difference. Jane Flax argues that feminist theory is necessarily post-modern in that it challenges the natural, fixed and universal definition of gender relations.[42]

Though the number of such feminists is very small, their contention is quite significant. To Patricia Waugh, feminism reacts against ideas emanating from the Enlightenment.[43] The notion of a universal rational subject is inherently masculine. But the difficulty with post-structuralism or post-modernism is that while they negate what is generally accepted, they do not give another meaning that would have finality in its implications. So Chris Weedon, a post-structuralist feminist, committed as it is to the principle of difference and deferral, never fixes meaning once and for all.[44] Niral Yuval-Davis coins the term 'transversal politics' in which perceived unity and homogeneity are replaced by dialogues which give recognition to the specific functionings of those who participate in them as well as to the unfinished knowledge that each such situated positioning can offer.[45]

The success of the feminist movement has certainly raised the status of woman in society and converted her into a 'new man' irrespective of the fact that much still remains to be achieved. The 'new feminism', as it may also be called, desires to see women as self-reliant in securing their aims with this impression in their minds that all men are irredeemably bad as sloganised by the Leeds Revolutionary Group in Britain. More and more success in this direction would certainly transform the state of affairs and create a wishful condition in which men, rather than women, have the problem. Some feminists have seen rationalisation as 'male logic', antipathetic to feminine feeling and intuition. Post-modernist literary criticism has provided feminists with a powerful conceptual framework to reveal the gender-bias in the use of language, to uncover new messages in and behind texts, and to attack traditional male-oriented canons of literary excellence.[46] Liberal feminism thus stands defeated whose champions ever insist that women's liberation would benefit men too.

---

41. J. Evans: *Feminist Theory Today*.
42. J. Flax: "Post-Modernism and Gender in Feminist Theory" in L. Nicholson (ed.): *Feminism/Post-modernism*.
43. Patricia Waugh: "Post-Modernism and Feminism" in S. Jackson and J. Jones (eds): *Contemporary Feminist Theories*, p. 177.
44. C. Weedon: *Feminist Practice and Post-Structuralist Theory*, p. 99.
45. N. Yuval-Davis and F. Anthias: *Women-Nation State*, p. 131.
46. Leach, *op. cit.*, p. 161.

Women Empowerment

Feminism is one of the highly political movements in terms of its attempt to effect social change for the sake of elimination of all kinds of injustice done to women in the name of gender discrimination. The contention of the feminists is that their desired goals cannot be achieved until women share power. After much struggle, the feminists could get the right to vote, but their repeated grouse is that they are under-represented in the legislative chambers and almost unrepresented in crucial decision-making bodies. So Brown argues: "More than any other kind of human activity, politics has historically been an explicitly human activity."[47] Carole Pateman attacks patriarchal system that is male-dominated and links it to the denial of citizenship for women.[48] Patriarchy is then seen as a private familial problem that can be overcome if public laws and policies treat women as if they are explicitly the same as men. Like Olympe de Gouges and Mary Wollstonecraft, Fraisse complains that although women took part in the bloody French revolution, the post-revolutionary regime excluded them from full political citizenship. She refuted Rousseau's argument that 'although women were precious half of the Republic, they made the customs while men made the laws'. Thus, she cried out that personal problems could be solved only through political means and political action.[49]

The feminists reject the notion coming down from the centuries that the personal and public affairs of life can be distinguished in the case of women. In 1792 Wollstonecraft argued: "I really think that the women ought to have representations, instead of being arbitrarily governed without having any direct share allowed to them and the deliberations of the government."[50] Kate Millett asserts that the issue of relationship between the two sexes should be studied in the light of politics what she calls 'informal' or 'institutional' politics.[51] Power-relations operate within primary and social relations as well as within more impersonal secondary social relations of the civil and political domain. In forceful words, Stacey and Price hold: "If women wish to make changes in the society they live in, they must seek and achieve power positions."[52]

The crux of all such arguments is that women must have a say in all social, cultural and political spheres like men, as only then the face of this informal or institutional politics can be changed. Phillips complains that it is patently and grotesquely unfair for men to monopolise representation.[53] If Rousseau argues that the will of a person cannot be represented by another person, so Phillips contends that the interests of the women can be represented only by them. If Mill says that the participation of women in politics would help in the creation of a civilised political culture, Hedlund argues that the

47. W. Brown: *Manhood and Politics*, p. 4.
48. Carole Pateman: *The Sexual Contract*, p. 17.
49. Cited in Freedman, *op. cit.*, p. 27.
50. *Ibid.*, p. 28.
51. Kate Millett: *Sexual Politics*, p. 34.
52. M. Stacey and M. Price: *Women, Power and Politics*, p. 189.
53. A. Phillips: *Feminism and Politics*, p. 229.

women would bring their experience of informal politics into the formal political arena and thus create a more open political culture.[54] Likewise, Anna Jonasdottir maintains: "Women must be visible politically as men, and be empowered to act in that capacity, because there is the continual possibility (not necessity) that they may have needs and attitudes on vital issues which differ from those of men."[55]

Politics is an activity centred on the theme of power. It is power and struggle for its sake. Hence, feminist movement has a patently political character. Since it aims at the presence of women in the legislative chambers and also in the decision-making bodies, it is also known as the 'politics of presence'. The empowerment of women would replace the 'politics of ideas' or mere debates on the social status or issues of women. A male-dominated family is patriarchal; a male-dominated state constitutes the case of public patriarchy. Even in the welfare state, hierarchies of power are male-dominated. "So women have moved out of their position of private dependency as men in the house into a postion of public dependency on the male-controlled state."[56]

Empowerment is envisaged "as an aid to help women to achieve equality with men, or at least to reduce gender gap considerably."[57] It would enable women to perform certain roles which they cannot perform without it. It is indicative of a shift in perspective or emphasis from welfare development to one of development of authoritative decision-making skills. "Empowerment strategies are varied and refer to those ones which enable women to realise their full potential. They consist of greater access to knowledge and resources, greater autonomy in decision-making, greater ability to plan their lives, greater control over the circumstances that influence their lives and, finally, factors which would free them from the shackles of customs, beliefs and practices."[58] New social movements are, by and large, of a defensive character, but they become of a marginally offensive character as well. As is the case with ecological and human rights movements, so is the case with the women's movements which "seek to improve women's position in the society itself, albeit at a time when the economic crisis is undermining women's economic opportunities."[59]

Critical Appreciation

The contributions of women in various walks of life cannot be lost sight of. A long list of eminent figures may be prepared to show the great role played by the women in the making of civilisation and culture of the people. A historian may refer to the names of great queens like Elizabeth I, Victoria and Elizabeth II of England, Christina

54. Cited in Freedman, *op. cit.,* p. 38.
55. K.B. Jones and A.G. Jonasdottir (eds): *The Political Interest of Gender*, p. 53.
56. Freedman, *op. cit.,* p. 44.
57. P.K.B. Nayar: "Empowerment of Women: Its Overall Perspectives" in K. Shanthi (ed.): *Empowerment of Women*, p. 24.
58. Rajkumari Chandrasekharan: "Education Empowers Women", *ibid.,* , p. 77.
59. A.G. Frank and Marta Fuentes: "Nine Theses on Social Movements" in Ghanshyam Shah (ed.): *Social Movements and the State: Readings in Indian Government and Politics,* Part 4, p. 41.

of Sweden, Maria Theresa of Austria and Catherine the Great of Russia. He may also refer to the names of great heads of governments like Golda Meir of Israel, Srimavo Bandarnaike of Sri Lanka, Indira Gandhi of India, Margaret Thatcher of Britain, Angela Merkel of Germany, Benazir Bhutto of Pakistan, Sheikh Hasina and Begum Khaleda of Bangladesh, and Y. Shinwatra of Thailand. He may also refer to the names of the Presidents or the heads of the states like Chandrika Kumaratunga of Sri Lanka, Meghawati Sukarnoputri of Indonesia, Pratibha Patil of India and E. J. Sirleaf of Liberia. A political theorist may admire the ideas of Rosa Luxemburg of Germany, Miss M.P. Follet of America and Hannah Arendt of England.

If the French revolution witnessed the assassination of men like King Louis XVI, Robespierre, Mirabeau, Danton and Mara, it also witnessed the same fate of women like Queen Mary Antoinette, Madame du Barry, Olympe de Gouges and Lucile Desmoulins. A. de Reincourt says: "Yet women did acquire equal respects in one respect—the right to have their heads chopped off like those of their male counterparts."[60] Joan of Arc of France and Laxmibai of India paid with their life for the sake of love for their country. Martin Luther shut the doors of Protestant church for women, but Mary Paker Eddy founded a church for her followers and thereby she solved the problem of women's place in the Christian religion. She undid Luther and Calvin and got the nickname of 'God-like man' and 'God-like woman', 'God anointed'. Germaine de Stail played a crucial part in the downfall of Napoleon Bonaparte and commented that the 'genius has no sex'. Like Socrates, Rosa Luxemburg paid the price with her life for the freedom of thought and expression. Many more brilliant names may be added to this catalogue to demonstrate the great services and sacrifices of women in the construction and reconstruction of human civilisation and culture. Memorable are the words of Rabindranath Tagore: "Deprived of *Shakti,* the creative process in society languishes and man, losing his vitality, becomes mechanical."

And yet the feminist movement may be said to suffer from certain weaknesses which may be enumerated as follows:

1. All categories of the feminists have sharp differences among themselves on many crucial issues. While the liberals feel satisfied if the women are enfranchised and they have their representation in the national legislature and in some important decision-making bodies, the socialists (Marxists) identify 'sex war' with 'class war' and so clamour for their abolition, while the radicals want to destroy male-dominance in every sphere. Family cannot be identified with a class and to think in terms of its abolition defies commonsense. Patriarchy is an age-old institution that cannot be terminated as desired by the radical feminists.

2. The feminists forget that, biologically or naturally, the women are weak and so they should stop at a point in demanding equality with men. The rash statement of Nietzsche should not be mercilessly discarded, rather it should be taken with a cool mind that "men are trained for war, and women for the procreation of

60. A. de Reincourt, *op. cit.,* p. 360.

the warriors." They should realise that hard and hazardous tasks are not meant for women. They may operate a computer, but they cannot defend the Siachen glacier. Only men can provide security to women. The feminists forget that in the name of equality, they want much more than that. They want to share all rights which are available to men and, at the same time, they claim for themselves all other privileges available to them since the dawn of civilisation. They would like to have administrative and police offices, but would shirk in leaving their homes after sunset. Chantal Mouffe calls it 'Wollstonecraft's dilemma'. As A. de Reincourt says: "In a nutshell, many contemporary women would like to have their cake and eat it too—share with the men the status, power and privileges that they apparently enjoy in social and professional life, while keeping all the special privileges that were allotted to women as compensation for having been virtually idled by the machine. This, of course, will never come to pass."[61]

3. The feminists should also keep in their mind the psychological fact that by nature women harbour feelings of grudge towards other women. This point may well be taken note of in the movement of the black feminists who have their grievances against white women. Schopenhauer is not wrong in his assessment: "The natural feeling between men is mere indifference, but between women it is actual enemity.... Even when they meet women in the street, women look at one another like Guelphs and Ghibbelines."[62] It is also a fact that the women lack in some other respects. For instance, their contribution is negligible in the field of scientific research. Marie Curie, who could win a Nobel prize by virtue of being a partner of her husband, said that 'women of genius are rare'. Such an impression was in the mind of Queen Victoria when she deprecated the movement for female franchise.[63]

4. The feminists take a wrong view of the patterns of social and political life of human beings. They ignore the reality of religious and cultural norms which determine the composition and operation of family life. The two sexes constitute a family, the family grows into a community for whose security and protection state ushers in. Division of labour becomes a natural development. Men and women put together manage all private and public spheres in their respective domains. The evil of male-dominance cannot be ignored, but to do away with it in entirety would be like jumping from a fry pan into the fire. The relationship between the two sexes should be of a positive not negative, or a cooperative not conflicting nature. It should be inspired by the bonds of reciprocity, tolerance, communion, concord and harmony between the two sexes.

---

61. *Ibid.,* p. 415.
62. Cited in A.de Reincourt, *op. cit.,* p. 316.
63. "The Queen is most anxious to enlist everyone who can speak or write or join in checking that mad, wicked folly of 'Women's Rights' with all its attendant horrors, on which her poor feeble sex is bent, forgetting every sense of womanly feeling and propriety. Lady Anderlay ought to get a *good whipping.*" *Ibid.,* p. 315.

5. Above all, the feminists, like the idealists and the anarchists, go to the extent of rambling in utopia. They look for a social and political order in which women have full equality with men and that they enjoy power after dismantling all bastions of male dominance. As Rousseau's natural born man would see the end of his chains in a community in which each citizen is a ruler and the ruled, or in Gandhi's Ram Raj there 'would be no distinction between a prince and a pauper and that justice would be done even to the dog', so the feminists have a dream of their own. For every action-oriented programme sky is the limit, but the feminists in their fit of zeal may desire to go beyond it.

Since nature has made the woman weak and also 'incomplete', the feminists should struggle for the achievement of equality for the women with a sense of caution. The Hindi word '*stree*' (woman) is such in which no letter is full. It is a collection of half letters which signifies that woman is just half and her fullness comes with her association with man. The English word 'femina' comes from Fe and Minus. Thus, the etymology of this word indicates that the element of 'minus' very much exists in the word 'femina' itself. What is needed, however, is that the liberation of women should not be done at the cost of dehumanisation of the existing society. In 1872 the Gordian brothers, the anarchists, established an association in Spain to realise the goal of 'gynatropism' which implied emancipation and humanisation of women.[64]

64. *Ibid,* p. 336.

14
Multiculturalism

Liberalism has seen its astonishing triumph in the age of globalisation and yet its critics have hit at its inadequacies by throwing light on certain new themes related to the 'politics of identity or recognition'. Multiculturalism is one of them. Its ardent advocates like Charles Taylor, Will Kymlicka and Bhiku Parekh lay stress on the fact that cultures have their unique and authentic essences. As such, liberal social and political orders should be based upon guaranteed basic freedoms having their source in the cultural contexts. Hence, multiculturalism having its core implication in the case of active citizenship or civic republicanism looks like hovering between the poles of liberalism and communitarianism.

Nature and Essential Implications

The phenomenon of cultural pluralism may be noticed in almost all countries of the world. It may be owing to many factors such as migration of the people whether as fleeing refugees or as inspiring visitors in search of work or some gainful engagement. The influx of such people and their contact or assimilation with the culture of the natives may be compared with the 'melting pot' or 'salad models'. That is, either such elements happily or willy-nilly merge themselves with the people of that country and thereby lose their distinct identity as may be noticed in the United States or it is also possible that such elements desire to maintain their distinct identity like the ingredients of a 'salad bowl' (Ashish Nandy) or a 'sandwitch' (Yogesh Atal) and thereby create the scenario of 'insider/outsider duality' (R.K. Merton). In fact, the present concern for multiculturalism in academic circles is attributed to this new and emerging phenomenon.

The 'insider/outsider duality' creates a situation of resistance as well as of resilience depending upon the attitude of such numerically smaller and diverse groups. Certain elements may adhere to their distinct identity of course, but with the change of time, such resistance becomes weak. The line of distinction between the 'insider' and the 'outsider' is gradually blurred. The element of innovation imperceptibly creeps into the core of the culture and thus the process of resilience remains at work. It denotes the capacity of a culture to withstand shock so as not to allow any kind of breakdown, rupture or deformation of the cultural system of a country as a whole. "Resilience may be equated with the pliancy of a bamboo—'bending with the storm but not breaking'. It is a synonym of 'homeostasis' or 'Gaia', springing back to former position: recidivism."[1]

A liberal-democratic order requires active participation of the people in the political process of the country. As such, active citizenship involves the stance of multiculturalism that provides ample material for the study of the politics of 'identity', or 'recognition', or 'difference'. It emerged as a theoretical stance through the activities of the 'Black Panthers' in the United States in the 1960s, but it, in a short course of time, covered all agitations of the excluded, marginalised or stigmatised sections of the society in other countries of the world. It hinted at the communal diversity usually arising from racial, ethnic, linguistic and sexual differences that created a typical consciousness among the people belonging to such groups. The movements of the Negroes, minorities, depressed classes, women, etc., appeared in the form of political assertiveness that sometimes became violent to the extent of breaking the bonds of national identity. The notable point is that such groups demonstrate their pride in their 'exclusive identity' which they like to preserve and then demand a proper place for themselves in the social and political set-up of the country.

Multiculturalism, therefore, attaches importance to the separate and distinct identity of certain neglected and stigmatised sections of the society. Its advocates proudly claim and desire to preserve their distinct recognition and, at the same time, struggle for having a respected place in the political community so that they are not treated as 'second-rate citizens'. The main features of this trend may be enumerated as follows:[2]

1. Distinctive cultures deserve to be protected or strengthened particularly when they belong to minority or vulnerable groups.
2. Such a position is based upon a belief in value pluralism, the idea that there is no single or overriding conception of good life, rather there are many competing conceptions.
3. Such groups are entitled for 'social justice' and so the state should adopt the policy of affirmative action for the benefit of the unprivileged sections of the society.
4. Such groups are no longer willing to be silenced or marginalised, or to be defined as 'deviant' simply because they differ in race, culture, gender, ability or sexual orientation from the so-called 'normal' citizens. They demand a more inclusive conception of citizenship which recognises (rather than stigmatises) their identities and which accommodates (rather than excludes) their differences.
5. It desires a pluralistic order ensuring differentiated citizenship.

It is obvious that multiculturalism is a new variety of liberalism that attaches particular significance to the rights and freedoms of the hitherto neglected, excluded

1. Yogesh Atal: "Culture and Human Development" in *Madhya Pradesh Journal of Social Sciences,* Ujjain, Vol. 11, No. 1,2006, p. 35.
2. Andrew Heywood: *Political Theory: An Introduction,* pp. 215-16.

and humiliated people and, at the same time, desires to maintain their distinct place in a pluralistic society and a democratic state. It rejects the case of a fascist system which imposes a particular kind of culture on all sections of the people; it also reacts against the tendency of forced assimilation of different stocks of people in a particular pattern of *vox* (community) by a dictatorial state. A system of equality of rights with the equality of worth and dignity of all the members of a political community should be maintained to realise the ideal of unity in diversity.

Multiculturalism, therefore, attacks the present order based on social and political injustice it also offers remedial measures for its eradication. It focuses on cultural injustices rooted in social patterns of representation, interpretation and communication, including cultural domination (being subject to patterns of interpenetration associated with another culture); non-recognition (being rendered invisible in the authoritative communicative practices of one's culture) and disrespect (being disparaged in stereotypical public cultural representations or in everyday life interactions. Its targets are status groups, defined by relations of recognition in which they enjoy lesser esteem, honour and prestige than the other groups. It aims to affirm group differences. The remedy is cultural or symbolic change to upwardly revalue disrespected identities and cultural products of maligned groups, or positively value cultural diversity.[3]

Liberalism and Its Inadequacy

Multiculturalism may exist and prosper only in a liberal-democratic order where essential freedoms of the people are legally recognised and the state has no power to suppress or virtually blot out the minorities. People belonging to multicultural groups have the right to preserve their distinct identity so much so that they enjoy the status of 'nationalities' in a nation-state. The state may recognise four languages as in Switzerland (French, German, Roman and Swiss), or two languages (English and French) as in Canada. It is also possible that in a pluralistic social order, the state may have only one national language as we may see in the United States and the United Kingdom. It is also possible that the state may put a ban on the wearing of a particular dress by a community (as the wearing of veil by the Muslim women in France) for the reasons of security. But the state should not dispense with the separate or distinct identity of multicultural groups. Only in a fascist system it may happen like the torture of the Jews in Germany, of the Kurds in Iraq, and of the Christians in Sudan and Lebanon.

A liberal-democratic state adopts a soft attitude towards various multicultural groups. At the same time, it is desired that distinct identities should have their volitional assimilation with the national mainstream. Still, there remains a possibility of some kind of discrimination against some groups or communities and the state is accused of 'benign neglect' towards them. For this reason, the communitarians (as Michael Walzer and A. Maclntyre) attack the liberal democratic order for ignoring the case of

3. Kymlicka: *Contemporary Political Philosophy: An Introduction* (Delhi: Oxford University Press, 2005), pp. 332-33.

the 'public good'. They redefine the premises of liberalism in a way that the interest of the individual is dominated by the consideration of the public good. Liberal majorities and communitarian minorities should enjoy equality in terms of rights, opportunities and positions of honour in the midst of a common national language and some common social institutions.

Obviously, multiculturalism desires a modified or revised liberal-democratic order that ensures 'civic nationalism' or 'societal culture'. That is, it calls for a territorially concentrated culture, centred on a shared language which is used in a wide variety of societal institutions in both public and private life (schools, media, law, economy, government, etc.). In other words, it "involves a common language and social institutions rather than common religious beliefs, family customs or personal life styles. Societal cultures within a modern liberal democracy are inevitably pluralistic, containing Christians as well as Muslims, Jews, and atheists; heterosexuals as well as gays; urban professionals as well as rural farmers; conservatives as well as socialists. Such diversity is the inevitable result of the rights and freedoms guaranteed to liberal citizens, particularly when combined with an ethnically diverse population. The diversity, however, is balanced and constrained by linguistic and institutional cohesion; cohesion that has not emerged on its own, but rather is the result of deliberate state policies."[4]

Multiculturalism may survive and develop only in a liberal social and political order. However, Bhiku Parekh (who worked as the Chairperson of the Commission for Racial Equality set up by the British Government) hits at its inadequacy.[5] He is of the view that all societies are multicultural and that this phenomenon shall survive in the times to come. It should not be studied with a sense of scorn or fear, because it is the way to properly understand human society. This multicultural perspective is a consequence of mutually constructive effects of mutually complementary visions. It may be noted in the following three directions:

1. Each community is rooted in a cultural context and its members are born and brought up in the same. They organise themselves in the same cultural structure, they attach value to it and thereby they maintain their distinct identity. It is, however, possible that sometimes they are critical of their own cultural contexts, or they go to the extent of emulating the cultural contexts of others. And yet they evaluate other cultural systems with the help of their own ethical standards.
2. Different cultures represent some patterns of 'good life' along with varying dimensions of its philosophy. It is, therefore, required that one should mix with the people of other cultures to expand his ethical horizon. He may have a view of 'good life' of his own, but he may expand or develop it after realising that no

---

4. *Ibid.*, p. 346.
5. Bhiku Parekh: *Rethinking Multiculturalism: Cultural Diversity and Political Theory* (Basingstroke: Palgrave Macmillan, 2000).

culture is either significant or insignificant in an absolute sense. Hence, he has no right to impose his value-judgement on others.

3. Putting aside the case of very primitive communities, Parekh argues that each developed culture is inherently plural and a constant interaction goes on between its varying traditions and currents of thought. It absorbs the traits of other cultures, albeit in an autonomous manner, and then gives a new shape or definition to its norms. Each culture affects other cultures and, at the same time, is affected by them. All epithets like Euro-centrism, Afro-centrism, West-centrism, etc., are baseless, because they falsify the total history of cultures.

No particular ideology can serve the purpose of multiculturalism in view of the fact that it lacks a holistic framework. Whether liberalism claiming itself to be based on the high ideals of liberty, equality, justice and humanism, or any variety of socialism (Fabianism or Communism) having its aim in the establishment of a society free from the evils of exploitation, oppression and injustice, take a partial view of the cultural reality, or present before us a partisan picture of 'good life'. Liberalism may, of course, be admired for advocating the values of human dignity, autonomy and egalitarianism, but it forbids their interpretation in a different way. As such, it becomes an ideology in its own right that makes its believers insensitive to the cultural norms and traditions of the marginalised sections of the society.

In this way, Parekh argues that liberalism draws a maginot line between the culture of the majority and that of the minority. It informs the members of the majority culture to be obstinate and egotist in their behaviour towards the people subscribing to other ways of life. What is, therefore, required is that multiculturalism should not be treated as a nightmare, rather attempts should be made to reshape social, political and economic institutions so as to preserve and nurture ethical traits of all cultures existing in the state. It is clear that he advances a defence of pluralistic perspective on cultural diversity and highlights the inadequacy of liberal multiculturalism. His view "is based upon a dialectical interplay between human nature and culture, in which human beings are culturally constituted in the sense that their attitudes, behaviour and ways of life are shaped by the groups to which they belong. The complexity of human nature is thus reflected in the diversity of cultures."[6]

Varieties of Multiculturalism

Multiculturalism may be seen in the existence of the 'minorities' of various hues in many states of the world. There may be 'national minorities' (as the Tamils in Sri Lanka, the Hindus in Pakistan and the Muslims in France), or 'immigrant groups' (as the Bangladeshis in India, the Muhajirs in Pakistan and the Chinese in Indonesia), or 'isolationist ethnic and religious groups' (as the Mexicans in the United States and the Jews in the Russian Federation), 'metics' or 'resident aliens' (as the Turks in Germany and the North Africans in Italy) and the 'African-Americans' or negroes in the States of USA. Examples may be multiplied and the points of difference in their status in

6. Heywood, *op. cit.*, p. 217.

different countries may also be noted. For instance, in some countries these people have rights equal to those of the citizens, or they may be victims of some kind of discrimination. They may have the status of 'stateless people' or 'partial citizens' as well.[7]

Such groups may feel like 'sub-state nations' or citizens deprived of former power, glory and status. Such people form their unions or organisations to fight for their specific interests. The question is as to what they should do to redress their grievances or to immunise themselves from the onslaught of injustice. Such groups may choose the course of leaving their country and taking shelter in some friendly country as was done by the Germans of Kazakhistan who, after the disintegration of the USSR in 1991, moved to Germany. It is also possible that they fight for 'autonomy' and may feel satisfied by having their institutions of governance at the local and regional levels like the Roman Catholics in Northern Ireland. Then, it is also possible that such groups have their integration with the majority culture on some better or fairer terms as we may see in the case of the French people in the English-dominated provinces of Canada. The last option is that such groups accept permanent marginalisation without murmur as the Tibetans in China.

This fact cannot be refuted that such 'minorities' have to suffer injustices of different kinds, for example, in the form of separate classes of the Turkish children in some states of Germany, or ban on wearing head scarf for the Sikh males in France or non-availability of citizenship of the United States to a foreigner on the ground of his ignorance of the English language and the like. The result is that the deprived and segregated sections of the people agitate and their struggle may assume the form of a civil war as happened in Serbia, Croatia and Kosovo of former Yugoslavia. The best way to deal with such sensitive problems is to create conditions so that such people join the national mainstream. At the same time, this point should be repeated that no association or group claiming its separate and distinct identity should be allowed to subvert the constitutional framework of the liberal-democratic nation-state. In the advanced democracies of the West it has been possible by making "a complex package of robust forms of nation-building combined and constrained by robust forms of minority rights."[8]

Multiculturalism and the Case of Human Development and Human Rights

The theme of multiculturalism has carved its place in the study of development in its revisited form. The idea of development, which was once confined to the economic domain, has now assumed a human face. In the case of the Third World countries, development became a sort of ideology for rapid, planned and directed cultural change. The newly independent nation-states sought to move in a pre-determined direction with defined goals and targets as well as with preconceived strategies. It created a revolution of rising expectations. But the results were frustrating. The process of

7. Jeff Spinner: *The Boundaries of Citizenship, Race, Ethnicity and Nationality in the Liberal State* (Baltimore: John Hopkins University Press, 1994).
8. Kymlicka, *op. cit.*, p. 365.

development, in fact, created wider disparities, broadened the divide between the rich and the poor sections of the people, and even falsified many tenets of modernisation. The institutions or the mechanisms imported from the advanced countries of the West failed to yield positive dividends.

This realisation led to the reconsideration of development strategies. That is why, the United Nations started talking in terms of human development. The World Summit on Social Development held at Copenhagen (1995) voted for a central role of culture. It was taken into recognition that the roots of social breakdown or disintegration were embedded in the cultural contexts. The result is that the word 'development' assumed a new meaning—enhancement of the effective freedom of the people involved to pursue whatever they have reasons to value. Good life is to be an ideal, but it may have numerous forms or norms. As the Report of the World Commission on Development says: "This view of human development (in contrast to narrow economic development) is a culturally conditioned view of economic and social progress. Poverty of life, in this view, implies not only lack of essential goods and services, but also lack of opportunities to choose a fuller, more satisfying, more valuable and valued existence. The choice can also be for a different style of development, a different path, based on different values from those of the highest income countries now. The recent spread of democratic institutions, of marked choices, of participatory management of firms, has enabled individuals and groups and different cultures to choose for themselves."[9]

Like development, the issue of human rights constitutes an integral part of the comprehensive study of multiculturalism. Laski says that a state is known by the system of rights it maintains and that such a system creates the conditions in which a person may have the best possible development of his personality. The Protection of Human Rights Act (1993) of India defines "human rights as those relating to life, liberty, equality and dignity of the individual guaranteed by the Constitution or embodied in the International Covenants." Thus, a positive approach to the subject of human rights "necessitates constructive reconciliation between individual and community, universality and specificity, and non-discrimination principle of equality and social justice."[10]

Obviously, such an interpretation contradicts the Benthamite principle of the 'greatest good of the greatest number' and instead endorses the view of John Stuart Mill that in a democratic system minorities must not be blotted out. The fact of social plurality or multiculturalism cannot be lost sight of in any political system whether democratic or not. The laws of the state must protect the interests of all whether those in majority or in minority. A situation should not be allowed to exist in which discrimination or protective discrimination of any kind creates inequality upon inequality. The commands

9. *Our Creative Diversity-Report of the World Commission on Culture and Development,* UNESCO, Paris, 1995, p. 22.
10. V.K. Tyagi: "Dynamics of Human Rights in a Federal Polity: The Indian Experience" in *Madhya Pradesh Journal of Social Sciences,* Ujjain, Vol. 13, No. 1, 2008, p. 2.

of the state affect different communities in different ways of course, but the salient fact should be borne in mind that the principles of liberal democracy and the universal agenda of human rights do not address the disadvantages to which minority groups are subjected.[11] Group-differentiated rights can only help rectify the disadvantage by alleviating the vulnerability of minority cultures to majority decisions. These external protections ensure that the members of the minority have the same opportunity to live and work in their own cultures as members of the majority. The principle of pluralism, therefore, renders the presumption of homogeneity and uniformity of cultural mode in a multicultural, multi-religious, multiethnic, multi-caste and multiregional society theoretically, empirically and operationally invalid."[12]

Multiculturalism has its blending with anti-colonialism and post-colonialism when its theorists stretch their canvas to compare the case of human rights with a sort of cultural or ethnic dominance. They question the relevance and value of human rights in modern, open and pluralistic societies. "In particular, they reflect a form of ethnocentrism, in which the norms and values of dominant cultural groups take precedence over those of minority cultural groups. Anti-colonial and post-colonial theories have at times portrayed the doctrine of human rights as an example of cultural imperialism."[13] They discover its panacea in the existence of active citizenship that may allow room for weightage in favour of certain minority groups. The traditional conception of citizenship "is based on the idea of universality, and derives its emancipatory character from the notion that disadvantaged groups may aspire to fulfil citizenship rights. Multiculturalists, however, argue that in view of the deeper cultural and moral diversity of modern societies, citizenship should be 'differentiated' to take account of the special rights of particular cultural groups."[14]

Critical Appreciation

The idea of multiculturalism has its positive and negative aspects. In its defence, it may be said that it enables the 'minorities' of any hue to preserve their distinct identity by living in a liberal-democratic state and also seek their development like other people in majority. It embodies the ideal of 'unity in diversity'. There may be many models of 'good life', but their operation is possible only in a multicultural order. The merit of everyone should be recognised regardless of the fact that he belongs to a 'minority' community. Such groups play a significant part in the nation-building process as well as in the operation of a pluralistic system. The communitarians are justified in dismissing the idea of the 'unencumbered self' and in arguing that the 'politics of the rights' should be replaced by the 'politics of the common good'.

11. Gurpreet Mahajan: *Identities and Rights: Aspects of Liberal Democracy in India* (New Delhi: Oxford University Press, 1998), p. 2.
12. Tyagi, *op. cit.,* p. 4.
13. Heywood, *op. cit.,* p. 191. Elsewhere, he says: To define certain values as 'established', 'traditional' or 'majority values' may simply be an attempt to impose a particular moral system upon the rest of the society." *Ibid.,* p. 271.
14. *Ibid.,* p. 219.

On the other side, multiculturalism foments anti-national tendencies. It is a great obstacle in the way of the realisation of the goal of national integration. The groups of the German people living in the states of Austria and Czechoslovakia supported Hitler's call for pan-Germanism and thereby Germany could swallow the whole of Austria and Sudetenland of Czechoslovakia. The groups of the Chinese people living in the countries of South-East Asia obdurately stick to their distinct identity and often create problems for the governments of Indonesia and Vietnam. Such groups may join hands with other secessionist and terrorist elements living abroad and then may create problems in a country like India and the Russian Federation.

Like nationalism and racialism, multiculturalism is just another form of collectivism that subordinates the rights and needs of the individuals to those of the social group. Thus, it threatens individual freedom and personal self-development. An Indian writer Amartya Sen in his book *Identity and Violence* (2006) calls multiculturalism as a 'solidaristic theory' which suggests that human identities are formed by the membership of a single social group. Thus, it leads to the 'miniaturization of humanity'; it also makes violence more likely as the people identify themselves alone with their monoculture and fail to recognise the rights and integrity of people from other cultural groups. Multiculturalism thus breeds a kind of 'ghettoisation' that diminishes, rather than broadens, cross-cultural understanding. The solidaristic thinking is also evident in ideas that emphasise the incompatibility of cultural traditions what S.P. Huntington calls 'clash of civilisations.'[15]

To sum up, the phenomenon of multiculturalism has negative and positive aspects. As Atal says: "Increasing geographical mobility and resettlement of migrant groups in different lands has made most cultures plural societies. The migrant groups evolve their own mechanisms to preserve their cultural identity and yet develop interfaces with the culture of the host society. The emerging culture of the immigrants is the result of sandwiching between the forces of the host culture and the parent culture. Since host cultures vary, the sandwich cultures of peoples originating from the same country but settled in different countries also differ. The existence of sandwich cultures will make cultures more diverse and heterogeneous."[16]

We may safely conclude that the spectre of multiculturalism elicits starkly different political responses. Its supporters highlight its personal and social advantages in stressing the extent to which human beings are culturally embedded. Hence, cultural diversity "promotes the vigour and health of society, each culture reflecting a particular range of human capacities and attributes. By contrast, its critics portray multicultural societies as inherently fractured and conflict-ridden, arguing that successful societies must be based upon shared values and a common culture."[17] One may fondly hope

15. Andrew Heywood: *Political Ideologies: An Introduction,* IV ed., 2011, p. 330.
16. Yogesh Atal: "Asian Cultures: What Destination?" in E.B. Masini and Yogesh Atal (eds.): *The Future of Asian Cultures,* Bangkok, UNESCO, 1993, p. 17.
17. Heywood, *op. cit.,* p. 49

that in the age of globalisation multiculturalism "would be superseded by a genuine form of cosmopolitanism. The differences of culture and nationality would be regarded as affairs of secondary importance, as everywhere the people would come to view themselves as 'citizens of the world' united by a common interest in addressing ecological, social and other challenges that are increasignly global in nature."[18]

18. Heywood: *Political Ideologies,* pp. 329-30.

15
Humanism

Like liberalism, humanism is a very flexible idea; a principle, a doctrine, a tendency, an outlook, and a way of life that may not be put into the category of an ideology. And yet this can be done if we take note of the fact that its adherents demonstrate their unshakeable love for the liberty and dignity of the individual. Its advocates denounce medieval times as 'dark ages', because during the long era of about one thousand years there was no light of learning or knowledge owing to the hold of Christianity that made everything God-centred. The existence of man as a rational creature was mercilessly ignored. The sun of knowledge arose after the fourteenth century when the pioneers of humanism recalled the ideas contained in ancient Greek and Latin classics and thereby they established the supremacy of man as a rational being. Physics replaced metaphysics and God-centredness was replaced by man-centredness. Spratt proudly declares: "We set forth in complete outline a definite ideology.... We want to open the frontiers, to open the windows, to let all the winds of the world blow over the land, the art, the literature, the science, the technology of the world, to let people know them and enjoy them and profit for them."[1]

Meaning and Nature: Humanism appeared as a movement representing an extensive change—almost in the nature of a profound mutation—in the realms of art, literature and philosophy. It occurred in Western Europe at the close of the Middle Ages and in early modern times. Its pioneers developed an increasing interest in Greek and Latin classics. They refuted the prevailing beliefs, rather myths, in supernaturalism as preached by the Christian Fathers on account of which it became indistinguishable from paganism. It is, therefore, correctly observed that, more than any other series of events, it signified a marked transition from medieval to modern times. Its spirit expressed itself in the form of a revolt against sacerdotalism, a layman's rebellion against the tyranny of the churchmen, a declaration of the independence of thought from the restrictions of ecclesiastical authority."[2]

Though humanism had its dominant place in the spheres of art, literature and philosophy, it covered political sphere as well. The pioneers invoked the teachings of great Greek thinkers that 'man is a rational being' and that 'he is the measure of all things.' Casting aside all whims of metaphysics, they laid stress on man's being the centre and the sanction of all affairs. In this new intellectual climate, it was felt that

1. M.N. Roy and Philip Spratt: *Beyond Communism,* pp. 22-28.
2. E.P. Cheysney: "Humanism" in *Encyclopaedia of the Social Sciences,* edited by E.A.R. Seligman, Vol. VII, p. 537.

if men were to lead their lives in fullness and freedom, they must be independent of the tyranny exerted by the church, the state and the society. It is a fact that scientific researches broke the shackles of medievalism and thereby played their part in the rapid growth of humanistic thought. It is also a fact that natural scientists regarded man as a creature whose life is governed by the inexorable laws of the material world. Hence, F.C.S. Schiller comments that "on its critical side, humanism was essentially a protest against the dehumanising and depersonalising freedom which seemed to characterise both the natural sciences and absolutist metaphysics."[3]

The history of humanism is quite old. In ancient Greece, philosophers like Socrates, Plato, Aristotle and Protagoras laid stress on the rational faculty of man that required freedom of thought and expression. It had its doom in the Middle Ages when the churchmen preached that 'God writes the destiny of man with His finger'. Thus, the 'man-centred' thought was replaced by the 'God-centred' dogma. St Augustine formulated the 'tale of two cities'—earthly and heavenly—and advised the religious heads to show the path of salvation to the laymen. Earthly city was thus subordinated by the heavenly city and thus the temporal sphere became the handmaid of the spiritual sphere. It implied that man could do nothing of his own by his will inasmuch as he was like an entity acting according to the will of God.

Renaissance occurred in the fourteenth and fifteenth centuries. It revived the traditions of the ancient Greek and Latin classics. It was admired as the 'rebirth of pagan antiquity'. In Italy Machiavelli identified destiny with a woman and advised man to keep it under his strong control. Secularism replaced theocracy which made the state independent of the control of the church. In England Hobbes condemned the hold of the religious heads in very harsh words so much so that Bishop Bramhall nicknamed him as the 'monster of Melmsbury'. In France, Rousseau and in Germany, Kant laid stress on the rational faculty of man. Such ideas not only awakened the dormant spirit of the individuals, it also inspired them to rise in revolt against absolutist hold of the monarchs and their privileged supporters.

It is due to the rising tide of humanism in early modern times that the English people fought against their king (Charles I) and executed him in 1649. They rejected the claim of the monarch that his rights had a divine origin, instead they established the tradition of political authority based on the will of the people. The Americans overthrew the hold of the British in 1776. The Delaration of Independence drafted by Thomas Jefferson affirmed that 'governments are instituted among men deriving their just powers from the consent of the governed'. In 1789 a violent revolution occurred in France where the people raised the slogan of 'Liberty, Equality, Fraternity'. They assassinated their Emperor (Louis XVI) in 1791. The Declaration of the Rights of Man and Citizen affirmed that "men are born, and always continue to be, free and equal in respect of their rights." These great events terminated the age of absolute monarchies and cleared the way for the advent of the democratic system based on the pillars of liberty and equality. In this way, the nineteenth and twentieth centuries witnessed the triumph of humanism.

---

3. *Ibid.*, p. 543.

Maxims of Humanism

1. Man is the central issue or a matter of main concern.
2. Man is the maker of his own destiny as well as of this world.
3. Man's experience is the source of all values.
4. Search for truth and freedom constitutes the basic urge of human progress.
5. Liberty and dignity of man should not be undermined, or suppressed or sacrificed at the altar of society or state or any other form of collective ego like nationalism or communism. Man should struggle for freedom in an ever-increasing manner.
6. Men have an inalienable right to overthrow an unjust political order.
7. Ringing out of the background of the law-governed physical nature, man is essentially rational. Reason is a biological property, it is not an anti-thesis of will.
8. Ideation is a physiological process resulting from the awareness of environment.
9. A social renaissance can occur through determined and widespread endeavour to educate the people as regards the principles of freedom and rational cooperative living.
10. Human knowledge is constantly evolving. Existing knowledge should be tested again and again, and changed according to new standards of rational thought. Socio-political institutions should be so adjusted.

Obviously, the spirit of humanism is contained in its firm adherence to the norms of a free and constructive life of man that alone can make greatest possible accomplishments. Here is a great ideal for the sake of which great figures like Socrates, Lincoln and Gandhi paid with their life. Thomas Jefferson of America affirmed: 'Give me liberty or give me death'; Olympe de Gouges of France in a similar tone affirmed: 'Woman has the right to mount to the scaffold'. The waves of humanism affected different segments of the people. The commoners raised their voice against the lords; the slaves opened their mouth against their masters; the dependent people staged their opposition to the hold of the colonialists; the women came forward with their demand for empowerment. The spirit of humanism is inherent in all movements for the liberty and dignity of the individuals. The zealous humanists now advocate social reconstruction of the whole world as a commonwealth and fraternity of free men by the cooperative endeavours of spiritually emancipated human beings. In short, humanism is the philosophy of freedom that "gives moral priority to the achievement of human needs and ends."[4]

4. Andrew Heywood: *Political Ideologies,* p. 257.

Some Important Aphorisms

1. Man is the measure of all things. (Protagoras)
2. Man is born free, but he is everywhere in chains. (J.J. Rousseau)
3. Treat each individual as an end in himself, not as a means to that end. (Immanuel Kant)
4. The proper study of mankind is man. (Alexander Pope)
5. We hold these truths to be self-evident that all men are created equal; that they are endowed by their Creator with certain unalienable rights; that among them are rights to life, liberty and the pursuit of happiness. (Thomas Jefferson)
6. Man is the root of all mankind. (Karl Marx)
7. Liberty is the power man has to do or forbear doing any particular action according to as he himself wills it. The end of law is not to abolish or restrain but to preserve and enlarge freedom. (John Locke)
8. The mere removal of compulsion, the mere enabling of a man to do as he likes, is in itself no contribution to true freedom.... The ideal of true freedom is the maximum of power for all members of human society alike to meet the best of themselves. (Thomas Hill Green)
9. Man's dearest possession is life, and since it is given to him to live but once, he must so live as not to be scared with the shame of a cowardly and trivial past, so live as not to be tortured for years without purpose, so live that while dying he may say: 'All my life and my strength were given to the first cause of the world—the liberation of mankind.' (V.I. Lenin)
10. We believe that it is the inalienable right of the Indian people, as of any other people, to have freedom and to enjoy the fruits of their toil and have the necessities of life so that they may have full opportunities of growth. (Jawaharlal Nehru)

Varieties: Humanism has its varieties—scientific, liberal, socialist, radical and ecological—each having its strong and weak points which may be discussed briefly as follows:

'Scientific humanism' appeared in the early modern period when social and political life of the people was set free from obscure and orthodox beliefs, and new light was shed on the conduct of human affairs. Men like Rousseau, Montesquieu, Diderot, Voltaire and Marquis de Condorcet of France, John Locke, Isaac Newton and David Hume of Britain and Immanuel Kant and G.E. Lessing of Germany, in particular, adopted a new outlook informed by reason and scientific research. It was known as

5. The 'creed of enlightenment' stressed the possibility of man's own intellectual planning of a society on rational grounds. It denied, therefore, the traditional authority of kings and the church. David Robertson: *A Dictionary of Modern Politics,* p. 165.

the 'age of enlightement'[5] in which its pioneers sought to establish a link between scientific inventions and human progress which led them to realise that human beings could make use of scientific methods to establish a rational world in which the ideal of human fulfilment could be materialised.

A critic may comment that rationalism, blended with scientism, procreates intellectualism of a very high order to the extent that it touches the verge of utopianism as we may see in the formulation of Rousseau's theory of 'general will' and Kant's design of 'perpetual peace' in the world. It may also create the tendency of anti-intellectualism that provides stuff to the discipline of social psychology. For example, Graham Wallas asserts that human actions are less informed by reason, but more informed by irrational forces like habits and natural instincts. Rational outlook may enable an economist like Adam Smith to justify the existence of the capitalist system operated by the 'invisible hand'. It certainly inspired early socialists to attack such a system in the name of its exploitative and oppressive nature leading to the dehumanisation of man.

Liberalism and humanism complement each other. Like twin concepts, their spirit is contained in the motto: 'Everything by man, for the benefit of man'. 'Liberal humanism' contends that in an environment of freedom, man can exercise his inner faculties to the best possible extent. Hence, Laski defines liberty as 'the eager maintenance of that atmosphere in which man may have the best possible development of his personality'.[6] It is possible only in the conditions of peace. Man knows it and so, for this sake, he may surrender his all rights in favour of a strong ruler (Leviathan), as Hobbes says. However, after the replacement of the horrible 'state of nature' by the commonwealth (collective name of society, state and government) the people may go to the extent of killing that Leviathan if he violates the terms of the social contract. Likewise, John Locke empowers his individuals to make 'an appeal to the heaven' (revolt) and thereby replace the unconstitutional government by a government based on the consent of the people.

However, the difficulty with liberal humanism is that its implications have a negative as well as a positive character. Negative liberalism insists on minimum possible interference of state in the liberty of the individuals. Mill contends that 'over himself, his own body and mind, the individual is sovereign'. Nozick cautions that the role of the state should be confined to that of a 'night watchman'. Hayek advocates the case of 'evolutionary rationalism' implying that the individual should strive for the development of his personality on his own. Such development with the help of state or some other social institutions, what he calls 'constructive rationalism', is against the law of nature. Opposed to it, positive liberalism lays stress on the role of the state in rendering socially useful services. In the words of R.M. MacIver, the function of the modern state is 'to protect the weak against the strong'. It may, however, be made clear at this stage that though positive liberalism moves closer to democratic socialism by emphasising increasing activity of the state for the sake of human welfare at the minimum possible cost of liberty of the individuals, it deliberately refrains from

6. H.J. Laski: *A Grammar of Politics,* p. 142.

converting a limited government into a total state as done by the fiery advocates of scientific socialism or communism. Hence, positive liberals like Harold Lasswell and John Rawls disdain the trend of identifying their brand of liberal humanism with any variety of socialism.

'Socialist (including Marxist) humanism' is similar to as well as different from liberal humanism in certain respects. In the nineteenth century many varieties of socialism emerged ranging from the utopian socialism of Robert Owen of England and St. Simon of France to the scientific socialism of Marx of Germany and Engels of England. All socialists condemn the conditions of exploitation and oppression of the peasants and the workers at the hands of the feudal lords and the industrial barons and instead present the picture of a new or ideal society in which man may lead a life of freedom and happiness. How can this new kind of society be brought about? While the 'utopian' socialists insist on peaceful ways of persuasion and the Fabians or the English socialists advocate constitutional methods, the Marxist-Leninists scoff at the possibility of peaceful methods and instead lay stress on the ways of a violent or bloody revolution.

In the view of the Marxian socialists, humanism "is an approach to society in which man's dignity and great value as an individual, as well as his right to free development are upheld, while the principles of equality, justice and kind treatment of one another are recognised as the norms in relations among the people. The existence of antagonistic classes, the alienation of labour and the estrangement of one person from another (the dehumanisation of society) are inter-connected. Marxism came out against all forms of the alienation of man, against the distortion of man's essence. To make relations among people really humane, social relations must be transformed and a level of production development achieved that would make it possible to eliminate the social division of labour prevailing under capitalism, which cripples man and would turn him from the means into the objective of social development. Socialist revolution is the first step in that direction. Socialism lays the foundation for tackling the great humanistic tasks facing mankind. It eliminates exploitation of man by man, liberates the working people from political and national inequality, abolishes the opposition between physical and mental labour, between town and countryside, does away with poverty and unemployment among the broad population and places the treasure of world art at their disposal."[7]

Socialism aims at the elimination of the conditions of exploitation and oppression in a new social order in which glorious human values of liberty, equality and fraternity or cooperation would prevail, but its significance is confined to the theoretical plane. The picture is different when socialism of this type is examined in a practical perspective. Socialist systems of any hue have failed to bring about the desired new social order in spite of various experiments made by the 'welfare state' in a democratic country or by a 'total state' in a communist country. In particular, the socialist system of a communist country killed human initiative that was called the 'loss of human capital'. Instead of

7. *A Dictionary of Scientific Communism* (Moscow: Progress Publishers, 1984), pp. 108-10.

having a happy leap of man from the 'kingdom of necessity' to the 'kingdom of freedom and happiness', man could see an unhappy leap from the kingdom of exploitation and oppression to the kingdom of complete servitude. Fortunately, it came to an end in the last decade of the last century signifying, what Zbigniew Brzezinski called, the 'grand failure'. Francis Fukuyama satirically termed it as 'end of history'.

M.N. Roy is a fiery advocate of humanism he calls by different names as 'new humanism', 'scientific humanism', 'integral humanism' and 'radical humanism'. His humanism is a vehement attack on the socialist system as established in the Soviet Union. It is based on his experiences that he had by virtue of his stay in that country in the 1920s and, more than that, his close association with great Marxist leaders like Lenin and Stalin. In course of time he felt disillusioned with it. He became a critical Marxist after 1930 and an anti-Marxist after 1940. According to his contention, humanism could have no place in a country having a thoroughly totalitarian system and where a fully state-controlled economy prevailed. Roy is also critical of liberal humanism that appreciates the system of parliamentary democracy. In it the government is limited and accountable of course, but it is operated by political parties dominated by some leaders imbued with a fascist mentality. Obviously, his radical humanism appears like a hard and soft critique of the socialist and liberal-democratic systems respectively.

Roy contends that humanism can prevail in a country where the individuals have freedom to develop their personality. The political system should be operated without political parties, but with the help of people's committees. There should be people's councils to guide and enlighten the people. Roy calls it 'cultural revolution' that should precede the establishment of 'organised democracy'. Economy should be cooperative. Such an ideal can be attained through the collective efforts of spiritually emancipated individuals committed to the creation of a world of freedom. As his Thesis No. 21 of the 'Principles of Radical Democracy' reads: "Radicalism integrates science into social organisation and reconciles individuality with collective life; it gives to freedom a moral-intellectual as well as a social content; it offers a comprehensive theory of social progress in which both the dialectic of economic determinism and dynamics of ideas find their due recognition; and it deduces from the same method and programme of social revolution in our time."

'Ecology' is the science of environment. It also deals with the relationship between physical organisms (human and non-human) and natural environment. Development is necessary for human welfare and happiness, but men should realise that the development of today should not be a disaster in time to come. Hence, the concept of sustainable development has come to be accepted. Human efforts should focus on maintaining the balance of nature and preservation of bio-diversity of the natural world. Man should realise that indiscriminate cutting of trees or emission of toxic gases or release of chemicalised water into the rivers pollute earth, air and water. It causes environmental degradation that becomes a potential danger to human and non-human existence. If this essential fact is ignored and the exploitation of natural resources goes on unchecked and indiscriminately, the consequence would be, what Garrat Hardin calls, 'tragedy of the commons'. Freedom of man does not mean freedom to damage natural environment. The statement of John Locke that 'men are the masters and possessors of nature' must

Some Important Statements

- The most important discovery of the Renaissance—more significant than the single work of art and painting—was the discovery of man.

William Ebenstein,
Great Political Thinkers, p. 278.

- Renaissance adhered to the worth and significance of man by making him once more a man in the fathomless universe.

R.H. Murray,
The History of Political Science from Plato to the Present, p. 106.

- We hold these truths to be self-evident that all men are created equal; that they are endowed by their Creator with certain unalienable rights; that among these are life, liberty and the pursuit of happiness. That to secure these rights governments are instituted among men deriving their just power from the cosent of the governed; that whenever any form of government becomes destructive of these ends, it is the right of the people to alter or abolish it, and to intitute a new government, laying its foundations on such principles, and organising its powers in such form, as to them shall seem most likely to affect their safety and happiness.

Thomas Jefferson,
American Declaration of Independence, 1776.

- And the more one thinks, the more one begins to examine existing conditions and to criticise them. And this often leads to a challenge of the existing order. Ignorance is always afraid of change. It fears the unknown and sticks to its rut, however miserable it may be there. In its blindness it stumbles on anywhere. But with right reading comes a measure of knowledge, and the eyes are partly opened.

Jawaharlal Nehru
Glimpses of World History, p. 276.

be re-interpreted in the light of modern conditions. Gandhiji says that 'mother nature can satisfy everybody's need; it cannot satisfy everybody's greed.' Since such considerations have not been in the past, men have taken a wrong view of freedom. Hence, David Ehrenfeld has called it 'arrogance of humanism'.

The concept of 'anthropocentrism' has come into currency. It implies that nature should be used as an instrument of human welfare and happiness. When it is realised that the protection of the natural world is essential for maintaining congenial conditions for human life and happiness, the goal of anthropocentrism coincides with that of eco-centrism having its synonym in scientific humanism. "Ecology, therefore, represents a new kind of politics, whose central vision is of nature as a network of precious but fragile relationships between human and non-human living species and the natural environment. Humankind no longer occupies centre stage, but is regarded as an inseparable part of nature".[8]

Critical Appreciation: Humanism is a creed of man's freedom and the development of his personality in an environment of liberty, equality and fraternity. Naturally it is a very fascinating ideology which attracts everybody whose soul inspires him to undertake constructive engagements for the good of the people at large. It seeks to demolish all barriers created by the society and the state that stand in the way of the creation of a 'commonwealth of free human beings'. The saga of humanism runs from the elimination of blind faiths or myths in supernatural objects, abandonment of outmoded social traditions, and destruction of dictatorial political systems to the establishment of open and pluralistic social orders of the day in which men feel capable of exercising their inner faculties for their own good as well as for the good of the society at large.

However, the difficulty with humanism is that it is so fluid and flexible that its specific dimensions or contours cannot be laid down. Its advocates range from the liberals who mounted on the gallows or took refuge by migrating to some other country so as to live in an 'open society' to the so-called humanists (communists) boasting of their 'closed' societies allowing no room for exploitation, oppression and alienation of the people. Liberalism and humanism are like synonyms and so the 'timeless quality' of this ideology is to break down the 'chains of slavery'. One may comment that it "seems to be not so much to build as to pull down, to remove obstacles which block human progress rather than to point out the positive goal of endeavour or fashion the fabric of civilisation."[9] But this bold fact cannot be lost sight of that "everywhere it is removing superincumbent weights, knocking off of fetters, clearing away obstructions.[10]

8. Andrew Heywood, *op. cit.,* pp. 257-58.
9. L.T. Hobhouse: *Liberalism,* pp. 14-15.
10. *Ibid.*

PART-II

Great Social and Political Thinkers (Western and Indian)

Political thought is thought about the State, its nature and its purpose. Its concern is with nothing else than the moral phenomena of human behaviour in society. It seeks not so much an explanation of the existence of the State as a justification of its continuance.

—C.L. Wayper,

Political Thought, p. vii.

16
Plato

Plato (427-347 B.C.) is regarded as the father of speculative political philosophy. His works represent an intoxicating mixture of philosophy and poetry, science and art, ethics and metaphysics, in a word, the whole life of a man. But their dialogue-form text sometimes makes it difficult to discover what his mouthpiece (Socrates) really wants to say. However, the most striking aspect of the works of Plato is the place of politics as a handmaid of ethics. His most important work—*The Republic* —is a great contribution to the subject of politics placed under the domination of ethics. The element of 'righteousness' constitutes the keynote of the whole treatise to jusify the case of an ideal state. True to say that, according to Plato, there "is no distinction, except one of convenience, between morals and politics. The laws of right are the same for classes and cities as for individual men. But one must add that these laws are primarily laws of personal morality; politics is founded on ethics, not ethics on politics".[1]

The Republic: The *Republic* of Plato touches every phase of the thought of his time and institutes an imposing compendium of Greek learning and culture. Commentators and textbook writers have used colourful phrases to highlight the real vlaue of this first important work on political thought. For instance, R. L. Nettleship describes it as "a dramatised philosophy of human life" and "really an attempt to interpret human nature psychologically; the postulate upon which its method rests is that all the institutions of society, class organisation, law, religion, art and so on, are, ultimately, the products of the human soul, an inner principle of life which works itself out in these outward shapes."[2] It is also said that the *Republic* "is a complete treatise in itself. Here we shall find his metaphysics, his theology, his psychology, his pedagogy, his politics, his theory of art."[3]

The keynote of the *Republic* is the principle of righteousness contained in Plato's peculiar notion of justice that is the end of the ideal state. It is based on the tripartite conception of human personality sanctioning the existence of three corresponding social classes on the principle of division of labour and specialization of functions. However, Plato's aristocratic bent of mind is discernible when he takes up the study of the two upper classes in his ideal state and suggests the application of subjective and

1. A.E. Taylor: *Plato: The Man and His Works,* p. 265.
2. R.L. Nettleship: *Lectures on the Republic of Plato,* p. 68.
3. Will Durant: *The Story of Philosophy,* p. 15.

objective institutions of education and communism respectively to keep the state in the hands of the uncorrupt and incorruptible guardians. The result is that the lowest class of the numerous many is reduced to the status of mere "onlookers" in the ideal state. We may, therefore, take note of Prof. Burnet's view with a reservation that the fundamental ideal of the *Republic* is contained in Plato's search for "conversion of the soul" in the first place and the "service of mankind" in the second. It is well admired by Prof. E. Barker as "an attempt at complete philosophy of man" and "a philosophy of mind in all its manifestations."[4]

Ideal State: The most outstanding contribution of Plato's political thought, as contained in the *Republic,* is the "representation of human life in a state perfected by justice and governed according to the idea of the Good." (Stallbaum). Here we find the model of a Utopia deprecated by the critics as a city in the clouds, a sunset fabric seen for an hour in the evening and then fading into the night, a city of nowhere, a state in the world of words. At the same time, it has been lauded as a perfect model for the actual state, an ideal political system to do away with the ills of a contemporary social order and, as such, "a city . . . . based on actual conditions; it is meant to mould, or at any rate to influence actual life."[5]

The ideal state of Plato is a three-class polity based on the scheme of separation of functions and specialisation of the job under perfect rulers having their souls subjectively refined by means of a very long course of education and practical training and objectively purified by a stern order of communistic life. The whole construction is based on a spiritual parallelism or an analogy drawn between the three elements of human personality and the three corresponding classes in the social organisation. As there are three elements in human personality—reason, courage and appetite, correspondingly, there should be three classes in the social order—rulers, fighters and husbandmen. Thus, the doctrine of the triplicity of the soul is the foundation of the *Republic.*

The construction of the ideal state is based on Plato's psychological method having support of his logical approach. He takes his start from this point of human personality that "states do not come out of an oak or a rock, but from the characters of men that dwell therein."[6] His study of the human soul (personality) leads him to take it as a heterogeneous whole of three elements—Reason, Courage, and Desire or Appetite. Each element of the soul has its distinct quality. While the element of desire or appetite is the ally of worldly pleasure and satisfaction, the element of courage or spirit issues in the form of chivalry, and finally, the element of reason enables one to understand the idea of the Good and Essence of Beauty. If so, there should be three separate classes in society in correspondence to the three elements of the soul; that is, one having the dominant element of desire must go to the economic class; then, one having the dominant element of spirit must join the class of the warriors, and, finally, one

4. E. Barker: *Greek Political Theory: Plato and His Predecessors,* p. 171.
5. *Ibi.d,* p. 277.
6. *Republic,* VIII, 544.

having the dominant element of reason must go to the class of the philosopher-rulers. So Socrates says: "Must we not acknowledge that in each of us there are the same principles and habits which there are in the state; and that from the individuals they pass into the state.?"[7]

Plato not only treats the human soul as a three-element whole, he takes up each of the elements beginning with the lowest (desire) and proceeds to the highest (reason) through the intermediary place of spirit in order to show how each of the three elements, in its turn, contributes its quota to the construction of the ideal state in the following manner.

1. First of all, Plato takes up the case of the economic class corresponding to the element of desire. In his view, it involves some form of association as the essential wants of society cannot be satisfied except by means of a common action. The production of goods for the satisfaction of the needs of the people relating to their diet, dress and living requires that one should do one's job in ample measure in order to confer upon others and, in turn, taking from them what pertains to reciprocal requirements. It leads to the coming up of the system of division of labour. The State has, thus, its binding force in economics.
2. Then, there is the intermediary class of the soldiers. A large territory is needed for the people to live in; its defence from external aggression is also needed. Thus, there arises the need for another class of fighters. The state, apart from being an economic organisation, also becomes a military community. Apart from the numerous class of the farmers and artisans carrying on the professions of agriculture and industry, there should be the class of the soldiers whose business is to make war both for the defence of the territory as well as for the securing of land needed for a self-sufficing life of the people. A very noticeable point at this stage is that while Plato leaves all economic life into the hands of the multitude, he prescribes education and training for the class of the soldiers whom he also calls "auxiliary guardians of the state." In this respect he is guided by the principal consideration that the business of conducting warfare cannot be left in untrained hands.
3. At the top there is the ruling class of the philosopher(s) to guide the nation. The perfect guardian is the watchdog of society identifying the "welfare" and "mishap" of all with his own welfare and mishap respectively. The philosopher-ruler is one whose soul has the dominant element of reason—an intellectual test of his philosophic power. The state, in the hands of Plato, thus becomes a rational organisation led by an all-wise ruler in addition to being an economic or military community. At the head of it, there is a philosopher-king representing the sovereignty of reason. Once again, a very striking point is that while Plato leaves all economics in the hands of the multitude, he lays extraordinary stress on the long education and practical training of the rulers coupled with a communistic way of their life. Plato's ruler is, therefore, a perfect embodiment of an infallible

7. *Ibid.*, IV, 435.

administrator. "Setting aside every other business, the guardians are to dedicate themselves wholly to the maintenance of freedom in the state, making this their craft, and engaging in no work which does not bear on this end."[8]

The end of the ideal state is contained in the principle of justice. It implies that each element should keep to its respective sphere in the social order. Specialisation is the only author of unity in a social organisation; naturally, the principle of division of labour and specialisation of functions can eliminate unlimited and destructive competition rampant in every imperfect state. "The intention was that . . . . each individual should always be put to the use for which Nature intended him, one to one work, and then every man would do his own business, and be one and not many; and so the whole city would be one and not many."[9]

The final authority of the ideal state is in the hands of a perfect guardian having a soul enlightened from within by virtue of a very long course of education and practical training coupled with a very austere life sans enjoyment of private property and family. The business of the perfect ruler "is the correct regulation of spiritual and physical needs of the individual and the human community."[10] It constitutes the fundamental doctrine of the *Republic,* as Nettleship observes, that governing authority "must be associated with broadest knowledge and culture, that the philosopher should be the statesman." Thus poet Shelley once admired Plato for "being perhaps first and last to maintain that a state ought to be governed not by the wealthiest, or the most ambitious, or the most cunning, but by the wisest." So says Taylor that Plato "suggested an authority whose personal insight with good creates the public tradition by which the rest of the society is to live."[11]

The theory of the ideal state, as propounded in the *Republic*, may be criticised on these grounds:

1. It is a city of nowhere, being a dream-state of Plato, a city laid up in the heaven and not on this earth. It all makes Plato a visionary philosopher fondly endeavouring to actualise the ideal picture of a super-state possible for the divines only.
2. The whole construction of the ideal state is based on an elaborate analogy between the human soul and the state. It may be said that while analogy is no argument, in this case analogy has been carried to the extreme so much so that in this ultimate analysis the two lower elements of human personality ensuing in the two lower social classes are starved. The final power is vested in the all-wise philosopher endowed with the supreme and infallible faculty of reason.
3. The way Plato ignores the class of the toilers and the artisans altogether and reduces the scope of his attention more and more from the class of the fighters to

---

8. *Ibid.,* III, 395.
9. *Ibid.,* IV, 423.
10. Zeller: *Outlines of the History of Greek Philosophy,* pp. 140-41.
11. Taylor, *op. cit.,* p. 282.

that of the philosophers is a clear mark of the fact that he "bisects the state into two halves" each with "its different temper and its different institution."

Among the recent critics, Karl Popper charges Plato with taking to the course of historicism. This programme "can be fairly described as totalitarian. And it is certainly founded on a historicist sociology."[12]

Justice: Justice, having its like meaning in the term "righteousness", is the hinge of Plato's political thought contained in the *Republic*. The sub-title of this work "concerning justice" is the very sign of the extraordinary importance that the author attaches to the end of the ideal state—justice. It is not at all to be treated like a legal concept; it has an ethical and a philosophic character. Plato does not take it as a matter relating to the proper enforcement of rights by a court. It simply means that one individual should perform only one function and the function that is best suited to his natural aptitude without meddling with the function of others. In other words, justice implies a life of the people conforming to the law of functional specialisation. Thus, Plato's conception of justice has a meaning of its own different from the one understood by the students of law and jurisprudence. "Justice is no mere function of the law courts: it is equality and its function. It is equality, for it means nothing more and nothing less than man's performance of the part which the purposes of society demand that he shall pay. It is function, his function, for only he can discharge it adequately."[13]

The original principle underlying Plato's scheme of specialisation is that one man should practise one thing only and the thing to which his nature is best suited. What Plato stresses is the point that "each individual should be put to the use for which nature intended him, one to one work, and then every man would do his own business, and the one and not many; and so the whole city would be one and not many."[14] Justice, thus, becomes the fulfilment of one's duty at a proper station. As Nettleship says: "When we call a man wise, we mean he has the power of understanding what is for his real interest as a whole man; when we call a state wise, we ought to mean that the men who have the gift for governing have their understanding entirely set upon the interest of the whole state. Again, a brave man is one who has the courage of his opinions, that is one who will carry out his principles, whether those principles are the result of his own reason or received from others; and a brave state is one where the men who have to defend it have the courage to carry out the laws and principles improved by constituted authority. Again, by a temperate or self-controlled man we mean not merely one who governs his appetites, but one in whose soul there is harmony and no internal conflict between different parts of the nature; and by a self-controlled state we mean in which social order is not merely preserved by the army and police, but rests upon genera! agreement."[15]

---

12. Karl Popper: *The Open Society and Its Enemies,* Vol. I, p. 87.
13. R.H. Murray: *History of Political Science from Plato to the Present,* p. 13.
14. *Republic,* IV, 423.
15. Nettleship, *op. cit.,* pp. 160-61.

Viewed in this context, justice demands uniform and correct regulation of both inward and outward aspects of human personality. In a real sense, it seeks to establish strict oneness between the life of action and that of contemplation. The full realisation of the principle of justice requires that the outward expression of human personality (that appears in the form of action) must mirror forth the image of the inward mode of thought, or the one being unjust will render the whole as unjust. Keeping this in view, Nettleship observes: "Real justice means not the mere doing of one's own business in the state, but such outward doing of one's own business as is an expression of a corresponding mode of action within the soul; if the outward action is really just, it means that the soul is just within, that like a just state the whole soul and the several parts of it perform their proper function in relation to one another."[16]

In order to offer a precise definition or explanation of "justice", Plato follows the method of taking up and then refuting certain contemporary notions with the sharpness of his arguments in the following manner:

1. First of all, he refutes the notion of *traditional morality* as represented by Cephalus (a metic living in the Peiraeus and the father of the orator Lysias) and a changed position of defence taken by his son Polemarchus. As a representative of the traditional morality, Cephalus defines justice as "speaking truth and paying debt." Carrying the point further, Polemarchus adds that justice being an art means "doing good to friends and bad to enemies." But Socrates (Plato) rejects this argument on the ground that justice is not an art or a technique but a quality of soul and a habit of mind connoting an idea of service to the whole society. Plato questions how it can be possible to have real distinction between a friend and a foe, and that it would never be an act pertaining to the principle of justice to restore weapons to a man who has gone mad even if he be their bonafide owner.
2. Then, Plato takes up the *radicalism* of the Sophists represented by Thrasymachus who defines justice as "the interest of the stronger." It simply means justification of the old idea of might being right and authority being based on force or selfish interests of the rulers. Taking a changed position, Thrasymachus holds that "injustice is better than justice as it brings wisdom, power and happiness." But Plato rejects all such contentions on the ground that they represent ethical nihilism and that they would create divisions and hatred and internecine quarrels leading to the destruction of the polity.
3. Finally, Plato takes up the *pragmatism* of Glaucon who holds that "it is better to be unjust than to suffer injustice as all benefits rest with the former." But Plato rejects it on the ground of being based on fear and having an artificial or conventional character. Instead he contends that justice is nothing but a natural, internal and right condition of human life.

It follows that justice, in the view of Plato, is something subjective; it has its place in soul and, as such, it is something natural commanding a man for having and doing

16. *Ibid.*, p. 160.

what is one's own in accordance with the best element of his personality, without allowing any intervention of one element into the domain of others. The underlying principle is to enjoin upon the individual a specific duty to be discharged at a specific station of social life.

Plato's theory of justice implying, what Irwin Edman feels, "name for that kind of individual life where every part of the soul does its own business, that life of the state where each individual and each class performs its appropriate function", may be subjected to the following lines of criticism:

1. It assigns a static character of life both to the individual and to the social order of which he is an integral part by condemning him to perform his specific duty at a specific station. Aristotle is, therefore, justified in disagreeing with the views of his teacher on the point of excessive uniformity of life.
2. The theory of justice is too passive in character. While it bids men to keep to their respective spheres, it provides no solution for dealing with a situation of conflict. Of course, it gives a medicine for curing a disease, but certainly gives nothing to alleviate the adverse condition if it happens to grow.
3. Last, and this also seems to follow from the above, the theory of justice confuses the boundary line between the objective world of law and the subjective world of morality.

The brunt of Popper's attack is that Plato's demand for justice "leaves his political programme at the level of totalitarianism; and we should have to conclude that we must guard against the danger of being impressed by mere words... Plato identifies justice with the principle of class rule and class privilege."[17]

Philosopher-King: If the principle of justice is the keystone of Plato's ideal state, the rule of an all-wise philosopher-king is the coping stone of the whole edifice. To Plato, the rule of the perfect guardian is the panacea of all social and political ills; it is the only efficacious cure for the principal evil of his days—division of every city into two, converting a state of the individuals into "a city of the swine." The construction of the ideal state culminates in uniting political power and philosophy in the hands of a superman who has sought the "salvation" or "purification" of his soul not by a ritual of ceremonial holiness but by means of a scientific curriculum of long education and practical training coupled with his life tied to the pattern of a very austere existence. Herein lies the only remedy for all ills—social and political. As Plato affirms: "Until philosophers are kings, or the kings and princes of this world have the spirit and power of philosophy, and political greatness and wisdom meet in one, and those commoner natures .who pursue either to the exclusion of the other all compelled to stand aside, cities will never have rest from their evils—nor the human race, as I believe, and then only will this our state have a possibility of life and behold the light of the day."[18]

---

17. Popper, *op. cit.*, pp. 90-91.
18. *Republic,* V, 473.

The construction of the ideal state is not merely confined to the affirmation of the rule of the philosopher-king, it also highlights the qualifications that the perfect ruler ought to possess and further develop to prove himself worthy of the great office. These are:

1. The ruler must be endowed with the faculty of reason giving proof of his full moral elevation like Wordsworth's "Happy Warrior." He must have the qualities of intellectual quickness and retentive memory giving proof of his eminence superseding all else.
2. A very long course of education and practical training is necessary for the all-wise ruler. A selective test at the age of 20 years will entitle only a few to have higher education; while another selective test finally at the age of 35 will work out the best over the better, leaving the latter to the category of the military officers and the former to rule and guide the nation after a stern apprenticeship of the next 15 years.
3. The rulers, apart from having their subjective purification by virtue of their long education and practical training, are commanded to lead a life of stern simplicity under the system of communism. In Plato's commonwealth there is no place for the rulers for the enjoyment of material possessions or women, including sexual pleasures, amounting to the condemnation of the fair sex to the life of drones into a body of working-bees.

Obviously Plato's philosopher-king is like a perfect statesman with a subjectively purified and objectively refined personality. He well knows when the existing order is failing to serve its purpose and in what way it can be reformed. He understands the Idea of the Good, Essence of Beauty and Quality of Temperance and, therefore, he is fit to rule and guide the nation. His philosophic nature has an ever-hungry fondness for knowing more and more about less and less and his search for knowledge is distinguished from other kindred forms of activity. It is all due to the supreme quality of his personality that enables him to understand that the perception of forms or principles "is, therefore, of vital importance for the governor; and if a man who possesses it can add to it what is called experience, he will have the essential requisites for good government."[19]

The fundamental political idea of the *Republic* contained in the doctrine that the governing authority must be associated with the broadest knowledge and, for that reason, the philosopher should be the statesman, may be criticised on these grounds:

1. There is the theoretical difficulty of having such a ruler as desired by the architect of the ideal state. It is doubtful that even after such a long life of exhaustive education and stern training, there would ever be a ruler free from all taints of a mundane personality.
2. A practical difficulty flows from the further examination of the above point. In practical terms, the philosopher-king will either be a monk or an ascetic or an

19. Nettleship, *op. cit.,* p. 198.

armchair recluse incapable of managing public affairs in as much as he would always be taking delight in the world of contemplation, or, on the other hand, he would be greatly different from what Plato really seeks, in case he has the courage to run the machinery of government like a competent administrator.

3. It may not be out of place to say that Plato's all-wise philosopher is an autocrat and thus, as Karl Popper says, Plato becomes the "enemy of an open society". The result of all this is that Plato's *Republic* becomes a romance under a monarch acting autocratically.

A critic of Plato like R.H.S. Crossman asks what kind of ills the great philosopher has in his mind when he exhorts his rulers to use strong medicine. In an answer to this, he emphasises that Plato means "propaganda, the technique of controlling the behaviour of the bulk of the ruled majority."[20] Popper deprecates it all as a profile of "totalitarian morality" that "over-rules everything, even the definition, the Idea of the philosopher."[21] One may say that the entire case of an all-wise philosopher-king is based on the "myth of blood and soil." Here we see that "Plato's utilitarian and totalitarian principles overrule everything, even the ruler's privilege of knowing, and of demanding to be told, the truth,"[22]

Education: If justice is the life-breath of the ideal state, a system of very long education and practical training is essential for the enlightenment of the soul. It provides training for a special purpose, and inculcates the spirit that keeps unselfishly to its performance as required by the principle of justice in the ideal state. Plato's emphasis is concentrated on the point: "A really good education will furnish the best safeguards. The one great thing is education and its nurture: if the citizens are well educated, they will easily see their way through other matters which I omit; such, for example, as marriage, the possession of women and the procreation of children, which will follow the general principle that friends have all things in common, as the proverb says."[23] In simple words, the whole process of education "is conceived as putting before the young all that is beautiful, noble, good and true and excluding and suppressing all that is ugly, unworthy, evil and false".[24]

It is clear that Plato takes the institution of education as a subjective instrument for bringing soul into that environment which is best suited for development in each stage of its growth. He is deeply impressed with the dictum of his teacher (Socrates) that "virtue is knowledge." He starts with a fundamental proposition and feels that virtue in a citizen may be cultivated only through a very good system of education. Thus, education as the fundamental premise of the *Republic* lays stress on shaping human nature in the right direction.

---

20. R.H.S. Crossman: *Plato Today,* p. 130.
21. Popper, *op. cit.,* p. 138.
22. *Ibid.,* p. 140.
23. *Republic,* IV, 423.
24. T.A. Sinclair: *A History of Greek Political Thought,* p. 148.

If education is so important for the state that culminates in the realisation of the Idea of the Good and makes the individual a useful member of society, it is understandable that its management cannot be left in the hands of private agencies. That is, Plato advocates a system of state-controlled education. He is the first great philosopher to tell in very clear terms that pedagogy is an exclusive function of the state. It is the first and foremost function of the state to terminate the commercialised monopoly of education and see that the citizens receive proper education that is in consonance with the harmony and well-being of the organisation.

Not a mere emphasis on the paramount need for a state-controlled system of education but, in addition to that, a detailed curriculum of subjects included strictly in accordance with the age and mental development of the students is the most striking feature of Plato's theory of education in the *Republic*. A modern reader of Plato's educational philosophy is bound to feel struck by the study of various courses at different stages which may roughly be grouped into two—elementary and higher.

The elementary stage begins from infancy and lasts till the age of 20. It has different phases. The first phase beginning from the early life of the child runs upto the age of 6 years in which lessons of religious truth and morality are imparted. In Plato's view, such an elementary teaching inculcates the quality of a simple and good life. However, the next phase begins from 7 and lasts till the age of 18. Here the inclusion of various subjects of study has been made with intellectual and physical considerations. The subjects of study are gymnastics and music. The former trains the body for the sake of the mind and elicits the qualities of courage and endurance so as to produce temper and spirit. Its study also includes the knowledge of medicines and dietetics. Music is taken by Plato in a wider sense. It includes both art and literature. It is meant to train the mind in order to develop the power of reason. It cannot give knowledge, though it may form right opinion. However, poetry is seen with disfavour, for it has an emotional rather than a rational appeal. The importance of mathematics is also somewhat emphasised, as the science of numbers is the mother of all sciences and arts. The final phase of this stage (from 19 to 20 years of age) includes teaching of the subject of military science in order to create the qualities of courage, endurance and discipline.

The higher stage of education beginning from the age of 21 and running till the age 50 is a privilege of the select few. It is meant for imparting vocational knowledge and practical training to the guardians alone. However, this stage has its own phases. The first phase covers the period of 21 to 30 years. During this period the selected students are educated in logic, higher mathematics and metaphysics. Much significance is attached to the study of subjects concerning warfare and public administration. Thus higher mathematics includes geometry and astronomy, while the scope of logic covers dialectics. The second phase of the higher stage covers a small period of five years. It ends at the age of 35 years wherein further study of the technical subjects included for the first phase of the higher stage is recommended. The third and final phase of this stage ends at the age of 50 years. During this period of 15 years, a stern training of practical statesmanship is prescribed for the higher guardians who are to rule and guide the nation after completing the age of 50 years.

Plato's theory of education may be subjected to the following lines of criticism:

1. While Plato nowhere talks about the exclusion of the economic class from the provision of education (as he certainly does in case of communism), his centre of attention is confined to the guardians rulers and the soldiers. It is a clear mark of his aristocratic approach.
2.. Plato confuses the line of distinction between man's life of action and that of contemplation. One may ask whether the whole plan of education is for a practical ruler or for a monk. Here "is a certain wavering between the ideal of action and that of contemplation."[25]
3. The whole system of education culminates in the establishment of the absolute rule of a perfect guardian whose authority is not, and cannot be, bound by the canons of law. In the view of Plato, "the all-wise ruler will not condescend to legislate about the ordinary dealings between man and man about insult and injury, and the commencement of action."[26]

Communism: The plan of communism is the second essential device suggested by Plato for the realisation of justice in his ideal state. In a real sense, both education and communism supplement each other. If education has the power to bring the soul into that environment which in each stage of its growth is best suited to its development, communism is the second effective agency whereby those material temptations are removed that divert it from living in a proper environment. Barker well points out that communism "is a heroic remedy for a desperate evil—the union of political power and economic temptation in the same hands."[27]

Plato's plan of communism has two varieties, distinct but integrally connected:

1. It prohibits private property for the guardians and provides common enjoyment of material goods for them. As Plato says: "And this agrees with the other principle which we were affirming, that the guardians were not to have houses or lands or any other property; their pay was to be their food, which they were to receive from the other citizens, and they were to have no private expenses: for we intended them to preserve their true character of guardians."[28] It implies that the use of private property whether houses, land or money, is forbidden to the guardians who are commanded to live in camps, tents and barracks and to have their meals at common tables like consecrated men sworn to simplicity. Their material requirements are to be met with the economic class consisting of artisans, farmers, traders, husbandmen and the like.
2. Plato's scheme of communism stands for the abolition of the private family system and its substitution by a community of wives for the guardians. As Plato says: "Both the community of property and the community of families, as I am saying,

25. Barker, *op. cit.,* p. 334.
26. *Republic,* IV, 25.
27. Barker, *op. cit.,* pp. 209-10.
28. *Republic,* V, 464.

tend to make them more truly guardians; they will not tear the city in pieces by differing about 'mine' and 'not mine'; each dragging any acquisition which he has made into a separate home of his own, where he has a separate wife and children and private pleasures and pains; but all will be affected as far as may be by the same pleasures and pains because they are all of one opinion about what is near and dear to them, and therefore they all tend towards a common end."[29]

The plan of communism, as suggested by Plato for the realisation of justice in his ideal state being a supplementary institution to the grand scheme of long education and training of the guardians, may be criticised on these grounds:

1. Aristotle is the first critic to raise serious doubts about the efficaciousness of a material remedy suggested by his teacher to cure a spiritual disease. The objections of Aristotle stand on Plato's mistaken view of the unity of the state. It is precisely the "whole" that Plato seems to misconceive by failing to see that, as Aristotle points out, the nature of the state "is to be a plurality and in tending to the greater unit, from being a state it becomes a family, and from being a family an individual; for the family may be said to be more than the state, and the individual more than the family."[30]
2. It may be commented, in line with the argument generally advanced against every socialistic and communistic system, that the abolition of private property would amount to the serious dilution of responsibility on the part of the rulers. More than that, Plato's scheme relating to the community of wives is sure to create confusion and disharmony in social order. It would make the guardians more unhappy and restive. Plato forgets the real and abiding significance of a family life based on permanent monogamous sexual relationship.

It is clear, therefore, that if a rigorous system of very long education and training is devised by Plato as a means of spiritual dieting for his guardians, a ruthless surgery of material ills is the essential concomitant for their external cure in Plato's therapeutics. Thus, the two institutions of education and communism are integrally connected for converting the "life of the swine" (corrupt rulers) into the "Victors of Olympia" (Perfect Guardians) who are the state by themselves in view of the fact that the third class of the husbandmen, artisans and toilers practically disappears from the scene of politics.

Idea of the Good: Underlying the whole scheme of Plato's ideal state is the "idea of the good." Plato says that there is a "form of good" which is to the object of knowledge and to know itself, for instance, what the sun is to visible objects and to sight. This is further explained by adding that the sun both makes the colours we see and supplies the eye with the source of all its seeing. In the same way, the "good" supplies the object of scientific knowledge with their being and renders them knowable. Moreover, as the sun is neither the colours we see nor the eye which sees them, so the "good" is something even more exalted than being. Later, he asserts that the sciences form a

29. *Ibid.,*
30. Aristotle: *Politics,* II, 126.

hierarchy which has its culmination in the actual apprehension of this transcendent good. Obviously, the "good" holds a pre-eminent place among "forms" so much so that we may even call it a "form" any more than we can call the sun a colour. However, there should be no doubt that the "form of good" "is identical with the supreme Beauty, the vision of which is represented in the *Symposium* as the goal of the pilgrimage of the philosophic-lover."[31]

Simply stated, "the idea of the good" implies the case of a virtuous life. This pattern of life can be obtained only when the individual has the right type of education and the state is ruled by a perfect guardian endowed with the capacity to understand and maintain the system of justice. In this way, education is the only instrument to realise the "idea of the good." That is, the realisation of the Idea of the Good may be said to have occurred "when the soul has adjusted itself to its environment, when it has seen the purpose which animates it all." In this way, the aim of education is not only to understand the world in the light of an end; it is also to gain the master-key of conduct and action, since all right conduct, and proper action will be conformed and directed to the end which is the end of all things. This is the real sense in which virtue is knowledge.[32]

It may, therefore, be said that such an interpretation of Plato is full of metaphysical and mysterious implications that can neither be explained nor proved. One may say that the distinguishing characteristic of the "form of good" is that it is the transcendent source of all the reality and intelligibility of everything other than itself. It even transcends the distinction between the value and existence—the essence and existence. Though Plato is said to have reconciled the elements of contradictions in his Idea of the Good, yet it may be said to have many philosophical surprises for us. None but a man of super-wisdom may see things through and then realise the Idea of the Good both for himself as well as for the members of his political community. Thus, a critic observes: "Neither Plato nor anyone else could tell another man what the good is, because it can only be apprehended by the most incommunicable and intimate personal insight. Thus, as it seems to me, metaphysically the Form of Good is what Christian philosophy has meant by God, and nothing else".[33]

The Laws: It is the last work of Plato, longest of all his writings and containing his latest and ripest thoughts on the subjects which he had all through his life most at heart—ethics, education and jurisprudence."[34] The peculiar thing about this work is not its almost monologue form because the treatment of the subject is from a relatively realistic point of view. That is, the idealism of the *Republic* is abandoned and the trend towards realism of the *Politicus* is further sharpened here. That is why, the *Laws* of Plato is described as a practical handbook on politics that "will not appeal to a reader who cares more for metaphysics and science than for morals and politics. More than

31. Taylor, *op. cit.*, pp. 186-87.
32. Barker: *The Political Thought of Plato and Aristotle,* p. 127.
33. Taylor, *op. cit.*, p. 289.
34. *Ibid,* p. 463.

any other work of Plato, the *Laws* stands in direct relation to the political life of the age in which it was composed and is meant to satisfy a pressing felt need."[35]

The time of the publication of the *Laws* is a matter of controversy. However, it is certain that it was written after 360 B.C. when Plato had not only entered the last phase of his life, rather he had become more experienced after his return from Syracuse. What caused such a change in his political thinking? Some reasons may be assigned for this. First, in 367 B.C., Plato visited Syracuse at the invitation of its ruler (Dionysius II) 'to turn his kingdom into a Utopia.' Plato accepted the offer, but he could not impress the arrogant prince with his ideas as contained in the *Republic*. The result was that the great philosopher returned like a frustrated teacher. Naturally, this bad experience made him aware of the realities of political life. Second, in the meantime, the intellectual atmosphere of the Academy had also changed. Aristotle had entered the Academy during the period of Plato's absence. Now the pupils of the great teacher had also become critical of some of his ideas contained in the *Republic*. It had its own impact upon the mind of Plato.

The political ideas of Plato, as contained in the *Laws*, may be briefly put as under:

Here Plato affirms supremacy of law over the ruler. It appears that he is now convinced with the unavailability of an all-wise statesman of his choice. Now a law-state combined with a mixed constitution comes to have a dominant place in his system. Moreover, while in the *Republic* he subordinated self-control to justice, now he subordinates justice to self-control. Obviously, he "is no longer an absolutist that he was when he wrote the *Politicus*...Plato, if he is still a physician of the States, has become a wise family doctor instead of a brusque consulting physician. He has a deeper knowledge of human nature; the lessons which he professes to derive from history in the third book of the *Laws* are really derived from the history of his own life."[36]

The system of education occupies a quite important place here as well. Although the general outlines of the curriculum, as including music and gymnastics, remain similar to those of the *Republic*, his distrust of the poets still issues in the most rigorous censorship of literature and art. Hence the education of the women equally with men remains an important part of the plan, and the education of all citizens is made compulsory. The changes are that now he gives more attention to the organisation of education and since the whole state is no longer an educational institution, he is obliged to consider the articulation of the system of education with the rest of government. Plato now undertakes to outline a system of publicly regulated schools having paid teachers to provide a fully outlined course of instruction for the elementary and secondary grades.

What engages our attention at this stage is that the idea of state-controlled system of education is not only retained, it is specifically put under the charge of a minister. The regulation and control of education is to be conducted by several judges, inspectors and

---

35. *Ibid.*
36. Barker: *Greek Political Theory: Plato and His Predecessors,* pp. 312-13.

examiners under the Education Minister who would conduct competitive tests and give away prizes. Once again, the curriculum provides for two stages. The primary education begins with childhood. In the cradle stage, the nurses attend children and teach shooting and jumping. After three, they are sent to village temples; after six, physical training begins and instructions are imparted in archery and riding. The secondary stage begins at ten and it includes the study of literature, music and mathematics. However, the most important feature of Plato's theory in this direction is that now education becomes a thoroughly state-controlled system covering all sections of the people. "The theory of education in the *Laws*, unlike that of the *Republic*, is the theory of a system of educational institutions."[37]

As regards social structure, the *Laws* offers a new theory of division of labour. Here the agriculture is marked out as the special function of the slaves, trade and industry as of the class of free men who are not citizens, while political functions are assigned only to the class of citizens alone. Here the economic part of the population is not composed of citizens at all. The status of women is exalted, because they are treated with men on an equal footing even for war purposes. The institution of marriage is to be shared by the rich and the poor for the benefit of the state, but the offsprings are to be treated for state purposes. An office of women overseers is also sanctioned.

Plato also suggests a number of useful checks on the operation of administrative machinery, The administrative arrangement is vested in a Board of Thirty Seven, having men of 50 to 70 years of age, who are to be chosen by election. This Board would exercise supervision and its orders are to be executed by an administrative council of 360 and its members are drawn on the basis of some election as well as lot. Here a jury system is also proposed. The great philosopher also suggests the formation of one more council consisting of 10 members for the purpose of ensuring proper and smooth working of the whole constitution.

However, the most interesting part of the *Laws* is retreat from communism as given in the *Republic*. The ban on private property and family system goes and yet communism in a drastically modified form remains. For instance, a common mess system for both the sexes is retained. Plato concedes to human frailty, in this regard, two main points—their love for private property and their attachment with private family system. Permanent monogamous unions under public supervision are accepted as the lawful form of marriage. With concession to private ownership of property, Plato unites the most stringent regulation of its amount and the use following in general the regulations as applicable in the state of Sparta.

The number of the people in the sub-ideal state is fixed at 5,040 and the land is divided into an equal number of allotments, that pass by inheritance, but can neither be divided nor alienated. The produce of the land is to be consumed in common at a public mess. In this way, property in land is equalised. The personal property is permitted to be unequal, but its amount is limited. Ownership of personal property is prohibited, if it is in excess of four times than the value of the plot of land. The purpose behind it seems

37. Sabine, *A History of Political Theory,* p. 84.

to be to control feuds between the rich and the poor which were very common in the days of Plato. However, he leaves much for the poor class by depriving any economic activity to the class of free men. The state is to have only token currency, the taking of interest for loans is prohibited; even the possession of gold and silver by the people is disapproved.

A brief look at the main ideas of Plato, as contained in this work, shows that now he switches over from the plane of idealism to that of realism and seeks to present the model of a sub-ideal state. As we shall see, it is the second best state of Plato that becomes the first best state at the hands of Aristotle. We may rightly say that here the state of Plato is a half-way house between the ideal and the real near enough to the actual conditions prevailing in contemporary Greece. Barker says that the scheme of Plato now represents a return to the general Greek idea of the rule of fundamental law.[38]

Critical Appreciation: On the whole, Plato's contribution to the stock of Western political thought is immortal. We may differ from his conclusions or solutions to social and political problems, but we may not ignore the salient fact that he started an important trend by aligning politics with ethics, thereby setting the idealist tradition in political philosophy. Moreover, he sought to regenerate society as a whole in order to establish a new kind of polity in it. Thus, political sociology, political economy, political psychology, political philosophy and political science all are combined in the system of Plato. It is well observed: "From Plato onwards, one of the distinctive marks of political philosophy was its approach to political society as a functioning system. Although Plato may have exaggerated the possibilities of a society achieving systematic unity, the greatness of the achievement was to point out that in order to think in a truly philosophical way, one had to consider society as a systematic whole".[39]

38. Barker, *op. cit.*
39. S.S. Wolin: *Politics as Vision,* p. 53.

17
Aristotle

The importance of Aristotle (384-322 B.C.) in the realm of Western political thought is due to his great work on the science of the state called *Politics*. However, the true significance of this work is a matter of dispute. A commentator like Taylor, following the line of Jowett, says: "No Aristotelian work is quite so commonplace in its handling of a vast subject as the *Politics*. In truth his interest in these social questions is not of the deepest."[1] Mcllwain holds: "For while there may be difference of opinions about the importance of the *Politics*, there can be very little concerning its difficulty: it is, if not the most important, by far the most puzzling of the classics of political philosophy."[2] However, Zeller holds that "the *Politics* of Aristotle is the richest treasure that has come down to us from antiquity and the greatest contribution to the field of Political Science that we possess."[3]

Origin, Nature and End of State: Distinguished from the belief of the Sophists, who regarded state as a historical institution having conventional origin, Aristotle, like Plato, subscribes to the doctrine of the natural origin of state having an ethical end contained in the principle of "good life." The way he proceeds to trace the biological and economic origins of the state is based on his maxim that "man is a social and political animal." The essential character of the state as a natural association and a moral organism has its succinct interpretation in his affirmation that the state and the individuals composing it "form an organic whole, for the state is as natural to man as the family or the clan; it is as natural as water to a fish, the medium without which human faculties can never come to their full compass."[4]

Like Plato, Aristotle advocates the organic theory of state by treating man as essentially a social and political being by nature and necessity. To him, therefore, the source of the origin of state finds place in the natural desires that compel a man to satisfy his economic wants and racial instincts. This very feeling drives man towards the family or household whose membership is shared by the free persons, male and female, and the slaves. When efforts are made to lead a better, or still better, life whose wants cannot be satisfied by the family, there comes into being a higher unit called the village. And the state is the name of a bigger unit that is the product of the same process.

1. A.E. Taylor: *Aristotle,* p. 85.
2. C.H. Mcllwain: *The Growth of Political Thought in the West,* pp. 50-51.
3. *Ibid.,* p. 50.
4. John Bowle: *Western Political Thought,* p. 53.

Hence, the state is the collection or assemblage of numerous families and villages whose organisation has been effected for the satisfaction of wants and the leading of a civilised life. The state is thus a culmination of man's achievement, and only its membership entails a perfect and fullest satisfaction of his wants and a realisation of his aims. The process of state formation thus begins with the individual and through the organisation of numerous families and villages finds its culmination in the *polis* or state. The motivating force behind this process is the set of human desires calling for the satisfaction of economic wants and the realisation of an ethical purpose—"good life."

If the state has its origin in human nature and not in convention, it is obviously a natural and not an artificial association. Aristotle has used the Greek word "koinonia" which, though taken to be identical with, is more than anything like friendship, fellowship, participation, community, communism, share-holding, partnership, reciprocity and the like. It is that sort of organisation whose spirit cannot be animated even by Platonic communism. It all implies a common participation not in mere life but in something higher, particularly in thought and conversation. The state is not merely an association, it is the supreme association; it embraces all other associations within its fold. It is a perfect organic whole, while other associations are just its integral parts. It is prior to the village, family and even the individual by virtue of nature, not time, though it has come into being much later. The family is prior to the state in time, but the state is prior to the family in nature. All the remaining associations find their perfection in the state, and none can retain its existence outside or independent of or separated from it; they can find the realisation of their objective only in the state and, as such, it would be a fallacy to say that man created the state because he wanted to satisfy his material needs like an irrational creature of the universe.

According to Aristotle, man is necessarily good and, therefore, it is the function of the state to encourage and promote his good qualities. The ideal life is the end of every association and, in this way, the state by virtue of being the supreme association has its supreme end. It is also its important duty to inculcate in man the feelings of leading a virtuous life. In this sense, the state is a moral association. Aristotle says: "A social instinct is implanted in all men by nature, and yet he who first founded the state was the greatest benefactor. For man, when perfected, is the best of animals, but when separated from law and justice, he is the worst of all; since armed injustice is the more dangerous, and he is equipped at birth with the arms of intelligence and with moral qualities which he may use for the worst ends. Wherefore, if he has no virtues, he is the most unholy and the most savage of animals, and the most full of lust and gluttony".[5]

The state is not merely an association but an organic compound in which the collection of parts does not create a mere aggregate but leads to a new and higher entity. The individuals, families and villages are the parts of the state, and every union has a particular relationship between the higher and the lower levels. The state is an organic collection of parts which are different from one another in every respect and are

5. *Politics,* I, 1252-53.

also subject to each other. In short, the state covers within itself all the parts of human association and, as a natural whole, embraces within its fold all as its component parts. The state thus represents an organic compound having the noble end of moralising the life of its individuals. Aristotle adds: "Every state is a community of some kind, and every community is established with a view to some good; the state of political community, which is the highest of all, and which embraces all the rest, aims and in a greater degree than any other, at the highest good."[6]

However, the theory of Aristotle on the origin, nature and end of the state may be criticised on these grounds:

1. It relies heavily on the factor of nature and necessity of man and ignores several other factors like consent, force, religion and the like that have definitely played their part in the evolution of the political community.
2. While Aristotle builds up the state out of its elements like the individual, the family and the village, he tells us nothing about the pre-historic phase of human existence.
3. It makes the individual nothing but a member of the political community without having any independent existence.
4. Being an ardent advocate of the organic theory, Aristotle makes a wrong distinction between the integral and contributory parts of the state. We are struck by the fact that, like his teacher, he excludes artisans, traders and all manual labourers from the share of the privilege of citizenship, because they have no time to take part in the deliberative and judicial functions of the state. Likewise, his idealisation of slavery (whereby he treats a slave as an irrational being meant for serving the household of freemen like a living tool) militates against the very spirit of the organic theory of state.

It may, however, be added that while criticising Plato's conception of the unity of state, Aristotle draws very close to his teacher in his final affirmations. It is evident from his assertion that the state "is moral and man is distinguished from beast by his power of seeing the difference not only between things beneficial and things harmful, but also between just and unjust, right and wrong. Any association of human beings, whether it be large or small, household or city, must be of this kind."[7]

Slavery: The study of slavery constitutes a very pertinent part of Aristotle's approach to the state. The analysis of Book I of *Politics* opens with the origin of state. As the state is made up of families, Aristotle, first of all, deals with the management of the household whose parts are persons composing it, including freemen and slaves and the instruments. Thus, he looks into the relationship between husband and wife, master and slave, father and child, and his particular attention devoted to the issue of relationship between the master and the slave, and the place of the latter in an

6. *Ibid*,. 1252.
7. T.A. Sinclair, *A History of Greek Political Thought,* p. 214.

ideal household ultimately results in his justification of the institution of slavery. The principal contribution of the author of the *Politics,* in this way, finds place in his advocacy of the principle of natural inequality of mankind sanctioning the rule of the few superiors over the many inferiors as both expedient and necessary. For this sake, Aristotle puts the following arguments:

1. It is impossible to lead a better life, even life as such, without a proper household consisting of articles and instruments of two types—living and dead. If the utensils and furniture constitute the inanimate part, the slave is the animate one. Thus, according to Aristotle, a slave is the living tool of the household.
2. The instruments of the household are meant for the discharge of certain specific functions. When the spindle, for example, is used, it makes something that is different from it in working. However, being an instrument of the household, of course, the slave is a tool of a different kind: he is an instrument of use—work. The slave "is an instrument not of production but of action not for making some particular article but to aid in the general conduct of life."[8]
3. The slave is a necessary living instrument of the household, it is proper as well as essential for him to act like a tool as per the will of the master.
4. Aristotle employs a psychological argument as well. Life is possible only in the union of the body and the soul and whereas the existence is determined by the union of the two, the soul is the master and body, its slave living under the control and direction of the former. Similar relationship exists between the master and the slave whose union determines the existence of the household.
5. The principle of natural inequality of mankind informs that when nature has made some people richer than others in matters of reason, knowledge and virtue, it has at the same time ordained that inferiors live under the subjection of the superiors. It is useful for both the master and the slave.
6. Aristotle's defence of slavery treats slave as a living instrument of the household working under the control of the master. The relationship between the master and the slave is, therefore, unequal in view of the fact that of all the household relationships, only this fails to rise to the level of *koinonia* (highest and best institution) as it is not at all a relationship of man with man; the slave is an instrument of the master rather than a man with his individuality.

Apart from justifying the institution of slavery in the name of natural inequality of mankind, Aristotle sanctions certain conditions that should be looked into. First, he does not recognise slavery by force. It can never be a just form of slavery in cases where strong and powerful persons enslave the weak or less powerful. In this way, the enslavement of the defeated people by the conquerors is unjustified, as the factor of physical strength is no proof of higher reason, virtue or excellence of a man. Second, it is equally undesirable that a Greek should enslave a Greek. It testifies to the prevalent notion of the Greeks that their Hellenic race was civilised, while others were barbarians.

---

8. Ross: *Aristotle,* p. 240.

Third, the master should never abuse his authority and if ever the slave covers up his deficiency and exhibits an equality of virtue or excellence with his master, he should be emancipated on payment. Aristotle even sanctions due punishment to a master persecuting his slaves. The master should behave like a 'friend' of the slave, he should not merely command but 'reason' with him and give him the hope of emancipation. Last, Aristotle rejects the case of slavery by inheritance.

Such an idealisation of the institution of slavery sounds very unnatural and unconvincing to a student of politics in modern times. Not only that, the arguments of Aristotle lack consistency. We may furnish the following points of criticism:

1. It is clear that nothing but a blind faith in the superiority of the Hellenic race sustains the line of defence taken by Aristotle. His assertion that a Greek should not enslave a Greek is altogether implausible. None would agree with the view of Aristotle that all Greeks were civilised and others barbarians.
2. The line of psychological argument, as advanced by Aristotle, based on the simile of soul and body is wholly inapplicable in this case; it is at the most like a forced insertion. It is quite ridiculous to say that while the master is a soul without a body, the slave is a body without a soul. Nor is the slave a mere instrument whether living or dead. As a matter of fact, no person should be regarded as simply a 'living tool.'
3. Aristotle's notion of some being superior to and therefore masters and of many being inferiors and therefore slaves contradicts his celebrated dictum of the *Ethics* that man is a rational being. If a man is a rational being, then every man, including the slave, is a rational creature. Even if he may be treated as a servant working under the control of the master, he cannot be taken like a mere tool of the household. A slave is a living person and for that reason he cannot be compared with the dead instruments of the household.
4. While one may admire Aristotle's injunction that a master should not abuse his authority and 'reason' with his slave like his friend, he may find fault with his notion of the slave's eventual emancipation on some payment. When every fruit of a slave's labour is taken away by the master, wherefrom any amount may fall into his hands so as to seek his emancipation. One may also ask that whereas a slave may be quite inferior to his master with regard to his rational development, can't he earn maturity of mind in due course so as to supersede even his master?
5. Above all, such an idealisation of slavery is without any plausible ground of defence in modern times. True that the institution of slavery in Greece was never as bad as it was in the days of Roman empire or as it obtained in the United States, yet it was not free from its own taints. Hence, such a justification of the evil institution of slavery can have no admirer in modern times. Moreover, the view of Aristotle looks like an attempt to cut the society into two unequal classes-one class of the freemen exploiting the other class of the slaves in the most malevolent manner. Ross thus remarks: "What cannot be commended in Aristotle's view, however,

> is his cutting of the human race in two with a hatchet. There is a continuous gradation of mankind in respect of both moral and intellectual qualities."[9]

Once again, we may take note of the fact that Aristotle's defence, even idealisation, of the institution of slavery serves his real purpose—justification of the rule of the privileged few. He mercilessly ignores even contemporary Greek conditions in which a section of the free people was in favour of progressive egalitarianism. Though he is said to have followed the course of empiricism, such a treatment becomes self-contradictory.[10]

Citizenship: Book III of *Politics* opens with its 'central and most fundamental part'[11] dealing with the question: What is a state? As Aristotle regards the state as an institution composed of the citizens, he looks into the issue of various qualifications that entitle one for the privilege of citizenship. However, he studies the problem very carefully and, though he recognises several difficulties in offering a precise and standard definition of the term, he endeavours to furnish his own view which, despite its being best applicable to the system of a democratic government, is 'most comprehensive'. The significance of Aristotle's definition of a citizen lies in giving a positive character to the concept by enjoining upon the holder of this great privilege the duty of taking active part in the deliberative and judicial affairs of the state. Thus, his standpoint, in a peculiarly Greek and particularly Athenian fashion, becomes analogous to what the great Athenian leader (Pericles) said: "We alone regard a man who takes no interest in public affairs not as a harmless but as useless character and if few of us are the originators, we are all sound judges of a policy."

With a view to give a precise definition of his own, Aristotle keeps different considerations in his mind and moves ahead by finding fault with all of them in this or that respect by means of following aporetic method. He does not recognise mere residence as the determining factor inasmuch as the population of a state consists even of the foreigners; nor is one regarded as a citizen who has no legal right except that of suing and being sued, for this right may be enjoyed even by the aliens under the provisions of a treaty; nor even a man born of free citizens becomes a citizen, because such a qualification may create difficulties when the character of the state is changed by a revolution. The determining factor, therefore, is active participation in the sphere of state activity. "There is nothing by which a citizen in the absolute sense is well marked off as participation in judicial power and public office." Aristotle also takes into the scope of his study the essential point that the definition of a citizen varies from one political system to another. That is, every political system has its own standard to define the quality of citizenship. It is owing to this reason that the definition of a citizen as applicable to a democratic system fails to be operative in a different form

9. Ross, *op. cit.,* p. 242.
10. It is difficult to appreciate the view of W.L. Newman that Aristotle deserves to be remembed more as a reformer than a defender of slavery. *The Politics of Aristotle,* Vol. I, p. 144.
11. Ross, *op. cit.,* p. 246.

of government. He who is a citizen in a democracy will often not be a citizen in an oligarchy. However, he makes it plain that his notion of a citizen is best applicable to a democratic order in view of the existence of deliberative and judicial offices of the state.

It follows that the ingredient of Aristotle's definition of a citizen lies in participation in legislative and judicial offices of the state. A citizen is one who takes part in the working of the ecclesia (assembly) and juries (court). That is, "the characteristic of the citizen proper is a share in the administration of justice and in the membership of the governing assembly."[12] Surprisingly, by taking an organic view of the state, Aristotle confines the privilege of citizenship to a very small section of the community.

The definition of a citizen, as given by Aristotle, inheres three important qualifications:

1. A citizen must have the double capacity of ruling as well as being ruled.
2. Aristotle's definition of an active citizen excludes the major class of the toilers for the reason of their having no capacity to rule. Because of having no time for taking part in the deliberative and judicial functions of the state, the toilers are deprived of the privilege and their sole concern remains with the job of carrying on their profession for the satisfaction of the economic needs of the people.
3. The privilege of citizenship is not available to the womenfolk. The world of a woman is confined to the household management and, as such, even freewomen have nothing to do with the performance of deliberative and judicial functions.

Such a view of Aristotle is partly original and partly eclectic. The definition of Aristotle exhibits an element of originality when we find that he excludes everyone, including a free Athenian male, from the privilege of citizenship in case he has no time or capacity to take part in the deliberative and judicial functions of the state. At the same time, his exclusion of the class of the toilers from the privilege of citizenship takes him very close to the world of the *Republic* of his teacher and thereby makes his notion of a citizen largely eclectic.

If we make a further comparison between the fundamental convictions of Plato and Aristotle in this direction, it appears that the treatment of the former is partly narrower and partly elevated than that of the latter. Its narrowness lies in the point that while Plato confers the privilege of citizenship of his ideal state on both the sexes and takes into consideration all the three classes, Aristotle includes only freemen having necessary leisure and capacity to take part in legislative and adjudicative functions of the state. On the contrary, Aristotle's treatment of the subject is more exalted. While Plato showers the privilege of citizenship indiscriminately on every member of his ideal three-class polity, Aristotle mentions certain precise qualifications that entitle only a freeman to enjoy the great privilege. However, a deeper examination reveals that the difference between the two is of a purely superficial nature as both, in the true

12. Ross, *op. cit.*, p. 247.

sense of the term, ascribe citizenship to the affluent freemen and ultimately prefer a variety of aristocratic citizenship.

Similar situation arises when Aristotle's view is compared with modern notion of citizenship. Here too his view looks partly narrower and partly exalted. It is narrower in the sense that it opens the privilege of citizenship to a very restricted class of the society, while modern conception of citizenship is based on the principle of universal adult suffrage. Conversely, Aristotle's conception is exalted in the sense that while modern view confers the privilege of citizenship on every Tom, Dick and Harry, Aristotle keeps it limited to only those who are in a position to take active part in the legislative and judicial functions of the state by virtue of their dual capacity for ruling as well as being ruled.

Finally, Aristotle takes up the issue of the identity of a good man and a good citizen. He is of the view that the two are not identical. Every citizen cannot have equal virtue and excellence as each has to perform different functions, even though he may share equal concern in the security and welfare of the state. Like citizenship, even the standards of virtue vary in excellence from one form of government to another. The virtues of a good ruler are different from those of a good citizen as he has to live and work in a world of different activity. Therefore, the virtues of a good man are identical with the virtues of a good ruler, though they may be different from the virtues of a good citizen.

That is, Aristotle lays down that the virtues of a citizen and those of a good man cannot coincide, unless we assume that in the good state all citizens must be good. In the perfect state, the good man is absolutely the same as the good citizen is only good relatively to his own form of government. Obviously, though one citizen may differ from another, yet the 'salvation' of the community is the task of all citizens. Therefore, all must have the virtues of 'good citizens'—thus, and thus only, can the state be perfect. It is only in the best state that the virtues of good man and a good citizen coincide, because only in it all the citizens are good men. As each government has a peculiar character which originally formed and which continues to preserve it, therefore the laws are to be used to mould the citizen to suit the forms of government under which he lives.

Aristotle's theory of citizenship may be criticised on the following grounds:

1. It appears from the tenor of Aristotle's argument that the very notion of a citizen as taken by him, is almost strange to modern political thought. By conferring the privilege of citizenship on a very limited class of freemen having leisure and capacity to take part in the deliberative and judicial functions of the state and thereby excluding the numerous class of the toilers, what to say of the slaves, he cuts the society into two parts and, more than that, condemns the larger portion to the position of mere means to the welfare of the very small class of the fortunate freemen. Such a view cannot be accepted in modern times when it is realised that every human being has his own moral potentialities and is capable of a life worth

living for himself and, for this reason, it is the function of the state to secure rights, both social and political, for all of its members from the humblest to the most privileged.

2. Though Aristotle claims his definition to be best applicable to a democratic system of government, in its essential character it is aristocratic. In the days of representative government when citizenship is conferred on every individual regardless of the distinctions of religion, caste, sex, economic position and the like, such a view of Aristotle fails to have any plausible argument. True that a mechanic or a toiler may not have time to sit in the assembly or in the court, there is no reason why he should not have the privilege of citizenship. We cannot appreciate the view of Aristotle that manual toil actually deliberalises the soul and thereby makes a man unfit for being enlightened. Thus, the view of Aristotle loses its relevance in a democratic state.
3. Herein we may also discover the case of imposed virtue for the sake of creating citizenship. Three things must combine to create a man a virtuous citizen—nature, habituation, and teaching. Children should be kept away from 'mean' manners and thoughts. Education should be imparted so as to produce virtuous ways of life. Everything is subordinated to the cause of the salvation of the community. A critic may, therefore, say that even intelligence is sacrificed at the altar of virtue in the system of Aristotle and, in this way, ominously, he "becomes a fore-runner of the case for cultural regimentation and censorship."[13]

However, one may discover a line of consistency in the thought of Aristotle. What we have said in the preceding sections, may be repeated here that Aristotle gives an aristocratic complexion to his conception of citizenship that fits well with his theories of state and slavery. The scope of citizenship is kept confined to a very small class of the virtuous people who are none else than the affluent and free males. The rest are ignored and rather condemned to manage menial and economic affairs of the community. However unjust and iniquitous it may be, a good citizen must acquiesce in the social structure in which he lives, he cannot challenge or change it. In addition, the state can justly use its machinery to ensure and perpetuate conformism. The ideal of citizenship fails to do justice to the individual.

Constitution: In Book II of *Politics*, Aristotle studies the term 'constitution' in a peculiar sense which seems outrageous to a student of the science of government in modern times. A constitution is defined by him "as the arrangement of magistracies in a state, and especially of the highest office. The nature of the constitution depends on the seat of authority."[14] It may, however, be added here that, while treating the term constitution in a peculiar sense, Aristotle is concerned only with the Hellenic race and with nothing beyond the changes that had occurred before him and possibly might have occurred in foreseeable future.

---

13. O.P. Bakshi, *Politics and Prejudice: Notes on Aristotle's Political Theory,* p. 39.
14. Ross, *op. cit.,* p. 250.

According to Aristotle, "constitution means a scheme of the arrangement of offices determining as to which of the citizenry shall hold highest offices and which of them the other offices of the state. A constitution is the arrangement of magistracies in a state especially of all. The government is everywhere sovereign in the state, and the constitution is in fact the government."[15] That is, to Aristotle, the arrangement of magistracies becomes another name of the constitution. Barker paraphrases: "Thus, the constitution may be fully defined as an arrangement of the offices of the state determining their distribution, the residence of sovereignty and the end of political association."[16]

The meaning of Aristotle in this regard is well explained by McIlwain who says: "But if the polity or constitution is so all important in fixing the character of the *polis,* we must know exactly what the polity is. Aristotle's central thought on this subject may be expressed in three propositions concerning it, and if we can fully understand their terms, most of the political ideas will be clear to us. They are these:

1. The *polity* (constitution) determines the character of the polis (state);
2. The *politeuma* (ruling party) determines the character of the polity;
3. The *polity* is a certain ordering of the inhabitants of the *polis*."[17]

In this way, the constitution is the political reflection of the way of life of the citizens. It signifies that a change in the constitution is naturally a consequence of the change in the way of life of the citizen-body. McIlwain further says: "The *polis* is a *koinonia* (association) of citizens under a constitution and it must follow that when this constitution changes its character, the *polis* itself ceases to be the same as that existed before, just as a chorus in a comedy totally changes its character and becomes a really different chorus if later used in a tragedy, although the members may remain precisely the same. This is equally true of the state. It is to the *politeia* or constitution that we must look for; if that changes, the state is changed, if it remains unaffected, the state persists through all other operations of place or constituent members. The *polis* is a *koinonia* and the *koinonia* is embodied in the *politeia*."[18]

It can be easily understood that the idea of Aristotle about the constitution of the state highly varies with the modern notion. It is true to say that, to a very great extent, both stand apart. The view of Aristotle is consistent with the modern notion to the extent the constitution is regarded as an order determining governmental offices. But, in modern times, it cannot be accepted that the constitution implies a manner of life as well and the view of Aristotle that any change in the constitution causes a corresponding change in the life of the people of the state. It cannot be appreciated by a student of politics in these days.

15. *Politics,* III, 1278b.
16. Barker: *The Political Thought of Plato and Aristotle,* p. 305.
17. McIlwain: *The Growth of Political Thought in the West,* p. 77.
18. *Ibid.,* p. 77.

Polity: One of the essential merits of Aristotle's *Politics* lies in considering the state in its ideal as well as real forms. In other words, Aristotle studies the case of an ideal state as a matter of aspiration; he also deals with the issue of the best attainable state, what he calls the "polity". For the sake of preliminary clarification, it should be pointed out at this stage that here polity is not to be taken as one of the six forms of states as mentioned in the classification of states; it is the name of a particular form of rule where power is in the hands of the middle class representing a wise synthesis of democratic and oligarchical elements with a weightier share of the former. Moreover, such a practicable state of Aristotle is different from his purely ideal state sketched elsewhere, where the supreme qualification of virtue entails the rule of the saints. As Barker points out: "The ideal state has for its aim the blessedness of a complete and active virtue, the achievement of a common good for the state which is also the supreme good of men. It is not so with the polity. The polity is modest and middling: It is content with a military form of virtue . . . The polity . . . will have the humdrum life of a quiet bourgeoisie: the ideal state is by comparison a communion of saints."[19]

In simple words, polity may be defined as "a mean between and a mixture of the oligarchic and democratic orders, and in which rich and poor alike share legal power."[20] That is, such a system of government is dominated by a well-to-do middle class that outnumbers both the very rich and the very poor and thereby saves the political order from the hazards of a purely democratic rule in the hands of the numerous poor and a purely oligarchic rule in the hands of a very small class of the very rich people. Aristotle describes the way of life of this ruling middle class as the life of moral virtue furnishing the mark of the "best attainable social life" and, for that reason, approximating, as far as possible, to the ideal state.

The case of polity as the best practicable state is based on a set of special benefits accruing to the people. These are:

1. It is a merit of the middle class that its members suffer the least from ambition, which both in military and civil spheres is dangerous to the states.
2. The middle class consists of equals and peers and thus it contributes to the security of the state along with its own security. The people of this class do not covet the goods of others; nor do others covet their possessions as the poor covet those of the rich. Neither plotting against others, nor plotted against themselves, they live in freedom from insecurity.
3. That polity is the most stable form of political system. It may be seen in this affirmation of Aristotle that constitutional stability and the concomitant phenomenon of the unification of political and economic power appear as conceptual manifestations of a consistently integrated pattern of thought.

---

19. Barker: *The Political Thought of Plato and Aristotle,* pp. 473-74.
20. W.T. Bluhm "The Polity in Aristotle's Ideal State Theory" in *Journal of Politics,* November, 1962, p 747.

4. It must also be considered a proof of the value of such a rule that the best legislators such as Solon, Lycurgus and Charondas belonged to the middle class.

Aristotle's treatment of polity as the best attainable state may be criticised on two grounds. First, the whole plan is not clear-cut. Though polity is taken by him as a blending of democracy and oligarchy and is supposed to be the most stable and secure form of government, it remains far from being either. It may be asked if such a kind of government would ever exist in the form desired by the author of the *Politics*. We find that Aristotle himself realises three cardinal difficulties in the way of its existence. Moreover, his statement that though polity is a very rare form of government or a government of very emphemeral duration always susceptible to be overstepped by a democracy or an oligarchy, it may hardly serve the purpose of being a standard for evaluating the merits of actual states. This line of objection leads one further to question whether Aristotle is a realist on this score, or whether he has unintentionally moved in the direction of constructing an ideal state like that of his teacher. In any case, the polity of Aristotle presents the case of his grossly stretched view of the excellence of middle-class rule.

Second, a student of political thought finds here a peculiar case of the dichotomy between two different and independent theoretical concerns—a value theory of an ideal state and a causal theory of the actual state. Polity neither remains a purely actual form of state in view of the great difficulties understood by Aristotle himself, nor does it attain the heights of a purely ideal state. So, it is neither here on earth like the commonwealth of Hobbes, nor does it find its place in the ideal *polis* of Plato laid up in the heavens. The real character of the state, as viewed by Aristotle, thus becomes a two-faced phenomenon. It leads a critic to point out: "We must begin by observing the peculiar Janus-face that the *Politics* presents as a whole gazing on the idealists as if it were a Platonic Utopia and on the realists as if a sober and empirical science and yet obviously being really both at once."[21]

Critical Appreciation: Plato and Aristotle deserve the credit for setting the idealist tradition in political philosophy. Despite differences in the views of the teacher and the taught, both take state as a moralising agency or "a partnership in virtue" which alone can ensure "good life" to its people. In this way, both make politics the handmaid of ethics. This tradition saw its startling break after the death of Aristotle. But it saw its resuscitation in the works of Rousseau in France in the eighteenth century. It saw its further elaboration in the works of Kant and Hegel in Germany and then of Green and Bosanquet in England. This point should, however, be noted that Aristotle is both an idealist and a realist and hence while he studies politics in ethical terms, he also studies it in empirical directions. For this reason, Dunning comments: "The capital significance of Aristotle in the history of political theory lies in the fact that he gave to politics the character of an independent science."[22]

---

21. Werner Jaegir: *Aristotle,* p. 264.
22. W.A. Dunning: *A History of Political Theories,* Vol. I, p. 49.

18
Church Versus State Controversy

The history of medieval political thought looks like an account of the two contending traditions hinging on the issue of Church-State relationship. While the earlier tradition finding its powerful expression in the works of St. Augustine and St. Thomas Aquinas, in particular, frankly defends the case of Church supremacy entailing the subordinate position of the State, the latter tradition finding its clear expression in the works of Marsiglio of Padua and William of Occam, in particular, defends the case of State as an independent institution in the wordly or secular matters. Hence, while the former tradition justifies the case of absolute power in spiritual as well as temporal matters of the Pope as well as the final authority of Christendom, the latter tradition repudiates the unassailable position of the Pope and seeks to place the State in an autonomous position. Naturally, the triumph of the latter tradition ushered in the emergence of a secular and sovereign nation-state after the decline of the Papacy in the fifteenth century.

St. Thomas Aquinas

St. Thomas, (1225-1274) a Christian philosopher known for his master work of synthesisation of medieval thought with the systematisation of Latin theology, is the best thinker of the best part of the Middle Ages. He belonged to the middle phase of the thirteenth century in which Europe had passed from the early phase of the Middle Ages, as a result of which intellectual liberation of the men of great personality and spirit of enterprise appeared on the scene. The real character of this period has rightly been described as "formative" and "architectural" in view of the remarkable fact that it "was an age in which men tried to move mountains. The Papacy and the Empire alike dreamed of universal jurisdiction; the universities, lately established, were packed with youth, anxious and determined to explore and master all the far continents of thought."[1]

Synthesised Politics: Also known by the titles of 'Christianised Aristotle of the Middle Ages', 'Angelic Doctor' and 'Sainted Aristotle of the thirteenth century', St. Thomas rendered his remarkable contribution by integrating diverse positions through rational interpretations in order to provide a new basis to the teachings of the Christian Church. The most crucial point before him was the question of establishing a reconciliation between faith and reason and he resolved the great crisis by arguing that the two were not conflicting terms, rather each had its own meaning and occupied a legitimate position in its own sphere. Following the traditions of his pagan predecessors

---

1. M.D.C. Arcy: *Thomas Aquinas,* pp. 3-4.

like Aristotle and the Christian theologians like St. Augustine, he argued that faith was the perfection of reason and, for this sake, it should rule the secular world until it had to give way to the faith that provided a dependable bridge between the mundane and heavenly worlds.

The edifice of medieval political thought stands on four pillars, namely, Aristotle's *Politics,* Roman Law, Bible and Teutonism—ideas of the German barbarian tribes that sacked the Roman Empire and thereby established the era of feudalism in Europe. The victory of the Arabs over the Iberian peninsula opened the gateway for the entry of the classics of pagan antiquity into Christendom. As a result, the translations of classical literature by the Arabs and the Spaniards contributed to the acquisitions of abundant knowledge of the ideas of the classical masters by the theologians of the Church. Thus, Aristotelianism was revived and Roman law Christianised to suit the purpose of Church Fathers. Moreover, with the settlement of the German barbarians and their gradual conversion to the religion of Christianity, the teutonic ideas no longer remained like a stock of heresy to the philosophers of the Latin Church.

1. The architectonic nature of the political philosophy of St. Thomas is traceable in following respects: his natural theory of state shows how he brought about a compromise between the tenet of Aristotelianism regarding the state as a natural institution and the teaching of his Christian predecessors treating it as a conventional association sanctified by the institution of the holy Church.
2. On the issue of slavery, he establishes a happy synthesis of the ideas of Aristotle and Christian Fathers by holding that while all men are equal in the eyes of God, they are not so in their capacity to reason. The inferior people should be placed under the charge of the superiors not for the sake of convenience or expediency but for the consideration of diminishing divine punishment for sin and achieving salvation.
3. It is further noticeable in his views on the issue of virtuous life. Aristotle described that the end of state 'is good life'; St. Augustine insisted that a life of virtues, as fostered and promoted by the state, must be interpreted in the light of the teachings of Christianity. The immediate end of the state is to preserve an orderly society by maintaining internal and external peace and by ensuring the satisfaction of man's corporal necessities. Its ultimate end, which gives true meaning to the common good, is the temporal perfection of its members. In order to pursue the latter goal, the state is enjoined upon to foster a virtuous life by promoting moral, intellectual and cultural achievements of man. Obviously, a life according to virtue is a life according to reason.
4. It is also traceable in the way he presents a Christianised version of the classification of law. He subscribes to the doctrine of a higher law to which the civil law of the state must conform for the sake of its validity. In his four-fold classification of law higher law, has three distinct varieties-Eternal Law, Divine Law and Natural Law. However, the essential ingredient of all the three is the same implying the existence of some supernatural agency ordaining a higher law commanding people to do this and avoiding that.

5. His conception of elective monarchy as better than royal government based on the principle of heredity is a mark of his debt to the idea of the Teutons. It is well inferrable from his views on the best form of government where we find him treating constitutional monarchy as the excellent form of rule by virtue of its combining within itself the best elements of monarchy, aristocracy and democracy.

It well demonstrates that St. Thomas synthesised the traditions of Greek scholars (particularly Aristotle), Roman jurists, Christian theologians, and also of the Teutonic races and in his ideas presented a unique fusion of their best elements. Hence, it is commented that St. Thomas 'represents the totality of medieval political thought'.[2]

Law: The distinctive contribution St. Thomas made to the development of medieval political thought is to be found in his comprehensive analysis of law. His main effort "was directed towards the development of a theory of law, and it is for this work that he is best known politically."[3] Commenting on the significance of this aspect of his political philosophy, Hacker points out: "His abiding claim to the attention of the students of political theory lies in his role as a legal theorist. Government, he says, must at all times operate under the rule of law. Law, for St. Thomas, is a far broader conception than used by legislators, lawyers or judges. His intention is to create a legal framework which will encompass the governance of all aspects of the universe. The system of law, then, does not specify behaviour for all circumstances, nor is it a catalogue of procedural rules. Rather, it is an over-arching scheme with several inter-related parts, each of which has a particular purpose."[4]

The meaning of law, as conceived by St. Thomas, is contained in his four-fold classification of law—Eternal, Natural, Divine and Human. He looks upon law as "the dictate of reason emanating from the ruler who governs a perfect community. Thus, eternal law is the divine reason that governs and orders the whole of creation. In other words, it is the eternal plan of God's wisdom and, for this reason, it is beyond human comprehension. It is the plan of Government in the Chief Governor from which all the plans of government in the inferior governors must be derived. In simple words, it is the reason existing in the mind of God by which the whole universe is governed. It regulates both earthly and heavenly spheres and both animate and inanimate kingdoms. As Aquinas in his *Summa Theologica* says: "The very idea of the government of things in God, the ruler of the Universe, has the nature of a law. And since the divine reason's conception of things is not subject to time but is eternal, therefore, it is that kind of law that must be eternal."

Natural law is a reflection of the divine reason in human beings. It is written in the heart of man and through his reason it enables him to recognise, understand and obey eternal law. As reason helps man to evolve certain general principles of conduct through his innate knowledge of what is good and bad and as these principles form the body of natural law, this law enjoins upon all to do that which is implied to give human

2. M.B. Foster: *Masters of Political Thought,* Vol. I, p. 238.
3. Judd Harmon, *Political Thought from Plato to the Present,* p. 128.
4. Andrew Hacker: *Political Theory, Philosophy, Ideology, Science,* p. 146.

inclinations their widest scope. In its fullness it remains in the mind of man. It is not fully comprehensible to him. In other words, it is the reflection of the eternal law in this universe or divine light by which a man is enabled to take part in the fulfilment of the divine plan. Since human reason is limited and imperfect and, owing to this, it is unable to understand all principles of natural law, divine law comes to meet the deficiency. It consists of direct revelation of the divine purpose to the saints—authors of the scriptures. The Ten Commandments are a clear example of this kind of law. Last, there is human law. It is derived from natural law and is valid to the extent it does not clash with the latter to which it is subservient.

The four-fold classification of law, as given by St. Thomas, in this way, links up the case of political obedience with the moral obligation of human beings. Dunning sums up the meaning of St. Thomas in these words: " The *lex aeterna* (Eternal Law) is the controlling plan of this universe existing in the mind of God; *lex Naturalis* (Natural Law) is that participation of man, as a rational creature, in the eternal law (or the divine reason), through which he distinguishes between good and evil and seeks true end. Human law is the application by human reason of the divine precepts of natural law to particularly earthly conditions. The divine law in the special sense is that through which the limitation and imperfections of human reasons are supplemented and man is infallibly directed to his super-mundane end—eternal blessedness; it is the law of Revelation."[5]

The master-classification of law, as given by St. Thomas, leaves some amount of confusion when we find that he gives no list of those principles that make up the law of nature. If the law of nature is immutable and universal and the civil law must conform to it for the sake of its validity, it ought to lay down some specific norms or frontiers understandable to man. The mere assertion that there is a higher law to which all civil law must conform is a vague and confusing idea, and a modern philosopher like Bentham was well justified in calling it "rhetorical nonsense upon stilts." The whole purpose of St. Thomas is to justify Papal supremacy.

Best Government: St. Thomas seems to follow the pattern of medieval thought that was, in general, oriented towards treating kingship as the ideal form of government. Agreeing with the trend of early medieval political thought laid down by his Christian predecessors, St. Thomas justified excellence of the monarchical form of government on three grounds—necessity for unity, analogy with nature, and experience. As the welfare of the community lies in the preservation of its unity and order, its integrity can best be achieved and maintained by a single ruler rather than by several persons in view of the fact that they may have their serious disagreements causing division and disintegration of political authority. Likewise, as art imitates nature, the political community should be the example of nature, where all objects are governed by one, as the heart is the principal mover of the body, and a single God is the ruler of the universe. Finally, experience shows that societies ruled by several persons are usually torn with dissensions.

5. W. A. Dunning: *A History of Political Theories,* Vol. I, pp. 192-93.

Apart from highlighting the significance of the monarchical form of government, and also hitting at its two serious defects, St. Thomas also studies the case of legal control to prevent the king from abusing his authority. He dismisses the remedy of tyrannicide as suggested by his predecessor—John of Salisbury. "Tyranny is not merely a public crime, but if there could be such a thing, a crime more than public." He clearly warns that it would be highly detrimental to the interest of the civil order if private individuals could assume the right to murder their king on the charge of his being a tyrant. He, however, recognises people's right to resistance in three situations—if the oppression of the king is of a very serious character; if there is a reasonable chance of revolt in getting success; and if there is an assurance that the revolution would not provoke greater social evils than those it desires to eradicate.

So deeply is St. Thomas afraid of the horrors of a revolution that he prefers to live under a tyrant rather than to have an uprising causing serious problems to the people. His advice is that a government, long established, should not be changed for light and transient reasons, and that the government should be so organised and conducted that the avenues of tyranny are plugged. That is, the powers of the king should be so "tempered" that they cannot easily lead to the rise of a tyrannical form of government. Thus, the best form of government, as suggested by St. Thomas, "can be described as a constitutional monarchy in which the concentration of the administrative power is combined with legal controls to prevent its arbitrary use."[6]

The preference of St. Thomas for a mixed form of government is supported by two considerations. First, he realises that, as a matter of political reality, forms of government must be suitable to the talents, culture and social maturity of the people. Second, he accepts the view of Aristotle as adopted by Polybius and Cicero that both monarchical and aristocratic forms overlook the fact that one man or a selected elite, no matter how virtuous, can never be as good as the whole community which comprises them as one of the parts. That is, St. Thomas subscribes to the law of cycle of the political systems that inevitably takes place in course of time, to replace one form of government with another having its worst form in the substitution of a royal form of government by a tyranny.

It is, therefore, reasonable to assume that St. Thomas believes in the excellence of the royal rule absolutely or ideally speaking. At the same time, he feels that in the practical order monarchy must give way to some mixed type which would embody a balancing of interests or forces. It is clear that the real preference of St. Thomas is for a limited or constitutional monarchy committed to the maintenance of the conditions of the public good.

Interpreted in this way, the main duties of the king become two-fold. First, he is responsible for the satisfaction of the material requirements of his people. To this end, St. Thomas suggests the securing of economic justice through currency control, price regulation, care of the poor and other measures for strengthening the system of agrarian

6. W.T. Bluhm, *Theories of the Political System,* p. 225.

economy. The king should take proper precautions against disintegrative tendencies created by trade and commerce, and also by the foreigners engaged in such pursuits. It also becomes his duty to provide suitable sites for the laying out of villages and towns after taking into consideration the factors of health, climate and environmental conditions. Besides, St. Thomas advises the monarch to establish suitable places of learning, markets, military training camps, churches and the courts. Finally, for the sake of proper administration, he makes it essential for his king to recruit very suitable persons. Second, after securing proper satisfaction of the material needs of the people, the king should be very particular in watching that the way is cleared for the realisation of the higher aims of life. The people should have their spiritual upliftment.

St. Thomas's view of the excellence of the elective monarchy—an idea he certainly borrowed from the tradition of the Teutons—has been misinterpreted as his dim acceptance of the doctrine of popular sovereignty if a critic carefully notes the fundamental feature of his political philosophy as being an earnest attempt to champion the cause of papal absolutism. One may hardly agree with the view of Prof. Barker that St. Thomas, like the Clerical thinkers of the Middle Ages in general, "is a Whig; he believes in popular sovereignty, popular institution of monarchy, a pact between king and people, and the general tenets of Locke." Any faint idea of contractual relationship subsisting between the king and his people signifying the doctrine of popular sovereignty can by no means be reconciled with the acceptance of divine authority overshadowing the jurisdiction of temporal power.

Secular Authority: If the state, according to St. Thomas, is an ecclesiastical institution, in the ultimate analysis the sphere of kingly authority is overshadowed by the priestly jurisdiction. It is then easily inferrable that this "Angelic Doctor" presents a well argued case in defence of papal absolutism. The case of papal absolutism placing secular authority under the domination of the Church is supported by the following arguments advanced by St. Thomas:

1. The subservient position of secular authority is conditioned by the very fact that its natural character is attributable to its existence by virtue of a divine plan. The institution of authority in the state is a God-given phenomenon. The authority of the state exists to make human life possible on earth; it is also required to create conditions for the fulfilment of the divine plan.
2. The higher position of the priest implying supreme position of the Pope is also supported by the natural law of gradation and hierarchy. For this St. Thomas takes the help of an analogy. As soul rules the body and God rules the universe, spiritual authority should rule the temporal sphere.
3. The theory of Two Swords, as enunciated by Pope Gelasius I, finds a peculiar twist at the hands of St. Thomas who, while agreeing with the dualist conception of authority, secular and spiritual, makes the former subservient to the latter.
4. The position of the State being subordinate to the Church is further determined by the emphasis of St. Thomas on the higher aim of human life—salvation.

5. The subordinate position of the secular authority is governed by St. Thomas's theory of determination of the legitimate frontiers of civil government.

It follows that St. Thomas takes an instrumental view of the state. It is to serve the individual in a particular way. It is not an end in itself but a means for serving the Church and embodying a higher purpose—the salvation of man. The laws of the state must conform to the precepts of the higher law whose interpretation is the concern of the priestly class having Pope at the top. We have already seen that the twofold function of the king concerning the material and spiritual domains of human life are specified by St. Thomas in a way that the latter well overshadows the former. In spite of having its separate area of activity, the state obviously becomes a subordinate department of the ecclesiastical organisation. In this way, the Church becomes the 'upholder' of state authority and by laying stress on the instrumental conception of the state, St. Thomas "makes it the pivot of his political doctrine."[7]

Critical Appreciation: No doubt, St. Thomas represents the totality of medieval political thought. He performed a miracle by fusing diverse tendencies into a single whole that led to the creation of a new trend known by the name of Thomism. It is a fact that he acted as a bridge in transmitting ancient and medieval ideas to the modern period. His contribution to the school of scholasticism and his best exposition of the four categories of law constitute the brilliant feature of medieval political philosophy. Barker says that Aristotle "taught St. Thomas and through St. Thomas he also taught Hooker who, in turn, was the judicious teacher of Locke."[8] The remarkable work of the fusion of the tenets of pagan Aristotle and Christian Augustine attributed to him the title of being the best prophet of scholasticism which "is the master-key to the understanding of medievalism."[9]

Marsiglio of Padua

If St. Thomas is known as the best advocate of the traditional doctrine of papal absolutism, Marsiglio (1270-1343) is regarded as the best exponent of the secularist tradition that eventually triumphed to entail the decline and fall of the papacy. Also known as Marsilio or Marsilius, he received his early education in his home town University of Padua in Italy—a prominent centre of learning that, like the University of Paris, was at that time known for being "infested" with Aristotelian teachings. On March 12, 1313, he was given the office of the Rector of Paris University where he gave lectures on natural philosophy and remained engaged in medical research and practice. However, what immortalised his name is his book titled *Defensor Pacis* (*Defence of the Peace*) completed on 24 June 1324, written with the help of his one-time teacher William of Brescia, also known by the nickname of John of Janduan. This work soon became a matter of controversial study and a subject of inquisitional proceedings. Pope John XXII (having his seat at Avignon) resented this book so much

7. Avelling: "St. Thomas Aquinas" in Hearnshaw, (ed.): *Social and Political Ideas of Some Great Medieval Thinkers,* p. 97.
8. Barker (ed.): *The Politics of Aristotle,* p. Ixii.
9. Avelling, *op. cit.,* p. 88.

that he called both the authors "the sons of the devil", "the sons of Belial", "pestiferous men", while his successor, Pope Clement VII, in 1343 denounced them as "the worst ever of the heretics."[10]

State: Marsiglio follows the Aristotelian tradition in comparing the state with a living organism consisting of many parts each of which must perform its function satisfactorily for the benefit of the whole body. As he says: "Even an animal that is well disposed in accordance with nature is composed of certain proportionate parts ordained to one another, which communicate their actions mutually to one another and to the whole, so a state that is well disposed and instituted in accordance with reason is constituted in a similar way." To Marsiglio, the state thus becomes a natural and organic whole represented by diverse social classes devoted to the purpose of promoting the good life and welfare of the people. From this point of the organic character of the state, Marsiglio picks up the thread that malfunctioning of any part of the organism is injurious to the whole structure. Hence, if a clergy transgresses his jurisdiction by interfering in secular affairs, the social organism suffers from strife and disorder. The concern of the priestly class is confined to the religious or spiritual sphere and, as such, this class is not entitled to interfere in the secular sphere.

Such a twist of the Aristotelian arguments enables Marsiglio to refute the doctrine of synthesis of reason and faith as expounded by St. Thomas. While "Sainted Aristotle of the thirteenth century" defended the higher position of the clergy by establishing a compromise between reason and faith in a way that the latter dominated the former, Marsiglio takes a different view by keeping reason and faith apart. A proper reconciliation of faith and reason is not at all essential, as the people may lead a good life without clerical intervention in their secular affairs.

Once again, while following the Aristotelian tradition, Marsiglio touches the issue of good life that is possible only in the state. However, he interprets "good" or "sufficient" life as one of economic and social security, and of the fulfilment of man's natural desires without particular reference to the ethical and moral values. To Marsiglio the state is primarily and mainly an agency for satisfying the material needs of the people and, therefore, his accent is on the useful (material) things of life with no mention of the state as the promoter of moral values. A clear line of anti-Aristotelianism is thus traceable in the political philosophy of Marsiglio by the very fact of his placing the state supreme over the church. We find that Marsiglio's theory of state discards the ethical orientation of Aristotelianism and the theological orientation of St. Augustine, and thus makes politics independent of its normative character.

By separating politics from ethico-theological predilections, Marsiglio denies any metaphysical character to the state. He asserts that the unity of the state consists in the acceptance by the people of a common government. In simple words, this implies that the state must be studied from a purely secular standpoint without any reference to the supernatural aspects of man's life. All references to the hand of some supernatural agency in the composition of the state or in laying down the norm of political obligation

10. Alan Gewirth: *Marsilius of Padua: The Defender of Peace,* Vol. I, p. 13.

should be discarded as they cannot stand to reason. "The divine creation, governance, and end of the world are no longer in any sense susceptible of rational proof, and consequently the entire divine order exercises no control whatsoever upon a political doctrine established by rational demonstration."[11]

Popular Sovereignty: The real concern of Marsiglio is not confined to the repudiation of all ethico-theological predilections with a resolve to uphold the supremacy of the state over the church, it also covers his assertion of the doctrine of popular sovereignty implying residence of legislative authority with the people. If the state is for the good of the people, its power should be in the hands of those who are concerned with the existence of unity and peace in the community. That is, the maintenance of peace and unity in the state is a concern of all, not of a single person, whether king or bishop or Pope. Thus, Marsiglio subscribes to the celebrated maxim that what affects all must be approved by all. The doctrine of people as legislator, as laid down by Marsiglio, stands on the support of his various arguments that may be enumerated as under:

1. Marsiglio asserts that people assembled in a body are wise judges of an issue and that they are more likely to act in the general interest than would one man or a few act. He agrees with the traditional arguments.
2. The doctrine of legislation by the people is in consonance with the idea of freedom. Freedom is indivisible. Man is free if all are free. As the law applies to all people, they should be the sovereign legislators. Even if one man or few could perform a better job as an object proof of the excellence of legislation by one or few persons, Marsiglio contends, it would still be better to vest the power in the people as a whole inasmuch as this is the best way to ensure their freedom.
3. Marsiglio asserts the doctrine of "trust in the majority." To him any sort of rule in the hands of a single ruler or of a few, howsoever good it might be, is bound to degenerate in the long run. Only rule in the hands of many or all is the best bulwark against degeneration of a political system into a perverted form of government.

Marsiglio's use of the term "weightier part" has given rise to a considerable difference of opinion about its interpretation. While his critics have interpreted it to construe as "an elite of the people" signifying his real preference for an aristocratic form of government, his admirers have taken it as "majority of the people" to assert his position as a democrat. A great authority on Marsiglio like Gewirth thus points out: "Marsilus' concept of the people as it emerges from these several aspects may be briefly summed up in the following characteristics. First, its basic units are not individuals but classes or functional groups. Second, none of these groups is to dominate the others, but all are to have a share in political authority. Third, the share accruing to each group is determined by both quantitative and qualitative standards which prevent the domination of respectively the honorabilities alone or the vulgus alone. Fourth, as a consequence, the people is the all-inclusive political body of the state; it is a corporate whole, a *universitas* which can act as one."[12]

11. H.J. Schmandt: *A History of Political Philosophy,* p. 171.
12. See Downtron, Jr. and Hart (eds.): *Perspectives on Political Philosophy,* Vol. I, p. 307.

Law: Marsiglio presents twofold classification of law—human law and divine law. Following the tradition of Aristotle, he defines human law as a command, permission, prohibition and the like given by a popular authority. It signifies a command for acts which are essentially good, a prohibition for acts which are essentially bad, and a permission for those which are ethically indifferent. The definition of human law has thus a double aspect—positive and negative. Positively, law is a command or an affirmative statute obliging its transgressor to punishment; it is a prohibition for certain acts that are essentially detrimental to the interest of the community. In a word, law is a coercive command. As Allen interprets: "Law is essentially adjustment as to what is just and advantageous to the community. It is an imperative expression of the common need, formulated by reason, promulgated by recognised authority, sanctioned by force."[13]

If law is a punitive weapon and the rule of law implies that laws rightly laid down must be dominant, it follows that the human law is basically different from the divine law. When Marsiglio puts the essence of law in being a coercive command, it well indicates that this command is given by someone who is a human authority. Obviously, Marsiglio brushes aside the agency of God as not relevant to his purpose. He intends to discuss the establishment of only those laws and governments which emerge immediately from the decision of the human mind. Gewirth thus analyses: "Law, hence, involves not merely coerciveness, even applied impartiality; it must emanate from those who have the authority to coerce. And this authority, as he subsequently shows, can belong only to the people. Hence, his full definition of law provides that it is the command of the whole body of citizens."[14]

The higher law is divine law that may be variously termed as the law of grace, evangelical law, new law, or law of eternal salvation. The real purpose of this law is to help men attain eternal salvation. It emanates from some supernatural agency having no coercive power like that of a government on earth. Moreover, the divine agency is essentially merciful and, as such, divine law is based upon the consideration that mercy rather than immediate punishment should be the prime factor in dealing with the sins committed by man. The human law has an imperative character as a result of which the wrong-doer is punished at the hands of the rulers on the earth; contrary to this, divine law has a noncoercive character and a wrong-doer might redeem himself by praying to God for mercy knowing that "the mills of God grind but slowly." Gewirth thus explains: "No man is to be judged irrevocably as a sinner in this world, for Christ mercifully allows sinners to repent and earn merit in the very end of their lives. Punishment for transgression in this world would hence seem to close books which, in fact, remain open to the very last."[15]

---

13. J.W. Allen: "Marsiglio of Padua" in Hearnshaw, *op. cit.*, p. 181.
14. Gewirth, *op. cit.*, p. 143.
15. *Ibid.*, p. 237.

It is to be noted here that while Marsiglio agrees with the existence of a higher law in the name of divine law, and thereby conforms to the medieval tradition of Christian theology, he takes a revolutionary turn by adding that divine law is not a mystic conception as taken by his predecessors, but a body of rules contained in the New Testament. Marsiglio thus makes the body of divine law quite specific by laying down the doctrine of accepting what Christ has said on this earth as well as by making a "literal" interpretation of his meanings in the light of prevailing circumstances. The very notion of the divine law thus assumes a material form at the hands of Marsiglio.

Government: Marsiglio considers elective monarchy with limited power as the best form of government. A monarchical government has the best executive capable of maintaining peace and unity in the state. It best guarantees peace through the maintenance of law and justice. Whereas legislation is the work of the people or a weightier part thereof, administration or the execution of the law is a concern of the monarch. It follows that Marsiglio regards the king as the best officer to implement the will of the people contained in the body of the statutes. However, in order to make his king's office in tune with the doctrine of general council, Marsiglio wants him to be elected by the people. The election of the ruler by the people follows in the first instance from the fact that the people make the laws. For law and ruler are correlative, since the law is to the ruler as form is to the matter; and those who generate a form determine also the matter of that form.

Apart from emphasising the elective nature of the king's office, Marsiglio further places his king under the legitimate authority of law. It implies that the rule of king is illegitimate unless he keeps himself under law like his subjects and thereby lends a democratic character to his form of government. Gewirth thus sums up: "He (Marsiglio) flatly rejects any ruler or government which is not under the law or not subject to correction by the people for transgressing the law, as well as any which is not made by the people."[16]

The idea of elective monarchy with limited powers, as conceived by Marsiglio, is basically different from Plato's notion of an all-wise philosopher-ruler; it also differs greatly from the notion of a virtuous ruler as advocated by the Christian theologians before him. The essential qualification of the king is not the element of virtue in him (superseding the virtues of all else), but his election by the people who are real legislators of the commonwealth. Moreover, Marsiglio makes no mention of the presence of "theological" virtues in his king. What he really desires is the administrative power of the state in the hands of a monarch chosen by the people to carry out their will. One may say that every king must invariably be endowed with three virtues—prudence, justice and equity—and Marsiglio's non-reference to them is liable to make even a non-virtuous man the king of the Christian commonwealth.

It appears that Marsiglio's doctrine of popular sovereignty embodied in the form of his idea of a people-legislator, and his preference for an elected king exercising limited powers signifies his attempt to lay down a glimpse of the doctrine of

16. *Ibid.*, pp. 240-41.

separation of powers and parliamentary supremacy.[17] His best form of government is a representative assembly consisting of the body of the believers (or their nominees) and having an executive (king) entrusted with the job of administering the laws for the sake of maintaining peace and unity in the state. It may, however, be pointed out that Marsiglio's whole picture is not very clear. The composition of his legislature (*Legislator Humanus*) and his executive (*Pars Principans*) has hardly any resemblance with modern organs of a democratic government. Mcllwain takes a very firm stand in rejecting the view that Marsiglio desires to say anything on the subject of the separation of powers or representative parliament as we take them today.[18]

General Council: Marsiglio takes a line of basic difference from all his Christian predecessors in defining the meaning and nature of the Church. To him, it means not an institution embodied in a single person like the clergy or the bishop, it signifies the whole body of the faithful people believing and invoking the name of Christ along with all parts of the whole body in every community, even the family. As such, the church comes to have a democratic organisation in which all believers share equal authority and, for that very reason, it is the whole body of the faithful that has the right to deal with important matters relating to the determination of the articles of faith, ex-communication of the heretics, election of the ecclesiastical office-bearers, including the Pope, and the like. It is obvious that such a revolutionary definition of the church "means not only that the church exists for all the faithful, but, even more important than that, the church is controlled by the faithful, not merely by the clergy or Pope".[19]

Such a definition of the church, as given by Marsiglio, subverts its entire hierarchical structure. The equalisation of the authority of the clergy and the bishop, including the Pope, with the whole body of the believers destroys the very basis of the superior, even supreme, position of the priestly class. It is obvious that such an interpretation of Marsiglio breaks the tradition whereby the priesthood loses its political or institutional authority to the whole body of the believers.

With a view to giving more weight to his conception of reforming the church by destroying the tradition of priestly supremacy, Marsiglio re-examines the question of relationship between the priesthood and the sacraments. He discards the view that a clergy is infallible. If any man can err, the bishop is no exception. Even the Roman bishop can sometimes err or be inclined by perverted emotions to do so. There can be no mediation of the clergy in relationship of man with God. "To err is human and to forgive is divine." As such, Marsiglio says, there is no difference between the layman and the clergy in matters of committing sins and seeking their forgiveness by God. If the Church is a congregation of all the believers and if this body alone has the right to choose its office-bearers, it implies that Marsiglio not merely refutes the traditional doctrine of papal absolutism, he assigns to the priestly class a mere advisory role to be performed under the over-riding control of the *universitas fidelium*.

---

17. F. Pollock: *An Introduction to the History of Science of Politics,* p. 87.
18. McIlwain: *Growth of Political Thought in the West.,* p. 307.
19. Gewirth: *op. cit.,* p. 263.

A very significant feature of Marsiglio's revolutionary doctrine desiring democratisation of the Church finds place in his sanction of coercive power to the body of the believers. That is, the jurisdiction of the entire body of congregation of the Church is not merely confined to the election of the office-bearers or in determining the articles of faith, it also covers certain areas where it can punish the wrong-doers for the sake of maintaining peace and unity in the Church having its integral connection with peace and unity in the State.

Critical Appreciation: It is clear that Marsiglio's political philosophy, as discussed in the preceding sections, "is a root and branch attack upon the ecclesiastical hierarchy and especially upon a papal *plenitude potestatis*."[20] We. have seen that the fundamental pursuit of this "best champion of the anti-papal tradition" was to destroy the myth of papal absolutism by means of a reconstructed version of Aristotelianism and a revisited interpretation of Christian theology. His views on the state as a natural association, his emphasis on the separation of reason from faith along with the Latter's position as being higher than the former, and, above all, his concept of the general council, all had very decisive effects in the direction of his repudiation of the traditional doctrines of the plenitude of powers (*plentitudo potestatis*) of the Pope. As a matter of fact, the real significance of Marsiglio lies in his being a revolutionary thinker of the later middle ages projecting certain ideas precursing modern political thought. That is why, he is described as the precursor of the great thinkers of the modern period like Hobbes, Locke, Rousseau, Montesquieu, Bentham and even Marx. The immediate impact of his ideas should be seen on the Leaders of the Conciliar Movement. For this reason, it is said that "Marsiglio not merely divined the Europe of his own day, but he also divined the Europe of the ages unborn."[21] "Many of the ideas of Reformation, and even many of the ideas of the French Revolution, were proclaimed, though in scholastic garb, by such men as Marsiglio of Padua."[22] The conceptions of Marsiglio "foreshadowed almost every point of modern political philosophy."[23]

---

20. G. H. Sabine: *A History of Political Theory,* p. 300.
21. R. H. Murray: *History of Political Science from Plato to the Present,* p. 81.
22. F.W. Maitland: "Introduction" in his English translation of O.V. Gierke's *Political Theories of the Middle Ages,* p. 5.
23. H.J. Laski: "Political Theory in the Later Middle Ages" in *Cambridge Medieval History,* Vol. VII, p. 629.

19
Machiavelli

Machiavellil (1469-1527) has rightly been called "a child of his own times." As the period of his life and work coincided with the glorious days of the Renaissance and as he vigorously represented the shade of New Learning in his writings, he is also known as the "Child of the Renaissance." Of course, the political ideas of Machiavelli were coloured by the conditions of his own days. However, to him, the most shocking factor was the unfortunate conditions of his beloved Italian peninsula where none of the rulers of Venice, Florence, Naples, Milan and the Papal States was able to consolidate its strength. Not only this, Italy was the battleground of intriguing and ambitious potentates, local as well as foreign, who had very little capacity to preserve or protect the integrity and independence of Italy from the aggressions of her belligerent neighbours. He also noted the unfortunate fact that during the period of constant disorder and internecine warfare, public morality was deplorably low, and an unscientific statecraft had become the sole arm of defence. The norms of public conduct declined so precipitously that the old institutions of the church and the empire were no longer able to evoke a spirit of unity and stimulate an interest in private and public morals.[1]

The Prince: This work of Machiavelli ascribes to him the title of being the maker of a new political science as Galileo is known for being the founder of a new science of nature. Herein we find the picture of a ruler—a despot capable of disciplining his subjects in a strong political organisation under his perfect leadership. Herein we find his dismal picture of the human nature that serves the very purpose of having an absolute ruler in the state. Most important of all, herein we find a set of specific injunctions that the ruler must observe for the consolidation of his power. It is this part of the work that ascribes to him the credit of being a great authority on the subject of statecraft. However, the underlying point ought to be borne in mind that all is written for the sake of his beloved country. "It is an essay on what makes for success in Italy from the point of view of Prince. It is an endeavour to show what a Prince must understand, what he must do and be, and what he must not do, in order to consolidate and extend his dominion. It has reference throughout to Italian conditions of the moment."[2]

---

1. What really influenced the mind of Machiavelli in this regard was the practical experience that he gained by virtue of his very close contact with the rulers of Germany (Emperor Maximilian), of France (Emperor Louis XII) and of Romagna (King Caesar Borgia) during the course of his ambassadorial assignments there. He drew many lessons from the achievements of Borgia in particular.
2. J.W. Allen: *A History of Political Thought in the Sixteenth Century,* p. 466.

The subject matter of *The Prince,* for the sake of a convenient study, may be classified into three heads—organisation of a strong central government, territorial expansion of the empire, and a passionate appeal to the ruler of his country to make his state powerful and great. First and foremost, the organisation of a strong central government is the *sine qua non* of restoring unity and strength in the state. For this purpose, Machiavelli advises his ruler to completely destroy the customs and institutions of a free people in order that he may begin again to create a new community not infected with the virus of freedom. Though the people are generally conservative, they admire great renovators like Moses, Curus, Theseus and Romulus, for the reformers succeed in altering the shape of a society by their tough endeavours. The ruler may make use of sheer treachery and brutality and other perfidious methods by his demonstrable skill. However, the use of such methods should run for a very short duration, as it is the affection of the people that has a long-term effect, and the ruler ought to win it as a remedial measure to surmount the impending crises.

Machiavelli also advocates the doctrine of divide and rule for the use of the ruler for consolidating his power. Feuds among the people and the nobility have always been there, and it is for the ruler to consolidate his power by playing off one against the other. The ruler must maintain his own strong army to beat the invaders. In settlement of disputes among his rivals and opponents, the ruler must possess and exercise the qualities of the lion and the fox. The element of fortune is elaborately discussed. He compares it with a woman and, for that reason, advises the ruler to keep it under his strong control. He admits the hand of accident in the rise and fall of the rulers; at the same time, he cautions his Prince against the insidious tendency of depending upon the element of chance without making use of his critical commonsense.

The second important part of *The Prince* contains Machiavelli's advice for the ruler to seek territorial expansion of his empire. The state should either expand or perish. War gives a natural outlet to the ebullient energy of the people; it also manifests a mark of patriotism in the hearts of the people. Security is impossible unless a state is stronger than its neighbours and, more than that, to be securely stronger, it must dominate, better conquer, others. In foreign affairs the ruler should make treaties and agreements but abrogate them whenever required in the national interest. If there is a war, the state should never remain neutral. It is always wiser to take sides in a war. Thus, the Prince should join hands preferably with a weaker party and win after conducting an honest struggle. A strategy of coalitions is better than a policy of letting alone in foreign policy situations, both offensive and defensive. Thus, the foreign policy of the state must be framed and practised in sheer consonance with the national interest.

The last part of *The Prince* seems to be like his passionate appeal to the ruler (Lorenzo de Medici of Florence in particular) to restore national unity and power. The author offers a bold proof of his patriotism by desiring his ruler to expel all aggressors and barbarians from the soil of his beloved country. In a roundabout reference to de Medici, he issues a powerful appeal: "You see how she prays to God daily to send someone to deliver her from the cruelty and insolence of the barbarians. You see how fain and ready she is to follow the banner if only it were set up."[3]

A word of caution may be given at this stage that *The Prince* does not at all reveal real preference of Machiavelli for any particular form of government. It appears from the general tenor of the discussion that this small book on the science of statecraft signifies Machiavelli's real preference for the rule of an absolute monarch. It is not so. The real purpose of *The Prince* is to offer specific counsels for the ruler to consolidate his power with a resolve to establish a stable and strong state. The ruler of Machiavelli means the government whether in the hands of one, or few, or many.

It is obvious that Machiavelli's theory of human nature is extremely pernicious. His political philosophy based on the principles of universal egoism and wickedness makes his name an anathema. It is certain that he takes a thoroughly wrong view of human nature; he was unmindful of the fact that if a man is not wholly good, he is not wholly bad either. Man has a social aspect of personality that brings him in natural association with other human beings and thereby seeks his co-operation in the pursuit of a common good. The result is that Machiavelli's thoroughly inaccurate judgement of human nature makes him the propounder of an immoral and inaccurate doctrine. According to Prof. Jaszi, "At the same time, by the passionate and enthusiastic glorification of political crime he must bear the responsibility of having made from the diffused crime of isolated princely criminal, a compact philosophical doctrine which corrupted public opinion in many parts of the world and which envenomed still more an unscrupulous political practice."[4]

The Discourses: Machiavelli's *Discourses*, a longer and more discursive work than his *Prince*, contains a very large number of observations on the excellence of a strong republican government. Rambling from one subject to another and then trekking back, it does represent an integral part of the general theory of the state as given by the Florentine when he lauded it as "a new route which had not yet been followed by anyone." The central theme of this work, though shrouded in a mass of miscellaneous reflections, is contained in all that has a direct as well as indirect bearing on what "constitutes political strength and stability."[5] For this very reason, Machiavelli looked into the history of the great Romans and then placed great emphasis on five cardinal qualities—virtue, religion, liberty, patriotism and maintenance of citizen-soldiery—that form the subject-matter of this great work.

In attempting to solve every problem relating to the instability and decline of a political order, Machiavelli comes to the conclusion that the well-being and development of any political society depends less on its institutions than on the spirit that stands behind them. Machiavelli calls this spirit by the name of *virtus* having its English version in "virtue." However, the meaning of this term at the hands of Machiavelli "has

3. *The Prince,* Ch. 25.
4. Geisar and Jaszi: *Political Thought from Plato to Jeremy Bentham,* p. 119.
5. Allen, *op. cit.,* p. 457.

many facets; basically it was Italianisation of the Latin word *virtus* and denoted the fundamental quality of man which enables him to achieve great works and deeds."[6]

A study of the glorious Roman history taught Machiavelli that what had made his country great in the past was nothing but this great quality of character. Thus, he insists that the determining quality of leadership is virtue. The sole reason for the decline and fall of the Roman glory should, according to him, be traced in the absence of the great quality of human character. For this he ardently desires that his people should not only take lessons from the pages of their glorious history, but must rather establish a perfect republic in the form of a unified body that by acting instinctively "generated the strength, single-minded will power, and vitality necessary for political success."[7]

Machiavelli's judgement of religion is strictly utilitarian. He calls religion, as prevailing in his times, a force of disunity and disruption. In his view, the right kind of religion can be of immense value in creating stability and strength in the state. He says: "As the observance of divine worship is the cause of the greatness of a state, so the contempt of it is the cause of its ruin. It implies that religion is not at all a superstition; it has its instrumental values. What is needed is a religion after the fashion of old Rome: a religion that teaches that he who best serves the state best serves the gods."[8]

Like virtue, the notion of liberty has a very complex connotation. It seems to consist essentially not in any mode or form of government but in a security for life, honour and property under law. In its widest sense, liberty includes everything relating to the rights of the people, freedom from oppression, a share in the direction of public affairs, security and discharge of public duties. It would not be incorrect to say that, according to Machiavelli, virtue, liberty and patriotism are interchangeable terms. Not only that, liberty also infers rule under a ruler of exceptional ability. A corrupt people cannot keep liberty as they lack the quality of public spirit; so liberty cannot be enjoyed by a disunited and insecure people. In short, men who have security, freedom from oppression and a burning sense of patriotism in their hearts encouraging them to take a positive part in the direction of public affairs, and worship the name of liberty.

Integrally allied with virtue and liberty is the notion of patriotism. The public spirit of the citizens rests on the sure foundation of their self-regard. It is the absence of this spirit of true public service that encourages the corrupt rulers to engage mercenary troops for suppressing the freedom of their own people. Similarly, it is the want of this quality that brings disunity and corruption in society, entailing its own decline and fall.

The last quality is the maintenance of a citizen-soldiery. The state must not at all depend upon the support of the mercenary troops as they are never loyal to any particular ruler. Machiavelli strongly enjoins upon the ruler to have a disciplined army of his own people whose hearts are filled with a deep sense of faithfulness to their country. For this, he recommends compulsory military training for all youths of the

6. Felix Gilbert: *Machiavelli and Guicciardini: Politics and History in Sixteenth Century Florence,* p. 179.
7. *Ibid.,* p. 191.
8. Allen, *op. cit.,* p. 459.

country. He warns: "Prince or Republic is much to be blamed if without an army of its own."[9]

If these are the cardinal factors that bring about strength and stability in the state, a republican system of government is decidedly the best form of government where these qualities have their best possible prospect of realisation. Machiavelli argues elaborately that a popular government of the republic is in every respect superior to that of the despotism of a single ruler. The worst form of government, according to him, is the rule of a despot. As he says: "The mass is wiser and more constant than a Prince."[10] Again, "I affirm that a people is more prudent, more stable and of better judgement than a Prince. Not without reason is the voice of people likened to the voice of God".[11]

It is said by critics that Machiavelli wrote handbooks for the "tyrants" with a view to pleasing his new ruler of Florence in particular. In general, both *The Prince* and *The Discourses* were intended to reveal the laws for the benefit of the usurpers and conspirators. In particular, the ambition of the younger Medici, first Giuliano and then Lorenzo, for founding a dynasty "stimulated Machiavelli to prepare a treatise on the policy to be followed by a new prince."[12] Summing up the general approach of Machiavelli, Butterfied points out: "His maxims were written for princes, usurpers, conspirators, soldiers and citizens in turn for princes rather than for the states, for princes even when their interests are not those of the state. Machiavelli is willing to tell the tyrant how to move if he wishes to increase his power or to destroy free institutions. At the crucial points his statecraft, in the *Discourses*, at any rate cannot take shelter behind a doctrine which judges conduct by reference to public good".[13]

Ethics and Politics: The distinctive aspect of Machiavelli's political philosophy becomes clear from his affirmation that while it is most praiseworthy for a ruler to be good, nevertheless he must remain prepared to set aside all moral considerations and employ every possible method of violence, cruelty, bad faith, intrigue and the like in preference to the maxims of religion and morality. It is frankly and emphatically sanctioned by Machiavelli in situations calling for the consolidation of power and expansion of the dominion. According to Machiavelli, a discreet ruler should particularly avoid the infamy of those vices which imperil the life of the state and thus be relieved of concern about those that are necessary for the sake of its preservation. In his own words: "Let a prince, therefore, aim at conquering and maintaining the state, and the means will always be judged honourable and praised by everyone, for the vulgar is always taken by appearances and the issue of the event; and the world consists only of the vulgar, and the few who are not vulgar are isolated when the many have a rallying point in the prince."[14]

9. *Discourses,* 1, 21.
10. *Ibid.,* I, 58.
11. *Ibid.,*
12. Gilbert, *op. cit.,* p. 161.
13. H. Butterfield: *The Statecraft of Machiavelli,* pp. 108-9.
14. *The Prince,* p. 66.

Obviously, in Machiavelli's system, moral judgments, religious precepts or ethical considerations are frankly subordinated to the exigencies of the political interests. Since the necessity of the existence and the preservation of the state are an object of fundamental concern, Machiavelli subordinates every consideration to the interest of the state and expatiates upon the dictates of unscrupulous patriotism. In his *Discourses* he says: "Where the safety of one's country is at stake there must be no consideration of what is just or merciful or cruel, glorious or shameful; on the contrary, everything must be disregarded save the course which will save her life and maintain her independence."[15] Likewise, he continues: "There is no disgrace in not keeping promises that were imposed on you by force and extorted promises that concern public interest will always without shame be broken when the power to enforce them is wanting."[16]

Moreover, Machiavelli not only separates politics from religion and ethics, he also adheres to the latter's instrumental value. He insists that the ruler should employ the norms of religion and ethics to influence his people for the sake of his own interest. The considerations of religion and ethics have no intrinsic or objective value of their own, rather they are valuable instruments of policy and, for this reason, the ruler should utilise them as a tool whenever so necessary. In no way, are they sacrosanct, because if the state were ever to observe them strictly, it would disintegrate owing to the overflow of the egoistic and aggressive tendencies of its own people. The science of statecraft thus demands that political authority should pay no regard for the qualms of conscience but adopt all means, even religious and moral, to pursue a policy pertaining to the strength and security of the state.

Machiavell's affirmations in this regard lay down his theory of double morality—private and public. He clearly suggests that the conduct of the people and of the state cannot be properly judged by the same canons of morality. It is wrong if one man kills another; but even the massacre is justified if by such action the ruler tends to promote public good. It follows that for the sake of public welfare the ruler should always be ready to do even dishonourable things.

In short, Machiavelli's total separation of politics from religion and ethics signifies his advocacy of the doctrine that *ends determine means:* nothing but consolidation of power ought to be the aim of the ruler; nothing but the realisation of this aim ought to be his commitment. As Allen says: "To be successful in politics, he asserts, you must be ever ready to deceive or to slaughter and, in fact, to commit any atrocity; and whether you call the doing of such things good or bad, does not alter the fact that the doing of them may, and often does, conduce to the general welfare of a political society."[17]

Machiavelli's total divorce of politics from religion and morals deprives the sphere of secular authority of many fundamental virtues. His thorough secularism looks barren and pernicious. Politics wholly deprived of the canons of religion and morality is a death-trap that kills the conscience of civilised people. Naturally, the secular authority

15. *Discourses,* III, 41.
16. *Ibid.*
17. Allen, *op. cit.*, p. 479.

cannot be divorced entirely from the discipline of ethics. So Allen says: "But what most of all shocked most people and made him seem to some terrible and to some contemptible, was that he seemed to teach that reason of state might justify every degree of treachery and brutality. To many he seemed to go further and to imply that the highest virtue was that quality which enabled a man, without fear or scruple, to deceive and assassinate, whether he could gain a desired end by so doing. He seems to have taken evil for good and to ask admiration for the worst deeds of worst men."[18]

Statecraft: The theory of statecraft, as given by Machiavelli, shows his keen interest in the subject of the pathology of states, the seamy side of politics and the conduct of government under emergency conditions. His observations, maxims and conclusions are addressed primarily to a ruler caught in an anomalous situation rather than to a king ruling safely in an established position. Indeed, he has little to say about normal governments in as much as for them no problem, as such, exists at all. He cites the cases of the Roman Emperors who had no need either for the Praetorian bands or a multitude of legions to defend them, for their own goodness and the affection of the people were like a sufficient defence. In his *Discourses* Machiavelli says: "For when people are well governed, they neither seek nor welcome any change of government."

The leading principles of statecraft, as propounded by Machiavelli, may be thus summed up:

1. The ruler should regard public welfare as his chief concern, or he would lose the affection of his people and have no effective remedy to deal with the matters of crisis. He should never take the risk of unpopularity or general opposition, or the enmity of a small faction of the nobles would assume formidable proportions.
2. The ruler should win the love of the people; or, in its absence, create an air of terror, but it is ruinous to be hated. To avoid the possibility of being hated by the subjects, he may even commit an outrage on the property or person of his people with or without plausible pretexts and thus suppress the element of popular contempt by generating the sense of fear.
3. The ruler should protect properly the person and property of his subjects as it inculcates the feelings of loyalty and promotes patriotism.
4. The ruler should be very ambitious in expanding his dominion. The security of the state is not possible unless the perpetually unsatisfied souls of the people are given to dominate, if not outrightly conquer, the neighbours. However, Machiavelli disfavours the idea of indiscriminate expansion; he desires that only those newly acquired territories should be placed under the rule of the prince where the people speak the same language and observe the same principles of religion and culture.
5. The ruler should be blamed if he is without an army of his own. He rejects the use of mercenary troops as they lack the sense of loyalty to the land. He even sanctions compulsory military training for all male youths of the country.

18. *Ibid.*, p. 471.

6. Machiavelli advises that the ruler should use force ruthlessly, exercise persuasion skilfully and act decisively. Mere force is not enough and, for this reason, he should use devices lulling his people into peace but without making any real concession for them. The ruler must possess the qualities of both the lion and the fox.

It is obvious that Machiavelli's theory of statecraft embodies a code of important principles which a wise ruler should follow in order to preserve and consolidate his power. The real purpose of Machiavelli, as already suggested, is to show that if these principles are strictly observed, they decidedly make a new prince look like a hereditary ruler and render him at once secure and firm in the state than if he were established there of old.. Undoubtedly he wrote for the ruler of his beloved state, but his principles of statecraft and statesmanship are of universal and eternal application and constitute a solid insurance against the future. It is well said: "It is not strange, therefore, that in a certain aspect his new statecraft was regarded as an insurance against the future. And since most of these discussions have been referred to the downfall of Italy and particularly the invasion of 1494, it was an insurance against the very kind of misfortune which the Italians of the kind seemed so ready to complain."[19]

Hence, it is clear that Machiavelli discovered a new route to politics by offering a new science of this subject. His writings "attempted to indicate to the prince those means that were compatible with the conditions of his time and with human nature. Even religion—for which he had a deep feeling though he was not outwardly pious—was subordinated by him, in matters of state, to the states' iron necessity and made into an instrument or tool of power. Indeed, Machiavelli is regarded as the inventor of the reason of state. Even so he can be said to have laid the foundations of modern tactics. . . . . Machiavelli enters on a new road leaving behind him the traditions and methods of humanist historiology."[20]

Machiavelli's theory of statecraft is very dangerous. If the state, in a correct sense, is the first condition of civilised life, it should never be treated as a machine of violence and coercion for the sake of fulfilling certain egoistic and wicked purposes of a man in power. He has ruthlessly ignored the aspect of noble statesmanship. He spent his power of writing on making the state strong and great by all possible means whether good or bad. Murray thus remarks: "In truth he committed the fundamental blunder of a low-strung mind; he mistook cunning for the craft of the statesman in the large sense of the terms. C.J. Fox reached the statesman-like standpoint when he enunciated the maxim that 'what is morally wrong can never be politically right,' an axiom that eternally condemns the Florentine."[21]

Critical Appreciation: On the whole, it may be said that no political thinker has been so persistently abused and so little understood as Machiavelli "whose enigmatic

---

19. Butterfield, *op. cit.*, p. 119.
20. *Encylopaedia Britannica,* Vol. XI, 1978 Ptg., pp. 229-30.
21. R.H. Murray: *History of Political Science from Plato to the Present,* pp. 128-29.

figure stood in the porch of the sixteenth century as a sinister rock of offence."[22] He is rightly remembered for exercising great influence both on political philosophy and the science of statesmanship and diplomacy. His use of empirical method, his thorough separation of politics from ethics and, above all, his alignment of political theory with political practice made his political ideas realistic by virtue of being empirically valid. Moreover, his doctrine of a secular, sovereign and national unitary state ascribed to him the title of being the "first writer to embark on the express task of describing the world politics as it actually operates."[23] It is well commented: "Niccolo Machiavelli is perhaps the most universally reprobated figure in the history of political literature. The men whose precepts are universally disavowed in principle, but regularly followed in practice".[24]

22. Allen, *op. cit.*, p. 447.
23. Andrew Hacker: *Political Theory*, p. 159.
24. C.C. Maxey: *Political Philosophies*, p. 126.

20
Hobbes

The most important place in the history of modern English political thought is occupied by Thomas Hobbes (1588-1679) who is rightly regarded as the originator of modern political philosophy. His *Leviathan* is regarded as the masterpiece on the subject of scientific politics. Prof. Michael Oakeshott has described it as "the greatest, perhaps the sole, masterpiece of philosophy written in the English language."[1] Macpherson says that it "still stands as the crowning achievement of his political science."[2]

Methodology: An important feature of Hobbes's political philosophy should be discovered in his method of study that indicates a startling break with tradition. Instead of taking the help of history or empiricism, as was done by Machiavelli and Bodin, he takes the help of physics and mathematics. He constructs his political philosophy on the basis of his postulates derived from the disciplines of natural sciences. It is said that after his "discovery of Euclid," he became clearly aware of the need for a new political philosophy. It taught him that the necessity and possibility of treating politics as a science was a matter of course. One may call it a novel experiment made by Hobbes in the sense that he showed the possibilities of presenting a social study like a 'demonstrable science.' Let us see the elements of physics (motion) and mathematics (numbers and figures) in the methodology of Hobbes as a result of which he secured the distinction of being a mechanistic materialist, and his political philosophy earned the reputation of being systematic, scientific and revolutionary.

The element of physics in the methodology of Hobbes is discoverable in his assertion that everything is to be explained in terms of motion. The explanation of Hobbes centres on the assumption that even the elements of our body that appear to be non-material like hopes, ideas, thoughts, fears, loves and hates "can be reduced to mere internal motions brought into play by the stimulus of an external body and eventuating in action on the outside world." Side by side with the element of physics is the element of mathematics. Hobbes accepts the excellence of geometry as it reaches absolutely demonstrable complex propositions. The science of geometry teaches how to start from self-evident propositions to reach the final point of proving a hypothesis. It is the science of geometry that teaches how to move step by step in the correct direction with the help of numbers to solve a theorem that in the end becomes a conclusive proof. The acceptance of the mathematical method is also accepted by Hobbes owing to his

1. Oakeshott: "Introduction" in his (ed.): *Leviathan,* p. viii.
2. C.B. Macpherson: "Introduction" in his (ed.): *Leviathan,* p. 22.

belief that it is based not on passion but on reason and, owing to this, a study of politics can, in a real sense, be immune from the traditional complexion of being an irrational discipline. "Political philosophy must be just as exact and accurate as the science of lines and figures."[3]

It follows that the system of Hobbesian politics is based on the natural sciences of motion and numbers in view of the fact that what occurs to him is that various forms of matter are distinguishable only by the differences of motion inherent in them, and that mathematical method can well be applied to the study of a problem relating to the disciplines of a social science. "A study of Hobbes's political philosophy, viewed from the angle of methodology, indicates that it may be called a three-part philosophy relating to physical phenomena, knowledge and sensation, and social phenomena. However, a better title that is ascribed to Hobbes's methodology is the resolutive-compositive method. While the resolutive part is the way to reach the required simple basic propositions, the compositive is the way to build the complex ones from those."[4]

Power: The grandest conclusion of Hobbesian politics finds place in his clearest and most perfect expression of the naturalistic conception of human nature when he tells us that man "desires power and ever greater power, spontaneously, and continuously, in one set of appetite, and not by reason of a summation of innumerable isolated desires caused by innumerable isolated perceptions."[5] As he confidently asserts: "I put for a general inclination of all mankind, a perpetual and restless desire for power, that, ceaseth only in death. And the cause of this is not always that a man hopes for a more intensive delight, than he has already attained to: or that he cannot be content with a moderate power; but because he cannot assure the power and means to live well, which he hath present, without the acquisition of more."[6]

While exposing the lineaments of "power", Hobbes takes care to define this term in a comprehensive way. To him power means some "future apparent good." As he says: "Natural power is the eminence of faculties of body or mind: an extraordinary Strength, Form, Prudence, Arts, Eloquence, Liberality. Instrumental are those powers, which acquired by these, or by fortune, are means and instruments to acquire more as Riches, Reputation, Friends, and the secret working of God, which men call Good Luck."[7] A clear inference from this explanation leads Hobbes to admit that the search for power is the root cause of competition among individuals. Interests collide in the race to acquire more and more riches, honours and commands and for this sake the competitors take to the means of killing, subduing, supplanting and repelling their opponents. Though the struggle for power has its incessant play among the competitors, Hobbes further tells us, it is also true that men like to live in peace in order to enjoy the iota of power they possess; it disposes them to live under a Common Power.

---

3. Leo Strauss: *The Political Philosophy of Hobbes*, pp. 136-37.
4. Macpherson, *op. cit.*, pp. 25-26.
5. Leo Strauss, *op. cit.*, p. 10.
6. *Leviathan*, Ch. 11.
7. *Ibid.* Ch. 10.

It is clear that Hobbes uses the word "power" in a very comprehensive sense. Power, though identifiable with anything like "future apparent good" has a very wide connotation. After making a thorough study of the political philosophy of the *Leviathan*, Macpherson comes to hold the view that Hobbes defines man's natural power "not as his faculties of body and mind, but as the eminence of his faculties compared with those of other men, and that his acquired powers are those he has acquired by means of that eminence. A man's power consists of the amount by which his faculties, riches, reputation, and friends exceed those of other men."[8] A proper study of the Hobbesian politics culminating in the construction of the commonwealth under a perfect sovereign ordaining all individuals to live in peace in order to avoid the "violent fear of death" leads to the conclusion that, in a strict sense, Hobbes's meaning of power "means specifically or only power over other men." Studied thus, one may partly accept the observation of Bluhm when he says that power, according to Hobbes, "does not mean only domination but, more broadly, the ability to secure a good. Wealth is power, friends are power, good luck is power."[9]

In appreciation of this, Prof. Oakeshott observes: "It is, indeed, of the greatest importance, for Hobbes' philosophy is, in all its parts, preeminently a philosophy of power precisely because philosophy is reasoning, reasoning the elucidation of mechanism and mechanism essentially the combination, transfer and resolution of force. The end of philosophy itself is power. Man is a complex of powers; desire is the desire for power, life the unremitting exercise of power, and death the absolute loss of power. And the civilised order is conceived as a coherence of powers, not because politics is vulgarly observed to be a competition of powers, or because civil philosophy must take its conception from natural philosophy, but because to subject the civil order to rational enquiry unavoidably turns it into a mechanism."[10]

Social Contract: Hobbes's procedure for fashioning the Commonwealth is geometrical in the sense that he takes his start from a blank page what he calls the 'state of nature', a hypothetical period of human existence without any institutions of society and state. The people living in this state of nature make a contract whereby they establish civil society under the rule of a perfect sovereign. Thus, the geometrical figure is completed. The start of Hobbes from a hypothetical state of nature culminates in the creation of Society, State, and Government all identifiable with what he calls the "Commonwealth." The use of geometrical procedure looks like the mathematisation of politics at the hands of Hobbes whose intent is evidenced from the admission that the "skill of making and maintaining Commonwealth consisteth in certain Rules, as doth Arithmetic or Geometry, not as Tennis-play or Practise only."[11]

It follows that the state of nature of Hobbes is a pre-social and pre-political phase simply for the reason of his geometrical procedure that informs him to begin with a

8. Macpherson, *op. cit.,* p. 35.
9. W. T. Bluhm: *Theories of the Political System,* p. 289.
10. Oakeshott, *op. cit.,* p. xxi.
11. *Leviathan,* Ch. 20.

hypothesis. As an advocate of macabre psychology, he starts from the axiom that mortal fear is the prime mover that issues in the form of vanity leading to internecine warfare as a result of which the law of struggle for power determines the relationship between master and servant. What strikes Hobbes so forcefully is the equality of men in the faculties of both mind and body, for despite certain obvious differences in physical and mental development, it seems to him that even the weakest "has the strength enough to kill the strongest, either by secret machination or by confederacy with others, that are in the same danger with himself."[12]

The only standard that determines the way of life in this horrible condition is the law of nature that means a set of rules based on the principle of expediency for the sake of self-preservation. It lays down that every man should seek peace and preserve it; if he cannot obtain it, he must defend it by all means at his command. It also states that man must be willing along with others; and in the interest of peace and self-defence he should forswear his right to all things, be content with as much liberty as he would allow others over himself and transfer some of his rights by a social contract. It enjoins that man should obey a covenant that he makes out of his own choice. Finally, the law of nature informs man to renounce feelings of pride, revenge, cruelty, avarice, etc. and fear no harm from the authority in whose favour the surrender of rights is effected. However, in the view of Hobbes, the observance of natural law is based on expediency and utility and, for this reason, the individual should follow its dictates only when his self-interest is thereby secured.

The escape from such a horrible condition in which man's life is "solitary, nasty, poor, brutish and short" is effected by means of a contract made by the "ideally reasonable men" when everyone says:" "I authorise and give up my right of governing myself to this man or to this assembly of men on this condition that thou give up the right to him and authorise all actions in the like manner."[13] By this contract everyone surrenders all his natural rights to a sovereign (King or Assembly) and thereby society, state, and government are established. The person or the assembly of persons to whom the rights are surrendered becomes the sovereign in the form of a masterless man and the covenanting individuals who agree to submit to the authority of the sovereign become loyal subjects. The sovereign is no party to this contract and the people take it upon themselves to render him their unquestioned obedience. With this, there comes into being a society having state and government. As Hobbes says: "This is the generation of the great Leviathan, or rather (to speak more reverently) of that Mortal God to which we owe under the immortal God, our peace and defence."[14]

A critical study of Hobbes's theory of social contract shows that it is false and absurd from the standpoints of history, philosophy and logic. The whole explanation is nothing but a fiction from the viewpoint of history. It is said that the state of nature presents a thoroughly wrong picture of man's primitive life. It also ignores the facts of

12. *Ibid.,* Ch. 13.
13. *Ibid.,* Ch. 17.
14. *Ibid.,*

sociology and anthropology which, as Cook says, reveal that men have always lived under some form of authority in a social organisation. The other points of attack are, indeed, very weighty. It is surprising to see how the ravening beasts living in a state of nature can think in terms of establishing a civil and political authority in order to terminate that horrible condition of continual warfare. It is never possible that a series of discrete individuals living in a state of perfect anarchy can be brought under an organised society with a despot sitting at the head. It can never be taken into conviction that the same individuals who at one moment were rushing to each other's throat, should fly into each other's arm with equal eagerness the following moment. The whole story looks as if it is based on a legendary conversion. Thus Vaughan says: "But if *Leviathan* is useless as a key to history, it is also fruitless as a theory of the state. The society called together by the covenant is no society at all."[15]

Sovereignty: Undoubtedly, Hobbes's theory of sovereignty is his greatest contribution to the discipline of Political Science. His affirmation of the headship of a masterless man—an artificial person who personates, not impersonates, every member of the Commonwealth, who formerly made up the headless multitude—makes a distinct improvement upon the theory of Bodin who subjected his sovereign to the Law of God, Law of Nature and Law of Nations and thereby, for any reason whatsoever, committed a serious contradiction in his doctrine of sovereignty.

According to Hobbes, the powers of the sovereign over all governmental functions are absolute. He is the sole legislator, principal executive and chief judicial officer. He hears and decides all controversies and makes a determination of facts and laws, controls the defence and levies taxes to support his administration, and chooses his own ministers and counsellors who are like his agents responsible to him alone. Besides, he has the power to reward and punish his subjects. The very creation of the institution of sovereignty makes it evident that, according to Hobbes, authority "must belong to the sovereign, for if his is the responsibility for governing and keeping the peace, which is the chief end of the state, he must control the means to that end." Hobbes thus affirms: "By the authority given him by every particular man in the commonwealth, he has the use of so much power and strength conferred on him that by error thereof, he is enabled to form the wills of them all to peace at home, and mutual aid against their enemies abroad. And in this consisteth the essence of the commonwealth; which (to define it) is one person, of whose acts a great multitude by mutual covenants with one another, have made themselves everyone the author, to the end he may use the strength and means for them all, as he shall think expedient, for their peace and common defence. From his institution of commonwealth are derived all the rights, and faculties of him, or them, on whom the sovereign power is conferred by the consent of the people assembled."[16]

Hobbes's theory of sovereignty may be criticised on some grounds. First, his theory of the rule of a masterless man is a clear attempt to justify the case of royal absolutism like that of Charles I whose obduracy led to the outbreak of the Civil War in England.

15. C.A. Vaughan: *Studies in the History of Political Philosophy,* Vol. I, p. 54.
16. *Leviathan,* Ch. 18.

Strangely enough, by means of such an affirmation, Hobbes cuts across the very theme of social contractualism. The state under the authority of the leviathan cannot reconcile itself with the fundamental principle of the theory of social contract signifying that the state is based on the free consent of the people. The result is that the people, in spite of being the makers of the sovereign authority, are reduced to the status of dumb-driven cattle in the system of Hobbes. The social contract of Hobbes reveals the substitution of one will for many wills into a common will what Rousseau calls the "general will." The result is, as Vaughan says, the society called together by the covenant is no society at all, because all the life "is gathered in one man at the head of it, the rest of the body is a dead weight, a mere unprofitable mass."[17]

Law: Hobbes's theory of law is a corollary to his theory of sovereignty and, as such, it precurses the analytical jurisprudence of John Austin. In this direction, Hobbes frankly repudiates Coke's elaborate conception of law as the artificial perception of reason suggested by the lawyers and the jurists and he holds that the only test is the sovereign's reason as embodied in his will. In other words, Hobbes asserts the same thing, what Austin said afterwards, that law is nothing but the command of the sovereign. Hobbes's theory of law bears the following salient characteristics:

First, law is the command of the sovereign. The sovereign alone can make it, but he is above it. Naturally nothing but the command of the sovereign can have the force of law. Custom is no law unless it becomes the sovereign's command. Properly speaking, Hobbes asserts, law is the word of him that by right has command over others. Second, law has a binding character. Hence, natural law and divine law are no laws owing to their indeterminate nature. Third, law must be rational. Sovereign's will alone is the standard of reason. Last, the sovereign is the maker and enforcer of law. He is above law.[18]

On the whole, the imperative jurisprudence of Hobbes seeks to justify the absolute character of sovereignty. The entire analysis is based on the assumption that the sovereign is the supreme law-maker who cannot do any injustice to his subjects, because he represents them. The sovereign may commit moral wrong, but he cannot do any legal injustice and he is responsible for his actions to God alone. This is very much like the doctrine that the king can do no wrong. In the words of Hobbes: "Covenants, without the sword, are but words, and of no strength to secure a man at all."[19]

Hobbes's theory of law has been criticised by the advocates of historical, philosophical and sociological schools. Both Savigny and Maine contend that the people themselves have been law-makers through the formation of habit and custom. Its sanction is not the coercive authority of the sovereign but a general sense of the right of society. According to Zane, the government "may superficially appear to make law as Hobbes and Austin mistakenly supposed, but it is the acceptance of the rulers

17. Vaughan, *op. cit.,* p. 54.
18. *Leviathan,* Ch. 17.
19. *Ibid.,*

by society that makes law and government. Duguit goes to the extent of saying that it is not the state which creates laws, but it is the laws which create the state. The truth is that even an absolute state cannot thoroughly undermine the standards of morality, culture and social behaviour. Law is not the only force; among other things, custom does have an important place. Recognising this fact, Maine says: "State has little power to make custom and perhaps even less to destroy it, although indirectly it influences the customs by changing the conditions out of which they spring."[20]

Right to Revolt: Of course, Hobbes holds his sovereign's authority absolute and unlimited, but he recognises only one exceptional condition in which resistance to state authority is justified. He recognises that every man has a right to disobey the sovereign, if he is commanded to kill, wound or maim himself or not to resist those that assault him; or to abstain from the use of food, air, medicine, or any other thing, without which he cannot live." Hobbes gives the reason that since men contract together to institute a sovereign only in order to save their lives, it cannot be maintained that they grant to the sovereign (whom they set up) the right to take away their lives.

The right to resistance, as recognised by Hobbes in one exceptional situation, is equally applicable to the case of sovereignty by "institution" as well as by "acquisition." The distinction between the two forms of sovereignty is made by Hobbes on the ground that while, in the former, men come together and establish the sovereign power by means of a social contract, in the latter, the sovereign acquires authority by conquest. Thus, there is a basic difference between the two forms of sovereignty in the sense that while in the former, men choose their sovereign for fear of one another and not of him to whom they institute, in the latter case they subject themselves to the new sovereign after feeling afraid of his coercive power. But the common point is that in both cases the motivating force is the "fear." "Whatever the method of establishment, afterward the power and authority of the sovereign is identical."[21]

It may be pointed out that Hobbes indirectly sanctions the case of an inevitable revolution. The very pretext of doing it for the sake of self-preservation is a sufficient excuse at the hands of the rebels to justify their move against the sovereign. If ever such a situation were created, it would appear that Hobbes, though quite unintentionally, desired the very revolution that he strongly detested. Thus, it is said; "Although revolution was forbidden by Hobbes's interpretation of natural right by giving 'sovereignty by institution' and 'sovereignty by acquisition', equal standing and by giving the subject no voice in the determination of the line of succession, Hobbes would seem to have made revolution virtually inevitable."[22]

Hobbes's theory of right to resistance brings about an element of contradiction and confusion in his general theory of sovereignty and government. If the sovereign has actual power to govern the state, as Hobbes thinks it requires to be governed, it is clear that the subjects' right to resist is non-existent. On the other hand, the sovereign

20. Henry Maine: *Ancient Law,* p. 160.
21. Le Cameron MacDonald: *Western Political Theory: The Modern Age,* p. 101.
22. *Ibid.,*

has no valid title to live in power in case he is too weak to be an efficient instrument of government. It follows that either the right which Hobbes assigns to the subjects is insignificant and meaningless, or the relation between sovereign and subjects is to result in chaos and anarchy. If right means power (as it does in Hobbes view), the subject has no right in either case whether the sovereign be strong or weak. If the sovereign is strong, the subjects clearly have no right to rebel and, on the contrary, if he is weak he is no sovereign at all and society thereby relapses into the state of nature in which no one has adequate means of protecting his life. W.T. Jones thus observes: "Either the subject has a right against his sovereign, or he has not. If he has not, Hobbes certainly should not say that he has the right. On the other hand, if he does have the right, Hobbes's major thesis—that the sovereign's power is, and must be absolute—is false. Hobbes cannot have it both ways at once. If the sovereign's power is absolute, it cannot be conditioned in any way; and if there is any sort of restriction or limitation on his power, it is not absolute."[23]

Critical Appreciation: If there are many points where Hobbes may be regarded as a Machiavellian thinker, there are other points as well which entitle him to be the founder of the prudential science of politics. His theory of sovereignty marked definitive improvement upon the contribution of Jean Bodin and thereby it presented a complete picture of monistic doctrine. His theory of law precursed positive jurisprudence of the analytical school of John Austin. Besides, his stress on the basically selfish nature of man had its clear influence on the hedonistic philosophy of David Hume and Jeremy Bentham. He turned the theory of social contract, an instrument of early liberalism, into a powerful defence of state absolutism at a time when the dogma of the divine right of kings was losing its ground. In short, Hobbes stands out as "the creator of a system. And he conceived this system with such imaginative power that, in spite of its relatively simple character, it bears comparision with even the grand and subtle creation of Hegel."[24]

---

23. W.T. Jones: *Masters of Political Thought,* Vol. II, p. 125.
24. Oakeshott, *op. cit.,* p. xv.

21
Locke

Neither Hobbes nor Rousseau but John Locke is the representative thinker of the social contract school for the simple reason that he keeps the sovereign power of the state with those who institute it and thereby saves the partners of a joint stock company from the totalitarian hold of their chosen manager. However, the writings of this great liberal political thinker, in a sense, should be read as companion pieces to those of Hobbes inasmuch as they were inspired by the same historical conditions and they shared the same rationalistic and mechanistic point of view. It is a different matter that Locke differed from Hobbes both in letter and spirit and, despite his drawing heavily from the storehouse of the *Leviathan*, he "never acknowledged his debt to Hobbes; in fact, he even denied it on at least one occasion, perhaps to avoid the distasteful label 'Hobbist'." The fact is that, like Hobbes, Locke wrote against a background of hectic political activity with avowed purpose of presenting a sensible defence of the "reasonable" revolution of 1688 that witnessed the voluntary abdication of James II and the accession of William and Mary as joint sovereigns to the throne of England according to the will of the Parliament. Thus, it is well said: "The theorist of the Revolution is Locke; and it was his conscious effort to justify the innovation of 1688."[1]

Social Contract: In common with other thinkers of his age, Locke seeks to explain the origin and nature of political authority within the framework of social contractualism. He starts with a hypothetical state of nature—a pre-political stage which "was a state of perfect freedom to order their actions, and dispose of their persons and possessions as they think fit, within the law of nature without asking leave or depending upon the will of any other man."[2] Obviously, it is not a state of perpetual warfare, as Hobbes tells us, rather it is a state of equality wherein all the power of jurisdiction "is reciprocal, no one having more than another."[3]

Locke points out that the state of nature is a state of liberty and not of license. Although in this pre-political stage man has full liberty to dispose of his possessions, he has no freedom to destroy himself or his neighbour. The law of nature prevails which obliges and teaches everyone that none has a right to harm another's person or goods. It sanctions that when all men are equal and independent and possess rights to life, liberty and property, none has the exceptional right to encroach upon the freedom

1. H.J. Laski: *Political Thought in England* (*From Locke to Bentham*), p. 28.
2. John Locke: *Second Treatise of Civil Government,* Chapter II.
3. *Ibid.*

of another. The observance of this law requires that all men be restrained from invading the rights of others. The law of nature wills the peace and preservation of all mankind and puts into the hand of everyone a right to finish the transgressor to a degree as it might hinder its violation. However, in the case of transgression, it sanctions that one man can come by power over another but only "to retribute to him so far as calm reason and conscience dictate, what is proportionate to his transgression, which is so much as may serve for reparation and restraint".[4]

If the state of nature is not a condition of violence and anarchy, it is also not a condition of Arcadian bliss. It is constantly upset by the corruption and viciousness of degenerate man. "The state of nature had the ill-condition which was full of fear and continual dangers and suffered from three main shortcomings—the non-existence of an established and settled legal system, the absence of an appropriate authority to execute the laws, and the want of an impartial judge to give and endorse just decisions. Hence, in order to escape from this ill-condition and gain certainty and security, men make a contract to terminate the state of nature and enter into the civil society or commonwealth. Thus, the men living in the state of nature, voluntarily compacted and agreed to join and unite into a community for their comfortable, safe and peaceable living, one amongst another, in a secure enjoyment of their properties and a greater security against any that are not of it."[5]

In Locke's view, the social contract terminates the era of statelessness and substitutes it by a civil society. Each individual agrees to give up some of the rights he possessed in the pre-political stage. This contract has two main features. First, it is no more than a surrender of some rights and powers so that man's remaining rights remain protected and preserved. Second, the contract is concluded for a limited and specific purpose and what is given up is surrendered to the community as a whole and not to a man (or the assembly of men) as Hobbes tells us. In this way, Locke holds that people are the real sovereign and the state exists for them, not *vice versa*.

Again, unlike Hobbes, Locke supposes the making of two contracts. The first is the social or express contract whereby civil society is established to meet the deficiencies of the state of nature. By it each individual agrees to give up not all his natural rights but the only one of interpreting and executing the law of nature and redressing his own grievances. Besides, the right is given to the community as a whole and that too on the understanding that the natural rights will be guaranteed and preserved. The second is the tacit or governmental contract. When civil society (state) is established, another contract is made by the community (in a corporate capacity) with a ruler (king) who takes upon himself the responsibilities of removing the ill-condition once existing in the state of nature. The second contract is implied and so subordinate to the first, because government has only a fiduciary power to act for certain ends and its acts are confined to securing them well. It also implies that if the government fails in this respect, people may dismiss it and substitute it by a new one.

---

4. *Ibid.*
5. *Ibid.*

Locke's theory of social contract is unsound from the historical, legal, logical and philosophical points of view. It attaches the stigma of "partnership" and thus reduces the state to the status of a limited liability concern. Hence, like Hobbes, Locke has been criticised for contributing to a "dangerous", "absurd," "fictitious" and "utterly false" theory of the origin and the nature of state. It may be argued that this theory represents a philosophy of the propertied and privileged class of which Locke himself was a member. His man living in the state of nature is a propertied gentleman who insists on his own rights and respects the rights of others, and he thinks in terms of entering into some contract simply because of his selfish interest. His ultimate preference for constitutional monarchy reveals his happiness over the victory of his class in the Glorious Revolution of 1688. In a word, the artificiality of the system of Locke is evidenced by his assertion that men are isolated individuals bound together just by the thread of a contract made for the sake of their self-interest, that is, the adequate protection of their natural rights relating to life, liberty and property. It is all unrealistic and, as Aaron says, it "fails to take into consideration the many ties, including race, geography and other things which hold the community together."[6]

Sovereignty: Locke's conception of sovereignty is quite different from that of Bodin and Hobbes. To him sovereignty is not absolute and indivisible, rather it seems to be divided between the people on the one hand and the rulers on the other. As already seen, the original or social contract is an agreement among the people to put an end to the state of nature and to substitute it by a civil society. This contract requires the consent of every member of the society. As a result of the second or governmental contract, the rulers are vested with certain powers and if they fail to carry out their obligations, they may be replaced by others without, in any way, affecting the basic character of society. In practice, this conception means that the people have sovereign authority in reserve, while the actual power is exercised by the government. In case the government violates trust, it becomes necessary for the people to withdraw their consent and change their government. Locke very clearly calls an arbitrary ruler a tyrant and empowers his people to overthrow his regime. He says: "Wherever law ends, tyranny begins, if the law be transgressed to another's harm and whosoever in authority exceeds the power given him by law, and makes use of force, has under his command to compass upon the subject which the law allows not, ceases in that to be a magistrate and acting without authority may be opposed, as any other man who by force invades the right of others."[7]

In other words, it implies that Locke makes his people a sleeping sovereign who let the government carry on sovereign authority within certain limits provided it does not abuse its power. The moment it does so, the sovereign people wake up from their slumber, overthrow their government and set up a new one in its place. Obviously, Locke's concern is not to exalt political authority but to describe its limitations. He maintains that the people form their government and so their rulers should not be

6. Raymond J. Aaron: *John Locke,* p. 287.
7. Locke, *op. cit.*

disobeyed. In case a ruler exercises his powers in a wrong way, he has no right to claim obedience, since he "is not the person the laws have appointed and consequently, not the person the people have consented to."[8]

Naturally the characteristic of Locke's state is that it is limited, not absolute. It is limited, because it derives powers from the people and because it holds power in trust for the people. It is limited, moreover, by natural law. Civil law is merely the statement of natural law in detail by means of authorised legislation. The true state is a constitutional state in which men acknowledge the rule of law, for there can be no political liberty if man is subject to the inconstant, uncertain, unknown and arbitary will of another. It should exist for the good of the people and depend upon their consent and should have a limited or constitutional authority, otherwise it loses its *raison d'etre* and can legitimately be overthrown.

Locke's theory of sovereignty is erroneous as well as pernicious. The very denial of the absolute and unlimited character of sovereignty is tantamount to its own negation. Calhoun is right in saying that sovereignty is a whole thing and to divide it means to destroy it. Not only this, Locke's conception bears very dangerous potentialities inasmuch as it opens the doors of rebellion or revolution at every turn and occasion. The sleeping sovereign or the people may break their sleep and overthrow their government whenever they are dissatisfied with it. In the last resort, it is just a licence for revolt or rebellion under any form of government. Always there is a a residual power in society to overthrow a particular regime and when Locke binds the right to revolution with the decision of the community, the position is made much more confused. In such a case, either it will be quite difficult, nay impossible, to determine when it is the act of the whole community, or the residual power in society will go unchecked and declare its act to be valid in the name of its being an act of the whole community. Finally, it has been pointed out that Locke cares little for the fact of legal sovereignty and dwells heavily on the side of political sovereignty. He hardly seems satisfied even with a full-fledged modern representative system of government. Dunning remarks that Locke "has no far-reaching theory of sovereignty."[9] The legislature in the first place is the legal sovereign. The king is not technically sovereign at all but as a title he is commonly called the sovereign. "The people, to whom the legislature is responsible, is political sovereign, but this sovereignty he regards as normally in abeyance, and it only takes effect when the government has been dissolved."[10]

Constitutional Government: Locke's political theory favours constitutional or limited monarchy. The government is different from the state, because it is a consequence of the second contract and its formation or dissolution does not at all affect the life of the state in the like manner. The government is also different from the society or community, because while the latter is really sovereign, the former has a mere fiduciary character. Besides, Locke also differentiates between the *de jure* and

---

8. *Ibid.*
9. W.A. Dunning: *A History of Political Theories,* Vol. II, pp. 359-60.
10. J.W. Gough: *John Locke's Political Philosophy,* pp. 114-15.

de facto governments. A *de jure* government is one that comes into being according to the established laws of the state and so its commands should be obeyed. But a *de facto* government is one which is an usurper of authority or which is not based on the consent of the people or which has violated the trust of the community and should thus be overthrown.

In the view of Locke, government is not only different from society and state; it also holds limited authority. It is made to accomplish certain ends. Locke vests supreme power in the hands of the people to remove or alter the government whenever they find it to have forfeited their trust. It should be noted that Locke assumes the making of a tacit contract by which the government is established and in order to clarify his point yet further, he uses the term "trust" to indicate the real relationship between the people and the government. His ultimate purpose is to justify the sovereign status of the people, and so the term "contract" is not appropriate in as much as it implies the standing of two parties at a pedestal of equality. Vaughan thus rightly suggests that by adopting the analogy of a trust rather than that of a contract, Locke "makes very fair provision not only for popular control of government, but also—what is yet more important—for a progressive extension of that control, as experience may dictate."[11]

It is obvious that in the political system of Locke the position of government is like that of a manager chosen by and accountable to the members of a joint stock company. The servant (government) cannot be treated as equal to that of the master (community) as his fundamental concern is to maintain the "trust" of his master. As Harmon says: "A contract between the two parties implies their equality and stipulates various rights and obligations pertaining to each. Hobbes rejects the use of contract between people and government because he does not wish to imply that people are the equal of government or that government has duties toward people. Locke's reasoning is the reverse of this. Government is not the equal of the people. It must be an agent of the people not a partner. The relationship between government and governed is analogous to that which exists between the parties in a legal trust. The government is the trustee who functions for and is responsible to the people who create the trust. Thus, the trustee or government has no rights equal to those held by the people, but only obligations to those for whom it acts as an agent."[12]

If the government has constitutional authority, its functions are also limited. According to Locke, its functions are confined to the protection and preservation of the life, liberty and property of the people. In this direction, it has to do three important things. First, it has to establish and make known to all persons the implications of the law of nature and this service is to be rendered by the legislative organ. Second. it has to provide an impartial authority to settle all disputes arising among persons in accordance with the established laws, and this business is to be performed by the judicial branch of government. Third, it has to safeguard the interest of its people against aliens and this work is to be done by the executive department.

11. C. E. Vaughan: *Studies in the History of Political Philosophy,* Vol. I, p. 147.
12. M. Judd Harmon: *Political Thought from Plato to the Present,* pp. 250-51.

Another important aspect of Locke's theory of government is that here he throws a faint light on the separation of powers and thus becomes a precursor of Montesquieu. He justifies the separation of legislature from the executive, because he fears that it "may be too great a temptation to human frailty, apt to grasp all power, for the same persons who have the power of making laws to have also in their hands the power to execute them."[13] Hence, he differentiates between three organs of government and calls them legislative, judicial and federative (executive) departments. The legislative power is placed in the hands of an assembly that meets periodically, but since the enforcement and administration of law is a continuous task, a power distinct from the legislature must live in ceaseless operation and this Locke decides in favour of the executive.

Locke's theory of government has been criticised on some grounds. It is said that a government of this type would be no government at all as regards its stability and efficiency. It would merely be a plaything in the hands of some "mischievous" leaders of the people. Its life would depend on the brink of revolution. Vaughan rightly fears that Locke "formulated not a theory of government but a theory of rebellion."[14] It is good to limit the authority of the government, but it is never wise to reduce it to the status of a fiduciary organisation. No government, even a democracy (constitutional government as envisaged by Locke), can ever be in a safe position to discharge its trust in a way that happens to secure general satisfaction. Obviously, Locke has underrated the importance of political organisation, Sabine aptly observes: "On the whole, Locke regarded the setting up of a government as a much less important event than the original compact that makes a civil society. Once a majority has agreed to form a government, the whole power of the community is naturally in them."[15]

Natural Rights: Locke's theory of individualism is based on his conception of natural rights. Dunning says that the most distinctive contribution of Locke to political theory "is his doctrine of natural rights."[16] His citizen has three rights relating to life, liberty and property; they are natural because they existed even in the pre-political stage. Their possession is enjoyed by the individual both in and out of the government. The individuals have these rights even before the making of the compact and they do not surrender or abandon them even after the formal inauguration of political authority. Obviously, in contrast to Hobbes and Rousseau, Locke does not write into the social contract that individuals must give up their rights to their sovereign at the time of entering into the community. In his view, the individual fully remains the master of his natural rights as in the state of nature so after the establishment of civil society.

In this direction, following implications may be drawn from Locke's affirmations:

1. Rights can be ascribed only to the individuals and not to their government and when Locke speaks of the rights of government or of any other body, he simply means by it "power" to perform a particular function.

13. *Second Treatise,* Chapter 12.
14. Vaughan, *op. cit.,* p. 150.
15. G.H. Sabine: *A History of Political Theory,* p. 534.
16. Dunning, *op. cit.,* p. 364.

2. Since rights are the possession of the individuals, they are held by all without any exception. There is complete equality in this respect. However, a right is different from a privilege, because the latter may be granted to a few people owing to some superior quality or virtue.
3. These rights are innate things conferred upon man by God and nature. Individuals continue to have them under any circumstance whatsoever. They existed in the state of nature, and they exist in the civil society without any reduction or restraint.
4. Locke asserts that the state should use its enforcement action to secure natural rights by giving them an official (legal) protection. By the contract each individual has given a right to the commonwealth to employ force for the execution of the will of the community.

In brief, Locke's theory of natural rights justifies that individual's rights to life, liberty and property are innate and so immutable, inalienable and permanent. The rights form an integral part of his personality and render to the government the character of a manager working with the trust of the people. However, a critic may argue that Locke's theory of natural rights takes a wrong view of social structure. Society is not a sand-heap of individuals but an organic compound in which the individual's rights cannot be studied in isolation. Rights have a social content and their legitimacy should thus be examined from the point of social expediency or interest. No right can have an absolute or transcendentalist character.

Property: Locke very strongly defends the institution of private property. Plato keeps his Guardians aloof from the possession of private property, because it obscures their reasoning power. Aristotle approves of it but fears that over-wealth becomes a cause of threat to political stability. St. Thomas Aquinas refuses to assert that private property is sanctioned by the law of nature and claims that it is an addition created by human legislators. Hobbes allows the people to keep their property, but he emphasises that the sovereign has every right to restrict the manner of its use and employment. Different from these standpoints, Locke appears as a powerful defender of the institution of private property. He says: "The great and chief end of men's uniting into commonwealth and putting themselves under government is the preservation of their property."[17]

Locke's defence of private property is based on the following arguments:

1. God "has put men on this earth and given them reason," so that they may make use of earthly resources to the best advantage of their life and convenience. The earth and all that is therein "is given to men for the support and comfort of their being." But the best way to accomplish this is to allow individuals to hold possession of the land and materials so that they will have the means and the incentive to turn each into usable commodities.
2. Locke propounds his labour theory of right to property. He asserts that man has a natural right to that with which he has mixed the labour of his body.

17. *Second Treatise,* Chapter 5.

3. Locke justifies private property on the ground of greater productivity. In his view, greater production raises the standard of living of the people and so. it is essential that the property holder must be industrious.
4. In Locke's view, property is based on consent. Division of labour and property was agreed upon when the people lived together and enlarged the use of their resources.
5. Locke's theory contemplates the case of an economic man—a man who will not waste his time and energy in unproductive activities.
6. Locke rejects the notion of acquiring property by means of physical force or conquest of the strong over the weak. He argues: "I may kill a thief that sets on me in the highway, yet may not take away his money; this would be robbery on my side."
7. Locke urges that the possession of private property should be coextensive with the capacity of making use of it. The reward of the property-owner is not to be more than what he and his family can actually use.

Locke's justification of private property is not only vague, ambiguous and full of important gaps at various stages, but it constitutes an idealisation of the capitalist economy. In other words, it is a naked defence of capitalism and, even from a capitalist point of view, the theory is defective in several respects. He forgets that the interplay of demand and supply amply governs the scope of production and consumption. Moreover, if the owners are merely allowed to keep as much in the way of profits as they can use, they will have no surplus cash for capital goods and so there will be no place for the role of investment funds in the productive process. His argument that "no more property than use prohibits unearned profits" which go to the investors, and since modern capitalist organisation is largely and mainly based on such an investment pattern, it is not difficult to find a place where Locke's thesis is incoherent even with the principles of modern capitalism. According to Hacker, "In Locke, therefore, we see the emergence of the politics of a capitalist society, the state must be strong enough to provide legal underpinnings for private investment and yet not so strong as to interfere with the free decisions of men who wish to risk their money to make a profit for themselves."[18]

Right to Revolt: In the political theory of Locke, the right to revolution finds a subterraneous manifestation. By strongly advocating the proposition that sovereignty is vested in the community, he insists that political authority is a "trust" which must be directed to the ends for which men abandon the state of nature and establish civil society. It, therefore, follows that if the government belies its trust or overacts its powers, the people have a legitimate right to resist its authority. They have every right to examine and determine if the government is justifying itself or not. Hence, if they find otherwise, they can remove an inefficient or oppressive government and establish a new one in its place. Locke says: "And thus the community perpetually retains a supreme power of saving themselves from the attempts and design of anybody, even if

18. Andrew Hacker: *Political Theory,* p. 269.

their legislators whenever they shall be so foolish or so wicked as to lay and carry on designs against the liberties and properties of the subjects."[19]

However, the right to resistance is to be exercised by the community or its majority only in the case of a specific breach of trust. It has two implications: First, the right should be exercised when the community as a whole or its majority is satisfied with its inevitable need. The revolution should not be an act of the caprice of a minority, for the contract is the action of the major portion of the people whose consent should likewise call for the dissolution of the compact. In the second place, there should be a concrete case to justify an invasion by the rulers over the legitimate rights of the people. Locke urges that if the majority of the people "are persuaded in their consciences that their laws, and with them, their estates, liberties, and lives are in danger, they will have every right to change the government for the sake of their safety and good."[20] Laski enumerates these contingencies in which a revolution could be justified in the Lockean sense. "The substitution of arbitrary will for law, the corruption of Parliament by packing it with the prince's instruments, betrayal to a foreign prince, prevention of the due assemblage of Parliament—all these are perversion of the trust imposed and operate to effect the dissolution of the contract. The state of nature again supervenes and a new contract may be made with one more fitted to observe it."[21]

While the process of election is a soft course, revolution is the reverse, and also a complementary, side of the supreme power of the people to rid themselves of an erratic political authority. Locke, well aware of this fact, therefore, prefers that the people "retain final power, but that they exercise it only occasionally in the election process, or, if absolutely necessary, through revolution."[22] Thus, Locke reserves to the community just a conditional right of revolution in case of an unpardonable breach of trust by the government. His pious phrase of "an appeal to the heaven" does not mean that the people are to wait passively the operations of divine justice on their behalf. He means that when no earthly judge exists before whom they can take their case, that is, when no constitutional channels of change exist, they must put their trust in heaven and believing in the rightness of their case, appeal to arms."[23]

Critical Appreciation: Locke is rightly regarded as the representative thinker of the social contract school. The political thought of modern times highlighting constitutional limitations on sovereign power, legal safeguards on individual liberty, security accorded to private property, fundamental rights emanating from the law of nature all are predicated largely upon the contributions of Locke. It is thus well commented that "the great debate inaugurated by the Reformation ceased when Locke had outlived the intelligent basis for parliamentary government."[24]

---

19. *Second Treatise,* Chapter 13.
20. *Ibid.,* Chapter 19.
21. Laski, *op. cit.,* p. 37.
22. Judd Harmon, *op. cit.,* p. 253.
23. W.T. Jones: *Masters of Political Thought,* Vol. II, p. 200.
24. H.J. Laski: *Political Thought in England* (*Locke to Bentham*), p. 61.

22
Rousseau

Jean Jacques Rousseau (1712-78) "still holds his place as one of the most outstanding and controversial political theorists."[1] His political ideas are traceable in *Discourse on the Moral Effects of Arts and Science* and *Discourse on the Origin and Foundation of Inequality among Men*. But his most important work is the *Social Contract* that, according to Rene Hubert, "is the very centre and keystone to the whole structure of political fabric." These works reveal his immortal contribution to the age of romanticism in literature, reason and reconstruction in the sphere of social and political ideas.

First Discourse: The central idea of Rousseau in this monograph finds place in his strong affirmation that states and civilisations tend to decay as they allow the development of arts and sciences that provide "conveniences" and "luxuries" and thereby create a materialistic outlook undermining virtues and morals. As he says: "As the conveniences of life increase, as the arts are brought to perfection, and luxury spreads, true courage flags, the virtues disappear; and all this is the effect of the sciences and of those arts which are exercised in the privacy of men's dwellings." Like a vehement critic of the model of materialistic civilisation, Rousseau goes on to assert that one should ignore the preachments of the philosophers and rely upon one's own conscience, instinct, feeling, faith and emotion. As he further says: "Why should we build our happiness on the opinions of others when we can find it in our own hearts? Let us leave to others the task of instructing mankind in their duty, and confine ourselves to the discharge of our own. We have no occasion for greater knowledge than this. Virtue! sublime science of simple minds, are such industry and preparation needed if we are to know you? Are not our principles graven on every heart: Need we do more to learn your laws, than examine ourselves and listen to the voice of conscience, when the passions are silent?"

The message of this work of Rousseau is, therefore, a plea "to return to the faith of fathers", "so beware of a too great preccupation with material values, and to reassert the values of faith, patriotism, and good citizenship."[2] As Rousseau says: "We have physicists, geometricians, chemists, astronomers, poets, musicians, and painters in plenty; but we have no longer a citizen among us or if there be found few scattered over our abandoned countryside, they are left to perish there unnoticed and neglected." It

---

1. R. D. Masters: *The Political Philosophy of Rousseau,* p. 303.
2. M. Judd Harmon: *The History of Political Thought from Plato to the Present,* p. 299.

implies that the proper standard, according to Rousseau is the creation of a natural man uncorrupted by the vices and luxuries of a materialistic civilisation. This, however, does not imply that Rousseau rejects the values of a modern civilised life and makes a clarion call of "return to nature." What he really desires is that modern civilised society must undergo a fundamental change in the direction of creating conditions whereby one may lead a new social life of a "wise" and "pure man."[3]

The *First Discourse* has been dubbed as the "poorest of his writings", "polemical, highly charged with emotion, and appears to have been hastily written."[4] It is also said that the refutations of Rousseau attempt to lay down upon all arts and sciences "an unreasonable burden of responsibility for all the ills of civilisation."[5] It is further said that Rousseau's essay of protest "is too short to allow the proper development of any of the suggestive insights which it contains."[6] As a result, his superficial denunciation of the materialistic civilisation "takes the place of detailed argument in too many instances. In spite of this, however, a number of elements in the discourse can be, and are, powerfully developed in Rousseau's greater works, and so stand out as the important parts of a defective whole. In conclusion, therefore, the *First Discourse* can be said to keep its place in the literature of protest; but it is not plausible enough to be taken very seriously as a contribution to philosophy."[7]

Second Discourse: It is his "first writing" in which he "completely developed his philosophical principles."[8] He describes it as "the work of greatest importance" that comes to us in the form of the result of his deep philosophical pursuits.[9] What Hobbes gives in his *Leviathan* and Locke in his *Second Treatise of Civil Government* with regard to the supposed nature of the pre-political phase and its termination by means of a social compact is given by Rousseau in his two works—the *Second Discourse* and the *Social Contract*. The *Second Discourse* looks like his attempt to provide an explanation of the origin of inequality among men that, in a real sense, becomes an essay on the origin of civil society necessitating the creation of political authority in due course when the noble conditions of Arcadian bliss and primitive simplicity are perverted by the savage conditions of cut-throat competition and internecine wars. In this way, the *Second Discourse* becomes a prelude to his *Social Contract*. Herein we find his philosophical description of what the social contractualists call the "state of nature" that is terminated by means of a social compact made by ideally reasonable people to establish political community. As he says: "To mediate on this great subject I travelled to St. Germain for seven or eight days. Deep in the forest I sought and found image of the first epochs. Whose history I proudly traced; revealed the little lies of men; I dared strip their nature nude, follow the progress of time and things, which

3. Masters, *op. cit.,* pp. 233-54.
4. Harmon, *op. cit.,* p. 298.
5. J. H. Broome: *Rousseau: A Study of His Thought,* p. 27.
6. *Ibid.*
7. *Ibid.*
8. Masters, *op. cit.,* p. 106.
9. *Ibid.*

have disfigured it, and comparing man's man with natural man, show them in man's supposed perfection the true source of his miseries."

A study of the *Second Discourse* illustrates the point that the creation of political community witnessed three revolutions. In the initial phase, man is neither moral nor immoral but amoral. He leads a life of simplicity and happiness. He is not a political creature. The first revolution takes place after the institution of family on a permanent basis that may be interpreted as the beginning of civil society. The establishment of permanent family relationship is described by him as 'reciprocal attachment'. As a result of the first revolution, there comes into being the state of inequality which is of two kinds—natural and moral. While the former consists of those differences such as age, physical strength and the qualities of mind and soul, the latter is established by man after entering into the phase of social existence.

The second revolution is brought about by the invention of agriculture and the fortuitous discovery of the usefulness of metals leading towards the specialisation of functions and division of labour. The creation of the institution of private property divided society into two classes—the rich and the poor—and thereby opened the Pandora's box of a highly competitive existence. While the poor struggled against the rich for the sake of earning the bare means of subsistence, the rich contended for the safety of their possessions.

It is clear that the creation of civil society, according to Rousseau, is effected by the force of inequality that produced conditions necessary for the artificial victory of the rich over the poor. One may say that it is like an *ad hoc* arrangement between the rulers and the ruled in as much as this state of life is not to exist for ever. The poor who willy-nilly succumb to the persuasion of the rich do it all not for the sake of throwing themselves into the frying pan after feeling fed up with the life of a competitive social environment, nor do they do it with the motive of getting back to the previous condition in case they ever feel fed up with the tyranny of a new social order, rather they do it with the hope of replacing this "bogus" arrangement with a better and nobler one by means of a social contract that becomes the central idea of Rousseau's *Social Contract*. As Hacker says: "The transition from the state of nature to society in the *Second Discourse* is political as well as social. And in building a state on top of society, men jumped out of the frying pan of cut-throat competition into the fire of political tyranny. This transition, then, is not a contract. It is informal and accidental, non-legal and in fact founded on a gigantic swindle. In no sense are rational or informed processes of consent at work, or in no sense are the resultant society and state to be considered legitimate institutions."[10]

Social Contract: Following the usual course of the social contractualists, Rousseau draws a soft picture of the state of nature in which man is neither moral, nor immoral, but amoral—"noble savage"—leading "a life of idyllic happiness and primitive simplicity." But this state could not have lasted for long. With the rise of civilisation, the institution of private property was established which brought forth "reason" in

10. Andrew Hacker: *Political Theory,* p. 301.

man and "inequality" in society. The "noble savage" enjoyed heavenly pleasures but private property entered like the Serpent in the Garden of Eden. It created a sense of jealousy and struggle, and substituted the condition of pristine self-sufficiency and happiness by the state of inequality and acknowledged usurpations. "What crimes, wars, murders, what miseries and horrors would have been spared the human race by him who, snatching out the stakes or falling in the ditch, should have cried to his fellows: "Beware of listening to this impostor; you are lost if you forget that the fruits belong to all and that the earth belongs to none."

These evils terminated the era of simplicity and happiness, and necessitated the formation of some political organisation. A return to the state of nature grew impossible because the world was too thickly populated to admit the roamings of the noble savage. As a result, the institutions of the family, private property, society, law and government had come to stay. It is thus obvious that, in Rousseau's view, the state is an evil to arrest the bigger evils. However, his view, as given in the *Emile*, becomes modified in the *Social Contract* when he comes to believe that the advantages of the civil society are greater than those of the state of nature. Hence, the people in that state of nature make a contract according to whose terms A, B, C, D, E etc., surrender their natural rights to the collective whole created by the union of A+B+C+D+E, etc. Like the men of Hobbes, they surrender all but, unlike them, they put their person and powers under the supreme direction of the collective whole which Rousseau calls the General Will. In his own words: "Then each of us puts his person and all his powers in common under the supreme direction of the General Will, and in our corporate capacity, we receive each member as an individual part of the whole."[11]

The making of this contract creates a political community and thereby turns individuals into citizens. By the terms of this contract they not only receive as much as they lose but, in addition, they acquire the common force to preserve what they individually had. The contract creates a moral and collective body with its own unity, common identity, corporate life and rational will. In this way, it terminates the state of nature and wholly transforms the character of the individuals who place themselves under the aegis of a democratic sovereign—the general will—an authority of the corporate whole of the community. They take equal membership of the community, submit to it and yet make themselves an integral part of the sovereign authority. In submission to this moral authority, they never feel subjection to an alien body, but to some authority, of which each is a part placed on an equal footing with others. Since they are both like an individual and a subject, so they remain both like a citizen and a sovereign and thus, while obeying the state as a citizen, they come to obey their own will incorporated in the general will along with the wills of others.

According to Rousseau, "The passage from the state of nature to the civil state produces a very remarkable change in man, by substituting justice for instinct in his conduct and giving his actions the morality they had hitherto lacked. Then only, when the voice of duty takes the place of physical impulse and right of appetite, does

11. *Social Contract,* Book I, Ch. VI.

man, who so far had considered only himself, find that he is forced to act on different principles and to consult his reason before listening to his inclinations. What man loses by the social contract is his natural liberty and an unlimited right to everything, he tries to get and succeeds in getting; what he gains in his civil liberty ... which is limited by the general will. We might, over and above all this, add to what man acquires in the civil state moral liberty, which alone makes him truly master of himself, for the mere impulse of appetite in slavery, while obedience to a law which we prescribe to ourselves is liberty."[12]

It is understandable that, like Hobbes and Locke, Rousseau starts from a hypothetical state of nature and formulates his theory of state on a purely imaginary foundation. The framework in which he seeks to answer the fundamental question of political obligation is really a hypothesis which cannot be proved by historical, philosophical, logical and legal standards. The result is that the significance of political institution is underrated and the theory leaves scope, although very little as compared to Hobbes and Locke, for the disobedience of governmental authority in the name of the general good.

General Will: General will is the will of the corporate body called the community and it stands for the common good and general welfare of the society as a whole. It supersedes the respective will of all those people who enter into social contract and agree to surrender all their powers to the community. The chief sanction or the characteristic mark behind it is not the number of persons willing it but the common good or general interest. However, it is not a mere compromise after the cancellation of pluses and minuses, it represents "a higher type of the will of the society," It represents common consciousness of the common good after discussion and proper deliberation. The only important thing about it is that it wills general, *i.e.,* common interest and not that what is willed generally, *i.e.,* by majority of the members of society. Barker puts it well: "When he (Rousseau) speaks of this general will, he uses the adjective to indicate the quality of the 'object' of this general will, he uses the adjective to indicate the quality of the 'object' sought, and not quality of the objects or persons by whom it is sought."[13]

An explanation of the general will indicates that it bears the characteristics of being rational or non-self-conflicting, indivisible or non-sectional, right or willing common welfare, inalienable or unrepresentable, permanent, non-impulsive and national. Such an explanation leads to several conclusions. First, the *body politic* taken as a whole may be regarded as an organised living body resembling that of a man and also being a moral entity possessed of a will. Second, the general will always tends to the preservation and welfare of the whole and every part. Third, it keeps all people in a particular relationship with all members of the political community. It is the source of law, justice and power. It constitutes popular sovereignty where the people are both the sovereign and the subject. Above all, it is always on the side of the general good.

12. Wright: *The Meaning of Rousseau,* p. 28.
13. E. Barker: "Introduction" to the English translation of *Social Contract,* p. xliv.

According to Prof. F.J.C. Hearnshaw, "It is always on the side which is most favourable to public interest so that it is needful only to act as justly to be certain of following general will."[14]

In this regard, however, Rousseau reaches very close to Locke inasmuch as he not only adheres to the fact of public good but, for practical purposes, believes in the superiority of numerical strength. Laski points out: "The general will, in practical, instead of semi-mystic terms, really means the welfare of the community as a whole, and when we inquire how the general will is to be known, we come, after much shuffling, upon the will of the majority in which Locke also puts his trust. Rousseau's general will, indeed, it at bottom no more than an assertion that right and truth should prevail; and for this also Locke was anxious."[15]

However, Rousseau's theory of general will may be criticised on the following grounds:

1. The idea of general will is too abstract and mystical. A will that is necessarily unidentifiable with the will of one, few, many, all, or even none, is no will at all. It indicates abstract theorisation. Besides, in a situation of conflicting opinions, who has the title to ascertain the characteristics of public good in varying and conflicting judgements of the people. It appears that Rousseau regards it as a sort of arithmetical balance to be arrived at by striking off the opposite judgements of this and that member of the political community representing a particular interest. Truly speaking, the process is dynamic. Roussean believes that collective opinion is not in the nature of a balance or average; it is more like the output of several factors. In brief, general will is purely an abstract notion based on the abstract theorisation of the author. Prof. L.T. Hobhouse rejects its premises by saying: "When it is will, it is not general; and when it is general, it is not will." Sabine also puts it thus: "The truth is that general will is abstract. How does this absolute right stand in relation to many and possible conflicting judgements about it? Who is entitled to decide what is right?"[16]
2. Rousseau's sanction that man may be compelled to obey the dictates of general will stands to contradict his theory of freedom. Force is the negation of freedom and its use cannot be reconciled with the fact of individual liberty in a way as he believes. It may never be in the interest of public welfare if the authority of the state is exercised tyrannically and, curiously enough, in the name of the community's good. Rousseau nowhere provides safeguards for the individual. His surrender is complete and so he keeps no weapon in his hands to resist the abused authority of the general will. The freedom of the individual is thus overridden by the freedom of the state and the state then gets a valid title to become even oppressive and

14. F.J.C. Hearnshaw: *Social and Political Ideas of the French Thinkers of the Age of Reason,* p. 102.
15. H.J. Laski: *Political Thought in England (From Locke to Bentham),* p. 52.
16. G.H. Sabine: *A History of Political Theory,* pp. 591-92.

tyrannical. Cole aptly questions: "What guarantee is there that the state, in freeing itself, will not enslave its members."?[17]

Sovereignty: Rousseau's sovereign is the creation of a social contract that terminates the state of nature and ushers in a political society in which the people are transformed from limited and stupid animals into active and intelligent citizens. The sovereign is neither one person (nor an assembly) like Hobbes's nor the community like Locke's; it is the general will—a will of the people standing for the good of the people. However, like Hobbes's, it is illimitable, infallible, indivisible, permanent, all-embracing and unrepresentable; and like Locke's, it is popular as it resides not in one person but in the community as a whole. Hence, in Rousseau's view, sovereignty is identifiable with the general interest of the community and it thus exhibits a compromise between the absolutism of Hobbes and the constitutionalism of Locke. In other words, like Hobbes, Rousseau regards sovereignty as absolute, unlimited, inalienable, permanent and indivisible; he does not vest it in a single person or an assembly of few persons and clearly differentiates between state and government and state and society. In his own words: "The social compact gives to the *body politic* absolute power over all its members. We can see from this that the sovereign power is absolute, sacred and inviolable, as it is, does not and cannot exceed the limits of general conventions, and that every man may dispose at will his goods and liberty as these conventions leave him."

A study of Rousseau's theory of sovereignty bears certain formidable proportions when we pass from a theoretical to a practical plane. His sanction of force to compel the obedience of general will destroys the whole fabric designed by him to safeguard the liberty of the people. As he clearly affirms: "In order then that the social compact may not be an empty formula, it tacitly includes the undertaking that whoever refuses to obey the general will shall be compelled to do so by the whole body. This means nothing less than that he will be forced to be free.... This alone legitimises civil undertakings which without it, would be absurd, tyrannical and liable to the most fruitful abuses."[18] Moreover, Rousseau himself recognises the practical difficulty of his thesis and so he sanctions that, for all practical purposes, majority opinion should be taken as indicative of the general will. Hence, he not only commits a sort of self-contradiction, rather he looks like authorising the majority to suppress the minority tyrannically and, curiously enough, in the name of public good. The result is that the gates of majority tyranny are opened and the minority has to suffer irrespective of the fact that its will may, in a certain case, pertain to the formation of general will.

Government: While Hobbes justifies absolute kingship and Locke favours constitutional monarchy, Rousseau's theory of government prefers direct democracy. However, he clearly differentiates between state and government and assigns a subordinate place to the latter. To him, government is simply an agent or a useful tool of the sovereign people. Not being a result of the contract, it has only limited authority

17. G.D.H. Cole: "Introduction" in his English translation of *Social Contract,* p. xxv.
18. *Social Contract,* Book I, Ch. VII.

derived from the sovereign people. Being devoid of any original power, its authority may be recalled by the sovereign people at any time. The subordinate character of the government is attested by the fact that, through periodic assemblies, the people decide about the desirability of the existing government and its personnel to continue in office. The sovereignty "belongs to the people in a corporate body while government is merely an agent having delegated powers which can be withdrawn or modified as the will of the people dictates. Government has no vested right whatsoever such as Locke's theory of contract had left to it, but it has merely the status of a committee."[19]

Rousseau also gives an account of the various forms of government and their excellence. He believes that their forms vary with the circumstances of time and place, and the number of persons holding and exercising executive authority. It is monarchy when the executive power is concentrated in the hands of a single person; it is aristocracy when it is put in the hands of a small number in which the number of private citizens is still more than the number of the magistrates; finally, it is democracy when it is vested in the whole people and exercised by them or by their majority. However, in this regard, two things should be noted. First, Rousseau points out that no form of government is absolutely static and one particular form may yield place to another in a greater or lesser degree. Second, he believes that certain maxims may be laid down to recognise the excellence of a particular form of government in the light of a particular time, place and other circumstances. Rousseau prefers aristocracy to monarchy, but he views aristocracy as a government of three types—natural, hereditary and elective. However, his real preference is for direct democracy existing in a very small state like Geneva of that time (his birthplace) where people may freely exercise their sovereign power.

Further, Rousseau says that the government means the executive alone. The legislative business is to be in the hands of the sovereign people who cannot part with their law-making power without curtailing their sovereign authority. The essence of legislation is will which is unrepresentable. It is thus perfectly obvious that Rousseau rejects the idea of representative democracy, for, in his own words, the deputies of the people "are not and cannot be its representatives." His ultimate choice is in favour of a small state consisting of about ten thousand people where a direct democratic system may successfully operate. In short, in his view, government is merely an agent of the people and not their master as Hobbes had done.

Rousseau's theory of government may be criticised from two points of view. First, his idea of true democracy insisting on perpetual town-meeting is, in a strict sense, utopian. Second, it cannot be admitted that government is merely an executive machinery having no concern with legislative business. Rousseau's conclusion can hardly be given a practical shape if it is acknowledged that the government is established merely for the sake of carrying out the will of the people. The works of legislation and execution are not so separable and thus the government is not like a policeman to carry out the will of the sovereign legislators, rather it has to keep and utilise its share in the

19. Sabine, *op. cit.*, p. 592.

work of law making. Conversely, the legislators' job is not merely to make laws, they are also concerned with their execution. Hence, it is untenable to point out that while the will of the legislature is general, in the case of the executive it is particular, and so the wills of both are different from each other. Rightly speaking, Rousseau's theory of general will "greatly diminished the importance of government."[20]

Master Legislator : From the foregoing account, it becomes clear that, in Rousseau's view, legislation is a vital function of the community brought into existence by the social contract. Nothing but manifestation of the general will can become law. Law, as such, deals with the good of the community and the conditions of civil society must be regulated only by it. Its concern is with the common cause and its formulation is a result of common endeavour. It, therefore, follows that law has two main characteristics, namely, the requirement of common welfare and common formulation, that is, the making of law necessarily involves participation of the members of the community for the cause of general good. Wright thus remarks that, in Rousseau's view, law exists only when all the people "act for all the people."[21]

Rousseau's legislator looks like Plato's philosopher-king in the framing of laws for the good of the community. However, there is a point of difference that while Plato makes his all-wise philosopher free from any over-riding authority in the name of his "omniscience," Rousseau makes the will of his wise legislator subject to the decision of the popular assembly. However, it does not take away the superior position of the legislator of Rousseau in view of the fact that he describes him (legislator) as having a superior intelligence which can survey all the passions of mankind, though itself exposed to none; an intelligence having no contact with our nature, yet knowing it to the full; an intelligence the well-being of which is independent of our own, yet willing to be concerned with it."[22] The legislator is called upon by Rousseau "to change, as it were, the very stuff of human nature; to transform each individual who in isolation is a complete but solitary whole, into a part of something greater than himself, from which, in a sense, he drives his life and being; to substitute a communal and moral existence for the purely physical and independent life with which all of us are endowed by nature."[23]

Obviously, the addition of legislators' element cuts much of the ground of Rousseau's theory of popular legislation. Certainly, in this respect, he draws inspiration from old Greek practice when distinguished foreign citizens were invited by popular bodies on important occasions. Rousseau was invited by Corsica and Poland on two occasions to serve as a constitution-maker. It is certain that a legislator of this type will act like Solon and Lycurgus, and in the name of his genius may coerce the wills of ordinary members of the popular assembly. In a political community based on the theory of general will, there is neither reason nor need to characterise the legislator as a "holy" or "super" man merely because of his genius or competence. According to W.T. Jones,

20. *Ibid.,* p. 593.
21. Wright, *op. cit.,* p. 78.
22. *Social Contract,* Book I, Chapter VII.
23. *Ibid.*

"Here again, as so often in Rousseau, we have a curious mixture of penetrating insight and fabulous nonsense."[24]

Freedom: Rousseau's deep love for individual liberty becomes obvious from the opening sentence of his *Social Contract:* "Man is born free, but he is everywhere in chains." In its original sense, it means that man ought to be free, independent and solitary (as this is the best life for him), but that the conventions and customs of society, the various regulations and restrictions which political and economic institutions involve, enslave him and cause his fall from his original and blessed state of freedom. But the subsequent and final meaning of this phrase, according to Rousseau, means that man ought to be free not in the sense of being able to do just whatever he wants, but in the sense of being an element in the general will of whose common life he is an integral part. At the same time, Rousseau asserts that man is seldom actually free, because modern states are really founded on force which is a negation of the real will of the people.

The freedom, in Rousseau's sense, is no more a licence and no longer the unrestricted conduct of a separate and independent individual. The freedom of the individual requires a kind of participation in a larger life which all the various physical organs share when they are functioning harmoniously in a healthy body. Obviously, it is not all the physical freedom to do whatever we can, as Hobbes asserted, it is not even the moral autonomy of the individual to judge and decide for himself which Locke advocated. Contradistinguished from the natural freedom of Hobbes and the moral freedom of Locke, Rousseau substitutes the conception of freedom not only compatible with, but actually implying, a certain kind of restraint. In his view, man is really free when, and if, his behaviour conforms to some pattern or model which he has set for himself, irrespective of the fact that this conformity involves considerable restraint of impulse and desires tending to lead him in opposite directions.

Remarkable is the fact that Rousseau's individual remains free in spite of the fact that he surrenders all his rights to the community. The reason is that surrender is not in favour of an alien authority but of a corporate body of which he himself is an integral part. Hence, the restrictions imposed on his liberty are self-imposed. The freedom of the individual is consonant with the good of the general body. It is no longer the unrestrained conduct of an isolated and independent individual; it is the rational freedom of an individual who leads a common life in organic relationship with his fellow-citizens, and whose welfare is integrally connected with the welfare of the whole community. The social compact thus successfully established a new kind of society in which the individual loses his precarious freedom "to do as he liked and gains the assured freedom to do that all consider right."[25]

Critical Apprecieation: Rousseau occupies a very important place in the history of modern Western political thought. His theories of general will and sovereignty represent a remarkable reconciliation of liberty and authority, and a peculiar

24. W.T. Jones: *Masters of Political Thought,* Vol. II, p. 593.
25. Wright, *op. cit.,* p. 28.

compromise between the views of Hobbes and Locke. He makes a sharp distinction between state and government, and also between sovereign law and governmental decrees. His sovereign law is the ancestor of the modern fundamental or constitutional law. He emphasises that the people are the ultimate source of all political authority; the government is merely an agent of the sovereign people; common welfare is the criterion of political existence; social life has got an organic character; liberty and authority are not antithetical to each other, and, as Green later said, "will, not force, is the basis of state." His whole thought can be epitomised in these words: "Political right can only replace the important traditional natural law teaching if utility can be combined with justice."[26]

26. Roger D. Masters, *op. cit.*, p. 303.

23
Bentham

A study of the important works of Jeremy Bentham (1748-1832) as *An Introduction to the Principles of Morals* and *Legislation* and *Fragment of Government* shows that he has freely borrowed ideas from Locke, Hume, Hartley, Voltaire, Barington, Helvetius, Montesquieu, Beccaria and Priestly in varying measures and made his own contribution to the school of utilitarian radicalism. It is, however, a different matter that his contributions have been differently evaluated by his critics. For instance, John Plamentaz is of the view that Bentham is "quite unwittingly trying to reconcile two couples of irreconcilable doctrines—egoistic hedonism with utilitarianism on the one hand and psychological system with an objective theory of morals on the other."[1] But C.L. Wayper says: "This is the greatest contribution of Bentham to political theory that he sees every question in terms of men and women whose lives it will affect and never in terms of abstraction."[2]

Utilitarianism: The political philosophy of Jeremy Bentham is based on the principle of "utility" in which he discovers a practical commandment as well as a scientific law, a proposition which is at one and the same time what is and what ought to be. He admires the psychological system of Richard Cumberland who refuted innate moral ideas of a rationalist doctrine and accepted the theory of general welfare. He also admires the views of Francis Hutcheson who in his *Moral Philosophy* urged that moral evil of an action "is as to the degree of misery and the number of sufferers so that action is best which accomplishes the greatest happiness of the greatest number." He also draws much inspiration from Priestley's *Essay on Government* in which it is given that the greatest happiness of the greatest number "is the great standard by which philosophy relating to that state must finally be determined." Then, from Hume, he gets the instruction of introducing the experimental method of reasoning into moral objects. Thus, he rejects the abstract notions of natural rights, social contract and metaphysical convictions and insists on the logic of usefulness, good and expediency. Naturally, the conclusions of Bentham become quite different from those of the social contractualists and the rationalists of the earlier centuries.

Bentham's utilitarianism has the following important features:

1. Bentham gives a peculiar meaning to the term "utility." To him utility means, positively speaking, all that is good, pleasant, useful, agreeable, advantageous,

---

1. Plamenatz: *The English Utilitarians,* p. 72.
2. Wayper: *Political Thought,* p. 106.

and beneficial; or negatively speaking, all that is the reverse of painful, useless, disadvantageous, bad and disagreeable. The characteristic mark of utility is, in simple terms, pleasure. Like an economist, he does not define utility as a want-satisfying power of a commodity; to him it is something synonymous with what is pleasant. In his own words: "An adherent to the principle of utility holds virtue to be a good thing by reason only of the pleasures which result from the practice of it: he esteems vice to be a bad thing by reason only of the pains which follow in its train."

2. Another important point is that, according to Bentham, utility possesses the power of motivation. That is, human actions are motivated by the consider-ation of pleasure and pain. Like the early Epicureans of Greece and the modern Hedonists of France, he believes that man by nature desires to do what seems pleasant to him and refrains from doing wherefrom he fears pain. He writes: "Nature has placed mankind under the governance of two sovereign masters, pain and pleasure. It is for them alone to point out what we ought to do as well as to determine what we shall do. On the one hand, the standard of right and wrong: on the other, the chain of causes and effects, are fastened to their throne."
3. Pleasures and pains differ in quantity not in quality. Playing pushpin is as good as reading poetry.
4. This enables Bentham to suggest that a felicific calculus may be established. He states it thus: "Sum up all the values of all the pleasures on the one side, and those of all the pains on the other. The balance, if it be on the side of the pleasure, will give the good tendency of the act upon the whole, with respect to the interests of that individual person; if on the side of pain, the bad tendency of it upon the whole. Take an account of the number of persons whose interests appear to be conceived, and repeat the above process with respect to each. Sum up the numbers expressive of the degrees of good tendency, which the act has, with respect to each individual, in regard to whom the tendency of it is good upon the whole; do this again with respect to each individual in regard to whom the tendency of it is bad upon the whole. Take the balance, which, if on the side of pleasure, will give the general good tendency of the act with respect to the total number of community of individuals concerned; if on the side of pain, the general evil tendency with respect to the same community."

Bentham is of the view that by means of computation, the formula of the "greatest good of the greatest number" can be laid down which signifies the maximum possible pleasure to the maximum number of persons. This should prevail. However, by doing this Bentham makes his utilitarianism universalistic and thus differentiates it from the egoistic hedonism of the Greeks. He realises that in a question relating to the happiness of one individual on the one side and that of the many on the other, the formula of the greatest happiness of the greatest number is the right answer. Thus, at the hands of Bentham, utilitarianism takes a benevolent and universalistic form.

Bentham's utilitarianism may be criticised on the following grounds:

1. Benthamite utilitarianism stands on the ethical and psychological foundations of hedonism which cannot be regarded as a sound moral philosophy. It certainly debases the character of human personality by regarding man as a "creature of feelings" and not of thought.

2. Bentham's assumption that pleasures and pains differ in quantity and not in quality from one another is also wrong. The pain and pleasure of one person are certainly different from the pleasure and pain of another. What is one man's food is another man's poison, and what is pleasant to a wise man is painful to a fool. In this regard, John Stuart Mill is right when he says: "It is better to be a human being dissatisfied than a pig satisfied; better to be a Socrates dissatisfied than a fool satisfied. And if the fool and the pig are of a different opinion, it is because they know only their own side of question."[3]

3. Bentham's felicific calculus is also absurd. The pleasures and pains are not concrete units which may be arithmetically counted. They are subjective and not objective things. Any such idea that they may be arithmetically computed and a formula may be established on that basis is nothing short of a mockery. Plamenatz finds it impossible not merely in practice but also in theory.[4]

However in appreciation of Bentham, Doyle says that he "did not wander into the labyrinth of abstract speculation."[5] Rightly speaking, Benthamism brought political theory back from the abstractions of the Age of Reason to the level of concrete realities. Hence, it has been said that Bentham's political philosophy was intensely humane and intensely practical being directly in touch with the living movements and interest of men."[6]

State: Like social contractualists, Bentham is not concerned with offering a plausible explanation of the origin of state, though he takes up the issues of its nature. He examines the nature of state from the utilitarian point of view and comes to hold that a political society is distinguished from a natural society in which a number of persons or subjects "are suffered to be in the habit of paying obedience to a person or an assembly of persons of a known and certain description (whom we may call governors). Such persons altogether (subjects and governors) are said to be in a state of political society."[7] Thus, natural society and political society are distinguishable on the ground that while, in the former, the subjects are not in the habit of obedience, they are so in the latter the reason for which should be traced in their realisation that state is an instrument to realise the principle of the greatest good of the greatest number.

---

3. Mill: *Utilitarianism,* pp. 17-18.
4. Plamenatz, *op. cit.,* p. 76.
5. P. Doyle, *A History of Political Thought,* p. 229.
6. W.L. Davidson, *Political Thought in England: The Utilitarians,* p. 29.
7. Bentham: *A Fragment on Government* (edited by W. Harrison), p. 28.

The principal features of Bentham's theory of state may be put as follows:

1. Like Plato and Aristotle, Bentham does not consider state as a natural association and, for this reason, prior to the individual. To him, the individual is prior to the state. State is not an instrument that promotes the personality of the individual, rather it is a contrivance to ensure his happiness. Since man is endowed with rational faculty, he lives in the state so as to seek pleasure and avoid pain. Obviously, state is the means to promote happiness of the individual. It has no integral relation with the moral life of the citizen. It seeks to change his behaviour; it cannot change him. It cannot help him to develop his character, to bring out the best that is in him. "For it is not the state that moulds the citizens, it is the citizens who mould the state."[8]
2. Bentham regards state as a law-making agency. The state is a group of persons organised for the promotion and maintenance of happiness; but for this end, it acts through law. By means of law, the state rewards or punishes so that the happiness is increased and the pain decreased. He urges that the law should take cognisance of bad actions and inflict punishment on the people so that the net balance of pleasure is increased and that of pain decreased. Mere morality is not sufficient and unless law comes into operation, bad things cannot be out of place. Only law being the command of the sovereign can secure habitual obedience of the people. So Bentham lays stress on the existence of a legal sovereign in the state.
3. Bentham's emphasis on law accompanies his repudiation of the phrase of natural law. He calls natural law simply as a phrase and natural rights as 'simple nonsense natural and imprescriptible rights, rhetorical nonsense, upon stilts'. For the abstract phrases of natural law and natural rights, he substitutes the practical norms of utility. Denouncing the abstract notion of natural law and rights, he says: "Absolute equality is absolutely impossible. Absolute liberty is directly repugnant to the existence of every kind of government."
4. Although Bentham repudiates the theory of natural law and rights, he asserts that all men are born free and equal. But, in this regard, his approach is neither rational nor metaphysical. He insists that all men are equal in the eye of law; all have equal rights as regards the promotion of happiness; and it is the duty of the state to ensure greater equalisation of property. If absolute equality is not possible, the state may do away with gross inequalities, for too great inequality is an insuperable obstacle on the road to the greatest good of the greatest number.
5. In this connection, Bentham also distinguishes between natural liberty and social liberty. He calls natural liberty as freedom to do whatever one wishes and civil liberty to do that is conducive to the formula of the greatest happiness of the greatest number. Natural liberty prevails in the forest, while civil liberty is a

8. Wayper, *op. cit.,* p. 98-99.

matter of social life and thus Bentham wants that the state should make laws whereby natural liberty is minimised and civil liberty is protected and promoted.

6. Bentham also sanctions right to resistance against the state. If the opposition produces less pain and thereby adds to the store of happiness, it is justified. If the individuals find it essential to resist political authority, i.e., if it is in their interest, they may adopt measures of resistance against the state.
7. Bentham assigns a democratic character to the state by holding it as a trustee for the happiness of the individuals. "The particular character assigned to the state centres around the function of the realisation of the principle of utility." Obviously, Bentham's explanation of the state is a complete statement in terms of his principle of utility, that is, greatest good of the greatest number, not confined to the vague generalities but demanding specific services. In short, to Bentham, the state is not a natural institution or a moralising agency as conceived by the Idealists or an instrument of public welfare as regarded by the Collectivists or an instrument of exploitation and oppression as denounced by the anti-authoritarians; it is an instrument to realise the principle of the greatest good of the greatest number. Moreover, as a legal reformer, he interprets security as the essential function of the state and for this he lays stress on the usefulness of the system of law.
8. Bentham accepts the usual classification of governments into three forms, namely, monarchy, aristocracy and democracy. But he prefers a democratic government where the realisation of the formula of the greatest good of the greatest number has the maximum possible chances. Only in a democratic government there is a reconciliation of the interests of the governors with those of the governed. Here public virtue or goodness of intention is more likely to be found, for the right of law-making resides in the people. Besides, democracy also breeds patriotism. A monarchy is, indeed, more powerful than all other kinds of government where all sinews are knit together in the hands of a single ruler, but there are imminent dangers of his employing that strength to improvident or oppressive purpose. So, in an aristocracy, there is less strength and honesty.

A study of Bentham's political theory in this regard leaves this strong impression that he ultimately prefers a democratic system for realising the principle of the greatest good of the greatest number. Obviously, such an affirmation becomes consistent with his moral theory. A problem arises as to how we may get the principle of utility realised by the political authority when the members of the government are naturally and primarily concerned with their own happiness. Bentham well studies this problem and he convincingly observes that only under a system of self-government, the interests of the governors and those of the governed would coincide. And if there is any problem in this regard, its only possible solution is to have a fully representative body.[9]

9. M.J. Rendall: *An Introduction to Political Thought,* p. 322.

Reforms: As already pointed out, Bentham was not a political thinker in the first instance. His main interest was law, and his coming into the field of politics and launching a vigorous movement for reforming legal and political institutions was a definite result of his frustration and disillusionment. The rejection of his plan of "Panopticon" by the government and his friendship with James Stuart Mill are the two important factors to which the cause of change in his thought should be attributed. As a matter of fact, he wanted to bring about drastic reforms in the legal, political and administrative institutions of his country and nothing but a grand failure in this regard pushed him towards a world of deep disillusionment and bewilderment. Thus, he took to the course of fighting for reforms with passion. He sharpened the trend of radicalism in contemporary English political thought, keeping which in view it is said that he gave English radicalism of the 18th and 19th centuries its theoretical formulation. (Halevy)

The reforms suggested by Bentham cover different fields like politics, education, legal system, administration, religion and the like. They may be summed up in the following manner:

1. In the sphere of politics, Bentham suggested universal manhood franchise to all tax payers, annual general election, unicameral legislature implying abolition of the House of Lords, a republican system desiring the end of monarchy, annual session of the Parliament, vote by secret ballot, equalisation of electoral districts, freedom of the press so as to publish parliamentary debates, a competitive examination for the recruitment of public servants, freedom of the representatives from the hold of the constituents, recall of public officials, existence of a code to limit the powers of the government, etc.
2. In the sphere of law and justice, Bentham emphasised the need for a civil and criminal code without unnecessary technicalities, redundancies and obsolete phraseology, making provisions of law in a simple and easily intelligible language, availability of legal texts to the common man easily and at a cheap price, quick and fair disposal of cases by the courts, constitution of single judge benches for expeditious adjudication of disputes and the like. We may also refer to his proposals like the institution of frugality banks, code of merchant shipping, introduction of health legislation, creation of public prosecutors, abrogation of usury loans, reform of the poor law, etc. Not only did he lay emphasis on the case of national law, but also on the codification of international law.
3. Bentham paid attention to the problem of proper punishment. The execution of justice should be exhibited to the people as far as possible so that the prospective wrong-doer may feel frightened. The main purpose behind meting out punishment to the wrong-doer should be to reform him so as to protect the happiness of society. For this sake, he advanced the plan of "Panopticon" or a semi-circular building of the prison house having the barracks of the criminals on the periphery and the seat of the superintending staff at the centre, so that all the activities of the prisoners may be watched by the jailor. The criminals should be given such training that

they become good people and when they are released, they should be given some useful employment.

4. Bentham also covered the sphere of education. Here he suggested that education should be such that goes to the advantage of the man as well as of the society. The imparting of education should be governed by the considerations of natural aptitude, age and capacity of the students. In particular, he laid stress on the education of the poor children. He insisted on suitable changes in the poor law of the country so that the state may give financial assistance to the education of poor children. His national education scheme is important in this regard.

5. Finally, the reform proposals of Bentham touched the sphere of religion. He criticised the sinecure and extravagant offices of the church. He also denounced the system of ecclesiastical peers in the House of Lords. In his view, the religious leaders hindered the intellectual progress by supporting beliefs contrary to the implications of the principle of utility.

Critical Appreciation: A brief review of the proposals advanced by Bentham amply illustrates that he was by all means a vigorous campaigner of reforms in all walks of life, so that the principle of utility may be applied for the regeneration of the whole people. Keeping this in view, W.A. Dunning compared Bentham with a "veritable bull that entered the china shop."[10] It is also said that Bentham's philosophy "was intensely humane and intensely practical being directly in touch with the living movements and interests of men."[11] E.M. Young comments that it "would be hard to find any corner of our public life where the spirit of Bentham is not working today."[12]

---

10. Dunning: *A History of Political Theories,* Vol. III, Ch. 6.
11. W. L. Davidson: *Political Thought in England: The Utilitarians,* p. 29.
12. Cited in Wayper, *op. cit.,* p. 83.

24
Mill

If Jeremy Bentham gave to his friend James Stuart Mill "a doctrine" and received in turn by the latter " a school," James's son (John Stuart Mill) (1806-1872) made it all in time with the needs and aspiration of the contemporary age and thereby won the credit of giving a positive turn to the prevailing thought of English liberalism. John Stuart Mill carefully took note of the fast changing social and economic conditions of his time and thereby sought to reinterpret the premises of English liberalism. It is because of this that his political ideas look like shifting from the plane of individualism or negative liberalism to that of collectivism or positive liberalism.

Modified Utilitarianism: A study of the political philosophy of John Stuart Mill begins with his work of modifying the basic premises of Benthamite utilitarianism. As pointed out above, the most important exponent of English utilitarianism after Bentham was not the father (James Stuart Mill) but the son (John Stuart Mill) who did the excellent work of modification of the premises of Benthamism. At the hands of John Stuart Mill, Benthamite utilitarianism witnessed a penetrating revision, so much so that even its foundations were changed. In proceeding as a modificator and a reformer, Mill acted as a most errant follower.

Mill's restatement of utilitarianism has the following main characteristics:

1. Mill repudiates the view that pleasures and pains differ in quantity and not in quality. To him the experience of human life suggests that pleasures and pains differ qualitatively as well as quantitatively. He argues that it "is better to be a human being dissatisfied than a pig satisfied; better to be a Socrates dissatisfied than a fool satisfied." He rejects the Benthamite dictum that the "quality of pleasures being equal, playing pushpin is as good as reading poetry" and holds that poetry as a source of pleasure is higher than the playing of an ordinary game. Naturally, Mill desires that man as a nobler and superior creature should pursue higher and real pleasures and avoid those that give happiness to a beast or a foolish person.
2. Mill refutes the logic of Bentham that pains and pleasures can be computed mathematically. In his view, the pleasures of a man are not objective or external units and thus the thesis of the felicific calculus is an absurd idea. When pleasures and pains differ both in quality and quantity, the necessary standards of computing cannot be operative and thus there can be no question of quantity. What means there are of determining which is the acutest of two pains or the interest of two

pleasurable sanctions except the general suffrage of those who are familiar with both?

3. Mill's utilitarianism is more benevolent and humanistic, for he narrows down the gulf between individual interest and general happiness. When there is a question of an individual's happiness and that of the others, Mill's utilitarianism requires him to be strictly impartial as a disinterested and benevolent spectator. Mill writes: "To do as you would be done by, and to love your neighbour as yourself, constitute the ideal perfection of utilitarian morality." Quite unlike Bentham, Mill recognises that not only external, but internal sanctions also constrain the individual to promote general happiness, because every individual possesses a feeling for the happiness of mankind."
4. Unlike Bentham, Mill pays regard to the intrinsic worth of human existence. Not self-realisation but the achievement of pleasure and the avoidance of pain is the object of human life according to Bentham, but by desiring that man should pursue a real and higher pleasure, Mill introduces the sense of dignity in man. He thus introduces a conception of the good life as something more than a life devoted to pleasures. This is to place moral ends above happiness which becomes not indeed a state of pleasure but a state of mind that ensues when one pursues some moral end. Maxey puts it thus: "Bentham's principle of utility, in a society of wolves, would exalt wolfishness; in a society of saints it would exalt saintliness. Mill was determined that saintliness should be the criterion of utility in any society whatsoever."[1]
5. One more point of retreat from Benthamite utilitarianism in Mill is visible in his defence of liberty. By seeing that all men are born in subjection. Bentham puts individual happiness under the stern subordination of the greatest good of the greatest number so much so that he empowers the majority to crush the happiness of the minority. On the contrary, Mill is a strong defender of individual liberty and is never prepared to see that it is crushed by the political authority. Particularly, in the self-regarding sphere, Mill wants no state intervention and sanctions such interference only when one man's freedom becomes a nuisance to the freedom of his fellow beings. Mill says: "The only point of the conduct of anyone, for which he is amenable to society, is that which concerns others. In the part which merely concerns himself, his independence is, of right, absolute."

The restatement of utilitarianism, as seen above, shows in a real sense that Mill "made it at once more humane and less consistent."[2] Of course, by making alterations, Mill made the premises of Benthamite utilitarianism soft and humane, yet the critics point out that it all meant confusion and abandonment of the basic premises. Instead of playing the role of a moderator and a reformer, Mill did the work of a destroyer. He introduced certain criteria which were quite opposed to the basic premises of

---

1. C.C. Maxey: *Political Philosophies,* p. 480.
2. Ivor Brown: *English Political Theory,* p. 119.

utilitarianism and he thus passed from making one standard after another. Wayper rightly says: "In all these alterations that he makes in Benthamism, Mill may think that he is defending it, but in fact he is destroying it."[3]

Liberty: It is in this background that Mill develops his thesis and with a Miltonian fervour advocates the cause of individual liberty. Following are the implications of Mill's doctrine of liberty:

1. Mill emphasises the necessity and desirability of diversity and originality which lead to the free play of individuality. In the presence of liberty, monotony and mediocrity diminish. Every individual keeps liberty to enrich his personality, but for this sake variety is essential. In his own words: "Such are the differences among human beings in their sources of pleasure, their susceptibilities of pain and the operation of their different physical and model agencies, that unless there is corresponding diversity in their modes of life, they neither obtain their fair share of happiness, nor grow up to the mental, moral and aesthetic level of which they are capable."
2. A very important feature of Mill's justification of liberty lies in his division of human actions into two parts. To him the actions of an individual are of two types—self-regarding, i.e., concerning none but himself alone, and others-regarding, i.e., affecting or likely to affect the life of others. The self-regarding sphere includes freedom of conscience, thought, opinion and expression. On the basis of this division, Mill insists that in the self-regarding sphere no external intervention is justified; but the state may interfere in the liberty of the individual when his behaviour becomes a nuisance to the liberty of his fellow beings. He thus says.: "The sole end for which mankind are warranted individually or collectively in interfering with the liberty of action of any of their member is self-protection. The only purpose for which power can be rightfully exercised over any member of a civilised community against his will, is to prevent harm to others . . . Over himself, his own body and mind, the individual is sovereign."[4]
3. One thing that Mill greatly apprehends is the force of majority tyranny or the oppressive weight of public opinion and he passionately stands against the pressure of public opinion and convention. In his view, it is the tendency of society to usually impose, by means other than civil penalties, its own ideas and practices as rules of conduct on those who dissent from time to time. The social tendency usually does much to fetter the development and prevent the formation of any individuality not in harmony with its ways, and compel all characters to fashion themselves upon the models of its own. The government is not justified in infringing the happiness of minorities by suppressing their views even when it is backed by the compact of men holding contrary views.

3. C.L.Wayper: *Political Thought,* p. 116.
4. Mill: *Utilitarianism, Liberty and Representatative Government,* pp. 72-73.

4. Another remarkable point about Mill's thesis is that he attaches certain qualifications and exceptions to his doctrine of liberty. To him the comprehensive meaning of liberty may be understood only by a man who holds natural faculties, i.e., he is not below a certain age-limit and that he possesses requisite character to enjoy it. In other words, the doctrine of liberty cannot be applicable to those who suffer from the deficiencies of mind, body and character.

It is said that Mill's statement of liberty "carried on and enriched a most valuable stream of English thought, at once lucid, practical and humane."[5] But his argument has been criticised for being negative, pessimistic, atomistic and empty. The following points may be raised in this connection:

1. It is said that Mill's statement does not find congruity with the fact of social harmony. It goes against a celebrated tradition of political thought that man's existence should not be studied in isolation. He wrongly assumes the case of individual liberty apart from his social existence.
2. Mill's rigid division of human actions into two parts is thoroughly unconvincing. There can be no water-tight division of an individual's actions. The distinction between self-regarding and others-regarding spheres cannot be worked out in practice, for whatever a man does, that has some direct or indirect bearing on his social behaviour. Obviously, committing suicide is a self-regarding action in Mill's view, but it can never be accepted that the state should do nothing to stop it. It has thus rightly been pointed out that the line between the two types of actions "is one which it is impossible to draw, and that, since we are members of one society, all our actions must necessarily affect in some degree the other members of that society."[6]
3. Finally, Mill's conception of state activity has been contested. The state is not a necessary evil, it is a welfare agency and its laws do not always curtail the liberty of the individual. He wrongly insists on the minimum possible state activity for the sake of maximum possible liberty of the individual. The new conception of state activity is that it should be enhanced for the sake of public welfare, no matter the liberties of the people may be circumscribed to the necessary or desirable extent.

Barker thus says: "Yet when all these allowances are made, it still remains true that Mill was a prophet of an empty liberty and an abstract individual. He had no clear philosophy of rights, through which alone the conception of liberty attains a concrete meaning; he had no clear idea of that social whole in whose realisation the false antithesis of 'State' and 'Individual' disappears."[7]

---

5. John Bowle: *Politics and Opinion in the Nineteenth Century,* p. 195.
6. Joad: *Modern Political Theory,* p. 28.
7. E. Barker: *Political Thought in England* (1848-1914), p. 4.

Democracy: Although Mill appears as a qualified admirer of democracy in his *Essay On Liberty,* in his *Considerations On Representative Government* he is a stern advocate of democracy, what he calls by the name of "representative government." He defines representative government as one in which the political power is exercised by the representatives periodically elected by and ultimately accountable to the people. But this definition embodies an implication which is quite different from the interpretation of other protagonists of democracy. He forcefully admires the excellence of representative government from moral and psychological points of view. "To him the test of good government lies in the effect that it leaves on its people. The first element of a good government is the virtue and intelligence of human beings composing the community. Hence, the most important point of excellence which any form of government can possess is to promote the virtue and intelligence of the people themselves."

It follows that the representative government can have an ideal character of its own if it is given a reformed shape and, in this direction, Mill insists on the following requirements:

1. He accepts the significance of minority representation and advocates the use of Hare Scheme or the proportional representation system. He desires that it is an essential part of democracy that minorities should be given proportionate and adequate representation.
2. He very strongly defends the case of female franchise in his work *The Subjection of Women* on the ground that it would wield a decisive influence in securing the enactment of advanced social legislation.
3. He favours the system of public voting. Rejecting the notion of secret ballot, he contends that the value and effectiveness of voting depends on the manner in which the right of voting is exercised.
4. He sanctions weighted suffrage. While recognising that the vote has a value which should be shared by all, he stresses that in the light of superior knowledge, education and intelligence, weightage should be given to some in comparison to those who are ignorant, stupid or of indifferent character.
5. He recognises the importance of educational qualifications. Unless a person has the minimum knowledge of reading, writing and elementary arithmetic, he should not be enfranchised. Moreover, he also makes it mandatory for the government to make suitable arrangements for this sake and deprive only those people of the franchise who fail to utilise the benefit of opportunity.
6. He justifies the imposition of property qualification as well. His contention is that the persons having property behave more responsibly than the propertyless ones, and when the representative assembly discusses a taxation measure, only persons having some property can show their sense of responsibility.
7. He insists on the gratuitous services of the representatives. He refutes the view that the parliamentarians should be compensated by way of salaries and allowances

in view of the heavy expenses incurred by them in their elections and valuable services which they in their daily career perform.

8. He lays emphasis on the independent role of the representatives. He does not consider the electorate as the controller or master of the representative or party rules as iron chains for him.
9. Finally, it may be mentioned that he disfavours pre-election commitments by the contesting leaders. He supports indirect election method on the plea that it acts as an impediment to the full sweep of popular passion. He insists on the election of the head of the executive from the party having majority in the legislature. He insists on optimum tenure of a legislative assembly being neither so short that the full conduct of the representatives may not be judged by the electors, nor so long that the delegates forget their responsibility and neglect the case of public good.

No doubt, Mill's thesis of representative government is a very thoughtful attempt to highlight the excellence of the popular system as well as offer a corrective for its weaknesses and inherent dangers. Mill detests a despotic system; he is also aware of the dangers of a paternalistic state and very seriously suggests certain attributes that may render to it an ideal character. The trend of utilitarianism may also be noted here, for he holds that democracy contributes to the happiness of the individual. However, more important is the fact that his benevolent approach overflows in supporting the case of democracy from a moral point of view. It is well said, "But Mill is a democrat above all not because he believes that democracy makes men happier, but he is convinced that it makes them better."[8]

Critical Appreciation: In short, both Bentham and Mill contributed significantly to the creed of utilitarian radicalism and thus in the nineteenth century they awakened interest in active politics, social reforms and beneficial legislation to an extent that had previously been unthought of. "The benefit is being felt today."[9] In appreciation of it, Brown comments that "the creed of utilitarianism, though long discredited, has in it the prospects of immortality."[10]

8. Wayper, *op. cit.*, pp. 117-18.
9. W.L. Davidson: *Political Thought in England: The Utilitarians,* pp. 249-50.
10. Iror Brown: *English Political Theory,* p. 129.

25
Hegel

Idealism in politics has its highest manifestation in the ideas of Hegel (1770-1831). His works are of a highly, philosophical nature in which politics is dominated by logic and metaphysics. His political ideas are traceable in numerous lectures that he delivered at the University of Jena between 1804-06 in which he touched upon the issues of ethics, logic and metaphysics, and thereby displayed his philosophy of nature and mind. However, what is really perplexing about Hegel is that he puts his ideas in very difficult language that is not intelligible to an average reader. It is also said that different works of Hegel lack consistency. J.H. Stirling in his monograph (*The Secret of Hegel*) feels nervous at the confirmation of endless jargon in the philosophical system of Hegel and remarks that there is "a scrutiny of thought so profound that is for the most part unintelligible."[1]

Dialectical Method: The political philosophy of Hegel shows on him a very penetrating influence of Aristotle, Rousseau, Kant and Fichte. But the peculiar thing about his political philosophy is that the answers to various political questions are given in a methodical manner. The novel feature of his political philosophy is the method to which he gives the name of dialectical idealism. For the sake of a convenient study, the salient features of his dialectical method may be put as follows under:

1. Like Fichte, Hegel believes that ultimate reality is "Reason", or "Spirit," but not "Matter." He describes it as "Absolute Idea" or "Reason" or "Spirit" and, contrary to the Kantian view, insists that there is nothing in the universe which the human mind cannot comprehend. Reason is something dynamic; it is essentially the principle of growth and development. The essence of reason which makes reality is self-consciousness and it has to pervade through several stages in an attempt to attain the highest form of self-consciousness of which it is capable.

2. If reason motivates the law of dialectic, it becomes a law of logic denying any distinction not only between the thought and things but between the thought of different persons. Like the earlier writers of ancient Greece, Hegel does not mean by dialectic the way in which opposite tendencies are adjusted in political life and history. He does not talk about the "law of pendulum," nor is it his purpose to say that historical changes proceed with the interaction of opposite forces; rather in his view, the dialectic constitutes a mechanism by which thought propels

1. Karl Popper: *The Open Society and Its Enemies,* Vol. II, p. 27.

itself, or the way in which reason progressively embodies itself in the institutions. Wright thus points out: "The dialectic begins with the most abstract conception of pure logic, that of mere being and terminates with the most concrete phases of thought, the philosophy of the Absolute Mind in its full comprehensiveness and concreteness."[2]

3. According to Hegel, there are three stages involved in the process by which reason moves through history and nature and they may be called thesis, anti-thesis and synthesis. The thesis passes into its anti-thesis with the result that synthesis takes place. But the synthesis becomes a new thesis and the process is repeated until all contradictions are resolved.

The Hegelian system of dialectic has been subjected to criticism by various schools of political philosophy as follows under:

1. The most important school is that of Marxism. Although Marx borrowed heavily from Hegel, he corrected his teacher. The system of triad is correct, but, according to Marxism, the motivating force is not reason but matter. Marx insists that matter is self-working and thus it has a motivating force within itself. Contrary to the metaphysics of Hegel, Marx insists that it is not the consciousness of man that motivates matter; on the contrary, "it is the material factors that influence human consciousness."[3] Marx thus retained the method but rejected the contention of Hegel. In one of his letters to Dr. Ludwig Kugelmann, Marx wrote in 1868 thus: "Hegel's dialectic is the basic form of my dialectic, but only after it has been stripped of its mystical form, and it is precisely this which distinguished my method."
2. Hegel's entire analysis is based on the premises of rationalism. Contrary to this, the modern school of psychoanalysis is not prepared to admit that reason is the only or decisively motivating factor. It is true that man is a rational creature, but elements of irrationality also influence his behaviour.
3. Finally, it may be pointed out that every kind of development does not take place in the way as the law of Hegelian dialectic tells us.

Freedom: Hegel's conception of freedom is entirely different from that of Kant, for while the latter treats it as a subjective and a limited phenomenon, the former considers it to be positive and objective. Drawing inspiration from Rousseau, Hegel treats freedom as the essence of man, the distinctive quality of human life, the renunciation of which is tantamount to the renunciation of humanity itself. He writes: "The notion of freedom must not be taken in the sense of the casual free will of each individual but in the sense of the reasonable will, the will in or itself. Hegel's approach is quite different from other German idealists also who conceived it to be an attribute or faculty of an individual person.[4] To Hegel man's freedom is associated with his life in society:

2. Wright: *History of Modern Philosophy,* p. 328.
3. Marx: *Capital,* Preface.
4. W.A. Dunning: *A History of Political Theories,* Vol. III, p. 155.

it no longer lies in obeying the dictates of self-imposed categorical imperative of duty. Hegel interprets it as one aspect of pure abstract intelligence: the idea of the will, as a last abstraction, is the free will that wills the free will. In Hegel's own phrase, it "is eternal, universal, self-conscious, self determining."[5]

The burden of Hegel's argument is that freedom consists in transcending the limitations imposed on us by our material and egoistic self and in realising the social aspects of our personality. In other words, it implies that the more we develop our rationality and spirituality, the more conscious we become of freedom in and around us. Obviously, Hegel does not follow the line of John Stuart Mill in taking freedom as something of a negative character implying absence of restraints. So, freedom does not signify the life of a man who has left this world like an ascetic. It implies two things: (i) it is the positive power of an individual to determine his actions actively, deliberately and consciously and, for this reason, distinguishable from anything like whim or caprice or sentiment and the like (ii) It is to be realised in relation to others, because relation to others is not merely a possibility but the necessity of mind, for it is by means of others and by means of sublation that mind preserves itself. Keeping it in view, Vaughan says that by freedom "is meant not the mere absence of external restraints: not the liberty of the individual to do what he wills with his own faculties and his own possessions—but the untrammelled development of man's powers, moral, intellectual and spiritual, according to the fundamental laws of our own nature."[6]

The first manifestation of will is law. Under this head, Hegel discusses the idea of personality, property and contract, and shows that all of them are the manifestations of free will. The second manifestation of will is the rules of inward morality. The final manifestation of will is the whole system of institutions and influences that make for righteousness in the nation-state. This is the sphere where mere externality of law and the mere inwardness of morality are reconciled. It is the sphere of concrete morality or conduct. It includes law, custom, sentiment and moral will.

With this interpretation of freedom Hegel exalts the nation-state. If state is the final embodiment of will, then no idea of force or contract can apply and the state must be envisaged not in terms of law or inward morality but as a custodian of social ethics—the highest expression of that social ethics at once precipitated in and enforced by social opinion which lies behind the life of the family, the political community itself.

Hegel's idea of freedom may be criticised on the following grounds:

1. Hegel offers a very confused as well as a perplexing meaning of freedom. It is full of paradoxes. To say that we are free only when we pursue our rational will embodied in the state and its institutions is to say that we have nothing like an independent choice of our own. Choice is the essence of freedom and to deny its place is to deny freedom itself.

---

5. *Ibid.,* p. 156.
6. C.E. Vaughan, *Studies in the History of Political Philosophy,* Vol. II, p. 153.

2. Such an idea of freedom in the realm of politics signifies nothing else than meek acceptance of the authority of the state. State and society become identifiable with each other, and an attempt to ignore the distinction between the two "may lead to unlimited state regulation of life."

Nation-State: Hegel's theory of state bears the salient characteristic of absolutism, etatism, authoritarianism. Every argument leads to the same goal and the result is that the imperfect institution of the state is first raised to the level of divinity, a mystic entity, an absolute idea, ethical substance, and then the same creation is proudly identified with the imperfect state of Prussia. It may rightly be asserted that all has been done to justify the glory and majesty of the Prussian state the reason for which should be traced in the historical movements of the nineteenth century.

If so, the state is an all-knowing, all-comprehending entity. In a real sense, the purpose of the individual cannot be contrary to or incompatible with that of the state. The individual realises freedom to the extent to which he identifies himself with the reason as manifest in the state and its institutions. The freedom of the individual thus lies in willing the purposes of the state as his own. Only in this way, he can be sure that he is willing what is rational. As the reason manifest in man may be imperfect or waived by his impulses and desires, the reason finally manifest in the state is always right and thus the only way to secure freedom from bondage to the irrational impulses and desires lies in voluntary submission to a more perfect impression of the reason manifest in the state. Analysing the meaning of Hegel, Wayper comments that the state "is the school-master which brings him knowledge of the Spirit, of Absolute Reason. His real will impels him to identify himself with the Spirit. The spirit is embodied in the state. Therefore, it is the real will to obey the dictates of the state."[8]

It follows that the state is an infallible institution. It can do no wrong and no plea of morality can frustrate or denounce its purpose. Nor is there any standard of international law or external morality that might bind the jurisdiction of state activity. Hegel thus repudiates the case of internationalism. There can be no ground, in theory or practice, for resisting the state's decrees in the internal or external spheres, for those over whom it exercises authority are not different from those who exercise it, and its decrees are inspired by the real wills of those who obey him, even though they obey unwillingly. Rejecting the idea of super-national authority, Hegel writes: "The nation-state is mind in its substantive rationality and is, therefore, the absolute power on earth. It follows that every state is sovereign and autonomous against the neighbours .... There is no Praetor to judge between states: at least there may be an arbitrator, mediator, and even he exercises his functions contingently, i.e, only in dependence on the particular wills of the disputants. It follows if the states disagree and their particular wills cannot be harmonised, the matter can only be settled by war."[9]

---

7. Barker, *op. cit.,* p. 54.
8. C.L. Wayper: *Political Thought,* p. 168.
9. Hegel: *Philosophy of Right,* paras 33-34.

In the same context, Hegel admires war and denounces the idea of world peace. In an emergency the state may do as it pleases, and as to what constitutes an emergency the state is to judge for itself. In theory at all times but in practice during war, the state may lawfully exercise complete power over the lives of its citizens.

Hegel's theory of state may be subjected to the following lines of criticism:

1. The Hegelian theory of state is too philosophical, abstract and metaphysical. Not only the phraseology is bombastic, but in very abstract terms he attributes to the state a personality of its own distinct from that of the nation and teaches us about its omnipotence, absolutism and divine character.
2. Hegel's repudiation of internationalism cannot be accepted. His idealisation of war and his denunciation of world peace as well as his rejection of international law and world morality are all wrong and pernicious.
3. Such an explanation of Hegel gives him the discredit of being the father of modern totalitarian ideologies.
4. Finally, Hegel creates a big mistake by identifying his ideal state with the imperfect state of Prussia.

In short, the Hegelian theory of state is too abstract and philosophical if seen from a theoretical standpoint; and if studied from a practical angle of vision, it furnishes a thoroughgoing defence of state absolutism. The difficulty is all the more increased when the ideal dimensions are blended with the non-ideal affairs of a particular state (Prussia) of which he was the official philosopher. Thus, an English critic strongly holds: "Just as in a simple religion, the powers that be are ordained of God, so with the metaphysician who starts from the belief that the things are what they should be, the fabric of social life and, in particular, the state system, is part of an order which is inherently rational and good, an order to which the lives of individuals are altogether subordinate .... The state is set up as a greater being, a spirit, a super-personal entity, in which individuals with their private consciences or claims of rights, their happiness or their misery, are merely subordinate elements."[10]

Critical Appreciation: The political philosophy of Hegel has been denounced for being too abstract and metaphysical, unintelligible to a man of average understanding as well as for offering a highly philosophical justification of state absolutism. At the same time, he has been lauded for inventing a method of social evolution which was borrowed by Marx and used in a revised form that came to be known by the name of dialectical materialism. The idealist tradition saw its highest water-mark in his metaphysical affirmations which were appreciated to such an extent by the English idealists like Green and Bosanquet that they came to be known as the "neo-Hegelians." Leaving aside the charge that Hegel wrote for the case of state absolutism, it cannot be denied that he did a great service to political thought by laying stress on the significance of nation-state without which man cannot realise his true nature and freedom.

---

10. L.T. Hobhouse: *Metaphysical Theory of State,* pp. 17 and 27.

26
Green

From Germany idealism went over to England and became popular in the writings of Green, (1836-1882), Bradley and Bosanquet. The English idealism, however, also acquired the name of Neo-Hegelianism for the simple reason that the English idealists drew heavily from the Hegelian system. The influence of Kant was there, but the influence of Hegel outweighed it. Yet it should be remembered that, in spite of this, British idealism could not abandon the native tradition of its liberalism. And if it was called Neo-Hegelianism, it was not at all Hegelianism, though it was much more than semi-Hegelianism or pseudo-Hegelianism. Among the English idealists Bradley and Bosanquet maintained closer affinity with Hegel as compared to Green, but even on them the stamp of English traditions survived as a result of which British idealism exhibited a fundamental continuity with the liberal thought coming from the days of Locke and Burke.

Political Obligation: Starting from a metaphysical foundation, Green comes to the conclusion that the basis of political obligation lies in human consciousness. The state is rooted in the will but it cannot be autocratic or misrepresentative, otherwise resistance to its authority is justified. This is very beautifully summed up by Barker in these words: "Human consciousness postulates liberty; liberty involves rights; rights demand the state."[1] Each phrase is meaningful and for this an explanation may thus be furnished:

(i) **Human Consciousness:** Green starts with a metaphysical proposition that consciousness is the distinctive characteristic of human beings. The quality makes humankind different from other species. It makes man conscious of other things as well as aware of his own self. It follows that man is something more than a mere part of nature, he is endowed with a free intelligence, a self-realising and self-distinguishing consciousness.

(ii) **Freedom:** Green's conception of freedom bears upon him the influence of Rousseau and Hegel. As a corollary to the above, he argues that human consciousness postulates freedom as the necessary condition of its very growth and expression. However, he takes a positive view of freedom, and in this respect his approach is distinctly different from that of Mill— the individualist, and Kant—the idealist. In one of his lectures delivered at Leicester in 1881, he defines freedom thus: "When

1. Barker: *Political Thought in England,* p. 23.

we speak of freedom as something to be so highly prized, we mean a positive power or capacity of doing or enjoying something worth doing or enjoying, and that too something that we do or enjoy in common with others. We mean by it a power which each man exercises through the help or security given to him by his fellowmen, and which he, in turn, helps to secure for them."

(iii) **Rights:** Then, liberty involves rights. From here Green proceeds to enunciate his theory of rights. The self-consciousness of man wills good both in respect of itself as well as of other selves. It wills the goodness of its relations with others; it wills the goodness of society which is constituted by such relations. Hence, when each recognises his own goodself and at the same time recognises the goodself of others, a system of rights comes into being. When an individual makes a claim out of his self-consciousness, he knows that it shall automatically be recognised by others, for the very claim stands for the good of his own as well as for the good of others.

(iv) **Need for Political Authority:** Like Rousseau, Green recognises the need for political authority. It is true that man, actuated by his selfless or real will, should move on the right path; he would not like to do or enjoy what is unworthy of doing or enjoying, but even then the selfish or the actual will might operate and then compel him to do or enjoy what is not worth doing or enjoying in common with others. Hence, rights need security, and for that sake, the state enters into the system of Green. If a man violates the system of rights, the state is there to use force against him so that the freedom is preserved. However, by using force, the basis of political authority is not changed, it is still the will of the people. The use of force by the state becomes essential in order to maintain the system of rights which the moral consciousness of the community makes up.

One more important point may be added here. When Green justifies that "will, not force, is the basis of state," he is not at all concerned with the problems of democracy or dictatorship. His purpose is to explain that whatever be the form of government, the basis of the state is neither force nor divine sanction but the consciousness of the people who are its citizens. He is simply content to analyse and elucidate the thesis implicit in the life of the existing states. Though Green's dictum that "will, not force, is the basis of state" is more clearly visible in a representative government, he is prepared to lay down that each state is based on the foundation of general will.

Like other idealists, Green may be criticised for overemphasising the fact of free will—a will that is spontaneous, subjective, internal. The school of modern pshyco-analysts is not prepared to accept that the individual is a mere creature of his rational will inasmuch as his life is also governed by irrational forces. The practical form of elections, propaganda, national movement and war all bear ample testimony to the fact that the people are motivated less by their faculty of rational will but more by their habits, emotions, instincts etc. Finally, he confuses the scope of state activity by calling the state "a society of societies." The result is that he now stumbles between the poles of monism and pluralism. In practice, such a state would have "a very confused area of activity."[2]

Rights : Green's theory of rights constitutes a very important aspect of his political philosophy. He rejects the Benthamite conception of the rights being the creation of a sovereign with power to inflict penalties in the event of their breach; he also repudiates the Lockean argument of their having a purely conventional character. In one more respect, his approach is different from that of Bentham; he disagrees with the view that natural rights are "nonsense." He retains the nomenclature of natural rights and reinterprets the idea in a way that is totally different from other protagonists of natural rights like Locke and Spencer. The reason for this should be traced in the elaborate expression of his standpoint in the general framework of his mataphysical and idealistic doctrine. The characteristics of Green's theory of rights may be thus enumerated:

1. Rights are created by the moral consciousness of the community and enforced by the state. When the claim of an individual arising out of his consciousness receives social consciousness, it is translated into a right. The foundation of rights lies in the capacity on the part of an individual of conceiving a good as the same for himself and for others, and of being determined to action by that conception. According to Green, "In analysing the nature of any right, we may conveniently look at it from two sides, and consider it on the one hand as a claim of the individual, arising out of his rational nature, of the free expression of some faculty; on the other, as a concession of that claim by society, a power given to the individual of putting the claim in force."
2. The rights may be termed natural in the sense that they are the necessary and indispensable means to an end which every rational and normal being should pursue for the fulfilment of his vocation in a rationally constituted society. Hence, the rights constitute the conditions under which the realisation of the moral capacity of a man is rendered possible.
3. Finally, the state does not create rights, it simply enforces and protects them. The rights arise out of the eternal self-consciousness of the individual and thus, assuming the shape of claims, receive moral recognition of the community as a whole. Hence, the state gives full reality to the rights already in existence. The rights are the product of an ideal society alone and so to call them pre-social is a contradiction in terms.

However, Green's theory of rights may be criticised for being inconsistent and confusing. Two difficulties arise in this regard. First, he nowhere draws up a list of rights which he would call natural or ideal. For this he may be condoned on the plea that no final list of natural or ideal rights can be prepared owing to the fact that social conditions change and the standards of morality change simultaneously. But the second difficulty stands out. If society considers something for the moral development of the people as necessary, but the people in their individual capacity think otherwise,

2. *Ibid.*, p. 68.

certainly a state of conflict would take place. The question arises as who is to be the judge of which natural or ideal rights are really necessary at a given time in a given society. Lancaster thus observes: "Green's treatment of the doctrine of natural rights is confused and inconsistent. He tries to draw distinction between it and what he regards as a correct explanation of the origin of rights, but in reality he accepts something like the usual theory."[3]

State Activity: In this respect, Green's views have been influenced by Kant's emphasis on the negative character of state activity as well as by the conditions of his own age which demanded a shift from an individualistic to a collectivistic trend. As a result, when Green insists that the effectual action of the state is necessarily to be confined to the removal of obstacles, or to the maintenance of conditions of life in which morality shall be possible, and morality consists in the disinterested performance of self-imposed duties, he also insists that the state should make positive attempts to remove three gigantic evils, namely, ignorance, pauperism and intemperance or drinking alcohol. In other words, Green's views on the character of state activity have both negative and positive aspects.

Negatively, the state should hinder the hindrances to good life, and do nothing to promote morality directly. Such is the nature of moral development that a person can achieve it for himself alone; it cannot be forced upon one from outside. All that the state can do is to secure that one's actions should conform to one's duties. Green holds that an act can be truly moral only when it is freely self-determined. "Now any direct enforcement of the outward conduct, which ought to flow from social interests, by means of threatened penalties—and a law requiring such conduct necessarily implies penalties for disobedience to it—does interfere with the spontaneous actions of those interests, and consequently checks the growth of the capacity which is in the condition of the beneficial exercise of rights. For this reason, the effectual action of the state, i.e., the community as acting through the law, for the promotion of habits of true citizenship seems necessarily to be confined to the removal of obstacles."

Positively, Green lays particular emphasis on the eradication of three gigantic evils by the state, namely, ignorance, pauperism and drinking alcohol. In his view, these three evils are so big that unless their eradication takes place by the action of the state, the promotion of morality among the citizens may not be possible. Hence, for this he emphasises the need for compulsory education, employment opportunities and prohibition. So firmly was he convinced of the pernicious effects of these evils that he took part in social campaigns and opened a coffee shop in Oxford to distract the attention of the drunkards.

It is clear that herein lies a philosophical justification of the idea of a welfare state. Green's anxiety for removing the gigantic social evils is so penetrating that it pushes him out of the philosophical orbit of idealism. Unlike Carlyle and Ruskin, who simply wrote on the ugliness and evils of industrialism, Green suggests concrete steps and

3. Lancaster: *Masters of Political Thought,* Vol. III, p. 244.

tries to work out a theory of state activity quite consistent with the actual conditions of his age.

Right to Resistance: The conditions of resistance arise out of the discrepancy between the natural rights of the ideal type and the actual rights recognised by the law of the imperfect state. In an un-Hegelian manner, Green sanctions qualified right to civil disobedience. He recognises the use of this right only when its necessity is warranted by social consciousness. However, he warns that there should be no breach of political obligation for the sake of disturbing social peace and harmony. The whole must not be sacrificed for the sake of the part, and the existing system of rights must not be disturbed for the sake of adding a new element to it owing to the risk of social disorder. The implication is that first a healthy public opinion be created and when the whole community becomes convinced with the need for civil resistance for the sake of public good, only then the right to resistance may be justifiably exercised. As he says: "The common good must suffer more from resistance to law or the ordinance of a legal authority until its repeal can be obtained. It is thus the social duty of the individual to conform and he can have no right that is against his social duty."[4]

Although an idealist, in Green the element of Kantian individualism outweighs the element of Hegelian absolutism. Green does not idealise the majesty of the state and sticks to the worth and dignity of the human person. As MacCunn says: "If it be individualism to see in every public movement the fate of human beings and in every controversy over institutions the weal or woe of fellow citizens, then there are few more declared individualists in political philosophy than T.H. Green."[5] Green's being more of a Kantian than that of a Hegelian is noticeable in these respects:

1. He regards the state not as an end in itself but a means to a higher end—full moral development of the people.
2. He adheres to the worth and dignity of man and is not prepared to sacrifice him at the altar of the state.
3. He emphasises the negative character of state activity and yet lays stress on the eradication of three gigantic evils (ignorance, pauperism and intemperance) for the sake of removing obstacles from the way of moral development of the people.
4. He recognises general will as will for the state, not of the state, and does not identify it with something in whose name so many crimes are committed by a dictatorial state.

---

4. T.H. Green: *Lectures on the Principles of Political Obligation,* Sec. 100. The meaning of Green is thus clarified by Barker: "We must not sacrifice what is almost the whole for the sake of a part: we must not risk social chaos, and the disturbance of the existing system of rights for the sake of adding a new element to the system. But when there is already implicit social acknowledgment of the claim to a natural right, we know that there is no possibility of such sacrifice or such risk. The same factor of a common social consciousness, which is the ultimate sustainer of legal rights, is here resisting legal rights for the sake of their greater perfection." *op. cit.,* p. 32.
5. Cited in Wayper: *Political Thought,* p 189.

5. He recognises the right to resistance or civil disobedience in certain circumstances.
6. His defence of natural rights reiterates the case of freedom of the individual.
7. He condemns war among nations in the name of the individual's right to life and advocates the case of internationalism.

Critical Appreciation: Green has produced a synthesis of individualism and idealism by recognising the worth and dignity of the individual and yet not seeing him as an isolated and therefore unrelated atom of society. The individual, nevertheless, remains the basis of his thought, though his free will is considered to be willing ideal objects alone. Barker observes: "He (Green) has seized the philosophy of Greece and Germany, and interpreted it for Englishmen with a full measure of English caution, and with a full reference to that deep sense of distrust and reason of state which marks Englishmen. Partly to this, and partly to the influence of Kant, we may ascribe his firm hold on the worth of the individual."[6] It is well commented: "Green's influence was all the greater in that, while acknowledging the correctness of Hegel's and the community, he idealised the state without deifying it and identifying it with absolute right."[7]

6. Barker, *op. cit.,* p. 46.
7. C.C. Maxey: *Political Philosophies,* pp. 509-10.

27
Lenin

The greatest leader and ideologue of the Marxist school in the twentieth century was V.I. Lenin (1870-1924) of Russia, described as a 'genius theorectician'[1] and 'a rare combination of a theorist and a man of action.[2] The thing that strikes our attention at the very outset is that since Lenin made some necessary revisions in the theory of classical Marxism in order to apply it to his country, his interpretations have not only been taken as an updated version of classical Marxism by his protagonists, but also as shrewd deviations from the teachings of Marx by his critics. However, before coming to this point of debate, it shall be better first to have a brief study of the views of Lenin on some important themes like state, Communist Party, revolution and imperialism as the final stage of capitalism.

State: Like Marx and Engels, Lenin regards state as an instrument of exploitation and oppression by one class over another. But his main contribution should be seen in his exposition of the nature of the state after the successful socialist revolution and its eventual 'withering away' to signify the life of a totally emancipated mankind. In his view, after the overthrow of the bourgeoisie, a 'quasi-state' of the workers would be established in place of the existing bourgeois state. This new state of necessity would be a classless organisation, but it would function as representative of the revolutionary working class. Thus, the state would ruthlessly suppress all reactionary and counter-revolutionary forces. In January, 1918 Lenin declared that the Bolsheviks "must break the old, savage, despicable and disgusting prejudices that only the rich can administer the state, since every rank and file worker who is able to read and write can do organisational work. There are masses of the people like that."[3]

The destruction of the capitalist state would lead to the construction of a new state (a socialist state) in the form of a 'quasi' or a transitional state. Power would be in the hands of the working class and the state would be used as an instrument to liquidate all reactionary and counter-revolutionary forces. It would be the 'dictatorship of the proletariat'. In declaring like this, Lenin is a dogmatic follower of Marx and Engels who repudiate the line of anarchism that state would be abolished just after the successful

---

1. Bukharin: *Lenin as a Marxist,* p. 5.
2. J.H. Hallowell: *Main Currents in Modern Political Thought,* p. 490.
3. Alexander Gray: *The Socialist Tradition,* p. 468.

revolution of the working class.[4] The new transitional state of the dictatorship of the proletariat has clearly nothing to learn from the old in the essential feature of being a class organisation and an instrument of suppression. "But indeed from the moment the dictatorship of the proletariat is acknowledged to be a kind of state, freedom is excluded: While the state exists, there is no freedom. When freedom exists, there will be no state."[5]

The dictatorship of the proletariat is not the end of class war, it is rather a continuation of the same in a different form and with a different goal. Now the class in power is at war against its enemy and is determined to crush and bury the enemy for ever so that it may never arise in the form of its anti-thesis. And the aim is to see the end of state itself. The state would perform certain functions like defence, security, communications, banking, etc. At the same time, it would be a proletarian democracy in fact. It would ensure participation of the workers through their free and voluntary association at all levels of administration. It would prohibit exploitation of any kind. It would remove all social and economic evils that prevail in a bourgeois state. All power of the working class would be in the hands of their only party (Communist Party) and the constitution would declare the state as 'the state of the workers and toilers'. Thus, Lenin could say that the Soviet democracy was million times more democratic than any bourgeois democracy of the world. "This was the first open assertion of the doctrine of parliamentary democracy."[6]

But the most striking feature of such a state is to act for its own end. It has to 'wither away' in the end so that the era of communism is ushered in with this principle: 'From each according to his ability, to each according to his needs'. As Gray puts: "The establishment of the dictatorship of the proletariat on the debris of the bourgeois state represents the point as from which the state should, in theory, begin to wither away. From that moment classes begin to disappear, and with the progressive disappearance of classes, the state and indeed, the party itself, suffer atrophy *pari passu*."[7] In short, in Lenin's view, the state in the form of dictatorship of the proletariat "is not communism; it is the period of transition in which the state is withering away."[8]

The implications of Lenin's theory of state may be thus enumerated:

1. The state is a special organisation of force; it is an organisation of violence for the suppression of the enemy class,

---

4. Lenin says that the error of the anarchists lies not in favouring the abolition of the state (for on this point he is at one with them), but in preaching that the state can be abolished overnight. *State and Revolution,* p. 46. Elsewehere he repeats that the mistake of the anarchists should not be defended. The state must be preserved during the period of transition. *The Task of the Proletariat in Our Revolution,* p. 16.
5. Gray, *op. cit.,* p. 16.
6. R.N. Carew Hunt: *The Theory and Practice of Communism,* p. 182.
7. Gray, *op. cit.,* p. 475.
8. G.H. Sabine: *A History of Political Theory,* p. 740.

2. The state is the armed and the ruling proletariat. Hence, it would exist in the transitional stage. To proclaim the withering away of the state prematurely would distort the historical process.
3. After the successful revolution, the party and the state would be inextricably interlinked. Class relationships would be exercised under the leadership of the Communist Party
4. At the same time, the state would create conditions of its own decomposition. It would establish a classless society that would find its culmination in a stateless condition of life.
5. The retention of the state during the transitional phase would be necessitated by the new conditions created by imperialism—the final stage of capitalism.

However, keeping in view the political development of Russia after the First World War, a critic may say that Lenin played fast and loose with what he preached and what he did. Crick says: "Fundamentally Lenin had rejected politics as a practical, natural, compromising and humane activity for the belief that history had created a single true ideology, immediately accessible only to the heightened consciousness of the vanguard of the working class and their leaders, and that it was in the future interest of the whole working class that this must be instituted by whatever means were needed. Human history was a history of violent class oppression, so that violence which hastened on the coming of a classless society and the famous 'withering away of the state' was not only justifiable in terms of the eventual lessening of human suffering, but was an 'historical necessity'. The present always had to be sacrificed for the future, and they were sure of the future. But the actual history of the Russan Revolution and the Soviet State disapproves any notion of predictable historical necessity."[9]

Communist Party: One important point where Lenin takes a line neither so boldly conceived nor so strongly appreciated by Marx and Engels is the role of the party of the workers (Communist Party). He lays special stress on the role of the Communist Party as 'vanguard of the working class'. It is the party that would indoctrinate the working class, organise the workers and prepare a secret plan of revolution. It would be 'a small and compact core of the reliable, experienced and hardened workers with responsible agents in the principal districts'. It would absorb all the best elements of the working class, their experience, their revolutionary spirit and their unbounded devotion to the cause of the proletariat. "But in order that it may be really the vanguard, the Party must be armed with a revolutionary theory, with a consciousness of laws of the movement, with a knowledge of the laws of the revolution...The Party must take its stand at the head of the working class, it must see ahead of the working class, lead the proletariat and trail behind the spontaneous movement."[10]

As a competent strategist and tactician, Lenin intoduces the following positive proposals in his view about the organisation and role of the Communist Party:

9. Bernard Crick: *Socialism,* pp. 60-61.
10. Stalin: *Foundations of Leninism,* pp. 105-06.

1. Given the Party's task of assuming the role of leading all exploited classes in the democratic revolution, it must have an all-Russian organisation.
2. The organisation should be composed of professional revolutionaries or such people who would devote themselves fully to party work and they would be fully trained.
3. The leadership would have to be chosen through the oligarchical principle of co-option. There would be election to all offices of the Party and full publicity of its activities would be made.
4. The principle of centralism would also work. It means that the highest unit of the Party under its supreme leader would take all decisions and issue directions that must be followed by all lower units of the organisation.
5. Since the Bolshevik Party had stagnated while remaining underground, he urged his followers to extend their bases, rally all organisations of the workers, and make the nucleus of the workers party broader and broader. And yet the idea of a 'clandestine party,' could not be fully abandoned.[11]

But the Communist Party becomes the state after the successful socialist revolution. It assumes all power in its hands in the name of the state of the workers and the toilers. Its size is constantly reduced so as to keep it as a body of the most faithful and most active members in the form of the 'rallying centre of the finest elements in the working class'. It would provide inspiration and leadership to the dictatorship of the proletariat. As Stalin affirms: "Not a single important political or organisational question is decided by the Soviets and other mass organisations without guiding directions from the Party."[12] Apparently the dictatorship of the proletariat is the dictatorship of the Communist Party, but Lenin says that its real implication is 'leadership of the Communist Party' in spite of the fact that the party runs the administration of the country with the help and cooperation of the Soviets, the trade unions and other mass organisations as 'transmission belts'.[13] In the words of A.G. Meyer: "Perhaps Lenin's most conspicuous contribution to twentieth century politics is his conception of the Communist Party as a creative history-making force and as the general stuff of the world revolution. In the Bolshevik movement he created the model on which many other modern totalitarian parties have been built. Lenin must, therefore, be considered a pioneer of the totalitarianism of our age."[14]

Revolution: How can a revolution be brought about? On this question, Marxism is both revolutionary and evolutionary. But Lenin sticks only to the side of a violent revolution. Taking lessons from the Paris Commune of 1871 and his abortive attempt of 1905, he very confidently asserts that the aim of a revolution can be achieved only by violent means. All tactics of a revolution are justified if they help in achieving the goal. The communists "should prepare a secret programme of insurrection and carry

11. Stalin, *op. cit.,* p. 35.
12. David McLellan: *Marxism after Marx,* p. 89.
13. *Ibid.,* pp. 134-35.
14. Meyer: *Leninism* (London: Westview Press, 1986), p. 19.

it out with the help of their most faithful and most committed followers."[15] In this connection, following important points emerge from what he asserts:

1. No revolutionary movement can be durable without a stable organisation of the leaders which preserves continuity.
2. The broader the mass which is spontaneously drawn into the struggle, which forms the basis of the movement and participates in it, the more urgent is the necessity for such an organisation, and the more durable this organisation must be, because the broader in mass, the easier it is for any demagogue to attract the backward sections of the mass.
3. Such an organisation must consist mainly of the people who are professionally engaged in revolutionary activities.

Lenin's ideas on revolution started from the orthodox tradition which he inherited from Plekhanov and more specifically from his examination of Russia's economic development. If deeply examined, his views are not different from those of Trotsky who insisted on the idea of a 'permanent revolution'. It is evident from Lenin's own statement: "From the democratic revolution we shall at once and precisely in accordance with the measure of our strength, the strength of a class-conscious and organised proletariat, begin to pass to the socialist revolution. We stand for uninterrupted revolution. We shall not stop half-way."[16]

The significant feature of Lenin's theory of revolution is that it takes into account the possibility of creating a revolution in any country of the world, if the leadership is capable of doing it. The role of the party as the 'vanguard of the proletariat' is very important. Though a party of the working class, it may include all revolutionary sections of the people who have full faith in or revolutionary devotion to the eventual triumph of socialism. In this way, Lenin "removed Marxian revolution as a possibility only in advanced capitalist societies and placed it within the realm of possibility for virtually any country, provided a revolutionary situation existed there and a revolutionary party was present that could guide the society on the road to socialism. By particularising Marxian analysis to Russia, Lenin taught that the Marxian model was useful in any society. It was a lesson that other revolutionaries, including the Chinese, were to learn well."[17]

Imperialism: Lenin calls imperialism the 'final stage of capitalism'. As he says: "Imperialism is capitalism in that stage of development in which the domination of monopoly capital and finance capital has taken shape; in which the export of capital has acquired preponderating influence, in which the division of the world by international trusts has begun; in which the partition of all the territory of the earth by the greatest

15. While clarifying the view of Lenin, Laski says: "There is no other way of breaking the class will of the enemy except by the systematic and energetic use of violence." *Communism,* p. 139.
16. David McLellan, *op. cit.,* p. 93.
17. A. S. Cohan: *Theories of Revolution,* p. 93.

capitalist countries has been completed."[18] With this point of view, Lenin called the First World War 'not a people's war' but an imperialist war and discovered its cause in the world of economics. It was a result of the clash among the capitalist countries of the world that had their vested interest in keeping their hold over as big a part of the world as possible for the sake of collecting raw materials therefrom and then flooding the markets with their finished goods so as to reap as much profit as possible. What Lenin really desired to emphasise was that the meaning of Marxism should be reinterpreted in the light of such development of capitalism in the twentieth century.

The following important implications may be drawn from this interpretation:

1. Capital has become international and monopolistic in its dominance.
2. Uneven economic and political development is absolute law of capitalism.
3. The export of capital has a preponderating influence.
4. There is the beginning of the division of the world by international trusts and cartels.
5. After the war, begins the partition of the world among victorious capitalist countries.

With such an interpretation of the growth of capitalism in its final form, Lenin could put his finger at the plight of the colonial countries of the world. He insists that the problem of a socialist revolution should be related to the problem of liberation from colonialism. Since the theatre of class struggle has shifted from the capitalist to the poor and backward countries of Asia and Africa, the possibilities of revolution may be explored there. Second, the system of imperialism has made the capitalist countries so rich that even the proletariat of these places has seen its 'bourgeoisification', a point that was taken by Engels. It has its adverse effect on the pace of a socialist revolution. "The solidarity of the working class is thus undermined, since a privileged upper stratum of the workers is enabled to live at the expense of the oppressed nations."[19]

Lenin As A Marxist: Now we may be in a position to examine the case of Lenin as a Marxist. In this direction, we have two different views. According to one view, Lenin is regarded as a true and dogmatic Marxist who interpreted and followed his teacher like a faithful disciple. On one occasion Lenin himself asserted: "You cannot eliminate even one basic assumption, one substantial part of the philosophy of Marxism (it is as it were a solid block of steel) without abandoning objective truth, without falling into the arms of the bourgeois reactionary falsehood."[20] Stalin could assert that Lenin neither repudiated any principle of Marxism, nor did he add any new one to the stock of Marxism. In his view, Leninism signifies three important points."[21]

18. Lenin: *Selected Works,* Vol. II, p. 709.
19. Gray, *op. cit.,* p. 464.
20. Lenin: *Collected Works,* Vol. XIII, p. 281.
21. Stalin, *op. cit.,* p. 13.

1. Leninism is the updated version of Marxism. What Marx and Engels said in the nineteenth century, Lenin could reinterpret it in the light of the astonishing developments of the twentieth century.
2. Leninism is the applied form of Marxism. What Marx and Engels wrote and said, Lenin put it into practice.
3. Leninism is the application of Marxism to the peculiar conditions of Russia.

But these contentions are not convincing to the critics who take Lenin as a shrewd leader and a theoretician who followed his master where he liked and freely changed his master's ideas where he felt so necessary for his purpose. Hallowell makes three important points in this direction.[22]

1. According to Marxism, a successful socialist revolution would take place only in a very advanced capitalist country, but Lenin could make it possible in a backward country like Russia with the use of the power of the peasantry. Marx had contended that following a revolution, the land should be immediately collectivised. On the other hand, Lenin argued that the discontent of the peasantry could be successfully utilised to bring about a socialist revolution and, as a matter of tactic, he encouraged the peasants to believe that following the revolution, they would become individual land-owners and for a time, following the Revolution, sustained them in that belief.
2. For the most part Marx favoured imperialism, since he believed that it would hasten the advent of socialism by extending capitalism to backward areas of the world and since socialism could only come into existence after capitalism had been established. On the other hand, Lenin believed that national revolts should be encouraged whether socialist in character or not, since any allies against the capitalists were useful whether strictly proletarian or not. Uppermost in Lenin's mind was the desire to bring about a successful revolution in Russia, and if Marxian theory had to be sacrificed or modified to that end, then he was willing to sacrifice or modify it.
3. The most significant way, however, in which Lenin differed from Marx was his interpretation of the role of the proletariat. According to Marx, the proletariat would become increasingly class conscious and militant as the contradictions in capitalism would become more and more apparent and acute. According to Lenin, the proletariat, if left alone, would develop only a trade union mentality. The working class is unable to develop a socialist consciousness of the irreconcilable nature of the class struggle unless it is impregnated with this consciousness from outside. This would appear to be a direct refutation of the Marxian thesis. Mistake or not, it was Lenin's belief that the proletariat had to be impregnated with the socialist consciousness, organised and led into revolution and the instrument for this purpose was the Communist Party.

---

22. Hallowell, *Main Currents in Modern Political Thought,* pp. 490-92.

No doubt, the revision of Marxism at the hands of Lenin looks like both an updated version of the ideas of the teacher as well as a shrewd modification of his preceptor's teachings for a certain purpose. The charge of 'careful opportunism' on Lenin cannot be entirely washed off. We may endorse the view of Sabine that "Lenin's Marxism presents the anomaly of being at once the most dogmatic assertion of orthodox adherence to the principles of the master and at the same time the freest rendering of it on points where circumstances required its modification."[23]

Critical Appreciation: Lenin gave to the world something new by putting the fundamental postulates of Marx and Engels, whom he reverently addressed as 'twin stars', into practice. No doubt, he was a great tactician and a competent strategist apart from being an excellent theorist. And it is for this reason that he had to make modificatory interpretations of Marxism. It is well observed: "Marx's statement that a socialist society can be established only in a highly civilised and industrialised country remains unrefuted in spite of Lenin's adaptation of Marxism to Russia. Yet, even if his is bastard Marxism, no one will minimise the significance of what he bequeathed to Russia and to the world."[24]

23. Sabine, *op. cit.,* p. 741.
24. Wayper: *Political Thought,* p. 230.

28
Gramsci

Once a member of the Italian Socialist Party and then a leading light of the Communist Party, Antonio Gramsci (1891-1937) is known for rehabilitating "the subjective or creative side of the Marxist thought."[1] His views are contained in his *Prison Notebooks* published after his death. In the phase of his early career, he developed appreciation for syndicalist or trade union movement launched by Sorel in France in the last phase of the nineteenth century, though the influence of the Hegelian historicism of Croce was also there. When the Labour Council sought to capture power in Turin, he appreciated the event and hoped that the Council movement would be the new proletarian state in miniature. When Lenin captured power in Russia in November, 1917, he described it as a revolution against Marx's *Capital* for being a spontaneous libertarian outburst. But when Lenin presented his thesis on the role of the Soviets (workers councils) in a socialist state, he lauded it.[2] In 1921 he founded the Italian Communist Party and declared that there was need for a homogenous and cohesive party with its own doctrine, tactics and rigid discipline. However, like Lukacs, he laid emphasis on the moral qualities of the party. His principles were imported into the Lyons' Thesis of 1926.

Role of Intellectuals: Gramsci has been called the theoretician of the 'superstructure' in which the intellectuals have the central place. He makes a distinction between mental and manual workers. As he says: "All men are intellectual, but not all men in the society have the functions of intellectuals." Everyone has some professional activity as a philosopher, an artist, a trader and the like, "participates in a particular conception of the world, has a conscious line of moral conduct and therefore contributes to sustain a conception of the world or to modify it, that is, to bring into being new modes of thought."[3] Further, each social class creates together with itself, organically, one or more strata of intellectuals which give it homogeneity and an awareness of its own function not only in the economic but also in the social and political fields."[4]

Gramsci draws a distinction between 'traditional' and 'organic' intellectuals. The former (as writers, artists, philosophers and particularly ecclesiastics) are those who consider themselves as autonomous of social classes and who appear to embody a

---

1. David McLellan: *Marxism after Mars* (London: Macmillan, 1979), p. 175.
2. *Ibid.*, p. 178.
3. Antonio Gramsci: *Selections from the Prison Notebooks,* p. 8.
4. *Ibid.*

historical continuity above and beyond social and political change. The notable point is that they survive even after the demise of the mode of production to which they owe their birth. The fact is that though they "remain linked to historically moribund classes, yet pretend to a certain independence that involves the production of a certain kind of ideology, usually of an idealist bent, to mask their real obsolescence."[5] Different is the case of the 'organic' intellectuals who are closely connected with a particular class and who articulate the collective consciousness of their class in the political, social and economic spheres. At the same time, they have a certain autonomy."[6]

Not the 'traditional' but the 'organic' intellectuals belonging to the class of the workers can create a socialist revolution. The production of its own organic intellectuals is a necessary condition for any successful revolutionary movement. The group of such inellectuals makes the party like a 'collective intellectual', a term coined by Italian communist leader (Togliatti), and may be called 'Modern Prince'. As he says: "The political party for some social groups is nothing other than the specific way of elaborating their own category of organic intellectuals directly in the political and philosophical field and not just in the field of productive techniques. These intellectuals are formed in this way and cannot indeed be formed in any other way, given the general character and conditions of formation, life and development of social group."[7]

Hegemony or the Notion of a Historical Bloc: "One of the main functions of the intellectuals, then, in addition to ensuring the economic organisation and political power of their class, was to preserve the hegemony of their class over society as a whole by means of a justifying ideology of which they were the agents."[8] Casually referred to in the Marxian tradition but frequently stressed by Lenin, hegemony has a very significant place in the writings of Gramsci. Literally, it means an overarching hold or influence of a particular class or of a particular variety of ideas which rule the society. But Gramsci takes it as "a process by which the proletariat gained leadership over all the forces (particularly the peasantry) opposed to capitalism and welded them into a new homogenous political-economic historical bloc, without internal contradictions."[9]

---

5. McLellan, *op. cti.,* p. 181.
6. *Ibid.*
7. Gramsci, *op. cit.,* p. 15.
8. McLellan, *op. cit.,* p. 184.
9. *Ibid.* Hegemony (from the Greek would hegemonia, meaning 'leader') in its simplest sense implies the ascendancy or domination of one element of a system over others (an example being the predominance of a state within a league or confederation). In Marxist theory the term is used in a more technical and specific sense. In the writings of Gramsci, it "refers to the ability of a dominant class to exercise power by winning the consent of those it subjugates, as an alternative to the use of coercion. As a non-coercive form of class rule, hegemony is typically understood as a cultural or ideological process that operates through the dissemination of bourgeois values and beliefs throughout society. However, it also has a political and economic dimension: consent, can be manipulated by pay increases or by political and social reform." Andrew Heywood: *Politics,* p. 201.

It creates the notion of a 'historical bloc' in which economic, social and ideological forces are combined in a temporary unity to change the existing social order.

Thus, hegemony implies the over-all hold of the intellectuals in power that imparts legitimacy to their rule. It is done by the intellectuals to justify the excellence of the capitalist rule; it may be done by the counter-intellectuals of the working class to legitimise the rule of the proletariat. Curiously, the hegemonic order appears to be based on the consent or acquiescence of the people in general. For this sake, the ruling class may use methods of force as well as persuasion and thereby exist like a guarantor of the interests of the society as a whole. In the view of Gramsci, it could be done by the capitalist class in Italy which purchased the consent of different classes as writers, artists, thinkers, literatteurs, priests, leaders of the political groups etc., or all subordinate groups and thereby they legitimised their otherwise illegitimate system. In this way, he solved the puzzle of the ability of capitalism to survive in the modern democratic systems. The notable point is that Gramsci "does not neglect the necessary element of force, he views it as dialectically linked with the struggle for hegemony in civil society: both persuasion and force were necessary in any revolutionary process."[10]

Civil Society and State: Gramsci's views on civil society differ from those of Marx and yet they converge when the state withers away and the society becomes both classless and stateless. To Marx the capitalist society is not a civil socety, because it is ridden with class conflicts as a result of which the class of the 'haves' exploits and oppresses the class of the 'have-nots'. The socialist society would be civil society by virtue of being classless and irresistibly moving towards the final goal of stateless condition of life. To Marx civil society implies the 'totality of economic relationships', but to Gramsci it refers to the 'superstructure' that is based on and that diffuses a particular ideology. Ideology performs the function of mediation between the existing economic structure and the state. It may be pointed out that Gramsci's civil society "denotes all the organisation and technical means which diffuse the ideological justification of the ruling class in all domains of culture."[11]

Since the capitalist society is legitimised by the ruling class by the diffusion of its ideology, its hegemony provides the 'ethical content of the state'. In his view, Fascism can create a fusion of civil society and the state. A socialist revolution may break this fusion. But the class of the proletariat would have to retain state during the period of transition so as to transform the bourgeois society into a socialist society. This phenomenon is called by Lenin as the 'new state', but Gramsci calls it 'statolatory'. A new ideology is imposed by the hegemony of the working class and the whole system of values undergoes a change from the kingdom of necessity to the kingdom of freedom and happiness. McLellan, therefore, aptly comments: "However much Gramsci might have deviated from Marx in his use of the concept of civil society, they were both

10. McLellan, *op. cit.,* p. 187.
11. *Ibid.,* p. 188.

agreed that the final aim was the reabsorption of political society by civil society in a classless society."[12]

Revolution and its Strategies: Like Lenin, Gramsci lays stress on the role of the Communist Party in bringing about the socialist revolution. While Lenin calls this party 'the vanguard of the proletariat', Gramsci calls it 'the modern prince'. It is a compact organisation rooted in everyday social reality and linked to a broad network of popular workers' unions, seeking to avoid inner party obstructions and demonstrating a disciplined unity in action. It is embedded in the masses. It is the galvaniser of struggles and a central bearer of critical and active consciousness to inflame the proletariat. It has its own group of 'organic' intellectuals who, with combative democratic tribunes, are engaged with the life of the masses and committed to the ideas of freedom, equality and solidarity. These intellectuals have their own 'ideology' aimed at freeing the working class from ideas that bind it to the existing political order. At the same time, it would bind all exploited, oppressed and unpriveleged sections of the people, or 'subaltern elements', so as to create a solid 'bloc' of the working class.

The 'organic intellectuals' of the Communist Party would continue their struggle on the cultural and political planes. In the capitalist society their main task would be to infuse a new culture in the working class through schools, churches, media and many other forms of social programmes. It would be like 'trench warfare' in the form of a cultural assult on the ideological supports of the aristocratic power. Obviously, it would be like a class war on the plane of ideas and values. Gramsci calls it 'war of position'. After being successful in this war, the 'organic intellectuals' would move towards insurrection or bloody revolution to overthrow the existing order. Gramsci calls it 'war of manouevre or movement'. However, he warns that the war of movement be launched when absolutely necessary. He has borrowed these terms from recent studies of military science to distinguish between a revolution and the condition preceding it.

It implies that a cultural revolution must precede an insurrection so as to make the socialist revolution a sure success. It is obvious that Gramsci rejects the view of Lenin that the Communist Party may stage a successful socialist revolution if its leadership is capable of that. He warns against the simplistic assumption that the Leninist strategy as exemplified in Russia could be applied unproblematically in all countries of the West. As he says: "The war of movement increasingly becomes war of position, and it can be said that a State will win war insofar as it prepares for it minutely and technically in peace time. The massive structure of the modern democracies, both as State organisations and as complexes of associations in civil society, constitute for the art of politics as it were the 'trenches' and permanent fortifications of the front in the war of position; they render merely 'partial' the element of movement which before used to be the 'whole' of war."[13]

12. *Ibid.*, p. 191.
13. Cited in McLellan, *op. cit.*, p. 190.

With this view Gramsci rejects the idea of 'permanent revolution' as advocated by Trotsky. Since the conditions of the countries of the world differ from one another, blind commitment to the idea of the export of revolution would be a grave mistake. A socialist revolution should be enacted in any country after ground is well prepared there in the form of a strong cultural revolution. Since Stalin attacked the thesis of Trotsky and he adhered to his thesis of 'socialism in one country', Gramsci came down in favour of Stalin who managed to defeat his rival and become the successor of Lenin. However, the most perplexing feature of his theory of revolution is that while he first lauded the Fascist coup of Mussolini as 'revolutionary' fostering the collapse of the traditional bourgeois order, he changed his view afterwards and called it 'reactionary' as it imposed a new variant of bourgeois ideology. Not only that, the Fascist regime purchased the acquiescence of various sections of the people by means of force and persuasion to legitimise their 'illegitimate' rule and thereby hampered the prospects of a socialist revolution there.

As a Neo-Marxist: Marxist thought underwent a serious revision in the twentieth century at the hands of leading theoreticians and leaders like Lenin of Russia, Gramsci of Italy, Lukacs of Hungary, Marcuse of Germany, Mao of China, etc. While Lenin and Mao claimed themselves as the dogmatic followers of Marx, others made no such pretence and they frankly justified their revision in the light of prevailing conditions of the twentieth century. Such thinkers contributed to the stock of modern Marxism, also known as Neo-Marxism. Though a Marxist, Gramsci sought to elaborate what was said by Marx in his *Eighteenth Brumaire* wherein he propounded the theory of 'relative autonomy' of state. In this connection, we may refer to these important points:

1. Gramsci does not agree with the 'economism' of Marx.[14] Not all social life is determined by the economic base. It is evident from his emphasis on the role of ideas of the intellectuals and the cultural pattern or value system of the people manifest in the forms of idology and hegemony.
2. Gramsci disagrees with the Marxian tenet of historicism that all development occurs in a single linear fashion. It is not necessary that socialism would come after the termination of capitalism and it would be replaced by communism in the final stage of social development. Fascism saved the tottering capitalist system of Italy and, more than that, the ruling class managed to make it 'legitimate' by purchasing the acquiescence of all sections of the people. He "emphasised the degree to which capitalism was maintained not merely by economic domination but also by political and cultural factors."[15]

---

14. Economism is a variant of Marxism which over-emphasises the determination of social life by the economic base and, therefore, under-estimates the influence of ideology and political action in the formation of history. It also embraces the view that there exists a set of objective laws of historical development. George Taylor: "Marxism" in R.E. Goodin and Hans-Dieter Klingermann (eds.): *A New Handbook of Political Science* (London: Oxford University Press, 1996), p. 252.
15. Heywood, *op. cit.*, p. 56.

3. Gramsci rejects the Marxian view that in every historical epoch the ideas of the dominant class rule. Instead he attaches importance to ideological superstructures *vis-a-vis* economic structure (implying autonomy of the state) and, more than that, his emphasis on hegemony displays the element of consent in civil society obtained not merely by the use of force. To Marx it is pure force, to Gramsci it is force as well as persuasion. The bourgeois class manages to maintain its hegemony by ideological manipulation rather than by coercion alone.
4. The concept of hegemony is crucial to the theoretical framework of Gramsci. Its aim is to redefine the nature of power in industrial society and a greater degree of importance to the struggle taking place at the ideological, political and cultural levels.[16] Hegemony is ethical-political, it must also be economic and must necessarily be based on the decisive function exercised by the leading groups in the decision-makers of economic activity.
5. The state consists of the entire complex of social, political and economic activities with which the ruling class not only justifies and maintains its dominance, but manages to win the active consent of those over whom it rules. The conception of power is broadened to include a vast array of institutions through which power relations are mediated in society as education, mass media, parliaments, courts—all activities and initiatives which form the apparatus of the political and cultural hegemony of the ruling class.
6. Within a wider and organic sense of struggle, Gramsci assigns an increasing level of importance to the role of 'organic' intellectuals who bring the masses into 'organic' relationship to constitute a solid 'bloc' of the working class. In this way, unity between economic activity and ideological superstructures is achieved.
7. Gramsci's views on the theme of revolution and its strategies differ from those of Marx patently as well as latently. In the view of Marx, revolution would occur automatically as a result of the class war. The exploitation of the working class by the capitalist class would push the former to the state of extreme misery, poverty and degradation. It would be a violent and bloody event. But Gramsci distinguishes betwen the cultural and political phases of the revolution and the role of the 'organic' intellectuals in them. First they would launch a revolution to change the existing unjust value system of the society what he calls the 'war of position', and then they would struggle to capture power of the state what he calls the 'war of manoeuvre or movement.' Hence, revolution would not be an automatic process. Like Lenin, he argues that it would be created. He even thinks about no possibility of a revolution in a capitalist society ruled by the Fascists who manage to establish their hegemony over all sections of the people. An illegitimate order is legitimised showing the application of the formula of 'reverse dialectic'.

16. Heywood, *op. cit.,* pp. 91-92.

Critical Appreciation: It is widely commented that with the exception of the great leaders of the Russian revolution like Lenin, Trotsky and Stalin, Gramsci has been the most original Marxist thinker.[17] But his thought looks like ridden with contradictions at different stages. His *Prison Notebooks* has references which are either vague at many places, or they deviate from the strictly Marxian path and take to a different course as a result of which it is decried by his critics as 'a monument of historical compromises'. This work has been a subject of intense debate and his legacy has been claimed as the inspirer of Eurocommunism popularised by Berlinguer of Italy and Carrillo of Spain in the 1970s. He may be credited with the task of reformulation of Marxism in a way that became the source of inspiration for the leading lights of the Frankfurt School and Neo-Marxism.

17. McLellan, *op. cit.*, p. 193.

29
Laski

H.J. Laski (1893-1950) holds the reputation of being the greatest teacher of Political Science of his age. He represented within himself the unique capability of being an excellent political scientist as well as a politician. The two World Wars had their definite impact on his life as a result of which his political ideas changed form one position to another. Luckily, his contact with eminent persons like Justice Holmes and President Roosevelt of America and with Prof. E. Barker and Prime Minister Attlee of England also imparted much to his practical approach. Besides, his career at the Harvard University and at the London School of Economics and Political Science enabled him to acquire a first-hand knowledge of the American and English institutions. It all made him a great teacher and a scholar as well as a politician. For some time he served as a member of the Fabian Society, but he passed the last years of his life in very close association with the Labour Party. The political ideas of Laski are contained in a good number of his books, pamphlets, articles, reviews, editorial comments, prefaces added to the works of others, etc,. He "was a scholar and a political philosopher; he was a politician, author, and journalist; he was above all a teacher and a friend. All these aspects of his personality were closely knit together by his conception of the task of an intellectual in society."[1]

Pluralism: Among the galaxy of political thinkers, Laski is ranked as a pluralist inasmuch as his main quest seems to be like that of a stern critic of the monistic doctrine of sovereignty.[2] Hence, the ideas of Laski represent a constant polemic against the mystic monism of sovereignty and they reveal an attempt to destroy the conception that the state in political theory is what the 'Absolute' is to metaphysics. In other words, he repudiates the view that the state is mysteriously one above all other human groupings and thus on account of its superior position and higher purpose it is entitled to the undivided allegiance of its people. Like J.N. Figgis, he contends that the state has developed out of the final break up of feudalism and thus the view cannot be magnified that the citizens must bow their heads before the supreme authority of the state. He,

1. Kingsley Martin: *Harold Laski: A Biographical Memoir,* pp. 256-57.
2. Pluralism is a political theory which sternly reacts against the monistic conception of sovereignty contained in the writings of thinkers like Bodin, Hobbes, Hegel and Austin. The main contention of pluralism is to deprive the state of its exclusive sovereign character. In part, it is a rationalisation of recent practical movements that "look in various ways towards a decentralised application of social control." Coker: *Recent Political Thought,* p. 508.

therefore, "attempts to destroy the monistic view by concentrating his critical fire on the concept of sovereignty."[3]

Laski's attack on sovereignty has two dimensions.[4] In the first place, he considers the existence of a legal sovereign nothing more than a fiction of logic. In his view, men do not merely obey the commands of their sovereign, they also pay allegiance to the rules and regulations of their various social groupings and associations. Even a sovereign law-making body like the English Parliament cannot do all what it wants or may want to do. Laski considers the concept of sovereignty both absurd and useless as a working hypothesis in any adequate political theory. He insists that it is unwise to dwell on the legal aspect of the sovereignty too much at the cost of its social and political aspects. Secondly, he argues that the monistic theory of sovereignty is absurd from an ethical point of view. He emphasises that the repeated surrender of the judgment of the conscience of the individuals necessarily implies an unquestioning obedience to the dictates of the state inasmuch it stunts the development of individual's personality and his moral stature.

The salient features of Laski's theory of sovereignty in this regard may be summed up as follows under:

1. As a pluralist, Laski attacks the validity of the doctrine that ascribes sovereign power only to the state. He appeals to the claims of individual conscience. He strongly urges that the state has no right to command allegiance of the individual unless his conscience so permits.[5] He says: "The claim of authority upon myself is....legitimate proportionately to the moral urgency of the appeal."[6]
2. To Laski the state is not the only association but one of the associations of society. The state does not exhaust the associative impulses of men. Since society is federal, the authority should also be federal. If the state is a reality, the associations are no less real than that. The state must compete with church, trade unions, employers' associations, clubs, friendly societies, political parties etc., but if there happens to be any conflict, the pre-eminence of state over other social institutions is justified only upon the superiority of its moral appeal in that case, otherwise the state is not all-in-all, since no association "can legislate the whole of myself."
3. In order to prove that the doctrine of sovereign state is practically untenable, Laski refers to actual instances of impotence of state in the face of determined resistance by groups within the State itself. According to him, during the First World War, the British Parliament lost heart to enforce anti-strike provisions of the Munitions Act against the defiant Welsh miners, or to put into operation the Irish Home Rule Act against the rebellious masses of Ulster. Similarly, in 1916, the association of

---

3. Laski: *Studies in the Problems of Sovereignty,* p. 208.
4. H.A. Deane: *The Political Ideas of Laski,* p. 13.
5. Laski: *The Foundations of Sovereignty and Other Essays,* p. 236.
6. Laski: *A Grammar of Politics,* p. 249.

railway employees in U.S.A., forced the Congress on threat of strike to pass a law prohibiting more than eight hours' work.

4. At a later stage, Laski shows a curious deviation when he explicitly modifies his stern pluralistic attitude by insisting that the sovereignty of the state is essential for the maintenance of class relations and the performance of civil and political responsibilities. Apparently, it indicates his shift to the school of Marxism. In the fourth edition of his great work, he even stresses that the "greatest weakness of the doctrine of pluralism lies in the fact that it does not sufficiently realise the nature of the state as an expression of class relations."[7] In a distinctly Marxian way, he adds that the state "is simply the executive instrument of the class in society which owns the means of production."[8]
5. Laski's attitude towards the state has a pragmatic character as well. Like Professors James and John Dewey of the United States, he evaluates the importance of the state in terms of the services it renders to its people. The state is not only one of the associations of the society, rather, according to him, as Duguit once said, it is 'a public service corporation'. Its value is to be judged by the adequacy of the services that it renders from time to time to the satisfaction and betterment of its people.
6. Finally, in the case of Laski, the state neither withers away as Marxian socialism predicts, nor does it happen to co-exist with other social groups and associations as Cole's guild socialism desires. The state, though one of the social groupings, exists on a higher and superior pedestal, because its membership is natural, compulsory and useful. It is natural, because man "finds himself in the modern world living under the authority of government and the objective to obey its orders arises from the facts of his nature."[9] Then, it is compulsory, because it "is the keystone of social arch. It moulds the form and substance of the myriad human lives with whose destinies it is charged."[10] Finally, it is useful, because it "becomes an organisation for enabling the mass of men to realise social good on the largest possible scale."[11]

Liberty: Laski bases his idea of liberty upon a broad and idealistic theory of the purpose for which the state exists inasmuch as he means by it the eager maintenance of that atmosphere in which people have the opportunity to be at their best selves. As such, liberty is a product of rights and is built upon the conditions essential for the full development of human faculties. It has the power to release their individuality and thus enable them to contribute their peculiar and intimate experience to the common stock of the society. In addition to this, according to Laski, liberty wields the capacity to know whether the decisions of the government are built upon the widest possible

---

7. Laski: *A Grammar of Politics* (1938), pp. xi-xii.
8. *Ibid.,* p. vii.
9. *Ibid.,* p. 17.
10. *Ibid.,* p. 21.
11. *Ibid.,* p. 25.

knowledge open to its members and prevent that frustration of creative impulse which destroys the social character of men. Laski holds: "Without rights there can be no liberty, because without rights men are the subjects of law unrelated to the needs of personality."[12]

According to Laski, liberty has three main characteristics:

1. It is a positive thing involving positive restraints. That is, it is not a thing of the woods; it lives within restraints.
2. It is a social and not an individual phenomenon. It should be studied taking the case of society as a whole. Individual has no liberty independent of his social life.
3. Liberty has a normative aspect and thus lays standard for the character of political authority.

Moreover, liberty has three aspects—private, political and economic.

1. Private liberty means the opportunity to exercise freedom of choice in those areas of life where the actions of the individual affect him alone. For instance, religion is a private affair and the state should not interfere in its domain.
2. Political liberty means the power to be active in the affairs of the state. Education and free press are its two essential conditions.
3. Economic liberty means an opportunity to feel reasonable security in the earning of one's daily bread. The people should be free from the constant fear of unemployment and insufficiency. It also implies democracy in the economic sphere.

In this regard, Laski also takes up the issue of the safeguards of liberty. The achievement of freedom by the people needs two special guarantees. First, there should be no special privileges creating an atmosphere of contingent frustration in society. It is immaterial that a particular individual has no desire to take full advantage of that access. However, its denial would mean sheer acceptance of that allotted station as a permanent conditon of his life and that, in turn, it is fatal to the spontaneity that is the essence of freedom. The habituated endurance of oppression in an atmosphere of frustrated impluse retards the growth of initiative and kills the habit of creativeness, thus incapacitating the individual to take advantage of his opportunities. The unprivileged life, over a period of decades and centuries, causes the loss of will and power of activity and in its place fills the element of fatalism or superstitions. Besides, the privileged position creates whim that those who possess it are themselves capable of freely moulding it. Laski rejects this argument by holding that such freedom is apt to be misutilised for personal gains, since the restraints may be manipulated for the sake of their own advantages. In an Aristotelian fashion, these privileged people will defend their security or, in the Macaulayan fashion will like to console the unprivileged in the name of their fortune. Hence, the enjoyment of liberty demands the absence of special privileges.

---

12. *Ibid.*, p. 142

The second safeguard is that the rights of some should not depend upon the pleasure of others. There should be equality with regard to the exercise of power and no group, or section of the society should be allowed to encroach upon the liberty of others. The political authority should plan certain principles of social action entailing the absence of those uncertainties which result in social loss and are deliberately planned to the individuals. Natural uncertainties are, of course, an exception but human uncertainties are definitely controllable and thus they demand their regulation by the state. However, in this direction, it is presupposed that the exercise of political authority should be unbiased and for this a system of rights is the best possible guarantee. Again, this guarantee implies the exercise of eternal vigilance.

The relationship between the liberty of the individual and the authority of the state is a very sensitive matter. To a negativist, the two are opposed to each other and so restraints, in view of their unavoidability, should be as little as possible. To a positivist, the two are not antithetical and so there may be as many restraints as are necessary in the interest of the society as a whole. Certain restraints on freedom add to man's happiness. The idea of liberty has to be understood in the context of social life. For once it is admitted that no man is sufficient unto himself; there must be rules to govern the habits of his intercourse. His freedom is largely borne from the maintenance of those rules. An individual abstracted from the society and his title to freedom outside the environment is devoid of any meaning. The need to give way to others, to accept, that is restraints upon our rights to unfettered activity is inherent in the nature of things. Laski hovers between the poles set by a negativist like Mill on the one side, and a positivist like Green on the other.

Equality: According to Laski, no idea is more difficult to be defined in Political Science than the concept of equality. He insists that equality does not mean identity of treatment, since there can be no such thing as long as people are different in matters of want, capacity and need. Nor does equality imply an identity of rewards. It, however, means a certain levelling process commanding that no man shall be so placed in society that he can overreach his neighbours to the extent which constitutes a denial of the latter's citizenship. Each individual should have equal prospects for the achievement of the best self. There is inequality if the voice of some is more weighty than that of others or is answered unequally by those who control political authority and who make the fulfilment of certain private desires in the name of public good."[13]

Laski's concept of equality bears the following salient characteristics:

1. It stands for the absence of special privileges. Each individual should be on an equal footing in the society. Particularly in the political sphere, it implies that the will of one should be equal to the will of another. It also signifies that there should be no discriminate selection in the conferment of public offices and that the authority of one employee should not be qualitatively different from that of another. Hence, Laski finds no justification in the retention of a hereditary second chamber like the House of Lords.

13. Laski: *A Grammar of Politics,* p. 150.

2. Equality requires equal opportunities open to all. However, it does not mean the identity of original chance, since the native endowments of every individual are not equal. What is needed is that at least all are given such training which seems in the light of experience more likely to develop their faculties to the full. Those circumstances should be created in which the training of mind becomes successful and which guarantees the fact that talent does not persist for want of encouragement.[14]

Property: Laski's concept of property is both a critique of the existing economic order and a justification of the existing institution of property largely on the Fabian lines of argument. To him, it is the institution of private property which guards man's root instincts of self-preservation. It emancipates him from the care of the morrow, the ghost of starvation, the dread of want, the yoke of involuntary work, the drudgery of undesired activity and the web of a grim routine. Positively speaking, it is a measure of security enabling the possessor to lead a comfortable life and seek intellectual attainments. However, Laski makes it clear that the number of such people in every society is always very small and the fortune of this type is a legacy not of some virtue or excellence of work but of a lucky descension an outrageous extortion.

At the same time, Laski undermines the significance of private property system in view of the fact that greater disparities of wealth are incompatible with social cohesion and that the domination of wealth leads to plutocracy. And although the power of combination or forming unions has enabled the labourers to protect their rights against the encroachments of the capitalist class, they have not been very useful in mitigating the unhappy circumstances on account of developing industrialism. Laski criticises the present capitalist system in the name of its wasteful and unplanned production entirely ignoring the facts of social utility.

Laski further points out that the evils of private property system weaken the foundations of society in an incessant manner. The arguments of the capitalists are entirely untenable and egoistic inasmuch as they are nothing but clever tricks to hide the facts of cruelty, exploitation and damage suffered by the community at their hands. Their activities destroy the good character of political life, pervert educational system and religious institutions, and certainly add to the insecurity of the well-ordered state. Hence, Laski says: "It remains historically obvious that a community divided into rich and poor is, when the latter are numerous, built upon the foundations of sand."[15] Laski warns that the capitalist hold is always pregnant with the germs of a revolution.

In addition to criticising the system of private property, Laski also gives justification of private property in some ways. In a Platonic manner, he rejects the apparent implications of various justifications employed by the lords of private property and then injects new implications in them according to his own standpoint in the following manner:

14. *Ibid.*
15. *Ibid.*

1. He adopts the psychological line of defence. It is said by the capitalists that the love of private property infuses an incentive to work. But he warns that the use of labour power and the exercise of such incentive must always be governed by the idea of social good. Thus, according to him, the present method is not a solution but a problem finding its appropriate solution not in the capricious interpretations of the capitalists as such but in the wider interests of the society.
2. He takes up the ethical line of defence. It is said by the capitalists that property is a return made to the individual for his efforts. It is ethically sound to duly reward the labours of a railway builder, radio inventor, island discoverer or a machine-maker. But he insists that there is definitely a flaw in this assumption inasmuch as when everybody makes efforts in various directions, the rewards appear to be unequal. To defend their position still more, the capitalists argue that this difference is due to natural variation in the ability and capacity of abstinence of the persons. But he rejects this assumption on the ground that the factor of abstinence is an obsolete and shameless argument and the factor of ability lies behind the mischievous capacity of reaping profits.
3. He takes up the philosophical line of defence. It is said by the capitalists that property is essentially a nurse of social virtues like generosity, inventiveness and energy. But he once again very easily dismisses this defence by holding that such virtues have been present only in the persons having no property.
4. He takes up the historical line of defence. It is said by the capitalists that all progressive societies have been constructed on the basis of private property. He at first agrees with this line of defence, but refutes it in the name of its being fallacious. In his view, this argument does not stand valid today as it was in the past. In the modern age, the conception of private property is necessarily bound to undergo change and its idealisation is thoroughly anachronistic like that of the practice of slavery. Today the right to private property cannot be treated as sacrosanct as it was possible in the days of Locke, since the modern state is under an obligation to mitigate the glaring inequalities of wealth.

The above explanation shows that Laski wants to give a new meaning to the celebrated concept of private property. He wants to see the retention of this institution but within the limits of social interest. He insists that the essential point in this regard is to keep a happy balance between private property and social service. Thus he puts: "The wider, moreover, the right of property, the less equal is the incidence of legislative benefit, and the less close is the relation between property and service."[16]

Rights: Laski defines rights as those conditions of social life without which no man, in general, can seek to be himself at his best. But, in this regard, he rejects the notion of any right that came into being in the pre-social stage; nor does he agree with the natural and immutable character of rights; nor does he support the view that rights imply power to seek a satisfaction of desires. However, he reinterprets the old theories

16. *Ibid.*, p. 93.

pointing out that rights are pre-political in the sense that whether they are recognised or not, they are there; they are historical in the sense that at some given period or place, they are demanded by the character of its civilisation; they are also natural in the sense that under certain limitations the facts demand their recognition. The rights have a content which changes with the times and places. In short, he contributes to the social utility theory of rights. In his view, rights are rights, because they are useful to the people living in the society and the state. As such, rights are built upon the utility to the individual and the community.

Laski's theory of rights has certain other aspects too. He calls certain rights as particular rights. These are:

1. Every citizen has a right to work which means the right to be occupied in producing a share of those goods and commodities which are useful for the society.
2. Every citizen has a right to adequate wages which means that all those who work must be given sufficient wages to maintain themselves.
3. Every citizen has a right to reasonable hours of work which means that he should be asked to put in that amount of work which does not exhaust him completely and thereby makes him unfit to fulfil his duties as a citizen.
4. Every citizen has a right to education which means that he should be given the minimum of education which is essential for the performance of his duties.
5. Every citizen has a right to political power which means that he should have the right to vote, to be elected, and also the right to assume governmental office and run the administrative machinery.
6. Every citizen should have the freedom of speech which means that he should have the right to ventilate his grievances and organise public opinion in his support.
7. Every citizen should be guaranteed the freedom of association and public meeting and be provided with judicial safeguards so that justice may be secured without fear or favour.
8. Every citizen has the right to private property limited only to that extent which is necessary for the growth of his personality and does not prove detrimental to the interest of the society.

Laski also deals with the right to resistance against the state. However, in this regard, he suggests four points. First, rights also imply duties inasmuch as they are real only to the extent they have been accepted by others as an obligation. Second, rights are co-relative with functions as the number of rights possessed by an individual must correspond to the contributions which he makes in person to the society. Third, rights are identical with necessity at a minimum level and it is the duty of the state to guarantee a certain minimum of rights without which it is impossible for the individuals to lead a creative life. Finally, he holds that a state is known by the rights it maintains.

It is the duty of the state to provide the individuals those outward environments which are essential for the development of their character. The citizen has claims upon the state and the latter must maintain his rights and guarantee him those conditions without which he cannot attain his best self. Hence, if the state violates them, the resistance by the people against its authority would be justified.

Finally, Laski deals with the question of safeguards. He dismisses the view that a bill of fundamental rights embodied in the national constitution is a sufficient safeguard, for although musty parchments do attach great sanctity, they cannot ensure their realisation. He also rejects the idea of separation of powers as a sufficient weapon for safeguarding the rights. But he puts three conditions by which rights of the individual can be safeguarded.

1. The state should decentralise its authority. When the people manage their own affairs, and have the functioning of authority before their own eyes, they will develop the capacity of resisting any abuse of authority that happens to arise.
2. The national government should work with the help of consultative bodies. To every department there should be attached a group of experts to the line whose duty is to advise on the problems facing it.
3. The state should not interfere in the internal affairs of various associations unless any group becomes a menace to its own existence.

Internationalism: Laski is a powerful advocate of international peace and goodwill. He is dissatisfied with the traditional doctrine of sovereignty which has made every state a master of its own activity even in those spheres which affect the life of the entire mankind. In this direction, he says: "The notion of an independent sovereign state is on the international side fatal to the well-being of humanity. The way in which the state should live its life in relation to other states is clearly not a matter in which the state is entitled to be the sole judge. The common life of states is a matter for common agreement between states. England ought not to settle what armaments she will erect and the immigrants she will permit to enter. These matters affect the common life of people; and they imply a united world organised to administer them. If men are to live in the great society, they must learn the habits of co-operative intercourse. In a world state, however, if built, and whatever the measure of decentralisation that obtains, there is no room for separate sovereignty."[17]

Laski's views on internationalism may be traced in his attack on the external aspect of sovereignty. Science and economics have changed the shape of the world. Modern science means a world market; world market means world interdependence; and, finally, world interdependence means world government. To act upon the consequence of tremendous syllogism is the only pathway to our security. As he says: "We are being rapidly driven to the point where, once we assume the sovereignty of the state, we have to infer the impossibility of those international institutions which the facts themselves

17. *Ibid.,* pp. 55-6.

are compelling us to establish."[18] Again: "Just as we spent the nineteenth century in thinking nationally and in completing the pattern of the institutions of national self-government, so we must spend the twentieth century in learning to think in international terms, in building as best as we may, the organs of that international community every year of whose delay in coming brings us so much nearer to disaster."[19]

State: Man is a social and political creature and so a social and political thinker gives his views on the theme of man in relation to his social and political existence. State is a natural association for the idealists like Plato, Aristotle, Rousseau, Hegel and Green; it is a conventional association for others like Hobbes, Locke, Mill, Spencer and Marx. Laski belongs to neither side. He recognises that state is a universal phenomenon in view of the salient fact that obligation to obey the dictates of state arises from the facts of human nature. Robinson Crusoe on his desert island, or Simon Stylites upon his pillar may defy the normal impulses which make them men, but for the vast majority to live with others is the condition of a rational existence. It implies that, in the view of Laski, state is neither a natural nor a moral but an essential association in which a man may realise his best self.

Laski's views on state may be analysed with the help of following significant points:

1. State is a part of society and its membership is also co-extensive with it, but it has its autonomous place. It may set the keynote of social order, but it is not identical with it. In personal composition the legal association (state) and the social organisation (society) are one, for they include the same body of persons. But in purpose, they are different, Society exists for a number of purposes, the state exists for a single purpose—enforcement of law. State is an association having coercive authority.
2. So the state is different from the government despite the fact that a theory of state is, at the same time, a theory of government. The state in practice is a body of men issuing orders and enforcing obedience to them. Its will is the decision arrived at by a small number of men to whom is confided the legal power of making decisions. The membership of the state is shared by all citizens, while government is a part of the state whose membership is available to those who work in some administrative capacity. Sovereignty is an attribute of the state, not of the government.
3. As a pluralist, Laski says that sovereignty should be shared by those social groups and associations which meet requirements of the people, but he does not appreciate the liquidation of the state as desired by the anarchists, the syndicalists or the communists. Like MacIver, he asserts that state is superior to but not supreme over other social associations. Social groups are real in the same sense as the state is real. That is, it has an interest to promote and a function to perform.

---

18. Laski: *Power Politics,* pp. 91-92.
19. Laski: *The State in Theory and Practice,* p. 223.

4. Then, as a Fabian, Laski frankly abandons the case of a *laissez-faire* state. He treats the state as a public welfare agency and for this reason favours the model of a functional state. That is, his principle of state action admirably balances the claims of the individual and society; his principle of individuality is uncompromising in its refusal to surrender the core of individuality expressed in the mind and conscience of the individual. So he says that state should increase its area of activity and thereby narrow the gap between the rich and the poor sections of the community. In his view, Marxism is mistaken in its inevitability of a violent revolution. So, Fascism constitutes the case of a counter-revolution.
5. Laski is an internationalist and, as such, he desires to put the sovereignty of the state under the control of some international organisation. No state has the right to make as many atom bombs as it likes and then to drop them whenever it so desires. It is dangerous to combine nationalism with sovereignty in a blind and aggressive form. We must contemplate nothing less than the establishment of a world legislature, directly responsible to the peoples of the world, a world police, a world judiciary. To this the experience of two World Wars and the incredible pace of scientific inventions have left us with no alternative.
6. The state is not infallible and the people may resist if they find that its authority lacks moral adequacy. The state ought to secure and maintain the conditions of self-realisation to the citizens. In case they find that their rights are not secured and that the state is acting contrary to the proper purpose of serving the community, the people have every right to resist it. The social conscience of the citizens is the surest guide to the conduct that the people should display in the face of events.
7. Last, the rejection of the general will of Rousseau or the 'social ethics' of Hegel is an important point in Laski's theory of state. The ideas of Rousseau and Hegel are quite abstract and so related to an abstract individual. That all men desire the 'good' of the society and the state must invariably act in the 'public interest' are vague expressions and so entirely useless for any practicable theory of state.

In short, Laski is both a pluralist and a democratic socialist. As such, he thinks about the state of concrete individuals "who realise that their good is involved in common good which their actual state is establishing."[20]

A critic may, however, comment that what is striking in the thought of Laski is that his views regarding the position of state change with the change of topic under consideration. In regard to the right or freedom of expression, the claims of society receive greater attention and the state becomes more prominent as the guardian or promoter of social welfare; inequalities of property lead to the frustration of personality and to rectify them, state saction would be necessary. Then, with regard to the right to resist, there is a generous statement of the claims of the individual to start with, but all circumspection is urged upon the individual in the exercise of the right, lest social

20. Laski: *State in Theory and Practice,* p. 61.

peace be disturbed. It is rare that the balance of the claims of the individual and the state is kept in view in considering each particular right. "Laski resembles Mill in this respect; Mill is at once an individualist and a socialist. The two elements stand unreconciled and unintegrated both in Mill and Laski."[21]

Critical Appreciation: In spite of the great influence that Laski exercised on contemporary political philosophy, it is beyond dispute that at various stages he assumed a shifty, self-contradictory, even utopian, stand. It appears that his ideas changed with the passage of time, and, whatever be the reasons for it, they make his whole approach towards the state philosophically inconsistent. The difficulty increases as we find him shifting from the plane of hard pluralism to that of soft absolutism of the state. As regards the case of sovereignty, he plays fast and loose with it. His hard attack on the sovereign character of the state is not justified. He forgets the fundamental fact that sovereignty, as Calhoun rightly says, is a whole thing and that to divide it is to destroy it. It is also said that Laski's theories of liberty, equality, property and rights do not fully cohere with his approach to the state. While dealing with all these themes he has dwelt on the utility of the state and adopted it as an instrument of social welfare. But when we notice the general tenor of his argument, it appears that he wants to keep the hands of the state off by warning against usurpation of the jurisdiction of other groups and associations of the society. However, Laski's ideas exercised such a tremendous influence that the days of his eminence became known as the 'Age of Laski'.

21. G.N. Sarma: *Political Thought of H.J. Laski,* p. 116.

30
Hannah Arendt

Born in a middle class Jewish family of Germany, Arendt (1906-75) left her country in 1933 for France apprehending the persecution of the Jews at the hands of the Nazis. For some time she stayed in England and then moved to the United States so as to live in an atmosphere of liberty and equality. She felt inspired by the existentialist thought of Martin Heidegger and Karl Jaspers that was lauded by her as 'thinking without barriers'. Like Hobbes, she suffered from fear psychosis that may be seen in her works.[1] Being a staunch lover of freedom, she took inspiration from Rousseau and Mill who idealised the system of democracy for being based on people's consent and civic republicanism. She is known for having capacity for sustained and powerful thought applied to some of the crucial problems of our times.

Critique of Totalitarianism: Arendt is sternly opposed to all kinds of totalitarianism, for it "impedes the progress of mankind, somnolences initiatives, and places dead weight and lumber on human freedom."[2] A totalitarian state is all-powerful that, in the words of its supreme leader like Mussolini and Hitler, can do no wrong. It may establish concentration camps, impose conscriptions and take any possible step to crush the liberties of the people. She lays stress on the point that it gags electoral process, subverts freedom of the press and unleashes a reign of terror. It boasts of creating equality that allows no room for liberty, fraternity and humanity. It is a system in which the masses are rendered superflous. Her *Origins of Totalitarianism* is a masterpiece work on this subject having many insights of which three, in particular, may be mentioned as follows:[3]

1. It creates a state of utter lawlessness and masquerades it as constitutionalism. The distinction between the party in power and the state is totally blurred.
2. An ideology is propagated as an instrument for manipulating and justifying absolute hold of a particular elite.[4]

---

1. Arendt's main works are *The Origins of Totalitarianism* (1951), *The Human Conditions* (1958), *On Revolution* (1962), *Eichmann in Jerusalem* (1963), *On Violence* (1970).
2. L. S. Rathore: "Hannah Arendt's Contribution to Political Theory" in J.S. Bains and R.B. Jain (eds.): *Perspectives in Political Theory* (Delhi: Radiant Publishers, 1980), p. 119.
3. Leonard Schapiro: *Totalitarianism,* p. 102.
4. Like Karl Popper and J.L. Talmon, Arendt views ideology as an instrument of social control to ensure compliance and subordination. Relying heavily on the examples of Mussolini's Fascism, Hitler's Nazism and Stalin's Communism, she describes totalitarianism as a 'closed system of thought' which, by claiming monopoly of truth, refuses to tolerate opposing ideas and rival beliefs. Andrew Heywood: *Politics,* p. 42.

3. Terror pervades everywhere that alienates the people even from their families and friends and converts them into meek citizens meekly obedient to the will of the state.

In the totalitarian system as a social and historical phenomenon of present times, all intermediate and secondary institutions between the 'leader' and the 'masses' are eliminated. In it the supreme ruler, unrestrained by legal, political and moral checks, rules by sheer terror. This ruthless and inhuman system retards human imagination and cripples the autonomy of the human soul. "The discretionary fetters and controlled bridles put by the totalitarian systems are injurious to the healthy development of the individual and full-blossomed advancement of mankind. Based as it is on terror and forcible subordination and servitude, it cramps human initiative, enslaves freedom and hurls the individual towards the worst kind of dependence and thraldom."[5]

As a serious patient of fear psychosis, Arendt traces the germs of totalitarianism in a set of ideas or formulations like pseudo-socialism of the Nazis or the theories of the American behaviouralists bereft of all normative considerations.[6] They make unsuccessful attempts to scientise social disciplines and make projections for the future which can never prove true. By obdurately sticking to the side of brute empiricism, they deliberately overlook the side of norms and values which alone can improve human conditions. The behavioural theories "have a hypnotic effect; they put to sleep our commonsense, which is nothing else but our mental organ for preserving, understanding and dealing with reality or factuality."[7]

Praxis or Purposeful Activity: In a highly philosophical style, Arendt distinguishes between various forms of human activity. It may be seen in her disinction between *vita contemplativa* (life of contemplation) and *vita activa.* (life of action). The latter implies three kinds of activities—labour, work and action. 'Labour' is an activity for any mundane purpose, like cooking food and consuming it for physical satisfaction. Its products are short-lived and are immediately consumed in the interests of the life process. 'Work' is a higher form of activity whose products last even after the passing away of the doer. Painting a scene or sculpting a statue are its instances. 'Action' is the best and the highest form of human activity. It has its manifestation in the form of noble deeds and services which have a moral effect and that is transformative of the existing norms of social order.

The threefold aspect of human activity assigns lowest place to labour, highest to the action, middle to the work. With this assertion, Arendt launches attack on thoroughly materialistic ways of life as appreciated by the Epicureans and the Utilitarians. What the people now living in industrial society call 'good life' is a collective entity of the consumers inevitably devouring more and more, and passively oscillating between the anodyne of routine and the shock of cheap sensation. Here we find a critique of human

5. Rathore, *op. cit.,* p. 116.
6. Hitler's Nazi Socialist Party and Stalin's Communist Party had nothing to do with the doctrine of socialism in the real sense of the term.
7. Hannah Arendt: *On Violence,* p. 8.

behaviour in a society of mere consumers where morality of classical type is altogether missing.

Labour, work and action make human life complete, but action has supreme place in this hierarchy. *Labour* is confined to the mundane conditions of human life, *work* is confined to the conditions of worldliness, but *action* is linked to the condtion of freedom and plurality. *Action* consists in doing something new or making some discovery or invention that is lasting and beneficial to mankind as a whole, Plurality means social life that is immune from the evil of isolation or alienation as a result of which the contribution of an individual is appreciated by the people. Only in a free and pluralistic order a person may make new experiments by his words and deeds and then win the admiration of his fellow beings. However, it is possible in an 'open' society where public space is ensured and the limited and rule-bound role of the state converts the aggregation of the individuals into civil society. The public sphere is the space that must not be taken as finally established, rather it should be recreated and renewed continually by the 'actions' of its members.

Conception of Modernity: Arendt regrets the victory of *animal laborns* over *homo fabor.* While the former refers to the values of labour, the latter refers to the values of freedom, plurality and solidarity sacrificed at the altar of productivity and abundance. In the modern age we find bureaucratic administration and elite domination as manipulation of public opinion, authoritarian and totalitarian forms of government based on naked terror and violence. We also find triumph of the materialistic ways of life implying replacement of freedom and plurality by homogeneity and conformity, alienation of man eroding all spontaneous forms of collective life. Her book on human conditions is a glorious attempt to criticise modern cultural orientations which create fundamental skepticism about the powers of the human mind to discover the nature of reality. She launches a scathing attack on rationalism and utilitarianism in the name of their adherence to the canons of science and traditional logic and instead appreciates the existentialist strain for having a deeper validity. With such an affirmation, she appears to be "first and foremost an effective moralist and the entire theory of modern culture is abundantly ethically loaded. She deplores the human condition in contemporary industrialised society and, directly or indirectly, suggests a full-fledged return to the classical tradition."[8]

Political Power, Identity and Citizenship: Arendt does not view politics as the 'last refuge of the scoundrels' as denounced by Samuel Johnson, or 'a second-rate form of human activity, neither an art nor a science, at once corrupting to the soul and fatiguing to the mind', as debunked by Michael Oakeshott. In *The Human Conditions* (1958) she says that politics is the most important form of human activity, because it involves interaction among free and equal citizens. It thus gives meaning to life and affirms uniqueness of each individual. To her, politics means power that should be exercised by those who are committed to maintain freedom of the people

8. Rathore, *op. cit.,* p. 123.

and the pluralistic character of society that makes their rule legitimate. It is the art of the possible to resolve conflicts.[9] It requires the existence of a public sphere or the 'space of appearance' built by free and active citizens ensuring the boons of liberty and equality.

In such an order alone, people can practise and regenerate politics by their 'actions'. Such people, inbued with the spirit of civic republicanism', can establish and perpetuate a really constitutioal order based on the recovery of a common shared world and the creation of numerous other 'spaces of appearance' in which they can disclose their identities. Only then the political society would exist along with civil society based on the values of freedom, reciprocity and solidarity. In such a society there should be no discrimination on any ground like religion or ethnicity, so that their differences as well as commonalities may emerge and become the subject of open and final debate.

Like Rousseau, Arendt desires that all citizens should actively participate in political affairs where decisions concerning all sections of the community are taken. Like Pericles of ancient Athens, she further says that if one is not present in such open spaces, one is not engaged in politics. Moreover, such an active citizen should understand the distinction between his private and public interests and, as a man of action, he should contribute his part to that which is in the public interest. It would protect and promote public freedom and happiness, and also generate and strengthen the sense of public agency and efficacy.

Politics means power and struggle for its sake for its proper/improper exercise. While Machiavelli and Hobbes make no distinction between the two, Rousseau and Kant differentiate and lay stress on the actions of the individual informed by his selfish and selfless wills, the latter prevailing over the former. It opens the issue of the 'legitimacy' of power. As she says: "Power springs up whenever people get together and act in concert, but it derives its legitimacy from the initial getting together rather than from any action that they may follow. It is the public support that lends power to the institutions of a country and the support is but the continuation of the consent that brought the laws into existence to begin with. All political institutions are manifestations and materialisations of power they petrify and decay as soon as the living power of the people ceases to uphold them."

---

9. Arendt is of the view that political power implies 'acting in concert'. Power is never the property of an individual; it belongs to a group and remains in existence only so long as the group keeps together. That is why, the heart of politics is often portrayed as a process of conflict resolution in which rival groups or competing interests are reconciled with one another. Politics is a particular means of resolving conflicts by compromise, negotiation and conciliation rather than through force or naked power. It is the 'art of the possible'. The very term 'political solution' implies peaceful debate and arbitration as opposed to what is often called a 'military solution'. Andrew Heywood: *Politics,* pp. 4 and 9. Such a note very much resembles the view of Bernard Crick who says that "politics is the activity by which differing interests within a given unit of rule are conciliated by giving them a share in power in proportion to their importance to the welfare and survival of the whole community." *In Defence of Politics,* p. 21.

As a powerful advocate of the liberal-democratic system, Arendt further argues that power is not the right of the rulers, but it is only that they exercise it with the consent or consensus of the people.[10] Power resides in the people who delegate it to their chosen representatives. Government is, therefore, the creation of the people active citizens or 'men of action'. Power stems from their consent and remains until that consent remains.

Arendt subscribes to the line of a neo-liberal like F.A. Hayek and a neo-Marxist like Herbert Marcuse who plead for a space or public sphere in which authority, religion and tradition have their final amalgamation. The present society of the 'consumers' should be converted into a community of human beings adhering to the values of classical morality. Marx says about the exploited, oppressed and degrading life of the workers in a capitalist society, but he also says about a new society (socialist society) in which efforts of the workers would be transformed from 'labour' into 'action'. Only the workers can change the pattern of life so as to replace the 'kingdom of necessity' by the 'kingdom of freedom and happiness.' Arendt argues that Marx's advocacy of a violent revolution to bring about the 'dictatorship of the proletariat' would assign "a bedevilling and repressive character stemming from his accepting man as a labouring animal now and a free being in the future."[11] But she asks a question as to why this may be possible in future, why not in the present by eliminating all vestiges of a totalitarian system and without showing the design of a classless and stateless society in the form of a projected paradise on earth.

In a society of human beings, freedom is meaningless unless it dignifies and transcends our present existence. The power of the state should be based on the consent of the people, what Rousseau calls 'general will' of the community, and it should be exercised in a way that the people may feel 'illumination'. The work of refinement may be done by the 'men of action' who adhere to the classical tradition of morality. In this way she edtablishes an organic link between politics and ethics. However, it may also be added that she is not a blind admirer of the past traditions. She wants to resuscitate what she finds fresh and genuine therein that can make past meaningful and present illuminating.

Critical Appreciation: Arendt appeared like a prolific writer in response to the conditions and requirements of her time. Though her works are appreciated for having the tinge of originality, it is difficult to place her in the category of a conservative, or a liberal, or a neo-liberal, or a communitarian thinker. Her sharp attack on all vestinges of a totalitarian system indirectly laid stress on the values of a free and open society. Instead of glorifying the democratic system like Mill and Bryce, she denounced the

10. The term 'consensus' means agreement, but it usually refers to an agreement of a particular kind. First, it implies a broad agreement, the terms of which are accepted by a wide range of individuals or groups. Second, it implies an agreement about fundamental or underlying principles as opposed to a precise or exact agreement. In other words, consensus permits disagreement on matters of emphasis or detail. Andrew Heywood, *op. cit.,* p. 10.
11. Rathore, *op. cit.,* p. 125.

totalitarian system in such harsh terms that implied the glorification of an open and pluralistic order. The peculiar feature of her writings finds place in an explicit attack on totalitarianism with implicit admiration of a truly democratic system. Hence, she may be admired for inaugurating the trend of neo-normativism. However, her triad of labour, work and action may be taken by a critic as confusing. It is different from Plato's triad of reason, courage and appetite that may be easily understandable to an average reader. The common point is that both make a philosophical effort to place the class of 'wise men' (Plato) or a class of 'men of action' (Arendt) at the top in the ascending hierarchy. Latently it is an attack on the ideas of Marx who attaches all importance to the role of the proletariat. The workers can create a crowd, Lenin's vanguards of the Communist Party can lead them to the path of revolution. But both Marx and Lenin mutilate the norms of good human life by appreciating the use of violence to establish dictatorship of the proletariat after the revolution. Arendt's bold expressions highlighting the evils of a totalitarian system emerged after the First World War may place her in the class of 'mass society theorists' (like Eric Fromm) who offered a set of ideas which inspired the 'new social movements'.[12]

12. Heywood, *op. cit.*, p. 285.

31
Hindu and Buddhist Political Traditions

Hindu Traditions of Dharamsastra and Arthasastra

The earliest phase of ancient India is known as the age of Dharamsastra of which Manu is the best representative. The names of Yajnavalkya and Parasar may also be referred to. This is the age when the sages compiled the Vedas on the basis of divine revelations or 'cosmic sounds of truth'. The Vedic literature included the *Shrutis* (what is heard) and *Smritis* (what is remembered) on the basis of which Manu, Yajnavalkya and Parasar composed their works. In this age, state existed in a very rudimentary form. Its origin was hailed as a divine dispensation by the invocation of which people were taught the lesson of obedience to the royal authority. A moral code was also provided to keep the ruler and the ruled within the bounds of righteousness (Dharma).[1] After the fourth century B.C., state had a developed form comparable to the city-states of Greece and Rome. Division of labour had become a settled feature of social life that was also deified by the sages. Public administration assumed a form of its own. Statecraft included diplomacy or maintenance of foreign relations. All this had a very clear exposition in the *Arthasastra* of Kautilya and, for this reason, this phase of ancient Indian polity is known as the age of Arthasastra. An account of the social and political life of the people of this period is contained not only in the works of great sages of India but also in the description of a Chinese traveller Fa Hsien (399-414 A.D.)[2]

The Hindu political philosophers conceptualised social and political life in terms of two central themes—*Dharma* and *Danda.* While *dharma* implied a moral code whose principle held the society together and bound the ruler by the canons of righteousness, *danda* implied discipline, force, restraint or punishment that was necessary to maintain peace and security by punishing the violators of the code of conduct. While the former specified the obligations of the ruler and the duties of the people so as to maintain the balance between the two, the latter dealt with the best ways of using the coercive power of the government. The two themes are integrally connected. It is a different matter

1. An account of the social and political life of the people in this phase is also contained in the description of a Greek traveller Megasthenes (327-25 B.C.).
2. R.S. Sharma in his *Aspects of Political Ideas and Institutions in Ancient India* describes six stages of the development of Indian polity. The age of Dharamsastra covers first and second stages. The age of Arthasastra covers last four stages having their distinct manifestation in the Mauryan and the Gupta periods.

that while in the tradition of *dharamsastra* more stress is laid on *dharma* and that overshadows the side of the *danda,* in the tradition of *arthasastra,* much stress is laid on *danda,* though its exercise is circumscribed by the canons of *dharma.* The reason for this should be traced in the changing conditions from simlicity to complexity. Hence, while the authors of the *dharamsastra* tradition were rather moralistic, those of the *arthasastra* tradition were realistic to the point of sometimes bordering on cynicism.[3]

The *dharamsastra* writers concentrated on exploring the *dharma* of individuals and social groups, including the government. They discussed the sources of *dharma* as well as what was to be done when these conflicted. And they also provided a detailed prospectus of duties. They were not moral philosophers but law-givers, and generally didactic and prescriptive. Since they did not concentrate on the government and attempted to provide a code of conduct covering the entire human life, they did not write books specifically on politics. Political *dharma* was incidental to the main concern and did not form a distinct and autonomous subject of investigation. In contrast to it, the authors of the *dharamsastra* were interested in the organisation and mechanics of *danda,* that is the way the government being the holder of it could be most effectively organised. They concentrated on the nature and organisation of government, the nature and mechanics of power, the way power is weakened and lost, the sources of the threat to government and the best way to deal with them, and so on."[4]

Differences between the two apart, they together constitute the tradition of Hindu political thought. In both traditions, the themes of *dharma* and *danda* have their place, the difference may be seen in their orientation. While the religious content is heavy in the former, the secular content overshadows *dharma* in the latter. Caste system remains the base owing to which while the Kshattriyas rule, the Brahmins act as their counsellers. It was upset by the Buddhist tradition that "replaced the Kshattriya-Brahmin alliance by the Kshattriya-Vaishya alliance under the former's leadership."[5]

Salient Features

Hindu political thought is as old as Hindu civilisation and it is traceable in many great works on Hindu religion and philosophy. For this reason, it is covered by metaphysical tapestry that informs a modern scholar to undermine it as mainly a theological exercise. Invocation to the divine power and its interference in the life of man is the foundation on which the premises of Hindu political thought stand. The Western writers may find much material here and wrongly compare it with the contributions of the Church Fathers of the early and later Middle Ages like St. Augustine, St. Ambrose and St. Thomas Aquinas, but the fact stands out that Hindu political thought has its own distinctive marks. All important issues of political philosophy such as the real basis of political obligation, proper relationship between the ruler and the ruled, ideal polity,

3. Bhiku Parekh: "Some Reflections on the Hindu Traditions of Political Thought" in Thomas Pantham and K.L. Deutsch (eds.): *Political Thought in Modern India,* p. 19.
4. *Ibid.,* p. 18.
5. *Ibid.,* p. 26.

legitimate function and powers of government and, above all, the very *raison d'etre* of the state are dealt with in the great works on Hindu political thought. As such, the study of Hindu political thought becomes "one facet of a vast and integrated system of reasoning which poses and interprets the very problem of human existence."[6]

The main features of this tradition may be pointed out as follows:

1. Politics is no longer treated here as an independent or autonomous discipline; it is like a handmaid of Hindu philosophy and metaphysics. The state is regarded as a divine creation bestowed upon the people to terminate the condition of complete anarchy or *matsyanyaya* (justice of the fish society). The ruler is there to establish and maintain justice which is given the name of Dharma. However, Dharma should not be taken as religion in the generally understood sense of term, it signifies the ways of righteousness as a whole. As D.M. Brown says: "Dharma is the core concept of Hindu political theory, profound in its implications and subject to varied definitions. Ultimately, it is more than law, for it is what underlies and creates law in the universe."[7] According to an Indian writer: "The conception of Dharma was a far-reaching one embracing the whole life of man. The writer on Dharmasatra meant by Dharma not a creed or religion, but a mode of life or code of conduct, which regulated a man's work and activities as a member of society and as an individual and was intended to bring about the gradual development of man and to enable him to reach what was deemed to be the goal of human existence."[8]

2. Since the state is a creation of God's blessing, it has a divine character. It is a natural as well as a moral organisation. Moreover, since it was bestowed on the people in response to their prayer by Lord Brahma, and since the people accepted their obligation towards the ruling authority on the condition of living under a proper and just rule of the monarch, it also signified a kind of contract between the ruler and the ruled. It is, therefore, obvious that the Hindu concept of the origin of state embodies the synthesis of divine origin dogma and the social contract theory as developed in Europe in the early modern period. In the "Santiparavam" of the *Mahabharata*, Bhisma says: "The people finding condition without political authority intolerable, approached God Brahma with the request: Without a Chief, O Lord, we are perishing. Give us a chief whom we shall worship in concert and who will protect us." Then God granted the request and appointed Manu to rule over them. "However, Manu hesitated to accept the appointment, as it would be very difficult to rule over people who 'are always deceitful in their conduct' until he was assured of the financial, moral and spiritual support of the people."[9]

---

6. D. Mackenzie Brown: *The White Umbrella: Indian Political Thought from Manu to Gandhi*, p. 6.
7. *Ibid.*, p. 15.
8. P.V. Kane: *History of Dharmasastra,* Vol. II, p. 2.
9. U.N. Ghoshal: *A History of Hindu Political Theories,* pp. 174-75.

3. It should also be noted that while Hindu political thought deifies and idealises the institution of monarchy, it never sanctions autocratic rule according to the whims and caprices of the head of the state. The ruler is bound to consult the state-priest as well as his ministers. Manu sanctions: "Without the *mantrins* matters of state should never be considered by the king alone, be he an expert in all the sciences and versed in policy. A wise king must always follow the opinion of the members of the council of *adhikarins* or ministers with portfolio of the President and the subjects. He must never follow his own opinion. When the sovereign becomes independent (of his council) he plans for ruin. In times he loses the state and loses the subjects."[10] The king is also commanded to lead a life of purity and complete temperance. So Kautilya sanctions: "Restraint of the organs of sense on which success in study and discipline depends, can be enforced by abandoning lust, anger, greed, vanity . . . . whosoever is of reverse character will soon perish, though possessed of the whole earth bounded by the four quarters."[11]
4. The Hindu tradition discards the system of democracy as it originated and developed in the West. The ruler belongs to the (a particular caste of the warriors) and his ministers or advisers belong either to his caste or to the caste of the Brahmins. The head-priest is a Brahmin. As a result of rigid caste system, the high offices of state cannot be given to the people of lower castes. The ruler belonging to the caste of Kshattriyas is the head of the state, but the priest belonging to the Brahmin caste holds a superior position as the spirit over the flesh.[12] And yet it should be noted that the two upper castes are never allowed to abuse their position and, for this reason, the charge of their being "undemocratic" fails to carry any weight. Since God Himself is seated on a throne under the cover of Truth signified by a "white umbrella" (*svet chhatra*) over his head, the earthly ruler is naturally bound by the law of *Dharma* by virtue of being the vicar of God on earth, enthroned by the state-priest with the invocation of religious precepts (*mantras*). "The priest held highest caste status and was identified ceremonially with the god Brahspati instead of with the temporal power Indra. His function was to interpret *Dharma* and preside over the rituals. Coronation by the priest was a necessary prerequisite to the exercise of royal power. In that ceremony, the *svet chhatra*, the White Umbrella, with jewelled handle, symbolised sovereignty or political power as was held over the head of the ruler as he took his place upon the throne."[13]
5. The Hindu tradition accords no place to the creed of state socialism as developed in the West in modern times. The rigid caste system flouts the principle of equality by assigning the last and the lowest place to the Sudras (menials and untouchables).

---

10. *Manusmriti,* VII, 58-59.
11. Shamasastry: *Kautilya's Arthasastra,* p. 10.
12. Coomaraswamy: *Spiritual Authority and Temporal Power,* p. 2.
13. Mackenzie Brown, *op. cit.,* p. 117.

All political privileges are available to the upper castes of the Brahmins and the Kshattriyas, while the Vaishyas (traders) are alloted an intermediary position. The females are also deprived of such privileges irrespective of their membership of any caste. The state is not commanded to undertake public welfare programmes to improve the lot of the underprivileged and the downtrodden. It may, however, be stressed that while Hindu political thought lays down the code of rights and duties for the two upper castes, it prescribes a set of duties for the remaining ones.

6. Hindu political thought identifies politics with *Rajniti* or policy of the state, and finds its substitute in the *Dandniti* which literally means the policy of rule and chastisement or punishment. This domain of political activity is confined to the males of the ruling class who know and understand the requirements of the polity and thereby adopt a suitable coercive policy for that purpose. It is not open for the people belonging to the non-ruling castes of the populace. The ruler is required to conduct the affairs of his state according to the canons of righteousness and, for that purpose, to punish the wrong-doers according to the principles of justice. An eminent Indian writer observes that *Dandniti* as politics "makes possible the acquisition of what has not been gained, the preservation of what has been acquired, the increase of what has been preserved, and the bestowal of surplus upon the deserving and the cause of worldly affairs, in short, depends upon it."[14]

7. A line of distinction should, however, be drawn between the nature of *Dharmasastra* and the *Arthasastra* traditions in a study of Hindu political thought. While the former constitute the codes of religion and morality, the latter deal with the science of statecraft and administration. The former lay down the higher law to which the law of the government must conform. But the two form part of the same end. "The easiest generalisation is to say that the *Dharmasastras* offer a system of law and organisation for the establishment of the Hindu state and social structure, whereas the *Arthasastras* provide working manuals to guide the ruler in the conduct of his daily affairs."[15]

In short, Hindu political thought is the oldest thought in the world in which fundamental questions relating to the origin and nature of political authority, the duties of the ruler towards the ruled and the obligations of the ruled towards their ruler, and, above all, the end of the state are raised and answered. A critic of the Western countries may fail to understand the greatness of the contributions of Hindu philosophers and seers because of his ignorance of the Sanskrit language as well as of his bias for not evaluating properly the ideas of non-Christian philosophers who produced such great works in pre-historic times. It is also true to say that several of the Hindu scriptures are full of contradictory ideas on many important themes, and their expression couched in metaphysical terms makes the whole case puzzling. Hence, a study of ancient Indian or

14. Ghoshal, *op. cit.*,
15. Mackenzie Brown, *op. cit.*, p. 10.

Hindu political thought should be made with this impression: "In general, the purpose of the Hindu state was to reinforce the moral codes of society and to insure justice among men, thereby guaranteeing the individual free opportunity to develop himself within the framework and recognised rules of his own caste Dharma."[16] A great Indian scholar throws light on the significance of Hindu thought in these words: "It is a chapter of the history of the human mind, full of vital meaning for us. The most ancient fancies sometimes startle us by their strikingly modern character, for insight does not depend on modernity."[17]

Manu

A study of Hindu political thought begins with Manu—the legendary figure known for giving a code (*Manusamhita*) laying down the principles of ideal monarchy.[18] We may also trace some principles relating to *Dandniti* and *Rajkala* (statecraft) in it. The state has a divine origin. As Manu says: "When creatures being without a king were through fear dispersed in all directions, the Lord created a king for the protection of his whole creation. Even an infant king must not be despised with an idea that he is a mere mortal; for he is a great deity in human form. Let no man, therefore, transgress that law which the king decrees with respect to those in his favour, nor his orders which inflict upon those in disfavour." But Manu is not a blind admirer or advocate of the institution of ideal monarchy. He defines the duties of an ideal king as follows:

1. The king has been created by the Protector of the castes and orders all of whom, according to their rank, discharge their several duties.
2. Let him daily worship the aged Brahmins, who know the Vedas and are pure, for he who always reveres aged men, is honoured even by the demons.
3. Let him, though he may be already modest, constantly learn modesty from them; for a king who is modest never perishes.
4. From those versed in the three Vedas let him learn the threefold sacred science—the primeval science of government, the science of dialectics, and the knowledge of the supreme Soul; from the people the theory of the various trades and professions.
5. Day and night he must strenuously exert himself to conquer his senses; for he alone who has conquered his own senses, can keep his subjects in obedience.

---

16. *Ibid.,* p. 21.
17. S. Radhakrishnan, cited *Ibid.,* p. 14.
18. "Mythologically, Manu is the father of the human race, the first law-giver. He is also regarded as the first and greatest of ancient Indian kings, the offspring of the Sun. Finally, he is said to be not a person at all, but a title given to great law-givers. The actual author or authors of the *Manusamhita* no doubt used the name of Manu to give authority to its rules, for early writers in the Orient often professed to be mere transmitters of ancient tradition and avoided claims to authorship." Brown, *op. cit.,* p. 27.

6. Let him carefully shun the ten vices springing from love and pleasure, and the eight proceeding from the wrath, which all end in misery. For a king who is attached to the vices springing from love and pleasure loses his wealth and his virtue, but he who is given to those arising from anger loses even his life. Hunting, gambling, sleeping by day, censoriousness, excess with women, drunkenness, an inordinate love for dancing, singing and music, and useless travel are the tenfold sets of vices springing from love and pleasure. Tale bearing, violence, treachery, envy, slandering, unjust seizure of property, revelling and assault are the eightfold sets of vices produced by wrath. That greediness which all wise men declare to be the root even of both these sets, let him carefully conquer; both sets of vices are produced by both. On a comparison between vice and death, vice is declared to be more pernicious; a vicious man sinks to the nethermost hell; he who dies, free from vice, ascends to heaven.
7. Let him appoint seven or eight ministers whose ancestors have been royal servants, who are versed in the sciences, heroes skilled in the use of weapons and descended from noble families and who have been tried. Let him daily consider with them the ordinary business referring to peace and war, the four subjects called the *sthana*, the revenue, the manner of protecting himself and his kingdom, and the sanctification of his gains by pious gifts. But with the most distinguished among them all, a learned Brahmin, let the king deliberate on the most important affairs which relate to the six measures of royal policy.
8. Let him, full of confidence, always entrust to the official all business having taken his final resolution with him, let him afterwards begin to act. He must also appoint other officials, men of integrity, who are wise, firm, well able to collect money and well tried. Among them let him employ the brave, the skilful, the high born, and the honest in offices for the collections of revenue, e.g., in mines, manufactures and storehouses, but the timid in the interior of his palace.
9. Let him also appoint an ambassador who is versed in all sciences, who understands hints, expressions of the face and gestures, who is honest, skilful and of noble family. With respect to affairs, let the ambassador explore the expression of the countenance, the gesture and actions of his confidential advisers, and discover his designs among the servants. Having learnt exactly from his ambassador the design of the foreign king, let the king take such measure that he does not bring evil on himself.
10. Let him make a town for the sake of his safety, protected by a desert or a fortress built of stone and earth, or one protected by water and trees, formed by an encampment of armed men or a hill fort. Let him cause to be built for himself in the centre of a spacious palace well protected and habitable in every season, resplendent with whitewash, and supplied with water and trees. Inhabiting that let him wed a consort of equal caste who possesses auspicious marks on her body

and is born in great family, who is charming and possesses beauty and excellent qualities.

11. Let him appoint a domestic priest and choose officiating priests who shall perform his domestic rites and sacrifices, let him obey the sacred law in his transactions with the people and behave like a father towards all men.
12. Let him cause annual revenue in his kingdom to be collected by trusted officials, let him obey the sacred law in his transactions with the people and behave like a father towards all men.
13. Let him honour those Brahmins who have returned from their teacher's house after studying the Vedas; for that money which is given to Brahmins is declared to be an imperishable treasure for kings.
14. Mechanics and artisans as well as Sudras who subsist by manual labour, he may cause to work for himself one day in each month.

Manu's Code lays down a number of principles relating to the proper determination and award of punishment by the king. His views on Dandniti may be enumerated as follows:

1. Having fully considered the time and place of the offence, the strength and the knowledge of the offender, let him justly inflict that punishment on those who act unjustly.
2. Punishment alone governs all created beings, punishment alone protects them, punishment watches over them while they sleep; the wise declare punishment to be identical with the law. If punishment is properly inflicted after due consideration, it makes all people happy, but inflictor of punishment should be such who is trustful, who acts after due consideration, who is wise and who knows the respective value of virtue, wealth and pleasure.
3. The whole world is kept in order by punishment, for a guiltless man is hard to find; through fear of punishment the whole world yields the enjoyment which it owes. They delcare the king to be the just inflictor of punishment who is trustful, who acts after due consideration, who is wise and who knows the respective value of virtue, wealth and pleasure.
4. A king who properly inflicts punishment, prospers with respect to those three means of happiness; but he who is voluptuous, partial and decietful will be destroyed, even through the unjust punishment which he inflicts.
5. Punishment possesses a very bright lustre, and is hard to be administered by men with unimproved minds; it strikes down the king who swerves from his duty, together with his relatives.
6. Punishment cannot be inflicted justly by one who has no assistant, nor by a fool, nor by a covetous man, nor by one addicted to sensual pleasures.

Finally, we may enumerate the views of Manu on the statecraft or the art of establishing and preserving a big and powerful empire as under:

1. Let the king having carefully considered each affair be both sharp and gentle, for only such a king is highly respected.
2. The highest duty of a Kshattriya is to protect his subjects, for the king who enjoys privileges is bound to discharge the duty.
3. He should gratify all subjects who come to see him by a kind reception and afterwards dismiss them; having dismissed his subjects, he should take counsel from his ministers.
4. Ascending the back of a hill or a terrace, and retiring there in a lonely place, or in a solitary forest, let him consult with them unobserved.
5. The king whose secret plans other people, though assembled for that purpose, cannot discover, will enjoy the whole earth, though he be poor in treasure.
6. Despicable persons, likewise animals and particularly women, betray secret counsel; for that reason he must be careful with respect to them.
7. At midday or at midnight, when his mental and bodily fatigues are over, let him deliberate either with himself alone or with his ministers on virtue, pleasure and wealth.
8. Let him not cut up his own root by levying no taxes, nor the root of other men by excessive greed, for by cutting up his own root or theirs, he makes himself or them wretched.
9. A king, who while protecting his people, is defied by foes, be they equal in strength or stronger, or weaker, must not shrink from battle, remembering the duty of a Kshattriya. Not to turn back in battle, to protect the people and to honour the Brahmins is the best means for a king to secure happiness.
10. As the weeder plucks up the weeds and preserves the corn, even so let the king protect his kingdom and destroy his opponents.
11. Let the king confiscate the whole property of those officials, who, evil minded, may take bribes from suitors and banish them.
12. After due consideration, the king shall always fix in his realm the duties and taxes in such a manner that both he himself and the man who does the work receive their due reward. As the leech, the calf and the bee take their food little by little, even so must the king draw from his realm moderate annual taxes. Let the king make the common inhabitants of his realm, who live by trade, pay annually some trifle, which is called a tax.
13. Let the king make peace when he is sure of his own gain and superiority in future and of inferiority at present; wage war when he thinks he is very strong to defeat the enemy; let him mark against the enemy when his enemy is well disposed

towards him and is comparatively superior, but remain neutral when he is weak in chariots and troops; let him divide their forces when he finds that his enemy is stronger in every respect, but take refuge with a rich and powerful king when he is very easily assailable by the forces of the enemy.

14. Let the king make use of all the four expedients, namely, conciliation, bribery, dissension and force. He should make use of all or anyone of them at a particular time, but the way of force should be resorted to as the last expedient.

15. Let the king strive after the acquisition of territories and countries that have not been conquered, and protect those that have been acquired. Let him abandon without hesitation even a rich and fertile land if this is required for his safety.

In the end, it may be said that Manu desires a stable social and political order. His society is a four-class system of castes which has a divine sanction, and the ruler belonging to the Kshattriya caste is commanded to maintain it. His state is not ruled by a power-hungry king. The monarch is bound by the canons of religion and morality and he is not advised to follow ruthlessly and relentlessly a policy of blood and iron as suggested by many subscribers to the Arthasastra tradition. His conclusion is that political wisdom consists in arranging everything so that the polity remains secure from any onslaught from the side of a friend or a foe and, as such, it "betrays the overwhelming influence of the traditional Smriti conception of a stable social order."[19]

Kautilya

Kautilya, also known as Chanakya and as the Prime Minister of the Mauryan Emperor, Chandragupta, is known for writing an immortal work on the science of public administration and the art of statecraft. Unfortunately the original work was untraceable until, in 1909, Prof. Shamsastry was able to trace its manuscript in a very old library in Tanjore without its first and last few pages—a fact which provides an excuse to some critics about the authenticity of its authorship. What is to be noted, however, in this connection is that though the Sanskrit word *artha* conveys the sense of wealth, *Arthasastra* means much more than being a treatise on the subject of revenue administration of the state. In a real sense, it covers the entire field of politics, public administration, statesmanship and statecraft. Moreover, Kautilya is not the originator of, or the first writer on this subject. Its traces may be seen in the works of Manu, Brahaspati and Usanas. But the notable point is that Kautilya's is the only complete work of its kind. It is not merely in respect of its range, but also in its worth and usefulness in regard to its application to the real problems of a polity and administration that it stands out as an incomparable work in ancient Indian political literature.

Like Manu, Kautilya regards the state as a divine creation, and defends the institution of ideal monarchy. He defines the duties of the monarch about enforcing the law on his subjects in accordance with all traditional usages. The king should disregard all customs that are harmful to his own interest or are opposed to *Rajdharma* (religion of state). He has no personal dislikes; it is the likes of his subjects that should be honoured

19. U.N. Ghoshal, *op. cit.,* p. 184.

and followed by him. In his view, a king is a visible dispenser of favours and disfavours and, therefore, he is in the position of gods—Indra and Yama respectively; he who despises him is visited with divine punishment. Thus the lowly folk should be silenced. The first and foremost function of the king is to abolish the condition of *matsyanyaya* or complete anarchy.

The king should follow Dandniti very judiciously. In his view, *danda* is the means of ensuring security and prosperity of the three sciences—Sacred Canon, Philosophy and Economics. In fact, *danda* is their root: the course of worldly affairs depends upon *danda*, and therefore he who seeks this course should constantly be ready to apply *danda*. In simple terms it means that the ruler should use *danda* for safeguarding the worldly existence of his subjects. It is also required that *danda* should be used very intelligently and wisely so that people retain their trust in government. It should neither be too harsh nor too mild. When *danda* is applied with sound knowledge of the canon, it confers the threefold end of life upon the people; when it is applied improperly under the influence of desire or anger or without knowledge it afflicts even the forest dwelling ascetics, not to speak of the householders; when it is not applied at all, it leads to the conditions indicated by the maxim of the larger fishes devouring the smaller ones. All this means that *danda* should be applied in a very judicious manner.

However, what makes the name of Kautilya a legend is his views on statecraft and diplomacy which may be enumerated as under:

1. The ruler should possess the qualities of high intellect, character and strong will power. He should be well educated and well versed in the disciplines of Religion, Philosophy and Economics.
2. The ruler should maintain his personal security that is a key to the security of the state.
3. The ruler should keep watch over the behaviour of his own officials as well as of his enemies by maintaining an elaborate system of espionage.
4. The ruler should observe and exploit popular superstitions for his own interests or ends.
5. The ruler should invariably guard and protect his subjects, loyal as well as disloyal, but he should seduce the subjects of his enemies.
6. The ruler should use the four expendients of conciliation (*sam*), bribery (*dam*), dissension (*bhed*) and punishment (*danda*) to deal with his rivals and enemies.
7. The ruler should win over his disaffected elements to his side by applying the rules of mob psychology.
8. The ruler should deal ruthlessly with social criminals and economic wrong-doers like corrupt judges and magistrates, false witnesses, crafty manufacturers, magicians, sorcerers, adulterators, poisoners, etc.

9. The ruler should appease with offers of wealth and honour those who have had some well-known cause to be disaffected, and impose punishment in secret on those who are for no reason disaffected or who are plotting against him.
10. The ruler should not use unscrupulous diplomacy to finish or assassinate the offenders so as to maintain the rule of his dynasty.
11. The ruler should not follow a policy which causes him loss but entails no such loss on the enemy, for it brings deterioration.
12. The ruler should achieve three successes (*siddhis*) or powers relating to his own energy, material resources and the counsel of his ministers.
13. During the times of financial crisis or emergency, the ruler may replenish his treasury by means of force and fraud through the agency of spies and state officials.
14. The ruler should attack the enemy when he is in trouble or when his enemy's people are impoverished and disunited.
15. A strong king should make peace with a weak enemy when the enemy's subjects are united; he should observe neutrality when he finds that war is of no advantage to him; he should take refuge with another king when he finds that his troubles are incurable.
16. The ruler should keep his army under a divided command as a sure guarantee against treachery.
17. When two kings are equally vulnerable, the ruler should attack the powerful but the unjust one instead of the weak and the just.
18. The ruler should fight treacherously when his enemy is strong and fight honourably when the enemy is weak, or may do so in the light of new conditions.
19. The ruler should use his spies to use poison, fire and force to cause instantaneous and widespread death of the enemy and his people. He should create disturbances in the land of the enemy by his untoward and wonderous power.
20. The ruler should pursue a foreign policy from decline to equilibrium and thereon to progress so as to become the ruler of the world. There are six forms of foreign policy. Of these agreement with pledges is peace; offensive operation is war; indifference is neutrality; making preparation is marching; seeking protection of another is alliance; and making peace with one and waging war with another is termed a double policy.

Some important points should be noted in the end. First, Kautilya does not justify the case of absolute and unlimited monarchy as we find in the case of Plato's philosopher-king or the Leviathan of Hobbes. His ruler is bound by a code of canons or laws and is also required to act in consultation with his ministers. The simile of Indra's having thousand eyes means a ruler be surrounded by a thousand advisers. Second, his ideas should not be regarded as the expression of cold and cynical realism as we find in the writings of Machiavelli. The ruler of Kautilya bears the qualities of a lion and a fox, by virtue of synthesising the traits of sharpness and gentleness, but he is required to observe the principles of social ethics or *Rajdharma*. It is, however, a different matter that, like Bhisma in the *Mahabharata*, Kautilya says that during times of grave emergency the interest of the state overrides the rules of traditional morality.

On the whole, Kautilya's *Arthasastra* finds a unique place in the literature on ancient Indian polity. It is free from the influence of mysticism and idealism, that is the outstanding feature of other Hindu writings. The work of Kautilya is a practical manual having a distinctly utilitarian character. The ruler of Kautilya is, therefore, provided a complete guide for establishing and preserving a big and powerful empire. The principles laid down by this peerless scholar of public administration, statesmanship and diplomacy have their eternal and universal relevance by virtue of having "the traits of extraordinary thoroughness, its eminent inductiveness and practical character, its unflinching logic and heedlessness of adventitious moral and religious standards, and its wide range of subjects and interest."[20]

Buddhist Tradition

Ample literature relating to the Buddhist tradition is contained in a number of books written in Sanskrit and Pali languages like *Vinaya Pitaka, Jatakas, Digh Nikaya,* grammar of Panini, commentaries of Patanjali, Aryadeva's *Chatuhsataka* and *Sukranitisara.* In many respects, this tradition resembles the Hindu traditions as sanctioned in the Brahamanic literature mainly contributed by Manu and Kautilya. However, a critic may comment that the Buddhist ideas about authority of the ruler and obligations of the ruled are not thoroughly consistent. The main features of the Buddhist tradition may be enumerated as follows:

1. It advanced a quasi-contractual theory of government. There was no state or government in the earliest stage of human life. Its origin finds place in the creation of authority to check and control the state of utter lawlessness that emerged with the creation of the institutions of private property and private family.
2. To manage the conditions, the people elected one of the noblest among them as the ruler, but he could exercise his authority in consultation with the people assembled in a *samgha.* However, this *samgha* did not include people in general, it was a gathering of noble families.
3. Kings are presented as gods by human convention to whom the obedience of the rulers becomes a matter of necessity. It signifies a kind of contractual relationship between the two. While the king is obligated to terminate the horrible state of anarchy (what Kautilya calls *matsyanyaya*), he is also bound to be virtuous and the people are commanded to render obedience to his authority. Aryadeva in his *Chatuhsataka* says about the supremacy of the people and the role of the king as

20. Rangaswami Aiyangar: *Ancient Indian Polity,* p. 35.

their servant. Moreover, like Kautilya, he in his *Sukranitisara* declares king to be a servant of the people with his one-sixth share of revenue received as his means of subsistence.

4. Politics is regarded as a dismal science or anti-thesis of ethics. Hence, *Asvaghosha* advocates complete separation of politics from ethics and *Aryasura* denounces politics for being dominated by the ends of wealth. The solution to this paradox is discovered in binding the ruler to the norms of righteousness and to the people by the obligation of obedience.

5 A description in the *Jatakas* and other Buddhist commentaries discloses that there were many small entities in the sixth century B.C. There was monarchichal system in some such entities, but most of them were *samghas* or republics. At that time, 12 *samghas* were very popular and vigorous as the Bhaggs, Bulis, Koliyas, Moriyas, Saikyas, Mallas, Licchavis and Videhas. The Licchavi republics were the best of all. So Buddha once uttered this prophetic note: "The republics would prosper as long as the Masters of their Assembly met frequently, showed reverence to age, experience and ability, transacted the state business in concord and harmony, and did not develop selfish parties engaged in unending wrangling for their narrow and selfish ends."[21]

6. These small entities were ruled by different types of groups and were known by different names as *ganas, samghas, srenis, puga, virata,* etc. In some there were war-lord kings, but in most of them were the self-governing 'multitudes' at which decisions were taken by the members in common. The striking point is that the government was dominated by the warrior class and so the privileges were available to the people belonging to the *rajkulas* (royal families).

7. Though these small entities *ganas* or *samghas* were like republics (to use modern term), the ways of their administration were not uniform. Panini refers to the working of the assemblies through the process of corporate decision-making that could be interpreted as government by discussion.[22]

8. The *samghas* were autonomous like guilds and corporations, but they were dominated by the wealthy persons. So the Vaishyas could have a share of power. It was like a contradiction, because Buddhism rejects caste system.

9. The concept of *Dhamma* prevailed which implied a code of basic social morality as enunciated by Lord Buddha.

10. It followed the Hindu tradition by binding the ruler with the canons of *Dhamma* and the destiny of man was determined by his action (Karma) of the previous life.

---

21. A.S. Altekar: *State and Government in Ancient India,* p. 379.
22. In his book *Buddhist India* Rhys Davids says that in the land of Buddha there were many populous territories which made public decisions in moots or assemblies.

Buddhism could not establish its lasting influence in India. It was brought back into Hinduism or Brahminism despite the fact that it had its sober influence on Brahminism that freed it from superstitions and rituals.[23] It is true that great debates and arguments were held in the Buddhist monasteries and at the meetings of the *samghas,* but new ideas, or old ideas in a new attire, were coming from the south and the west, the simplicity of the Buddhist thought was being gradually affected. Perhaps, there were two main influences which tended to deflect Buddhist thought in the same direction —Brahmanic and Hellenic.[24] The Buddhist tradition looks like a break from the Hindu tradition. In fact, it reconstituted the Hindu traditions. It had its effect on the Hindu traditions as well as a result of which, in course of time, the two became intermingled.

23. Jawaharlal Nehru: *Glimpses of World History,* p. 37.
24. *Ibid.,* p. 82.

32

Syed Ahmed Khan

Sir Syed (1817-98) is rightly lauded as the 'father of Muslim renaissance in modern India'. If Raja Ram Mohun Roy, Vivekanand and Dayanand awakened the Hindus and exhorted them to abandon their evil practices and superstitions, Sir Syed exhorted the Muslims to do likewise. He counselled them to modernise their society by having a rationalistic approach to religion and by learning English language. It is said that he had written a commentary on the Bible and the Koran (which remained unpublished) for which he was called a 'heretic' by his co-religionists. He laid stress on synthesising the old and new learning so as to secularise the system of education. No doubt, these were quite revolutionary ideas at that time. It is well commented that the Aligarh Movement launched by him "was a deliberate counterpoise to the stand of the Muslim revivalists like Haji Shariat Ullah, Dudhu Miyan and to the Ahl-i-Hadis movement. Syed Ahmed wanted to give the place of pride both to secular modern education and to Islamic theology."[1]

Socio-Religious Reform: As already pointed out, Sir Syed did a lot for awakening the Muslims from the slumber of ignorance and lethargy. For this purpose, he founded a school at Aligarh that soon became the Mohammedan Anglo-Oriental College with a view to popularise scientific and rationalistic knowledge of the West. In 1886 he founded Muslim Educational Conference to generate enthusiasm for social, economic and intellectual development of his co-religionists. In his book on the *Causes of the Indian Revolt* (1858), he regretted the deplorable condition of the Indian Muslims "for being under the influence of false and meaningless prejudices who do not understand their own welfare. In addition, they are more jealous of each other and more vindictive than the Hindus and suffer more from a sense of false pride. They are also poorer and for these reasons I fear that they may not be able to do much for themselves."

Sir Syed discovered its way out in the provision of new learning and loyalty of the Muslims to the British rule. The British rulers had deliberately repressesd the Muslims to an even greater degree than it had repressed the Hindus and this repression had especially affected those sections of the Muslims from which the new middle class might have been drawn. On the one hand, Sir Syed as an ardent reformer wanted to reconcile modern scientific thought with Islamic theology, on the other, he was convinced that he could uplift the Muslims through cooperation with the British rulers. Hence, he sought to dispel the general impression of the English rulers that not all the Muslims had taken part in the Mutiny and that all Muslims did not harbour the feelings

1. V.P. Varma: *Modern Indian Political Thought,* p. 429.

of enmity towards the British rulers. It is evident from the fact that one of the declared objects of the Aligarh College founded by him "was to make the Muslims of India worthy and useful subjects of the British Crown."[2]

Loyalty to the British Rule: After the Mutiny of 1857, the Indian Muslims "had hesitated which way to turn."[3] Sir Syed showed the way that the Muslims should regard the British rulers as their real well wishers. In his book *The Loyal Mohammedans of India,* he strongly tried to refute the impression of an Englishman like Lord Ellenborough that the "race of the Muslims is fundamentally hostile to us." Another Englishmen W.W. Hunter frankly endorsed that after the Mutiny, the British "turned upon the Muslims as their real enemies."[4] To change the hard anti-British sentiments of the Muslims of that time was really a gigantic task and Sir Syed managed to do it. He refuted the common notion that the Mutiny was the result of a conspiracy planned by the Muslim elites who had felt insecure at the diminishing influence of the Moghul monarchs.

However, its better manifestation may be seen in the pro-colonial role of Sir Syed for which he was well awarded. In 1869 he was awarded the Order of the *Star of India* from the British government. "In 1878 he welcomed Lord Lytton's repressive Vernacular Press Act as a liberal measure. In 1883 he asked the Muslims not to agitate for the Ilbert Bill, since it was being actively opposed by the Europeans. He actively opposed the Congress from the beginning, first on the basis of an upper class alliance of the Hindus and the Muslims and later on the basis of Muslim communalism. Throughout he preached that the British rulers were the guardians of Muslim interests. He declared the British to be *khilafatullah* or God's representative on earth, who should reward Muslims for their loyalty."[5]

Communal Unity: Sir Syed is known for his secular orientations by virtue of espousing the cause of Hindu-Muslim unity. In one of his powerful orations delivered at Patna on 27 January, 1883, he said: "Just as the high caste Hindus came and settled down in this land once, forgot where their earlier home was and considered India to be their own country, the Muslims also did exactly the same thing—they also left their climes hundreds of years ago and they also regard this land of India as their own . . . But my Hindu brethren and my Muslim coreligionists breathe the same air, drink the water of sacred Ganga and Jamna, eat the products of the earth which God has given to this country, live and die together . . . I say with conviction that if we were to disregard for a moment our conception of Godhead, then in all matters of everyday life the Hindus and Muslims, really belong to one nation (*kaum*) . . . and the progress of the country is possible only if we have a union of hearts, mutual sympathy and love . . . . I have always said that our land of India is like a newly wedded bride whose two beautiful and luminous eyes are the Hindus and the Mohammedans; if the two exist in

---

2. Jawaharlal Nehru: *The Discovery of India,* p. 365.
3. *Ibid.,* pp. 364-65.
4. W.W. Hunter: *The Indian Mussalmans,* p. 147.
5. Bipan Chandra: *Communalism in Modern India,* pp. 104-05.

mutual concord, the bride will remain for ever resplendent and becoming, while if they make up their mind to see in different directions, the bride is bound to become squinted and even partially blind."

No doubt, the secular orientations of Sir Syed were haunted by the phobia of Hindu dominance that may be traced in his gospel of Muslim isolationism. He advised his coreligionists to preserve their distinct and separate identity and it could be possible by keeping themselves aloof from the Hindu-dominated Indian National Congress and to maintain their firm and unflinching loyalty to the British rule. The educational complex founded by him at Aligarh "became the nerve-centre of Muslim educational, cultural and even political activities in the late nineteenth and early twentieth centuries. Along with encouraging the Muslims to take to English education, he advised his co-religionists to refrain from confronting the British rulers till they had been able to overcome their backwardness. In the interest of the empire the first three Principals of the M.A.O College "were only too eager to play their part in keeping the Muslims away from the main socio-political interests of the country."[6]

Sane and Loyal Nationalism: Sir Syed was a nationalist. He resented that the Englishmen were not prepared to treat the Indians with a sense of equality. So he walked out from the Agra Durbar in 1883 as in the seating arrangement the chairs for the Europeans were placed on the platform and those for the Indians down below. He raised the issue that there should be legislative councils in the country with representation to the Indian people so as to establish a vital communication link between the rulers and the ruled. His admiration for the British rule or his attempt to make the Indian Muslims loyal to the British raj should not be taken as inconsistent with his stand as a nationalist in view of the fact that even the leading lights of the national movement like Dadabhai Naoroji, Sir Pherozeshah Mehta and Surendranath Banerjea subscribed to the motto of M.G. Ranade that British rule was like a divine dispersation. Sir Syed did the same, though for different reasons.

As a nationalist, Syed Ahmed insisted on attainment of equality with the ruling class to be reinforced by strong Hindu-Muslim unity. In his book *Tahzibul Akhlaq,* he says: "No nation can acquire honour and respect so long as it does not attain equality with the ruling race and does not participate in the Government of its own country. Other nations can have no respect for Mussalmans and Hindus for their holding the position of clerks or similar other petty posts. Rather, that Government also cannot be looked upon with respect which does not give due respect to its subjects. Respect will be commanded only when countrymen will be holding positions equal to those of the ruling race. The Government have in sincerity good faith and justice given the rights to their subjects in every country to attain such equality. But for Indians there are many

---

6. S.K. Bandopadhyaya: *Mohammed Ali Jinnah and the Creation of Pakistan,* pp. 11-12. Rajendra Prasad prefers to place greater blame on the three English Principals (Beck, Morrison and Archbold) of the M.A.O. College who by their shrewd activities managed "to create the gulf which, with some interruptions, has gone on widening ever since." *India Divided,* p. 99.

difficulties and obstacles. We must work with determination and perseverance and should not keep back on account of the fear of any trouble befalling us."[7]

Elsewhere, he adds: "The word nation (*kaum*) applies to people who inhabit a country . . . . Remember that Hindu and Mussalman are religious words; otherwise, Hindus, Mussalmans and even Christians who inhabit this country all constitute on this account one nation. When all these groups are one nation, then whatever benefits the country, which is the country of all of them, should benefit all . . . . Now the time has gone when only on account of differences in religion, the inhabitants of a country should be regarded as of two different nations."[8] On another occasion, he asserted: "Just as the Aryan people are called Hindus, even so are also Mussalman Hindus, that is to say, inhabitants of Hindustan." While addressing the Hindus of Punjab, he said: "The word Hindus that you have used for yourself is, in my opinion, not correct, because that is not in my view the name of a religion. Rather every inhabitant of Hindustan can call himself a Hindu. I am, therefore, sorry that you do not regard me as a Hindu, although I too am an inhabitant of Hindustan."

However, his attack on the Indian National Congress created by A.O. Hume as a Hindu-dominated organisation having the seeds of an anti-British movement and then his attempt to create a counterpoise in the form of United India Patriotic Association in 1888 is differently evaluated.[9] It was indeed, his notable contribution that his idea of associating the Indian people with the administration under the Crown found its historic expression in the Royal Proclamation of Queen Victoria in 1858 and that laid the foundation for 'reasonable constitutional reforms' in times to come. Lord Reay, the then Governor of Bombay, appreciated these words of Sir Syed: "Most men agree, I believe that it is conducive to the welfare and prosperity of government indeed it is essential to its stability, that the people should have a voice in its councils. It is from the voice of the people that government can learn whether its projects are likely to be well received. This security can never be acquired unless the people are allowed a share in the consultation of government. The men who have ruled India can never forget that they were here in the position of foreigners . . . . The security of government is based on its knowledge of the governed as well as its careful observance of their rights and privileges."[10]

---

7. M. Tufail Ahmad: *Mussalmanon ka Roshan Mustakbil* (Urdu), pp. 281-82.
8. *Ibid.,* p. 107.
9. Sir Syed was not opposed to the Indian National Congress, because he considered it a predominantly Hindu organisation; he opposed it because he thought it was politically too aggressive (though it was mild enough in those days) and he wanted British help and cooperation." Nehru, *op. cit.,* p. 365. But a Marxist like M.N. Roy comments: "Those of the Hindus who inaugurated the agitation for representative government and social reforms were intellectual bourgeoisie, whereas the Aligarh alumni, on whom were showered the good grace of the British Government, belonged to the landed aristocracy with social and political tendencies predominantly feudal. Elements so diverse socially could not unite in a national movement." *India in Transition,* p. 223.
10. Syed Ahmed Khan: *Causes of the Indian Revolt,* p. 12.

Critical Appreciation: Sir Syed deserves to be remembered as a great social reformer and a political regenerator. As B.M. Malabari did a lot for reforming the Parsee society, or Dayanand did the same for the Hindus, Sir Syed did the same for the Muslims. It is a different matter that his bold programmes of reform were opposed by a section of the Muslim community having their seat at Deoband. His opposition to the Indian National Congress failed to have a wide impact as quite a large number of Muslims joined it. Keeping it in his view, Nehru says that the influence of Ahmed Khan "was confined to certain sections of the upper classes among the Muslims, he did not touch the urban or rural masses."[11] And yet it cannot be denied that he was a great patron of learning. He founded in 1864 Scientific Society at Aligarh on the lines of the Royal Asiatic Society at Calcutta. He founded a school that soon became a college (and later Muslim University) at Aligarh that is recognised as a great centre of learning for the benefit of all people irrespective of their religion, race or nationality.

Sir Syed's Aligarh movement had the twin merit of being pro-British and anti-Congress along with having reformist overtones. He looked at the British rule as the saviour of the Muslims from the dominance of the Hindus as well as a protector and promoter of the interests of the Muslims. His movement "was based on the 'emancipatory', 'democratic' and 'progressive' characterisation of the British rule. It was essentially reformist in matters of religion and social customs and its objective was to show that Islam does not conflict with progress and reason."[12] But he apprehensively looked at the Indian National Congress that "conducted itself on the complacent assumption that all Indians profess the same religion, speak the same language, have the same way of life, that their attitude to history is similar and is based upon the same historical traditions. For the successful running of democratic government, it is essential that the majority should have the ability to govern not only themselves but also willing minorities."[13]

Sir Syed was a nationalist of course, but he espoused the cause of fragmented or sectarian nationalism. He preached the gospel of Muslim isolationism or exclusivism that found its bold manifestation in the two-nation theory of Jinnah and eventually resulted in the partition of the country in 1947. In exact opposition to what Sir Syed often reitertaed, Maulana Abul Kalam Azad stressed that every Indian was a member of the Indian nation and could not, by virtue of a common bond of religion, separate himself from the larger Indian society and claim the status of separate nationhood. Not only this, Sir Syed never sought to make himself the man of the masses like so many leaders of the Indian National Congress. Moin Shakir comments: "Sir Syed appears to have been more concerned with protecting the interests of the aristocracy rather than propounding the Islamic notion of equality."[14]

---

11. Nehru, *op. cit.*, p. 366.
12. Moin Shakir: "Dynamics of Muslim Political Thought" in Thomas Pantham and K.L. Deuschts (eds.): *Political Thought in Modern India,* p. 149.
13. *Ibid.*
14. *Ibid.*, p. 152.

33
Vivekanand

In the history of modern Indian political thought Swami Vivekanand (1863-1902) (whose real name was Narendra Nath Dutt) occupies a significant place for the reason of giving a new orientation to the cause of nationalism through the message of Hindu religion in the true sense of the term. Apparently he looked like a 'cyclonic Hindu' and 'a Hindu Napoleon'; his concept of religion had secular implications which made him a socio-religious reformer as well as a political philosopher. His messages influenced a section of the Congress leaders who were called 'extremists' and who played a significant part in transforming the character of the freedom struggle. His casual attack on the activities of the Indian National Congress in the form of ignoring the interests of the poor and backward sections of the people and his stress on the theme of social equality amounting to the elimination of exploitation of the poor at the hands of the rich people, infused the element of socialism in his political philosophy. The most notable point is that "while Ram Mohan Roy and Gokhale believed in England's Mission to India, Vivekanand like Dayanand Saraswati and Mahatma Gandhi believed in India's message to the West."[1]

Religious Nationalism: Nationalism is the synonym of patriotism or love for the country that unites the people of a particular stock by awakening common political consciousness. It is reinforced by social, economic and political sources. Ranade and Naoroji dwelt on the economic sources; P.M. Mehta, W.C. Bonnerjee and S.N. Banerjea made use of the political sources. But Vivekanand found its real place in social or religious foundations. Hence, the Swami may be credited with arousing spiritual or religious nationalism in India and, for this sake, he drew abundant material from her glorious past. He made religion the backbone of national life and realised that the greatness of our nation could be rebuilt on the foundations of its past greatness. Thus, a spiritual or religious theory of nationalism may be regarded as his "first contribution to political theory."[2]

The concept of religion and religious life was linked in Vivekanand's view with the mode of life based on the principles of peaceful cooperation of all men, of their equality and mutual respect. This distinctive feature "is inherent in the Indian people, for that enormous people is the only one in the entire history of mankind that never left the boundaries of the country to conquer other peoples, although it was itself permanently the object of plunder and oppression. In India religious life forms the

1. V.P. Varma: *Modern Indian Political Thought,* p. 109.
2. *Ibid.,* p. 117.

centre, the keynote of the whole music of national life. So social reform has to be preached by showing how much more spiritual a life the new system will bring, and politics has to be preached by showing how much it will improve the one thing that the nation wants—its spirituality."[3]

In other words, religion has to be the principal and leading force in implementing all social changes in India. As Hinduism has been the religion since ancient times, it alone is capable of rousing the people. It should not be forgotten that the Hindu "lives religiously". It should, however, not be taken that he was a sectarian or a communalist. He resorted to religion as a means of awakening national consciousness, because he saw no other source or instrument for his purpose. The goals of socio-political reforms required their own specific means of attainment, but under the Indian conditions there was no other choice. On one occasion he said: "If you want to speak of politics in India, you must speak through the language of religion."[4]

As a matter of fact, to Vivekanand religion signified the eternal principles of moral and spiritual development. An organic growth of the nation required cultivation of the virtues of service and sacrifice in the people. Spirituality and religion meant the realisation of this principle and was never to be identified with social dogmas, ecclesiastical formulations and obsolete traditions of the society. As Varma says: "Vivekanand's soul, like that of Bankim, was lit with the luminous vision of Mother India as a deity and the conception of India as the visible expression of that divine mother has been the basic concept in the writings and the utterances of the early Bengali nationalists and terrorists."[5]

The message of Vivekanand had an electrical effect on a section of the young nationalists who swelled the ranks of the 'extremist school'.[6] His utterances "made him an embodiment of the highest ideas of the renaisscant Indian nation."[7] He is the first Indian who questioned the superiority of the West and instead of apologising for his religion and defending it against the attack of the critics, boldly asserted its spiritual pre-eminence and incomparable greatness."[8] However, the men of Marxist disposition take it otherwise. M.N. Roy says that Vivekanand's messages built orthodox nationalism of the declassed young intellectuals organised into secret societies advocating violence and terrorism for the overthrow of the British rule."[9]

Metaphysics of Monism: Vivekanand preached monism of the Advaita philosophy of the Vedanta. He was convinced that it alone could be the future religion of thinking humanity. Vedanta was not only spiritual but rational in harmony with a scientific investigation of external nature. This universe has not been created by extra-cosmic

---

3. Vivekanand: *Complete Works,* Vol. III, p. 220.
4. Vivekanand: *My Life and Mission,* p. 8.
5. Varma, *op. cit.,* p. 117.
6. Romain Rolland: *Life of Vivekanand,* Vol. I, pp. 165-66.
7. R.C. Majumdar, Raichaudhary and Datta: *An Advanced History of India,* p. 876.
8. Tara Chand: *History of the Indian Freedom Movement,* Vol. II, p. 416.
9. M.N. Roy and Abani Mukherji: *India in Transition,* p. 193.

God, nor is it the work of any external genius or supernatural force. "It is self-creating, self-dissolving, self-manifesting, One Infinite Existence, the Brahma. The Vedanta ideal was of the solidarity of man, his inborn divine nature; to see God in man is the real God-vision; man is the greatest of all beings. But the abstract Vedanta must become living-poetic in everyday life; out of hopelessly intricate mythology must come concrete moral forms; and out of bewildering Yogiism must come the most scientific and practical psychology."[10]

Whether the external conforms to the internal or the internal to the external, whether matter conforms to the mind or mind to the matter, whether surroundings mould the mind or the mind moulds the circumstances, it is a very old question and still remains unanswered. However, Vivekanand is not a dualist like Hegel (who says about the primacy of mind or spirit) and Marx (who says about the primacy of matter), he is a monist and holds that both are one and live side by side, though externally independent of each other. Neither mind is derived from matter, nor matter from mind. The dualists take a wrong view of the phenomenal and noumenal worlds. One party wants to explain the whole universe by a portion of it which is external, the other by another portion which is internal. Both of these attempts are impossible. Mind and matter influence or explain each other. The only explanation is to be sought for in something which will embrace both matter and mind.

It is all in spite of the fact that while the internal or noumenal is unchanging and indestructible, the external or the phenomenal is changing and destructible. Vedanta also says about the rise and fall, or the existence of two sides as a result of which development proceeds everywhere through contradictions between good and evil, joy and sorrow, life and death. "In the very nature of things it is impossible to have only one side on earth for ever. The universe moves in the cycle of wave forms. It rises, reaches its zenith, then falls and remains in the hollow, as it were for some time, that is in the simplest, most elementary state, once more to rise, and so on. As he says: "The history of the nations is like that: they rise and they fall; after the rise comes a fall, again out of the fall comes a rise, with greater power. This motion is always going on. In the religious world, the same movement exists. In every nation's spiritual life, there is a fall as well as a rise."[11]

With this standpoint, Vivekanand made a critical analysis of the social and political decline of India. India had fallen because she had narrowed herself, gone into her shell and lost touch with other nations, and thus sunk into a 'mummified' and 'crystallised' civilisation. Caste which was necessary and desirable in its early forms, and meant to develop individuality and freedom, had become a monstrous degradation, the opposite of what it was meant to be, and had crushed the masses. Caste was a form of social organisation which was and should be kept separate from religion. Social organisations should change with the changing times."[12]

---

10. Jawaharlal Nehru: *The Discovery of India,* p. 357.
11. Vivekanand: *Complete Works,* Vol. IV, p. 116.
12. Nehru, *op. cit.,* p. 357.

Humanitarian Socialism: Affirmation of socialist values is contained in the political philosophy of Vivekanand and yet he cannot be included in any category of the doctrinaire socialists. On one occasion, he affirmed: "I am a socialist not because I think it is a perfect system, but half a loaf is better than no bread. The other systems have been tried and found wanting. Let this one be tried if for nothing else, for the novelty of the thing." His socialist ideas may be seen in his stress on liberty, equality and appeal to the rising of the masses along with their emancipation from the curse of poverty and exploitation.

Liberty of thought and action is the only condition of life, of growth and well being. 'Where it does not exist, the man, the race, and the nation must go'. If examined deeply, his concept of freedom or liberty assumes a metaphysical character when he affirms: "There is the human spirit to rebel against nature's laws. . . . We are born rebels . . . . No laws for us. As long as we obey the laws, we are like machines, and on goes the universe, and we cannot break it . . . . Freedom is the song of the soul. Bondage, alas to be bound in nature, seems its fate."[13] According to his affirmation, the concept of God emanates from the concept of the freedom of the soul. "With the conception of God as a perfect free Being, man cannot rest eternally in this bondage. . . . . The conception of God, therefore, is as essential and as fundamental a part of mind as is the idea of bondage. Both are the outcome of the idea of freedom."[14]

The whole universe in its constant motion represents the dominant quest for freedom. The light of liberty is the only condition of growth. It is well observed: "To advance towards freedom—physical, mental and spiritual—and help others to do so is the supreme prize of man. Those social rules which stand in the way of the unfoldment of this freedom are injurious, and steps should be taken to destroy them speedily. Those institutions should be encouraged by which men advance to the path of freedom."[15]

Liberty also implies fearlessness, strength and capacity for resistance. 'If there is a sin in this world, it is weakness; avoid all weaknesses, weakness is death'. He exhorted the people to be bold. 'What our country wants now are muscles of iron and nerves of steel, gigantic wills which nothing can resist, which can penetrate into the mysteries and the secrets of the universe, and will accomplish their purpose in any fashion, even if it meant going down to the bottom of the ocean and meeting death face to face.' Hinduism was to be made aggressive. He asserted that *abhayam* (fearlessness) 'is the essence of the Vedic and Vedantic scriptures. The dynamic gospel of *Bhagwad Gita* lays stress on manliness'. This strength must come to the people through education. 'The will is stronger than anything else. Everything must go down before the will, for that comes from God. . . . a pure and strong will is omnipotent.'

Equality is the necessary complement of liberty. So Vivekanand laid stress on the elmination of untouchability. For this religion should not be blamed. The people create such social evils. The masses must be awakened first. The masses are the backbone of

13. Vivekanand: *Complete Works,* Vol. I, pp. 334-35.
14. *Ibid.,* pp. 335-36.
15. Romain Rolland: *Life of Vivekanand,* Vol. II, p. 753.

the country. They produce wealth and food. If the masses are ignored and humiliated, they cannot contribute to the growth of national strength. The masses live in the cottages; they should be elevated. On one occasion, he said: "I consider that the great national sin is the neglect of the masses, and this is one of the causes of our downfall. No amount of politics would be of any avail until the masses in India are once more well educated, well fed, and well cared for. They pay for our education, they build our temples, but in return they get kicks. They are practically our slaves. If we want to regenerate India, we must work for them."[16]

The socialistic affirmations of Vivekanand find place in his bold affirmation that four evils should be eradicated at the earliest—priestcraft, poverty, ignorance and tyranny. If a person pays no heed to them, he is a traitor. He accused the Indian National Congress of being pro-rich or a body of persons 'who are morally and spiritually dead' and so he asked as to what it had done for the masses. The poor and the distresed people must be helped, rather worshipped. It is known as his doctrine of *Daridranarayan.* Moreover, his emphasis on the rule of the masses in future is known as his message of *Shudra Raj* or Shudrocracy. The rule of the masses has already taken place in the Western countries and it is being vigorously preached by the socialists, anarchists, nihilists, etc. The masses are the vanguards of the social revolution that is to come. "The first glow of the dawn of this new power has already begun to break slowly upon the Western world and the thoughtful are at their wits end to reflect upon the final issue of this fresh phenomenon."[17]

Vivekanand's assertion that religion and nationalism could not be understandable to the hungry and the naked people was really a socialistic affirmation which inspired the leaders of the national movement to think in terms of redefining their purposes and goals. The task of rendering humanitarian and philanthropic activities was taken up by the leaders of the Ramakrishna Mission. But a critic of Marxist orientation may discover some point of attack in that Vivekanand offered no course or strategy to implement what he so ardently desired. "Vivekanand's programme of national reconstruction is a half-way house compromise. It stops in the middle. Oppening the eyes of the toilers so that they can realise the cause of their poverty and exploitation and wake up like a giant all these are very good and necessary too. But then what? What is the means for achieving their salvation, what is the path before them?"[18]

However, such criticism is not well grounded. Vivekanand was not a political leader like Lenin of Russia or Mao of China who offered their ideas and then sought to put them into practice. He was a *swami,* (monk) a socio-religious reformer like Ram Mohan Roy and Dayanand who delivered messages and then inspired the people to follow and implement them. He was a social and political philosopher, not a practitioner of his ideas like Nehru and Gandhi.

16. Vivekanand: *Complete Works,* Vol. V, p. 132.
17. *Ibid.,* Vol. IV, pp. 467-68.
18. B.K. Roy: *Socio-Political Views of Vivekanand* (New Delhi: People's Publishing House, 1986), p. 57.

Universalism: Vivekanand is the first great religious leader who delivered messages not only to the people of his country but for the people of other countries as well. He travelled to the United States and many other countries where he spoke on religion and philosophy and thereby impressed a very large number of people. This was given the name of his 'world mission'. He looked at the welfare of his country in a way that covered the good of the entire humankind. The problems of the Indian people were the problems of all people and so their solution could be possible at the international level. Even in politics and sociology, the problems that were only national twenty years ago could be solved when looked in the broader light of international grounds. 'International organisations, international combinations and international laws are the cry of the day'. Taking inspiration from Vedanta philosophy, he affirmed; "I am throughly convinced that no individual or nation can live to holding itself apart from the community of others, and wherever such an attempt has been made under false ideas of greatness, policy or holiness, the result has always been disastrous to the secluding one."

India had much to give to the West in the form of spirituality, but it also had much to take from the West in the form of material benefits. For this friendship and equality were required. 'If you want to be equal with an American or an Englishman, you will have to teach as well as to learn. The 'divinity of man' should be recognised. The real man lay behind all artificial differences of religion, race, caste, land, etc.' Herein we find a faint reflection of the message of Ram Mohan Roy's universalism and a clear forecast of the 'universal man' of Tagore whose intimate vision was essential for the realisation of universal brotherhood. "At a time when the world was convulsed with scepticism, nilhilism and materialism, as an Advaitist, Vivekanand stood for the resuscitation of the universal religious spirit. For him the awakening and liberation of India was to be a stage for the realisation of universal love and brotherhood."[19] Vivekanand's world mission is differently evaluated. While Nehru comments that he "grew progressively more international in outlook,"[20] M.N. Roy debunks it as 'spiritual imperialism or the romantic vision of conquering the world by spiritual superiority'.[21]

Critical Appreciation: Great are the contributions of Vivekanand not only for the people of our country but for the entire human race. His bold affirmations created aggressive nationalism that was adopted by the 'extremist' leaders of that time like Tilak, Lajpat Rai and B.C. Pal. Hume had founded the Indian National Congress with a view to 'save the British Empire' and the 'moderate' leaders of that time became his faithful disciples. It was, in the words of Hume, 'sane and loyal nationalism'. It was given an assertive form by the Swami and which found its faithful adherents in the 'extremist' leaders. The second wave prevailed over the first wave. Gandhiji borrowed much from the extremists, but he refined their methods with his novel techniques of non-violence and *satyagraha.* It may be called the third wave which judiciously assimilated the ideological contents of the 'moderates' and the 'extremists' and yet

19. Varma, *op. cit.,* p. 122.
20. Nehru, *op. cit.,* p. 358.
21. Roy and Mukherji: *India in Transition,* p. 193.

imparted a new dimension to them that saw its triumph in the independence of the country in 1947.

Although Nehru was critical of the social and economic philosophy of the Hindu revivalists and 'extremist' leaders in general, he lauded the contribution of Vivekanand in particular. According to him, Vivekanand "was one of the great founders, if you like you may use any other word, of the modern national movement of India, and a great number of people who took more or less active part in the movement at a later date drew their inspiration from him. Directly or indirectly, he has powerfuly influenced the India of today."[22] More colourful is the observation of Rolland who says: "From his ashes, like those of the Phoenix of old, has sprung anew the conscience of India—the magic bird—faith in her unity and in the Great Message, brooded over from Vedas times by the dreaming spirit of his ancient race—the message for which it must render account to the rest of mankind."[23]

22. Jawaharlal Nehru: *Sri Ramakrishna and Swami Vivekanand* (Calcutta: Advaita Ashram, 1960), pp. 6-7.
23. Romain Rolland: *The Life of Vivekanand* (Almora: Advaita Ashram, 1953), Vol. I, p. 7.

34
Aurobindo

Aurobindo Ghose, widely known as Sri Aurobindo, (1872-1950) has a significant place in the galaxy of modern Indian thinkers by virtue of his metaphysical interpretations of important social and political themes. Before being a *rishi* (seer) in his *ashram* at Pondicherry, he was associated with the revolutionary movement of the extremist leaders like Tilak and Bipan Chandra Pal. It may be seen in his link with Lotus and Dagger Society (a secret body at London) and then with Anusilan Samiti—a secret body at Calcutta. As an extremist leader, he decried the affirmations of moderate leaders like Naoroji, Pherozeshah Mehta and Surendranath Banerjea and nicknamed their organisation as 'Indian Un-National Congress'. Like other extremist leaders, he sternly opposed the partition of Bengal in 1905. In his booklet *Bhowani Mandir,* he exhorted his followers to use the methods of passive resistance and violence to throw out the Demon seated on the bosom of the Mother. Mother Shakti demanded the blood of the devotees for Her release from the bondage. On account of being involved in such activities, he was caught and prosecuted. He passed two years in the Alipore jail at Calcutta. After his release in 1910, he shifted his place to Pondicherry where he built his *ashram* (abode) and then became a *rishi.* Now he wrote a number of books and articles with his idealistic approach on social and political themes in highly philosophical and poetic tones. It is well observed: "Samkara was a philosopher and Tagore was a litterateur, but Aurobindo was both."[1]

Spiritual Nationalism: Nationalism is a sentiment or a mentality that informs the people of a particular stock to unite and thereby have a state of their own. It is anti-bondage. It emerged in Europe in the modern age with the rise of nation-states. It entailed the doom of Christendom that had so far been under the absolute sway of the Roman Pope. In the countries of Asia and Africa, nationalism emerged as a force to overthrow the rule of the colonialists. So it became anti-foreign rule or anti-colonialism. In India it emerged after the 'great upheaval' of 1857 and it took an organised form after the establishment of the Indian National Congress in 1885. Many leaders emerged on the scene with their divergent views. While some leaders (like M.G. Ranade, Dadabhai Naoroji, and G.K. Gokhale) laid stress on economic factors as exploitation of the country to drain away her wealth to England, others like (P.M. Mehta, and S.N. Banerjea) laid stress on political factors like subjugation of our country by means of force. Different from both, some leaders (like Swami Vivekanand and Tilak) invoked

1. V.P. Varma: *Modern Indian Political Thought,* p. 327.

spiritual force to strengthen the bonds of nationalism. Aurobindo's name has its place among those who spiritualised nationalism and politics.

In Aurobindo's view, nationalism is a religion sustained by the force of Divinity. It creates unity among the people which should be regarded as Divine Unity. God sends a super-man (*Virat Purush*) who unites the people and who raises the banner of revolt to get redemption from alien bondage. India is not merely a geographical expression but Motherland of all her children who are equal regardless of their faith or caste or creed. All should act according to the law of *Swadharma* and thus no section of the society should be suppressed.

The essential feature of Aurobindo's such a metaphysical interpretation is that he aligns it with universalism. He discards the case of exclusive and aggressive nationalism as preached by Herder and Hitler of Germany. His concept of nationalism is soft and enlightened and he links it with cosmopolitanism in the style of Tagore and Gandhi. As he says: "Nationalism is simply the passionate aspiration for the realisation of the Divine Unity in the nation, a unity in which all the component individuals, however various and apparently unequal their functions as political, social and economic factors, are yet really and fundamentally one and equal. In the idea of Nationalism which India will set before the world, there will be an essential equality between man and man, between caste and caste, between class and class, all beings, as Mr. Tilak has pointed out, different but equal and united parts of the *Virat Purush* as realised in the nation."

Herein we may find a fine synthesis of great elements of Indian culture with the values of universalism or cosmopolitanism. As Varma says: "Nationalism is not the last category of Aurobindo's political philosophy. He has been one of the earliest prophets of human unity. He has a vision not of the mechanical political unity of man, but dreamer of an inner oneness of all human beings. All kinds of separations and dividing walls are to crumble and man is to be united in an inward fraternity. Co-operation, mutuality, reciprocity, forbearance and love are to be the key factors moulding the lives of men."[2]

The idea of a super-man (*Virat Purush*) as its architect may not be understandable to a person of average comprehension. His message that man should evolve beyond mind to the super-mind is like a brilliant prescription for those who are above the animal level of human existence. Nationalism has been a great force all over the world, but in most of the cases it has played a negative or destructive role which informs Tagore to desire 'a world not fragmented by narrow domestic walls.' Enlightened nationalism, as appreciated by Woodrow Wilson and Jawaharlal Nehru, has its own form whose triumph may be seen in the creation of international organisations after the First World War. But spiritual nationalism is just a vision of the philosophers that gives refreshing touches to the academics of world peace and progress.

Swaraj: Indian national leaders often talked about Swaraj (self-rule), but there was a great divergence in their views. Not only this, none was clear about the implications of

2. Varma, *op. cit.,* p. 317.

Swaraj in the long phase of our freedom struggle until Jawaharlal Nehru, Sardar Patel and Subhas Chandra Bose defined it in terms of 'complete independence'. Naoroji, Surendranath Banerjea and Gokhale thought of Swaraj in terms of the 'Self-rule within the Empire'. Annie Besant, Jinnah and Tilak identified Swaraj with Home Rule or half-independence only in the internal sphere of administration. Gandhi thought of 'self-rule within the Empire if possible, without the Empire if necessary.' Different from all is the view of Aurobindo. When he was actively involved in the extremist movement, he meant by Swaraj termination of the British rule by all possible means whether passive resistance or insurrection. But after being a *rishi,* he imparted a spiritual meaning to it in the visionary style of Tagore.

The point to be especially noted here is that while the national leaders of the moderate and extremist schools thought about Swaraj in mundane terms, Aurobindo spiritualised its meaning and connected it with spiritual Swaraj all over the world. By Swaraj he means an ideal condition of spiritually emanicpated human beings living in a nation-state of their own and the state itself living in a free union of such states. It is evident that at the lower level, Swaraj desires a community of spiritually enlightened citizens of a nation-state and at the higher level a world community of spiritually emancipated humankind.

For Aurobindo, the emancipation of India was essential for fulfilling her destiny as a spiritual guide to humanity. India must play a seminal role in the spiritual regeneration of humanity.[3] As he says: "Swaraj is the necessary condition in order for India to accomplish the work for which she is destined. The success of the national movement, both as a political and a spiritual movement, is necessary for India and still more necessary for Europe. The whole world is interested in seeing that India becomes free so that she may become herself. "Swaraj cannot be fully realised by political independence alone, however, but in the resumption of her role as a spiritual guide to mankind. Swaraj is the fulfulment of the ancient life of India under modern conditions, the return of the *satyuga* of national greatness, the resumption by her of the great role of a teacher and a guide, self-liberation of the people for the final fulfilment of the Vedantic ideal in politics; this is the true Swaraj for India."[4]

Aurobindo's conception of Swaraj has a metaphysical nature in view of the fact that he integrates it with his conception of nationalism that is integrally connected with religion. "In his writings we find the gospel of nationalism as a pure religion suited to the needs of the time."[5] He wanted the great values of Indian culture and ethics like *Dharma, Tapasya, Jnanam* and *Shakti* "to become the dynamic galvanisers of a rejuvenated nation. Nationalism aligned with Swaraj is not the last category of his political philosophy. In a highly philosophical tone, he clears the conception of Swaraj

3. K.L. Deutsch: "Sri Aurobindo and the Search for Political and Spiritual Perfection" in Thomas Pantham and Deutsch (eds): *Political Thought in Modern India,* p. 198.
4. Aurobindo Ghose: *Sri Aurobindo Birth Centenary Library* (Pondicherry, 1972), Vol. 15, p. 902.
5. Ronaldshay: *The Heart of Aryavarta,* p. 128.

for India sustained by the forces of nationalism and religion (Hindu).[6] In appreciation of it, a noted English leader commented that Aurobindo "made the connection between his devout Hinduism and his strenuous nationalism clear."[7]

Since Aurobindo had remained actively associated with the revolutionary movement before his being a *rishi,* his conception of Swaraj looks like a unique blending of India's freedom from the British rule with the metaphysical projection of a spiritually free humanity. Thus, while the first phase of his conception (relating to India's freedom from the British Raj) is clear and easily understandable, it is not so with the later phase of his thought. Swaraj becomes an Absolute Ideal in the end and becomes a pleasant dream for the men of philosophical disposition.

State: Aurobindo desires a state that has its place in a free world union. State is a part of society which is organic and has a soul and the individual is also a spiritual self. Autocracy kills the spiritual self, hence state should have a democratic set up. State is known as a coercive organisation, but he sanctions use of force against erring and recalcitrant physical individuals, not against spiritually oriented persons who by obeying the dictates of, what Rousseau calls, the 'general will' can do no wrong.

To Aristotle, state is the supreme association having its goal in ensuring 'good life' to its people. But to Aurobindo, it is an ideal institution having its final place in the free world union. Such a state ensures Swaraj (self-rule) that guarantees spiritual freedom and equality to all. However, it is necessary that all people have their spiritual development so that they no longer live, in the words of Plato, in 'a city of the swine.' As he says: "I again call on those nobler spirits among us who are working erroneously, it may be, but with incipient or growing sincerity and nobleness of mind, to divert their strenuous efforts from the promotion of narrow class interests, from silly squabbles about offices and salaried positions, from a philanthropy laudable in itself and worthy of rational pursuit, but meagre in the range of benevolence and ineffectual towards promoting the nearest interest of the nation, into that vaster channel through which alone the healing waters may be conduited to the lips of their ailing and tortured country."[8]

In empirical terms, such a state of Aurobindo is democratic, but in normative terms it is an ideal having spiritually emanicpated people like Rousseau's civic republicans of a 'community'. Moreover, the goal of such a state is to join the free world union set up on a federal basis. As he says: "The ultimate result must be the formation of a World-State and the most desirable form of it would be a federation of free nationalities in which all subjection or forced inequality and subordination of one to another would have disappeared and, though some might preserve a greater natural influence, all would have an equal status. A confederacy would give the greatest freedom to the nations constituting the World-State."[9]

---

6. Varma, *op. cit.,* p. 317.
7. J. Ramsay MacDonald: *The Awakening of India,* p. 182.
8. Varma, *op. cit.,* p. 304.
9. *Ibid.,* p. 307.

Such affirmations of Aurobindo place him in the category of great idealists like Kant, Green and Gandhi. A critic may point out that, instead of establishing an ideal state of his conception on this earth, he takes the existing state to mystical heights. The whole description becomes like a piece of fantastic academic exercise relishable only to those who are well enlightened and think in terms of the struggle of ideas, in the words of M.N. Roy, at the human level of existence.

Integral Sociology: Aurobindo's sociological views are directly linked with his philosophical vision. The individual is the ultimate foundation of human society, the focus around which and for the sake of which all human institutions are created and exist. The family, various social organisations, nations and other 'aggregates' are all merely a means for the greater satisfaction of the individual. In the family he experiences spiritual and physical pleasures. In the public organisations, there is a less intimate but broader field of endeavour for the individual and his instincts—satisfaction of emotions involved in social life, communication within a collective, joint efforts, exchange etc. In the nation, he finds the means for satisfying even more remote feelings and interests —power, politics, etc.

Man is not merely a social being, he is rather an autonomous, independent individual regarding his life as the centre of the universe. He views man's individual being, his material practice and thinking, not as a concrete manifestation of social being but rather as a 'separate existence' based on the development of his life, satisfying his mental tendencies, emotional and vital needs and physical being according to his own desire governed by the reason."[10]

In Aurobindo's view, society develops from the less complicated forms of 'aggregate states' to the more complicated ones (horde, tribe, race, class, state, nation, empire) and in the future a world union. The highest form of this 'aggregate state' is in our period the 'nation', for it ensures in the best way the individual's psychical unity, consolidating the people physically and politically in defence of their interests. Moreover, the emergence of the nation is the result of the operation of the objective law of nature. For this reason all modern attempts to destroy by force or undermine the nation are stupid and futile.[11]

It is a fact that the purpose of society is to provide the necessary conditions for the achievement of human ideals. It follows that the ideals of society are to be derived from a correct understanding of the 'real' characteristics of human existence. As Aurobindo says: "The object of all society should, therefore, be and must become, as man grows conscious of his real being, nature and destiny and not as now only a part of it, first to provide the conditions of life and growth by which Individual Men—not isolated men or a class or a privileged race, but all individual men according to their capacity—and the race through the growth of its individuals may travel towards the divine perfection. It must be possible, secondly, as mankind generally grows more and more near to some figure of the Divine in life."[12]

10. Aurobindo Ghose: "The Human Cycle" in *Selected Works,* Vol, XV, p. 149.
11. *Ibid.,* p. 48.
12. Sri Aurobindo: *The Human Cycle,* Pondicherry Ashram, 1962, pp. 83-84.

As for man's actual inequality, it is the result of the imperfection of the 'aggregate' (economic, political and other types of associations) in which the individuals have so far united to attain their personal goals. It is precisely under the conditions of imperfect 'aggregate states' that such intolerable evils emerged as oppression, racial discrimination, lack of rights, poverty, etc. His conclusion is that the principal contradiction of human life is between individual and society, or aggregate, and this contradiction can be resolved if all men learn the ideal law of social development and if each individual restructures his practical life in accordance with that law. However, a 'spiritualised society' can and must be built only within the framework of the entire humanity. To achieve this goal all nations, as the most stable 'psychical communities' of individuals, must unite themselves in a single World State—a "world union founded upon the principle of liberty and variations in a free and intelligent unity."[13]

In an explicit political application of his vision, Aurobindo contends that there is an inherent relationship between liberty, equality and fraternity what, in the words of Ernest Barker, constitutes the theme of justice in a society. Not only this, the synthesis may exist in their proper and harmonious blending. None of the three should stretch itself at the cost of the other or others. When liberty is taken to the extreme, it creates the situation of 'competitive individualism' in liberal democratic societies. When equality is taken to its extreme, it first arrives at strife and then constitutes an artificial and a machine-made society as obtaining in socialist countries. In the spiritualised society, the fulfilment of the individual and the community can emerge only through a supermental (supermind) consciousness and power where the predominance of fraternity or brotherhood allows the union of the impulses for freedom and equality. Fraternity is grounded in the spirit and without it neither liberty nor equality can be actualised.[14]

Critical Appreciation: The social and political thought of Aurobindo is so mystical that it is far away from the world of reality as it prevails and, for this reason, it is hardly of any significance to one who tries to take things in their practical perspective. Hence, a critic observes: "It must be clearly stated that the enunciation of the deeper elements of the Indian value system by Aurobindo remains confined to an esoteric circle, not only because it was couched in the most obscure language, but also because no attempt had been made to link it to any concrete plan of action or to the concrete issues raised by the fulfilment of human needs. He did not take into account the real determinants of the social situation which the historical process had created at this point of time, nor did he provide the precise action required to remove the poverty of the teeming millions, the gap between the proclaimed ideals and their practice."[15]

A critic having his mind set on the philosophy of materialism would easily say that all ideas of Aurobindo are too idealistic and metaphysical having nothing to do with the world of reality. Such arguments may be furnished by anybody who desires

13. Aurobindo: *The Ideal of Human Unity,* p. 234.
14. *Ibid.,* pp. 546-47.
15. V.R. Mehta: *Beyond Marxism: Towards an Alternative Perspective,* p. 58.

to see and describe things in their realistic form. Different is the case of Aurobindo who has contributed to the philosophy of spiritual evolutionism like Vivekanand, Tilak and Gandhi. He could well establish a synthesis of the East and the West in his highly philosophical descriptions. It is well ohserved: "The vision of man and the world emerging from Aurobindo's synthesis of the East and the West will remain an inspiration for generations of men and women in their quest for wisdom, peace, harmony and joy."[16]

16. P. Puligandla: *Foundations of Indian Philosophy,* p. 268.

35
Gokhale

Gopal Krishna Gokhale (1866-1915) occupies an important place in the galaxy of great Indian nationalist leaders called the 'moderates' or 'liberals' owing to their differences with a group of other leaders called 'extremists' or 'militants'. While the former expressed their faith in British sense of justice and fairplay and subscribed to P.M. Mehta's slogan of 'Reform, Reform, Reform', the latter denounced the British raj for political subjugation and exploitation of the country and raised the slogan of 'Swaraj, Swadeshi and Boycott'. While Gokhale is known for being a leading light of the former, Tilak deserves the same for being the arch-priest of the latter. Gokhale served as a teacher of History and Economics at the Fergusson College of Poona and edited a journal of the Poona Sarvajanik Sabha (*Sudharak*). In 1905 he formed the Servants of India Society whose constitution reflected his deep sense of idealism and loyalty to the British Raj. As a true disciple of M.G. Ranade, he adhered to the path of constitutionalism which found its best expression in his occasional speeches and writings. The pandemonium at the Surat Congress (1907) informed him about the deficiency of proper rules and regulations necessary for the working of a national organisation. So he drafted the Constitution of the Indian National Congress that was adopted at the Madras Congress in the following year. It is true that he appreciated the British Raj, his utterances were punctuated with ironical remarks hitting at its shortcomings. He "wrote in his gently ironical way of the inscrutable wisdom of Providence which had ordained the British connection for India."[1]

Liberal Nationalism: The early Indian national leaders began their career with three cardinal principles—admiration of India's connection with the British rule on account of their faith in British sense of justice and fairplay, demand for more and more reforms for the betterment of the country, and use of peaceful and constitutional means to prosecute their movement. Gokhale subscribed to this tradition set by his predecessors like P.M. Mehta, Naoroji, W.C. Bonnerjee, S.N. Banerjea, etc. These leaders had been brought up in the Westernised environment and were said to have drunk the 'new wine of Western learning', or they had been a class of citizens 'Indians in blood and colour, but English in taste, opinions, in morals and intellect'. It was remarked that they "had plucked with both hands the fruits of the trees of Western knowledge, as they were the humble students of Kant, Spencer, Burke and Mill."[2]

---

1. Jawaharlal Nehru: *The Discovery of India,* p. 307.
2. Valentine Chirol: *Indian Unrest,* p. 24.

Like the pioneers of Indian renaissance (as Raja Ram Mohan Roy, Sir Syed Ahmed Khan and M.G. Ranade), Gokhale admired the British raj for establishing 'rule of law' in the country under whose auspices India could have her all-round progress. To him it was like 'a divine dispensation'. In his budget speech in the Imperial Legislative Council (1903), he said: "The India of the future under Providence, will not be an India of diminishing plenty, of empty prospect, or of justifiable discontent; but one of expanding industry, of awakened facilities, of increasing prosperity, and of more widely distributed comfort and wealth. I have faith in the conscience and purpose of my own country and I believe in the almost illimitable capacities of this. But under no other conditions can this future be realised than the unchallenged supremacy of the Paramount Power, and under no other controlling authority is this capable of being maintained than that of the British Crown."[3]

Like liberal leaders, Gokhale demanded reforms. In his presidential address delivered at the Kashi Congress (1905), he presented a list of nine demands which are as follows:

1. Expansion of the Legislative Councils raising the number of elected members to one-half, requiring the budgets to be passed by them.
2. Inclusion of at least 3 members in the India Council of the Secretary of State
3. Creation of advisory boards in all districts to advise the Collectors in matters of administration.
4. Recruitment of judges from the bar.
5. Separation of executive and judicial functions.
6. Reduction of military expenditure.
7. Extension of primary education.
8. Facilities for industrial and technical education, and
9. Eradication of rural indebtedness.

These demands "represent in a summarised form the political philosophy of the Indian moderates."[4]

Gokhale appreciated the Indian Councils Act of 1909 and, with Surendranath Banerjea, he lauded its enactment as 'their crowning success'. The then Secretary of State (Lord Morley) and the Governor-General (Lord Minto) were so impressed with the ideas and role of Gokhale that they asked him for sending some proposals to be accommodated in the next constitutional dispensation for the country. Thus, he drafted a list of such proposals in 1915 that is known as his 'political testament'. It had proposals like inclusion of three members in the 6-member Executive Council of the Governor-General, expansion of the Central Legislative Council to have 100 members with 80 elected members, extension of local self-government, introduction

---

3. *Speeches of G.K. Gokhale* (Madras: G.A. Natesan and Co., 1920) p. 88.
4. V.P. Varma: *Modern Indian Political Thought,* p. 193.

of provincial autonomy, commissions in the army and navy to be given to the Indians, etc.[5]

Despite the fact that Gokhale was a great liberal leader, who admired the British Raj and subscribed to the path of constitutionalism in demanding reforms for the country, he was a perfect nationalist too. In his mild tone, he criticised the role of white bureaucracy that demoralised the Indian people and led a life of extreme lavishness at the expense of the highly poor and starving conditions of the teeming millions. In 1897 he appeared before the Welby Commission, and frankly said: "The excessive costliness of the foreign agency is not, however, its only evil. There is a more evil which, if anything, is even greater. A kind of dwarfing or stunning of the Indian race is going on under the present system. . . . The full height to which our manhood is capable of rising can never be reached by us under the present system. The moral elevation which every self-governing people feel cannot be felt by us. Our administrative and military talents must gradually disappear owing to sheer disuse, till at last our lot as hewers of wood and drawers of water in our own country is stereotyped."[6]

The notorious event of the Partition of Bengal in 1905 infuriated Gokhale to an extent that, like an extremist, he nicknamed Viceroy Lord Curzon as 'India's Second Aurangzeb' and he preferred the course of *swadeshi* to be adopted. This was the first occasion when the moderates as well as the extremists with one voice demanded cancellation of this partition that was done not for the sake of administrative efficiency and economy (as officially claimed) but to weaken the rising power of Indian nationalism. And yet Gokhale did not convert himself into an extremist. He did not subscribe to the path of boycott of foreign goods. He managed to persuade Naoroji to be the President of the Indian National Congress at the Calcutta Congress of 1906 and thereby he could defeat the ambition of Tilak who wanted to grab this high post. Again, at the Surat Congress of the following year, he sided with his moderate colleagues who managed to choose Rash Behari Ghose as the President against the wishes of Tilak. However, it should not be assumed that he was a reactionary or anti-nationalist leader. On the contrary, he with his colleagues "represented at that time the most progressive force in the Indian society."[7]

Economic Nationalism: As a disciple of M.G. Ranade and as a student of G.V. Joshi, this teacher of Economics at the Fergusson College of Poona made use of powerful economic arguments to hit at the drawbacks of the British rule and to draw attention of the Government towards agricultural and industrial development of the country. Though a leading light of the moderate school, he did not hesitate in attacking the economic policy of the Government in his budget speeches delivered in the Imperial

5. These proposals were drafted by Gokhale in consultation with P.M. Mehta and Sir Agha Khan. It was kept like a secret and so these proposals could see light of the day in 1917. However, it was somehow leaked. So 19 members of the Central Legislative Council submitted their own proposals in this regard. It is known as the Memorandum of Nineteen (1916).
6. Cited in Tara Chand: *The History of the Freedom Movement in India,* Vol. II, pp. 572-73.
7. R.P. Dutt: *India Today,* p. 322.

Legislative Council wherein he launched vehement attack on the budget and demanded several measures to alleviate the economic ills of the country. On various occasions, he demanded cut in military expenditure, reduction of land revenue, curtailment of import duty, abolition of salt tax, raising level of the limit of income tax and the like. He insisted that the money thus saved should be spent on the activities of public welfare. Such criticisms could shock the framers of the budget of the Government of India. In 1904 Edward Law, the then Finance Member, cried out in exasperation: "When he (Gokhale) takes his seat at this Council table, he perhaps unconsciously adopts the role and demeanour of the habitual mourner, and his sad wails and lamentations at the delinqencies of the Government are as piteous as long practice and training can make them."[8]

Gokhale fully subscribed to the 'economic drain' theory of Naoroji implying that the British rulers were taking away the wealth of this country and that was the real cause of India's poverty. For this he called British rule as 'un-British'. Hence, he appreciated the call for 'swadeshi' given by the extremist leaders. He courageously pointed out that the British rulers had converted this country into their colony so as to exploit and take away her resources to the benefit of their own country. To them India was like a *kamdhenu* or the milch cow for England. He condemned the use of Indian army and revenues for the purposes of expansion of the British empire in Asia and Africa as being another form of economic exploitation.

The economic views of Gokhale had negative as well as positive aspects. While he demanded that the British Government should not do this or that to consolidate its colonial hold, it should also do much for the welfare of the masses. It should take steps to help the people in establishing their industries and to give them adequate protection. It should take measures to prevent famines, to provide irrigation facilities and to eliminate rural indebtedness. It should provide medical facilities and primary education. Since he had raised such points in the Central Legislative Council, he was unofficially declared as the 'leader of the opposition'. It enhanced his reputation as a great parliamentarian as well. As his biographer says: "Like Byron, he could have said that he woke up one fine morning and found himself famous."[9]

Such points were raised by other national leaders of that time as well like Naoroji, Dinshaw E. Wacha and R.C. Dutt, but Gokhale's presentation overshadowed all. It appeared that "the nature of economic policies advocated by the Indian national leaders from 1880 to 1905 gave to those years the character of being the period of economic nationalism."[10] Gokhale realised that the revival of handicraft industries destroyed by the rulers of the East India Company was not inevitable in the age of machine-made goods, so he demanded that the British Government should make alternative arrangements to restore indigenous economy. The state by a judicious system of protection should then ensure conditions under which new infant industries could grow

8. Bipan Chandra and others: *India's Struggle for Independence,* p. 122.
9. B.R. Nanda: *Gokhale: The Indian Moderates and the Raj,* p. 138.
10. Bipan Chandra: "Economic Nationalism" in Sekhar Bandyopadhyay, (ed.): *Nationalist Movement in India: A Reader,* p. 19.

up, and until the new industries could stand on their legs, it was the duty of the State to have the protection wall around them.

One important point to be noted here is that in the struggle for independence, economic issues had their natural entanglement with political issues and so Gokhale not only raised demands for the agricultural and industrial development of the country, he also desired that the British government should do the needful and also train the Indian people to move ahead in the same direction. It is true that the leaders of the Congress did not place economic issues in the forefront as they were more concerned with political issues. It is for this reason that the demands for economic reforms were raised after about a decade of the formation of the national organisation. So Swami Vivekanand accused the Congress of being a party of the rich people who were like dead weights and who never bothered for the good of the poor and the distressed people. Such a view was rather rash and mistaken as the Swami did not look at the things from close quarters. Like other national leaders stressing economic issues of that time, Gokhale's criticisms of the British rule as well as his suggestions for remedying the matters by new economic policies was basically anti-imperialist. Gokhale with such leaders "demanded fundamental changes in the existing economic relations between India and Britain. Even when their political demands were moderate, their economic demands were radically nationalist."[11]

Good Government: The issue of good government had been taken up by a number of social and political philosophers. Though national leaders of the first and second generations loudly talked of *swaraj,* they never presented a picture of the polity to be established after the achievement of self-rule. Credit should be given to Gokhale who took up this issue and gave four tests of a good government. These were:

1. "What measures the government adopts for the moral and material improvement of the mass of people and, under these measures, I do not include those applicances of modern government which the British Government has applied in this country, because they were appliances necessary for its very existence, though they have benefited the people, such as the construction of the Railways, the introduction of Posts and Telegraph, and things of that kind. By measures for the moral and material improvement of the people, I mean what the Government does for education or sanitation and for agricultural development and so forth."
2. "What steps the Government takes up to give us a large share in the administration of our local affairs—in municipalities and local boards."
3. "What voice the Government gives us in its Councils—in those deliberative assemblies where policies are considered."
4. "We must consider how far Indians are admitted into the ranks of public services."[12]

11. *Ibid.*
12. V.P. Varma, *op. cit.,* pp. 195-96.

The first test is the most important of all. Gokhale is perhaps the first national leader who stressed the point of moral improvement of the people of the country. He charged the British rule with the crime of infusing a sense of inferiority in the minds of the people. The English rulers had showed their racial arrogance at the time of the Ilbert Bill controversy in 1883. Even after that they continued to treat the Indians as 'hewers of wood and drawers of water'. In his presidential address at the Kashi Congress (1905), he said: "On the moral side the present situation is steadily destroying our capacity and dwarfing us as men of action. On the material side, it has resulted in a fearful impoverishment of the people. For a hundred years or more, now India has been for members of the dominant race, a country where fortunes were to be made to be taken out and spent elsewhere."

Nation-Building: India is a land of many religions, creeds, castes, communities, languages, dialects and ways of life. It is called her diversity. Hence, the English writers dismissed the claim of the India as being a nation, even a nationality. In 1883 Sir John Seeley remarked: "The notion that India is a nationality rests upon that vulgar error which Political Science principally aims at eradicating . . . . India is not a political but only a geographical expression like Europe and Africa. It does not mark the territory of a nation and a language, but the territory of many nations and many languages."[13] More emphatic was the comment of Sir John Strachey: "This is the first and most essential thing to learn about India that there is not and never was an India, possessing according to European ideas, any sort of unity—physical, social, political or religious; no Indian nation, no people of India, of which we hear so much."[14]

This was, indeed, a formidable challenge that our national leaders faced and gave a befitting reply to their critics. In his presidential address at the first session of the Indian National Congress held at Bombay in December, 1885, W.C. Bonnerjee called this organisation as 'National Assembly of India'. Gokhale took up this challenge and boldly responded by hitting at the racial arrogance of the Englishmen and the autocratic hold of the white bureaucracy. He defined *'swadeshi'* as the call of patriotism that was another name of nationalism. In his presidential address at the Kashi Congress (1905), he said that the idea of *swadeshi* or 'one's own country' "is one of the noblest conceptions that have ever stirred the heart of humanity."

However, Gokhale found two obstacles in the way of achieving the goal of national integration—issue of the minorities and the pitiable conditions of the depressed castes. The Muslim League had demanded reservation of seats in the Legislative Councils on the plea of the Muslims being in minority. The Indian Councils Act of 1909 had provided them such reservations along with separate electorates. It was stoutly condemned at the annual session of the Congress held at Lahore in December, 1909 and a resolution was passed to scrap it at the earliest possible moment. Gokhale was a party to it. But as an enlightened nationalist, he realised its urgency and so he discovered a possible way out. In a note submitted to the Secretary of State for India (Lord Morley), he proposed

13. Seeley: *The Expansion of England,* pp. 254-57.
14. Strachey: *India-Its Administration and Progress,* p. 5.

to throw open a substantial number of seats on a territorial basis, in which all persons qualified to vote should take part without any distinction of religion, race, creed, etc. And then supplementary elections should be held for the minorities which numerically or otherwise are important enough to need special representation; these supplementary elections should be confined to the minorities only. He appreciated the role of Jinnah in establishing communal unity and called him its 'ambassador'.

The second obstacle was the pitiable condtion of the depressed classes that was a consequence of the caste system of the Hindu society. So he raised his voice for the eradication of the evil of untouchability that stood in the way of social equality. In his address at the Dharwar Social Conference held on 27 April 1903, he said: "I think all fair-minded persons will have to admit that it is absolutely monstrous that a class of human beings, with bodies similar to our own, with brains that can think and with hearts that can feel, should be perpetually condemned to a life of utter wretchedness, servitude, and mental and moral degradation, and that permanent barriers should be placed in their way so that it should be impossible for them ever to overcome them and improve their lot. This is deeply revolting to our sense of justice."

Gokhale and Gandhi: Gandhi called Gokhale his political 'guru', but he did not prove himself as his blind disciple. He took inspiration from Gokhale's insistence on peaceful and constitutional methods, but he relied more on the method of passive resistance of Tilak, though he refined it with the techniques of *ahimsa* and *satyagraha.* In this respect he did not honour the advice of Gokhale.[15] The times had changed and after the tragedy of Amritsar, Gandhi had become patently anti-British. Thus, he rejected the idea of self-rule within the Empire so assiduously preached by Gokhale. However, he followed the line of his 'guru' more vigorously in working for the cause of communal unity and upliftment of the depressed castes.

When Gokhale was active in the freedom movement of India, Gandhi was at work in South Africa. Whenever it could be possible, Gokhale took the chance to see Gandhiji in South Africa on his way to England by ship. Not only this, he insisted that he (Gandhiji) should come to India to work for the cause of motherhood. Gandhiji came to India on a short trip at the invitation of Gokhale. He attended the Calcutta session of the Indian National Congress presided by D.E. Wacha in December, 1901 as a guest and put some resolutions also which were passed in a hurry owing to shortage of time. Then, just after a couple of days, he with Gokhale attended the Delhi Durbar (January, 1902) organised by Viceroy Curzon. He came to India in January 1915 to undertake the big mission that Gokhale had desired for him. He visited Poona to meet his 'guru'. After a couple of months, he left for England. But by the time he came back, Gokhale had left this world. He paid his tribute to his 'guru' in these glorious words: "Sir Pherozeshah Mehta seemed to me like the Himalaya, and Lokmanya like the ocean. But Gokhale was like the Ganges. One could have a refreshing bath in the holy river. The Himalaya was unscaleable, and one could not easily launch forth on the sea, but the Ganga invited one to its bosom."[16]

15. Valentine Chirol: *India- Old and New,* p. 297.
16. M.K. Gandhi: *The Story of My Experiments with Truth,* Vol. I, pp. 415-16.

Critical Appreciation: The moderate leaders of the Indian National Congress laid the foundation on which their successors worked and could be successful in reaching the desired goal. Since Gokhale was the leading light of the moderate school, his contribution is, indeed, monumental. The extremist leaders of that time rashly and mistakenly evaluated the performance of Gokhale and his followers, but with the passage of time they came to understand matters in real perspective. The situation underwent a big change after the First World War, but that did not make the philosophy of the moderates out of date. Even Tilak adhered to the path of constitutionalism when he insisted that the Montford Reforms should be tried and, for that reason, the path of responsive cooperation or non-cooperation should be adopted. The Swarajists also adhered to the same path. They entered the Legislative Councils to win *swaraj* by following the strategy of sabotage there. Though in 1919 Gandhiji had advised to non-cooperate with the Reformed Councils, he advised Jawaharlal Nehru to fight elections under the Government of India Act of 1935 so as to show the real position of the Congress in the country. Though a life-long rival of Gokhale, Tilak said these memorable words at the funeral of his departed colleague: "The diamond of India, this jewel of Maharashtra, this prince of workers, is taking eternal rest on the funeral ground. Look at him and try to emulate him."[17]

17. Bipan Chandra and others, *op. cit.*, p. 123.

36
Tilak

A study of Indian nationalism shows that it was apparently political; inherently it was economic as well, if we examine the ideas and the role of some great leaders like M.G. Ranade, Dadabhai Naoroji, R.C. Dutt and G.K. Gokhale. If studied more deeply it had spiritual dimension as well having its place in the metaphysical interpretations of Swami Vivekanand and Aurobindo. All these aspects have their place in the social, economic and political ideas of Bal Gangadhar Tilar (1856-1920), reverentially addressed as the 'Lokmanya'. Like Ram Mohun Roy, Ranade and Sir Syed Ahmed Khan, Tilak was an admirer of the British raj for its glorious role in modernising social, economic and political conditions of our country. And yet, different from them, he boldly preached the gospel of *swaraj* (self-rule), albeit within the British Empire. Feeling dissatisfied with the policies, programmes and methods of the moderate leaders of the Indian National Congress (like P.M. Mehta, Naoroji, W.C. Bonnerjee, S.N. Banerjea, G.K. Gokhale, etc.), he fearlessly advocated the path of 'extremism' that could not be identified with terrorism or revolutionary leftism. With Lala Lajpat Rai of Punjab and B.C. Pal of Bengal, he formed a small group of his own that came to be known as the trio of 'Lal, Bal, Pal'. By imparting the quality of political assertiveness, he transformed the character of the freedom struggle and prepared a solid base on which Gandhiji could take the movement to a successful end.

Extremist Nationalism: Tilak was a nationalist of a very high order. He could synthesise the Western concept of nationalism as given by Burke of England, Mazzini of Italy and Fichte and Herder of Germany with its Indian version as given by Bankim and Vivekanand.[1] Being a leader of the first generation of the Indian nationalists, he expressed his appreciation of the British rule that established parliamentary institutions like Central and Provincial Legislative Councils under the Act of 1861 and introduction of indirect election system for some of the unofficial seats in them under the Act of 1892. He appreciated election of Naoroji to the House of Commons in 1893. He endorsed 'economic drain theory' of Naoroji that caused poverty of the Indian people.

---

1. In his books like *The Orion* (1893) and *Arctic, The Home of the Vedas* (1898), Tilak proves Indians as the descendants of the Aryans belonging to Arctic whose *rishis* had composed the *Vedas*. His *Gita Rahisya* is regarded as the masterpiece work which inspired the leaders of the extremist school. It expounds his philosophical views in the most complete and systematic form. V. Brodov: *Indian Philosophy in Modern Times* (Moscow: Progress Publishers, 1984), p. 305.

Not only this, being a devout Hindu, and a Maharashtrian, he invoked historical and mythological sources to strengthen the bonds of nationalism among the people of his country. For this, we may refer to Shivaji Mela and Ganesh Utsav which he organised to awaken the people in the desired direction.

Since Tilak was under the impact of Western education, he showed his commitment to the liberal values of constitutional government. He gave the slogan of 'swaraj as our birth-right', but it implied country's 'freedom within the Empire'. The notorious event of the Partition of Bengal (1905) shocked him so much that he advocated the course of passive resistance. Because of the change in the political atmosphere of the country following the Bengal partition, Tilak with his followers laid stress on the use of his 'extremist' methods.[2] The Calcutta Congress of 1906 (presided by Naoroji) passed resolutions in favour of *swaraj, swadeshi,* boycott and national education. It showed growing influence of the fiery nationalism of Tilak that had a more volatile expression in the following year at the Surat Congress. Not satisfied with the election of Rash Behari Ghose at the defeat of his candidate (Lala Lajpat Rai) but feeling afraid of the motives of the moderates to upset what had been done at the last session of the Congress, Tilak created pandemonium as a result of which the session had to be abruptly adjourned. Tilak with his followers left the Congress. It came to be known as the Surat split.

Tilak who, like other intellectuals of that time, had admired the Royal Proclamation of Queen Victoria (1858) as the 'magna carta' of the Indian people, and the establishment of a constitutional order ensuring freedom of the people, struggled for the freedom of the press censored by the Indian Newspapers (Offences to Incitement) Act of 1908. As a fiery nationalist, he published his articles in his *Kesari* and *Mahratta* which were taken as 'rebellious notes' and for which he was charged with sedition and sentenced for six years and a fine of one thousand rupees.[3] Hence, he passed the period of internment in the Mandalay jail of Burma. However, after his return to India in 1914, he again became active in politics. He supported the Home Rule Movement of Annie Besant.

Nationalism implies love for and devotion to the motherland with a sense of pride. Tilak realised that it required awakened awareness that could be created through national education. So this item was included in the resolutions passed at the Calcutta Congress of 1906. It also required that the people, in the words of Swami Vivekanand, should be 'bold'. Hence, Tilak organised *akharas* or wrestling grounds in various parts of Maharashtra so as to train people in the art of fighting. Behind it was his belief that nationalism could be developed by fostering among the people the feeling that they

2. This event shocked Tilak so much that he denounced the action of Viceroy Lord Curzon "and, in the zeal of his love for the country, spoke like an extremist in bidding good bye to all hope of cooperating in any way with the bureaucracy in the interest of the people." Stanley Wolpert: *Tilak and Gokhale: Revolution and Reform in the Making of Modern India,* p. 176.
3. In 1882 Tilak was sentenced to four months' imprisonment for his publicistic articles that outraged the colonialists. In 1897 he was sentenced to eighteen months of imprisonment on the charge of his involvement in the Poona Conspiracy Case.

had common interests to be pursued and realised through united political action. He used social movements (like Poona Sarvajanik Sabha) as a means to foster the feeling of nationalism among the people.

It is, therefore, well pointed out: "Tilak's conception of Indian nationalism was an amalgam of diverse strands of thought; pride in the legacy of ancient India, appreciation of the role of British rule in bringing about the political and administrative unification of the country, appreciation of Western learning and science, recognition of economic exploitation by foreign rulers, and the recognition of the need to form a national political movement of the people across the barriers of race, caste, religion and sex."[4] However, since Tilak often invoked the messages of Hindu epics like *Ramayana, Mahabharat* and *Bhagwat Gita,* and Hindu rulers like Ashok and Shivaji, it was misunderstood by the non-Hindu writers. Valentine Chirol accused Tilak of making the national movement 'Brahmanical' and Zacharias commented that 'Tilak was the spokesman of an anti-Muslim retaliation'.[5]

Swaraj: It literally implies self-rule or independence of the country from foreign domination. But the concept had different implications if we compare the views of eminent nationalists like Naoroji, Tilak, Annie Besant, Gandhi, Motilal Nehru and Jawharlal Nehru. To some it meant 'self-rule within the British empire' (Naoroji); to some it meant Home Rule or 'freedom in the internal sphere' (Annie Besant), to some it meant 'self-rule within the Empire if possible, without the Empire if necessary' (Gandhi); to some it meant 'Dominion Status' (Motilal Nehru); and to some it meant 'complete independence' (Jawaharlal Nehru). These implications changed with the growth of the national movement. Since Tilak belonged to the first generation of the Indian nationalists, he subscribed to the view of Naoroji. However, with a distant view, he appreciated Home Rule as a midway achievement, because 'freedom was its soul'.[6]

Tilak raised the slogan of 'swaraj as our birth right' and valiantly fought for its sake so much so that he published notes in his *Kesari* and *Mahratta* which were taken as 'rebellious' and for which he had to undergo imprisonment of six years. Because of his strong advocacy, the Calcutta Congress of 1906 (presided by Naoroji) passed a resolution in favour of *swaraj.* In 1907 after the Surat split he founded his New or Nationalist Party and defined its goal as achievement of *Swaraj.* In a thundering voice, he said: "The point is to have the entire control in our hands. I want to have the keys of my house and not merely one stranger turned out of it. Self-government is our goal. We want control over our administrative machinery."[7]

---

4. N. R. Inamdar: "The Political Ideas of Lokmanya Tilak" in Thomas Pantham and K.L. Deutsch: (eds.): *Political Thought in Modern India,* p. 115.
5. Zacharias: *Renascent India,* p. 121. An Indian Marxist comments: "The reactionary forces contributing to the doctrine of 'integral nationalism' stood revealed when Tilak declared that Indian nationalism could not be purely secular, that it must be based on Hindu orthodoxy." M.N. Roy and Abani Mukherji: *India in Transition,* p. 186.
6. Cited in Inamdar, *op. cit.,* p. 114.
7. Cited in V.P. Varma: *Modern Indian Political Thought,* p. 236.

In political terms, to Tilak *Swaraj* meant democratic system as well. He admired British parliamentary system and desired that it should prevail in our country. Hence, he appreciated the system of indirect election to the Central and Provincial Legislative Councils under the Indian Councils Act of 1892. He could have his seat in the Bombay Legislative Council in 1896 after winning his case in the Bombay High Court, since at that time the election was to be confirmed by the Governor who was reluctant to do it. Democracy means freedom of the people and denial of arbitrary rule. It permits use of constitutional methods. Hence, the people should not only be united, they should carry on their struggle by peaceful means. After the Calcutta Congress passed the resolution in favour of *Swaraj,* he stressed that "while the people may pray and petition to the Government as a part of the constitutional agitation and seek the redressal of grievances or the fruition of political aspirations, the nation will merely rely on its own endeavours to accomplish the object. Swadeshi, boycott and national education are the three most potent weapons given in our hands by the National Congress, and with these we must establish Swaraj."[8]

It may be mentioned that Tilak recognised four connotations of *Swaraj.* First, it means that the rulers and the ruled belong to the same country, religion and race. Second, it refers to a well-governed state or a system of rule of law. Third, it means a government promoting the well being of our people. Fourth, there should be a government elected by and responsible to the people.[9] The last connotation was dearest to him. As he wrote: "Liberty is an adjunct of the soul. Where there is liberty, there is soul. It is an eternal doctrine and it is not afraid of anyone. Political philosophy must end in this very doctrine."[10]

Social reform movement was at its height during the days of Tilak. Men like Naoroji, Malabari, Phule, Ranade and Dayanand had done a lot of work in this direction. As a lover of freedom of the people, he tried to associate social reform with his political programme. He realised that social reform was an integral part of his campaign for self-rule. His plan for reform involved three necessary steps—popular education coming from the people and thus being moral and democratic, following the ideals of Indian civilisation of cooperative social organisation, and concentration for the political goal of *Swaraj.* "With the attainment of *Swaraj,* the necessary steps for social reform might be taken, supported by education and popular consent, based on the classical values and the ideals of India's own way of life."[11]

Tilak's concept of *Swaraj* had not only a political aspect aiming at the freedom of the country from foreign rule, it had moral and metaphysical aspect as well. As he says: "Our life and our *Dharma* are in vain in the absence of *Swaraj.*" Mere replacement of the bureaucratic rule by the rule of the people was not *Swaraj.* It implied establishment

8. *Ibid.,* p. 238.
9. Inamdar, *op. cit.,* p. 114.
10. Tilak: *Writings and Speeches,* p. 111.
11. T.L. Shay: *The Legacy of the Lokmanya,* p. 189.

of a democratic system in the real sense of the term. Hence, it "meant a revolutionary recasting of those forms to accord with the Indian civilisation's value system; it meant the remaking of the state so that it would fulfil the purposes and become the embodiment of Swaraj as it was in the Indian civilisation. Swaraj was the restoration of political order so that it would accord with the cosmic order, and so that individual lives might be assisted in attaining to the purposes of life. Tilak always insisted, 'Swaraj is the foundation'."[12]

Tilak not only dreamt of a Swaraj of his choice, he also laid stress on the means of its realisation. In this respect he disagreed with the methods of the moderate leaders who advocated the course of peaceful and constitutional methods like making prayers, sending petitions or waiting on the high officials of the British government. Instead he advocated the course of agitational methods like organising the people, taking out processions, raising loud slogans, crying for swadeshi and boycott. Such methods certainly took the struggle to the masses and thereby broadened the base of national movement. Democratic Swaraj was the opportunity for spiritual Swaraj for all people. Swaraj, he often asserted, was the 'natural consequence of dilligent performance of duty'. Thus, united popular action, properly led into into proper channels could bring about the desired change. Shay, therefore, well observes: "Tilak was the first political leader to break through the routine of its somewhat academic methods, to bridge the gulf between the present and the past, and to restore continuity to the political life of the nation. He developed a language and a spirit, and he used methods which Indianised the movement and brought it into the masses."[13]

Passive Resistance: The moderate leaders of the Indian National Congress always advocated the use of peaceful and constitutional methods for the achievement of their demands for 'reforms'. The extremist leaders like Tilak, Lajpat Rai and B.C. Pal endorsed the course of extremism as advocated by Vivekanand and Aurobindo. The partition of Bengal infuriated the leaders of the national movement so much that even the moderates drew closer to the line of Tilak's passive resistance implying self-denial and self-abnegation or no cooperation to the oppressive rulers of the land.[14] In a message delivered to the members of his New or Nationalist Party formed in 1907, he said: "So many of you may not like arms, but if you have not the power of active resistance, have you not the power of self-denial and self-abnegation in such a way as not to assist the foreign government to rule over you? This is boycott and this is what is meant when we say, boycott is a political weapon. We shall not give them assistance to collect revenue and keep peace. We shall not assist them in fighting beyond the frontiers or outside India with Indian blood and money. We shall not assist them in carrying on the administration of justice. We shall have our own courts and when the

12. *Ibid.,* p. 103.
13. *Ibid.,* p. 107. J.S. Hoyland mistakenly comments that Tilak "had been coquetting with doctrines of physical force." *Gokhale,* p. 25.
14. Valentine Chirol makes an absurd comment that Tilak "had been first to create the atmosphere which breeds murders." *India,* p. 122.

time comes, we shall not pay taxes. Can you do that by your united efforts. If you can, you are free from tomorrow."[15]

The course of passive resistance involved many measures to achieve the goal of freedom like boycott of foreign goods, use of home-made articles, non-payment of taxes, no cooperation to the British rule and the like. But Tilak never advocated the course of a violent or bloody revolution. His message was that if the British government did anything unconstitutional, the people of India had the right to undo it in a similar unconstitutional manner. After about a decade and a half, Gandhiji followed into the footsteps of Tilak with his novel techniques of non-violence and *satyagraha.* He confessed that Tilak "breathed into us the spirit of *swaraj.* And in all humility I claim to deliver his message to the country as truly as the best of his disciples. But I am conscious that my method is not that of Tilak."[16]

Congress Democratic Party: Tilak's concept of Swaraj implied 'self-rule within the Empire'. He supported the Home Rule Movement of Annie Besant as it desired 'independence of the country in the internal sphere' that could be stretched further in time to come and that the 'spirit of freedom' was inherent in it. It became more obvious when at the Amritsar Congress (1919) he opposed Gandhi's programme of non-cooperation as it would rupture India's link with the British Empire. Instead he advocated the course of 'responsive' cooperation or non-cooperation. It meant cooperation to the British government where it was right, non-cooperation where it was wrong. So he insisted that the Congressmen should accept the Montford Reforms (Government of India Act, 1919) and enter the Legislative Councils so as to test it. As he was afraid of Gandhi's programme of non-cooperation to be adopted by the Congress at its forthcoming annual session, he formed his Congress Democratic Party in early 1920.[17]

The social and political ideas of Tilak have a clear manifestation in the *Manifesto* of this paty. It reads: "The Congress Democratic Party, as the name denotes, is a party animated by feelings of unswerving loyalty to the Congress and faith in Democracy. It believes in the potency of democratic doctrines for the solution of Indian problems and regards the extension of education and political franchise as two of its best weapons. It advocates the removal of all civic, secular and social disabilities based on caste or custom. It believes in religious toleration, the sacredness of one's religion to oneself, and the right and duty of the State to protect it against aggression. This Party supports the claim of the Mohammedans for the solution of the Khilafat question according to Mohammedan dogmas and beliefs and the tenets of Koran."

15. Cited in Inamdar, *op. cit.,* pp. 119-20.
16. *Ibid.,* p. 119.
17. A little before his death, Tilak's last coherent utterance was that "Gandhi should be regarded as a political power and not be lightly thwarted or opposed by the Nationalists, lest they should find themselves in a minority and lose their lead in politics." Cited in Judith Brown: "The Mahatma and Modern India" in Sekhar Bandhopadhyay (ed.): *Nationalist Movement in India* (New Delhi: Oxford Univ. Press, 2009), pp. 57-58.

"This Party believes in the integration or federation of India in the British Commonwealth for the advancement of the cause of humanity and brotherhood of mankind, but demands autonomy for India and equal status as a sister-state with every other partner in the British Commonwealth including Great Britain. It insists on equal citizenship for Indians throughout the Commonwealth and effective retaliation whenever it is denied . . . . . This party proposes to work the Montford Reforms Act for all its worth and for accelerating the grant of full responsible government, and for this purpose, it will, without hesitation, offer cooperation or resort to constitutional opposition, whichever may be expedient and best calculated to give effect to the popular will."

This party failed to do anything because of the death of Tilak on 31 July, 1920. However, it had its effect on the leaders of the Indian Liberal Federation (formed in 1918) like Surendranath Banerjea, C.Y. Chintamani, K.V. Raghunath Reddy, etc. who took part in the provincial elections of 1920 and then occupied the seats of the ministers holding charge of the 'transferred' subjects. It had its partial effect on the Swaraj Party as well (formed in 1923) whose leaders as C.R. Das, Motilal Nehru, N.C. Kelkar, etc., took part in the elections of 1923. But they declined to accept any ministerial post, for their object was to non-cooperate from within. The experiment of council-entry miserably failed. The Liberals resigned their ministerial assignments in disgust and the Swarajists abandoned their 'in and out' strategy after realising its futility. One may say that the formation of the Congress Democratic Party manifested realism of Tilak's leadership; it did not compromise with the ethics of Gandhiji. So it was displaced by the leaders of the Congress in a short time to come. However, the watchword of this party was significant: "Educate, Agitate and Organise'.[18]

Tilak and Gokhale: Both have their significant place in the galaxy of Indian nationalists. However, the line of difference between them is drawn on the point of Gokhale being a great moderate leader and Tilak for being a great extremist leader. In spite of the fact that both were Maharashtrians and belonged to the caste of Chitpavan Brahmins and both served as teachers at the Fergusson Collge of Poona for a number of years, temperamentally they were poles apart. Gokhale followed the line set by Mehta, Naoroji, Bannerjee and the earlier leaders of the Indian National Congress who, being the loyal followers of Ranade, regarded British rule as a 'divine dispensation' and strove for reforms. They invariably advocated the path of constitutionalism. But Tilak followed the line of Vivekanand and Aurobindo and advocated the use of extremist methods like organising people, taking out processions, raising loud slogans, staging boycott of foreign goods and passive resistance in the form of non-cooperation. Since the moderate leaders did not appreciate the ways of the extremists, they opposed Tilak who could not grab the office of the President at the Calcutta Congress of 1906. Gokhale and others resisted again as a result of which Tilak's candidate (Lala Lajpat Rai) saw his defeat at the hands of Rash Behari Ghose at the Surat Congress in the following year.

18. Shay, *op. cit.*, p. 146.

The points of difference between the two great leaders are thus summed up by an eminent historian of the Congress: "Gokhale's plan was to improve the existing Constitution, Tilak's was to reconstruct it. Gokhale had necessarily to work with the bureaucracy, Tilak had necessarily to fight it. Gokhale stood for cooperation wherever possible and opposition wherever necessary, Tilak inclined towards a policy of obstruction. Gokhale's prime concern was with the administration and its improvement, Tilak's supreme consideration was with the Nation and its upbuilding. Gokhale's ideal was love and sacrifice, Tilak's was service and suffering. Gokhale's method sought to win the foreigner, Tilak's to replace him. Gokhale depended upon others' help, Tilak upon self-help. Gokhale looked to the classes and the intelligentsia, Tilak to the masses and the millions. Gokhale's arena was Council Chamber, Tilak's forum was the village *mandap.* Gokhale's medium of expression was English, Tilak's was Marathi. Gokhale's objective was Self-Government for which the people had to fit themselves by answering the tests prescribed by the English, Tilak's objective was Swaraj which is the birth right of every Indian and which he shall have without let or hindrance from the foreigner. Gokhale was on a level with his age, Tilak was in advance of his times."[19]

However, a serious examination of this theme shows that the differences between the two have been exaggerated. Gokhale was a great moderate leader of course, who did not appreciate the doings of Tilak like raising loud slogans of *swaraj* in the sessions of the Congress and disruption of the proceedings of the Surat Congress, yet he followed the line of Tilak in attacking the misdeeds of the British rulers, though in mild tone. For instance, he appeared before the Welby Commission in London in 1897 and presented his thesis before it, loaded with facts showing lavish and highly expensive life of the English bureaucrats and compared it with the starving conditions of about 75 per cent of the people of India. Like other extremists, he condemned the partition of Bengal and nicknamed Viceroy Curzon as the 'Second Aurangzeb'. In his presidential address at the Kashi Congress (1905) he endorsed Tilak's idea of *swadeshi.* He appreciated the passage of resolutions on *swaraj, swadeshi,* boycott and national education at the Calcutta Congress of 1906. It shows that Gokhale was like a mild extremist. On the other hand, after his return to India in 1914, Tilak became a moderate leader owing to his old age and health failure caused by his long internment in the Mandalay jail. He supported the Home Rule Movement of Annie Besant, but he stoutly opposed Gandhi's programme of non-cooperation. Instead he came forward with the proposal of 'responsive' cooperation or non-cooperation in response to the prevailing situation. Not only this, he formed the Congress Democratic Party in early 1920 to have an alternative arrangement to Gandhi's call of non-cooperation implying ban on Council-entry. In short, despite the fact that Gokhale is known as a moderate leader and Tilak is known for being an extremists leader, the difference between the two is one of degree, not of kind.

Tilak and Gandhi: A comparative study of these two great national leaders shows that between them the points of resemblance are many, the points of difference are

19. Pattabhi Sitaramayya: *The History of the Indian National Congress,* Vol. I, p. 99.

few. Both were great and fiery nationalists; both had a vision for the future of India; both favoured methods of mass protests against misdeeds of the British rulers; both adopted the course of passive resistance; above all, both raised the demand for *swaraj*. However, the points of difference between the two may be pinpointed as follows:

1. Tilak was a fiery extremist who preferred the course of passive resistance in the form of adoption of *swadeshi,* boycott of foreign articles, non-payment of taxes, non-cooperation to the foreign rulers and the like. Gandhi also adopted this course, but he bracketed it with his techniques of *ahimsa* and *satyagraha.* It is rightly remarked: "For Tilak *Ahimsa* could at best be only a policy, but for Gandhi it was a matter of absolute faith."[20]
2. Tilak's concept of *swaraj* implied 'self-rule within the Empire'. Gandhi also said it, but after the Jallianwala Bagh tragedy, his mind was changed. At the Amritsar Congress (1919) he identified British rule with 'Satanic rule' to which no cooperation should be given. But Tilak opposed it. He adhered to his course of 'non-cooperation where the British rule was wrong, cooperation where it was right'. While Gandhi counselled the idea of no Council-entry with a view to reject the Montford Reforms, Tilak advanced the idea of Council-entry to test the reforms so as to clear the way for the inauguration of better reforms under a new constitutional dispensation. Gandhi's non-cooperation was one-dimensional. To Tilak, cooperation, non-cooperation, limited cooperation and responsive cooperation or non-cooperation were all necessary techniques of the struggle.
3. Both were idealists in their own right. They had a vision of the future of the country. While Tilak's idealism was blended with political realism, Gandhi's idealism was reinforced by insistence on ethical consistency. It is due to this that while the secularism of Tilak was blended with Hindu orthodoxy at the root, Gandhi's idealism was unadulterated.

Such lines of difference apart, it may be safely pointed out that Tilak prepared the base on which Gandhi could raise superstructures with his novel techniques of non-violence and *satyagraha.* It is well observed: "Tilak was the Lokmanya, Gandhi was the Mahatma. Each fulfilled the obligations of his Swadharma . . . . . Tilak and Gandhiji taught the classical message of perfect yourself, dedicate yourself to the highest aspirations of man, live in Truth, live in our True Nature, strive for the fulfilment of the Purpose of Life. Their political philosophy was founded on the philosophy of life. Self-reliance, courage and willingness to sacrifice motivated each man and was a part of their message to all men. The willingness to act, to meet the challenges of the world and to make of the world a better place in which to live guided each man and was a part of the message of each. They each relied upon the people, their wisdom and their willingness to act, to bring about the common goal."[21]

---

20. Varma, *op. cit.,* p. 255.
21. Shay, *op. cit.,* p. 158. Prof. V.P. Varma well observes: "Tilak was Karmayogin and Rajpurusha, Gandhi was a Mahatma and Dharamatma." *op. cit.,* p. 258.

Critical Appreciation: Great is the contribution of Tilak to the cause of India's struggle for independence. In his magnificent role one may discover the tenets of his social and political philosophy which has been differently evaluated by the writers of contemporary Indian history and politics. Since Tilak followed the line of Vivekanand and Aurobindo, and he took inspiration from the Hindu epics and thereby organised people in the garb of religious festivals, the non-Hindus misinterpreted it as 'the Hinduisation of national movement'. Jawaharlal Nehru comments: "Socially speaking, the revival of Indian nationalism in 1907 was definitely reactionary."[22] It is, likewise, pointed out that this trend "not only inevitably weakened the advance of the political consciousness and clarity of the movement but also divided the advancing forces. The programme of social reaction alienated many who could have been ready to accept the reactionary and metaphysical rubbish which was being offered as a substitute for leftwing movement."[23]

It is not an easy task to properly evaluate the place of Tilak in the history of modern Indian political thought. An English journalist (Valentine Chirol) may make a prejudiced statement that Tilak was the 'prince of the Indian unrest', but all right-minded people would agree with Gandhi ji's statement that Tilak was the 'maker of modern India.' No doubt, Tilak changed the course of national movement, he transformed the character of the Indian National Congress; above all, he defined the term *swaraj* in his own way and made it realisable by the techniques of passive resistance which were refined by Gandhiji. Gandhiji admired Tilak as 'an ocean' and frankly expressed his debt to the 'lion of Maharashtra'. He was an idealist of course, but his idealism was reinforced by political realism. Notable is the fact that he "never tolerated the degeneration of realism into the apotheosis of the cult of power, force and success. Hence, his school of political thought can be characterised as nationalism founded upon 'democratic realism."[24]

---

22. Nehru: *An Autobiography,* p. 24.
23. Rajni Palme Dutt: *India Today,* p. 328. The Marxist writers fail to properly understand the ideas and role of the great Indian nationalist leaders, because they try to examine everything with a rigid viewpoint set by Lenin and his followers. So V. Brodov says: "Tilak made careful and vigorous preparations for the revolution he expected. However, being an idealist in his view of social phenomena, he could have no clear and distinct idea about the nature and motive forces of this revolution, making grave mistakes in his practical actions. For example, endeavouring to attract to his side the broad popular masses, to take the lower classes by the hand, as he was wont to put it, Tilak appealed to their religious feelings rather than class consciousness. . . . . Failure to understand the true role of the popular masses in history led Tilak and his followers to a tactical error. Instead of creating a political party out of the best members of the working class and the poorest peasants, a party that could work out a concrete programme for the national liberation struggle, that could organise and inspire the people and lead them in the battle for carrying out that programme, they expended their strength in appeals for spiritual remoulding of man (of all Indians) and in organising this remoulding according to the principle: 'first in the heart and then in being of the world." *Indian Philosophy in Modern Times,* pp. 307-09.
24. Varma, *op. cit.,* p. 260.

37
Iqbal

Basically a poet and a philosopher and then a lawyer and a politician, Mohammed Iqbal (1873-1938) occupies a place of distinction in the galaxy of the distinguished intellectuals of our country. His social, political and economic ideas ranging from liberalism to socialism may be traced in his long and short poems, quartrains and couplets written in Persian and Urdu languages, though one may also refer to some of his important writings, speeches and occasional correspondence available in the English language. However, what makes him a unique as well as a controversial figure is his drastic change from a nationalist to a communalist platform and, more than that, his role in sharpening the implications of the 'two-nation theory' that became the ideological basis of our country's partition in 1947. The doctrine of ego or selfhood (*khudi*), with which his name is so prominently associated, finds its practical manifestation first in his own role as a politician (1926-36) and then in the search for a 'great leader' of his choice (Jinnah) (1937-47) a 'perfect man' (*mard-i-kamil*) or a super-man (*mard-i-momin*) who played his distinctive part in laying the foundations of the Muslim State of Pakistan.

Philosophy of the Self and Selfhood : The most outstanding feature of Iqbal's social and political philosophy should be traced in his idea of the self (*khudi*) that has been mistakenly termed as 'ego' by a number of Western writers and commentators on this subject like R.A. Nicholson and A.J. Arberry.[1] The power of the self has its best expression in the personality of an individual in so far as he is the centre of energy and activity. In other words, it presents itself as a significant unity in the form of all embracing concrete self—the ultimate source of all individual life. However, the remarkable point about Iqbal's philosophy at this stage is that he gives a new direction to the tenets of Islam as a religion by characterising this force of the self as something progressive and practical. The real meaning of *khudi* is, therefore, not identifiable with the doctrine of 'ego' as understood in the West and is certainly the anti-thesis of anything like self-negation, self-abnegation and self-abandonment.

1. Iqbal has also used the word 'ego' in some of his English writings for want of a better substitute. In 1937 in a note dictated to Nazir Niyazi, Iqbal explained the meaning of *khudi* in these words: "Metaphysically, this word is used in the sense of indescribable feelings of 'I' which ethically, as used by me, means self-reliance, self-respect, self-confidence, self-preservation, even self-assertion when such a thing is necessary in the interest of life and power to stick to the cause of truth." *Iqbal: His Art and Thought,* (Lahore, Seikh Muhammed Ashraf, 1944,) pp. 238-44.

Iqbal imparts a particular meaning to the terms like self (*khud*) and selfhood (*khudi*) having their negative side in selfless (*bekhud*) and selflessness *(bekhudi*). It is distinctly contrary to the Sufi thought of some Muslim seers and intellectuals who, in their own ways, subscribed to the Hellenistic doctrines of pantheism.[2] It is also opposed to the Hindu philosophy of Vedanta. He does not accept the view of life as a mere illusion (*Maya*) as conceived by the Hindu philosophy, nor does he endorse the Buddhist philosophy of luxuriating in the eternal joys of salvation (*Nirvana*). Instead, like a devout Muslim with an enlightened mind, he focuses on the potentialities of a dynamic society as understood by the Prophet of Islam. In this way, his real endeavour "is to remove all corrupting and stagnating influences on the dynamics of a religion-bound society like Islam, in particular, so that it might secure its pristine glory and sanctity. Obviously, a religion like Islam becomes a dynamic force in Iqbal's political philosophy through the doctrine of *khudi.* "[3]

The power of the self is the centre of energy and, as such, it is the cause of all social progress. Man struggles against the odds of his life for the sake of achieving the goals of his existence and this is because of the existence of this power within him. As he himself says: "The life of ego is a kind of tension caused by the ego in invading the environment and environment invading the ego."[4] The existence of this ego manifests itself into sensation, feelings, emotions and ideas which continually shape as well as change it. Again: "Man marches ahead to receive over fresh illuminations from an Infinite Reality which every moment appears in a new glory, and the recipient of divine illumination is not merely a passive recipient. Every act of the ego creates a new situation and thus offers further opportunities of creative unfolding."[5]

It implies that man has within himself a unique power by which he may comprehend reality and realise the goals of his life. By virtue of this, he becomes a self-contained exclusive centre both physically and spiritually.[6] He draws closer and closer to God until he becomes 'the most complete person.'[7] In this direction, Iqbal himself says: "The end of the ego's quest is not emancipation from the limitations of individuality; it

2. Prof. V.P. Varma presents a different point when he says that though Iqbal makes a transition away from pantheism in his philosophical development, some of his ideas and statements retain pantheistic influence. To substantiate his statement, he cites this statement of Iqbal: "Nature is to the Divine Self as character is to the human self. In the picturesque phrase of the *Koran,* it is the habitat of Allah." *Modern Indian Political Thought,* (Agra: Lakshmi Narain Agarwal, 1980), p. 446 n 2.
3. In appreciation of it, Asif Khan says: "This essentially progressive and practical outlook of Islam had an appeal for him which none of the Western thinkers could claim for themselves." *Same Aspects of Iqbal's Thought,* (Lahore: Islamic Book Service, 1977,) p. 19.
4. Iqbal: *Religious Reconstruction of Islam,* (Lahore, Sheikh Muhammed Ashraf, 1958,) p. 102.
5. *Ibid.,* p. 123.
6. Hafeez Malik: *Muslim Nationalism in India and Pakistan,* (Public Affairs Press, Washington, D.C., n,y), p. 244.
7. M. Aziz Ahmad: *Iqbal's Political Theory,* (Lahore: Sheikh Muhammed Ashraf, 1944), p. 239.

is on the other hand, a more precise definition of it. The final act is not an intellectual act but a vital act which deepens the whole being of the ego and sharpens his will with the creative assurance that the world is not something to be merely seen or known through concepts but be made and remade by continuous action."[8] If so, philosophy "is an intellectual view of things—it does not care to go beyond concepts which can reduce all the rich variety of experience to a system. It sees Reality from a distance as it were. Religion sees closer contact with Reality. The one is theory, the other is living experience, association, intimacy."[9]

The doctine of the self is as old as the Hindu scriptures. In the West, its reflections may be traced in the works of Descartes and Nietzsche. However, being a true Muslim, Iqbal frankly refutes the line of atheism finding its culmination in the philosophy of Nietzsche.[10] He belongs to the category of modern Indian romanticists having their spiritual home in the East like Aurobindo, Tilak, Tagore and Gandhi with this marked difference that while for all others it is the Indian motherland, to him it is the Arabia of the times of the Prophet of Islam. The influence of the Western philosophy is there, but his frank criticism of the Western civilisation smacks of his disavowal of the secularistic approach of the Western thinkers. His real source of inspiration is the holy *Koran* that informs him to warn his co-religionists about the post-Reformation developments of the Christian community in the West and instead adhere to these words of the Prophet: *Takhallaqu bi-Akhlaq Allah* (Create in yourselves the attributes of God.). At one place, he says: "Humanity needs three things today—a spiritual interpetation of the universe, spiritual emancipation of the individual, and basic principles of universal import directing the evolution of human society on a spiritual basis."[11]

A necessary concomitant to the development of the self is, therefore, man's turning towards God. Faith, not reason, is the foundation of selfhood and mystic experience. Disagreeing with a rationalistic approach to his religion as done by some leading Muslim figures like Sir Syed Ahmed Khan, he contends that scientific experiment alone is not the key to inner knowledge. The foremost element in the modern Western culture is the dominance of reason, but in reality faith or intuition is the senior partner in the joint firm of intellect and faith.[12] According to *Javed Nama* of Iqbal, there are three stages in the evolution of the ego: (*i*) The realisation of the creative possibilities of the ego is the first stage of individuality. (*ii*) Then comes the second stage of sociality

---

8. Iqbal, *op. cit.,* p. 199.
9. *Ibid.,* p. 61. Elsewhere Iqbal says: "Never imagine that self is a farm without any produce. When yourself becomes mature, it is immortal, for the separation of true lovers is itself a union."
10. Iqbal calls Nietzsche 'a mad man of Europe' for his atheistic pronouncements. This is inspite of the fact that he borrows from him the idea of a superman (like Napoleon). For this, Iqbal may be described as the 'diluted edition of Nietzsche'. See P.S. Muhar: "The Political Philosophy of Sir Muhammed Iqbal" in *Indian Journal of Political Science,* Vol XVIII, July-December, 1957, p. 176.
11. Iqbal, *op. cit.,* p. 170.
12. Muhar, *op. cit.,* p. 180.

as now ego is seen in the context of other egos. (*iii*) Last comes the stage in which God is realised and the ego is viewed in the perspective of divine consciousness. "By being steadfast before the eternal light of God one can become powerful and thus partly like the omnipotent God."[13]

Obviously, Iqbal's philosophy of ego is based on this assumption that primacy lies not with brute force but with the power of spirit within the personality of man. The emergence of great figures like Rumi, al-Ghazali, Mahmud Ghaznavi, Nadir Shah, Napoleon, Ghalib, Mussolini, Lenin, etc., owes its source to this power of the self. Such a doctrine, grounded in a spiritual ethos, is inherent in these affirmations. First, man is a creature endowed with infinite power. Second, it is by subduing matter, an obstacle in the flow of life, that the human ego achieves its growth and expansion. Third, the human self possessed of infinite potentialities seeks its fulfilment in a holistic view of the society where the whole is larger than the total of its parts. Last, the birth of Islam is the birth of inductive intellect. In short, for Iqbal, the individual is the measure of all things by virtue of being endowed with the power of the self, and the life of the community is the essential framework within which it operates for the sake of having its outward manifestation.[14]

The power of the self may be seen in the behaviour of Satan who chastises the angels for doing nothing except eulogising the greatness of the Creator. Not only that, the sharpness of the ego enthuses Satan to enter into a dialogue with the faithful angels and even the Creator, in so far as the role of man in the construction of human society, as a result of Adam's expulsion from the Garden of Eden at his (Satan's) behest, is concerned. A man conscious of his inner potentialities may claim credit for his own part in the construction and re-construction of this world and thereby raise himself to the level of the vice-regent of God. It is obvious that Iqbal interprets the Sufi doctrine of *insan-al-kamil* (perfect man) in his own way. It teaches that "everyman is potentially a microscope and that when he has become spiritually perfect, all the divine attributes are displayed by him so that as a saint or a Prophet he is the God-man, the representative or the vice-regent of God on earth."[15]

The striking impression is that the real purpose of Iqbal is to awaken the power of *khudi* in man and thereby enthuse him to play his part in the reconstruction of society on the lines of Islamic theology as done by the Prophet and his followers. This is the way a person may become *mard-i-momin* (qualified or complete man) like Moses and Muhammed and may earn the eternal gratitude of his fellow-beings. As Dr. Nicholson observes: "The appearance of the divine vice-regent will be the beginning of a new age. He will be the glory of the world, and the soul of the universe. Pitching his tent in this

13. Varma, *op. cit.,* p. 450. See the English translation of *Javed Nama* by A.J. Arberry, (London: George Allen and Unwin, 1966).
14. M.A. Siddiqui: "Iqbal and Marxism" in A.A. Ansari (ed.): *Iqbal: Essays and Studies,* (Delhi: Ghalib Academy, 1978), pp. 308-310.
15. Refer to 'Introduction' by Dr. R.A. Nicholson in his English translation of Iqbal's *Asrar-i-Khudi* (Secrets of the Selfhood), pp. 78-79.

wide world, he will execute the command of Allah all around. A number of beautiful worlds will spring up and blossom from the meadows of his thought. He will infuse everything with the melody and radiance of youth. He will give humanity a message of happiness. He will offer a warning as a soldier, as a marshal and as a prince. His knowledge will be unfathomable and time will be under his domination. He will give new explanation of our life and its dreams, its mysteries and inspirations. The function of present sick race of mankind is dependent upon the ideal of a coming humanity, the supermen. They will bring once more the days of peace to those who seek battle in the world."[16]

National Identity of the Indian Muslims: An awareness of a separate Muslim national identity in the Indian sub-continent can be traced back to the thoughts of el-Biruni of the eleventh century. Such a consciousness sustaining itself on the force of a particular faith was later stressed by Majaddid Alf Thani. However, its recent instances can be traced in the socio-religious reform campaigns launched by Shah Waliullah of the eighteenth and Sir Syed Ahmad Khan of the nineteenth centuries. In the present country this trend was followed by many prominent figures of this community like Sir Aga Khan, Sir Muhammed Shafi, Sir Salimullah Khan and a host of others adorning the ranks of the Muslim League. This trend of exclusiveness and separatism found its manifestation in the call for separate nationalism of the Muslim people and eventually it became the ideological basis of the two-nation theory of Jinnah. However, it is Iqbal who "deserves the credit for visualising a Muslim state with a clear notion of an ideology it must adhere to. Though primarily a poet and a philosopher, we also owe to him first and formal enunciation of the two-nation theory."[17]

Overtones of communalism appear in the social and political philosophy of Iqbal after the withering away of the Khilafat movement in 1924. He then began talking about the welfare of the Muslim *millat* (nation) requiring the leadership of a charismatic personality. What had remained in his heart for the many years now emerged in the form of his endeavour for the good of his co-religionists.[18] There is no doubt that by virtue of his philosophical training, his deep knowledge of Islamic history and culture and

16. *Ibid.*, p. 83. Explaining the meaning of Iqbal, Dr. M. Aziz Ahmed points out: "The vice-regent of God is the completest ego on earth. The goal of humanity is a combination of the highest power and the highest knowledge. The vice-regent is, therefore, the real ruler of mankind; his kingdom is the kingdom of God on earth. Out of the richness of his nature he lavishes the wealth of his life on others, and brings them nearer and nearer to himself." Refer to his paper titled "Iqbal's Political Theory" in *Iqbal as a Thinker: Essays by Eminent Scholars* (Lahore: Sheikh Muhammed Ashraf, 1944), p. 242.
17. Asif Iqbal Khan: *Some Aspects of Iqbal's Thought,* (Lahore: Islamic Book Service, 1977), p. 91.
18. For instance, on one occasion, Iqbal advised his co-religionists to break down the idols of colour and blood and be immersed in the *millat* (brotherhood of Islam) so that there might not be left distinct people as Turani, Irani and Afghani." See Karl von Vorys: *Political Development in Pakistan,* (Princeton: Princeton University Press, 1965), p. 40.

his keen political insight, he was able to visualise the real goal of the Indian Muslims much before his chosen follower (Jinnah) came to dominate the scene in 1937. Hardly a few years after the creation of the Muslim League in 1906, he, like preceding leaders of the Aligarh movement, had expressed his fears about the domination of the Hindus over the Muslims. It shows that a great poet and philosopher knighted for his poetry in 1922 fell prey to the mischievous divide and rule policy of the colonial masters.[19]

A fundamental change occurred after 1925 when this poet-philosopher emerged as a politician so as to translate his philosophy of *khudi* and *millat* into an ideology for the welfare of his own community according to the injunctions of Islam. Our study at this stage finds its first concrete instance in his election to the Punjab Legislative Council in 1926 on a ticket of the Unionist Party. It enabled him to organise the people of his *millat* on a common platform so as to prepare them for the contemplated ordeal. His attitude towards the initial endeavours of Jinnah bringing about communal amity was wary, and he even scoffed at Jinnah's title as 'the ambassador of Hindu-Muslim unity'. The reason behind this is that Iqbal never had the illusion that the Hindus and the Muslims, two separate nations, could have a common goal. On the other hand, he wanted to bring the Muslims of India on a common platform, to make them a force to be reckoned with.[20]

By this time, it became quite clear that Iqbal was totally committed to the well-being of the Indian Muslims and he channelised all his energies towards that end.[21] In the debates of the Punjab Legislative Council he laid stress on bettering the lot of the Muslims in particular. In 1928 he passed critical remarks on the deliberations of the Nehru Committee for ignoring his plea of a consolidated Muslim state in the North-Western part of India on the ground of its being a very 'unwieldy unit'. However, with a view to meet such a difficulty, he suggested exclusion of the Ambala division as well as of some other contiguous areas predominantly peopled by the non-Muslims from the proposed unit of North-West India. In January, 1929 he attended the Muslim Conference in Delhi (held under the presidentship of Sir Aga Khan) and made significant contribution to its deliberations. These instances make it quite clear that even before his presidential address at the Allahabad session of the Muslim League in December, 1930, Iqbal had assumed an attitude basically different from one of stern

19. D.H. Bhutani hints at the influence of the Arya Samaj movement in Punjab in addition to the role of British colonial policy. As he says: "Being a genius he (Iqbal) had all the crankiness of that class. Being a Punjabi, he was greatly affected by the virulence of the Arya Samaj movement, which was really a reaction against Muslim fanaticism; he imagined that the Hindus were out to exterminate Islam and the Muslims. The truth really was that the imperial power was, by a variety of techniques and methods and devices, making the leaders of the Hindus and the Muslims dance like marionettes, and Iqbal joined the mad dance." *The Future of Pakistan,* (New Delhi: Promilla and Co. Pub., 1985), p. 103.
20. Asif Iqbal Khan, *op. cit.,* p. 75.
21. *Ibid.,* p. 74.

patriotism of the pre-1905 period[22] and sought to defend this change in his views due to 'maturity of his thinking'.[23]

The most important event, in this direction, is the role of Iqbal as a Muslim ideologue at the Allahabad session of the League when in his presidential address he presented 'a rough sketch of what became the Pakistan project'.[24] In very clear terms he said : "I would like to see the Punjab, North-West Frontier Province, Sind and Baluchistan amalgamated into a single state. Self-government within the British empire, or without the British Empire, the formation of a consolidated North-West Indian Muslim state appears to me to be the final destiny of the Muslims at least of North-West India."[25] Again, "The life of Islam as a cultural force in this country very largely depends upon its centralisation in a specific territory."[26] Reacting sharply to the proposal of Rt. Hon'ble Sir Srinivas Sastri that by insisting on the creation of an autonomous Muslim state, the Muslims would have to exert pressure on the Government of India in times of emergency, Iqbal observed that they were prompted by a genuine desire and that their wish for free development would essentially remain impossible under the type of military government contemplated by the nationalist Hindu politicians who wanted to secure permanent communal dominance in the whole of India.[27] He concluded his address with these forceful words: "Hold fast to yourself; no one who erreth can hurt you, provided you are well-guarded."[28]

The contents of this important address of Iqbal have been evaluated in different terms by some writers to save the name of the great poet-philosopher from being associated with rank communalism in the evening phase of his life.[29] Such endeavours,

22. Thus, Jawaharlal Nehru in one of his letters to Padmaja in 1929 said: "I have never met Iqbal. He has always been one of the many problems I could not solve. How can a real poet be so extra-ordinarily communal and narrow-minded and earthly? And yet he happens to be both." See S. Gopal (ed.): *Jawaharlal Nehru: An Anthology,* (Delhi: Oxford University Press, 1980), p. 580.
23. In an interview given to the *Bombay Chronicle* in September, 1931, on the occasion of his departure to England as a member of the Muslim delegation to take part in the Second Round Table Conference, Iqbal said: "In my college days I was a zealous nationalist which I am not now. The change is due to mature thinking." *Letters and Writings of Iqbal,* compiled and edited by Bashir Ahmed Dar (Karachi: Iqbal Academy, 1967), pp. 58-59.
24. Ian Stephen: *Pakistan,* (London: Ernest Benn, 1963), p. 75.
25. Syed Sharifuddin Pirzada: *Foundations of Pakistan* (All-India Muslim League Documents), Vol. II (1924-47), (Delhi: Metropolitan Book Co., 1982), pp. 153-71.
26. *Ibid.*
27. *Ibid.*
28. *Ibid.*
29. For instance, Prof. P.S. Muhar says that Iqbal "did not want to surrender the unity of India by creating two independent states of India and Pakistan as was done later in 1947. All that he wanted was that an autonomous Muslim state (province) in the North-West be brought into existence, so that the Muslims could develop their culture and personality unhindered by the Hindu majority. He did not extend this principle to the Muslims of united Bengal." *Op. cit.,* p. 185. Compare it with the view of Freeland Abbot who says: "Like Waliullah, Iqbal's problem was how to assure a healthy religious climate in India

however, fall flat if we study his real role in the events of the following years. He took part in the Second Round Table Conference of 1931 and then in the third Round Table Conference of 1932 held in London as a member of the Muslim delegation.[30] On 21 March, 1932 he presided over the meeting of the All-India Muslim League held in the city of Lahore and in his address said : "The whole community needs a complete overhauling of its mentality in order that it may again become capable of feeling the urge for fresh desires and ideals . . . Concentrate your whole ego on yourself alone, and ripen your clay into real manhood if you wish to see your aspirations realised."[31]

A distinct improvement upon what Iqbal had said in his presidential address at the Allahabad session of the League about the creation of a compact Muslim state in the North-West part of India occurred in 1937 when he converted his scheme of such a compact state into that of a greater Muslim state so as to cover the Muslim-majority province of Bengal as well. Now his idea of a state based on the two-nation theory covered other parts of the country as well on the logic of saving his co-religionists from any possible domination of the non-Muslim people (particularly the Hindus) of the land. In a confidential letter (dated 10 November, 1937) he wrote to Jinnah: "To my mind the new constitution (Act of 1935) with its idea of a single Indian federation of the Muslim provinces . . . is the only course by which we can secure a peaceful India and save the Muslims from the domination of the non-Muslims. Why should not the Muslims of North-West India and Bengal be considered as nations entitled to self-determination just as other nations in India and outside India are?"[32]

Search for a Charismatic Leader: Iqbal was a great ideologue of course, but he lacked the quality of a capable political leader. He could find faults with the leadership of Sir Fazl-i-Hussain and Sikander Hayat Khan of the Unionist Party of Punjab and yet he wanted to find a man of his choice who could realise what he had contemplated and expressed through the medium of poetry. This he could discover in the personality

---

for Muslims. Searching to ensure Muslim solidarity in his time he urged the creation of a separate Muslim state in the North-West India." *Islam and Pakistan,* (Cornell: Cornell University Press, 1968), p. 165. "The seeds of Pakistan can be found in Iqbal's address." Hafeez Malik, *op. cit.,* p. 241.

30. When the Third Round Table Conference was going on in London in 1932, at a meeting in the House of Commons the Aga Khan, poet Iqbal and historian Shafaat Ahmed Khan stressed "inherent impossibility of securing merger of Hindu and Muslim political, or indeed social, interests" and the "impracticality of ever governing India through anything but a British agency." Bipan Chandra: *Communalism in Modern India,* (Delhi: Vikas 1984), p. 107.
31. Asif Iqbal Khan, *op. cit.,* pp. 75-76.
32. Hector Bolitho: *Jinnah: Creator of Pakistan,* (London: John Murray, 1954), p. 114. In this letter Iqbal frankly stressed the point that Muslim India could solve her problems but for that it would be necessary to redistribute the country and to provide one or more Muslim states with absolute majorities. Keeping this in view, Prof. V.P. Varma comments that thus Iqbal "became the spiritual and ideological protagonist of the Pakistanist separatism." *Op. cit.,* p. 457.

of M.A. Jinnah. During the period of 1930-34 he enriched the Muslim League with an ideological sharpness. At the same time, he was determined to involve Jinnah in whom he had seen the model of his superman. During the period of his sojourn in England (1930-34), he often pleaded his case with Jinnah and wrote fine couplets in appreciation of the latter's loftiness of vision, depth of insight and capability of leadership. In this mission he eventually succeeded when Jinnah assumed the leadership of the Muslim League in 1937 that took part in the provincial elections held under the Act of 1935. Relying upon his own experinces of the past, he advised Jinnah against having any electoral understanding with the leaders of the Unionist Party. Though Jinnah had his own way in clear violation of his mentor's advice, Iqbal "stood steadfast with Jinnah in those trying days and helped him to charter the course of Indo-Muslim politics."[33]

Subsequently, Jinnah realised his mistake and drew closer to Iqbal while doing the needful for the betterment of the lot of his people at the behest of his mentor. The proposal of Iqbal for a separate Muslim state could convince Jinnah only after the most astounding defeat of the Muslim League in the elections of 1937. It provided a favourable occasion for Iqbal to take Jinnah under the cover of his ideology. In a confidential letter addressed to Jinnah (dated 28 May, 1937), Iqbal said : "After a long and careful study of the Islamic law I have come to the conclusion that if this system of law is properly understood and applied, at least the right to subsistence is secured to everybody. But the improvement and the development of the *Shariat* of Islam is impossible in this country without a free Muslim state or states."[34] Again, "If such a thing is impossible in India, the only other alternative is civil war which, as a matter of fact, has been going on for some time in the shape of Hindu-Muslim riots. I fear that in certain parts of this country, e.g., North-West India, Palestine may be repeated."[35] Above all, he argued : "In these circumstances, it is obvious that the only way to a peaceful India is the redistribution of the country on the lines of social, religious and linguistic affinities."[36]

---

33. *A History of Freedom Movement,* published by the Pakistan Historical Society, Karachi, 1963, Vol. III, Part III, p. 315.
34. *Islamic Culture* (Lahore), October, 1943, Vol. XVII, No, 4. Jinnah wrote a 'Foreword' to the published letters. Herein he expressly says that Iqbal's views were substantially identical with his own and that they ultimately found expression in the Resolution passed on 23 March, 1940, *Ibid.,* p. 466. Subsequently, on 21 June, 1937 Iqbal wrote another letter to Jinnah stating that his idea of having a separate Muslim state had the appreciation of Lord Lothian along with his comment that it would take about 25 years to occur." *Letters of Iqbal to Jinnah,* (Lahore: Sheikh Muhammed Ashraf, 1943).
35. *Ibid.*
36. *Ibid.* On one occasion Iqbal said: "India is an Asia in miniature, India is a continent of human groups, belonging to different races, speaking different languages and professing different faiths." F.K. Khan Durrani: *The Meaning of Pakistan,* (Lahore: Sheikh Muhammad Ashraf, 1946), p. 156.

It all shows the great and abiding impact of Iqbal's two-nation theory on the mind of a superman of his choice like Jinnah. So deep was the impact of this emphasis that the vision of a separate state of the Muslims stood before the eyes of his ambitious disciple after the shocking experiment of provincial elections and it came to have its manifestation in the historic resolution adopted at the Lahore League of 1940. The speech of Jinnah delivered on this occasion should be studied in the context of what his mentor (Iqbal) had been doing for the last ten years in particular. Iqbal created the path, Jinnah treaded it. And so if Jinnah became the father of Pakistan, Iqbal deserves the credit of being its ideological patron-saint. Its endorsement can be seen in the statement of a leading League leader given in 1945: "Thoroughly aware of the Western learning and leanings, their merits and demerits, he (Iqbal) felt the supreme necessity of reconstructing Islamic thought in modern times and has eminently done so in his forceful poems, so that now the entire Muslim intelligentsia, who demands Pakistan,... is inspired by Iqbal. Anyone, therefore, who wishes to gauge Muslim feelings today must acquire the acquaintance of Iqbal."[37]

Iqbal died in 1938 leaving behind his 'qualified man' who gave a concrete shape to the vision of his mentor at the Lahore League in 1940 and then struggled for the materialisation of a dream that could be a possibility in 1947. Though a man of ego, Jinnah paid his glowing tributes to Iqbal on 25 March, 1940 in these words: "In April 1931,1 thought of transforming the Muslim League which was then only an academical institution into a parliament of Muslim India. From that time to the end of his life Iqbal stood like a rock by me."[38] While speaking on the Iqbal Day at Lahore in 1944, he said: "Although a great poet and philosopher, he was no less a practical politician. With his firm conviction of faith in the ideals of Islam, he was one of the few who originally thought over the feasibility of carving out of India such an Islamic state in the North-West and North-East zones which are historic homelands of the Muslims."[39] In 1947, Jinnah frankly acknowledged: "To me, he (Iqbal) was a friend, a guide, and a philosopher and during the darkest moments, through which the Muslim League had to pass, he stood like a rock and never flinched one single moment."[40]

Critical Appreciation: Iqbal's contribution to the Persian and Urdu poetry is undoubtedly great. However, some weak points may be traced when we examine his metaphysics as applied to politics for no other reason than to strive for the betterment of his co-religionists through the instrumentality of a superman. To throw light on the inner potentiality of man is really creditable—it highlights the spirit of the renaissance. A critic may point out at this stage that as this element is hidden in the personality of every individual, how can Iqbal's doctrine of *khudi* be reconciled with the super-ego

37. Z.A. Suleri: *The Road to Peace and Pakistan* (Lahore: Sheikh Muhammad Ashraf, 1945), p. 64.
38. See Khwaja Abdur Rahim (ed.): *Iqbal: The Poet of Tomorrow,* p. 6.
39. See Asif Iqbal Khan, *op. cit.,* p. 78.
40. *Ibid.,* p. 90. Also see Vahid: *Iqbal: His Art and Thought,* (Lahore: Sheikh Mahammed Ashraf, 1944), p. 29.

of a Big Blond Beast. Plato, Machiavelli, Hobbes and Nietzsche may be criticized for being state absolutists, but their conclusions are not inconsistent with their basic theoretical assumptions. The difficulty with Iqbal is that, in spite of his advocacy of spiritual democracy and as a supporter of Islamic theocracy, he does not sanction sovereignty of the people. He does not sponsor the ultimateness of the power of a popular parliament even in secular matters. "Thus instead of extending the implications of social democracy of Islam and thus giving to the people of the Muslim countries a liberating vision of the democratic ideal, Iqbal championed the reactionary and medievalist and even fascist cult of the hero."[41]

Without accepting Hegel's dialectical idealism, Iqbal concurs with his (Hegel's) concept of an organic absolute ego. This is due to his unflinching faith in Islamic theology that becomes the source of contradiction between his metaphysical philosophy and political theory. The conscious individuality of man or *khudi* cannot be reconciled with the collectivity as contained in the concepts of the *Millat* and the *Shariat*. And if Iqbal tries to do it, his attempt is a failure on theoretical as well as practical planes. It is a different matter that a devout Muslim may close his eyes to this point of weakness and prefer to pay all respect to the contributions of a great leader of his community.

But a critical student of political theory would agree with this remark of Prof. Varma that Iqbal "was trying to ride two horses. As a Muslim, he wanted to accept the basic theological tenets of the *Koran*. As a philosopher he adhered to an absolute organic idealism. The duality of standpoints is the main reason why he does not provide a clear ontological status of the finite ego. This philosophical confusion is responsible for a political confusion . . . . The fundamental difficulty of Iqbal's political philosophy is that he is trying to do the impossible—neither on the basis of the Koranic concept of the theocracy nor on that of absolute idealism is it possible to assert the claims and rights and potentialities of the ego."[42]

Iqbal appears like the Dante of Islam in justifying the absolute hold of a royal person on some mystical grounds. Like St. Thomas Aquinas, he manufactures certain scholastic arguments to reconcile the features of modern knowledge with medieval Muslim theology. The result of this is that like Dante and More, he comes to offer the picture of a Utopia—though a theocratic one—inspired by the vision of a new world-wide state with its capital at Mecca and embracing all Muslims without any barriers of race and language. Only such a model can be congruent to the principle of *Tauhid* or the unity of Godhead. One may comment that in such a polity, religion and politics are indissolubly blended. More than that, in such an order there is hardly any place for democracy, even spiritual democracy by allowing room for diverse patterns of life. All power rests with the chosen class of the devout Muslims marked not by their power of the ego living and working under the command of a superman endowed with a super ego, and all devoted thoroughly to the cause of thc *millat*. Obviously, like Hobbes and

41. Varma, *op. cit.,* pp. 457-56.
42. *Ibid.,* pp. 458-59.

Hegel, Iqbal "is, in the last analysis, the champion of a totalitarian state. At the best if there is democracy, it is only for the elite."[43]

It may also be added that, in a way, Iqbal belongs to the class of Plato, Machiavelli and Nietzsche who sought amelioration of all problems—political, social and economic—in the leadership of a superman. Plato's philosopher-king is an all-wise person capable of establishing 'justice' in the ideal state; Machiavelli's prince is a super-hero combining the virtues of a lion and vices of a fox and therefore capable of restoring the grandeur of a strong Roman state; Nietzsche's Big Blond Beast has every *title* to command total allegiance from the healthy instinct of the masses; Iqbal's *mard-i-momin* is the vice-regent of God by virtue of having the most volatile power of *khudi* dedicated to the cause of the welfare of the *millat* according to the tenets of faith. More than that, he goes to the final length of crying for a separate and sovereign homeland of the co-religionists, because this ideal cannot be realised in a secular country with the majority of people professing a different faith. However, different from all Western thinkers like Plato, Machiavelli and Nietzsche, Iqbal first sets for himself that role and then looks for a hero of his choice to be on the stage so as to complete the show for the lasting satisfaction of his chosen audience. For this aim he exalts the part of Satan in awakening the inner potentiality of Adam that opened the way for the creation of a new life on this earth. What Satan did to Adam, Iqbal did to Jinnah.

In the end, Iqbal's genius as a poet of nationalism deserves appreciation of every Indian, but his part in providing an ideological sharpness to the concept of a separate and sovereign homeland of the Indian Muslims makes him a controversial figure in our country. It is a different thing that while his first part is non-controversial in India, the second part has the same position in Pakistan. By emphasising the principle of *khudi*, he could influence a very large number of the Indian people; but by giving it a different direction, he imparted sharpness to the pernicious theory of two nations and thereby earned for himself a place in the heart of the people of Pakistan. He could win over an ambitious person like Jinnah and make him eat the forbidden fruit. Jinnah who had decried the scheme of separate electorates under the Act of 1909, who had urged his followers to fight shoulder to shoulder with the Congress and other Hindu majority organisations in India, and for all such acts who was widely known as the 'ambassador of Hindu-Muslim unity' and, above all, who had rejected the Pakistan project of Rahmat Ali and others by treating it as 'children's chimera' ultimately became the 'father of Pakistan'.

---

43. Muhar, *op. cit.*, p. 187.

38
M.N. Roy

Once a nationalist-anarchist, then a Marxist, then a critical Marxist and, finally, a radical humanist, Roy (1886-1954) occupies a significant place in the galaxy of modern Indian social and political thinkers. His ideas are contained in many of his writings, most important of which are *Scientific Politics* (1942), *New Orientation* (1946), *Beyond Communism* (1946), *New Humanism* (1947), *Science and Philosophy* (1947), *Radical Humanism* (1952) and *Reason, Romanticism and Revolution* (two volumes) (1952). Apart from being a great social and political thinker, he remained engaged in active politics by virtue of his association with the Russian Communist Party led by Lenin and Stalin, Chinese Communist Party led by Mao and Indian National Congress led by Gandhi and Nehru. However, the puzzling feature of his career is that his ideas changed after every decade or so as a result of which one cannot make a coherent description of his social and political philosophy.

Critique of Marxism: Roy who was once a Marxist in the early phase of his life became a critical Marxist in the end. He finds fault with the main tenets of Marxism. He discards some and revises some other tenets of Marxism. Instead of rejecting the premises of materialism altogether, he tries to synthesise them with the chords of idealism. Thus, he looks like a neo-Hegelian. He decries materialism of Marx for being dogmatic and unscientific. His main points of attack may be noted as under:

1. Roy is critical of the Marxian rejection of the autonomy of the human being. Marx's philosophy of materialism neglects the creative role of the human subject. The economic interpretation of history is deduced from a wrong interpretation of materialism. It implies dualism, whereas materialism is a monistic philosophy. History is a determined process, but there are more than one causative factors. Human will is one of them and it cannot always be referred directly to any economic incentive.[1]

2. The dialectical materialism of Marx is dialectical only in name; dialectic being its corner-stone, it is essentially an idealistic system. Dialectic is a category of idealistic logic. The laws of the dynamics of the ideas cannot be called dialectical. For instance, the transition of ideas from domocracy to socialism was not dialectical but continuous. The ideas have their autonomy and logic which is not dialectical but dynamic.[2]

---

1. Roy: *Reason, Romanticism and Revolution,* Vol. II, pp. 216-17.
2. *Ibid.,* p. 186.

3. Marx's economic interpretation of history is defective in one more respect. Before man became a *homo economicus* in quest of economic amenities, he was inspired and guided by biological considerations. The early activities and struggles of the human species were centred on finding out the means of subsistence. Thus biology, not economics, dictated the early activities of mankind.[3]
4. In Roy's views, ethical foundations of Marx are very weak. Marx contends that in the process of struggle with nature, man changes his own nature. With the change in the modes of production and exchange of goods, the whole cultural setup undergoes a change. It shows that Marx hints at the total malleability of human nature. Roy insists that no sane ethics can be built without the acceptance of some constant elements in human nature which make essential the realisation of some permanent values.[4]
5. Marx's theory of class war is wrong, because it takes a false view of the reality of social life. The existence of the middle class cannot be lost sight of and that the social classes live in harmony despite the fact that there are occasional frictions or fights between different social segments. A social cohesive bond has always been operative.
6. One contradiction in Marxist historiolgy arises from Marx's attempt to combine the belief in history and cosmos as a determined process with the enunciation of the teleological concept of the freedom of revolutionary will and action in changing the texture of that process. Thus, Roy says that materialistic determinism and revolutionary teleology cannot be reconciled.[5]
7. Roy finds fault with the Marxian prediction that revolution would establish 'dictatorship of the proletariat' and that the process of making a classless society would eventuate into the emergence of a stateless condition of life. Instead, he argues that for creating a new world of freedom, revolution must go beyond economic reorganisation of society. Freedom does not necessarily follow from the capture of political power in the name of the oppressed and exploited classes and abolition of private property in the means of production.

Despite his attack on the tenets of Marxism, Roy remains like a modified Marxist in view of the fact that he subscribes to the philosophy of materialism on the basis of which scientific laws of social progress may be discovered and formulated. In his rejection of the Marxian tenets, we may also notice his "restatement of the propositions of Marx."[6]

Radical Humanism: Roy's philosophy of humanism is known by many names as radical humanism, new humanism, scientific humanism and integral humanism. The

3. V.P. Varma: *Modern Indian Political Thought,* p. 501.
4. *Ibid.,* p. 502.
5. *Ibid.,* p. 504.
6. *Ibid.,* p. 513.

keynote of his philosophy is an urge for human freedom that implies realisation of the creative faculties of man. Scientific knowledge alone can help to restore this freedom. It liberates man from the time-honoured prejudices about the essence of his being and the purpose of his life. Man has blind faith in forces beyond his comprehension and control until knowledge illuminates his path. When the light of truth makes his innate rationality more manifest, he can discard old hypotheses based on ignorance. In this regard, his ideas are summarised in the *22 Theses of Radical Democracy* (1948) the important of which may be enumerated as follows:[7]

1. Man is the archetype of society. Cooperative social ralationships contribute to develop individual potentialities.
2. Quest for freedom and search for truth constitute the basic urge of human progress. The quest for freedom is the continuation of a higher level of intelligence and emotion of the biological struggle for existence.
3. The purpose of all rational human endeavours, individual as well as collective, is attainment of freedom in an ever-increasing measure. Freedom is progressive disappearance of all restrictions on the unfolding of the potentialities of the individuals as human beings, and not as cogs in the wheels of a mechancial social organism.
4. Arising out of the background of the law-governed physical nature, the human being is essentially rational. Reason, being a biological property, is not the anti-thesis of will. Intelligence and emotion can be reduced to a common biological denominator. Historical determinism, therefore, does not exclude freedom of the will.
5. Ideation is a physiological process resulting from the awareness of the environment.
6. For creating a new world of freedom, revolution must go beyond economic reorganisation of society.
7. Communism or socialism may conceivably be the means for the attainment of the goal of freedom. How far it can serve the purpose, must be judged by experience.
8. The state being the political organisation of society, its withering away under Communism is a utopia which has been exploded by experience.
9. The function of a liberating and revolutionary social philosophy is to lay emphasis on the basic fact of history that man is the maker of his world—man as thinking being, and he can be only so as an individual.
10. Education of the citizen is the condition for such a reorganisation of society as will be conducive to common progress without encroaching upon the freedom of the individual.

7. See J.C. Johari: *M.N. Roy: The Great Radical Humanist,* pp. 228-34.

11. Radicalism integrates science into social organisation and reconciles individuality with collective life; it gives to freedom a moral-intellectual as well as a social content.
12. Radicalism starts with the dictum that 'man is the measure of everything', or that 'man is the root of all mankind'. It advocates reconstruction of the world as a commonwealth and fraternity of free men by the collective endeavour of spiritually emancipated moral men.

Such principles of radical democracy, as enunciated by Roy, place him in the category of great lovers of human freedom like Thomas Jefferson and John Stuart Mill. Here we may also take note of his idea of universalism or an ideal picture of the entire human race as contemplated by Rousseau, Green, Aurobindo and Tagore. Marx virualised a fully emancipated man in the classless and stateless communist society; Roy finds it in a society reorganised by spiritually liberated human bings. The society as conceived by Jefferson and Mill is an empirical entity, the society as conceived by Roy is an abstraction. However, the brilliant aspect of Roy's radical humanism is that it has a refreshing touch, because it "enunciates the supremacy of the eternal urge of freedom."[8]

Scientific Politics: Roy's theory of politics, what he termed 'scientific politics', is contained in his three books—*Scientific Politics, New Orientation* and *Beyond Communism.* It finds place in the post-Marxian phase of his intellectual career when he was in search of seeing something beyond communism. The keynote of his writings in this regard is to suggest that politics should be guided by a scientific philosophy of life. The stress of Roy "is on the social foundations of scientific propositions. He means by it a system of political propositions based on the recognition of the class character of the upholders of different ideologies."[9]

Plainly stated, Roy's theory of scientific politics aims at the rejection of spiritualism, nationalism, communism and even socialism as such and instead appreciation of materialism alone. He calls all other philosophies as 'heresies' or 'antiquated creeds of the twentieth century' and declares materialism as the only 'possible philosophy, for it represents the knowledge of nature as it really exists—knowledge equated through contemplation, observation and investigation of the phenomena of nature itself. Obviously, it implies his relentless attack on the premises of religion and metaphysical philosophy what he calls the 'embodiment of human ignorance'. Religion made man a spiritual slave. Man was given to understand about the existence of life after death, about the possibility of a life in heaven for those who obeyed the commands of the religious leaders, about the need for passive obedience to the decrees of the king who was like the vicar of God on earth.

Freedom of the individual is one of the central themes of Roy's scientific politics. He would call any theory reactionary and antiquated which attempts to sacrifice the

8. Varma, *op. cit.,* p. 512.
9. Roy: *Scientific Politics,* pp. 55-56.

individual at the altar of a 'collective ego' like nationalism, communism and fascism. As he says: "In the modern world since the middle of the nineteenth century, the individual has completely disappeared not only from the frankly reactionary political thought but also from the so-called progressive and liberating political ideologies."[10] He further says that nationalism is like a collective ego at whose altar human beings are sacrificed. "Nationalism cannot be reconciled with radicalism. A conscious nationalist will reject radicalism and be an honest counter-revolutionary, a conscious Fascist."[11]

Roy is an uncompromising critic of communism as well. There can be no freedom in the era of 'dictatorship of the proletariat' and that a classless society would be stagnant. In such a society the law of dialectic would not operate as a result of which "progress would come to a standstill and the humanity will die."[12] The state can never disappear unless human society will revert to the state of savagery. A political system and an economic experiment which subordinates the man of flesh and blood to the imaginary collective ego, be it a nation or a class, cannot possibly be the suitable means for the attainment of the goal of freedom."[13]

In short, the scientific politics of Roy is another name of his humanist politics. In its appreciation, it may be said that by virtue of being well acquainted with the inadequacies of various current 'isms', Roy wanted "to place before the tormented humanity a new outlook."[14] Nevertheless, it cannot be lost sight of that the solution offered by Roy to the 'crisis of the present century' is highly speculative. Like great idealists, instead of giving anything of practical value, he finishes himself as an academic recluse. Rejection of Marxism and yet appreciation of materialism in such a bold form looks like a bundle of contradictions. As a critic says: "Renouncing Marxian dialectic was his first sin which is responsible for the chain reaction of his subsequent sorrows."[15]

Partyless Democracy: The idea of partyless democracy is quite old. It was enunciated by the founding fathers of the American republic like George Washington, James Madison and Thomas Jefferson in the last phase of the eighteenth century. They denounced party politics of the European countries and, instead, desired to have a democracy without the role of 'mobs and factions indulging in violence'. In India this idea was faintly mooted by Mahatma Gandhi shortly before his death that was developed by his followers like Acharya Vinoba Bhave and Jayaprakash Narayan afterwards. However, credit goes to Roy who dissolved his Radical Democratic Party on December 29, 1948 and in his concluding speech at its Calcutta session, declared: "We must show in action that power is not the only incentive for political action. Unless the urge for freedom is wide awake in individual men and women, democracy is not

---

10. Roy: *Beyond Communism,* p. 132.
11. Roy: *New Orientation,* p. 42.
12. Roy: *New Humanism,* p. 150.
13. *Ibid.*
14. Roy: *New Orientation,* p. 19.
15. R.K. Awasthi: *Scientific Humanism,*. p. 74.

possible . . . . . In this way the radical humanist movement will revaluate ancient values and create the atmosphere of an intellectual resurgence preparatory to the creation, by self-reliant man, of a free, happy and harmonious social order."[16]

It is clear that Roy's thesis of partyless democracy has two facets—denunciation of the party system and projection of a new social order in which there is no room for the scramble for power. His indictment of party politics has these salient points:

1. Roy rejects the view that democracy cannot be operated without the mechanism of political parties. Parties are relatively a recent phenomenon peculiar to the past hundred years or more, while politics is as old as organised social life.
2. Political parties indulge in the scramble for power. They work on this assumption that no change in society can be brought about without a particular group of people coming to power. The basic aim of a political party is to gain power. Elections are fought for this very cause. Thus party politics leads to concentration of power and hence carries in it the germs of the destruction of democracy.
3. Party rule means mis-representation of the people. The party system destroys democracy by denying the individuals any significant opportunity for effective participation in the management of public affairs. Power is vested in the people for the sake of name; in fact, it is used and abused by few great leaders of the political parties.
4. Party rule signifies rule of the minority. In fact, a popular government represents only the party which controls it and the membership of even the largest party is only a small fraction of the people.
5. Political parties work for the good of the leaders in the name of the good of the people. It leads to dishonesty and corruption in administration and public life.

On the basis of these points, Roy says: "Everywhere political parties are formed not with the object of practising democracy, but of capturing power. They are guided by the dictum that the end justifies the means, and the means often amount to the corruption and destruction of democracy, as contemporary and past experience in many countries shows."[17]

Roy is not merely critical of the party system, he also suggests a design of his own social order in which rule of the self-seeking opportunist party politicians is replaced by the role of the educated and enlightened people. It would be a thoroughly decentralised order in which most of the functions of the present state would be performed by the free and voluntary associations (cooperative societies) of the enlightened people. In such a new social order, the state "will become no more than a clearing house of information, an advisory and administrative machinery to coordinate and supervise policies framed directly by the people as a whole operating through local people's committees. That is

16. Roy: *Politics, Power and Parties,* pp. 112-13.
17. *Ibid.,* p. 67.

how the state will become identical with society, its functions confined to an overall co-ordination and harmonisation of social life in a country as a whole."[18]

A critic may say that Roy's criticism of party politics is unduly harsh. He may also comment that the alternative of a new social order, as suggested by him, is quite utopian. His attack on the party system has its merit of course, but his hope of running a democractic system without the role of political party cannot be put into practice. It is just like his negative contribution that takes him very close to the Anarchists, Guild Socialists, Syndicalists and Sarvodayists who hopefully visualise a new social order run by the operation of free and voluntary associations of the people. Roy left the Indian National Congress in 1940. Then he formed his Radical Democratic Party that saw its rout in the general elections of 1945. He dissolved it in 1948. It may be argued that when the power was actually transferred to the Indian National Congress by the British Government in 1947, Roy realised that in the field of power politics his future was sealed. "Out of frustration, therefore, he is said to have developed the theory of partyless politics and politics without power."[19]

Humanist Economy: Roy's economic philosophy shows his disagreement with all the existing schools like capitalism, socialism, communism, fascism and democratic socialism. However, it also shows his reinterpretation of classical liberalism in a way that the essential points of economic development are reconciled with the values of human freedoms. The tenets of cooperative farming and cooperative economic decentralisation are welded together in a peculiar way that the economic order, as desired by him, represents the reconstruction of Indian economy vis-a-vis the reconstruction of Indian polity. Thus, economic democracy "is integrated with political democracy in a way that competition is replaced by cooperation, planning is reconciled with freedom and, above all, cooperative socialism is offered as a substitute to communism on the one side and to capitalism on the other."[20]

Before presenting the picture of an economic system based on the theses of his radical humanism, Roy rejects various principles of economy. In the first place, he rejects the principle of capitalist economy on the ground that its motto of 'free enterprise' falsifies the ideal of human freedom. Its justification of 'free competition' leads to gross economic inequalities and exploitation of man by man. This unfortunate state of helplessness kills the spirit of democracy and creates an atmosphere favourable for the rise of collectivism. The socialist system of economy is equally bad, because it increases the role of the state in the economic sphere that kills the initiative of the people. "The abolition of private property, state ownership of the means of production and planned economy do not by themselves end exploitation of labour, nor lead to an equal distribution of wealth."[21]

18. *Ibid.*, p. 84.
19. G.P. Bhattacharjee: *Evolution of the Political Philosophy of M.N. Roy.*, p. 196.
20. K.C. Jena: *Contribution of M.N. Roy to Political Philosophy,* p. 445.
21. Roy: *New Humanism,* p. 40.

More harsh is his attack on the communist system of economy which prevailed in the former Soviet Union at that time. In it the liberty of the individual is mercilessly crushed by an all-powerful state determined to bring about a new social order by means of centralised planning. The system of mixed economy as appreciated by democratic socialism is equally bad, because exploitation of man by man goes on even in a welfare state. It is a hotch-potch of capitalism and socialism. It cannot succeed in avoiding contradictions and chaos of capitalism, and the dangers and defects of state socialism. Apart from this, Roy rejects the system of Gandhian economy in the name of its being obsolete, reactionary and a demonstration of economic ignorance. He ridicules *charkha* (spinning wheel) as the wasteful employment of labour.

Roy is not merely a vehement critic of the prevailing economic systems, he offers his own scheme of a new economic order having its hallmarks in cooperation, decentralisation and planned development. The entire economic activity should be conducted by cooperative societies at all levels—local, regional, provincial and national. The network of consumers' and producers' cooperatives built up from the bottom to the top should be protected and assisted by the state. In order to be flexible, planning should be from the bottom and that too through the network of cooperative societies. It would eliminate exploitation of man by man and guarantee a progressive standard of living. Economic liberation of the masses is essential. Active participation of the people would be ensured through the network of people's councils which would disseminate knowledge. Such a new society would be democratic—politically, economically as well as culturally.[22]

A critic may say that while Roy's attack on the prevailing systems of economy is understandable, his picture of a new order based on cooperative economy is too hazy having its parallel in the guild commonwealth of G.D.H. Cole. In theory he presents a praiseworthy utopia, where man is the maker of his destiny; planning is combined with democracy and individual freedom; where man has the responsibility for his choice of relief and conduct; and his inventiveness and initiative, his varied resourcefulness and personality are not swamped. But when faced with brass facts of reality, where one has to go to details? Such a theory gives rise to a host of confusions and disagreements.

Critical Appreciation: The social and political philosophy of Roy looks like a brilliant mixture of his attack on the prevailing schools of thought on the one hand and a fine storehouse of confusions and contraditions on the other. While his 'friends' admire him for presenting an unusual mixture of reason, romanticism and revolution, and for resisting everything which poisons or suffocates the living centre of personal being, his 'foes' go to the extent of saying that he failed in building up a system of thought like Hobbes and Marx, and that his path to success was dogged by several failures and frustrating experiences of his long political life. A critic may, therefore, comment that while the destructive side of his social and political philosophy is clear, its constructive side is too vague and hazy. Varma rightly calls him an 'Ethical Revisionist.'[23]

---

22. Awasthi, *op. cit.,* pp. 247-48.
23. V.P. Varma, *op. cit.,* p. 513.

Roy's long political career is like a saga of his intermittent failures and frustrations that occurred owing to his highly egotistic and rash temperament. It is because of this that he shifted from one plane to another until he could find solace in his rationalism known by different names coined by him and subject to different laws of objectivity and subjectivity. Hence, Kaviraj calls it 'heteronomous rationalism'. Owing to this, there could be no consistency in his social and political ideas ranging from his advocacy of the twentieth century Jacobinism to his participation in the elections of 1945 through his Radical Democratic Party signifying his acceptance of the path of constitutionalism. His stubborn rationalism made him incapable of understanding the spiritual power of Gandhi and the political power of Nehru. If studied deeply, one may say that his radical humanism was a resuscitation of the rationalist humanism of the European renaissance. Keeping such points in his view, Kaviraj comments: "Roy was a living paradox. His heresies from Marxism of the Comintern are usually given the greatest amount of critical attention. But it is perhaps this peculiar combination of political radicalism and philosophical heteronomy which explains the futility of his politics."[24]

24. Sudipta Kaviraj: "The Heteronomous Radicalism of M.N. Roy" in Thomas Pantham and K..L. Deutsch (eds.): *Political Thought in Modern India,* p. 213.

39

Ambedkar

What Mahatma Jyotiba Phule said and did for the welfare of the depressed classes and his companion Gopal Baba Walangkar advanced it in the nineteenth century, was accelerated in a more vigorous form by B. R. Ambedkar (1893-1956) in the twentieth century. He is known for being a great champion of social justice. He struggled for the cause of the 'untouchables' (*dalits*) and for this sake he denounced Hindu scriptures for deifying caste system. However, he gave a political turn to the cause of social justice by demanding separate electorate system for the advancement of the socially downtrodden classes. As a stern critic of the Hindu religion, he found solace in the teachings of Gautam Buddha. In 1951 he established Indian Buddhist People's Union and edited a book (*Buddha Upasna Path*). In 1955 he established Indian Buddhist League. He embraced Buddhism in 1956. At the Kathmandu meet he was honoured as the 'New Buddha' where a large number of his followers felt pride in glorifying him as Buddhisttava of the twentieth century.

State and Government: Ambedkar is an advocate of social welfare state that ensures the boons of liberty, equality and justice to all irrespective of their religion, creed or caste. The three aims of the State are:

(a) To maintain the right of every subject to life, liberty and the pursuit of happiness along with free speech and free exercise of religion,

(b) To remove social, political and economic inequality by providing better opportunities to the estranged communities, and

(c) To make it possible for every subject to enjoy freedom from want and fear.

It requires a responsible government intended to:

(a) prevent the majority from forming a government without giving any opportunity to the minorities to have a say in the matter,

(b) prevent the majority from having executive control over administration and thereby make the tyranny of the minority by the majority impossible,

(c) prevent the inclusion by the majority party in the executive representatives of the minorities who have no confidence of the minorities, and

(d) to provide a stable executive necessary for good and efficient administration.

Democracy: Like John Stuart Mill, Ambedkar is a reluctant democrat. He does not appreciate democracy as such as established in our country. In his view, democracy rests on four premises:

(a) The individual is an end in himself.

(b) The individual has certain inalienable rights which must be guaranteed to him by the Constitution.

(c) The individual should not be required to relinquish any of his constitutional rights as a condition precedent to the receipt of privileges.

(d) The state shall not delegate powers to private persons to govern others.

Besides, social democracy should have these premises:

(a) On a constitutional basis, all social inequalities and privileges should be abolished so that there may not be any discrimination on artificial grounds.

(b) By statutory measures untouchability along with all inabilities connected with it should be eliminated.

(c) Fundamental rights should be guaranteed to all people without any discrimination.

(d) There should be effective implementation of the Uniform Civil Code.

Religion: Religion is not contained in the observance of certain rituals or the manner of worshipping God or some supernatural forces. In the view of Ambedkar, religion has four essential elements:

(a) That the society must have either the assertion of law or the sanction of morality to hold it together. Without either of them, society is sure to go to pieces.

(b) Religion must be in accord with science. It must be understandable by rational approach.

(c) The religious code must recognise the fundamental tenets of liberty, equality and fraternity.

(d) Religion must not sanctify or ennoble poverty. Renunciation of riches by those who have it may be a blessed condition of life.

All these points are contained in Buddhism. Keeping it in view, it is observed by an Indian writer: "A well-ordered society based on religious consciousness of things to be pursued that are for the benefit of all is the central theme of Ambedkar's concept of religion."[1]

Nationalism: Like many leaders of the Indian freedom movement, Ambedkar is a nationalist, though his version of nationalism has a particular tinge. According to him, it "is a feeling of consciousness of a kind which, on the one hand, binds together those who have it so strongly that it over-rides all differences arising out of economic conflicts or social gradations and, on the other hand, secures them from those who are not of their kind."[2] To the leaders of the Indian freedom movement, nationalism had anti-British orientation whose victory was visualised in the liberation of the country from foreign rule. But Ambedkar goes a step ahead. To him nationalism meant

1. D.R. Jatav: *The Political Philosophy of B.R. Ambedkar,* p. 33.
2. Cited in Rajendra Prasad: *India Divided,* p. 9.

emancipation of the Indian people from the yoke of British colonialism as well as the liberation of the depressed classes from the unjust hold of the upper castes of the Hindu society. He protested against the external domination of the British as well as against internal oppression of the upper castes. As he asserted: "Unless the Indian people secured political power and unless that power were concentrated in the hands of the socially oppressed sections of the Indian society, it would not be possible completely to wipe out all social, legal and cultural disabilities under which that section suffered."[3]

Caste System: The fourfold division of the Hindu society into castes has been in existence since ancient times. Ambedkar's views in this regard have two layers. First, he forcefully puts forward the view that the *Sudras* once belonged to the Kshattriya caste and they were relegated to the status of untouchables by the conspiracy of the Brahmins who placed themselves at the highest pedestal of the social order. Second, he seeks redemption of the *Sudras* in the annihilation of the caste system itself. He not only inspires the Untouchables to organise and agitate, he also finds solace in Buddhism where caste system has no place.

As a great scholar of history and law, Ambedkar invokes scriptural and historical evidence to assert that the *Sudras* were not dark-skinned aboriginals enslaved or subordinated by the Aryan invaders, rather they were the Aryans who belonged to the Kshattriya solar dynasty. The subordinate status of the *Sudras* was brought about by a bloody battle between Sudas (the king of *Sudras*) and Vasistha. Due to social vicissitudes and changes of fortunes, they became degraded from their Kshattriya status. The Brahmins hatched a conspiracy to degrade them by denying *yajnopavita* (thread) to them and to learn Sanskrit language. The low status of the *Sudras* was a creation of the Brahmins who justified it in their mischievous interpolations.[4]

Ambedkar was not a mere social and political thinker like Plato, he was also a practitioner of his ideas like Gandhi. He organised the *Sudras* and encouraged them to agitate for their rights. In December 1927 he launched a movement in Mahad as a result of which the *Sudras* got right to take water from the Chowder tank. He took his followers to the Parvati temple in Poona and Kala Ram temple in Nasik and thereby broke the ban on their entry. On the occasion of the Mahad agitation he burnt *Manusmriti* and exhorted his followers: "My final word of advice to you is: educate, agitate and organise. Have faith in yourself. With justice on our side, I do not see how we can lose our battle for freedom. For, our battle is a battle not for wealth or for power. It is a battle for freedom. It is the battle for the reclamation of the human personality." It was acclaimed as the 'first untouchable liberation movement'.[5]

Ambedkar wanted retention of the caste system for the welfare and advancement of the *Sudras*. For this sake, he struggled for providing them communal electorates and reservation of posts in public services. At the same time, he wanted a casteless society to emancipate the *Sudras* from the curse of inhumanity. Here one may find a

---

3. D.R. Jatav, *op. cit.*, p. 53.
4. Ambedkar: *Who Were the Sudras?*, p. 155.
5. Gail Omvedt: *Dalit Visions*, p. 44.

striking difference between the views of Ambedkar and Gandhi. Gandhi appreciated the *varnashram* system on the plea that it led to functional specialisation, but he also insisted that there should be no hierarchical order to place any caste at the top and others in the middle or at the bottom. Not only this, he more forcefully insisted on the abolition of untouchability. Varma observes that Ambedkar's conversion to Buddhism "shows that he contemplated a future for the Untouchables somewhat in separation from the broad stream of the Hindu society. Gandhi did not want to disrupt the organic structure of the Hindu society. It may, however be noted that the approach of Buddhism to social problems was only half revolutionary, because it was also half conservative. Buddhism seeks to liberalise the structure of the caste indirectly by ignoring the case of considerations in the Samghas as well as in the lay community. But it did not make a protracted and a radical attempt to root out caste itself."[6]

Ambedkar's views on the caste system and its place in the Indian polity are diabolical. On the one hand, he talks about the 'annihilation of caste system', on the other hand, he desires protection and promotion of the Dalits under the patronage of the British rule. It is evident from his enunciation of a set of following principles, standards and goals relating to the removal of untouchability as well as improvement of the lot of the Dalits by the role of a welfare state under the British hold.

1. Untouchables must possess pride and self-respect, must dissociate themselves from the traditional bonds of Untouchable status.
2. Untouchables must become educated, not only to literacy but to the highest level.
3. Untouchables must be represented by their own representatives at all levels of government.
4. The government must take responsibility for the welfare of all its people, creating special rights for those to whom society has denied education and educational opportunities.
5. All forms of caste must be abolished. The functions of the Brahmins as priests should be performed by the trained persons from any caste under state supervision.[7]

A comparison of the views of Gandhi and Ambedkar on the issue of caste system shows that, inspite of sharp divergences, they converge in the end. To begin with, Gandhi touched upon untouchability alone, while leaving the other rules of the caste intact. Then, through his temple-entry movement, he began advocating inter-mingling and interdining as well. More than that, he insisted that the only marriage he would solemnise in his *ashram* was one between a Dalit and a Savarna, thus calling into question the very basis of the caste system itself. All such efforts had their natural place in the programmes of Ambedkar. One may, however, find a difference in their tone and temper. What Gandhi said and did humbly, Ambedkar did the same with an angry

6. V.P. Varma: *Modern Indian Political Thought,* pp. 569-70.
7. Eleanor Zelliot: "The Social and Political Thought of Ambedkar" in Thomas Pantham and K.L. Deutsch (eds.): *Political Thought in Modern India,* pp. 172-74.

and retaliatory tone. While Gandhi laid stress on the amelioration of the conditions of the Dalits, Ambedkar looked into the historical roots of this evil so as to win his point without bothering for its consequences that might cause caste conflicts. One may easily discern that Ambedkar's insistence was unduly vindictive.

The line of sharp differences between the two may thus be traced in their different approach and temper. Gandhi's view was very broad that covered the cases of all sections of the backward people, while Ambedkar's view was limited to the Dalits that made him the Messiah of their cause. It is an irony of history that they were opponents with the same goal. An Indian historian well observes: "Although they were rivals in the life time from the vantage point of history, one can clearly see that Gandhi and Ambedkar played complementary roles in the understanding of an obnoxious social institution. For no upper caste Hindu did as much to challenge untouchability as Gandhi. And Ambedkar was, of course, the greatest leader to emerge from within the ranks of the Dalits."[8]

Republican Party: The social and political ideas of Ambedkar may also be seen in the principles of his Republican Party that he formed in 1950 to replace his Independent Labour Party. These were:

1. It will treat all Indians as not only being equal before law but also being entitled to equality and will accordingly foster equality where it does not exist and uphold it where it is denied.
2. It will regard every Indian as an end in himself with a right to his own development or his own way and the state only as a means to that end.
3. It will sustain the right of every Indian to freedoms—religious, moral, political and economic—subject to such limitations as may arise out of the need for the protection of the interests of the other Indians or the state.
4. It will uphold the right of every Indian to equality of opportunity subject to the provision that those who have had none in the past shall have priority over those who had it.
5. It shall keep the State ever aware of its obligations to make every Indian free from want and fear.
6. It will insist on the maintenance of liberty, equality and fraternity and will strive for redemption from exploitation of man by man, of class by class, and of nation by nation.[9]

8. Ramchandra Guha: "They were Rivals but with the Same Mission" in *The Hindustan Times* (New Delhi), 26 October, 2014, p. 14.
9. Jatav, *op. cit.,* pp. 235-36. That Ambedkar was a nationalist is evident from two facts. First, in 1930 at the Depressed Classes Conference in Nagpur, he urged independence for India—the first Untouchable leader to urge British to leave. Second, though a strong critic of the Indian National Congress, after independence he "fell under the sway of the dream of a new united and progressive India, and abandoned many of his more radical convictions as he steered the Constituent Assembly through the process of agreeing on a Constitution." Zelliot, *op. cit.,* pp. 164 and 169.

Critical Appreciation: Ambedkar is rightly regarded as the great advocate of social justice who played a pioneering role in the sphere of Dalit resurgence in India. What was launched by Phule and Walangkar in the nineteenth century was given a vigorous form by Ambedkar in the twentieth century to an extent that he became the 'stormy petrel of Dalit resurgence'. A critic may not appreciate some of his views (as destruction of the caste system, over-zealous criticism of Hinduism and his peculiar interpretation of nationalism indirectly suggesting emancipation of the Dalits from the 'colonial' hold of the savarnas), but none can deny that Ambedkar "was the social prophet of the Untouchables. He denounced the monstrous inequalities and calumnies which Brahmanical Hinduism had heaped upon the Untouchables."[10] He "was not an arm-chair political philosopher, but a man of action, a political leader of the Depressed Classes in India. His political ideas have come to be formulated in the light of his social ideas."[11] Ambedkar deserves to be recognised as the 'modern Manu' (law giver) for his work in piloting the Constitution of independent India through the Constituent Assembly, as well as, in Nehru's words, for being a symbol of revolt against all oppressive forms of Hindu society."[12]

10. V.P. Varma, *op. cit.,* p. 570.
11. Chandra Bharill: *Social and Political Ideas of B.R. Ambedkar,* p. 183.
12. Zelliot, *op. cit.,* p. 161.

40
Nehru

Jawaharlal Nehru (1889-1964) occupies a very significant place in the galaxy of modern Indian social and political thinkers for being first a man of very high ideas and ideals, and then their translator into practice. Influenced by many ideas and ideologies of the nineteenth and mid-twentieth centuries like Marxism, Communism, Fabian Socialism and Gandhism, he managed to carve out a way of his own by accepting essential elements of some and rejecting some essential elements of others. He played a very important role in the freedom struggle of the country and managed to synthesise liberal nationalism of Gokhale with assertive nationalism of Tilak and then to synthesise both with the non-violent nationalism of Gandhiji. The novel point to be noted is that while he agreed with many like Vivekanand, Tilak, his father (Motilal Nehru) and Gandhiji on certain points, at the same time he disagreed with them on certain other points and thereby managed to present a clear picture of his own social, political and economic thought. He was associated with the Madras-based Theosophical Society of Annie Besant and the Bombay-based Home Rule League of Tilak in the early phase of his career, he switched over to a different plane in the later years of his career when he did not join the Swaraj Party led by C.R. Das and his father, and refuted the demand for Dominion Status. Instead, he raised the demand for *purna swaraj* (complete independence). It shows that in the second phase of his career, he "acquired a deeper appreciation of Indian history and philosophy, and enriched the basis for subsequent thought and action."[1]

Liberal and Assertive Nationalism: Nationalism implies deep love for and devotion to the motherland. It also implies *Swaraj* or self-determination as well as all-round development of the country. It takes inspiration from past history and traditions of the land and aspires for carving out a place of honour for the motherland in the comity of nations. Ever since the formation of the Indian National Congress, our great leaders were prosecuting national movement, but their views and strategies required change from time to time. This is the reason that the second generation of leaders came forward with its new demands in a vigorous form for which they were called 'extremists' in contrast to their predecessors called 'liberals' or 'moderates'. Then came Gandhi with his new ideas and strategies signifying a peculiar assimilation of both—constitutionalism of the former and passive resistance of the latter along with their refinement with his novel techniques of *ahimsa* and *satyagraha.* Nehru emerged on the scene with a personality of his own after 1920 when he found this or that fault with such

1. Michael Brecher: *Nehru: A Political Biography,* p. 181.

forms of nationalism. He openly criticised the working of the Indian National Congress and sought to push the freedom movement towards enlightened secularism, democratic socialism and internationalism. That is, he desired "introduction of a secular, rational, scientific and international outlook as the essential ingredients of Indian nationalism."[2]

The predecessors of Nehru had taken political and economic issues to strengthen the case of Indian nationalism; they scarcely touched foreign issues having their impact on the growth of our nationalism. Different from them, Nehru chose three foundations for nurturing the theory and practice of nationalism—moral, economic and political. On the moral plane, he denounced the way of racial arrogance shown by the Englishmen in our country. On some occasions he referred to the Ilbert Bill controversy and ill-treatment meted to the Indians at the hands of the 'white' rulers of the country. On the economic plane, he threw light on the exploitation of the country by the British merchants. On the political plane, he condemned the state of slavery created by the colonial masters. For this sake, he raised the demand for *swaraj*. But his *swaraj* meant complete freedom of the country in internal as well as external spheres. What more, he desired integration of the case of India's slavery and exploitation with other countries of the world groaning under colonial subjection.

In February, 1927 Nehru participated in the session of the League Against Colonial Oppression and Imperialism held at Brussels. He said: "We cannot tolerate any longer the state of slavery, because it is a question of life and death for us. For us in India freedom is a pressing necessity. . . . . We want the fullest freedom for our country, naturally of course not only for the internal control, but freedom also of making connections with our neighbours and other lands as we wish."[3] On this occasion, he forcefully asserted that "our national movement must be uncompromisingly anti-capitalist, anti-feudal, anti-bourgeoisie and, of course, anti-imperialist. Its sole objective "should be the establishment of a democratic socialist republic in independent India'.[4]

One more aspect of Nehru's nationalism deserves to be mentioned. It is his furious attack on the evil of communalism, whether of the Hindus or of the Muslims, that not only weakened the force of our nationalism by creating divisions and conflicts in the society at large but also by having clandestine link with British colonialism. The Muslim League was a pampered child of the colonial masters on whose demand the Indian Councils Act of 1909 had granted reservation of seats and separate electorates to the Muslims in the Central and Provincial Legislative Councils. It was extended to other minorities under the Government of India Act of 1919. It was further extended to the Depressed Castes under the MacDonald Award of 1932. So, in his presidential address delivered at the Lucknow session of the Indian National Congress held in April, 1936, he said: "It is significant that the principal communal leaders, Hindu or Muslim or others, are political reactionaries, quite apart from the communal questions.

2. R.C. Pillai: "The Political Thought of Jawaharlal Nehru" in Thomas Pantham and K.L. Deutsch (eds): *Political Thought in Modern India,* p. 261.
3. B.N. Pande: *Nehru,* pp. 122-23.
4. Nehru: *The Unity of India,* p. 166.

It is sad to think how they have sided with British imperialism in vital matters, how they have given approval to the suppression of civil liberties, how during these years of agony, they sought to gain narrow profit from their group at the expense of the larger cause of freedom."

Nehru understood the fact of India's 'unity in diversity' and so he firmly believed in the objectivity of the fundamental unity of India nurtured in her cultural foundations which were not religious in the narrow sense of the term. He accepted that, in spite of numerous diversities, there is a running unity throughout Indian history. He was also inspired by the concept of cultural pluralism, and synthesis and synthetic universalism propounded by Tagore and had no appreciation for the assimilative-integral religious approach to nationalism as taken by Dayanand, Vivekanand and Aurobindo.[5]

Purna Swaraj: It literally means self-rule or emancipation from alien domination. Although this word was invoked by many great leaders of the Indian National Congress, none but Nehru deserves the credit for giving it a precise connotation. Despite the fact that Tilak often said that 'swaraj is my birth right', he did not specify its full implications. He appreciated the case of India's 'self-rule within the Empire'. In 1916 he supported the Home Rule Movement of Annie Besant that desired India's independence in internal sphere. At the special session of the Indian National Congress held at Calcutta in September, 1920, Lala Lajpat Rai in his presidential address explained that "this word was deliberately chosen for its ambiguity in order to enable the Indians to remain within the projected Commonwealth, or to leave it according to their choice."[6]

Gandhiji could make a slight change in the concept of *swaraj* when he defined it 'within the Empire if possible, without the Empire if necessary'. He himself "never defined it, never elaborated it, never visualised it even to himself."[7] Nehru took note of this fact and at one stage he commented that Gandhi "was delightfully vague on the subject and he did not encourage clear thinking about it."[8] Motilal Nehru laid stress on Dominion Status that meant a little short of complete independence. In a mood of exasperation on 23 March 1927, he said: "I do not think there is one man among the old or the new sort of Congressmen who will not go into fainting on hearing the words 'complete independence' for India."[9]

Though Nehru rejected the first part of Gandhi's idea of 'Swaraj within the Empire', he accepted its second part relating to 'Swaraj without the Empire if necessary'. It implied what he termed Purna Swaraj or complete independence. He joined the Independence of India League formed by Srinivas Iyenger in 1927 that came forward with the demand for complete independence. When Subhas Chandra Bose joined it, the trio became a force to be reckoned with. The Madras Congress held in December,

5. V. P. Varma: *Modern Indian Political Thought,* p. 558.
6. Daniel Argov: *Moderates and Extremists in Indian National Movement,* p. 188.
7. Pattabhi Sitaramayya: *The History of the Indian National Congress,* Part I, p. 376.
8. Nehru: *An Autobiography,* p. 76.
9. J.N. Brown: *Gandhi and Civil Disobedience,* p. 12.

1927 passed a one-line resolution to this effect. But in the following year the Calcutta Congress endorsed the demand for Dominion Status as preferred by Motilal Nehru who presided this session. The Nehru Report of 1928 also demanded the same for India. As Jawaharlal Nehru and Subhas C. Bose were the members of this All-Parties Committee set up under the headship of Motilal Nehru, they opposed it.

Jawaharlal Nehru had the chance to make complete independence the goal of the Indian National Congress at its annual session held at Lahore under his presidentship in December, 1929. On this occasion he boldly affirmed: "We have much controversy about independence and Dominion Status, and we have quarrelled about words. But the real thing is the conquest of power by whatever name it may be called. I do not think that any form of Dominion Status applicable to India will give us real power. A test of this power would be the withdrawal of the entire army of occupation and economic control. Let us, therefore, concentrate on these and rest will follow easily. We stand, therefore, today for the fullest freedom of India. This Congress has not acknowledged and will not acknowledge the right of the British Parliament to dictate to us in any way."

Mere such declaration at the Lahore Congress or passage of a resolution to this effect was not enough. Nehru realised it and so he wrote a pledge that was taken at Lahore on 26 January, 1930. It read: "We believe that it is the inalienable right of the Indian people as of any other people, to have freedom and to enjoy the fruits of their toil and have the necessities of life so that they may have full opportunities of growth. We believe also that if any Government deprives the people of these rights and oppresses them, the people have a further right to alter it or abolish it. The British Government in India has not only deprived the Indian people of their freedom, but has based itself on the exploitation of the masses, and has ruined India economically, culturally and spiritually. We believe, therefore, that India must sever the British connection and attain Purna Swaraj or complete independence."

Enlightened Secularism: Nehru's views on secularism may be traced in his concepts of nationalism, democracy and socialism. In a literal sense, secularism desires separation of politics from religion and ethics. However, it does not desire irreligiousity. Religion is a private affair. Everyone should enjoy freedom of conscience. He may profess faith in any religion and may also convert as per his choice. However, it is required that one should not be superstitious or a blind follower of any faith. The state should treat all religions as equal and there should be no discrimination among the people on the basis of religion, race, creed, caste, etc. The state should be neutral in regard to religions. Above all, people of all faiths must play their part in the all-round development of the country.

In the view of Nehru, a secular state is always a democratic state in which rule of law prevails. Hence, there should not be separate personal laws for the Hindus or the Muslims or the Christians and the like. Not only this, social evils as those of untouchability or caste discrimination should also be removed. Economic disparities inflate the conditions of communalism. Hence, the evil of poverty should be eliminated.

The formula of 'one person, one vote' should be implemented, but there should be no communal electorate system. In a speech delivered at Aligarh on 24 January, 1948 he said: "It is not possible for us to go back to a conception that the world has outlived and that is completely out of tune with modern conception. The Government of a country like India with many religions that have secured great and devoted following from generations can never function satisfactorily in the modern age except on a secular basis."[10]

Democratic Socialism: Nehru was a socialist by conviction without being a degmatic follower of any of its varieties. In this regard his views range from the poles of Marxism-Leninism to that of the Fabianism or English variety of democratic socialism and yet assume a form of their own that may be called 'Nehruism'. In Marxism, as he says, he could find 'comfort and hope', but in its applied form (Marxism-Leninism or communism) he could find a parallel of Fascism. Being under the influence of Gandhiji, he described any communist movement as the 'enemy' of nationalism. But he did not agree with the economic ideas of Gandhiji and virtually treated them as 'utopian'. As a matter of fact, he drew closer to the English variety of socialism as a result of which some writers have preferred to call him the 'Indian Fabian'.

In the initial phase of his career, Nehru developed liking for the scientific approach of Marx. As he says: "A study of Marx and Lenin produced a powerful effect on my mind and helped me to see history and current affairs in a new light much in the Marxist philosophical outlook."[11] But he could discover fallacies in the theories of Marx and Lenin that appeared with the growth of democracy and transformation of the capitalist system itself. Thus, the old emotional attachment of Nehru with Marxism and Leninism declined and he could identify communist system of Russia with fascist system of Italy. So his biographer observes: 'Nehru is a convinced socialist, but he is not a Communist. The record of word and deed is clear on this point. He drank deeply of Marxist literature in the thirties, but he never became intoxicated. Indeed, at the very height of his attraction to Communism, he remained the sceptic, impressed by certain social achievements but repelled by their method, influenced by the Marxist interpretation of history but unalterably opposed to its dogma enamoured of Communist ideals but distressed by Communist practice."[12]

Though Nehru discarded the path of Marxian socialism, he drew close to Fabianism in which socialism could be happily integrated with the premises of democracy. The noteworthy point at this stage is that he found in this variety of socialism a remedy

10. Nehru: *Independence and After,* (Speeches edited by J.S. Bright), p. 123. Nehru's resolution on Fundamental Rights and Economic Policy adopted at the Karachi Congress of March 1931 contained many principles of secularism as freedom of conscience, free profession and practice of any religion subject to public order and morality, protection of the culture of the minorities, no discrimination in public services on the grounds of religion, race or caste, and no restriction on such grounds in matters of use of roads, wells, schools and other places of public resort.
11. Nehru: *The Discovery of India,* pp. 29-30.
12. Michael Brecher, *op. cit.,* p. 233.

to solve social and economic problems not only of India but of the whole world. The Karachi Congress had passed his resolution on Fundamental Rights and Economic Policy having many important items as living wage for industrial workers, limited hours and healthy conditions of work, social security, protection of women workers and maternity relief, protection of trade union rights, reduction of rent and land revenue, imposition of progressive tax on agricultural income, graduated inheritance tax, etc.

It shows that by now Nehru had made up his mind to radicalise the policies and programmes of the Congress Party. At the Lucknow Congress (1936), he declared that "socialism is a creed which I hold with all my head and heart."[13] He integrated the struggle for national liberation with the philosophy of socialism when in his presidential address he said: "I work for Indian independence because the nationalist in me cannot tolerate alien domination. I work for it even more because for me it is the inevitable step to social and economic change. I should like the Congress to become a socialist organisation and to join hands with other forces in the world who are working for the new civilisation."[14]

Impressed with the socialist ideas of Nehru, some Congress leaders as Jayaprakash Narayan, Asoka Mehta, Acharya Narendra Deva, Yusuf Mehrally, etc., had formed Congress Socialist Party in 1934 and they had desired that Nehru should become its president. But sensing the displeasure of Gandhiji at its creation, he refused to join this body, though it continued to operate as a pressure group inside the national organisation and Nehru remained the source of inspiration to its leaders.[15]

The socialist ideas of Nehru have their clear reflection in the provisions of the Constitution of India. Its Part IV having Directive Principles of State Policy was described by Dr. Ambedkar as the 'charter of social and economic democracy in India'. Nehru established Planning Commission in 1950 to put his socialist ideas into practice. In 1955 the Congress at its Avadi session adopted the goal of 'socialist pattern of society'. It was the basis on which the Planning Commission prepared the Second Five Year Plan that incorporated provisions for the creation and growth of the public sector. Zamindari was abolished in Bihar and Uttar Pradesh. Feeling afraid of the power of the judicial review of the Supreme Court and High Courts, the Nehru government made First Constitutional Amendment Act in 1951 that inserted Ninth Schedule. It provides that any law or regulation of the State becomes immune from judicial scrutiny if it is included in this schedule of the Constitution.

It is true that Nehru was critical of the capitalist system. It is equally true that he was not in favour of complete nationalisation of private property. He disfavoured Gandhi's

13. Nehru: *India and the World,* p. 83.
14. *Ibid.,* pp. 83-84.
15. This bloc of the Congressmen was like a ginger group within the national organisation with which Nehru's emotional sympathy was too obvious. It was given the name of 'Congress left'. When Nehru defined the Government of India Act of 1935 as the 'charter of slavery', they happily endorsed it and raised the call for complete independence with great vigour. At the Lahore meeting, the CSP leaders adopted a detailed programme based on the Karachi resolution of Nehru. L.P. Sinha: *The Left Wing in India,* pp. 444-45.

idea of 'trusteeship'. He chose the middle course. Let the private sector and the public sector exist side by side. Let private property system remain, but under strict control of the state. If necessary, private property should be nationalised in the public interest by the authority of law and on the payment of compensation. This system came to be known as Nehru's model of 'mixed economy'. Surprisingly, while he disfavoured the Russian pattern of 'command economy' set up by Stalin, he favoured the Chinese pattern of mixed economy set up by Mao. The reason behind it is that he wanted to follow the ideals of socialism by maintaining the system of democracy. "He wanted to remove the evils of capitalism from democracy by adopting socialist principles. And socialism, for him, largely meant the addition of economic democracy to political democracy."[16]

Parliamentary Democracy: As already pointed out, Nehru was a strong advocate of democracy. It may be traced in his bold criticism of all kinds of dictatorial and authoritarian systems and instead his strong defence of the freedom of the individual. His resolution on Fundamental Rights and Economic Policy contained several items relating to the freedom of the individual as freedom of speech and expression, right to form associations and combinations, freedom of conscience, freedom from arrest and arbitrary detention, equality before law, protection of the rights of the minorities, etc. Suppression of the fundamental rights of the people makes the government dictatorial as may be seen in a communist country like Russia. As he says: "To crush a contrary opinion forcibly and allow it no expression, because we dislike it, is essentially exactly of the same genus as cracking the skull of an opponent, because we disapprove of him."[17]

In this respect, Nehru followed the Gandhian line of unbreakable nexus between end and means. Right means should always be adopted to achieve a right end. It may be possible only by following the ways of non-violence. Let the people enjoy freedom, but it should be regulated by the norms of social discipline. Its exercise should be allowed in the larger context of social responsibility. Democracy alone can guarantee equality of rights and opportunities for all in political and economic fields and ensure freedom for the individual to develop his personality. In this respect, he looks like a powerful defender of the representative or popular government like John Stuart Mill and Lord James Bryce. As he says: "My roots are still perhaps partly in the nineteenth century and I have been too much influenced by the humanist liberal tradition to get out of it completely."[18]

Nehru appreciated the role of the opposition in democracy. Only free and fair elections can reveal the mandate of the people. Hence, the party that secures absolute majority in the popular chamber forms the government, while other parties form the opposition. The role of the opposition is to keep the government on the right track.

16. R.C. Gupta: *Indian Freedom Movement and Thought: Nehru and the Politics of 'Right' Versus 'Left'* (1930-47), (New Delhi: Sterling Publishers, 1983), p. 282.
17. Nehru: *The Unity of India,* p. 67.
18. Nehru: *An Autobiography,* p. 591.

There should be no opposition for the sake of opposition. Hence, the members of the opposition should observe the norms of decency or discipline. Only then parliamentary democracy may operate well. Such type of democracy "is not something which can be created by some magic wand. . . . . Parliamentary democracy naturally involves the methods of action, peaceful acceptance of decisions taken and attempts to change them through peaceful ways again."[19]

Scientific Humanism: The renaissance occurred in Europe in the fifteenth century. It delivered the message of man's creative potentialities and encouraged him to think in a rational manner. Thus, it informed men to shake off medieval superstitions. Scientific inventions of Copernicus, Galileo and Newton created a miracle in changing the minds of men. Now emerged the modern age. People developed scientific temper and spirit of enquiry. The pioneers of this movement stressed that man was the creator of his own destiny as well as of the whole world. It occurred in India in the nineteenth century in the form of social and religious reform movements in which great leaders like Raja Ram Mohan Roy, Vivekanand, M.G. Ranade, Dayanand, Mahatma Phule, Syed Ahmed Khan etc., played a notable part.

Humanism lays stress on the freedom and dignity of the individual and desires a political system based on the consent of the people. It informs man to be critical in evaluating prevailing systems in their social, economic, cultural and political aspects and to modernise them in the light of the changing times. Its keynote is 'ring in the new, ring out the old'. Let the individual remain engaged in the quest for freedom and let the free individuals create a synthesis of humanism and scientific spirit. As an advocate of humanism, Nehru says: "It is the scientific approach, the adventurous and yet critical temper of science, the search for truth and new knowledge, the refusal to accept anything without testing and trial, the capacity to change the previous conditions in the face of new evidence, the reliance on observed fact and not on pre-conceived theory, the hard discipline of the mind all this is necessary, not merely for the application of science but for life itself and the solution of its many problems."[20]

Nehru thought that the better type of modern man is practical and pragmatic, ethical and social, altruistic and humanitarian. However, man is governed by practical idealism for social betterment or for the good of the humanity as a whole. The ideals which move the mind represent the spirit of the age that may be called *Yugadharma.* This view "has discarded to a large extent the philosophical approach of the ancients, their search for ultimate reality, as well as the devotionalism and mysticism of the medieval period. Humanity is its god and real service is its religion." But the scientists should also note that they do not have the monopoly of truth; that nobody has a monopoly, no country, no people, no book. Truth is too vast to be contained in the minds of human beings, or in books however sacred."[21]

19. Nehru: *Independence and After* (Speeches edited by J. S. Bright), p. 56.
20. Nehru: *The Discovery of India,* pp. 623-24.
21. Nehru: *Speeches,* Vol. III, p. 433.

Internationalism: Nehru was a fiery advocate of world peace. So he attacked blind and aggressive nationalism of the Italians and the Germans who dreamt of conquering the whole world. Nationalism should be enlightened so that it may be harmonised with internationalism that desires peace and security all over the world. Internationalism stands for peaceful and cordial relations among all nations of the world and so it insists on pacific settlement of disputes. It also lays stress on the creation of some international body to maintain peace and security and prevent the outbreak of a great war that brings untold suffering to mankind. Nationalism can thrive and prosper in the garden of internationalism.

Nehru's internationalism cannot be taken as similar to the idea of cosmopolitanism or universalism as advocated by Ram Mohan Roy, Tagore and Gandhi. The very word 'international' presupposes the existence of nationalism. Let there be many nations of the world with their distinct social and cultural orders or ways of collective life, but all should live in a secure atmosphere of peace, cooperation and goodwill. The idea of universalism or cosmoplitanism desires amalgamation of all nations of the world into a harmonious whole in which all distinctions of land, race, blood, religion, caste, creed etc., disappear. A critic may easily comment that while the idea of universalism or cosmoplitanism is like the sweet dream of a philosopher or a poet, the idea of internationalism is realistic and one could see its triumph in the twentieth century. Taking note of this fact, Nehru says: "But real internationalism is not something in the air without roots or anchorage. It has to grow out of national cultures and can only flourish today on basis of freedom and equality."[22]

Gandhi and Nehru: A comparative study of the two great leaders relating to their role in the freedom movement and also relating to their social, political and economic ideas shows many points of resemblance and difference, both running concurrently. Nehru joined the non-cooperation movement in 1921 and he felt highly optimistic of the advent of 'Swaraj within a year' as often exhorted by Gandhiji. But he felt annoyed when Gandhiji abruptly stopped this movement after the Chauri Chaura violence in February, 1922. In his words, it happened at a time when "we seemed to be consolidating our position and advancing on all fronts."[23] And yet he appreciated the strategy of non-coperation to terminate the 'Satanic rule'. He did not join the Swaraj Party formed by his father (with C.R. Das) in 1923 that had taken to the anti-Gandhian line. The Nagpur Congress (1920) had passed Gandhiji's resolution demanding 'Swaraj within the Empire if possible, without the Empire if necessary'. Nehru disagreed with its first part, but he accepted its second part and converted it into his demand for 'purna swaraj' in 1927. By this time Gandhiji also displayed his agreement with what Nehru demanded and so he moved a resolution that was passed at the Lahore Congress of 1929.

---

22. Nehru: *The Discovery of India,* p. 600.
23. Nehru: *An Autobiography,* p. 81.

However, the point of sharp difference between the two may be traced in their different versions of socialism. While Gandhi advocated the idea of 'trusteeship', Nehru preferred the ideology of Fabianism. Gandhi desired that private property system should be retained, but the mentality of the owners should be transformed so that they regard themselves as the custodian of what belongs to the society. Nehru regarded it as 'utopian'. Instead he preferred the ideology of socialism that, in the view of his mentor (Gandhiji), was 'Western' and thoroughly materialistic. But Nehru had deep regard for the sentiments of Gandhiji. When Jayaprakash Narayan formed his Congress Socialist Party in 1934 and desired to see Nehru as its president, Gandhiji expressed his displeasure at it. Sensing the mind of Gandhiji, Nehru declined to join it despite the fact that the leaders of the CSP continued to regard him as their 'intellectual god-father'. Nehru criticised the Government of India Act of 1935 as 'charter of slavery' and, as the President of the Indian National Congress, he refused to take part in the elections to the Provincial Legislative Assemblies. However, at the behest of Gandhiji he changed his stand. The Congress participated in the elections and owing to the great influence of Nehru, that he could establish by his whirlwind tour of the country, it formed its governments in 8 out of 11 provinces.

When the Second World War broke out in 1939, Gandhiji advised Congressmen to help the British as *ahimsa* required to do so in the event of 'enemy's being in difficulty', Nehru and Maulana Azad (who was the President of the Indian National Congress in 1940) opposed it. After a little interval, Gandhiji agreed with the views of Nehru and Azad that no cooperation could be given to the British Government unless it cleared its 'war aims' and assured its resolve to free India after the War. When Gandhiji launched his Quit India Movement in 1942, Nehru and all leaders of the Congres took part in it and most of them remained behind the bars.

One more point where Nehru did not agree with the views of Gandhiji was related to the issue of taking freedom struggle to the Indian native states. Gandhiji often insisted that there should be no interference in the affairs of the states as their rulers were Indians, while our struggle was against the British. For instance, in order to settle the issue of Rajkot in 1938, he preferred the course of *satyagraha* that was done first by Kasturba and then by Kripalani. But Nehru and Subhas C. Bose (who was the President of the Congress at this time) did not appreciate this move. Bose went to the extent of calling it 'a flea-bite'. Without bothering for the views of Gandhiji, Nehru worked as the president of All-India States People's Conference that was a federation of various *mandals* and *samitis* operating in the native states and fighting for the introduction of constitutional reforms there. The most crucial point of difference between the two great leaders arose in June 1947 on the issue of country's partition. While Gandhiji had often asserted publicly that partition would take place on his dead body, Nehru with Patel accepted the Mountbatten Plan. The helpless Mahatma was on the dais when the AICC at its Delhi meeting on 15 June 1947 passed a resolution in its favour. He preferred to keep quiet in the face of powerful orations of Nehru and Patel hinging on the plea of an unfortunately optionless situation before them.

Apart from this, Nehru tried to follow the advice or Gandhiji at many times as he was deeply impressed with his three great contributions—fearlessness, novel techniques of non-violence, and moral approach to politics. Like Vivekanand, Gandhiji exhorted the countrymen to be bold and to fight against injustice of any kind. But, unlike any other great leader of the country, he always advised to stick to the path of non-violence. Though Nehru often disliked this counsel of Gandhiji, in a fit of rashness he succumbed to it after a short interval. For instance, he had criticised the abrupt stoppage of the non-cooperation movement by Gandhiji; after some time he appreciated Mahatma's wisdom and described him as 'the best physician' of the country. The line of difference between the two on this count may be seen in the fact that while Gandhiji treated non-violence as a matter of faith, Nehru accepted it as a matter of policy or strategy. However, Nehru always adhered to the moral path that his mentor showed to his people.

Differences between the two may be seen in their economic ideas as well. While Gandhiji prefered simple rural economy based on *charkha* and cottage industries, Nehru favoured heavy industrialisation and urbanisation on a large scale as existing in developed countries of the world. Gandhiji never favoured the idea of zamindari abolition, but Nehru did it. Nehru hated poverty but he preferred wealth, if not its concentration, Gandhiji disliked poverty as much as he disliked the excess of wealth.

In short, Gandhiji was an idealist who took things to a mystical height, for instance in his concept of Ram Raj, Nehru was a practical idealist who studied things from a scientific outlook for which he expressed his debt to Marx. Thus while a critic may discover many points of a utopian nature in the social and political philosophy of Gandhiji, he may not trace any such point in that of Nehru. In 1934 earthquake took a heavy toll of life in Bihar, Gandhiji discovered its reason in the practice of untouchability by the people for which they were punished by God. Tagore dismissed it with a word of ridicule and Nehru followed him. However, he frankly acknowledged that this 'reactionary' leader "knows India, understands India, almost is like a peasant of India, and has shaken up India as no so-called revolutionary has done." Praiseworthy is the comment of an English Fabian: "What is outstanding in the leadership of Gandhi and Nehru is the keenness and subtlety of intellect, the depth and refinement of the emotional life of these two men, compared not only to the brutality and ultracoarseness of Mussolini and Hitler, but even to the conventional outfit, in thought and feeling, of Churchill and Roosevelt."[24]

Critical Appreciation: Great is the contribution of Nehru to the freedom struggle of the country as well as to the stock of social, political and economic thought of modern India. A critic may say that his over-optimism in taking the country towards socialism in the national sphere and his idealism in the management of India's relations with foreign countries proved counter-productive. He followed the model of a welfare state as established in Britain after the Second World War. But the growth of the public sector and enhancement of the role of the state in rendering socially useful services resulted in growing corruption and maladministration with which the country

24. Statement of Beatrice Webb given on September 24, 1940, in her *Diaries,* Vol. 54, p. 176.

is suffering now. However, it cannot be denied that through his writings, utterances and actions he "wanted to bring a traditionalist under-developed society and economy from the bullock-cart stage to the age of atomic reactors. He wanted the development of representative institutions, parliamentary democracy, planned social and economic change, socialism and internationalism."[25]

25. V. P. Varma: *Modern Indian Political Thought,* p. 566.